glossary of art architecture and design since 1945

Third edition

Revised, enlarged and illustrated

JOHN A. WALKER

Foreword by Clive Phillpot

LIBRARY ASSOCIATION PUBLISHING
L O N D O N

Published by

Library Association Publishing Ltd
7 Ridgmount Street
London WC1E 7AE

Published simultaneously in the United States of America by

G. K. Hall & Co
70 Lincoln Street
Boston
Massachusetts 02111

First published 1973
Second edition 1977
This third revised, enlarged and illustrated edition 1992

British Library Cataloguing-in-Publication Data
Walker, John A.
Glossary of art, architecture and design since 1945 – 3rd ed.
I. Title
709
ISBN 0–85365–639–8

Designed and typeset by **AND Association, London.**

Printed and made in Great Britain by **Butler & Tanner Ltd, Frome, Somerset.**

ACKNOWLEDGEMENTS

This book would not have been possible without the help of the many people who provided information and advice. My thanks in particular to Dawn Ades, Vicki Bailey, Jon Bird, Guy Brett, David Cheshire, Emmanuel Cooper, Toni Del Renzio, Rita Donagh, Ken Friedman, Peter Gidal, David Harding, Brian Hatton, Michael Hazzledine, Judy Hoffberg, Sylvia Katz, Irene Kotlarz, Simon Lewandowski, Jeanie Lowe, Peter Moore, Clive Phillpot, Gerald Shepherd, Bette Spektorov, Michael Strain, Heather Strutt, Necdet Teymur and Lisa Tickner.

Thanks are also due to the staffs of Middlesex Polytechnic art library, the Victoria & Albert Museum National Art Library, the Tate Gallery Library and the RIBA Library; to Barbara Jover for her editorial encouragement; to Jenni Boswell-Jones and Ismail Saray for their design skills; to Roderick Coyne for his architectural photographs, Paul Barritt for technical assistance; and, finally, to all the artists, designers, photographers, galleries and organizations who kindly supplied photographs and gave permission for their use.

Every effort has been made to trace and credit the producers and copyright holders of the images used in this book. The author apologises for any omissions or errors.

FOREWORD

The 1980s have come and gone since the publication of the second edition of John A. Walker's *Glossary of Art, Architecture & Design Since 1945* and many new terms have been washed up on the shore of history. One, Neo-Geo, was so euphonious that it quickly accumulated mileage – despite a tenuous connection with some of the art it purported to describe – still appears in print, and even entered popular culture with a gratuitous mention in the 1987 movie *Batteries Not Included.* A good label is hard to find, so 'Neo-Geo', like 'Cubism' for example, may not disappear in spite of its limitations.

While the imprecision of such words in labelling disparate works and ideas may mislead, their limitations may eventually become irrelevant if they remain in circulation, since they can frequently come to function solely as mnemonics or shorthand for the complicated phenomena that they designate. The word 'Cubism' is likely to conjure up, even in the mind of a relatively uninformed reader, more than just those few paintings in which motifs have been simplified into illusionistic cubic forms. But the ink is dry on Cubism, and countless publications and exhibitions have established a widely-shared understanding of its parameters and meaning. By contrast, whether Neo-Geo finally enters the vocabulary of art history or not, it is certainly too early to say that its meaning is fixed. Therefore the existence of a glossary such as this, which literally documents the origins and initial meanings of such terms, benefits not only those who wish to communicate with some exactitude, but also those who wish to unravel critical shorthand or to match one usage against others.

Britain and the rest of Europe have for many years been warmed by a Gulf Stream of art magazines, exhibitions, catalogues, and artists from the United States, consequently the British origins of the *Glossary* throw a useful light on the international currency and validity of the numerous art labels spawned there since 1945. This vantage point also facilitates the expansion of the familiar pantheons of artists associated with movements or styles originating in the United States with other practitioners, whether from Britain or further afield. In addition, of course, those terms that have originated in Britain and elsewhere in Europe are explicated for North Americans.

While the purveyors and consumers of art language in many countries will find this book valuable, so too will those who seek order and relationships among the plethora of neologisms, in particular the thesaurians and classifiers. Indeed, among those professionally concerned with relations of terms, especially librarians, the hiatus of more than a decade between editions of the *Glossary of art, architecture and design since 1945* has been disconcerting. Turning to 'Walker' for explanations of recent terminology had become a less frequent activity. There will, therefore, be a warm welcome for this edition, which will diminish only when rumbles about a fourth edition increase to a roar.

Since our guide through this thicket of recent art terminology is a glossarial artist who is also alert to irony and possessed of a keen critical intelligence, reading the *Glossary* is not only informative but also pleasurable and thought-provoking. John A. Walker is also well aware that even an A–Z guide conceals as much as it reveals; he has therefore helped us to unlock the hundreds of other terms embedded in the alphabetical matrix by providing us with a comprehensive index to his remarkably wide-ranging researches into recent art, architecture and design.

Clive Phillpot
Director of the Library
The Museum of Modern Art
New York

INTRODUCTION

It is a basic characteristic of human culture that language changes as society changes. A survey and analysis of the new, specialist terms employed in any intellectual field will, therefore, serve as a precise index of the major and minor developments taking place in that field.

New inventions and technologies provide new tools for artists and always give rise to new words. In the 1977 edition of this book the terms 'Computer Art', 'Electronic Art', 'Holography', and 'Laser Art' all appeared. Naturally these entries needed extending in the light of expansions in these areas during the '80s, but also new entries were needed on 'Copy Art', 'Quantel Paintbox' and 'Telematics'. Design based upon computer models became more and more commonplace in the realms of architecture and industrial design, while new interactive computer and laser disc technologies made possible human participation in completely simulated realities. During the '80s the writings of Jean Baudrillard influenced the work of both visual artists and critics. His terms 'Simulation, Simulacra and Hyperreality' became fashionable as the second-order worlds of the mass media and computer models threatened to replace first-order Nature.

'Video Art' dated from the mid '60s but it too benefited from technological advances in the '70s and '80s: the appeal of much 'Rock' and 'Scratch Video' depended upon the remarkable special effects and image manipulation made possible by more sophisticated TV editing suites. The public became much more aware of these creative forms of video not only because of the efforts of museum curators in mounting video exhibitions and installations, but also because of the increase in TV output and channels (terrestrial, cable and satellite) and the developments in home video facilities (video-recorders/cassettes).

Scientific ideas probably had less impact on the visual arts than technology; however, the fascination with the concept of chaos in the realms of science and mathematics spilled over into the arts as critics and artists alike responded with delight to the beauty and infinite regress of 'Fractal Geometry'. A fashionable philosophical term of the '80s was 'Deconstruction' but no two writers seemed to agree what it meant when translated into architecture, painting or sculpture.

In the 1977 edition a few geographical terms were included, i.e. 'Bay Area Figuration', 'Chicago School', 'Düsseldorf School', 'New York School', 'SoHo', 'Washington Colour School', 'West Coast School'. The advent of the term 'East Village Art' signified the continuing importance of some districts of New York, but the promotion of the label 'School of London' by Ron Kitaj and others signalled a British challenge to New York's hegemony. Glasgow too emerged as a significant centre for the art of painting (the so-called 'New Image Painting' of Ken Currie, Peter Howson, *et al*). 'Latin American Art' also demanded a place as European and American curators and critics belatedly paid homage to the work of modern South American artists.

Although the 'WestKunst' of Europe and North America remained dominant throughout the '80s, the artworld increasingly developed a global perspective. Books appeared on the 'Township Art' of Black South Africa; the 1989 *Magiciens de la Terre* show in Paris was the first exhibition that intended to be worldwide in scope; and artists working with global computer networks instituted participatory works that temporarily overcame space and time and dissolved the boundaries between nations. 'Globalization' also meant that phenomena such as 'Hybrid Culture' and 'Cross-Overs' became more common as different peoples and cultures interacted in the metropolises and media networks of the world.

As in the past, many artists found it helpful to band together, either in pairs – 'Art in Ruins', 'Komar & Melamid' – or in groups – 'Grey Organization', 'Group Material', 'Guerrilla Girls', 'Information Fiction Publicité', 'Ionist Art Group', 'KOS', 'Mülheimer Freiheit', 'Mutoid Waste Co', 'Survival Research Laboratories', 'Textruction'. Thus the pervasive individualism of modern fine art practice was modified, to some degree, by the increasing popularity of 'Collaborations' of various kinds. Warhol's and Basquiat's was only the most famous. However, artists as a whole still found it difficult to act collectively: the attempts to establish a British Artists Union in the '70s met with only limited success and the '80s witnessed a shift away from trade unions towards professional organizations (e.g. 'International Artists' Association', 'National Artists Association').

Perhaps the most striking linguistic development between the time of the first edition of this book (1973) and the present moment, was the emergence and rise to dominance of the term 'Post-Modernism' and its variants. This concept generated such a huge literature, there is no doubt that a major paradigm shift took place within the visual arts. Even so, the Post-Modernist claim that it marked the end of the sequence of avant garde movements associated with Modernism appears dubious. Time has not stopped flowing nor has it ceased to be unidirectional: the '80s witnessed the emergence of new movements and artistic groups (e.g. 'Neo-Expressionism' and 'Neo-Geo') as new generations of artists reacted against the dominant styles of their predecessors in the time-honoured fashion of rebellious youth. Success in the art market requires that new art show signs of difference, so young artists are compelled to seek it.

A proliferation of 'posts' and 'neos' within Post-Modernism indicated that genuine originality was at a premium. Terms like 'Copy Art', 'Media Art', 'Plagiarists' revealed the extent to which new art borrowed from the art of the past or from contemporary mass media imagery. Artists associated with these tendencies often justified their re-use of existing imagery as subversive and critical. Another positive justification for the recycling of images and materials was furnished by the green movement. The latter gave rise to the terms 'Green Architecture and Design', and to British groups like 'Reactivart'. The present concern for the natural environment can be traced back to the late '60s and hence it preceded the popularity of the word 'green' (as the presence of the terms 'Ecological Architecture and Art' in the 1977 edition of my book indicated).

Certain tendencies within the visual arts since 1945 overlap the divide between Modernism and Post-Modernism. For instance, there is a strong line of continuity between the 'Junk Culture/Sculpture', 'Combine Paintings' and 'Assemblage Art' of the late '50s and the 'Creative Salvage', 'New British Sculpture' and 'Mutoid Waste Co' of the '80s. Obviously, this particular artistic trend reflects the wider social fact that the wave of consumerism which began in Britain in the '50s is still with us and generates ever more waste matter.

The Post-Modernist loss of faith in the idea of progress in art gave rise to a plethora of blatantly backward-looking tendencies: 'Arcadian' and 'Cultured Painting', 'New Classicism', 'New Futurism', 'New Spirit', 'Neo-Expressionism', 'Brotherhood of Ruralists' ... all of which could be subsumed under the general headings of 'Historicism' and 'Retro'. The rejection of the 'Machine Aesthetic', and the functionalism/purity of form associated with Modernism also prompted a revival of interest in decoration, hence the vogue for 'Ornamentalism' in architecture and design, and the welcome given to American 'Pattern Painting'. British architects founded the organization 'Acanthus' to restore decoration and craft skills to an honoured place in architectural design.

Also during the '80s, many museums and galleries mounted historical shows that re-examined the groups and movements of the '50s and '60s. For instance, 'Arte Povera', 'CoBrA', 'Conceptual Art', the 'Direct Art' of the Viennese Aktionismus, 'Fluxus', the 'Independent Group', 'Neo-Romanticism', 'Nouveau Réalisme' and the 'Situationists'. Only 'Tachisme' seems to have been overlooked by ambitious curators and art historians.

Although the advent of Post-Modernism and associated terms like 'Pluralism' marked a more sophisticated understanding of the complexity and heterogeneity of contemporary culture, it was in certain respects the sign of a reaction against the radical initiatives of the '60s and '70s intended to subvert and transform the artworld, the private gallery/public museum infrastructure. In fact, increased affluence, communication and travel in the developed countries of the world strengthened the art market and official art institutions. During the '80s terms such as 'Art Fairs', 'Art Agencies', 'Artist-in-Residence', 'Business Sponsorship', 'Commodity Aesthetics', 'Saatchi Collection' ... signalled the growth in importance of private sector support for the arts and the application of publicity methods derived from the worlds of business and commerce. Relatively speaking, public sector support for the arts declined but the bureaucracy associated with it did not, hence the appearance of terms like 'Arts Administration' and 'Artocrats' (see under Arts Administration).

A more subtle instance of cultural change was detectable in the gradual shift of emphasis from 'Community Art' in the '70s to 'Public Art' in the '80s. 'Public' is a broader concept than 'community'; it implies a blander, less committed kind of art. The concept of community fared better in the field of architecture during the '80s when Rod Hackney, a leading advocate of 'Community Architecture', was made President of the Royal Institute of British Architects. Several organizations dedicated to fostering Public Art were established, e.g. 'ArtAngel Trust' and 'Public Art Development Trust'. Of course, contemporary Public Art can still be critical in its content and intention but the radical tendencies occur more in the ephemeral forms of Public Art than in the permanent forms, e.g. 'Billboard' and 'Projected Art'. Involving ordinary people in the making of art and directing art towards disadvantaged groups had been the hallmarks of Community Art. Something of these ideals persisted in the vogues for 'Art Therapy', 'Hospital' and 'Prison Art'.

For those who welcomed the radical, utopian and experimental movements and initiatives of the '60s, the evidence of current art terminology is discouraging. During the '70s and '80s the radical impulses of the '60s faltered and withered away in the more hostile economic and political climate, or they had to adapt, to allow themselves to be incorporated into official structures, in order to survive. For instance, 'Alternative Spaces' either had to close or to gain the support of Arts Councils and/or sponsors. In Britain the 'Free Form Arts Trust' began as a community arts organization in the late '60s. Unlike many similar organizations it has survived, but it has had to devise commercial strategies (such as a hoardings mural painting service to developers) in order to subsidize its more community-orientated projects.

Blacks, feminists and gays were three minorities that developed a new self-awareness in the late '60s. They did manage to strengthen their positions in the following two decades. More and more 'Black Art' shows were held, more and more galleries specializing in this kind of art were opened and self-help organizations such as 'Obaala' were founded. Meanwhile theorists debated such concepts as 'Negritude' and 'Orature'. The literature on 'Feminist Art' and aesthetics grew dramatically and important institutions such as the 'National Museum of Women in the Arts' and the 'Women Artists' Slide Library' were established in Washington and London respectively. Disquieting for some feminists, however, was the emergence of 'Post-Feminist Art'. 'Gay Art' was defined via several exhibitions and books but during the '80s the gay community was devastated by the deadly disease Aids and had to mobilize to combat it; hence the 'Art Against Aids' campaign in New York.

Gallery environments and site-specific works pre-dated the '80s, but in that decade 'Installations' and 'Site-Specific Art' became much more fashionable as artists became increasingly conscious of physical contexts. These forms of art apparently resisted the art-as-portable-commodity syndrome, but the Saatchis proved that even an Installation consisting of sump oil could be purchased. Viewing sculptures in natural settings proved increasingly popular as more and more 'Sculpture Parks' were opened to the public in Europe and North America.

Dramatic social, political and economic changes took place in the Soviet Union and Eastern Europe in the late 1980s. During the preceding period of oppression, many Soviet artists became exiles. Some managed to make successful careers in the West; the duo 'Komar & Melamid' for instance. Once the barriers to trade and travel were dismantled, a market in Russian art developed in the West. The radical changes in the USSR were reflected in the arts by the shift from 'Unofficial Soviet Art' to 'Sovart' (the name of an organization for exporting Soviet art: see under Unofficial Soviet Art). In the West 'Political Art' became accepted by the art market as a viable genre. This tended to blunt the critical edge of committed work. Nevertheless, many artists continued to protest against injustice, e.g. 'Artists Against Apartheid'.

Arguably, it was architecture and design that proved more glamorous and significant in the '80s than the arts of painting and sculpture. Indeed, the '80s were dubbed the *design decade*. In Britain, the designer-businessman Terence Conran and the design historian Stephen Bayley assiduously promoted the cause of industrial design via the 'Conran Foundation' and the Boilerhouse Project series of exhibitions held at the troubled Victoria & Albert Museum; they also established a new museum of design in London's 'Docklands'. Museums attracted enormous numbers of visitors but experienced crises of funding, management and direction; they were also the target of much critical analysis – witness the term 'New Museology'.

Neville Brody emerged as the decade's most influential graphic designer and the magazine whose layout and typography he designed – 'The Face' – founded by Nick Logan in 1980, for a time, lived up to its claim to be the best-dressed magazine in the world. 'Gridniks' was the neologism the British style expert Peter York coined to describe the new breed of graphic designers. Books on 'Cult Objects' such as 'Filofaxes' appeared (even *Marxism Today* published an article analysing this key yuppie accessory of the '80s). Concurrently, American and British design historians established scholarly societies and journals where they discussed such terms as 'Product Environment' and 'Product Semantics'.

Fusions and cross-overs were endemic in the realms of design, craft and art. Many instances of 'Architects' and 'Artists' Furniture' were recorded in several books and an American critic invented the ugly term 'Usable Art'. In New York 'Art et Industrie' encouraged artists and designers to swap roles, while in Britain various fine artists contributed to a show of 'Conceptual Clothing'.

'Post-Modernism' was a term that proved indispensable to writers in the realms of architecture and design. Charles Jencks, the architectural critic based in London and author of several books on 'Post-Modern Architecture', proved to be a prolific inventor of new labels. 'Abstract

Representation' was one of his more gnomic formulations. Jencks was not content merely to write about architecture, he also wanted to design it; hence his 'Symbolic Architecture' building projects. Within Post-Modernism, according to Jencks, 'Modernism' could continue as one of the many stylistic options, hence 'Late-Modern Architecture' and the continuation of 'High-Tech' in the work of such British architects as Norman Foster and Richard Rogers. In reaction to the vogues for 'Techno Functionalism', 'High-Tech', 'High-Touch' and 'Minimalist Design', there emerged in the '80s a new tendency towards colour and softness variously called 'Boldista' (in Italy) and 'Soft Design/Tech'.

'Japanese Design/Style' constantly set new standards in terms of product quality and innovation. In Milan 'Post-Industrial Design' was manifested in the colourful and kitschy furniture of the group 'Memphis', while in Britain nostalgia prevailed in the sphere of interior design, e.g. 'English Style', 'Laura Ashley Style', 'New Georgians'. However, outside the home 'Street Fashion' flourished and a renaissance took place in 'Retail Culture/Design' as the appeal of 'Lifestyle' lured more and more to the new, lavish hypermarkets and shopping malls. Barbara Kruger's slogan piece *I shop therefore I am* was never more apt.

Deciding what terms to include in this new edition proved problematical not only because of the sheer volume of new labels, but also because the dividing line between the traditional fine arts and mass cultural forms became more and more blurred. The term 'Comic Art', for example, has a double signification: it can refer to comics as art in their own right or to works of fine art whose iconography is based on comics. Some nations (e.g. Japan, France) rate comics much more highly than others so their status as art varies from country to country. The advent and subsequent popularity of 'Graphic Novels' tackling serious themes and written for adults, was a sign that comic books were capable of becoming high culture.

It was also symptomatic that one of the most innovative and popular forms of expression during the '80s was 'Animation' because animated films and videos involve a mix of media both traditional and modern: they combine drawing, modelling and film or videotape, words and images, music and movement. They also offer multiple possibilities in terms of how they are made and distributed, and in terms of the social purposes they serve, i.e. they can be drawn painstakingly by hand or rapidly with the aid of computers; they can be produced by individual art students or by teams of artists employed by Hollywood studios; they can appear in the cinema and on TV; and they can serve the ends of education, entertainment, propaganda, commerce and art. For all these reasons, it appears that Animation exemplifies the condition of contemporary visual culture more than the traditional forms of painting and sculpture.

For this new edition the vast majority of existing entries have been revised and updated. Some lesser-used and out-of-date terms have been deleted and several of the older ones have been shortened. In most cases, however, expansion has been necessary in respect of both entries and bibliographies in order to take account of artistic developments and publications since 1977. A number of new entries have been added to fill gaps for the period 1945 to 1977 and over 150 brand-new entries have been included to take account of terms that have appeared in the literature of art and design since the last edition. The general bibliography still consists of books giving national and international surveys and it is still arranged chronologically in date of publication order so that texts referring to the most recent trends in art and design appear last, but for greater convenience items have been rearranged under three headings: art, architecture and design. Unlike previous editions this one is illustrated. Assuming a picture really is worth a thousand words, the addition of images showing particular examples should significantly improve the book's usefulness.

INSTRUCTIONS FOR USE

When seeking a term, first look in the main A~Z sequence. If the term cannot be found, try the index at the back of the book because the term you require may be subsumed under another heading. **Numbers given in the index refer to A~Z entries not pages.**

Alphabetical filing is word by word rather than 'all through'. Groups and organizations commonly referred to by their acronyms rather than by their full titles (e.g. APG, KOS, SPADEM, TAC) have been entered under those headings and they have been treated as words for filing purposes.

Bibliographical citations at the foot of each entry refer to books, exhibition catalogues and periodical articles. They are given as fully as information permits and listed in date order so as to generate a chronological sequence of publications. The citation order for periodical articles is as follows: Author, title of article, name of periodical, (country of origin if an obscure journal), volume number (in bold), issue or part number (in brackets), month, year, page numbers. If no place of publication for books and catalogues is given, then it should be assumed to be London.

'See also' references at the foot of each entry provide a third system of connections. Their purpose is to draw the reader's attention to similar or closely related terms.

1 **ABORIGINAL ART**

(Also Abo Art, Dreamings) This term refers both to the 'primitive', 'stone age' arts and crafts of the native, nomadic tribes of Australia before the advent of British colonial rule and to works produced by Aborigines in recent decades. During the 1970s and '80s contemporary Aboriginal Art achieved a remarkable critical and financial success via exhibitions in Australia, Europe and the United States. In part this was due to the promotional efforts of the Aboriginal Arts Board of the Australia Council, to the work of the Aboriginal Arts Centre, Adelaide, and to the activities of various organizations marketing 'traditional' work made with modern artists' materials.

Originally the native tribes of Australia did not have a word for art or a specialist group called artists. However, they did make visual artefacts with animal and human images or geometric ornament, e.g. sand, bark and rock paintings, wood and rock carvings. They decorated tools and weapons such as paddles, shields and boomerangs; they also painted their bodies and engaged in sacred ceremonies, song cycles and dances ('corroborees') that involved the use of ritual figures and objects.

Modern Aboriginal artists, who are mainly men, respond to two cultures: their own tribal traditions and the influences of modern art and white culture. Many such artists adapt their own traditions in order to preserve them (on the grounds that 'cultural revival is survival') and to remind white viewers and collectors of the past crimes of Europeans and the Aborigines' present-day claims for land rights. Sales of paintings and tourist craftwork provide a much-needed source of income for Aborigines.

In the 1930s Albert Namatjira (1902–59) of the Aranda tribe who lived near the Hermannsburg Mission, Central Australia, was encouraged to take up painting by the water colourist Rex Battarbee. Other Aborigines followed suit and the Hermannsburg School came into being. Namatjira's work was non-Aboriginal in style. Later, in 1971, Aborigines in the Western Desert were introduced to painting with acrylics on canvas by Geoff Bardon. This gave rise to so-called 'Papunya painting'. Aboriginal paintings (i.e. those based on native culture) are normally executed flat on the ground and usually employ an iconography of dots, circles, semi-circles, parallel lines and schematized snakes. Popular colours are white, ochre, brown and red. The paintings resemble aerial views of stone age settlements. Part of their appeal to white collectors is their visual similarity to abstract art. Abo painting is not in fact abstract: it is based on myths and stories called 'Dreamings', e.g. the dream of the possum. Not all symbolic meanings are revealed to white viewers.

During the '80s Aboriginal Art and white Australian art was shown side by side for the first time in Europe and in 1986 the Ramingining Performance Group presented a post-funeral cleansing ceremony in public at the Sydney Biennale. Aboriginal painters were also represented in this exhibition. Well- known Aboriginal artists include: Gordon Bennett, George Milpurrurru, Sally Morgan, George Mung Mung, Trevor Nickolls, Lin Onus, Jimmy Pike, Paddy Japaljarri Sims, Rover Thomas, Michael Nelson Tjakamarra, Clifford Possum Tjapaltjarri, Charlie Tjapangatti, Patricia Torres, Paddy Fordham Wainburranga and Uta Uta Tjangala Yumari. Rikki Shields is an Aboriginal artist who has employed modern media such as photography and film. Some white artists in Australia have also been influenced by Aboriginal designs so 'aboriginality' is no longer confined to the native people.

In 1990 a festival of Aboriginal culture called 'Tagari Lia: My Family' featuring paintings, sculptures, prints, films, videos, photographs, dances, songs, plays, poetry readings and talks by both outback and urban artists was held at the Third Eye Centre, Glasgow. The festival was claimed to be the most comprehensive survey presented outside Australia.

● See also Black Art, Ethnic Art, Hybrid Culture.

● R Berndt (ed) *Australian Aboriginal Art* (Sydney, Ure Smith, 1964).

● S Nairne & others *State of the art: ideas and images in the 1980s* (Chatto & Windus/Channel 4 TV, 1987).

● P Sutton (ed) *Dreamings: the art of Aboriginal Australia* (NY, The Asia Society Galleries, 1988).

● M West (ed) *The inspired dream: life as art in Aboriginal Australia* (Brisbane, Queensland Art Gallery, 1988).

● T Fry & AM Willis 'Aboriginal Art: symptom or success?'

Art in America **77** (7) July 1989 108–16, + 159–63.

● J Ryan *Mythscapes: Aboriginal Art of the desert* (Melbourne, National Gallery of Victoria, 1989).

● R Benjamin 'Report from Australia: Aboriginal Art: exploitation or empowerment?' *Art in America* **78** (7) July 1990 73–81.

● A Bourke (curator), L Onus & T Smith (essays) *Contemporary Aboriginal Art 1990 from Australia* (Sydney, Aboriginal Arts Management Association; Glasgow, Third Eye Centre Publications, 1990).

2 ABSOLUTE ARCHITECTURE

A proposal for a pure, non-objective and purposeless architecture made by Walter Pichler and Hans Hollein in 1962. Such architecture would be the antithesis of functionalism; its form would be dictated by the individual architect's imagination, not by utilitarian requirements. In other words, this kind of architecture aspired to the condition of fine art or music. The term was also used by the innovative and individualistic American architect Bruce Goff (1904–82) for whom it served as an ideal; he imagined non-functional buildings or 'walk-in sculptures' that were simply formal explorations of space and structure.

● See also Conceptual Architecture, Radical Design, Utopian Architecture.

● V Conrads (ed) *Programmes and manifestos on twentieth-century architecture* (Lund Humphries, 1970).

● D de Long *Bruce Goff: toward Absolute Architecture* (Cambridge, Mass, MIT Press, 1988).

3 ABSTRACT EXPRESSIONISM

(Also American-Type Painting) A major movement in American painting dating from the 1940s and '50s; the first to be acclaimed and imitated throughout the world. The term 'Abstract Expressionism' was first used in the 1920s to refer to the work of Kandinsky; Robert Coates of the *New Yorker* applied it to American painting in 1945. (Clement Greenberg was the critic who, following Patrick Heron, forwarded the term 'American-type painting' in a 1955 *Partisan Review* article.) The movement's name suggested it was a synthesis of two earlier idioms – abstraction (Hans Hofmann's work derived ultimately from Cubism) and expressionism – but this was an over-simplification because several other influences were also crucial to its formation: surrealism, Oriental calligraphy, Mexican and Works Progress Administration mural paintings and 'primitive' art.

The principal Abstract Expressionists were Arshile Gorky (regarded as a transitional figure), Jackson Pollock, Willem de Kooning, Franz Kline, Mark Rothko, Barnett Newman, Clyfford Still, Philip Guston, Robert Motherwell, Mark Tobey, Theodore Stamos and Adolph Gottlieb. They did not subscribe to a single style but did fall into two main camps: the gestural or action painters (Pollock, de Kooning, Kline) and the colour-field painters (Rothko, Newman, Still). They also tended to work in an all-over manner on large canvases (reflecting the influence of mural painting) and to stress the creative act or process of painting.

Their paintings often appeared to be completely abstract but this was a misleading impression because most of the Abstract Expressionists did not seek total abstraction: de Kooning painted women and landscapes, even late Pollock drip paintings included figuration, and the majority of the artists laid great stress on 'subject matter', i.e. tragic and timeless themes represented via a type of indirect symbolism called 'ideographs' (defined by Newman in 1947 as characters, symbols or figures suggesting the idea of an object without expressing its name). An artschool Newman, Rothko and Still established in 1948 was called, significantly, 'Subjects of the artist'.

Although Mark Tobey worked on the West Coast, Abstract Expressionism was primarily a New York phenomenon – consequently in the '40s the term 'New York School' was synonymous with the movement. The literature on Abstract Expressionism is now vast; the bibliography below ignores catalogues and monographs on individual artists in order to concentrate on books providing general surveys.

● See also Abstract Imagists, Abstract Sublime, Action Painting, All-Over Painting, Automatic Art, Calligraphic Painting, Colour-Field Painting, Drip Painting, New York School, Process Art, Tachisme.

● B Newman *The ideographic picture* (NY, Betty Parsons Gallery, 1947).

● P Pavia 'The unwanted title: Abstract Expressionism' *It Is* (5) Spring 1960 8–11.

● I Sandler *Abstract Expressionism: the triumph of American Painting* (Pall Mall Press, 1970).

● M Tuchman (ed) *The New York School: Abstract Expressionism in the '40s & '50s* (Thames & Hudson, 1970).

● D Ashton *The life and times of the New York School* (NY, Viking Press/Bath, Adams & Dart, 1972).

● C Greenberg 'American-Type Painting' (1955) – in – *Art and culture* (Thames & Hudson, 1973) 208–29.

● E Cockcroft 'Abstract Expressionism: weapon of the cold war' *Artforum* **12** (10) June 1974 39–41.

● S Foster *The critics of Abstract Expressionism* (Ann Arbor, Michigan, University of Michigan Research Press, 1981).

● R Hobbs & G Levin *Abstract Expressionism: the formative years* (Ithaca, New York, Cornell University Press, 1981).

● A Cox *Art-as-politics: the Abstract Expressionist avant garde and society* (Ann Arbor, Michigan, University of Michigan Research Press, 1983).

● S Guilbaut *How New York stole the idea of modern art* (Chicago, University of Chicago Press, 1984).

● W Seitz *Abstract Expressionist art in America* (Cambridge Mass, Harvard University Press, 1984).

● M Auping & others *Abstract Expressionism: the critical developments* (Thames & Hudson, 1987).

● 'New myths for old: redefining Abstract Expressionism' *Art Journal* **47** (3) Fall 1988.

● D & C Shapiro (eds) *Abstract Expressionism: a critical record* (Cambridge University Press, 1990).

● S Polcari *Abstract Expressionism and the modern experience* (Cambridge University Press, 1991).

4 ABSTRACT EXPRESSIONIST CERAMICS & SCULPTURES

In the mid 1950s a group of West Coast artists emerged – Billy Al Bengston, Mike Frinkens, John Mason, Jim Melchert, Kenneth Price and Peter Voulkos – who produced experimental ceramics and polychrome sculptures which, according to John Coplans writing in 1966, was strongly influenced by Abstract Expressionism. Nicolas and Elena Calas also identified certain other American sculptors whose work during the late '50s and early '60s emulated the qualities of improvisation and loose structure characteristic of Abstract Expressionist paintings, i.e. Richard Stankiewicz, John Chamberlain, Mark di Suvero and Claire Falkenstein. These sculptors rejected the traditional methods of sculpture – carving and modelling – preferring instead to assemble pieces from junk materials. Of the Abstract Expressionists themselves, Barnett Newman and Willem de Kooning have produced sculptures.

● See also Assemblage Art, Funk Art, Junk Sculpture.

● J Coplans 'Abstract Expressionist ceramics' *Artforum* **5** (3) November 1966 34–41.

● N & E Calas 'Abstract Expressionist sculpture' – in – *Icons and images of the sixties* (NY, Dutton, 1971) 50–8.

5 ABSTRACT ILLUSIONISM

(Also Perverse Perspectives) A tendency in American abstract painting of the mid 1960s, noted by Barbara Rose in October 1967, marked by a return to illusionism. The painters concerned – Darby Bannard, Ron Davis, Jules Olitski, Frank Stella, Larry Zox and others – used such pictorial devices as two-point perspective, orthographic drawing, and cool/warm colour contrasts in order to achieve depth effects. Lucy Lippard called this new, incongruous illusionism 'perverse perspectives'. It incorporated, she said, 'the statement of the flat surface of a painting' and the 'counter statement of an inverse perspective that juts out into the spectator's space'. In 1972 the English critic Bryan Robertson also employed the term 'Abstract Illusionism' to characterize the sculptures of Kenneth Draper, Nigel Hall and William Tucker and the paintings of Paul Huxley and Bridget Riley.

● See also Op Art.

● L Lippard 'Perverse Perspectives' *Art International* **11** (3) March 20 1967 28–33, + 44.

● B Rose 'Abstract Illusionism' *Artforum* **6** (2) 1967 33–7.

● B Robertson *British sculpture* '72 (Royal Academy, 1972).

6 ABSTRACT IMAGISTS

A term derived from an exhibition organized by the American art historian H. H. Arnason in 1961. It is a somewhat contradictory label since 'abstract' suggests 'no image' while 'imagist' suggests 'representation'. The term was intended to distinguish the non-expressionist artists of the abstract expressionist movement – Mark Rothko, Barnett Newman, Adolph Gottlieb, Ad Reinhardt and Clyfford Still – from those like de Kooning, Pollock and Kline who favoured a gestural mode of painting. The artists in question produced canvases with large, flatly painted areas of colour and sign-like motifs suggestive of some kind of symbolic content. 'Quietistic' and 'colour-field' were other labels applied to this kind of art. Arnason's show also included works by a younger generation of abstract artists, e.g. Kenneth Noland, Frank Stella, Ellsworth Kelly, and consequently the term has been deemed to apply to them too.

● See also Abstract Expressionism, Action Painting, Colour-Field Painting.

● H Arnason *American Abstract Expressionists and Imagists* (NY, Guggenheim Museum, 1961).

7 ABSTRACT IMPRESSIONISM

Elaine de Kooning coined this term in 1951 to describe paintings with a uniform pattern of brushstrokes, which retained the optical effects of impressionism while dispensing with its representational content. One consequence of the success of the abstract expressionist movement had been a re-evaluation of the large-scale, all-over paintings by Claude Monet. In 1956 Louis Finkelstein called Philip Guston's paintings 'Abstract Impressionist' in order to distinguish them from the more violent action painters. Two years later the British Arts Council supported an exhibition organized by Lawrence Alloway entitled 'Abstract Impressionism' which included works by Bernard and Harold Cohen, Nicholas de Staël, Sam Francis, Patrick Heron, Pierre Tal Coat, Joan Mitchell and Jean-Paul Riopelle. Aldo Pellegrini, the Argentine critic, also applied the label to a group of French abstractionists – Jean Bazaine, Alfred Manessier and Gustave Singier – whose paintings were popular in the immediate post-1945 period.

● L Finkelstein 'New look: Abstract Impressionism' *Art News* **55** (1) March 1956 36–9, 66–8.

● E Corbett *Abstract Impressionism* (South Hadley, Mass, Mount Holyoke College, 1957).

● L Alloway *Abstract Impressionism* (Arts Council of Great Britain, 1958).

● A Pellegrini *New tendencies in art* (NY, Crown, 1966).

8 ABSTRACT LANDSCAPE

(Also Dépaysage, Paysagisme Abstrait) A mode of painting practised in the mid 1950s by a number of artists belonging to the School of Paris, i.e. Roger Bissière, Vieira da Silva, James Guitet, John Koenig, Pierre Tal Coat and Zao Wou-Ki. Michel Ragon, the French critic, coined the term 'paysagisme abstrait' in 1956 to characterize abstract paintings which by their naturalistic colours and atmospheric use of tones suggested natural landscapes. In some instances the 'landscape' referred to was an internal, mental one rather than an external one. Bissière (1888–1964) always used nature as a starting-point and therefore denied that his paintings, despite their lack of recognizable objects, were abstract.

● See also Abstract Impressionism, All-Over Painting.

● M Ragon *Vingt cinq ans d'art vivant* (Paris, Casterman, 1969).

9 ABSTRACT REPRESENTATION

Title of a thematic issue of *Architectural Design* edited by Charles Jencks. The conjunction of 'abstract' and

ABSTRACT LANDSCAPE ROGER BISSIERE, 'Paysage' (1956). Oil on canvas, 18" x 22". Photo: courtesy of Hanover Gallery, London.

'representation' was paradoxical because normally the two words would be considered mutually exclusive. 'Abstract' was equated with modern architecture because it made an ideal of pure, geometric forms or those composed according to logical systems, while 'representation' was equated with post-modern architecture because it marked a return to analogies, figuration, symbolism and ornament. Abstract Representation, therefore, was conceived of as a synthesis of late-modern architecture (or 'the new abstraction') and post-modern architecture (or 'the new representation'). According to Jencks, the synthesis was exemplified in the 1980s work of Hans Hollein and Michael Graves. Their architecture combined the rational clarity of abstractionism with the accessibility of the best of post-modernism. It also involved 'veiled representation', i.e. representation was present but abstracted to avoid being too obvious.

● See also Analogical Architecture, Figurative Architecture, Late-Modern Architecture, Post-Modern Architecture, Symbolic Architecture.

● C Jencks (ed) 'Abstract Representation' *Architectural Design* **53** (7/8) 1983.

10 ABSTRACT SUBLIME

(Also American Sublime) A term used by the American critic Robert Rosenblum in 1961 in reference to paintings by certain members of the abstract expressionist movement. Barnett Newman had previously employed the word 'sublime' in connection with his own work in 1948, having been influenced by Edmund Burke's theory of the contrast between the beautiful (smoothness, gentle curves, polish, delicacy) and the sublime (terrible objects, obscurity, solitude, vastness). Rosenblum found similarities between paintings of the sublime in nature by such romantic movement artists as James Ward, Casper David Friedrich and J. M. W. Turner and paintings by the abstract expressionists Jackson Pollock, Mark Rothko, Newman and Clyfford Still. This parallel has also been discussed by Lawrence Alloway.

● See also Abstract Expressionism.

● 'The ides of art 6: opinions on "what is sublime in art?"' *Tigers Eye* **1** (6) December 1948 46–56.

● S Monk *The sublime: a study of critical theories in eighteenth-century England* (Ann Arbor, Michigan, University of Michigan Press, 1960).

● R Rosenblum 'The Abstract Sublime' (1961) – in – *New York painting and sculpture 1940–70* by H Geldzahler & others (Pall Mall Press, 1969) 350–9.

● L Alloway 'American Sublime' *Living Arts* (2) 1963 11–22.

11 ACANTHUS

The acanthus is a Mediterranean plant much used in architectural decoration. For this reason it was adopted as the name for a nationwide network of twelve British, medium-sized, independent architectural practices – Acanthus Associated Architectural Practices Ltd – dedicated to the principle of working with artists and craftspersons for the purpose of raising the standards of design and craft in architecture. Acanthus was established in 1986. George Ferguson of Ferguson Mann, Bristol was the founder and first chairman. In 1988 Acanthus organized a conference in Edinburgh on the theme of artists and architecture. Acanthus claims to represent an attitude towards architecture, not a style; it respects the past without reproducing it and stands for permanence rather than fashion in design.

● See also Art & Architecture.

▨ G Ferguson 'A new beaux arts?' *Town & Country Planning* **57** (5) May 1988 13–45.

▨ A Armstrong 'Design network' *Traditional Homes* **4** (12) September 1988 88–91.

ACANTHUS DAVID WRIGHTSON, Michael Balston (designers for Balston Lawrence & Wrightson) & John Shuffleton (sculptor for Rattee & Kett), 'Triton's Head' (1985). Produced for the Landscape Ornament Company. Photo: ACANTHUS.

12 ACME

The ACME Housing Association was a charitable organization established in London in 1972 for the purpose of obtaining living and studio spaces for artists by renting short-life property and buying old buildings. In 1976 ACME opened a gallery in Covent Garden to display works by members.

▨ *The ACME Housing Association* (ACME, 1976).

13 ACTION ARCHITECTURE

An expression coined by the American architect George Kallmann in 1959 to describe the work of a new generation of architects who sought 'fierce, direct and brutal action in design', who used materials 'as found', and who responded to particular situations. (Clearly, the concept of Action Architecture was comparable to that of action painting.) According to Peter Collins, the term referred to architecture created with the aid of sketches rather than exact working drawings. Charles Jencks, on the other hand, defined it as 'the generation of form through the repetition and development of an idea'. A building influenced by these ideas was the Boston City Hall (1964–9) by Kallmann, McKinnell & Knowles.

● See also Action Painting.

▨ G Kallmann 'The "Action" architecture of a new generation' *Architectural Forum* **111** (4) October 1959 132–7, 244.

▨ P Collins *Changing ideals in modern architecture* (Faber & Faber, 1965).

▨ C Jencks *Modern movements in architecture* (Harmondsworth, Penguin Books, 1973), 226–8.

14 ACTION OFFICE

A flexible system of office furniture for individuals or companies, capable of being arranged in a variety of configurations. It was designed in 1964 by the American architect George Nelson for the furniture manufacturer Herman Miller Inc., after a research study into the work patterns of American business executives conducted by Robert Propst.

● See also Bürolandschaft.

▨ G Nelson 'Action Office' *Architectural Design* **36** (2) February 1966 101.

▨ R Cuddon 'Design review: office furniture' *Architectural Review* **140** (837) November 1966 369–70.

15 ACTION PAINTING

(Also Gestural Painting) Harold Rosenberg, a critic writing for *Art News,* invented this term in 1952 to describe works by certain members of the abstract expressionist movement: Jackson Pollock, Franz Kline, Willem de Kooning and Jack Tworkov. The painting of these artists was improvisational in character and depended upon the unconscious as a source of inspiration: it extended into oil painting the automatic drawing/writing technique favoured by the surrealists. Paintings were gestural in the sense that they consisted of a loose structure of brushmarks or dripped skeins of pigment reflecting emphatic movements of the painter's hand, arm and indeed the whole body. The term also referred to the existential act of painting; the process of making became as important as the end result. (The question 'when can a painting be regarded as finished?' was a major talking point at the time.) Rosenberg considered the canvas an arena within which the painter could perform, the result being not so much a picture as an event. To which Mary MacCarthy riposted: 'you cannot hang an event on a wall, only a picture'. Rosenberg's conception of abstract expressionism was contested by his main critical rival Clement Greenberg who proposed a different account of the movement.

● See also Abstract Expressionism, Automatic Art, Drip Painting, Process Art, Tachisme.

● H Rosenberg 'The American Action Painters' – in – *The tradition of the new* (Thames & Hudson, 1962) 23–39.

● — 'The premises of Action Painting' *Encounter* **20** (5) May 1963 47–50.

● — 'Action Painting: crisis and distortion' – in – *The anxious object: art today and its audience* (Thames & Hudson, 1965) 38–47.

● M Rowell *La peinture, le geste, l' action: l' existentialisme en peinture* (Paris, Éditions Klincksieck, 1972).

16 ACTIONS

(Or Aktionen) The word 'aktion' has been popular in German art circles at least since the publication of *Die Aktion* (1911), the magazine of German expressionism. It means 'activity', 'process', 'undertaking'. In the context of German and Austrian art of the '60s and '70s it referred to a form of event similar to the Happenings of New York. In Bern an art gallery – the 'Aktiongalerie' – was devoted to this kind of work. Austrian artists belonging to the 'Weiner Aktionismus' movement advocated 'material action'. To this end they organised rituals which, they claimed, were real (direct, literal events) as against the pretended reality of theatrical performances. Actions often implied a social and political consciousness among artists: the idea that art could be used to intervene in society to change it for the better. Joseph Beuys founded a political party and in such Actions as the one at the Tate Gallery in 1972 he involved the public in a debate about politics, art and education. Beuys also called this kind of activity 'social sculpture'.

'Action' was also a word popular with community artists in Britain (e.g. the London groups Action Space – founded in 1968 and led by Ken Turner, and Inter-Action) and with radical groups in the USA (e.g. Guerrilla Art Action).

● See also Community Art, Direct Art, Fluxus, Guerrilla Art Action Group, Happenings, Haus-Rucke- Co, Inter-Change, Performance Art, Process Art.

● W Vostell *Aktionen: Happenings und demonstrationen seit 1965* (Hamburg, Rowohlt, 1970).

● *Joseph Beuys Aktioner Aktionen* (Stockholm, Moderna Museet, 1971).

● F Popper *Art – Action and participation* (Studio Vista, 1975).

● J Schilling *Aktionkunst* (Frankfurt, Bucher Verlag, 1978).

17 ACTUAL ART

A type of street art or happenings performed in Prague in the mid 1960s by a number of Czechoslovakian artists calling themselves 'Art of the Actual' or 'Group Actual'. They were led by Milan Knizak and participants included Sona Svecova, Vit Mach and Jan Trtilek. The Czech authorities were disturbed by the 'live art' activities of Group Actual and in 1973 Knizak was arrested and spent time in prison for his allegedly anti-revolutionary attitude.

● See also Actions, Happenings, Living Art, Street Art.

● A Kaprow *Assemblage, Environments and Happenings* (NY, Abrams, 1965) 299–310.

● M Knizak 'Actual in Czechoslovakia' *Art & Artists* **7** (7) October 1972 40–3.

● (Special issue on Czech art) *Schmuck* January 1974.

18 ADHOCISM

A term coined by Charles Jencks in 1968 to describe a method of architectural design in which each part of a building, or complex of buildings, was produced in an 'ad hoc' manner, i.e. separately by a specialist or an expert with little regard to the conception as a whole. Architects, Jencks claimed, no longer needed to design new forms because they could collage buildings together from ready-made materials, parts and prefabricated units selected from catalogues. Adhocism also meant improvisation, the rapid solution of design problems with whatever was at hand. The term 'bricolage' derived from the anthropologist Claude Lévi-Strauss was also invoked. (A bricoleur was an odd-job person or handyman.)

● See also Creative Salvage.

● C Jencks 'Criticism: Adhocism on the South Bank' *Architectural Review* **144** (857) July 1968 27–30.

● C Jencks & N Silver 'The case for improvisation' *Architectural Design* **42** (10) October 1972 604–7.

● —*Adhocism* (Secker & Warburg, 1972).

● R Banham 'Arts in society: Bricologues à la lanterne' *New Society* **37** (717) July 1 1976 25–6.

● D McConaghy 'The limitations of advocacy' *RIBA Journal* **80** (2) February 1972 63–6.

19 ADVOCACY PLANNING

An American concept dating from the 1960s: the term was first used by the planner Paul Davidoff. It denotes planning and architectural design done on behalf of minority or deprived groups within cities, especially when fighting against unfavourable redevelopment schemes and plans for motorways. Socially conscious individuals and groups such as ARCH represented – as legal advocates do – the views of ordinary people when negotiating with planning authorities.

● See also ARCH, Community Architecture, Participatory Design, Social Architecture/Design.

● P Davidoff 'Advocacy and pluralism in planning' *Journal of the American Institute in Planning* **31** (4) November 1965 331–8.

● 'Advocacy planning: what it is, how it works' *Progressive Architecture* **49** September 1968 102–15.

● 'Advocacy: a community planning voice' *Design Quarterly* (82/83) 1971.

20 AFFICHES LACÉRÉES

(Also Affiches Déchirées, Affichistes, Décollage) The peeling, torn or lacerated posters found on walls and hoardings in major cities have fascinated a number of European artists in the twentieth century. These damaged surfaces exposing several layers of fragmented, jumbled images and words were removed and collected by certain artists and included in exhibitions of the Nouveau Réalisme movement during the early '60s at which time they were praised by the critic Pierre Restany. Raymond Hains, a French photographer, began collecting torn posters in Paris in 1949; later he was joined by Jacques de la Villeglé. In 1959, another Frenchman, Francois Dufrêne became interested, especially in the reverse sides of posters. Two Italians – Mimmo Rotella and Alberti Moretti – also became affichistes independently of the French during the 1950s, as did the German Wolf Vostell (he was in Paris in the mid '50s).

The affichistes employed various methods: posters were selected and then removed as found, or via the process of 'décollage' (literally 'unpasting'): posters were torn down and then reconstituted on canvas; in some

AFFICHES LACÉRÉES WOLF VOSTELL, 'A LOS TORROS' (1961). Décollage 120cm x 200cm. Photo: Galerie Baecker, Bochum.

instances their backs were rubbed to generate new images. Rotella later devised a method of photographing décollages onto sensitized canvas.

To some extent tattered posters resembled the abstract shapes of action and tachist paintings but since fragments of lettering and popular imagery often remained, they also had affinities with concrete poetry and pop art. The various affichistes differed in their intentions: some were intrigued by torn posters as aesthetic compositions while others viewed them as a means of undertaking a critique of advertising and, by defacing them and tearing them down, making a protest against consumer society.

Léo Malet, a surrealist, claims to have originated the idea of décollage in 1934. It was a word Wolf Vostell found useful when he participated in the Fluxus movement in Germany during the '60s. For Vostell 'décollage' meant more than merely tearing, overpainting and burning posters: it signified the destruction associated with human behaviour (e.g. car crashes) and the dissolution inherent in life itself. In response to this insight, he devised a series of mixed-media, chaotic destructive events which he called 'Décoll/age-Happenings'. He also edited a magazine entitled *Décoll/age* which featured his own work and that of his Fluxus colleagues.

● See also Actions, Billboard Art, Concrete Poetry, Demontage, Destructive Art, Fluxus, Happenings, Nouveau Réalisme, Pop Art.

● *Décoll/age* (Cologne, (1–7) 1962–9).

● P Restany *Rotella: dal décollage alla nuova immagine* (Milan, Edizioni Apollinaire, 1963).

● W Vostell 'Dé-coll-age' *Art & Artists* **1** (5) August 1966 9–10.

● J de la Villeglé 'L'Affiche Lacérée: ses successives immixtions dans les arts' *Leonardo* **2** (1) January 1969 33–44.

● L Malet 'A new art medium (1): how poetry devours walls' *Leonardo* **2** (4) October 1969 419–20.

● W Vostell *Décoll/agen 1954–69* (Berlin, Galerie René Block, 1969).

● J Merkert 'PreFluxus Vostell' *Art & Artists* **8** (2) May 1973 32–7.

● T Trini *Rotella* (Milan, Giampaolo Prearo Editore, 1974).

● S Peters 'Vostell and the vengeful environment' *Art in America* **63** (3) May–June 1975 50–1.

● J-B Lebrun 'Les "affichistes" de la rage à la froideur' *XXe Siécle* **37** (45) December 1975 63–72.

● B Schwabsky & S Hunter *Rotella: décollages 1954–64* (Milan, Studio Marconi/Electa, 1986).

● 'Les Affichistes' *Opus International* (112) February–March 1989.

● C Fournet & F-J Pirion *Villeglé: la peinture dans la nonpeinture* (Paris, Marval, 1989).

● C Phillips 'When poetry devours the walls' *Art in America* **78** (2) February 1990 138–45.

21 AIR

The initials of two organizations, one American and one British. AIR (USA) – Artists in Residency, housing the Women's Art Registry – was founded in 1972 by Susan Williams and Barbara Zucker. AIR was one of the consequences of the emergence of the feminist art movement in the late 1960s. It is a women artists' co-operative and gallery. In 1977 Slyvia Sleigh painted an 'AIR group portrait' depicting leading members of the co-operative.

AIR (UK) – Art Information Registry – was a London organization founded in October 1967 by Peter Sedgley, Stuart Brisley and others in order to provide a channel between artists and their public, and to act as an alternative to the commercial gallery system. The registry, or artists' index, consisted of slides, photographs, press cuttings, catalogues and biographical details relating to over 500 British artists. For a time AIR published a directory of addresses (*Airmail*) and a newsletter. An exhibition space – the AIR Gallery – was also opened which mounted shows of work by members and by young, unknown artists. During the 1980s, when the gallery was run by Sara Selwood and Jenny Lockwood, it encouraged live art, performance, video and installations concerned with social and political issues. Owing to lack of public funds the gallery closed in March 1989. Selwood and Lockwood responded by founding 'Art & Society', a 'non-venue art agency' for the purpose of organizing projects in collaboration with other bodies on such themes as human rights and the problems of immigrants.

● See also Alternative Spaces, Feminist Art, SPACE.

● S Braden 'A.I.R. R.A. R.I.P? S.P.A.C.E.D.' *Time Out* (84) September 24–30 1971 20–1.

● *Report on Art Information Registry 1967–71* (AIR, 1971).

● D Palazzoli 'Minus times equals plus' (AIR, USA) *Domus* (520) March 1973 47–9.

● C Cumberlidge 'As one door shuts' *Independent Media* (89) May 1989 17.

● S Selwood & J Lockwood 'Art & Society' *AND Journal of Art & Art Education* (20) 1989 42–3.

22 AIR ART

(Including Blow-up Art, Gonflable Art, Inflatable Sculpture, Sky Art/Sculpture) A broad category encompassing a variety of structures and activities which have in common the fact that they exploit the possibilities of compressed air, or the natural forces of the wind, usually in association with plastic envelopes of different kinds. Air Art can be regarded as a sub-species of kinetic art since movement is normally involved. It gained attention as a result of three exhibitions held in the late 1960s: (1) 'Structures Gonflables' (Paris, Musée d'Art Moderne, 1968); (2) 'Air Art' (Philadelphia Arts Council, 1968); (3) 'Inflatable Sculpture' (New York, Jewish Museum, 1969). Amongst the artists participating in these shows were Charles Frazier, Hans Haacke, Les Levine, David Medalla, Robert Morris, Otto Piene and Andy Warhol. Most were not specialists in Air Art but Piene, a German working in the United States, had been obsessed with sky works for some years. Apologists for Air Art found precedents in the art of Leonardo, Duchamp, Klein and Manzoni. The significant qualities of Air Art were its public character (sky works can be seen by thousands), its participatory potential (the appeal of inflatables to children and athletic adults), and its contribution to the anti- or post-object trend in the art of the late '60s.

Artists committed to this form of art, like Piene or Graham Stevens (of the Eventstructure Research Group), tended in their excitement at its future prospects to make exaggerated claims that, for instance, air structures were cultural expressions of the energy continuum of the universe, or that they had a revolutionary potential for social change. Most Air artists demonstrated a strong interest in science and new technologies (particularly video, computers, lasers, telecommunications, spaceships and satellites).

During the 1980s the term 'Sky Art' seemed to become more popular than Air Art: in 1981, '83 and '86 the Center for Advanced Visual Studies at MIT organized conferences and exhibitions of 'Sky Art' which brought together artists and scientists from many countries, while in 1982 a Sky Art conference was held at Ars Electronica, Linz, Austria. Sky Art encompassed such activities as flying kites, firework displays, using aircraft to draw smoke patterns in the sky or to pull banners with poems on them, projecting laser light beams, using solar power to generate burn images, employing slowscan radio and television transmissions, seeding clouds with crystals (Eugene Malic, the artist–pilot responsible for the latter, belonged to the Enigmatic Art Group, protoArt and called his work 'ecological aesthetics' and 'weather art'). It was only to be expected that many Sky artists would extend their interests to outer space: they proposed interstellar broadcasts, spaceship sculptures, employing satellites for photographic projects or designing satellites as works of art. Some of these artists employed the term 'Space Art'.

● See also Ecological Art, Electronic Art, Environmental Art, Eventstructure, Holographic Art, Kinetic Art, Laser Art, Pneumatic Architecture, Soft Art, Space Art, Technological Art, Telematics, Utopie Group.

● W Sharp 'Air Art' *Studio International* **175** (900) May 1968 262–5.

● J Glusberg 'Air Art one' *Art & Artists* **3** (10) January 1969 40–9.

● N Frackman 'Inflatable Sculpture' *Arts Magazine* **44** (1) September–October 1969 55.

● G Stevens 'Pneumatics and atmospheres' *Architectural Design* **43** (3) March 1972 165–71.

●— 'Blowup' *Art & Artists* **7** (2) May 1972 42–5.

● O Piene *More Sky Art* (Cambridge, Mass, MIT Press, 1973).

● H Woody 'Kinetic environmental art: Sky Sculpture' *Leonardo* **7** (3) Summer 1974 207–10.

● *Sky Art conference '81* (Cambridge, Mass, CAVS/MIT, 1981).

● *Sky Art conference '82* (Linz, 1982).

● *Sky Art conference '83* (Cambridge, Mass, CAVS/MIT, 1983).

23 ALCHIMIA (Also Studio Alchymia) An Italian design co-operative of architects and designers influential in the late 1970s and early '80s. It was established by Alessandro Guerriero in Milan in 1976 and participants included Alessandro Mendini, Ettore Sottsass and Andrea Branzi. The name 'Alchimia' was selected to suggest mystery and magic; in Italian the word means 'alchemy' but also

ALCHIMIA Adriana Guerriero of Alchimia sitting on the 'Proust' armchair, 1978 (Bau Haus Collection, 1979) designed by ALESSANDRO MENDINI. Photo: Fruitmarket Gallery, Edinburgh, 1989.

'deception, falsification'. One aim of Alchimia was to manufacture and sell experimental designs, not just conceive them. The products they made were post-modernist in their ironic use of historical styles, inappropriate decorative fabrics, pastel colours, irrational shapes and references to pop culture. Alchimia marked a reaction against the uniformity and dullness of international product design. Rejection of the principles of modernism was indicated by the irreverent 'Bau Haus' collection of 1979. Mendini, a theorist and editor of the magazines *Domus* and *Modo,* specialized in 'false' and 'infinite' furniture intended to amaze and provoke, while Branzi proposed a 'Gallery of Copyism', i.e. second-hand furniture painted with pastiches of Kandinsky and Mondrian. Sottsass departed in 1981 to found Memphis.

● See also Italian Craze, Memphis, Post-Modernism, Radical Design.

● B Radice *Elogia del banale* (Milan, Studio Forma, 1980).

● A Branzi *The hot house: Italian new wave design* (Cambridge, Mass, MIT Press, 1984).

● S Casciani & P Bontempi *Alchimia* (Milan, Idea Books, 1985).

24 ALL-OVER PAINTING

Works avoiding any kind of central composition or concentrations of forms into areas of special interest to create figure/ground effects and hierarchies of forms. They are usually painted in a flat, uniform manner or with accents distributed evenly across the surface of the canvas, filling it up to the framing edges. The term has been applied to the drip paintings of Jackson Pollock and also the late works of Claude Monet. The scientist C. H. Waddington found a link between all-overness in art and in science: i.e. the everywhere-dense continuum of events concept that replaced the 'billiard ball' atomic theory of matter.

● See also Colour-Field Painting, Drip Painting, Monochromatic & Monotonal Painting, Non-Relational Art.

● 'Panel: All-Over Painting' *It Is* (2) Autumn 1958 72–7.

● C Waddington *Behind Appearance...* (Edinburgh University Press, 1969).

25 ALLIANCE GRAPHIQUE INTERNATIONALE (AGI)

An organization founded in 1950 by two Swiss graphic designers Donald Brun and Fritz Bühler and three French designers Jean Colin, Jacques Nathan-Garamond, and Jean Picart Le Doux. They felt the need for an association that would facilitate international contacts and exchanges of ideas amongst creative graphic artists. AGI holds congresses that take place in different countries every year; it also mounts exhibitions of the work of members.

● R de Harak (ed) *Posters by members of the Alliance Graphique Internationale 1960–85* (NY, Rizzoli, 1986).

● F Henrion *AGI annals: Alliance Graphique Internationale 1952–87* (Rotovision, 1989).

26 ALTERNATIVE ARTS

An all-woman, community organization founded in London in 1970 promoting popular entertainments in public places, e.g. street theatre, Punch & Judy shows, displays of magic, fire-eating, breakdancing, and so forth. In 1988 the director of AA was Maggie Pinhorn. From the mid 1970s AA events took place in the Covent Garden area but in 1988 they were forced to move to Carnaby Street.

● See also Community Art, Public Art, Street Art.

● M Kennedy 'Street impresarios bow out of Garden' *Guardian* December 2 1988 8.

27 ALTERNATIVE SPACES

Galleries and other exhibition spaces providing an 'alternative' to public museums and commercial art galleries; a visual arts equivalent to fringe theatre. The expression itself has been credited to Brian O'Doherty, an American artist–critic who was head of the visual arts section of the National Endowment for the Arts. Such spaces proliferated in major cities, particularly in the USA, during the 1970s as the number of arts graduates exceeded the market's capacity to absorb them. Derelict or disused shops, warehouses and lofts were frequently adapted for the purpose and sometimes spaces doubled as studios.

Alternative Spaces were usually run by groups of artists on non-profit-making lines and were financed via grants from public funds. (They have also been called 'artist-oriented service organizations', 'artists' playgrounds'.) Generally their purpose was to display new, experimental art by unknown artists or to present thematic shows, or programmes of dance, music and videos, or performance pieces, or mixed-media installations, or site-specific works that were temporary and nonsaleable. Some were devoted to the needs of particular social groups, e.g. women artists, while others specialized in the kind of art they promoted, e.g. book art.

A notable British example of an Alternative Space was The Gallery established at 65a Lisson Street North London, in 1972 by the artist Nicholas Wegner who was later joined by another British artist Vaughan Grylls. At the outset humorous exhibitions were devised which satirized trends in contemporary art, but later on serious shows were mounted of the work of artists like Grylls, John Latham, Rita Donagh and Steve Willats. Influenced by the example of Warhol, Wegner and Grylls developed a distinctive style of black-and-white photodisplays. Over 30 shows were put on and most involved collaborations between the 'directors' of The Gallery and the exhibiting artists. Wegner also promoted the idea of 'standard art'. Although influential for a time in the '70s, The Gallery could not be sustained without sales or grants and so it was forced to close in 1978.

Because of their dependence upon subsidies, goodwill and volatile groups, Alternative Spaces tended to be shortlived. Some, however, did survive and became part of the established system. Although conceived as something different from mainstream commercial galleries, Alternative Spaces often served the former as testbeds for new art. The Alternative Spaces took the risks and the commercial galleries then creamed off the best new talent. Institutionalization and bureaucracy were also dangers that threatened the inventiveness and radical politics of Alternative Spaces. According to some observers, the formation of a national organization of Alternative Spaces in the USA in 1982 marked the end of the critical thrust of the movement.

● See also AIR, Artists' Space, Arts Lab, East Village Art, Installations, SoHo, SPACE.

● P Patton 'Other voices, other rooms: the rise of the Alternative Space' *Art in America* **65** (4) July–August 1977 80–9.

● D Phillips 'New faces in Alternative Spaces' *Art News* **80** (9) November 1981 90–100.

● M Delahoyd 'Seven Alternative Spaces: a chronicle 1969–70' *Alternatives in retrospect* (NY, New Museum, 1981).

● J Baer 'After the fire is gone' *ZG* (9) 1983 25.

● N Wegner *Depart from zero: the development of The Gallery, London, 1973–8* (The Gallery Trust Publications, 1987).

● J Walker 'A short history of The Gallery' *AND Journal of Art and Art Education* (15/16) 1988 47–9.

---

28 | **ANALOGICAL ARCHITECTURE** — A term used by the Italian architect Aldo Rossi to describe his own work of the 1970s. Rossi welcomed the fact that his designs suggested analogies with other structures – vernacular architecture, engineering works, famous buildings of the past, or even natural forms. He was inspired by Jung's reflection that analogical thought was 'a meditation on themes of the past, an interior monologue ... archaic, unexpressed and practically inexpressible in words'. Analogical Architecture also appears to have been a working method, part of Rossi's imaginative process, in the sense that designs evolved

according to the associations, memories and correspondences they evoked. Analogies, Rossi contended, were the essence of architecture's meaning.

● See also Rational Architecture, Symbolic Architecture, Tendenza.

● A Rossi 'An Analogical Architecture' *A & U (Architecture & Urbanism)* (65) May 1976 74–6.

● A Ferlenga (ed) *Aldo Rossi: architettura 1959–87* (Milan, Electa, 1987).

---

29 | **AND ASSOCIATION** — A non profit-making, British association of artists, designers and educationalists founded by Jenni Boswell-Jones, Roderick Coyne and Ismail Saray in east London in 1981 for the purpose of mutual aid, and to encourage discussions about current social issues amongst left-wing artists, art educationalists, students and the public at large. Members of AND have given their support to many radical causes as well as designed posters, banners, catalogues and publications of all kinds. Art education has been of particular concern to AND: they participated in the pressure group AD 2000 which protested about cuts in British fine art educational courses in the mid '80s. More recently, in response to the Gulf

AND Front cover of *AND Journal of Art & Art Education* (11/12) 1987. Front cover montage of a still from 'State of the Art' and an image (detail) from 'A World's Waste' exhibition of artists responses to Nuclear Reprocessing.

War, AND organised an Artists Against War group. In conjunction with the Committee Against the War in the Gulf, an exhibition "Come and See" evolved and was held at the Kufa Gallery in London 1991.

Since 1983 the central activity of AND has been the publication of the magazine entitled *AND Journal of Art and Art Education* (co-edited by Jenni Boswell-Jones and Ismail Saray). The magazine extends the objectives of the Association in providing a platform for artists, practitioners and critics who support AND's aims.

● See also Political Art.

30 ANGRY PENGUINS

Title of a journal edited by Max Harris and John Reed published first in Adelaide and then in Melbourne in the 1940s (nine issues 1940–6) which acted as a focus for contemporary literary and visual art activities. It was also the title of an exhibition of Australian art shown at the Hayward Gallery, London in 1988. The show featured works by the Angry Penguins Group – Sidney Nolan, Arthur Boyd, John Perceval, Albert Tucker and Joy Hester – whose aggressive and critical paintings were often expressionistic/primitivistic in style, and works by the rival group of social realists – Noel Counihan and Yosl Bergner, championed by the art historian Bernard Smith. Both groups wanted to establish an authentic Australian art free from the influence of European abstraction and surrealism.

● See also Antipodeans.

● M Ryan (ed) *Angry Penguins and Realist painting in Melbourne in the 1940s* (Hayward Gallery/South Bank Centre, 1988).

31 ANIMATION

Today several different kinds of animated films and videos exist: short cartoons and personal statements, full-length features made for cinema-goers, educational and training films, TV commercials and programme titles, rock music videos. The prime aim of the art of animation is to render movement via a sequence of still images – usually drawings – which are then photographed on to film and a sound-track added. (Exceptionally, some animation techniques do not employ a camera: images are drawn or scratched directly onto the film itself.) Another technique using a camera involves a single object or set which is adjusted slightly between one frame and the next to produce a sense of movement or metamorphosis in the finished film. This kind of animation can be either two-dimensional (e.g. paper cutouts) or three-dimensional (e.g. models, puppets). Some artists and independents photograph paint or sand images on back-lit plates of glass. Because this technique is practised directly under the camera it is called 'direct animation'.

Animation is extremely costly, labour-intensive and time-consuming because of the huge amount of hand-work involved. Exactly what impact computer graphic machines and laser discs will have on the processes and economics of animation in the future remains unclear.

Animated films can be abstract or figurative; animation can also be combined with live-action footage (witness the acclaimed movie 'Who framed Roger Rabbit?' (1988) with animation by Richard Williams). Representational animation rarely aims for naturalism in spite of the need for movements to be convincing. Indeed, the constructed nature of animation means that it lends itself to formal and technical invention and to caricature, fantasy and surrealism.

As a technique, animation developed in the late nineteenth century and reached a high point of popular appeal in the 1930s and '40s with the cartoons and feature-length films of the Walt Disney Studio. The cartoon form developed in Hollywood from 1910 onwards. It was designed specifically for mass production. Drawing styles were simplified and standardized so that teams of animators could be employed and techniques divided into many stages. A standardized genre developed – character animation, comedy, stereotypes, the family audience – that was elaborated and perfected by Disney.

Large-scale animated films depend upon the skills and labour of many specialists; however, animation is also a form which, like painting, can be highly individualistic. One dedicated person can write a script, produce a storyboard, draw the images, film them, record the soundtrack, and complete the camerawork and editing. Eastern European animators such as the Czechs Jan Svankmajer and Jiri Barta are noted for their idiosyncratic, melancholy, critical or surreal films. A highly praised example

ANIMATION CAROLINE LEAF, Still from 'The Street' (1976). Paint on backlit glass. Photo: the artist/National Film Board of Canada.

of a personal film motivated by ecological concerns was Frederic Back's 'The man who planted trees' (1987); this film took five years to make.

A distinction is often made between entertainment films and 'experimental animation'. The latter was the title of an American book by Robert Russett and Cecile Starr first published in 1976. It discussed the work of such artist–animators as Hans Richter, Leopold Survage, Viking Eggeling, Robert Breer, Paul Sharits, John Whitney, Stan VanDerBeek and Ed Emshwiller, from the 1920s to the '70s. The pioneers of the '20s generally came from a fine art background and their aim was to animate abstract art, to produce a visual equivalent of music, or to achieve a new synthesis of colours, shapes and sounds. Russett and Starr were obviously distinguishing this kind of animation from 'commercial' animation (an art/mass culture opposition). However, the assumption that only artist–animators experiment is dubious. Arguably, animation is virtually unique in its conjunction of traditional artistic skills (drawing, puppet and model making, storytelling) and modern mass media technology (film, sound recording, computers), and in the interaction it permits between the realms of avant garde art and popular culture. Experiment and innovation take place across the whole range of animated films.

Britain has a long tradition of animation. In the 1930s Len Lye, Norman McLaren (of the GPO film unit), George Pal and Anthony Gross became noted for their experimental approach to the medium. In 1954 the partners Halas and Batchelor were responsible for 'Animal Farm' (based on Orwell's novel), the first British animation feature film. During the '60s British-based animators – George Dunning, Bob Godfrey and Richard Williams – worked on the Beatles' 'Yellow Submarine' (1968). British animation has proved buoyant in the '70s and '80s as a result of commissions from advertising, pop music and television. A highlight of the '70s was Terry Gilliam's collage animation for the TV comedy series 'Monty Python'. Notable examples of animated pop videos included Elvis Costello's 'Accidents will happen' (1978–9) with computer animation by Annabel Jankel and Rocky Morton (Cucumber Studios) and Peter Gabriel's 'Sledgehammer' with stop-motion animation by the Brothers Quay amongst others.

Computers have been the major technological development of recent years. They promise to end the laboriousness of hand-drawn, cel (short for celluloid) animation but it is also feared they will not be able to rival its special quality. Even so, award-winning computer animations have been produced by the American John Lasseter ('Tin Toy', 1987) at Pixar. Ray Harryhausen is a famous American model animator whose career was inspired by the 'King Kong' movie of 1933. An artist praised for combining model animation, folklore and the Japanese tradition of puppetry is Kihachiro Kawamoto.

Contemporary animators are usually trained in artschools (such as the Royal College of Art, or the West Surrey College of Art, Farnham, whose course began in 1969), work on commission for commerce, broadcasting or Hollywood, and they also make personal films. In the United States animation skills are taught at the California Institute of the Arts and at the Rhode Island School of Design. One showcase for new work of all kinds is the biannual International Festival of Animation (currently organized by Irene Kotlarz); in 1987 and '89 the Festival was held in Bristol. Channel 4 television has also been important as a patron: during the '80s it commissioned some of the best independent animation; it also transmitted documentary programmes about animation. This Channel seems set to continue its interest into the '90s.

Animation archives have been established in museums such as MoMA, New York and exhibitions of examples of drawings and artwork by animators have been held in a number of art galleries and sold to collectors and museums. In short, the artistic achievements of animation are increasingly being recognized and celebrated.

● See also CalArts, Disneyana, Expanded Cinema, Rock Video, Underground Film.

◉ G & D Peary (eds) *The animated cartoon* (NY, Dutton, 1980).

◉ D Crafton *Before Mickey, the animated film 1898–1928* (Cambridge, Mass, MIT Press, 1982).

◉ 'The Bristol Animation Festival' *Direction* November 1987 19–52, + *Direction* November 1989 35–65.

◉ C Solomon (ed) *The art of the animated image* (Los Angeles, American Film Institute, 1987).

◉ R Noake *Animation* (McDonald, 1988).

◉ R Russett & C Starr *Experimental animation: origins of a new art* (NY, Da Capo Press, rev ed 1988).

32 ANONIMA

A group of American painters – Ernst Benkert, Francis Hewitt and Edwin Mieckowski – who operated as a research team. The name of the group was derived from the Italian word 'anonima' which means 'incorporated'. It was selected in 1964 though the artists had known each other since 1957. Anonima was established in Cleveland; they exhibited work in London and Warsaw in 1966, and moved to New York in 1967. Members set themselves a rigorous programme of research into perceptual problems related to painting. Their works were abstract and executed in a hard-edge style. Examples were reproduced in their own irregularly issued journal *Anonima* (1963–) and in books on optical art.

● See also Collaborations, Hard-Edge Painting, Op Art.

● *Anonima Group* (ICA, 1966).

● H Raleigh 'Anonima Group' *Leonardo* **2** (4) October 1969 423–30.

33 **ANONYMOUS DESIGN**

Title of an exhibition held in 1974 at the Louisiana Museum, Humlebæk (near Copenhagen) consisting of examples of mass-produced household goods and utensils on which no designers' names appeared. The products were selected on the grounds that they possessed 'genuine character, good form, fine performance and honest use of materials'. The opposite of 'anonymous' or 'non-conscious' design has been called, by Umberto Eco, 'identified design', i.e. 'design which is the outcome of an expressed theory and of a practice in which the object aims to exemplify explicitly its author's theory'.

● See also Architecture without Architects, DIY, 'Good Design', Popular Art.

● 'Anonym Design' *Louisiana Revy* **14** (3/4) April–August 1974 1–28.

● S Hansen 'Anonymous design' *Mobilia* (228/229) July–August 1974 2–9.

● U Eco 'Phenomena of this sort must also be included' – in – *Italian reevolution: Design in Italian society in the eighties;* P Sartago (ed) (La Jolla, California, La Jolla Museum of Contemporary Art, 1982) 129.

34 **ANONYMOUS SCULPTURE**

A description applied by Bernhard and Hilla Becher to certain types of industrial structure – gas holders, kilns, silos, water towers, pithead winding towers and so on – which they regard as exhibiting sculptural qualities. With their camera the Bechers have assiduously documented hundreds of examples of these structures in Europe and the United States and displays of their photographs have been mounted in dozens of art galleries. To illustrate the minor variations within types, the Bechers produce display panels consisting of a series of photos of one kind of structure. The somewhat surprising popularity of these images in avant garde art galleries and magazines was due to the vogues for serial imagery, documentation and photo-works during the '60s and '70s.

● See also Photo-Works, Serial Art.

● B & H Becher *Anonyme Skulpturen: eine typologie technischer bauten* (Düsseldorf, Art Press, 1970).

● *Bernd & Hilla Becher* (Arts Council of Great Britain, 1974).

● B & H Becher *Photographs 1957–75* (Cologne, Rheinland-Verlag, 1975).

● — *Water towers* (Cambridge, Mass., MIT Press, 1988).

ANT FARM 'Media burn' (1975). Cow Palace, San Franciso. Photo: Ant Farm.

35 ANT FARM

A group of 'environmental nomads', that is, American architects, designers and others from a variety of backgrounds, formed in San Francisco in 1968 by Doug Michels and Chip Lord. Its strange name came from a remark that the only interesting things in architecture were happening underground 'like an ant farm'. Besides architecture, Ant Farm was concerned with educational reform, communication, graphics, film, 'life-theatre' and high art. They described themselves as a family and attempted to create a common lifestyle as an alternative to existing socio-economic systems. Their projects were featured in underground magazines but also in *Architectural Design* and *Progressive Architecture*. Ant Farm projects included domes, inflatables and a media van equipped with video. Ant Farm's most notorious works were: (a) 'Cadillac ranch' (Amarillo, Texas, 1974), a row of vertical cars half buried in the earth, and (b) 'Media burn' (Cow Palace, Texas, 1975) – a car used to destroy a barrier of TV sets.

● See also Air Art, Conceptual Architecture, Underground Art, Video Art.

◗ T Albright 'Ant Farm' *Rolling Stone* (48) December 13 1969 36.

◗ 'Conceptual architecture' *Design Quarterly* (78/79) 1970 5–10.

◗ G Celant 'Ant Farm' *Casabella* (376) April 1973 27–31.

◗ Ant Farm/Chip Lord *Automerica: a trip down US highways from World War Two to the future* (NY, Dutton, 1977).

36 ANTI-ART

(Including Anartism & Anti-Art Art) Most critics regard this notion as having originated with dada, the iconoclastic European movement which repudiated the art and culture associated with the bourgeoisie because it held that class responsible for the horrors of the First World War. The invention of the term itself has been credited to Marcel Duchamp, an artist who has been called 'the master of Anti-Art'. Art is a social institution and the power to determine what is and is not art normally rests with the artworld. So while Duchamp's gesture of drawing a moustache on an image of the Mona Lisa counts as art, a vandal's defacement of the painting does not. The recuperative power of the institution of art is such that most attacks upon it by artists are transformed into art within a few years: hence the paradoxical phenomenon of Anti-Art Art. This was the fate of Duchamp's ready-mades. Logically speaking, Anti-Art Art must be against itself therefore it is, so to speak, suicidal: witness the self-destroying machines built by Jean Tinguely.

Since art is not a fixed and static concept, new art often extends into areas previously considered non-art. Cultural conservatives tend to greet all new movements as Anti-Art because the new inevitably puts into question traditional assumptions about the nature of art. There is some justification for this reaction because avant garde movements do break with the past and do tend to denigrate earlier and rival forms of art. Various kinds of marginal visual culture have also been labelled Anti-Art, e.g. graffiti was so considered by Herbert Marcuse. Gregory Battcock proposed that underground sex comics were Anti-Art or 'outlaw art' because they transgressed accepted standards of morality. The American writer on aesthetics George Dickie subscribed to the view that art is a social institution; for him Anti-Art consisted in activities that manipulated the norms of the artworld but failed to provide any art. He cited the art gallery performances of Vito Acconci as an example. Groups of intellectuals motivated by politics, such as the Situationists, were Anti-Art in the sense that they wanted to dissolve or abolish the category altogether. Arguably, bad art is the commonest form of Anti-Art.

● See also Artworld, 'Bad' Painting, Destructive Art, Graffiti, Situationists.

◗ B Taylor 'Art-Anti-Art' *Listener* November 12 1959 819–22.

◗ H Rosenberg *Artworks and packages* (NY, Dell, 1964).

◗ N Calas 'Art intervenes, Anti-Art interrupts' *Art International* **13** (1) January 1969 21–4.

◗ G Battcock 'Marcuse and Anti-Art' part 1 *Arts Magazine* **43** (8) Summer 1969 17–9; part 2 *Arts Magazine* **44** (2) November 1969 20–2.

◗ U Meyer 'The eruption of Anti-Art' – in – *Idea Art: a critical anthology* G Battcock (ed) (NY, Dutton, 1973) 116–34.

◗ G Dickie 'What is Anti-Art?' *Journal of Aesthetics & Art Criticism* **33** (4) 1975 419–21.

◗ H Parmelin *Art Anti-Art: Anartism explored* (Marion Boyars, 1977).

◗ S Home *The assault on culture: utopian currents from lettrisme to class war* (Aporia Press & Unpopular Books, 1988).

37 ANTI-FASHION

A term used by Ted Polhemus and Lynn Proctor to describe those forms of clothing which avoid the dynamic of constant change typical of the fashion industry. Examples include industrial/protective clothing, 'classic' designs such as the dark suit of the city businessman, and military uniforms. Function is normally more important than style in the case of Anti-Fashion clothes. However, they are not 'timeless' because they do alter periodically or evolve slowly.

◗ T Polhemus & L Proctor *Fashion and Anti-Fashion:*

an anthropology of clothing and adornment (Thames & Hudson, 1978).

38 ANTI-FORM

A term used by the American artist Robert Morris and others to describe sculptures of the late 1960s which foregrounded materials, gravity and process, in reaction to the geometric, predominantly rectangular forms of previous abstract sculpture, in particular minimal art. Allan Kaprow insisted that no sculpture can be against or without form and suggested that 'anti-form' meant 'anti-geometry'; he also argued that a similar approach to art developed in happenings. An exhibition with the title 'Anti-Form' was held at the John Gibson Gallery, New York, in October 1968; it included work by Eva Hesse, Robert Ryman and Richard Serra. The expression 'Anti-Form' was also used widely in Europe as a broad label to encompass the various new tendencies in avant garde art (e.g. arte povera, earth art, etc.) which followed the fashion for minimalism.

● See also Happenings, Minimal Art, Post-Minimalism, Process Art.

● R Morris 'Anti-Form' *Artforum* **6** (8) April 1968 33-5.

● A Kaprow 'The shape of the art environment: how anti-form is "Anti-Form"' *Artforum* **6** (10) Summer 1968 32–3.

● M Kozloff '9 in a warehouse' *Artforum* **7** (6) February 1969 38–42.

● G Muller 'Robert Morris presents Anti-Form: the Castelli warehouse show' *Arts Magazine* **43** (4) February 1969 29–30.

39 ANTIPODEANS

A group of seven Australian painters exhibiting at the Victorian Artists Society's galleries in Melbourne in August 1959. The artists concerned were Arthur and David Boyd, John Brack, John Perceval, Clifton Pugh and Charles Blackman (all from Melbourne) and Robert Dickerson (from Sydney). Following several group discussions, a manifesto – 'The Antipodean Manifesto' – was written by the art critic and historian Bernard Smith. The purpose of the show was to counteract the dominant international tendency towards abstraction (e.g. tachism, abstract expressionism) by presenting paintings that were 'figural' – i.e. emphasizing the role of the image, myth, the representation of the Australian landscape and life in the Antipodes. However, the artists also wanted to avoid the opposite extreme of naturalism and socialist realism.

Much later Alan McCulloch, author of an encyclopedia of Australian art, employed a similar label 'Antipodean School' to encompass a far wider range of Australian artists.

● See also Angry Penguins.

● *Antipodeans* (Melbourne, Victorian Artists Society, 1959).

● B Blackman 'The Antipodean affair' *Art & Australia* **5** (4) March 1968 608–16.

● A McCulloch 'Antipodean School' *Encyclopedia of Australian art* vol 1 (Melbourne, Hutchinson, 1984) 32–5.

● B Smith 'The Antipodean Manifesto' & 'The truth about the Antipodeans' – in – *The death of the artist as hero: essays in history and culture* (Melbourne, Oxford University Press, 1988) 194–213.

40 APG

(Artist Placement Group) A visionary project launched in 1966 by the British artists John Latham, Barbara Steveni, Jeffrey Shaw and Barry Flanagan. Others joined later, including David Hall and Stuart Brisley. The function of APG – which was funded for a time by the Arts Council – was to act as a mediating mechanism between artists and non-art organizations, specifically to 'place' artists for specific periods within industries, businesses, universities, government departments, etc. The aim was to resolve the alienation of artists from society by placing them within the centres of power. As 'incidental persons' whose insights encompassed the needs of the whole of society, artists were judged capable of transcending the short-term goals and divisions of existing organizations. Placements were to be undertaken not primarily to generate art objects but in order to achieve social change. Sculptures, films and so forth were produced but APG artists were expected to enter organizations without any preconceptions about end results so that the work undertaken was a response to specific contexts.

An APG exhibition took place at the Hayward Gallery in 1971 and many other shows and public meetings were held in Britain and in Europe during the '70s. APG has aroused much adverse criticism in the art press but it did arrange a number of successful placements and the idea of artist placement has become commonplace in the British artworld. Since the 1960s, APG has functioned sporadically, i.e. whenever finance was available.

Recently, a new name has been adopted: O+I (Organisation and Imagination).

● See also Artist-in-Residence, Community Art.

● J Walker 'APG: the individual and the organisation, a decade of conceptual engineering' *Studio International* **191** (980) March–April 1976 162–72.

● B Steveni 'Artist Placement: APG 1966–83' *Aspects* (24) 1983 5–7.

● — 'Will art influence history?' *AND Journal of Art & Art Education* (9) 1986 14–21.

41 ARAU

(Atelier de Recherche et d'Action Urbaine) A Belgian protest group founded in the 1970s, headed by Maurice Culot, and concerned with issues of mass housing, modern architecture and urban renewal. ARAU concerns have been made public via the journal *Archives d'Architecture Moderne* (October 1975–).

42 ARCADIAN PAINTING

Paintings dating from the 1970s and '80s by such artists as Lennart Anderson, Milet Andrejevic, Edward Schmidt, James Lecky, Paul Resika and Thomas Cornell representing the mythical realm of Arcadia (figures in landscape settings, scenes of pastoral simplicity). A return to classicism and traditional modes of painting associated with post-modernism. An exhibition of this type of work was held at the Robert Schoelkopf Gallery in New York in 1982. An English artist with a comparable interest in classical themes is Stephen McKenna. The Scottish artist Ian Hamilton Finlay also employs the classical style (often with irony) in his Temple Garden sculptures and he has been featured in the *New Arcadians Journal* issued by the New Arcadians, a Yorkshire group consisting of the writer Patrick Eyres and the painters Ian Gardner and Grahame Jones.

● See also Cultured Painting, New Classicism, Post-Modernism.

● *Contemporary Arcadian Painting* (NY, Robert Schoelkopf Gallery, 1982).

● G Tapley 'The Arcadian ethos in contemporary painting' *Arts Magazine* **57** February 1983 124–5.

● C Jencks 'The classical sensibility' *Art & Design* **3** (7/8) 1987 48–67.

43 ARCH

(Architects' Renewal Committee in Harlem) A New York organization established by the architect C. Richard Hatch in October 1964. Hatch, Jack Bailey and others were concerned about the people living in the rat-infested slums of Harlem and sought to mobilize the local community in order to generate designs and planning proposals for the renewal of housing. Workshops were also established for architectural students in order to expose them to the problems of the poor. Following Hatch's initiative, similar groups were founded in other American cities. ARCH was an early example of community architecture and participatory design.

● See also Advocacy Planning, Community Architecture, Participatory Design, Social Architecture/Design.

● A Lopen 'Harlem's streetcorner architects' *Architectural Forum* **123** (5) December 1965 50–1.

● C Hatch 'Urban renewal in Harlem' *Zodiac* (17) 1967 196-8.

44 ARCHIGRAM

An organization of architects, designers and environmental researchers led by Peter Cook, based in London and the United States, that was operative in the 1960s and early '70s. Members included Warren Chalk, Ron Herron, Dennis Crompton, David Greene and Mike Webb. *Archigram Magazine* or manifesto was published from 1961 onwards. As Cook explains, the title 'came from the notion of a more urgent and simple item than a journal, like a telegram or "Aerogramme" hence "Archi(tecture)-gram"'. However, the group itself was formed two years later in reaction to what members perceived as the sterility of post-1945 British architecture.

Archigram delighted in inventing experimental projects – plug-in cities, clip-on architecture, capsule dwellings, instant and walking cities– inspired in part by the advanced technology of the American space programme. Change, mobility and flexibility were key concepts. They were also interested in architecture as communication, environments that were responsive and reflected the new age of leisure. They also subscribed to the expendability aesthetic of the pop design of the '60s. Their futuristic ideas were communicated via lively texts, collages and graphics.

In 1970 Archigram won first prize in an international competition for the design of an entertainments centre at Monte Carlo (the project was in the end cancelled) and in 1973 an exhibition of their work was held at the ICA, London. In the mid '70s members of Archigram designed a swimming pool for the singer Rod Stewart and stage sets for the rock group Queen. The Archigram group have been called 'the Beatles of architecture'. Archigram was above all an architectural 'think-tank' and as such stimulated and influenced subsequent generations of architects. The design of the Pompidou Centre in Paris has been cited as one popular building that owed much to the imagination of Archigram.

● See also Conceptual Architecture, Expendability in Design, Experimental Architecture, Mobile Architecture, NATO, Pompidou Centre, Pop Design.

● 'Archigram Group, London: a chronological survey' *Architectural Design* **35** (11) November 1965 534–5.

● *Archigram book* (London, Faber & Faber/Mass, MIT Press, 1970). Reprint of *Archigram Magazine* issues 1–8.

● P Cook & others (eds) *Archigram* (Studio Vista, 1972).

45 ARCHITECTS' FURNITURE

Many modern architects have wanted to design every aspect of their buildings including fixtures and fittings, interiors and furniture. The highly original and fine quality furniture of such architects as Charles Rennie Mackintosh and Frank Lloyd Wright has long been famous. Individual chairs designed by architects have also attained the status of classics: e.g. the 1929 Barcelona chair by Mies van der Rohe. Via the agency of reproduction such classic designs are made available to a wide public long after they were created and outside the context for which they were originally made. Post-1945 examples of architects' chairs include: Eero Saarinen (1910–61): pedestal chair (1955–7); Charles Eames (1907–78): lounge chair (1956); Arne Jacobsen (1902–71): egg armchair (1959); Piero Gatti, Cesare Paolini and Franco Teodoro: sacco easy chair (1969); Frank O'Gehry: wiggle dining chair (1971–2); Michael Graves: lounge chair (1982).

● See also Artists' Furniture.

◉ M Page *Furniture designed by architects* (NY, Whitney Library of Design, 1980).

◉ *Furniture by architects* (Cambridge, Mass, MIT Press/Hayden Gallery, 1981).

◉ M Emery *Furniture by architects: 500 international masterpieces of twentieth-century design and where to buy them* (NY, Abrams, 1983).

46 ARCHITECTURE MACHINE

Title of a book by Nicholas Negroponte (Assistant Professor at the School of Architecture and Planning, Massachusetts Institute of Technology) in which he described a research project concerned with the role of artificial intelligence in architectural design and planning. Negroponte and the Architecture Machine Group were concerned with far more than computer-aided design: they wanted to see the computer fully integrated into the design process. In reality the 'architecture machine' was a computer linked to various peripherals. The aim of the research was to give computers the same behavioural abilities as human beings, i.e. sensors, intelligence, the ability to cope with a complex, uncertain and changing environment, so that they could learn by interaction with reality and engage in dialogue with designers. If such machines could be built, then computers would become partners in design rather than simply sophisticated design tools.

● See also Computer-Aided Design, Environmental Design, Participatory Design, Soft Architecture.

◉ N Negroponte *The Architecture Machine: toward a more human environment* (Cambridge, Mass, MIT Press, 1970).

◉ — & L Groisser 'Sector: the semantics of Architecture Machines' *Architectural Design* **XL** September 1970 466–9.

◉ — 'Aspects of living in an Architecture Machine' – in– *Design participation*; N Cross (ed) (Academy Editions, 1972) 63–7.

47 ARCHITECTURE WITHOUT ARCHITECTS

Title of an exhibition of photographs, collected over 40 years by Bernard Rudofsky, held in New York in 1965. They illustrated a wide variety of shelters and other structures – caves, earthworks, tree houses, tents – used or built by people with no professional architectural training, i.e. early, ancient and tribal peoples, nomads and peasants. Other terms for such structures include 'anonymous', 'exotic', 'indigenous', 'non-pedigreed', 'primitive', 'rude', 'rural' and 'vernacular'.

● See also Anonymous Design, Earth & Earthwork Architecture, Fantastic Architecture.

◉ S Moholy-Nagy *Native genius in anonymous architecture* (NY, Horizon Press, 1957).

◉ J Fitch & D Branch 'Primitive architecture and climate' *Scientific American* **207** December 1960 134–44.

◉ B Rudofsky *Architecture without Architects* (NY, MoMA, 1965).

◉ L Wodehouse 'Indigenous architecture' *AAQ* **7** (3) July–September 1975 23–8.

◉ B Rudofsky *The prodigious builders* (Secker & Warburg, 1977).

◉ *Indigenous architecture worldwide: a guide to information sources* (Detroit, Gale Research, 1980).

◉ E Guidoni *Primitive architecture* (Faber & Faber, 1987).

48 ARCHIZOOM

(Studio Archizoom Associati) A group of six Florentine architects and designers – Andrea Branzi, Gilberto Corretti, Paolo Deganello, Massimo Morozzi, Dario and Lucia Bartolini – founded in 1966. The work of Archizoom was representative of the anti-functional, supersensualist trend in Italian design: futuristic plans for a 'No-stop city'; 'Dream Beds' reflecting the influence of Pop culture and kitsch. It was featured in exhibitions of 'Superarchitecture' and in such magazines as *Domus, Casabella, Architectural Design* and the Milanese magazine *In*.

● See also Conceptual Architecture, Italian Craze, Radical Design, Supersensualists.

◉ 'Conceptual architecture' *Design Quarterly* (78/79) 1970 17–21.

◉ Archizoom Associates 'Residential parkings, nostop city, climatic universal sistem' *Domus* (496) March 1971 49–55.

◉ C Jencks 'The supersensualists' Part 2 *Architectural Design*

ARPILLERAS Patchwork showing Chile's economic dependence on the dollar. Vampire bats represent the four members of the military junta. (1976?) Photo: Chile Solidarity Campaign, London.

49 ARCOLOGY

A new conception of architecture involving a fusion of architecture and ecology proposed by Paolo Soleri, an Italian architect resident in the USA. Arcology was Soleri's solution to the urban problems of the twentieth century; he advocates vast vertical megastructures capable of housing up to three million. One of Soleri's visionary projects – Arcosanti, a structure resembling a small hill town set in the Arizona desert – is slowly being constructed by student and volunteer labour. The aim is to create a self-sufficient community based on a huge greenhouse powered by solar energy.

● See also Ecological Architecture, Megastructures.

● P Soleri *Arcology: the city in the image of man* (Cambridge, Mass, MIT Press, 1969).

● H Skolimowski 'Paolo Soleri: the philosophy of urban life' *AAQ* **3** (1) Winter 1971 34–42.

● D Wall *Visionary cities: the arcology of Paolo Soleri* (Pall Mall Press, 1971).

● R Banham 'Arts in society: the mesa Messiah' *New Society* May 6 1976 306–7.

● I S Gardiner 'Rocky mountain utopia' (Arcosanti) *Observer Magazine* March 22 1981 54–7.

50 ARLIS

(Art Libraries Society in the United Kingdom and the Republic of Ireland) A society founded in London in 1969 'to promote art librarianship particularly by acting as a forum for the interchange of information and materials'. Membership is open to individuals and institutions in Britain and Ireland. Between 1969 and '76 ARLIS published a newsletter but from Spring 1976 it was largely superseded by a more scholarly periodical, the *Art Libraries Journal*. As a result of the founding of ARLIS in Britain a similar society was established in North America: ARLIS/NA. The latter publishes the journal *Art Documentation*. Both societies regularly organize conferences.

● C Phillpot 'ARLIS: the Art Libraries Society' *ARLIS/NA Newsletter* **1** (2) February 1973 2–3.

51 ARPILLERAS

(Also Chilean Patchworks) In Chile after the violent military coup of 1973 destroyed the democratically elected Marxist government, groups of poor women living in the shanty towns around Santiago began to make small pictures by sewing scraps of waste cloth together, using old flour sacks for the base. These patchworks, by women untrained in art but with some craft skills, were a means of expressing their solidarity and their daily experiences, and a form of cultural resistance to an oppressive regime. In style the images were child-like: flat, bright colours and mixtures of patterns. Some had three-dimensional elements, e.g. pockets in which tiny figures could be placed. They depicted scenes of everyday life, scenes of torture and also symbols of hope, and dreams of plenty. The pictures brought them income by being sold abroad via the agency of the Catholic Church. Exhibitions of patchworks were also circulated in Europe in the late 1970s in order to publicize events in Chile. Many Western critics, feminists and other viewers found them highly attractive, decorative and moving. Postcards of the Arpilleras were also sold to raise money for exiled resistance organizations. Sensitive to the critical content of the patchworks, the Chilean authorities labelled them 'Tapestries of defamation'.

● See also Feminist Art, Naive Art, Political Art, Popular Art.

● 'Patchwork from Chile' *Crafts* (32) May–June 1978 30–3.

● 'Chilean patchwork pictures' *Index* **7** (5) September – October 1978 30–5.

● G Brett 'Patchwork pictures from Chile' *Black Phoenix* (1) Winter 1978 19–22.

● E Moya-Raggio 'Arpilleras: Chilean culture of resistance' *Feminist Studies* **10** (2) Summer 1984 277–90.

● G Brett 'All this we have seen' – in – *Through our own eyes: Popular art and modern history* (Heretic/GMP Publishers, 1986) 28–53.

● M Agosin *Scraps of life* (Zed Press, 1987).

52 ART AGAINST AIDS

Umbrella title for 72 shows organized by Ann Livet and Stephen Reichard, held in New York galleries during 1987, for the benefit of the 'Foundation for Aids Research'. The appearance of the disease Aids in the 1980s resulted in many thousands of deaths in the United States. Artists who have died of Aids include Keith Haring, Robert Mapplethorpe and Philip Core. Since homosexuals in the New York artworld were particularly at risk, efforts were made to mobilize the arts to combat the disease and public prejudice against Aids sufferers. Sales of works of art raised funds for research and for victims. Artists also designed placards, posters, leaflets, neon signs, and stickers, painted murals, wrote electronic billboard messages, etc., to protest, to raise consciousness, and to demand more central and local government help, and to urge drug companies to release new drugs. Artists such as Keith Haring, Jenny Holzer, Barbara Kruger, Ross Bleckner, the group Gran Fury, and the critic Douglas Crimp were involved. Video artists and film-makers like Ray Navarro and Ellen Spiro also contributed by documenting Act Up (Aids Coalition To Unleash Power) street demonstrations. Their aim was to produce an alternative to mainstream media coverage of Aids. Since their work was stylish, they were called 'MTV activists' (MTV = Music Television; Navarro preferred 'More Than a Virus activists'). Aids also became a subject for art: Bleckner painted memorials for the victims of Aids; Don Moffett, a photographer, produced photo-text works based on gay pornography to address the issue of sex and to counter the new puritanism.

The largest work associated with the Art Against Aids campaign was the Aids Memorial Quilt. The quilt was begun in San Francisco in 1987. It consisted of 13,000 panels each one created to commemorate a life lost to Aids. When completed the quilt weighed 16 tons and covered 14 acres. It has been described as 'the largest piece of folk art in the world'.

Meanwhile, in Britain, Gilbert & George mounted an exhibition to assist 'Crusaid' which raised half a million pounds. Other shows held in 1990 included: 'Art-Aid for Crusaid', Broughton House Gallery, Cambridge, and 'Ecstatic antibodies: resisting the Aids mythology', Ikon Gallery, Birmingham.

● See also Gay Art, Gilbert & George, Political Art.

● R Rosenblum & others *Art against Aids* (NY, 1987).

● S Evans 'Act Up' *Artscribe International* (73) January–February 1989 82–3.

● *Gilbert & George for Aids exhibition* (Anthony D'Offay Gallery, 1989).

● C Reid 'Art & politics: beyond mourning' *Art in America* **78** (4) April 1990 50–7.

● S Gupta & T Boffin *Ecstatic antibodies: resisting the Aids mythology* (Rivers Oram Press, 1990).

53 ART AGENCIES

(Also Artists' Agencies) Since the late 1960s a number of organizations have been founded with the aim of acting as a bridge between artists and others – businesses, architects, individual patrons, local authorities, community groups – who might wish to buy works of art, or to commission works, or to employ artists. (The objective is to provide visual artists with the same kind of services as literary agents provide for writers.) British examples included: the Artists' Agency, Sunderland; the Yorkshire Contemporary Art Group; Projects U.K., Newcastle upon Tyne; APG; and the Artangel Trust, London. These organizations are generally financed from public arts funds and run by people trained in arts administration. They offer advisory and consultancy services to clients and generally stimulate art activities. In particular they are interested in public projects beyond the gallery and the museum. Some maintain image banks in the form of slide collections.

● See also AIR, Alternative Spaces, APG, Artangel Trust, Arts Councils, Women Artists Slide Library.

● A Moszynska 'Art at work' *Art Monthly* (80) October 1984 32–3.

● A Wheeler & R Padwick 'Initiators and enablers: the growth of Art Agencies' *Artists Newsletter* October 1986 20–1.

54 ART & ARCHITECTURE (A&A)

In 1982 following a conference held at the ICA, London, some British artists and architects formed the Art & Architecture Group which subsequently became Art & Architecture, a non-profit-making limited company. As the name suggests, the aim of A & A was to foster the collaboration of architects, artists and craftspeople. A & A organized seminars, workshops and exhibitions, maintained an index of practitioners (published as a register), and issued a newsletter. In 1984 the chairman of A & A was Colin St John Wilson. Also during the '80s a course concerning art and architecture was established at Canterbury College of Art.

● See also Acanthus, Artangel Trust, Collaborations, Public Art, Public Art Development Trust.

55 ART & LANGUAGE (A&L)

An Anglo-American grouping of artists who worked collaboratively, which made a significant contribution to the conceptual art movement of the period 1966–75. (The work began in 1966 but the group was not formally

ART & LANGUAGE 'Portrait of V.I. Lenin in the style of Jackson Pollock III' (1979). Enamel paint on paper. Photo: Lisson Gallery, London.

constituted until 1968.) British participants included Michael Baldwin, Terry Atkinson, David Bainbridge and the art critic/historian Charles Harrison. American participants included Ian Burn, Sarah Charlesworth, Joseph Kosuth and Mel Ramsden plus the Australian Terry Smith. (The membership of A & L fluctuated continuously.) Following critiques of minimal art, A & L adopted language as their main means of expression. In 1969 they began to issue a journal entitled *Art-Language* whose obscure and difficult discourse was influenced by British analytical philosophy and several other academic disciplines.

Analysis of the concept art was extended to the broader socio-economic context in which it was marketed, and so a gradual politicization (i.e. Left-wing) occurred (see, for instance, the US publication *The Fox* (three issues 1975–6)). From the mid 1970s onwards A & L fragmented due to ideological disagreements. Terry Atkinson left to pursue an independent career as a socialist painter. During the 1980s the British branch of A & L exhibited paintings produced in response to the popularity of neo-expressionism but the content and style of these canvases were still dependent upon the conceptual critique of contemporary art and its institutions which was the hallmark of the group.

● See also Conceptual Art, Neo-Expressionism, Political Art.

● P Maenz (ed) *Art & Language* (Cologne, Dumont, 1972).

● *Art & Language 1966–75* (Oxford, MoMA, 1975).

● C Harrison & F Orton *A provisional history of Art & Language* (Paris, Éditions E Fabre, 1982).

● C Harrison/Art & Language *Confessions: incidents in a museum* (Lisson Gallery, 1986).

● C Harrison *Essays on Art & Language* (Oxford, Blackwell, 1991).

56 ART AUTRE, UN

(An other art) Title of a book by the French writer Michel Tapié published in 1952. In the same year a Paris exhibition featuring works by a number of non-geometric abstract and semi-abstract avant garde painters, mostly European – Karel Appel, Camille Bryen, Alberto Burri, Jean Dubuffet, Jean Fautrier, Willem de Kooning, Georges Mathieu, Jean Paul Riopelle and Wols – was organized with the same title. In his text Tapié also employed the term 'l'art informel' and the literature is rather confused as to the usage of the two labels. Tapié claimed that post-'45 trends indicated a complete break with traditional modes and the primary characteristics of this 'other art' were the relinquishing of all forms of control, vehement expressive brushwork, an uninhibited use of materials, formlessness. According to some of Tapié's critics, the term is synonymous with tachisme while others think it is so broad as to be almost meaningless. Even so, it gained currency. In 1955, for instance, Reyner Banham began speaking of 'Architecture Autre' in reference to the work of R. Buckminster Fuller.

● See also Art Informel, Tachisme.

● M Tapié *Un Art Autre* (Paris, Gabriel - Giraud, 1952).

● —*Morphologie Autre* (Turin, Edizioni d'Arte Fratelli Pozzi, 1960).

● R Banham *The new brutalism: ethic or aesthetic* (Architectural Press, 1966) 68–9.

57 ART BANK

Name of a large store of visual art located in Ottawa, Canada; also the name of an imaginative scheme of patronage with the aims of assisting living artists and increasing the level of appreciation of art. The Art Bank was established in 1972 by the Canada Council. Works of art were bought from Canadian artists after selection by a jury of their peers, placed in the Bank and then leased to federal premises throughout the country. In effect the Art Bank was a nationwide picture loan scheme.

● 'The Canadian cultural revolution' *ArtsCanada* **32** (3) Autumn 1975 1–92.

● R Bongartz 'Banking art in Ottawa' *Art News* **76** (4) April 1977 80–4.

A term meaning 'raw, uncultured art' devised by the French artist Jean Dubuffet who was an avid admirer and collector of all kinds of rough, unsophisticated visual expressions – graffiti, paintings and drawings by mental hospital patients, by children, outsiders, prisoners, primitives – in short by all those who created outside the context of the artworld in order to satisfy their own private, psychic needs. In 1948 he along with André Breton, Michel Tapié and others founded a society – Compagnie de L'Art Brut– to further the study of 'unpractised' art and a year later he organized an exhibition of his collection at the Galerie René Drouin, Paris. (In 1972 the collection was donated to the city of Lausanne, Switzerland.) Dubuffet liked raw art for its originality, innocent vision, directness of technique, use of unconventional materials, and lack of inhibition in respect of subject matter. He emulated these qualities in his own paintings and sculptures. For instance, he experimented with materials such as sand, ashes and vegetable matter to generate rough textures in which he scratched childlike images, and thus his own work also came to be known as L'Art Brut. What Dubuffet was seeking to avoid through his cult of the primitive, were the habits and fashions of mainstream, professional fine art – what he called 'cultural art' and others named 'tame art'. However, Dubuffet's own highly successful art gallery and museum career surely demonstrates that no such escape is possible at least for trained, professional artists.

● See also Art Therapy, Graffiti, Hospital Arts, Matter Art, Outsider Art, Prison Art.

● J Dubuffet *L'Art Brut préféré aux arts culturels* (Paris, Compagnie de L'Art Brut, 1949).

● G Limbour *Tableau bon levain à vous de cuire la pâte, L'Art Brut de Jean Dubuffet* (Paris, Éditions René Drouin/NY, Pierre Matisse Gallery, 1953).

● *L'Art Brut, fascicules 1–8* (Paris, Compagnie de L'Art Brut, 1964–6).

● *L'Art Brut* (Paris, Musée des Arts Decoratifs, 1967).

● *Catalogue de la collection de L'Art Brut* (Paris, 1971).

● M Thévoz *Art Brut* (Academy Editions, 1976).

● 'Primitivism and Art Brut' *Aftermath: France 1945–54: new images of man* (Barbican Centre for Arts, 1982) 73–117.

● A Weiss (ed) 'Art Brut: madness and marginalia' *Art & Text* (27) December–February 1987–88 (Special issue).

A New York collective committed to innovative design founded in 1977 consisting of 12 artists sponsored by the gallery owner Rick Kaufman. The collective have designed a variety of objects combining elements of

ART BRUT Le voyageur Français, 'Composition with flowers' (1902?). Watercolour. Collection: Compagnie de l'Art Brut, Lausanne, Switzerland.

art, architecture and furniture. Howard Meister, an artist–designer, specialized in metal constructions he called 'dangerous furniture', while Main and Main (Terence and Laura) generated surrealistic chairs in vivid colours.

● A Fawcett & J Withers 'Art et Industrie' *The Face* (32) December 1982 4–6.

(Also Art Expo, Kunstmarkt) Large-scale international gatherings of art dealers/galleries for the purposes of publicity and sales; the artworld equivalent of business trade fairs and motor shows. Such events are generally held in huge exhibition halls. Each gallery rents a stand, so physically the typical Art Fair resembles a maze of small rooms. Since dealers in all kinds of art – from avant garde to kitsch, from the good to the very bad – attend, the visitor encounters an unusually wide cross-section of contemporary art. By banding together for a special occasion, the galleries attract far more attention than they would separately. One aim of the fairs is to extend the audience and market for art but at the same time trading also takes place between dealers from different countries. Some visitors to fairs are disturbed by the hard-sell, culture-as-commerce, art-as-commodity atmosphere.

The first Art Fair dates from 1967 when 18 German dealers founded the Cologne Art Fair. Since then fairs have proliferated and take place annually in Düsseldorf, Basel, Zürich, Paris, Chicago, London, Bath, Milan and Los Angeles. In October 1973 the European Art Dealers Association was founded in imitation of the American Art Dealers Association.

Illustrated catalogues are normally on sale at Art Fairs and the shows themselves are often reviewed in the art press.

● See also Business Art, Commodity Aesthetics.

● G Jappe 'Art fairs – vanity fairs?' *Studio International* **186** (961) December 1973 244–5.

● H Haacke *Artfairismes* (Paris, Pompidou Centre, 1989).

● G Watson *Art in Ruins: Lies in ruins* (London, ICA, 1986).

● M Dickson 'White trash: Art in Ruins' *Variant* (Glasgow) (3) Autumn 1987 18–19.

● S Gassert *Art in Ruins: New realism* (Gimpel Fils, 1987).

furniture, stuffed animals, kitsch images and raw materials – often refer to contemporary art and architecture. Objects tend to be used allegorically and the exhibits comment on current political and theoretical issues. Emphasis on fragments, recycled goods, the relation of the past to the present, and ruins reveals a pessimistic, post-modernist consciousness at work. Art in Ruins have also published a number of artists' books and contributed art criticism to several journals.

● See also Book Art, Collaborations, Installation, Post-Modernism.

61 ART IN RUINS

A name adopted by two British artists, Glyn Banks and Hannah Vowles, in 1985. (They have collaborated since 1977 and previously employed the term 'Common Knowledge'.) Art in Ruins specialize in mixed-media installations which take place in galleries, museums and other, non-art spaces. Their installations – consisting of such items as wall paintings, found objects,

62 ART INFORMEL

An extremely broad term employed by the French writer Michel Tapié in his book *Un Art Autre* (1952) to characterize certain tendencies in the European art of the late 1940s and the '50s towards a mainly abstract but non-geometric style. The label appears to encompass work also described as tachisme, matter art, and lyrical

ART IN RUINS GLYN BANKS & HANNAH VOWLES, 'New realism: from the Museum of Ruined Intentions' (1987). Detail of mixed-media installation. Photo: Gimpel Fils Gallery, London.

abstraction. These tendencies arose in Europe at the same time as abstract expressionism/action painting in the USA and there seemed to be stylistic similarities between them. English writers have generally translated 'informel' as 'informal' (thus 'L'Art Informel' becomes 'Informalism').

Tapié's meaning is hard to discern because of the high-flown poetical manner of his writing: 'When form, transcended, is heavy with the possibilities of becoming...'. Literally, 'L'Art Informel' means 'art without form' and descriptions such as 'shapeless', 'intuitive', 'psychic improvization' were applied to the paintings of such 'authentic individuals' as Wols, Hans Hartung, Jean Fautrier, Henri Michaux, Jean-Paul Riopelle, Georges Mathieu and Alberto Burri.

Italian artists – Burri, Lucio Fontana, Emilio Vedova and Tancredi Parmeggiani – contributed much to L'Art Informel and several exhibitions surveying the movement have been mounted over the years. According to the critic Maurizio Calvesi, 'Informel is not simply a synonym for "without form", but signifies "nonformal"; it implies the negation of form as a category or value that remains distinct from reality, even though it may represent it. It denies the idea of form as something created according to plan. Informel is dominated by the direct communication of the "sign", the artist's gesture...'

● See also Abstract Expressionism, Action Painting, Art Autre, Lyrical Abstraction, Matter Art, New Informalists, Tachisme, Zen 49.

◉ J Paulham *L'Art Informel* (Paris, Gallimard, 1962).

◉ D Durbé & M Calvesi *L'Informale in Italia fino al 1957* (Livorno, Palazzo Communale, 1963).

◉ *Aspetti dell'Informale* (Milan, Palazzo Reale, 1971).

◉ R Barilli *Informale, oggetto, comportamento* 2 vols (Milan, Feltrinelli, 1979).

◉ R Barilli & F Solmi (eds) *L'Informale in Italia* (Bologna, Galleria Communale d'Arte Moderna, 1983).

◉ W Holler *Das Informal in der Europäischen Druckgraphik: Sammlung Prelinger* (Munich, Staatliche Graphisme Sammlung, Neue Pinakothek, 1985).

◉ *Informale in Italia* (Lucerne, Kunstmuseum, 1987).

◉ M Calvesi 'Informel and abstraction in Italian art of the fifties'– in– *Italian art in the 20th century* E Braun (ed) (Royal Academy/Munich, Prestel, 1989) 289–94.

63 ART SCHOOLS

Although some major artists (e.g. Francis Bacon) and designers have succeeded without receiving any formal training, the vast majority of professional practising architects, designers and artists have been educated at specialist schools, colleges and institutes. It follows that these institutions have had a crucial influence upon con-

temporary art and design. Furthermore, in Britain during the post-1945 era, part-time teaching in Art Schools provided a vital, hidden form of patronage for hundreds of artists. Artists too have been involved in the many government investigations into the future of art education: witness the famous Coldstream reports of the 1960s.

Since many creators feel that art cannot be taught, the presence of so many Art Schools in Europe and North America is somewhat paradoxical; a considerable literature exists about what should be taught to students. Some schools teach skills that can be traced back to the academies of Renaissance Italy (e.g. life drawing), while others embrace modern scientific ideas (e.g. cybernetics). Students employ brushes and computers; ancient and modern practices exist uneasily side by side. Since fine art in particular is hard to justify economically, these courses regularly come under threat – hence the numerous magazine and newspaper articles about crises, cuts and closures.

Some sociological studies of art students have been published and some general histories of art and design education exist, and there are also articles and books about notable individual schools such as the Bauhaus, Hornsey and the Royal College of Art, but there is a lack of a comprehensive study describing the influence of course contents and teaching methods on the subsequent development of art, design and architecture. However, one topic explored by several writers in the mid '80s was the link between British Art Schools and the pop music industry.

● See also Basic Design, Black Mountain College, Cal Arts, Goldsmiths, New Contemporaries, Related Studies, St Martin's School of Art Sculptors, Ulm.

◉ Staff & students of Hornsey College of Art *The Hornsey affair* (Harmondsworth, Penguin Books, 1969).

◉ S Hannema *Fads, fakes and fantasies: the crisis in the artschools and the crisis in art* (MacDonald, 1970).

◉ S MacDonald *The history and philosophy of art education* (University of London Press, 1970).

◉ G Battcock (ed) *New ideas in art education* (NY, Dutton, 1973).

◉ C Madge & B Weinberger *Art students observed* (Faber & Faber, 1973).

◉ D Rushton & P Woods (eds) *Politics of art education* (Studio Trust, 1979).

◉ K Baynes (ed) *Young blood* (Lund Humphries, 1983).

◉ S Frith & H Horne *Art into pop* (Methuen, 1987).

◉ J Walker 'The art school connection' – in – *Cross-overs: art into pop, pop into art* (Comedia/Methuen, 1987) 15-36.

(Related terms: Insane/Mad Art, Pathologic/ Projective/ Psychiatric/ Psychoneurotic/ Psychopathological/ Psychotherapeutic/ Psychotic Art, Remedial Art, Schizophrenic Art) In the twentieth century doctors and psychiatrists working in mental institutions have encouraged their patients to make 'art' in the form of drawings, paintings, ceramics, and sculptures. Such work serves as therapy for patients and as an aid to diagnosis for doctors. The assumption is that art is an externalization or objectivification of inner experience, that 'spontaneous' art in particular involves a process of free association or play which enables the unconscious to become visible. The fact that visual art is a non-verbal form of communication is considered an advantage. Taking part in activities with others also enables withdrawn patients to resocialize.

Tutors, mainly women, trained in art rather than medicine are employed in mental institutions to organize workshops, to supervise patients and to give them technical help. (They may also lead discussion sessions about the work on an individual or group basis so that the patients themselves can gain insight into their condition.) Although art therapists are not doctors, they are expected to have some knowledge of psychology and psychotherapy. Since the mid 1970s art therapy has also been practised in some American and British schools for the benefit of difficult or disruptive children.

In Britain a course to train art therapists is provided by St Albans School of Art. (It is also concerned with the application of art to health in a more general way, e.g. the design needs of the physically handicapped.) The course was established by Edward Adamson who has been called 'the father of art therapy in Britain'. For 30 years he ran the art studios at Netherne Hospital and preserved 60,000 paintings. A gallery was opened in Ashton, Northamptonshire in 1983 to display work from the Adamson Collection. Recent decades have seen an expansion and growing professionalization of art therapy. Several journals devoted to the subject have been founded: *American Journal of Art Therapy* (1961–); *Art Psychotherapy* (1973–), *Japanese Bulletin of Art Therapy* (1969–), *Inscape* (1962–). The latter is issued by BAAT– the British Association of Art Therapists.

Classic texts on the art of the insane were written decades ago by Ernst Kris and Hans Prinzhorn. Contemporary art therapists generally rely upon the established body of Freudian and Jungian theory, but they also refer to the writings of Melanie Klein, Anton Ehrenzweig and D. Winnicott. Concepts such as dreamwork, free association, empathy, introjection, projection and transference are routinely employed by art therapists.

Many exhibitions of art by mental patients or disturbed children have been held but most of this work does not count as 'art' as far as the artworld is concerned because (a) it is not made by professionally trained artists; (b) it is not of high enough aesthetic quality; and (c) it does not contribute to the public issues and discourse of contemporary art. However, modernism's interest in 'primitive' forms of expression did lead to an appreciation of the art of children and the insane. Furthermore, some insane people were previously artists (e.g. Richard Dadd) or were capable of producing high-quality work.

In terms of mental health, the line between normality and abnormality is uncertain. Analysts often perceive neurotic symptoms in the work of famous artists such as Leonardo and Michelangelo who are not otherwise considered mentally ill. There are also cases of artists (e.g. Van Gogh) whose mental disturbances were episodic. In some instances insanity seems to stultify creativity, while in other instances it liberates it. The precise influence of madness upon art is, therefore, complex and problematical. The popular cliché that madness culminating in suicide is somehow an essential prerequisite for great art is an idea that should be resisted.

Psychoanalysis, as a mode of interpretation, has been applied to art and creativity in general, i.e. to sane as well as to insane art. Arguably, all art is to some degree therapeutic both for its makers and for society at large.

● See also Art Brut, Freudian Aesthetics, Hospital Arts, Jungian Aesthetics, Outsider Art.

● H Prinzhorn *Artistry of the mentally ill...* (Berlin, Springer Verlag, 1972), first published 1922.

● F Reitman *Psychotic Art* (Routledge & Kegan Paul, 1950).

● E Kris *Psychoanalytic explorations in art* (Allen & Unwin, 1953).

● N Kiell (ed) *Psychiatry and psychology in the visual arts and aesthetics: a bibliography* (Madison & Milwaukee, University of Wisconsin Press, 1965).

● R Pickford *Studies in Psychiatric Art* (Springfield, Illinois, Charles S Thomas, 1967).

● *Art & mental health* (Commonwealth Institute, 1968).

● E Adamson 'Art for mental health'– in– *The social context of art* J Creedy (ed) (Tavistock, 1970).

● P Pacey 'Remedial art' *ARLIS Newsletter* (9) October 1971 10–4.

● — *Remedial Art: a bibliography* (Hatfield, Hertfordshire County Council Technical Library & Information Service, 1972).

● M Vernon & M Baughman 'Art, madness and human interaction' *Art Journal* **31** (4) Summer 1972 413–20.

● W Anderson (ed) *Therapy and the arts: tools of consciousness* (NY, Harper & Row, 1977).

● O Billig & B Burton-Bradley *The painted message* (NY, John Wiley, 1978).

● A Robins *The artist as therapist* (Human Sciences Press, 1987).

● T Dalley & others *Images of art therapy: new developments in theory and practice* (Tavistock, 1988).

● C Case & T Dalley (eds) *In the picture* (Routledge, 1989).

● A Gilroy & T Dalley (eds) *Pictures at an exhibition* (Routledge, 1989).

● J MacGregor *The discovery of the art of the insane* (Princeton University Press, 1989).

● D Waller *Becoming a profession: the history of art therapy in Britain 1940–82* (Routledge, 1991).

65 ART ULTRA

Title of an exhibition of American decorative art and furniture dating from the period 1946–59, organized by Steve Starr, held at the Hyde Park Center in Chicago in 1983. The term refers to decorative art that was 'ultra-modern'. Reflecting the affluence of post-war America, and the new scientific and technical developments of the era, designers such as Charles Eames, George Nelson, Royal Haeger, Eero Saarinen and others took advantage of new materials and manufacturing processes to design lamps, vases, ashtrays, chairs and tables that looked like giant amoebas, DNA molecules, Sputniks and so forth.

● See also Austerity/Binge, Contemporary Style, Free Forms, Populuxe.

● *Art Ultra: decorative arts & furnishings from 1946–59* (Chicago, Hyde Park Art Center, 1983), brochure.

66 ART WORKERS' COALITION (AWC)

An association of radical American art workers – artists, critics, architects, film-makers, museum employees – founded in New York in 1969. Members of AWC were critical of the capitalist gallery/dealer establishment and the 'star' system of promoting artists. They demanded reforms in the way museums were being administered, more representation in exhibitions of women artists, equal rights for black and Puerto Rican artists, and an end to the war in Vietnam. AWC organized strikes, sit-ins and demonstrations and it was associated with other movements and groups such as the New York Strike, Guerrilla Art Action and Art Workers United. According to Lucy Lippard, by the end of 1971 the AWC 'had died quietly of exhaustion, backlash, internal divisions and neglect by women'.

● See also Artists' Unions, Black Art, Guerrilla Art Action Group, Political Art.

● L Picard 'Protest and rebellion: the function of the Art Workers' Coalition' *Arts Magazine* **44** (7) May 1970 18–24.

● T Schwarz 'The politicization of the avant garde II' *Art in America* **60** (2) March–April 1972 70–9.

● L Lippard 'The Art Workers' Coalition: not a history' – in– *Get the message? A decade of art for social change* (NY, Dutton, 1984) 10–22.

67 ARTANGEL TRUST

A British, non-profit-making, 'outreach' organization founded in April 1985, based in London, for the purpose of supporting and commissioning new public art in unusual locations. There is a commitment to take art out of the museums and to foster work which makes political or social interventions in both urban and rural environments. Artangel is funded by private sources and by corporate enterprises and it encourages temporary and site-specific works in preference to the traditional types of public sculpture (i.e. stone and bronze statues and monuments). Examples include: images by Les Levine (1985) and Barbara Kruger pasted up on billboards; images projected on to buildings by Krystof Wodiczko (1985); messages flashed up on 'Spectacolor' – an animated display board in Piccadilly Circus – by Ann Carlisle and Jenny Holzer (1988). The director of Artangel in 1988 was Roger Took.

● See also Billboard Art, Projected Art, Public Art, Site-Specific Art, Street Art.

● I Hunter 'The Artangel Trust' *Artists' Newsletter* March 1987 23.

68 ARTE DEBOLE

(Weak Art) In 1989 four Italian artists – Renato Alpegiani, Luigi Antinucci, Renato Ghiazza and Gian Carlo Pagliasso – exhibited in London under the title 'Arte Debole'. They showed mixed-media constructions, reliefs and sculptures employing kitsch and popular culture materials, objects and iconography, e.g. imitation brick surfaces and decorative ironwork. Illusionistic or simulation devices were frequently employed. This tendency in art dated from 1986 and was manifested in a series of shows held in Turin. The term itself derived from the 'weak thought' concept of the post-modern theorist Gianni Vattimo. The work displayed was a paradoxical response to 'an age of decline' and 'the death of time'. According to Viana Conti, Arte Debole was art that could not 'make up its mind' nor 'find a name for itself'. Arguably, these deliberately synthetic contrivances were not only weak in thought but in aesthetic merit too.

● See also Kitsch, Post-Modernism, Simulation/ Simulcra/ Hyperreality.

● G Vattimo *Il pensiero debole* (Milan, Feltrinelli, 1983).

M Roberts 'Arte Debole' *Flash Art* (Italian ed) (138) April 1987 72–3.

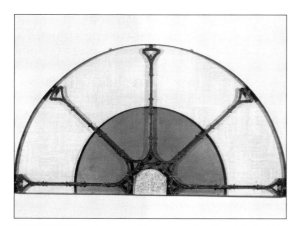

ARTE DEBOLE LUIGI ANTINUCCI, 'For a restructuring of aesthetics' (1988). Mixed-media construction. Photo: Flaxman Gallery, London.

● V Conti & others *Arte Debole – murmurs* (Turin, Gianfranco Zani, 1988), broadsheet.

● G Vattimo *The end of modernity* (Polity Press, 1988).

● M Campitelli & P Bellasi *Arte Debole: beyond the rest* (Flaxman Gallery, 1989).

69	ARTE POVERA

(Poor or impoverished art) A term devised by the Italian critic Germano Celant in 1967 to characterize certain works by Italian artists exhibiting at the Galleria La Bertesca, Genoa. Artists such as Mario Merz, Michelangelo Pistoletto, Pino Pascali, Gilberto Zorio, Giovanni Anselmo, Aligheri Boetti, Giulio Paolini and Jannis Kounellis have been associated with arte povera (lower case letters were used to indicate a modest status). Originally then it was an Italian phenomenon, but in a book he edited in 1969 Celant claimed that it was international by illustrating works by Carl Andre, Joseph Beuys, Robert Morris and other non-Italians. In his text Celant also listed a series of alternative terms: actual art, anti-form, conceptual art, earthworks, impossible art, micro-emotive art, raw materialist art which signified that his category was a broad one encompassing several international trends in the art of the '60s. Celant's label stressed the unworthiness (i.e. non-fine art) of the materials used–coal, sand, earth, twigs, cement, felt, rubber, rope, newspapers, old clothes, etc. Piles of materials were often simply dumped on the floors of galleries but generally installations consisted of strange combinations of different materials and irregular forms. Most arte povera was temporary in character. Also, its creation frequently took place at remote sites; consequently; its occurrence was only made permanent and known to the public via documentation which was then shown in galleries or published in books. Some arte povera reflected a new romanticism/primitivism: natural materials, rural settings, the artist as magician or alchemist working with the elements (water, snow, ice, grass) and forces of nature (gravity, wind, growth).

Although during the '60s arte povera was claimed to be 'non-saleable', most of the artists associated with it became commercially successful. A renewed interest in arte povera was demonstrated in 1984–5 when historical and contemporary exhibitions were held in Turin, Madrid and New York. Again it was Celant who provided the main critical support.

● See also Anti-Form, Conceptual Art, Earth & Land Art, Ecological Art, Installation, Matter Art, Minimal Art.

● G Celant (ed) *Arte povera* (Milan, Mazzotta, 1969); English edition *Art povera...* (London, Studio Vista/NY, Praeger, 1969).

● — (ed) *Arte povera: histories and protagonists* (Milan, Electa, 1985).

● — (ed) *The knot: arte povera at P.S.1* (NY, P.S.1 & Institute for Art & Urban Resources/Turin, Umberto Allemandi, 1985).

● S Westfall 'Anything, anytime, anywhere: arte povera at P.S.1' *Art in America* **74** (5) May 1986 132–6, + 169.

● G Celant *Arte povera* (Turin, Umberto Allemandi & C, 1990).

70	ARTHROPODS

Invertebrate animals with articulate, segmented bodies and limbs; a term applied by Jim Burns in 1972 to a number of experimental design groups because 'their members are articulated or interconnected for singular purposes of environmental creation, while still being segmented into their individual personae as artists, architects, designers, planners or performers'. The groups in question included: Ant Farm, Archizoom, Coop Himmelblau, Eventstructure Research Group, Experiments in Art & Technology, Haus-Rucker-Co, PULSA, and Superstudio.

● J Burns *Arthropods: new design futures* (NY, Praeger/London, Academy Editions, 1972).

71	ARTIST-IN-RESIDENCE

A form of patronage for living artists which became popular in Britain during the 1970s. Art centres, galleries, colleges, universities, schools, prisons, and other public organizations, invited artists to take up residence for a few weeks, a few months, or even a year. Living accommodation, studio space and funding were supplied by the host organization (or organizations because sometimes several were involved in one residency). Financial support was also supplied by regional and national arts councils. In return, artists were expected to open their studios, to give talks and tuition, and to hold exhibitions. Clearly, the aim of these schemes was to bring artists and a particular fraction of the public closer together, to increase the understanding and appreciation of contemporary art. For a detailed account of one such residency at Cambridge University, see the three extracts from Ian Breakwell's diary listed below. Residencies often posed severe problems of communication for both artists and clients; see Timothy Hyman's report of his year-long residency in Lincoln.

● See also APG, Community Art.

● I Breakwell 'From a Cambridge diary' (Part 1) *Art Monthly* (56) May 1982 6–10; (Part 2) (57) June 1982 8–10; (Part 3) (58) July–August 1982 8–13.

● T Hyman 'Out of the frying pan into the fire: an artist in residence at Lincoln' *Artscribe* (51) March–April 1985 66–7.

● A Rogers 'Considering residencies' *Art Monthly* (109) September 1987 5–7.

● 'Studios International: residency schemes home and abroad' *Alba* (10) Winter 1988 39–42.

● D Dahl *Residencies in education: setting them up and making them work* (Sunderland: AN Publications, 1991).

72 ARTISTS AGAINST APARTHEID (AAA)

Pop musicians and visual artists from around the world willing to perform and produce work to publicize and raise funds in support of the cause of black freedom in South Africa. When a concert was held in June 1988 at Wembley Stadium, London, to honour the 70th birthday of the imprisoned ANC leader Nelson Mandela, images by such artists as Sue Coe, Ralph Steadman, Keith Haring and John Muafangejo surrounded the stage and were seen via worldwide TV by an estimated audience of one billion. Other fine artists produced films and videos to be shown between acts but the TV companies censored them (they were only seen by the stadium audience). Previously, a number of exhibitions had been mounted by AAA, e.g. in Paris at the Fondation Nationale des Arts Plastiques (1983) and in London at the Royal Festival Hall (1985). These shows featured works by such British artists as Conrad Atkinson, Gavin Jantjes, Sokari Douglas Camp and Peter de Francia.

● See also Black Art, Political Art, Township Art, Video Art.

● *Art contre apartheid* (Paris, Fondation Nationale des Arts Plastiques, 1983).

● 'Artists Against Apartheid: cultures of resistance' *Fires: art/culture/politics* (2) Autumn 1986 14–20.

● W Mandela *Free Nelson Mandela festival concert book* (Penguin Books, 1988).

● 'Nelson Mandela: birthday video tribute' *AND Journal of Art & Art Education* (18/19) 1989 15–19.

73 ARTISTS' FOUNDATIONS

A number of wealthy modern artists, mindful of the struggles endured by many young and poor artists, have established foundations and charities in order to help their less fortunate colleagues. Others have made wills leaving money or an estate for the same philanthropic purpose. Examples include: Robert Rauschenberg's Change Inc; the Adolph & Esther Gottlieb Foundation; the Pollock–Krasner Foundation; the Andy Warhol Foundation; the Henry Moore Sculpture Trust.

● W Robinson 'Artists turn philanthropic' *Art in America* **78** (7) July 1990 152–3, + 184.

74 ARTISTS' FURNITURE

(Also Artist-Furniture, Fantasy- Furniture, Furnitur-Related Art, Furniture-Sculpture) During the 1980s many American and European fine artists made or designed items of furniture and these were celebrated in books and exhibitions. The artists included Richard Artschwager, Larry Bell, Philip Garner, James Hong, Jörg Immendorff, Donald Judd, Kim MacConnel, A. R. Penck, Paula Sweet, Reiner Ruthenbeck, George Sugarman and Jack Youngerman. Several precedents existed for this development in the history of twentieth-century art, e.g. Gerrit Rietveld's famous de Stijl painted wooden armchair of 1917, Salvador Dali's 1936 sofa in the shape of Mae West's lips, the '60s kitsch interiors of Claes Oldenburg. The artists of the '80s explored the full gamut of furniture types: bookcases, chairs, couches, tables and lamps; screens proved popular with painters because they could paint images on them. The New York artist Colette specialized in womb-like environments made from ruched silk and satin. Stylistically, the objects tended to reflect that of the artist's fine art work. Some items were one-off and handmade, while others were designed for limited-edition production. They differed from conventional furniture by being more original, bizarre even, in form and in the materials employed. Sometimes the furniture was figurative, e.g. 'Big Julie' (1982), a reclining chair by Alan Siegel, was shaped like a woman. Objects were often intended to be looked at rather than used; indeed, some were non-functional. Artists' Furniture was an ambiguous, hybrid phenomenon: artists delighted in making sculpture masquerading as furniture or deforming furniture so that it acquired the status of art.

● See also Architects' Furniture, Usable Art.

● T Simpson *Fantasy Furniture: design and decoration* (NY, Reinhold, 1968).

● D Domergue *Artists design furniture* (NY, Abrams, 1984).

● H Mous *Het Meubel Verbeeld: furniture as art* (Rotterdam, Museum Boymansvan Beuningen, 1988).

ARTISTS' FURNITURE H. R. GIGER, 'Environment, Restaurant Nouvelle, Zürich' (1983). Photo: Galerien R. P. Hartmann Munich & U. Steinle, Zürich.

75 ARTISTS' INTERNATIONAL (AI)

An organisation of Left-wing, politically committed, commercial and fine artists, designers and critics founded in London in 1933 whose name was redolent of the International congresses held by Communist parties. Founding members included: Clifford Rowe, Misha Black, James Fitton, James Boswell, Betty Rea, Pearl Binder and Francis Klingender. AI's aims were to unite all artists against war, fascism and colonialism; to form working units of artists willing to produce artworks and visual propaganda, to organize exhibitions, and to maintain contact with similar organizations in other countries. Art – mainly social realist in style – and agitprop imagery were to be harnessed to the cause of the emancipation of the working class. In 1935 the AI was renamed the 'Artists' International Association' (AIA) in order to widen membership to include any artists willing to form a popular front against fascism and war.

AIA had regional groups and was an extremely active body which published a bulletin, mounted exhibitions, organized lectures and art classes. Its members produced drawings, prints, posters, paintings, sculptures, cartoons and banners; they participated in demonstrations and raised money for many causes. During the late 1930s and the period of the Second World War, AIA concentrated on taking art to the people. In 1953 the political clause in the AIA's constitution was deleted and this signalled the end of the radical movement though the name continued to be used for a non-political exhibiting society with a gallery in Lisle Street, London, until this closed in 1971.

● See also International Artists' Association, National Artists Association, Political Art.

● *Artists' International Association: the first five years* (AIA, 1938).

● T Rickaby 'The Artists' International' *Block* (1) 1979 5–14.

● L Morris & R Radford *The story of the AIA 1933–53* (Oxford, Museum of Modern Art, 1983).

● R Radford *Art for a purpose: the Artists' International Association* (Winchester School of Art Press, 1987).

76 ARTISTS' SPACE

A non-profit-making exhibition space established in 1973, financed by grants from national and state arts funds, and one of the best known of New York's 'alternative' galleries. The purpose of the gallery was to give one-person shows to young, unknown, 'unaffiliated' artists.

A slide bank was established and initially exhibitors were selected by a changing panel of established artists. Irving Sandler, art historian and critic, was closely involved in the setting up and running of the gallery. The director of Artists' Space from 1975 to 1980 was Helene Weiner.

● See also Alternative Spaces.

● D Seagrief 'Creativity at work: Artists' Space' *Studio International* **187** (967) June 1974 274–5.

● T Grace 'Artists' Space' *Art Journal* **34** (4) Summer 1975 323–6.

77 ARTISTS' UNIONS

At different times in different countries artists have banded together in order to form unions for the purpose of improving their conditions of employment and social status. In the United States a union was formed in 1934 and it published a magazine entitled *The Art Front*. In Holland the BBK (Beroepsvereniging Beeldende Kunstenaars) dated from the immediate post-1945 era, while in England a union seeking affiliation to the TUC (Trades Union Congress) was first mooted in 1971. In Ireland the Artists Collective of Northern Ireland was established in 1981. Unlike the Artists' Unions of the West, that of the USSR was a state-approved body. It was established in the 1930s and for decades it exercised a virtual monopoly and control over Soviet artistic production.

Within free market economies Artists' Unions are highly problematical because of the individualism of most artists and the fact that they are not employees in the same sense as office and factory workers. However, some unions have been successful in obtaining improvements for artists, especially in those cases in which negotiations took place with government-arts funding bodies. Given the difficulties encountered in trying to organize the artists of Britain into a union in the 1970s, efforts during the '80s were directed towards the formation of professional associations.

● See also Artists' International, International Artists' Association, National Artists Association, Unofficial Soviet Art.

● S Davis 'The artist today. From the standpoint of the Artists' Union' *American Magazine of Art* **28** August 1935 476–8, + 506.

● 'The Artists' Union' *Studio International* **183** (944) May 1972 p 192.

● P Fuller 'United artists...?' *Art & Artists* **7** (4) July 1972 12–14.

● 'The Artists' Union: a statement' *Art & Artists* **7** (5) August 1972 12–13.

● S Braden 'Exhibitions: dispute in the art industry' *Time Out* (132) August 25–31 1972 37.

● 'Union now!' *Art & Artists* **7** (6) September 1972 10–13.

● G Monroe 'The Artists' Union of New York' *Art Journal* **32** (1) Fall 1972 17–20.

● 'The artist as an individual: the Artists' Union in Holland' *Studio International* **186** (957) July–August 1973 2–3.

● J Walstra 'Concerning the Dutch Artists' Union' *Studio International* **186** (961) December 1973 p 217.

● 'Artists as militant trade union workers during the great depression' *Archives of American Art Journal* **14** (1) 1974 7–10.

● M Field 'Artists in the United Kingdom...' *AND* (10) 1986 10–11.

78 ARTLAW SERVICES

A British charitable organization established in 1978 to provide legal advice and help, education, publications and research on all matters affecting the visual arts. Owing to lack of funds the Service had to close its office in 1983. One of the main achievements of Artlaw Services was the highly informative series of articles written by Henry Lydiate published in *Art Monthly* discussing a wide range of legal and financial problems which artists encounter in their professional practice. (The articles continued to appear after the office closed.) An Arts Law Centre was also founded in Australia in 1983.

● H Lydiate 'The present status of Artlaw' *Art Monthly* (85) April 1985 40.

● F Feldman, S Weil & S Biederman *Art Law: rights and liabilities of creators and collectors* 2 vols (Boston, Mass, Little, Brown & Co, 1986).

79 ARTOLOGY

A new term proposed by the French critic Paule Gauthier in 1973. By adding the suffix '-ology' (a science or branch of knowledge) to 'art' Gauthier arrived, by analogy with musicology, at the science and theory of art. Artologists would be those who studied art and were knowledgeable about it without being practising artists. Artology would encompass art history, criticism and connoisseurship but it would be distinguished from aesthetics in not being concerned with beauty in nature. In addition, Artology would take account of the insights of other disciplines, e.g. anthropology, linguistics, Marxism, philosophy, psychology, semiotics and sociology.

● See also Marxist Aesthetics, New Art History, Paraesthetics, Semiotics, Structuralism & Art/Design.

● P Gauthier (Artology) *Cimaise* (110/111) January – April 1973 97–8.

● A Goodwin 'What is Artology?' *Art International* **19** (3) March 20 1975 47–8.

80 ARTS ADMINISTRATION

A growth area in the decades since 1945. The expansion of visual arts activities has involved the establishment of many new funding bodies, arts councils, institutions, organizations, art centres and galleries, which in turn has led to the need for professionally qualified managers, administrators and fund-raisers. In London the City University provides a course to train such people. The increase in the numbers of arts administrators prompted the invention of the term 'artocrat', a synthesis of 'art' and 'bureaucrat'.

● See also Arts Councils, Business Sponsorship.

▒ A Geracimos & G Marzorati 'The artocrats' *Art in America* **66** (4) JulyAugust 1978 100–8.

▒ J Pick *Arts Administration* (E & F Spon, 1980).

▒ — *Managing the arts? The British experience* (Rhinegold Publishing Ltd, 1986).

81 ARTS COUNCILS

Most developed countries now have state bodies – councils or ministries of culture – responsible for funding and fostering the living arts within their own borders. Separate organizations usually exist with responsibilities for promoting national cultures in foreign lands (e.g. the British Council). The Arts Council of Great Britain was established in 1946 and is funded by the Treasury via the Department of Education and Science; its annual budget has gradually increased year by year. Its responsibilities include opera, music, literature, theatre and ballet, besides painting, photography, film and sculpture, hence its financial support for fine artists, touring exhibitions, etc. is only a small part of its outlay. The Council's headquarters are located in London but there are a number of Regional Arts Associations (RAAs) which foster the arts in the provinces. It is part of the policy of the Council to purchase works of art from living artists and hence a considerable body of material now exists – the Arts Council Collection – from which touring exhibitions are regularly mounted.

Public subsidies for the arts are in themselves highly controversial and even when such expenditure is accepted, how and to whom monies should be distributed are a constant source of disputes, consequently the Arts Council and its policies are continually being criticized. Details of the ACGB's activities, expenditures and policies can be found in its annual reports and in its periodic publications.

In the United States the equivalent body is the NEA – the National Endowment for the Arts – an independent federal agency located in Washington DC founded in 1965 under the administration of President Lyndon B. Johnson. Its mission is 'to foster the excellence, diversity and vitality of the arts ... and to help broaden their availability and appreciation'. Matching awards are made to non-profit, tax-exempt arts organizations of outstanding quality if they can raise funds elsewhere, and fellowships are given to artists of exceptional talent. The NEA is directed by a chairperson (appointed by the President) and advised by a National Council on the Arts with a rotating membership. The major funding programmes of the NEA are advised by panels of experts in the various arts. The NEA's budget for 1989 was $169,090,000.

● See also Arts Administration, National Campaign for the Arts.

▒ E White *The Arts Council of Great Britain* (Davis-Poynter, 1975).

▒ J Minihan *The nationalization of culture: the development of state subsidies to the arts in Great Britain* (Hamish Hamilton, 1977).

▒ *Arts Council Collection* (Arts Council, 1980).

▒ R Hutchison *The politics of the Arts Council* (Sinclair Browne, 1982).

▒ N Pearson *The state and the visual arts* (Milton Keynes, Open University Press, 1982).

▒ *The glory of the garden* (Arts Council, 1984).

▒ *A great British success story* (Arts Council, 1985).

▒ R Shaw *The arts and the people* (Jonathan Cape, 1987).

▒ L Biddle *Our government and the arts: a perspective from the inside* (NY, American Council for the Arts, 1988).

82 ARTS LAB

A phenomenon of the alternative or counter culture of the late 1960s. Jim Haynes (b. 1933), an American resident in Britain from 1956 to '69, established the first Arts Laboratory in Drury Lane, Covent Garden, London in 1967. By the end of '69 over 150 had been founded throughout Britain. Arts Labs were committed to avant garde, experimental activities across a range of media: theatre, films, rock music, visual art and so on. They were intended to serve as fun alternatives to the more staid and specialist cinemas and art galleries and they were often run as private clubs to avoid censorship problems; some provided workshop facilities. Arts Labs were short-lived because of a lack of funds but they set the pattern for the multi-function art centres that were to succeed them.

● See also Alternative Spaces, ICA, Underground Art.

▒ P Fryer 'The Arts Laboratory' *New Society* October 26 1967 p. 557.

▒ H Judson 'The Arts Laboratory: swinging smorgasbord' *Life* May 13 1968.

▒ J Allen 'The Arts Lab explosion' *New Society* November 21 1968 749–50.

▒ N de Jongh 'Lights out for the Arts Lab' *Guardian* October

21 1969 11.

▪ J Haynes 'Arts Lab: a fortress and haven for adult games' *Ark* (45) Winter 1969 2–28.

▪ R Neville *Playpower* (J Cape, 1970).

▪ J Haynes *Thanks for coming!* (Faber & Faber, 1984).

83 ARTSPEAK

A term devised by John A. Walker in 1976 (following the example of George Orwell's 'newspeak') to describe the obscure, convoluted and tortured language typical of so much contemporary art writing. Also the title of a magazine published by Art Liaison Inc., New York and a dictionary of art written by Robert Atkins.

▪ J Walker 'Internal memorandum' *Studio International* **192** (983) September–October 1976 113–18.

▪ R Atkins *Artspeak: a guide to contemporary ideas, movements and buzzwords* (NY, Abbeville Press, 1990).

84 ARTWORLD

A topic discussed by several American aestheticians. Arthur C. Danto defined it as 'an atmosphere of artistic theory, a knowledge of the history of art', whereas George Dickie saw it as the social institution responsible for defining art. Sociologically, the Artworld can be defined as the totality of people and institutions specializing in art: i.e. artists, art historians, critics, dealers, curators, patrons, collectors, arts officials, art tutors ... galleries, museums, arts councils, auction houses, artschools, etc. It is an international network or subculture (with headquarters in New York) which has most of the power to determine what is and what is not art, which artists are successful and which are not. Arguably, this state of affairs is unhealthy because art ought to be the concern of a wider cross-section of society.

● See also Conceptual Art.

▪ A Danto 'The Artworld' *Journal of Philosophy* 1964 571–84.

▪ G Dickie *Art and the aesthetic: an institutional analysis* (Ithaca, Cornell University Press, 1974).

▪ A Silvers 'Artworld discarded' *Journal of Aesthetics & Art Criticism* **34** (4) Summer 1976 441–54.

▪ H Becker *Artworlds* (Berkeley, University of California Press, 1982).

▪ L Alloway *Network* (Ann Arbor, Michigan, University of Michigan Research Press, 1984).

▪ R Hagenberg *Untitled '84: the Artworld of the '80s* (NY, Pelham Press, 1984).

▪ D Crane *Transformation of the avant garde: the New York Artworld 1940–85* (Chicago, University of Chicago Press, 1987).

▪ H Pindell 'Art (world) and racism' *Third Text* (3/4)

Spring–Summer 1988 157–90.

85 ARUP

A famous international group of consulting engineers founded by Sir Ove Arup (b. 1895) in Britain in 1946. Later, in 1963, Arup was joined by the architect Philip Dowson. The group provides expertise across a range of disciplines. During the 40-year period 1946–86 15,000 commissions were undertaken; they included buildings, bridges, roads, masts, oil rigs and exhibition structures. Notable projects were: Coventry Cathedral, the Sydney Opera House, the Pompidou Centre, Paris, the Hong Kong Bank, the Lloyds Building and Broadgate Offices, London.

● See also Coventry Cathedral, Pompidou Centre.

Ove Arup & Partners 1946–1986 (NY, St Martin's Press/London, Academy Editions, 1986).

▪ 'Sir Ove Arup' – in – *Contemporary Architects* A Morgan & C Naylor (eds) (Chicago & London, St James Press, 2nd ed 1987).

86 ASPEKT GROUP

At the 'Free Berlin Exhibition' of 1972 ten participants formed a group and adopted a common programme. The best known of the artists concerned were Bettina von Arnim, Peter Sorge and Hans-Jürgen Diehl. What they shared was a commitment to a social/critical realist form of art, one which would attempt to record the present epoch through depicting contemporary life and events. The artists organized exhibitions with titles like 'Principle of realism', 'Metropolis' and worked together at the Bethanien Art Centre in Berlin. Stylistically their paintings and drawings owed a debt to the earlier critical realism of Otto Dix and George Grosz – precise, 'overfinished', illustrative and descriptive renderings; the work also had affinities with the modern realist art of East Berlin. But in order to go beyond the limits of single images several of the artists used triptychs, or multi-panelled formats, or a montage of images. Besides direct observation, imagery was derived from mass media material and from visions of the future.

● See also Capitalist Realism, Critical Realism, Political Art.

▪ E Roters *Aspekt Groszstadt* (Berlin, Kunstlerhaus Bethanien, 1977 /Edinburgh, Talbot Rice Art Centre, 1978).

▪ I Davies 'Berlin realism today and its legacy' *Artscribe* (13) August 1978 29–34.

▪ S Kent & others *Berlin, a critical view: Ugly realism '20s – '70s* (ICA, 1978).

The name of a magazine and a place. *Aspen,* the magazine, was first published in New York in 1965 by Phyllis Johnson. It was promoted as 'the magazine in a box' because its contents appeared in various physical formats to match its interdisciplinary and multi-media approach to the arts.

Aspen, the place, is a ski and tourist resort in Colorado which was once a silver-mining town. Walter P. Paepcke, head and founder of the Container Corporation, held a design seminar there in 1951 and it subsequently became an annual event which attracted leading architects, designers and design theorists from around the world. In 1955 the conference was formally incorporated as an independent and non-profit-making corporation: International Design Conference in Aspen (IDCA). Discussions at Aspen have covered architecture, graphics, industrial and interior design, environmental planning and British design.

● R Banham (ed) *The Aspen papers: twenty years of design theory from the International Design Conference at Aspen* (Pall Mall Press, 1974).

● J Allen *The romance of commerce and culture: capitalism, modernism, and the Chicago – Aspen crusade for cultural reform* (Chicago, University of Chicago Press, 1983).

The term 'assemblage' was first used in a fine art context by Jean Dubuffet to describe his own work in 1953. He preferred it to collage because he thought the latter should be restricted to cubism. Assemblage is a technique or method similar to montage – constructing a work from various bits and pieces – while Assemblage Art describes the end results of that process. This form of art marked a departure from traditional artforms. Objects were made from various materials and items of junk; they were mixed-media works or composites and thus they transgressed the purity of medium aesthetic and blurred the difference between painting and sculpture. This kind of art was especially fashionable in the late 1950s and early '60s. W. C. Seitz's 1961 survey show entitled 'Art of Assemblage' illustrated the historical origins of Assemblage Art in cubism, dada, futurism and surrealism and the range of work being produced in Europe and America. Amongst the contemporary artists featured were Jean Dubuffet, César, Bruce Connor, Joseph Cornell, Ed Kienholz, John Latham, Louise Nevelson, Robert Rauschenberg and Daniel Spoerri.

During the 1980s a renewed interest in making objects from waste materials was evident in the work of a number of British artists and designers (see, for example,

ASSEMBLAGE ART JOHN LATHAM, 'Painting is an open book' (1961). Relief made from books, plaster on board, hessian bond, 1524mm x 914mm x 203 mm. Photo: Lisson Gallery, London.

Creative Salvage, Mutoid Waste Co and New British Sculpture). Historical curiosity was also indicated by the 1988 exhibitions 'Lost and found in California: four decades of Assemblage Art' organized by several private California galleries.

● See also Arte Povera, Combine Paintings, Environmental Art, Junk Culture/ Sculpture, Neo-Dada, Object Art, Packaging.

● W Seitz *The Art of Assemblage* (NY, MoMA, 1961).

● A Kaprow *Assemblage, environments, happenings* (NY, Abrams, 1965).

● S Star *Lost and found in California: four decades of Assemblage Art* (LA, Shoshana Wayne & other galleries, 1988).

The International Association of Art Critics was founded in 1949 to further the activity and profession of art criticism. Annual congresses are organized and the

Association publishes a review (AICARC). The headquarters of AICA are in Paris where a documentation centre is maintained. A special number of AICARC, to be published in 1991, will celebrate 40 years of the work of the organization.

90 ASSOCIATION OF ART HISTORIANS (AAH)

An organization founded in Britain in 1974 by art historians teaching in universities, art colleges and polytechnics or working in museums. Its aim is to advance the study of the history of art and to further the professional interests of members. The AAH holds annual conferences with book fairs and it publishes a newsletter plus the academic journal *Art History* (**1** (1) March 1978–).
● See also Artology, Design History Society, New Art History.
● J White 'The Association of Art Historians' *Times Literary Supplement* (3811) March 21 1975 313.

91 ASSOCIATION OF ILLUSTRATORS (AOI)

A British organization with headquarters in London, founded in 1973, dedicated to the promotion of the art and profession of illustration. By 1989 membership exceeded 1,000 and included, besides illustrators, art directors, art buyers, designers, agents, tutors and students. AOI facilitates contacts between clients and freelance illustrators, maintains an image bank in the form of slides, sponsors competitions, mounts an annual exhibition of the work of members and publishes a catalogue of all items displayed. It also provides financial advice, maintains an art gallery, publishes a monthly journal and *The Illustrator's Survival Guide,* and holds meetings to encourage discussion of all aspects of illustration.

92 ASTRATTO-CONCRETO

(Abstract-Concrete) A variety of abstract art appearing in Italy in the 1950s produced by the artists Afro Basaldella, Renato Birolli, Antonio Corpora, Antonio Scordia, Filippo Santomaso and Enzo Brunori. Although their paintings were abstract, the use of naturalistic colours and organic shapes evoked landscapes and subjective emotions. The movement was promoted via the writings of the critic Lionelli Venturi. The same critic was also supportive of Gruppo Degli Otto Pittori Italiani, a coalition of nonfigurative painters exhibiting at the Venice Biennale in 1952. The latter group included a number of the artists listed above.
● See also Concrete Art.
● E Braun (ed) *Italian art in the 20th century: painting and sculpture 1900–1988.* (London, Royal Academy/Munich, Prestel-Verlag, 1989).

93 ATELIER D'ART ABSTRAIT

A French teaching and research organization devoted to the cause of constructivist and abstract art which existed from 1950 to 1952. It was founded by Jean Dewasne and Edgard Pillet. Participants included the artists Victor Vasarély, Auguste Herbin and the critic Michel Seuphor.
● See also Constructivism.

94 ATELIER POPULAIRE

(People's Studio) Students of the École des Beaux Arts, Paris involved in the revolutionary events of May 1968 set up a workshop to issue political posters produced by means of the silkscreen process. The designs and captions were very simple, telegraphic even, printed in a single colour on a white ground. Their content was critical of government policies and police brutality. In order to avoid the errors of 'cultural art', designs were subject to group discussion and published anonymously. Before the workshop was closed by the riot police in June, 350

ATELIER POPULAIRE 'The police post themselves in the Beaux Arts, the Beaux Arts post in the street' (1968).

different posters were designed and 120,000 copies distributed and pasted up on the walls of Paris.

● See also Political Art, Popular Art, Prop Art, Silk-Screenprinting.

● *Text and posters by Atelier Populaire: posters from the revolution, Paris, May* (Dobson, 1969).

● J Montgomery 'Defense d'afficher' *Art & Text* (16) 1984 32–42.

● M Rohan (compiler) *Paris '68: graffiti, posters, newspapers, and poems of the events of May '68* (Impact Books, 1988).

95 ATELIER 17

A famous print studio and group workshop established by the British-born painter and engraver Stanley Hayter (1901–88) which was used by many leading modern artists. The first Atelier 17 was founded in Paris in 1927. When Hayter moved to New York in 1941 he started a second studio there and it functioned until 1955; Hayter returned to Paris in 1950 and opened his first studio again.

● See also Paddington Printshop, Tamarind Lithography Workshop, Tyler Graphics.

● S Hayter *New ways of gravure* (Oxford University Press, 1966).

● J Moser *Atelier 17* (Madison, Wisconsin, University of Wisconsin, Evehjem Art Center, 1977).

● P Hacker (ed) *The renaissance of gravure: the art of S W Hayter* (Oxford, Ashmolean Museum, 1988).

96 AUSTERITY/ BINGE

A term coined by Bevis Hillier in order to characterize the British decorative arts of the 1940s – a period of austerity – and the 1950s – a period of 'binge' or affluence. According to Hillier, these arts showed that the antiseptic functionalism typical of modern design before 1939 had been rejected. People in the post-war period favoured motifs and fads that were much more whimsical and popular, e.g. mermaids, winged horses, balloons, abstract amoeba shapes, heraldry, canal boat painting, the circus, fairground art and so on.

● See also Art Ultra, Contemporary Style, Fairground Art, Populuxe.

● B Hillier *Austerity/Binge: the decorative arts of the forties and fifties* (Studio Vista, 1974).

97 AUTO-ART

An abbreviation of 'autobiographical art', Peter Frank's 1976 term for the confessional, narcissistic self-portraiture of artists like Laurie Anderson, John Baldessari, Chris Burden, Julia Heyward, Urs Lüthi, Roger Welch and Hannah Wilke. A show called 'Choices' held in New York in 1986 also featured artists – Abramovic, Alex Grey, United Art Contractors, Ian Wilson and others – who made art from everyday experience. This work too was dubbed 'autobiographical' and also 'egocentric art'. (NB If 'auto' is regarded as short for 'automobile', then the term 'Auto-Art' could also describe the decoration and customizing of motor cars; see Car Culture and Customizing & Custom Painting.)

● See also Body Art, Photo-Therapy, Story Art.

● P Frank 'Auto-art: self indulgent? And how!' *Art News* **75** (7) September 1976 43–8.

● M Tucker *Choices: making an art of everyday life* (NY, New Museum of Contemporary Art, 1986).

98 AUTOMATIC ART

Paintings, drawings or writings produced while their makers are in a state of distracted attention such as a day-dream or light trance. Doodles are an everyday example of this phenomenon. Automatic drawings have been made by people under hypnosis and by psychics/mediums claiming to be under the sway of spirits from another realm. Automatism – the technique or method of Automatic Art – has been regarded by many modern artists, e.g. surrealists, abstract expressionists and tachistes, as a way of bypassing the control of the conscious mind in order to liberate material from the unconscious. (André Breton first used the phrase 'pure psychic automatism' in a 1924 surrealist manifesto.) However, the sameness of doodles suggests that they are the result of physiological motor activity and that therefore they are unlikely to provide any profound insights from the unconscious. (The word 'automatic' implies 'routine', 'machine-like'. Many would regard these characteristics as negative if manifested in art. For this reason certain artists responded sardonically to the 1950s' vogue for Automatic Art by automating it, e.g. Jean Tinguely's drawing machines called 'metamatics'.) The surrealists, of course, devised a whole range of means to subvert the rational: they used dream images, techniques such as frottage, grattage, fumage and décalcomanie, and also 'surrational' automatism. The latter derived from Freud's notion of 'free association': it involved beginning with a mark, a form or an image and developing it through a chain of unplanned associations. Yet another way in which modern artists achieved Automatic Art was by accepting the results of chance procedures, e.g. Hans Arp and Sophie Taeuber-Arp made collages during the First World War by allowing pieces of torn paper to fall on to a surface; therefore, the collages' compositions were determined automatically.

● See also Abstract Expressionism, Action Painting,

Automatistes, Process Art, Tachisme.

● A Breton 'First surrealist manifesto' – in – *Surrealism* by P Waldberg (Thames & Hudson, 1965) 66–72.

● D Menzel 'Doodling as a form of art' *Leonardo* **1** (2) April 1968 175–7.

● A Gauld 'Automatic Art' *Man, Myth & Magic* (7) 1970 189–93.

● J Wechsler 'Surrealism's automatic painting' *Art News* **76** (4) April 1977 44–7.

● M Sawin '"The third man", or automatism American style' *Art Journal* **47** (3) Fall 1988 181–6.

99 AUTOMATISTES, LES

Name of a group of Canadian abstract painters active between 1946 and '51 whose work has been variously described as surrealist, action painting and lyrical abstraction. The group was formed in Montreal by Paul-Émile Borduas (1905–60) and its members included Jean-Paul Riopelle, Fernand Leduc, Albert Dumouchel and Jean-Paul Mousseau. The name of the group dated from 1947: the critic Tancrède Marsil supplied it after a Borduas painting entitled 'Automatisme 1. 47'. Clearly, these artists were strongly influenced by the surrealist method of automatism. In 1948 Les Automatistes caused a scandal by publishing a manifesto – 'Refus Global' – which advocated liberation from established conventions and which was critical of Canadian life and the Catholic Church. Works by members of the group were featured in exhibitions held in New York and Paris from the late '40s onwards and Borduas and Riopelle both moved to Paris in the '50s.

● See also Action Painting, Automatic Art, Lyrical Abstraction, Tachisme.

● E Turner & G Viau *Paul-Émile Borduas 1905–60* (Montreal, Museum of Fine Arts, 1960).

● G Robert 'École de Montreal' *Cimaise* (75) February – April 1966 24–36.

● *Borduas et Les Automatistes: Montreal 1942–55* (Montreal, Musée d'Art Contemporain/Paris, Galeries Nationales du Grand Palais, 1971).

● F Gagnon 'Pellan, Borduas and the Automatists: men and ideas in Quebec' *ArtsCanada* (174/175) December –January 1972–3 48–55.

100 AVANT GARDE ART

(Also Vanguard Art) One of the most discussed and controversial concepts in the discourse of modern art criticism. The French term 'avant garde' means 'the advanced guard of an army'. This military metaphor was first applied to art and literature by utopian socialist writers in France during the early nineteenth century. Initial-

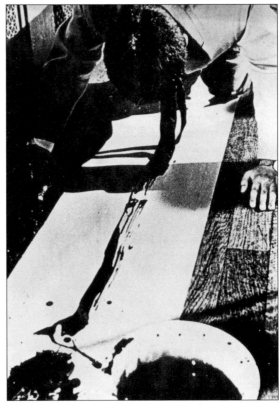

AVANT GARDE ART NAM JUNE PAIK 'Zen for head', Fluxus Festival, Wiesbaden, (1962).

ly, artistic radicalism was closely linked with political radicalism but this connection was not always maintained later on. Art could be radical in political terms or in formal/aesthetic terms (or both). Renato Poggioli has claimed that the Avant Garde originated in romanticism and that it is characterized by: (1) activism (taste for action, dynamism, exploration); (2) antagonism (against the past, tradition, and the social order); (3) nihilism (destructiveness, infantilism, extreme behaviour); (4) agonism (romantic agony, pathos, tension, sacrifice); (5) futurism (pre-vision, prophesying the art of the future).

Avant Garde Art can be briefly defined as that art of the current moment that is more advanced in concept, more experimental, more extreme in technique, more difficult in language, than all other types of art. It is a subspecies of modern art, the cutting edge of modern art. Avant Garde Art opposes both academic art and mass culture or kitsch, it often sets out to shock the bourgeoisie or the general public and tends to appeal to a minority audience of intellectuals. Since the 1840s there has been a succession of new artistic waves or Avant Garde movements – realism, impressionism, symbolism, fauvism, cubism, dada, futurism, etc. – so many in fact that the cult of the new and the different came to constitute a tradition. This produced a paradoxical, doublebind situation in which young artists were expected to rebel against rebellion (i.e. the Avant Garde itself). It became very difficult for young artists to top what had gone before. Their attempts to do so became absurdly extreme, so much so that Robert Hughes declared the Avant Garde was exhausted and bankrupt. An alternative was to renounce the premises of the Avant Garde altogether, hence the advent of post-modernism and the trans-avant garde.

● See also Modern Art, Modernist Painting, Post-Modern Art, Trans-Avant Garde.

● C Greenberg 'Avant Garde and kitsch' (1939) – in – *Art & Culture* (Thames & Hudson, 1973) 3–21.

● D Egbert 'The idea of "Avant Garde" in art and politics from the work of Henri de Saint Simon...' *American Historical Review* **73** 1967 339–66.

● R Poggioli The theory of the Avant Garde (Cambridge, Mass, Belknap Press/Harvard, 1968).

● T Hess & J Ashbery (eds) *The Avant Garde* (NY, Newsweek, 1969), *Art News* annual 34.

● D Egbert 'The idea of the Avant Garde in art and politics' *Leonardo* **3** (1) January 1970 75–86.

● R Hughes 'The decline and fall of the Avant Garde' *Time* December 18 1972 40–1.

● N Hadjinicolaou 'On the ideology of Avant Gardism' *Praxis* (6) 1982 38–70.

● P Wollen 'The two Avant Gardes' – in– *Readings and writings* (Verso/NLB, 1982) 92–104.

● P Burger *Theory of the Avant Garde* (Manchester University Press, 1985).

● R Kraus *The originality of the Avant Garde & other modernist myths* (Cambridge, Mass, MIT Press, 1985).

● E Timms & P Collier (eds) *Visions and blueprints: Avant Garde culture and radical politics in early 20th-century Europe* (Manchester University Press, 1988).

B

101 'BAD' PAINTING

(Also Punk Art, New Wave and Stupid Painting) Title of an exhibition curated by Marcia Tucker held at the New Museum, New York, in 1978 featuring the work of Neil Jenney, William Wegman, Robert Chamless Hendon, Joan Brown and Jim Chatelain.

At any one time the majority of art produced is bad. This is especially the case in amateur art and in the tourist kitsch art sold on park railings. 'Bad' Painting, however, is not of this kind; it is work by professionally trained fine artists which self-consciously tries to be bad. There is a risk here: 'Bad' Painting may degenerate into genuinely bad painting. Art critics face the difficult task of distinguishing between good 'Bad' Painting and bad 'Bad' Painting.

'Bad' Painting was a reaction to 'good' painting which had become too bland and predictable. In other words, the deliberate cultivation of badness was an attempt to renew the shock-value and interest of contemporary art by breaking what was probably modernism's final taboo. Peter Plagens characterized 'Bad' Painting as 'what looks like inept drawing, garish or unschooled colour, tasteless or trivial or bizarre imagery, odd and impractical assemblage, manically vigorous or disinterested paint application, dubious craft and materials, and a general preference for squalor over reason'. Amongst the artists Plagens cited were: Julian Schnabel, David Salle, Donald Sultan, Jonathan Borofsky, George Baselitz, Robert Colescott, Jedd Garet, Malcolm Morley, Karen Carson and the Hairy Who artists of Chicago. Art-historical precedents for the vogue for 'badness' were to be found in the late work of Picasso, De Chirico and Guston. Picabia, according to Plagens, was 'probably the best "bad" painter who ever lived'.

● See also Chicago Imagists, Kitsch, New Image Painting, Punk.

● C Barrett 'Are "bad works of art" works of art?' *Philosophy and the arts* Royal Institute of Philosophy Lectures Vol 6 1971– 2 (MacMillan, 1973).

● M Tucker *Bad Painting* (NY, New Museum, 1978).

● S Kent 'Time out with the Burberry brigade' *Time Out* 1– 7 June 1979 12– 13.

● P Plagens 'The academy of the bad' *Art in America* **69** (9) November 1981 11– 17.

● Q Bell *Bad art* (Chatto, 1989).

102 BANDE DESSINÉE (BD)

Literally 'a band or strip of drawings'. The French term for comic strips/books or 'graphzines' or graphic novels, especially those whose layout is based on the visual conventions of the cinema. (They have been compared to the storyboards used in the early stages of film-making.) In France (and in Japan) this type of popular culture is produced for adults as well as for children. Celebrated fictional heroes of La Bande Dessinée include Tintin and Astérix. An important magazine featuring this type of work – *Metal Hurlant* – was founded in 1975 by Jean-Pierre Dionnet and the artists Jean Giraud and Philippe Druillet. Other noted graphic artists were Serge Clerc, Frank Margerin, and the illustrators who constituted the Bazooka Group, i.e. Kiki and Loulou Picasso, Olivia Clavel and Kim Bravo.

Bande Dessinée has been dubbed 'the ninth art' and 'sequential art'. A journal providing critical evaluations of the form is *Les Cahiers de la Bande Dessinée*. In countries such as France and Belgium the comic is taken seriously as an artform in its own right, hence the museums and study centres devoted to it: at Angoulême in France there is a Centre National de la Bande Dessinée et de l'Image (CNBDI); an international comics festival is held annually at Angoulême; the Centre Belge de la Bande Dessinée, Brussels, Belgium was opened in 1989. It has 25,000 examples.

● See also Comic Art, Comix, Graphic Novels, Narrative Figuration/Painting.

● P Couperie & others *Bande Dessinée et figuration narrative* (Paris, Musée des Arts Decoratifs, 1967).

● G Blanchard *La Bande Dessineé: histoire des histoires en images de la préhistoire à nos jours* (Verviers, Gerard Marabout Université, 1969).

● P Fresnault-Deruelle *La Bande Dessinée: l'univers et les techniques de quelques 'Comics' d'expression Française* (Paris, Hachette, 1972).

● 'La résistance graphique' *The Face* (29) September 1982 46– 51.

Banners are pieces of cloth decorated with emblems and mottoes, attached to poles, which are employed as rallying points and as a form of public display; they are often carried, for example, in processions and marches. Banners are ancient forms of communication having been used by royalty, the military and the Church since feudal times. In the post-1850 period they are chiefly associated with trade unions because the new labour organizations of the Victorian era developed the habit of commissioning Banners to proclaim their existence, aims and ideals. They would then be carried to mass meetings, on May Day parades and on demos/marches. In the years before the First World War, suffragettes were another social group who generated Banners to aid their cause. Most trade union Banners were designed and made by the London firm of George Tuthill (ironically, a non-unionized workshop). A number are preserved in the collection of the National Museum of Labour History in Manchester. Since the Arts Council regards Banners as craft not art, it has been reluctant to give grants for their restoration. Three contemporary artists who have designed Banners for trade unions are Ken Sprague,

Andrew Turner (British) and Jer O'Leary (Irish).

An entry on Banners is warranted here by the revival of interest in the form brought about by the Banner Arts Project, London, founded by John Dugger in 1978. Dugger, an American artist resident in Britain from 1968 to '88, designed and made huge Banners (normally divided into vertical strips) for use at political rallies, sports events, community festivals and trade fairs. Commercial commissions enabled Dugger to subsidize community and fine art Banners. His designs were generally extremely simple, decorative with flat, bright colours; their style reflected the influence of Oriental art and the late paper cut-outs of Matisse.

● See also Community Art, Feminist Art, Political Art, Public Art.

○ J Gorman *Banner bright: an illustrated history of the Banners of the British trade union movement* (Allen Lane, 1973).

○ 'Banner Arts Project' *Art Monthly* (25) 1979 8.

○ A Turner 'Towards a new trade union Banner art' *Artery* (18) June 1980 9–11.

○ D Boshier 'Interview with John Dugger' *Real Life* (15) Winter 1985–6 10–14.

○ F O'Toole 'Jer O'Leary, trade union Banners' *Circa* (27) March–April 1986 35–6.

○ L Tickner *The spectacle of women: imagery of the suffrage campaign 1907–14* (Chatto & Windus, 1988).

○ V Shakespear 'Fly the flag' *Design* (499) July 1990 21–4.

(Also Basic Course) Basic Design courses consisted of practical exercises concerned with line, form, space, colour, tone, three-dimensional construction, visual perception and observation, undertaken by art students in British art and design colleges from the 1950s onwards. They were intended to provide students with a grounding in the fundamentals of visual design no matter what specialism they later adopted. British Basic Design courses were derived from the preliminary course taught by Johannes Itten at the Bauhaus in the 1920s and '30s. Paul Klee's *Thinking Eye* writings were also important and books about growth and form in nature. Basic Design courses were established in London, Leeds and Newcastle upon Tyne by such artist– tutors as Maurice de Sausmarez, Harry Thrubron, Tom Hudson, Victor Pasmore and Richard Hamilton. Pasmore claimed that Basic Design courses provided, for the first time, a scientific basis for art training. The idea of a uniform basic training persists today in British art schools in the form of foundation years. During the 1960s Pasmore's scientific analogy was fulfilled in the many 'visual research' departments that were established.

Basic Design has been criticized on the grounds that it

BANNERS JOHN DUGGER, 'El Salvador Vencera' (1982). Banner in use at a rally held in Trafalgar Square, London. Photo: John Dugger.

was analytic rather than synthetic, that the formal exercises were undertaken in a political and social vacuum, that they encouraged abstraction at the expense of representation and, in the United States, minimalism. Some students were also confused by the fact that such modern exercises took place alongside ancient academic practices such as life drawing and still life painting.

● See also Art Schools.

● *The developing process* (Newcastle upon Tyne, Durham University, 1959).

● M de Sausmarez & others 'A visual grammar of form' Part 1: *Motif* (8) Winter 1961 3–29; Part 2: *Motif* (9) Summer 1962 47–67.

● —*Basic Design: the dynamics of visual form* (Studio Vista, 1964).

● W Huff 'An argument for Basic Design' *Architectural Design* **36** (5) May 1966 252–6.

● R Banham 'The Bauhaus gospel' *Listener* September 26 1968 390–2.

● P Jones 'The failure of Basic Design' *Leonardo* **2** (2) April 1969 155–60.

● E Sonntag 'Foundation studies in art' *Leonardo* **2** (4) October 1969 387–97.

● J Walker 'The basic faults of the Basic Design courses' *Art Monthly* (46) 1981 27–8.

● *The continuing process: the new creativity in British art education* 1955–65 (London, ICA, 1981).

● E Forrest 'Harry Thrubron at Leeds...' *Journal of Art & Design Education* **4** (2) 1985 147–67.

BAY AREA FIGURATION RICHARD DIEBENKORN, 'Reclining nude pink stripe' (1962). Oil on canvas. 31" x 25". Photo: Waddington Gallery, London.

105 BAY AREA FIGURATION

A description applied to the late 1950s and early '60s work of a number of West Coast American painters – Elmer Bischoff, Richard Diebenkorn and David Park – who had studied or taught at the California School of Fine Arts, San Francisco (where Clyfford Still and Mark Rothko had also taught in the late 1940s). These artists painted figurative and landscape subjects but their manner of painting was influenced by the gestural style of abstract expressionism. The New York critic Clement Greenberg called this kind of work 'homeless representation'.

● See also Abstract Expressionism, West Coast School.

● P Mills *Contemporary Bay Area Figurative painting* (Oakland, California, Oakland Art Museum, 1957).

● — 'Bay Area Figurative' *Art in America* **52** (3) June 1964 42–5.

● T Albright *Art in the San Francisco Bay Area 1945–80* (Oakland, California, Oakland Museum, 1985).

● C Jones *Bay Area Figurative art 1950–65* (Berkeley, California, 1990).

106 BEHAVIOURAL ART

During the late 1960s and early '70s, the British artist Stephen Willats, founder and editor of *Control Magazine,* engaged in a new form of art based on the concepts and techniques of cybernetics and the behavioural social sciences. (As a student Willats had been influenced by his tutor Roy Ascott who, in his writings, employed the term 'Behaviourist Art'.) Acting on the premise that the purpose of art is to change human understanding and behaviour, Willats organized several projects involving members of the general public belonging to different social groups, in which he used market research, social survey and feedback methods as artistic strategies. The projects were intended to raise the consciousness of the participants in regard to their physical and social environments. In 1972 Willats founded a short-lived association called the 'Centre for Behavioural Art' at Gallery House, London.

The label 'Behavioural Art' was also used as the title of an event held at the Galeria Remont, Warsaw in 1976. Using their own bodies a number of Polish artists staged performances based on the 'grammar' of human behaviour; their aim was to reveal the unconscious emotional significance of bodily gestures.

A theorist who has reflected on the relation between biology, behaviour and art is Morse Peckham. He con-

 ART THEORY AND PRACTICE

CONTROL MAGAZINE ISSUE EIGHT

BEHAVIOURAL ART Cover of *Control Magazine* (8) 1974 with photo-work by STEPHEN WILLATS.

cluded that the biological, adaptive function of art is to serve as a rehearsal for novel problem situations we are likely to face in reality.

● See also Body Art, Cybernetic Art, Participatory Art, Performance Art, Sociological Art Group.

 M Peckham *Man's rage for chaos: biology, behaviour and the arts* (Philadelphia, Chilton, 1965).

 R Ascott 'Behaviourables and futuribles' *Control* (5) 1969 14.

 S Willats 'The artist as a structurist of behaviour' *Control* (5) 1969 16– 17.

 G Battcock 'Toward an art of behavioural control' *Domus* (513) August 1972 44– 6.

 R Brooks 'Behavioural Art' *Studio International* **951** (185) January 1973 27– 8.

 S Willats *The artist as an instigator of social changes in social cognition and behaviour* (Gallery House Press, 1973).

 ––*Art & social function* (Latimer New Dimensions, 1976).

 'Behavioural Art' *Musics* (9) September 1976 20– 1.

107 BENSON & HEDGES CAMPAIGN

A striking series of posters, magazine and cinema advertisements for a British brand of cigarettes which became famous in the late 1970s and early '80s. The 'hero' of the commercials was a gold pack which initially appeared in a variety of settings pictorially and iconographically resembling traditional oil paintings. Then the design was revamped in terms of modern art with surrealism and pop art being used to generate bizarre and puzzling images with no slogans or copy. Gallaher Ltd was the client, Collett Dickenson Pearce & Partners the ad agency and Alan Waldie the art director who commissioned several photographers and film-makers. In 1978 the posters were given an award by the Design Council and in 1984 another award was given for the cinema commercial 'Salvage' directed by Hugh Hudson. The adverts proved influential on cigarette advertising in general and spawned imitators such as the Silk Cut series employing slits in the manner of Fontana's spatialism. They were also subject to critiques by Left-wing theorists, parodied by the cartoonist Steve Bell, reproduced in art books, and sold as postcards in arts centres.

● See also Billboard Art, Pop Art, Spatialism.

 'Campaigns: what makes advertising art?' *Zoom* (1) 1978 6– 9.

 J Walker 'All that glitters..' *Camerawork* (15) September 1979 4– 5.

 G Mermoz 'Benson & Hedges' *Novum Gebrauchsgraphik* **52** (6) June 1981 32– 7, 59– 60.

 B Hatton 'A woman is just a woman, but a good cigar is a smoke' *ZG* (7) 1982 1– 2.

 'What the lens can't do, the brush can' *Design & Art Direction* May 1983 44– 8.

 J Williamson '...but I know what I like' *Consuming passions: the dynamics of popular culture* (Marion Boyars, 1986) 67– 74.

108 BIBA

A series of London fashion boutiques dating from the 1960s, and a department store open between 1973 and '75 (the old Derry & Toms building, Kensington High Street, an art deco classic designed by Bernard George in 1933). Biba, the store, was famous for its glamorous decor, extravagance, oddity and the stylishness of its goods (a mixture of Victoriana, art nouveau, art deco, camp, kitsch and Hollywood), and for the unhelpfulness of its shop assistants. Biba was the creation of the fashion designer Barbara Hulanicki; everything in stock was an expression of her personal taste.

● See also Camp, Kitsch, Pop Design.

 B Hillier 'Look at Biba' *Sunday Times* September 9 1973 43– 5.

 A Best 'Biba' *Design* (300) December 1973 38– 43.

 P Norman 'The battle for Biba' *Sunday Times Magazine* September 28 1975 40– 5.

 J Truman 'The rise and fall of the Biba empire' *The Face* (41) September 1983 18– 21.

● B Hulanicki *From A-to-Biba* (Hutchinson, 1983).

109 BIGOS

A group of Anglo-Polish artists founded in Britain in November 1985. Its name derived from a Polish dish made from a variety of ingredients. These artists had no common style or subject; they employed different media and tackled various themes including the issue of national identity. They issued a newsletter, organized exhibitions and visited Poland. Members of Bigos included: Andrzej Borkowski, Kasia Januszko, Simon Lewandowski, Karen Strang, Stefan Szczelkun, and Silvia Ziranek.

● See also Hybrid Culture.

● *Bigos: artists of Polish origin* (Brixton Gallery/The Crypt St George's Church, 1986).

110 BILLBOARD ART

An expression used by various writers to describe the imagery found on the huge, freestanding advertising signs or hoardings found in most countries but especially in the United States. An alternative term is 'skyline painting' and in France the word 'gigantisme' is also employed. Billboards are wooden structures designed to display bills or posters, most of which are photographic images printed in large editions. However, some hoardings are painted by professional commercial artists whose names are not generally known. These sign painters normally employ a photo-realist mode of representation. (James Rosenquist, the American pop artist, worked as a billboard painter early in his career.) Some billboards also incorporate elements which project beyond their framing edges, or even three-dimensional projections, to heighten the sense of realism or illusion. (Richard Smith's shaped canvas pieces of the early 1960s were influenced by such structures.)

Billboards have been used over several decades by fine artists in order to reach a wider audience than that available via art galleries, e.g. Yoko Ono and John Lennon, Joseph Kosuth, Daniel Buren, Ian Colverson, Denis Masi, Les Levine, Barbara Kruger, Peter Dunn and Loraine Leeson.

● See also Benson & Hedges Campaign, Environmental Art, Free Form Arts Trust, Photo-Realism, Public Art, Shaped Canvas, Street Art, Supergraphics.

● T Street-Porter 'Skyline painting' *Design* (300) December 1973 56– 9.

● L Rubenstein 'Big art: the art of the billboard' *Graphis* **34** (199) 1978– 9 448– 57, + 465.

● S Henderson & R Landau *Billboard Art* M Feldman (ed) (Angus & Robertson, 1981).

● L Levine *Blame God: billboard projects* (London, ICA, 1986).

Wei Yew (ed) *Gotcha! The art of the bill board* (Edmonton, Alberta, Quon Editions, 1990).

111 BIOTECTURE

A term combining 'biology' and 'architecture' coined by Rudolf Doernach. It meant architecture as an 'artificial super system', as 'live, dynamic, mobile, fantastic, environment systems'. Charles Jencks, the architectural critic, writing at the end of the '60s predicted that in the 1990s biology would become 'the major metaphor'. He had already identified a 'biomorphic school' or movement which included the work of Antonio Gaudi and Paolo Soleri. As an example of architecture influenced by biology, one can point to the huge city designed by Soleri which resembles the form of a tree and grows slowly in an evolutionary way.

In a theoretical paper published in 1972 the Italian Carlo Americo Lenzi employed the terms 'bioarchitecture' and 'biological architecture'. He defined bioarchitecture as 'a system of town planning and of architecture exclusively programmed on a biological base ... adapted to the ecological characteristics of every environment so as not to alter the free progression of micro and macro evolution'. His paper was concerned with design in relation to 'biotic communities' (e.g. a university city) and their interactions; it was illustrated with diagrams and photographs of models. According to Lenzi, bioarchitecture could solve all urban problems.

● See also Arcology, Ecological Architecture, Utopian Architecture.

● R Doernach 'Biotecture' *Architectural Design* **36** (2) February 1966 95– 6.

● C Jencks *Architecture 2000: predictions and methods* (Studio Vista, 1971).

● C Lenzi 'Bioarchitecture or biological architecture' *L'Architectura* **17** (10) no 196 February 1972 676– 85.

112 BLACK ART

(Related terms: Afro-American Art, Afro-Caribbean Art, Afro-Asian Art, Neo-African Art, Negro Art, Ethnic Art, Minority Art, Third World Art, NonEuropean Art) The term 'Black Art' is highly contentious and problematical. For example, is it appropriate to call people 'black' whose skins are brown and yellow? Since the art of white-skinned peoples is not generally called 'White Art', the very existence of the term 'Black Art' indicates a situation of discrimination and racism.

In its most general sense Black Art means 'the art of dark skinned peoples' whether living in Africa, India, the

Americas or Europe. However, this definition is so broad as to be uninformative. 'Black Art' refers primarily to the visual culture of dark-skinned people living as minorities in countries where there is a white majority (e.g. the USA and Europe). The deliberate adoption of the term by artists from those minorities signals a consciousness of racial pride and separateness which can be traced to the Civil Rights and Black Power movements in the USA during the 1960s. However, since black people obviously share in the general culture of Western society, Black Art must be further defined as that art which in terms of subject matter and style draws upon experiences specific to being black in a white-dominated society: for example, the 1977 mixed-media performance by Rasheed Araeen (a Pakistani artist who came to Britain in 1964) entitled 'Paki Bastard – portrait of the artist as a black person'.

Araeen saw Black Art as a unifying political concept and he defined it as 'a specific historical development within contemporary art practices (which) has emerged from the joint struggle of Asian, African and Caribbean people against racism, and the art work itself explicitly refers to that struggle. It specifically deals with and expresses a human condition, the condition of Afro-

Asian people resulting from their existence or predicament in a racist society or land, in global terms, from Western cultural imperialism.' Not all Asian artists living in Britain who drew upon the cultures of ex-colonies such as India shared Araeen's political view of art (Anish Kapoor, for instance).

Debates about Black Art and the vexed question of whether or not there is a Black aesthetic have a longer history in the USA. Since 1968 a number of American museums and galleries have mounted shows of Black Art. The Whitney Museum in New York, for instance, organized one in 1971. A showplace for Black Art called 'Studio Museum' was established in Harlem in 1968. Washington DC has a large black population and its black artists Sam Gilliam, Alma Thomas and Carroll Sockwell became internationally known. In 1987 the exhibition 'Choosing: an exhibit of changing perspectives in modern art and art criticism by Black Americans 1925–85' was held at the Howard University's art gallery, Washington DC.

For artists of African descent FESTAC '75 – the second world festival of Black and African arts – held in Lagos, Nigeria in 1975 was of particular significance. One of its purposes was to enable them to experience 'a

BLACK ART DONALD RODNEY, 'The lords of humankind' (detail) (1986). Paint on suspended cloth, an installation at the Elbow Room, London. Photo: Ann Cardale, courtesy of the artist.

return to origin'.

In Britain during the 1970s and '80s a considerable number of Black artists became familiar names in the artworld: Araeen, Frank Bowling, Gavin Jantjes, Sokari Douglas Camp, Veronica Ryan, Lubiana Himid, Donald Rodney, Marlene Smith, Mark Fairington, Eddie Chambers, Keith Piper, Sutapa Biswas, Shirazeh Houshiry, Sonia Boyce. In this period too magazines were published (*Black Phoenix* three issues 1978– 9; *Black Arts in London* 1987– ; *Third Text* 1987–) and groups/organizations founded (Blk Art Group, 1981; Pan-Afrikan Connection, 1982; OBAALA, 1981) and galleries opened (Black Arts Gallery, 1983; Creation for Liberation, 1983) and a significant number of shows mounted. White liberal guilt amongst arts bureaucrats ensured increased public funding for Black Arts festivals and activities.

While the category Black Art has a value in assisting self-definition and self-determination, and in encouraging Black artists to 'take as their themes Black history, culture, politics and people' (Chambers), it also has certain drawbacks. It can, for instance, create a ghetto in which artists isolate themselves from the rest of society (separatism). Is Black Art only to be for a Black public? Such a ghetto can be unwelcoming to sympathetic whites and to artists who are the result of mixed parentage and whose identities are thus torn between black and white.

● See also Artists Against Apartheid, Carnival, Ethnic Art, Negritude, OBAALA, Orature, Township Art.

● F Bowling 'Critique discussion on Black Art' part 1 *Arts Magazine* **43** (6) April 1969 16– 20; part 2 *Arts Magazine* **43** (7) May 1969 20– 3; part 3 *Arts Magazine* **44** (3) December– January 1969– 70 20– 2.

● A Werner 'Black is not a colour' *Art & Artists* **4** (2) May 1969 14– 17.

● H Ghent 'Notes to the young Black artist: revolution or evolution' *Art International* **15** (6) June 20 1971 33– 5.

● J Chase *The Afro-American artist* (NY, Holt Rinehart & Winston, 1972).

● A Gayle (ed) *The Black aesthetic* (NY, Anchor Books, 1972).

● L Sims 'Black Americans in the visual arts: a survey of bibliographical material and research sources' *Artforum* **11** (8) April 1973 66– 70.

● A Shields 'Is there a Black aesthetics?' *Leonardo* **6** (4) Autumn 1973 319– 23.

● C Hilliard 'Black Arts festival' *Africa* (39) November 1974 63.

● *Two centuries of Black American art* (Los Angeles County Museum of Art, 1976).

● E Fax *Black artists of the new generation* (NY, Dodd Mead, 1977).

● S Lewis *Art African American* (NY, Harcourt Brace Jovanovich, 1978).

● R Araeen & Guy Brett *Rasheed Araeen: Making myself visible* (Kala Press, 1984).

● K Owusu *The struggle for Black Arts in Britain* (Comedia, 1986).

● *From two worlds* (Whitechapel Art Gallery, 1986).

● A Gamble '"Choosing": defining a Black American aesthetic' *New Art Examiner* **14** (10) June 1987 28– 30.

● M Campbell & others *Harlem renaissance: art of Black America* (NY, Abrams, 1987).

● E Chambers & J Lamba *The artpack: a history of Black artists in Britain* (Chambers & Joseph/Haringey Arts Council, 1988).

● K Owusu (ed) *Storms of the heart* (Camden Press, 1988).

● R Araeen (curator) *Essential Black Art* (Chisenhale Gallery/Kala Press, 1988).

● E Chambers (curator) *Black Art: plotting the course* (Oldham Art Gallery, 1988).

● P Failing 'Black artists today: a case of exclusion' *Art News* **88** (3) March 1989 124– 31.

● R Araeen & others *The other story: AfroAsian artists in postwar Britain* (Hayward Gallery/South Bank Centre, 1989).

113 BLACK MOUNTAIN COLLEGE (BMC)

A famous American art education institution located at Black Mountain, North Carolina open between 1933 and '56. The BMC was noted for its experimental methods and the number of leading American artists who taught or studied there. The College was kept deliberately small in order to reduce administrative work; its aim was to integrate academic work and community life, and to establish an equality between staff and students. A key feature of the BMC was the variety of arts taught and the degree of interaction between them that was encouraged. Josef Albers was director at one stage and amongst the artists associated with BMC were John Cage, Robert Rauschenberg, Robert Motherwell, Philip Guston and Willem de Kooning. Several magazines were published by the College: *Jargon Press, Origin,* and *Black Mountain Review.*

● See also Art Schools.

● J Evats 'Black Mountain College: the total approach' *Form* (6) December 1967 20– 5.

● M Duberman *Black Mountain* (Wildwood House, 1974).

● M Harris *The arts of Black Mountain College* (Cambridge, Mass, MIT Press, 1987).

114 BLACKS IN ART

Iconographic studies of black people in Western paintings, prints and sculptures. A notable contribution to this type of text was a book by Dr David Dabydeen (a poet and lecturer in Caribbean studies at Warwick University) about images of blacks in the work of Hogarth. Social and economic analyses also revealed that the fortunes of many leading British patrons of the arts were based on colonial trade and the exploitation of black slave labour on West Indian plantations.

● See also Black Art.

● L Bugner (ed) *The image of the black in Western art* (Cambridge, Mass, Harvard University Press, 1976), volume one of a multi-volumed work.

● A Locke *The negro in art* (NY, Hacker, 1979).

● D Dabydeen *Hogarth's blacks: images of blacks in eighteenth century English art* (Dangaroo Press, 1985).

● A Boime *The art of exclusion: representing blacks in the nineteenth century* (Thames & Hudson, 1990).

115 BMPT

The initial letters of the surnames of four French artists – Daniel Buren, Olivier Mosset, Michel Parmentier, Niele Toroni – who began to collaborate in 1967. The products of BMPT represented the degree zero of painting: minimal, abstract canvases with banal designs – stripes, dots, circles – made quickly by mechanical and repetitive methods. Any one of the group could have done these 'paintings' since they were so simple, impersonal and without skill. Evidently, a critique of individualism, authorship and the art of painting was intended. Since the works of art were deliberately uninteresting, what remained of interest were the theoretical explanations governing their behaviour.

● See also 'Bad' Painting, Collaborations.

M Claura 'Paris commentary' *Studio International* **177** (907) January 1969 47– 9.

J Clair *Art en France: une nouvelle génération* (Paris, Chêne, 1972).

J-M Poinset 'A propos de BMPT' *Opus International* (61/62) January– February 1977 24– 6.

116 BODY ART

(Also Body Sculpture, Bodyworks, Corporal Art) An international trend in Western, avant garde art, dating from the late 1960s, which combined aspects of sculpture, performance, process and conceptualism. During the late '60s a widespread interest in the human body developed: encounter groups, body painting and tattooing, nudity in the theatre, 'Hair', drag shows, scientific and academic research into the languages of gestures and postures. Body Art was simply one facet of this cultural phenomenon.

Sculptors in particular have a special relationship with the human body, and consequently it was a logical step for them to turn to their own bodies as material, treating them as both subject and object. Amongst those categorized as Body Artists were Vito Acconci, John Baldessari, Giorgi Ciam, Terry Fox, Rebecca Horn, Urs Luthi, Barry Le Va, Bruce McLean, Bruce Nauman, Dennis Oppenheim, Gina Pane, Klaus Rinke, Keith Sonnier and William Wegman. The role of the body was also vital in the material actions or direct art of the Viennese artists Günter Brus, Rudolph Schwarzkogler, Arnulf Rainer and co. Body Art varied from artist to artist but certain themes recurred: narcissism, masochism, sexuality, and transvestism. In the name of art, human flesh was subjected to a host of indignities and even life itself was put at risk (e.g. the work of Chris Burden). Critics found precedents for Body Art in the oeuvres of Duchamp, Klein and Manzoni.

Since Body Art performances were transitory, photography, film and videotape became important in terms of documentation. Some works were planned as interactions between the artist and the recording medium. Given the difficulties of mounting a survey of Body Art, it was only in 1975 that the first mixed exhibition took place (at the Museum of Contemporary Art in Chicago). Three years earlier the ICA in London had organized a programme of lectures and events concerning the body as a medium of expression. A group called Body Arts at Large (BAAL) assisted with the programme.

● See also Direct Art, Gilbert & George, Living Sculpture, Nice Style, Performance Art, Process Art.

● W Sharp 'Body works' *Avalanche* (1) Fall 1970 147.

● 'Body works' *Interfunctionen* (6) September 1971 233.

● C Nemser 'Subject-object: Body Art' *Arts Magazine* **46** September– October 1971 38– 42.

● 'Le corps' *Chroniques de l'Art Vivant* (40) June 1973.

● (Special issue on Body Art) *Data* **4** (12) Summer 1974.

● L Vergine *Il corpo come linguaggio (la 'Body-Art' et storie simili)* (Milan, Giampaolo Prearo Editore, 1974).

● J Benthall & T Polhemus (eds) *The body as a medium of expression* (Allen Lane, 1975).

● I Licht *Bodyworks* (Chicago, Museum of Contemporary Art, 1975).

● L Lippard 'The pains and pleasures of rebirth: woman's Body Art' *Art in America* **64** (3) May– June 1976 73– 81.

● N Calas 'Bodyworks and porpoises' *Artforum* **16** (5) January 1978 33– 7.

● R Brain *The decorated body* (Hutchinson, 1979).

● *Body Art magazine* (Braintree, Essex, 1988–).

● T Polhemus *Body styles* (Luton, Lennard/London, Channel 4 TV, 1988).

117 BOLDISTA

(Or Boldism) A tendency within Italian design of the mid 1980s. In Bologna 15 designers and architects, including Maurizio Castelvetro, Bepi Maggiori, Maurizio Corrada, Dante Donegani and Ernesto Spiccilota, issued a manifesto extolling the virtues of small-batch or flexible manufacturing. Computer-aided design and manufacture, they argued, enabled a new level of variety and innovation in the appearance of goods. Their metal chairs, clothes, masks, furnishings and interiors exhibited a fascination with streamlined forms symbolic of the speed and fluidity they sought in their approach to design.

● See also Italian Craze, Styling.

● S Hayman 'Expo: Boldism' *The Face* (88) Aug 1987 54–7.

118 BOOK ART

(Also Artists' Books, Book as Artwork, Bookworks) Books are complex, multimedia products. They overlap the categories of literature, art and design because they are linguistic/literary entities and visual/material artefacts. Furthermore, book production is an industry in which many divisions of labour occur: authors, editors, illustrators, designers, typesetters, printers, papermakers, binders ... all make their specialist contributions. Hence the phrase 'the art of the book' can refer to high achievement in any or all of these specialities. Problems of classification result because if the skill is that of an author then the book is a work of literature, while if the skill is that of an illustrator then it is a work of visual art. Examples of the latter are collected by museums like the Victoria & Albert and displayed as objects in showcases.

Past examples of the art of the book include the illuminated manuscripts of the Middle Ages, the early printed bibles of Gutenberg, the total design concept of William Morris' Kelmscott Press publications, and the luxurious 'livres d'artiste' associated with School of Paris figures like Bonnard, Matisse and Dufy. However, the term 'Book Art' as used in avant garde circles means something different: publications by individuals or small groups of people whose background is the visual fine arts rather than poetry or literature. Their publications are usually small in size, slim, white, often effete pamphlets, journals or booklets issued in small editions and marketed via art galleries rather than bookshops. Although cheaper than paintings or prints, such books can seem expensive when compared to mainstream books. Frequently, the text and illustrations are minimal and while visual/material factors are generally foregrounded, many are not splendid examples of typography, printing or binding. What gives Bookworks their particular value are the qualities of ingenuity, originality, perceptiveness of the artistic ideas informing them.

The term 'Book Art' was first employed by Clive Phillpot in 1973 though Harold Rosenberg had used it earlier in the title of an essay about 'art-book art' (i.e. art as experienced only via reproductions). Some critics use 'Book Art' and 'Artists' Books' synonymously, while others restrict the former to books in which the form was intrinsic to the work from the outset, and restrict the latter to publications documenting a work executed in a medium which has an independent status, e.g. photography. (A set of photos can be presented in an exhibition or in book form.) Books-as-art shade into books-as-documen-

BOOK ART BEN LANGLANDS and NIKKI BELL, Three works (left to right): 'The British Museum', 'The Round Reading Room', 'The Panopticon' (1987). Wood products, glass, AC lacquer. 40cm x 30cm x 5cm. Photo: Langlands & Bell.

tation of performances, and into books-as-vehicles for texts and images. They began to appeal to artists in considerable numbers in the 1960s because they could be produced relatively cheaply and disseminated internationally. Some artists became fascinated by the form of the book and started to explore it in terms of narratives or other sequences, diptychal images, physical materials, word/image relations, and so on.

Since the early '70s exhibitions of Book Art too numerous to list have been held in Europe and the United States. Some private galleries have also been founded which specialize in the genre, e.g. 'Book Works', London, 'Franklin Furnace', New York. In New York a 'Center for Book Arts' exists which organized the first National Conference on the theme of Book Arts in the United States in 1990. Many contemporary artists have produced, illustrated or contributed in some way to books, but only a few have devoted themselves to books to the exclusion of all else. Artists noted for a significant number of Bookworks include Ian Breakwell, Marcel Broodthaers, John Cage, Ian Hamilton Finlay, Hamish Fulton, Gilbert & George, Sol Lewitt, Richard Long, Tom Phillips, Tony Rickaby, Dieter Rot, Ed Ruscha, Telfer Stokes, and the team of Ben Langlands and Nikki Bell. Obviously, the style and content of the Bookworks artists make tend to reflect the kind of art they normally produce. Certain movements, however, have encouraged the issuing of publications, e.g. conceptual art and Fluxus, and so have given rise to specific styles of design and presentation.

Books can serve as the subject matter for paintings – witness several of Van Gogh's pictures – or as the subject for sculptures – witness Anslem Kiefer's 'The High Priestess' (1985– 9), a massive metal bookcase laden with books made from lead. Old books can also serve as a material from which to make sculptures or reliefs. One artist who has mutilated hundreds of books in order to construct assemblages out of them is John Latham.

● See also Assemblage Art, Conceptual Art, Concrete Poetry, Copy Art, Magazine Art, Mail Art.

◦ G Celant 'Book as artwork 1960– 70' *Data* **1** (1) September 1971 35– 49.
◦ *Book as artwork 1960-72* (Nigel Greenwood Inc Ltd, 1972).
◦ *Artists' Books* (Philadelphia, Moore College of Art, 1973).
◦ *Artists' Bookworks* (British Council, 1975).
◦ *Artists' Books* (Arts Council of Great Britain, 1976).
◦ *Bookworks* (NY, MoMA, 1977).
◦ *Artwords and Bookworks* (Los Angeles Institute of Contemporary Art, 1978).
◦ T Whitfield 'Vigilance: an exhibition of Artists' Books exploring strategies for social change' *Artforum* **9** (11) September 1980 68– 9.
◦ *Bookworks: sculptural books by twenty artists* (Bracknell, Berks, South Hill Art Centre, 1981).
◦ C Courtney 'New York Artists' Books' *Art Monthly* (70) October 1983 9– 10.
◦ — 'Artists' Books in Britain' *Art Monthly* (72) December– January 1983– 4 20– 1.
◦ S Turner & I Tyson *British Artists' Books since 1970* (Lund Humphries, 1984).
◦ C Courtney 'Book Works anniversary' *Art Monthly* (87) June 1985 31– 2.
◦ J Lyons (ed) *Artists' Books: a critical anthology and source book* (Utah, Peregrine Smith Books, 1985).
◦ A Moeglin-Delcroix *Livres d'Artistes* (Paris, Centre Georges Pompidou/Éditions Herscher, 1985).
◦ A Brall *Kunstlerbucher/Artists' Books* (Frankfurt, Verlag Kretschmer & Grossman, 1986).
◦ *Turning over the pages* (Cambridge, Kettles' Yard, 1986).
◦ A Götz (ed) *The Books of Anselm Kiefer* (Thames & Hudson, 1991).

119 BOROUGH GROUP

(Also Borough Bottega, Bomberg School) A group of young, London-based painters whose work was influenced by the art and teaching of David Bomberg (1890– 1957). Between 1945 and '53 Bomberg taught an art class at the Borough Polytechnic, London. His students included Cliff Holden, Dennis Creffield, Dorothy Mead, Leslie Marr, Anthony Hatwell (the only sculptor), Peter Lasko, Gustav Metzger, Frank Auerbach and Leon Kossof. (The latter two artists did not, however, participate in Borough Group shows.) Bomberg's wife Lilian was also a painter and a member of the Group. The first exhibition of the Borough Group – founded in 1946 – was held at the Archer Gallery, London, in 1947. Others took place at different venues in '48 and '49. Catalogues were issued and some contain introductions by Bomberg on his aesthetic principles, the key one being the search for the 'spirit in the mass'. In 1953 the group was reconstituted as the Borough Bottega and exhibited at the Berkeley Galleries; a final show took place at Walker's Galleries in 1955. The drawings and paintings of the Group were figurative (about figures, landscapes and still lifes) but verged on abstraction. Drawings tended to be in charcoal with emphatic lines. Paintings tended to be expressively executed, heavily worked, dark in colour, oily, with thick impasto and bold brushstrokes.

◦ C Holden 'David Bomberg: the artist as teacher' *Studio International* **173** (887) March 1967 136– 43.
◦ R Cork *David Bomberg* (New Haven & London, Yale University Press, 1987).
◦ *Spirit in the mass: the Borough Group with Bomberg* 1946– 51 (Fine Art Associates, 1989).

The new capital city of Brazil located in the interior of the country was planned by Lúcio Costa in the 1950s. Brasilia became famous for the monumental modernist architecture (constructed between 1957 and '61) designed by the Brazilian architect Oscar Niemeyer. Despite its bold and visually striking structures, Brasilia also became noted as a symbol of the failure of modernism. Two cities came into being: the centre consisting of a lake, a cathedral, a national theatre, a presidential palace and other public and government buildings, and the outskirts of the favela or shanty town consisting of the dwellings of the poor.

● See also Latin American Art.

● W Stäubli *Brasilia* (Leonard Hill, 1966).

● R Spade *Oscar Niemeyer* (Thames & Hudson, 1971).

● D Epstein *Brasilia, plan and reality, a study of planned and spontaneous urban development* (Berkeley, University of California Press, 1973).

● J Holston *The modernist city: an anthropological critique of Brasilia* (Chicago, University of Chicago Press, 1990).

A small German electrical company based in Frankfurt, run by Artur and Erwin Braun, which during the mid and late 1950s became famous for its distinctively designed products. Max Braun AG made transistor radios, TV receivers and kitchen appliances. Several of the designers employed – Otl Aicher, Fritz Eichler and Hans Gugelot – had been trained at the Ulm school of design and they applied the school's ethos of uncompromising modernity and rationality to the design of Braun's products.

In 1955 Dieter Rams was appointed chief designer and he developed an 'in-house' look, i.e. all the company's products seemed to belong to the same family. The Braun style, as it has been called, was characterized by economy, clarity and simplicity, order and harmony, undecorated forms that were sculptural or geometric or based on a grid pattern, white surface finishes with grey or black detailing. Braun products were aimed at the top end of the market and they won prizes at several exhibitions; however, some critics considered they exemplified 'a chilly good taste'.

● See also 'Good Design', Gridniks, Ulm.

● R Moss 'Analysis – the Braun style' *Industrial Design* **9** (11) November 1962 36– 47.

● A & P Smithson 'Concealment and display: meditations on Braun' *Architectural Design* **36** July 1966 36– 23.

● W Schmittel *Design: concept, form, realisation* (Zürich, ABC Edition, 1975).

● I Franksen & others *Design: Dieter Rams &* (Berlin, IDZ, 1982).

Title of an important exhibition of British design organized by the Council of Industrial Design and held at the Victoria & Albert Museum, London, in 1946. After the shortages of the war years, crowds attended the V & A to see consumer goods that were at that time not generally available to the British since the export market was more important than the home market; consequently the exhibition was renamed 'Britain can't have it'.

Forty years later in 1986 a hindsight exhibition was held at the Royal College of Art entitled 'Make or break' which looked back at the 1946 show and posed the question: 'did Britain succeed in making it? – in the double sense of succeeding in the export market and in sustaining its manufacturing base. The answer was 'yes and no'.

● See also Austerity/Binge, Utility.

● Council of Industrial Design *Britain can make it* (HMSO, 1946).

● P Sparke (ed) *Did Britain make it? British design in context 1946– 86* (Design Council, 1986).

BROTHERHOOD OF RURALISTS GRAHAM OVENDEN, 'Peter and Juliette Blake' (1974-8). Oil on canvas, 48 x 36". Photo: Piccadilly Gallery, London.

123 BROTHERHOOD OF RURALISTS

A group of British landscape and figure painters – Ann and Graham Arnold, David Inshaw, Peter Blake, Jann Haworth, Annie and Graham Ovenden – formed in 1975 and exhibiting together at the Royal Academy summer show the following year. Their name clearly derived from the Pre-Raphaelite Brotherhood. These artists made a decision to move from the city to the country and to paint pictures celebrating 'the spirit of the country'. They drew upon such sources as Laurie Lee, Thomas Hardy, Shakespeare, Lewis Carroll, Stanley Spencer and Richard Dadd. Critics whose commitment was to avant garde art viewed them as reactionaries producing whimsical, academic and finicky paintings.

● See also Figurative Art.

● B Moynahan 'Brotherhood of Ruralists' *Sunday Times Magazine* October 3 1976 78– 84.

● N Usherwood *The ruralists: paintings, drawings and objects by the Brotherhood of Ruralists and their circle* (Bristol, Arnolfini Gallery; London, Lund Humphries, 1981).

124 BÜROLANDSCHAFT

A sophisticated form of office planning developed in Germany during the late 1950s and early '60s by the specialists in office organization Eberhard & Wolfgang Schnelle, and subsequently copied by businesses throughout the world. 'Bürolandschaft' – literally 'office landscape' – exploited the possibilities of open-plan offices (these had previously been developed in the USA before 1940). Departments and furniture were disposed according to the flow of paperwork, information and staff. A casual look resulted which seemed to echo the soft lines of a landscape, an impression reinforced by the liberal use of potted plants.

● See also Action Office.

● F Duffy 'Skill: Bürolandschaft' *Architectural Review* **135** (804) February 1964 148– 54.

● C Ray Smith 'Bürolandschaft USA' *Progressive Architecture* **49** (5) May 1968 174– 7.

● 'Chaos as system' *Progressive Architecture* **49** (10) October 1968 160– 9.

● F Duffy *Office landscaping: a new approach to office planning* (Anbar Publications, 2nd ed 1969).

● P Howard 'Office landscaping revisited' *Design and Environment* Fall 1972 40– 7.

● A Boje *Open- plan offices* (Business Books, 1972).

125 BUSINESS ART

A cynical philosophy expounded by the American artist Andy Warhol (1928– 87) 'Business Art is the step that comes after art. I started as a commercial artist, and I want to finish as a business artist ... being good in business is the most fascinating kind of art ... making money is art and working is art and good business is the best art.'

Another meaning of 'Business Art' is 'art for businesses'. In 1978 the Royal Academy in London founded the Business Art Galleries in order to market contemporary art, in particular to help public bodies and private companies acquire examples of contemporary art for their premises (an 'art-for-offices' scheme). Eventually, the Business Art Galleries became an independent company with their own exhibition space called The New Academy Gallery.

● See also Business Sponsorship, Commodity Aesthetics, Neo-Geo, Pop Art.

● A Warhol *The philosophy of Andy Warhol (from A to B and back again)* (NY, Harcourt Brace Jovanovich, 1975) 92.

126 BUSINESS SPONSORSHIP

(Also Corporate Art/ Patronage) A private sector form of patronage which became more fashionable during the 1980s as a consequence of cuts in public sector arts subsidies instituted by Right-wing regimes. Some businesses are willing to support exhibitions, festivals and other cultural activities in return for publicity and corporate image enhancement. Others are willing to purchase or rent works of art (e.g. 'art-for-offices' schemes) in order to improve working environments. In Britain an Association for Business Sponsorship of the Arts (ABSA) was founded in 1976. However, the practice of Business Sponsorship is not new: the tobacco firm Peter Stuyvesant has been assisting the arts through its Foundation since the 1960s (it supported the New Generation exhibitions at the Whitechapel Art Gallery). Also, artists-in-industry type schemes have existed for several decades. In the United States the practice is older still: during the 1930s Walter Paepcke of the Container Corporation of America began to commission modern artists to produce prestige advertisements; he also supported Moholy-Nagy and the new Bauhaus in Chicago, and in the 1940s he sponsored festivals and cultural gatherings at Aspen in Colorado. Initially, the aim of bringing commerce and culture together was to humanize business, but in the end art's function was to make business more effective.

From the artists' and art organizations' points of view, additional finance is welcome and plural funding means they are not so vulnerable to cutbacks in one sector. Nevertheless, there are numerous drawbacks to Business Sponsorship which disturb many in the artworld: sponsorship accounts for only a small percentage of total arts funding and is usually one-off, short-term or irregular;

BUSINESS SPONSORSHIP ARTISTS SUPPORT PEACE, 'Die In' demonstration at the Tate Gallery, 1986, to protest at the sponsorship of Kokoschka show by United Technologies. Photo: Roger Foss.

curators and artists have to spend a great deal of time and effort looking for funds; culture becomes conservative because businesses tend to support safe, mainstream events, and are therefore unwilling to fund exhibitions of new, experimental or critical art; ethical/political issues arise: living artists who are against war dislike the use of art to enhance the image of companies which manufacture weapons of war – 'using the arts to sell death' (Sir Roy Shaw). (In Britain a group called 'Artists Support Peace' demonstrated outside the Tate Gallery when exhibitions supported by the United Technologies Corporation – who helped to make cruise missiles – took place in the mid 1980s.) Finally, there is the objection that sponsorship is part of an insidious process whereby everything in society becomes commercialized until in the end it changes what it supports (e.g. an orchestra dressed in the colours of the company sponsoring the concert).

● See also APG, Artist-in-Residence, Arts Councils, Aspen, Corporate Design, New Generation.

◉ Association for Business Sponsorship of the Arts (publications include: a Sponsor's Guide, a Sponsorship Manual, Annual Reports, and Bulletin/newsletter).

◉ A Osborne *Patron: industry supports the arts* (London, 1966).

◉ C Georgi *The arts and the world of business: a bibliography* (Metuchen, New Jersey, Scarecrow Press, 2nd ed 1979).

◉ D Petherbridge 'Patronage and sponsorship: a special supplement' *Art Monthly* (38) July– August 1980 3– 22.

◉ J Allen *The romance of commerce and culture* (Chicago, University of Chicago Press, 1983).

◉ *Corporate ARTnews* **1** (1) May– June 1984 (an American subscription journal published by *Art News*).

◉ A Moszynska 'Patronage: United Technologies Corporation' *Art Monthly* (76) May 1984 30– 1.

◉ F Brauer 'What price arts sponsorship?' *Art Monthly* (88) July– August 1985 35.

◉ V Januszczak 'Art for sale' *Guardian* February 15 1986 11.

◉ 'The ethics of sponsorship' *Arts Express* (28) June 1986 8– 11.

◉ N Harris & M Norelli *Art, design and the modern corporation* (Washington DC, Smithsonian Institution Press, 1986).

◉ A Frean 'Cash culture' *Fires* (3) Spring 1987 43– 4.

◉ S Turner *Practical sponsorship* (Kogan Page, 1987).

◉ R Martorella *Corporate art* (New Brunswick, Rutgers University Press, 1990).

127 CALARTS

(California Institute of the Arts) An important art educational institution for the visual and performing arts situated on a 60 acre campus at Valencia, near Hollywood. CalArts dates back to 1961 when the Chouinard Art Institute merged with the Los Angeles Conservatory of Music. Funding was provided by Walt Disney and his Estate and family have close connections with the Institute; CalArts graduates in film and animation have entered the film industry in Hollywood. The Institute has schools of art, dance, film/video, music, theatre and critical studies. It also encourages interdisciplinary and intercultural activities. In the early 1970s Judy Chicago and Miriam Shapiro set up the first feminist art programme in America at CalArts; staff and students from this programme devised the influential 'Womanhouse' environment of 1972. In terms of the visual arts there has been a strong conceptual/theoretical emphasis due to the presence of the artists Michael Asher and John Baldessari on the staff. Some viewers found the work produced somewhat arid, hence the label 'Low Cal Art'. Two noted American painters of the 1980s who trained at CalArts were Eric Fischl and David Salle. The Institute publishes a news and information broadsheet entitled *CalArts Current*.

● See also Art Schools, Disneyana, Feminist Art.

● P Selz & H Seldis 'West Coast report: CalArts' *Art in America* **57** (2) March–April 1969 107–9.

● 'California Institute of the Arts: prologue to a community' *Arts in Society* **7** (3) Fall–Winter 1970.

● J Halas 'California Institute of the Arts' *Novum Gebrauchsgraphik* February 1987 36–43.

● *California Institute of the Arts Admission Bulletin 1989–90, 1990–91* (Valencia, CalArts, 1989).

128 CALLIGRAPHIC PAINTING

During the 1950s, at the time of the heyday of abstract expressionism, action painting and tachisme, a number of painters in Europe and the United States produced gestural paintings that evoked the direct brushwork of Oriental calligraphy.

Some of these artists were directly influenced by the calligraphy of the East, while others produced canvases which simply resembled it. Mark Tobey (1890–1976), the American West Coast painter, was an example of the former: he learnt about calligraphy through a friend, Teng Kuei, in the 1920s, visited Japan, and developed a form of miniature calligraphy he called 'white writing'. Ulfert Wilke, Morris Graves, Julius Bissier and Henry Michaux also belonged to this category. Examples of the latter included Franz Kline, Robert Motherwell, Bradley Walker Tomlin and Hans Hartung.

● See also Action Painting, All-Over Painting.

● L Alloway 'Sign and surface: notes on black and white paintings in New York' *Quadrum* (13) 1962 49–62.

● F Legrand 'Peinture et écriture' *Quadrum* (13) 1962 4–48, 179–85.

● G Nordland 'Calligraphy and the art of Ulfert Wilke' *Art International* **15** (4) April 20 1971 21–4.

● M Sullivan *The meeting of Eastern and Western art* (Thames & Hudson, 1973).

129 CAMBRIDGE SEVEN

A famous American architectural and design partnership – Cambridge Seven Associates – founded in 1962 in Cambridge, Massachusetts and New York by five young architects – Louis Bakanowsky, Peter Chermayeff, Alden Christie, Paul Dietrich, and Terry Rankine – and two graphic designers – Ivan Chermayeff and Thomas Geismar. Charles Redmond joined in 1970. Cambridge Seven have not limited themselves to the design of buildings: they have designed graphics, transport interiors (e.g. DC-10 aircraft, 1967), furniture, exhibitions (e.g. United States Pavilion, Expo '67, Montreal, 1964) and made films. They have advocated an integration of the various arts and stressed the need for buildings to be considered as elements in a total environment rather than as isolated structures.

● '7 a Cambridge, alcune opere' *Domus* (542) January 1975 91–2.

(Special issue) *Space Design* (Tokyo) October 1983.

130 CAMP

(Also Camp Architecture/ Art) According to Susan Sontag, Camp is a taste or sensibility characteristic of certain groups in twentieth-century society, a private code among urban cliques – historically homosexual – a form of dandyism in an age of mass culture. It is also a quality discoverable in objects just before they become fashionable. Camp taste delights in artifice, theatricality, exaggeration, playfulness, everything unnatural. An overblown, rhetorical style such as the baroque, for instance, has been described as being 'Camp about religion'. Kitsch objects have often appealed to Camp taste on the grounds that 'they're so bad they're good'. The origins of the word 'Camp' are uncertain: Roger Baker thought it derived from the Italian 'campeggiare' (to stand out from a background) while Alan Brien preferred the French verb 'se camper' (to posture boldly); both had theatrical associations.

Camp taste is considered to have begun with the eighteenth- century vogues for Gothic novels, Chinoiserie, caricature and fake ruins. In the twentieth-century the work of such artists as Aubrey Beardsley, Duggie Fields, Erté, David Hockney, Marie Laurencin and Andy Warhol has appealed to Camp taste. Some artists may be said to specialize in Camp Art: the British sculptor and jewellery maker Andrew Logan, for instance. He became notorious in the 1970s for organizing the 'Alternative Miss World Contests'(i.e. hilariously funny, drag versions of the 'Miss World' beauty competitions). Even certain kinds of architecture have been identified as Camp. According to Charles Jencks, who distinguished between high, middle and low Camp, the signs of such architecture were 'failed seriousness' and 'chaoticism' (i.e. a confusion of styles). Three of the buildings he cited were Ed Stone's Cultural Centre in Washington (1964–71), Bruce Goff's Bavinger House (1957) and Philip Johnson's New Harmony church, Indiana (1960).

● See also Kitsch, Pop Architecture.

◉ A Brien 'Campers courageous' *Harpers Bazaar* **64** (1) April 1961 138.
◉ 'Playboy after hours: Camp' *Playboy* September 1965 27–8.
◉ 'Camp' *Listener* October 20 1966 572–3.
◉ C Isherwood *The world in the evening* (Harmondsworth, Penguin Books, 1966).
◉ A Brien 'Private view: camper's guide' *New Statesman* June 23 1967 873–4.
◉ S Sontag 'Notes on Camp' – in – *Against interpretation* (Eyre & Spottiswoode, 1967) 275–89.
◉ R Baker 'Anatomy of Camp' *Queen* February 19 1969 48–51.
◉ A Carmines 'Keep the Camp fires burning' in *The image maker*, R Henderson (ed) (Richmond, Virginia, John Knox Press, 1971) 63–5.
◉ C Jencks 'Recent American architecture: Camp – Non-Camp' – in – *Modern movements in architecture* (Harmondsworth, Penguin Books, 1973) 184–237.
◉ 'Carry on camping' (Andrew Logan) *The Face* (20) December 1981 28–30.
◉ M Booth *Camp* (Quartet, 1983).
◉ P Core *Camp: the lie that tells the truth* (Plexus, 1984).

131 CAPITALIST REALISM

A name given to paintings and graphics by three West German artists – Konrad Fischer-Lueg, Sigmar Polke and Gerd Richter – which commented critically upon contemporary personalities and events. This type of work dated from the early 1960s and had some affinities with pop art. A demonstration/ exhibit entitled 'Demonstration für den Kapitalistischen Realismus' was held at the Mobelhaus Berges, Düsseldorf, in 1963. The term 'Capitalist Realism' ironically echoed the label 'Socialist Realism'.

● See also Critical Realism, Political Art.

◉ *Neo Dada, Pop, Décollage, Kapitalistischer Realismus* (Berlin, René Block Galerie, 1964).
◉ *Grafik des Kapitalistischen Realismus* (Berlin, Edition René Block, 1971).

132 CAR CULTURE

A term used by several writers to sum up the human behaviour associated with automobiles. Roland Barthes has argued that the motor car is the modern day equivalent of the great Gothic cathedrals of the feudal period. As designed artefacts invested with human dreams, desires and values (mainly those of men), motor cars are themselves material, visual embodiments of culture. Their forms and styles frequently symbolize aggression, power, speed, mobility, sex, social status and wealth. Particular makes of car are often associated with particular social groups and hence are one manifestation of lifestyles and sub-cultures. Some individuals personalize standard models by customizing them or by adding stickers and knick-knacks. Certain manufacturers have commissioned fine artists to decorate their cars, hence the term 'auto-art', e.g. BMW racing cars whose bodies were painted with designs by the American artists Alexander Calder, Roy Lichtenstein, Robert Rauschenberg, Frank Stella and Andy Warhol. The vehicles were displayed in an 'Art Cars' exhibition to mark the opening of a BMW showroom, Park Avenue, New York, in 1986.

From time to time a particular make of car becomes a cult object; a famous British example was the Morris Mini introduced in 1959 and designed by Alec Issigonis.

Some makes of old cars have become collectors' items: they are treated as valuable antiques and preserved in museums. Exhibitions celebrating cars and leading automobile companies such as Fiat increasingly take place in public design and science museums. Car Culture also encompasses secondary materials such as pictorial advertisements, photographs, magazines and films about cars and car designers, e.g. 'Tucker' (Lucas Film Ltd, 1988) directed by Francis Ford Coppola.

Motor cars have frequently served as the subject matter for paintings. Car styling was one of the topics discussed by the members of the Independent Group and some of Richard Hamilton's early pop paintings were inspired by the exotic styles of American cars in the 1950s. Andy Warhol's photo- silkscreened images of horrific car crashes in the 1960s highlighted one negative consequence of automobiles. Motor cars have also served artists as materials for making works of art, e.g. the assemblage artist John Chamberlain made sculptures from crushed auto bodies, while Arman embedded whole cars (58 of them) in a huge concrete tower he entitled 'Long term parking' (1982, located in a park at Jouy, France).

● See also Cult Objects, Customizing & Custom Painting, Hi-Way Culture, Lifestyle, Styling, Sub-culture.

◉ R Barker & A Harding (eds) *Automobile design: great designers and their work* (Newton Abbot, David & Charles, 1970).

◉ P Roberts *Any colour so long as it's black: the first fifty years of automobile advertising* (Newton Abbot, David & Charles, 1976).

◉ L Setright *The designers* (Weidenfeld & Nicolson, 1976).

◉ D Tubbs *Art & the automobile* (Guildford, Lutterworth Press, 1978).

◉ M Haslem *The amazing Bugattis* (Royal College of Art/Design Council, 1979).

◉ A Anselmi (ed) *Carrozzeria Italiana: advancing the art and science of automobile design* (Milan, Automobilia, 1980).

◉ B Laban *Chrome: glamour cars of the fifties* (Orbis Publishing, 1982).

◉ S Bayley *Harley Earl and the dream machine* (NY, Knopf, 1983).

◉ *The automobile and culture* (Los Angeles, Museum of Contemporary Art, 1984).

◉ F Basham & B Ughetti (photos) & P Rambali (text) *Car Culture* (Plexus, 1984).

◉ S Bayley *Sex, drink and fast cars: the creation and consumption of images* (Faber & Faber, 1986).

◉ D Barry *Street dreams: American Car Culture from the '50s to the '80s* (MacDonald/Orbis Publishing, 1988).

◉ J Flink *The automobile age* (Cambridge, Mass, MIT Press, 1988).

◉ C Edson Armi *The art of American car design* (Pennsylvania

State University Press, 1989).

◉ A Nahum *Alec Issigonis* (Design Council, 1989).

133 CARDBOARD ARCHITECTURE

A polemical term invented by the American architect Peter Eisenman in the late 1960s. He chose the word 'cardboard' because in architectural discourse it had derogatory connotations. Eisenman intended it as 'an ironic and pre-emptory symbol' for his argument, which was that the relation between form and function was more complex than modernist theory acknowledged. Cardboard – as used in models/the design process – clarified the logical way formal/spatial relationships could be explored without regard to the actual materials finally used or to the function of the building.

Charles Jencks also used the term in respect of the '60s' work of the American architect Louis Kahn and also the work of architects he influenced. According to Jencks, Kahn's architectural models recalled the drawings of Palladio – flat masonry surfaces ruptured by black, geometric holes – giving rise to an architecture resembling the honeycomb structures of cardboard boxes (e.g. Dacca Assembly building, Bangladesh, 1962–8). The influence of this style extended to the Philadelphia School, the New York Five and Robert Venturi.

● See also New York Five, Rational Architecture.

◉ P Eisenman 'Cardboard Architecture: house 1' – in – *Five architects* K Frampton & others (NY, Oxford University Press, 2nd ed 1975) 15–37.

◉ C Jencks 'Irrational rationalism: the Rats since 1960' – in –*The Rationalists: theory and design in the modern movement* D Sharp (ed) (Architectural Press, 1978) 208–30.

134 CARNABY STREET

An unprepossessing street in the Soho district of London which became famous during the mid 1960s as the centre for boutiques and shops selling 'gear' – clothes, records, posters and souvenirs – in the pop idiom. John Stephen, the menswear designer dubbed 'the King of Carnaby Street', opened his first shop there in 1957. The Union Jack was the emblem most frequently on display. The street's reputation as part of 'the scene' or 'swinging London/sixties' and its colourful and vulgar merchandise attracted tourists from all over the world. In 1988–9 the street was in the news again for selling Nazi-inspired material.

● See also Kitsch, Pop Design.

◉ K & K Baynes 'Behind the scene' *Design* (212) August 1966 18–28.

◉ C Hughes-Stanton 'What comes after Carnaby Street?'

Design (230) 1968 42–3.

● T Salter *Carnaby Street* (Walton on Thames, M & J Hobbs, 1970).

135 CARNEGIE INTERNATIONAL

A large-scale exhibition of contemporary painting and sculpture from around the world held at the Museum of Art, Carnegie Institution, Pittsburgh, every three years. The first one was held in 1896.

● J Lane & J Caldwell (eds) *Carnegie International 1985* (Pittsburgh, Museum of Art, Carnegie Institution/Prestel Verlag, 1985).

136 CARNIVAL

(Also Mas' from 'Masquerade') A communal and public form of festivity and merrymaking which takes place annually and normally involves a street procession with dancers, exotic colourful costumes, floats, and bands and/or sound systems. Carnival is an ancient phenomenon which probably derives from pagan fertility rites. In Catholic countries it is associated with the period before Lent when meat-eating is about to be given up. Cities such as Rio de Janeiro, Venice, Nice, Pasadena, New Orleans, Port of Spain and London mount Carnivals which are world famous but thousands of small towns and districts have them too. Carnivals can be considered a collective form of folk, community or popular art but the most ambitious are not simply spontaneous creative expressions on the part of the individuals – on the contrary, they are the result of months of design and preparation by Carnival organizations and participating groups. The Mas' groups compete with one another to design and make the best costumes and floats. Patronage also occurs in that the groups are often supported by wealthy businessmen. Variations in style and content result from the fact that different themes and concepts are adopted every year. Furthermore, some designers are full-time professionals. A case in point was Peter Minshall, a white designer famous for his stunning contributions to Trinidad's Port of Spain Carnival. Minshall also worked in Britain and was trained, in fact, at the Central School of Art, in London, as a theatre designer. He considered his costumes a form of kinetic sculpture because they had to be able to move with the bodily rhythms of the dancer/wearer.

Government agencies are sometimes involved in the funding of Carnivals. London's Notting Hill Gate Carnival, for example, has received grants from the Arts Council. This Carnival – now one of the largest street festivals in Europe – originated in the black West Indian immigrant community in London in the mid 1960s. Its costumes have been displayed in an exhibition held at the Royal Festival Hall; there are also plans for a Carnival museum in order to preserve the best costumes since otherwise the aesthetic achievements of Carnival are transitory. All these developments point to a raising of the cultural and artistic status of Carnival. While the degree of creative imagination and skill exemplified by the best artefacts of the major Carnivals merits the description 'art', this is hardly true of most local Carnivals which tend to be an unholy mix of amateurism, advertising, mass culture stereotypes and kitsch.

Carnival has frequently been conceived by anthropologists and Left-wing theorists as a quasi-revolutionary phenomenon, i.e. a ritual of protest, a world-turned-upside-down scenario. They are certainly occasions when the pleasure principle replaces the reality principle, when role reversals occur, and when there is a temporary suspension of social divisions, but most Carnivals are sedate affairs which affirm rather than challenge the status quo. Indeed, they could be regarded as a social safety valve. Even when protest does occur, it usually takes the form of crime committed against other revellers or riots directed against the police.

● See also Black Art, Community Art, Popular Art, Public Art, Scenography, Street Art.

● E Hill *The Trinidad Carnival: mandate for a national theatre* (Austin, Texas, University of Texas Press, 1972).

● J Murray 'Mas' man' (Minshall) *Observer Colour Supplement* August 19 1979 23–7.

● D Duerdon 'The meaning of Carnival' *New Society* August 21 1980 357–9.

● C Gutzmore 'The Notting Hill Carnival' *Marxism Today* August 1982 31–3.

● J Walker 'Carnival and contradiction' *Performance Magazine* (28) February–March 1984 32–4.

● U Eco & others *Carnival!* (The Hague, Mouton, 1985).

● W Harris *Masquerading: the art of the Notting Hill Carnival* (Arts Council & MAAS, 1986).

● K Owusu & J Ross *Behind the Masquerade: the story of Notting Hill Carnival* (Arts Media Group, 1988).

137 CAYC

Initials standing for Centro de Arte y Comunicacion. A South American interdisciplinary research organization established in Buenos Aires, Argentina, in 1968; its director was Jorge Glusberg. CAYC was composed of artists, sociologists, psychologists, mathematicians and art critics and it mounted exhibitions on such themes as the relation of art to society, science and technology (e.g. art and cybernetics).

● *CAYC: Museo de Arte Moderna do Rio de Janeiro* (Buenos Aires, CAYC, 1978).

138 CENTER FOR ADVANCED VISUAL STUDIES (CAVS)

This centre is part of the Massachusetts Institute of Technology, Cambridge, Mass., USA. It is concerned with research and experiment into all aspects of art and creativity in relation to science, technology, the environment and communications media. CAVS was founded in 1967 by the Hungarian-born artist Gyorgy Kepes (b. 1906). He was its director and driving force from '67 to '74. His successor was the German artist Otto Piene (ex-member of Zero and specialist in 'sky' art). Over the years CAVS has given fellowships to a large number of artists. It has also fostered collaboration and dialogue between artists and scientists, organized lecture series, symposia, events, exhibitions and issued publications. CAVS awards a Master of Science in Visual Studies.

● See also Air Art, Environmental Art, Technological Art, Zero.

● D Davis 'Gyorgy Kepes: the new landscape' – in – *Art & the future* (Thames & Hudson, 1973) 115–19.

● J Benthall 'Kepes' Centre at MIT' *Art International* **19** (1) January 20 1975 28–31, + 49.

● *Otto Piene und das CAVS* (Karlsruhe, Badischer Kunstverein, 1988) (an exhibition organized by the Deutscher Kunstlerbund, Berlin).

CENTRE DE RECHERCHE D'AMBIANCES BERNARD LASSUS, 'Garden of the creepers' (1980). Drawing, competition entry for project for the Parc de la Villette, Paris. Photo: Lassus & Stephen Bann.

139 CENTRE DE RECHERCHE D'AMBIANCES (CRA)

Bernard Lassus, a French kinetic sculptor and ex-pupil of Léger, established the CRA and became its first director in 1962. CRA was intended as an interdisciplinary organization bringing together specialists from architecture, psychology, sociology and poetics in order to achieve a comprehensive approach to the problems of environmental design. Lassus believed that humankind was evolving towards a 'global landscape, a continuum: an artificial environment which by virtue of its size will necessarily become more natural for us than what we call Nature'. His aim was to overcome the nature/culture opposition by developing mediating elements between natural and constructed forms. In practice this involved the fusion of the roles of sculptor and architect, the use of light, colour and visual games as a means of enlivening the urban environment. Underlying the work of the Centre was a search for general laws which would enable the solution of problems of form and construction on any scale, hence the investigation of 'Habitants-payagistes' (dweller-landscapes), the study of existing human modifications of the landscape. In 1969 Lassus was appointed Professor of Architecture at the École de Beaux Arts, Paris, and in 1975 a retrospective exhibition of his work was held at the Musée des Arts Décoratifs, Paris. During the late 1970s and early '80s Lassus designed a number of imaginative environmental projects gardens, parks and 'micro-landscapes' – including the award-winning 'Garden of Returns' (1982) for the Corderie Royale, Rochefort.

● See also Ecological Art, Environmental Art/Design.

● B Lassus 'Environments and total landscape' *Form* (UK) (5) September 1967 13–15.

● S Bann 'Bernard Lassus: Ambiance' *Art & Artists* **6** (3) June 1971 20–3.

● — 'De l'oeuvre d'art paysage global' *L'Oeil* (215) November 1972 52–7.

● — 'From kineticism to didacticism in contemporary French art' *Studio International* **185** (953) March 1973 105–9.

● B Lassus *Paysages quotidiens de l'Ambiance au démesurable* (Paris, Musée des Arts Décoratifs/CCI, Centre Beaubourg, 1975).

● 'France: Bernard Lassus: the garden of the anterior' *Studio International* **193** (986) March–April 1977 150–2.

● B Lassus & S Bann 'The landscape approach of Bernard Lassus' *Journal of Garden History* **3** (2) 1983 79–107.

140 CHICAGO IMAGISTS

(Also Hairy Who, Imagist Art, Monster School, Who Chicago) Chicago's visual artists of the post-1945 era began to gain national recognition in 1959 when a group of them were included in the New York show 'New Images of Man' and were labelled the 'Monster School'. (Chicago's contribution to modern architecture had been recognized much earlier.) By the mid '60s a coherent group was associated with the Hyde Park Art Center, assisted and promoted by its director Don Baum. This group exhibited – often as the 'Hairy Who' – in shows throughout the United States and in South America. The best known of these artists were Gladys Nilsson, James Nutt, Edward Paschke, Karl Wirsum and H. C. Westerman.

Chicago art tended to be viewed as deliberately anti-New York art. According to J. Allen and D. Guthrie, it lay 'somewhere in the overlap between the primitive, the naive, and popular kitsch', while Max Kozloff maintained that it was characterized by a 'chronic quoting of motifs, unwitting or conscious parodies of styles, and various uncertainties of tone'. Often, works were concerned with personal fantasies of sex and aggression towards authority figures. They borrowed images from juvenilia, comic strips and 'trash treasures'; hence the terms 'Imagist Art' and 'Chicago Imagists'. A substantial exhibition of the work of the Hairy Who was shown in London in 1981 at the Camden Arts Centre.

● See also Fantastic Art, New York School.

● F Schulze 'Chicago' *Art International* **11** (5) May 20 1967 42–4.

● — 'Art news in Chicago' *Art News* **70** (7) November 1971 45–55.

● — *Fantastic images: Chicago art since 1945* (NY, Wittenborn, 1972).

● M Kozloff 'Chicago art since 1945' *Artforum* **11** (2) October 1972 51–6.

● J Allen & D Guthrie 'Chicago-regionalism?' *Studio International* **186** (960) November 1973 182–6.

● *Who Chicago? An exhibition of contemporary Imagists* (Sunderland, Ceolfrith Gallery/London, Camden Arts Centre, 1980–1).

● D Adrian & R Born *The Chicago Imagist print: ten artists' work, 1958–87, a catalogue raisonné* (Chicago, David & Alfred Smart Gallery, University of Chicago, 1987).

141 CINÉTISATIONS

Bizarre images of contorted and shattered buildings produced by the French kinetic sculptor Pol Bury in 1966 by the simple device of cutting or stamping out a series of concentric circles at key points in photographs, engravings, or reproductions of architectural subjects. The resulting rings were then remounted slightly askew. This utterly destroyed the stability of the buildings. Bury enlarged his pictures and transferred them onto canvas or

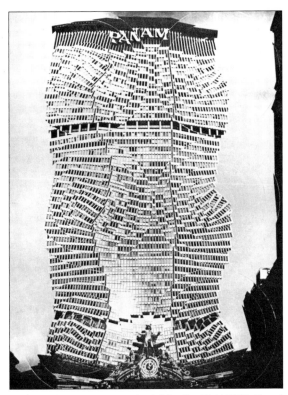

CINÉTISATIONS Pol Bury, 'Pan Am building New York' (1964). Treated photograph. Photo: Bury.

lithographic plates. The terms 'Cinétisme' and 'Art Cinétique' were also employed in respect of Victor Vasarely's op art pictures because they created an impression of movement and flicker.

● See also Kinetic Art, Op Art, Photo-Montage.

● *Pol Bury* (NY, Lefèbre Gallery, 1966).

● S Watson Taylor 'Pol Bury Cinétisations' *Art & Artists* **1** (10) January 1967 8–13.

142 CITY WALLS

An artists' co-operative founded by Jason Crum in New York in 1969 with the encouragement of the urban planner David Bromberg. Members included Robert Wiegand, Mel Pekarsky, Richard Anuskiewicz, Tania and Allan d'Arcangelo. The aim of City Walls was to improve the urban environment by decorating blank walls with colourful abstract murals painted in a hard-edge style. By 1974 over 35 examples had been produced. This type of art provoked adverse criticism from community muralists because of its 'cosmetic' character, its lack of figurative, social content and its failure to relate to the lives of local people.

● See also Community Art, Environmental Art, Hard-Edge Painting, Public Art, Street Art, Supergraphics.

● 'Painting for City Walls: the Museum of Modern Art, New

York' *L'Architecture d'Aujourdhui* (145) September 1969 91–4.

● L Alloway 'Art' *The Nation* September 21 1970 254.

● — 'Art' *The Nation* September 25 1972 252–3.

● E Cockcroft & others *Toward a people's art: the contemporary mural movement* (NY, Dutton, 1977) 38–42.

143 CLASP

(Consortium of Local Authorities Special Programme) In the late 1950s a number of British local authorities co-operated for reasons of economy and efficiency in the production of school buildings using a pre-fabrication system of construction first devised by Donald Gibson in Nottingham and later developed by C. H. Aslin in Hertfordshire. A CLASP school exhibited at the Milan Triennale in 1960 excited the admiration of Italian architects. A second consortium formed by other authorities gave rise to the acronym SCOLA.

● See also Prefabs, Social Architecture/Design, Systems Architecture.

● Ministry of Education *The story of CLASP* (HMSO, 1960).

● R Banham 'On trial 4: CLASP' *Architectural Review* **131** (783) May 1962 349–52.

● F Gnecchi-Ruscone 'CLASP in Italy' *Architectural Review* **133** (795) May 1963 319–20.

144 CLUSTER

A term much in vogue in architectural and planning circles during the 1950s. The urbanist Kevin Lynch first discussed the concept in an article published in 1954. It referred to a type of city layout that had many small centres instead of a nodal point surrounded by concentric rings and a radial road pattern. In 1957 Alison and Peter Smithson defined a 'Cluster' as 'a close knit, complicated, often moving aggregation, but an aggregation with a distinct structure'. Denys Lasdun's residential towers designed from 1953 onwards were also called 'Cluster blocks'. Sibyl Moholy-Nagy used 'Cluster' to mean groups of houses scattered haphazardly in the twilight zone between cities and the open countryside.

● See also Collective Form.

● K Lynch 'The form of cities' *Scientific American* **190** (4) 1954 54–63.

● A & P Smithson 'Cluster patterns' *Architecture & Building* **31** 1956 271–2.

● — 'Cluster city: a new shape for the community' *Architectural Review* **122** (730) November 1957 333–6.

● 'Cluster blocks...' *Architectural Design* **28** (2) February 1958 62–5.

● S Moholy-Nagy *Matrix of man: an illustrated history of the urban environment* (Pall Mall Press, 1968) 241–82.

145 CNAC

Initials standing for 'Centre National d'Art Contemporain', a French institution established in 1967 by the Ministry of Cultural Affairs for the purpose of organizing exhibitions, publishing catalogues and documenting current art and artists on an international scale. CNAC is located within the Pompidou arts complex in Paris.

● See also Pompidou Centre.

● B Hunnisett 'Centre National d'Art Contemporain, Paris' *Arlis Newsletter* (9) October 1971 2–3.

146 CoBrA

A group of European artists founded in Paris in 1948 by the Danish painter Asger Jorn, the Dutch painter Karel Appel, the Belgian artist Corneille and Jean Atlan and Pierre Alechinsky. Other participants included Egill Jacobsen, Lucebert and Karl H. Pedersen. They considered themselves the representatives of an International of experimental art sympathetic to expressionism and surrealism but opposed to geometric abstraction. The name of the group was derived from the initial letters of the three capital cities where key members lived: Copenhagen, Brussels, Amsterdam. The paintings of CoBrA somewhat resembled American abstract expressionism: a mixture of abstraction and figuration, vehement brushwork and powerful colours. However, they also employed thick impasto combined with crude child-like drawing and found inspiration in primitive art and folk art. 'Nordic Expressionism' is how some critics have characterized the art of the CoBrA group. Exhibitions of the works of CoBrA artists were held in Amsterdam in 1949 and in Liège and Paris in 1951. The group also published a magazine –CoBrA Revue – which ran for eight issues. The lifespan of the group was only three years but it subsequently proved to be one of the most influential of the post-1945 era.

● See also Experimental Group, Situationists.

● *CoBrA 1949–51* (Amsterdam, Stedelijk Museum, 1962).

● L Alloway 'Danish art and primitivism' *Living Arts* (1) 1963 44–52.

● *CoBrA 1948–51* (Rotterdam, Museum Boymans-van Beuningen, 1966).

● *Gruppe CoBrA und andere maler* (Kiel, Kunsthalle, 1974).

● W Stokvis *CoBrA* (Amsterdam, De Bezige Bij, 1974).

● *CoBrA 1948–51 Bulletin* (Paris, Éditions Jean-Michel Place, 1980).

● *CoBrA 1948–51* (Paris, Musée de la Ville de Paris, 1983).

● J-C Lambert *CoBrA* (Sotheby Publications, 1983).

● E Flomenhaft *The roots and development of CoBrA art* (Long Island, Fine Arts Museum, 1986).

● W Stokvis *CoBrA prints, CoBrA books* (NY, Franklin Furnace, 1986).

● *CoBrA: forty years after* (Amsterdam, Nieuwe Kerk, 1988).

147 COCA-COLA COLLECTIBLES/ DESIGN

The products, graphics and advertising associated with the giant American corporation Coca-Cola merit attention here for several reasons: their memorable design and powerful corporate identity, the fact that many early Coke artefacts have become collectors' items, and the fact that several pop artists (e.g. Clive Barker, Charles Frazier, Marisol, Mel Ramos, Andy Warhol) have depicted the Coke bottle as a prime emblem of American popular culture. Coca-Cola is a fizzy drink made from coca leaf and kola nut which is now consumed worldwide. The liquid itself was designed (to a secret formula) by a pharmacist called Pemberton in Atlanta during the late nineteenth century. Since that time it has been redesigned and various other drinks added to the range (e.g. diet Coke). The famous curlicue trademark was the creation of Frank M. Robinson, while the equally famous bottle was designed by Alex Samuelson and T. Clyde Edwards in 1915; its shape was later refined by Raymond Loewy. In 1986 the 'megabrand' Coca-Cola was the subject of an exhibition mounted by the Boilerhouse Project at the Victoria & Albert Museum.

● See also Corporate Design, Cult Objects, Pop Art, Pop Design.

● C Munsey *The illustrated guide to the collectibles of Coca-Cola* (NY, Hawthorn Books, 1972).

● P Watters *Coca-Cola: an illustrated history* (NY, Doubleday, 1978).

● S Bayley *Coke! Coca-Cola 1886–1986* (Boilerhouse Project/Victoria & Albert Museum, 1986).

● A Hoy *Coca-Cola: the first hundred years* (Atlanta, Coca-Cola, 1986).

● T Oliver *The real Coke* (Elm Tree Books, 1986).

● F Palazzini *Coca-Cola superstar: the drink that became a business empire* (Columbus, 1989).

148 COLLABORATIONS

During the Italian Renaissance paintings were often executed by several artists. It is only since an individualistic mode of artistic production became the norm during the modern era, that artistic collaboration – defined by Dan Cameron as 'to work in combination towards a unified action' – came to be viewed as something unusual. However, it should be acknowledged that modern artists have been willing to join together to form groups and movements, to publish manifestos and magazines, to mount exhibitions and to run alternative spaces and self-help organizations. (Witness the New York group –

active in the early 1980s – called Collaborative Projects Inc., or simply Co-Lab.) Many modern painters and printmakers have also worked in tandem to achieve high-quality prints. Furthermore, there have been instances of collaborations between artists and architects despite the tendency in modern times for the various arts to develop separately. In 1981 the Architectural League in New York mounted a centennial exhibition about artist–architect collaborations.

Three years later a show of twentieth-century artist collaborations was held at the Hirshhorn Museum, Washington. Recent examples of such collaborations have included David Salle/Julian Schnabel, Andy Warhol/Jean-Michel Basquiat. According to Cameron, collaborations must be temporary arrangements between two or more independent artists; he therefore excludes the long-term co-operative projects of groups like Art&Language and such artist duos as Gilbert and George, Komar and Melamid. Stefan Szczelkun is an Anglo-Polish performance artist whose book *Collaborations* documents over a decade of activities with other artists and groups.

● See also Alternative Spaces, Art & Language, Artists' Unions, Atelier 17, Gilbert & George, Group Material, Komar & Melamid, KOS, Public Art, Tyler Graphics.

● W Sheard & J Paoletti (eds) *Collaboration in Italian Renaissance art* (New Haven & London, Yale University Press, 1979).

● B Diamonstein (ed) *Collaboration: artists and architects* (NY, Architectural League/Watson-Guptill Publications, 1981).

● C Saft *Artist and printer: printmaking as a collaborative process* (NY, Pratt Graphics Center, 1981).

● G Jones 'Collaboration, a dirty word?' *Art Monthly* (53) February 1982 8–9.

● S Block 'The why and how of collaboration' *High Performance* **7** (2) 1984 10–13, + 81.

● D Cameron 'Against collaboration' *Arts Magazine* **58** (7)

COLLABORATIONS JEAN-MICHEL BASQUIAT & ANDY WARHOL, '1984' (1984). Acrylic on canvas 76" x 114". Photo: Mayor Rowan Gallery, London.

March 1984 83–7.

● C Jencks 'A modest proposal: on the collaboration between artist and architect' – in – *Art within reach* P Townsend (ed) (*Art Monthly*/Thames & Hudson, 1984) 15–19.

● C McCabe *Artistic collaborations in the twentieth century* (Washington DC, Hirshhorn/Smithsonian, 1984).

● R Fine & others *Gemini GEL: Art and collaboration* (Washington DC, National Gallery of Art/NY, Abbeville Press, 1985).

● S Szczelkun *Collaborations* (Routine Art Co/Working Press, 1988).

● M Robinette 'Collaboration: impossible dream or achievable reality?' *Circa* (45) May–June 1989 18–22.

149 COLLAGE CITY

In a 1975 special issue of *Architectural Review* Colin Rowe and Fred Koetter argued that existing cities consist of a jumble of partially realized set pieces – i.e. a collage – and that this reality should be seen as a positive feature because it gives pleasure to city dwellers. The authors concluded that planners should give up the idea of total control and cease dreaming of utopian solutions to urban problems because even if they could be realized they would be unsatisfactory.

● See also NATO, Urbanism, Utopian Architecture.

● C Rowe & F Koetter 'Collage City' *Architectural Review* **158** (942) August 1975; *Collage City* (Cambridge, Mass, MIT Press, 1978).

150 COLLECTIVE FORM

A term devised by the Japanese architect Fumihiku Maki in the 1960s. It stemmed from the fact that architects and town planners often have to cope with complex agglomerations of buildings, highways and greenspaces not just isolated buildings. Maki defined segments of the total form of the city as 'Collective Form' and he identified three compositional methods for establishing them: (1) compositional form; (2) megaform; (3) group form.

● See also Megastructures, Metabolist Group.

● F Maki *Investigations in Collective Form* (St Louis, Washington University School of Architecture, 1964).

● — & M Ohtaka 'Some thoughts on Collective Form' – in – *Structure in art and science* G Kepes (ed) (Studio Vista, 1965) 116–27.

● — 'The theory of group form' *Japan Architect* February 1970 39–42.

151 COLOUR-FIELD PAINTING

A label that was applied to paintings by a generation of American artists – Morris Louis, Kenneth Noland, Jules Olitski and Gene Davis – exhibiting in the late 1950s and early '60s. Exponents of hard-edge painting, e.g. Ellsworth Kelly, were sometimes included in the category and the term was also applied retrospectively to the abstract expressionist paintings of Barnett Newman, Clyfford Still and Mark Rothko. Newman was considered the originator and chief exponent of Colour-Field. The meaning of the term was complicated by the fact that critics also spoke of 'colour painting' or 'chromatic abstraction' and 'field painting'. 'Colour-Field' was clearly a combination of the two. Field painting began with Jackson Pollock's all-over drip paintings in which the canvas was treated as a continuous or extended plane, as a single unit so that figure and ground carried equal value. Colour-Field painters replaced tonal contrasts and brushwork by solid areas of colour or, in the case of the acrylic stain painting of Louis, with thin washes of pigment. These tended to extend across the canvas from edge to edge with the implication that they extended into the space beyond the painting's framing edge.

In no longer treating the picture space as a box or window-like cavity, Colour- Field Painting departed radically from the depth/illusionistic tradition of Western oil painting. According to Peter Plagens, a field of colour did have a shallow depth (in contrast to a spot of colour which appeared to sit on the surface of the canvas). However, what Colour-Field Painting lacked in depth, it made up for in breadth: most exponents favoured large, long canvases that were intended (in the case of Newman) to be viewed at close quarters so that they would engulf the spectator's whole field of vision. In these circumstances the fields of brilliant, saturated colour had a dramatic optical and emotional impact. Because this kind of painting 'enveloped' the spectator, it was also described as 'environmental'.

● See also All-Over Painting, Drip Painting, Hard-Edge Painting, Monochromatic & Monotonal Painting, Non-Relational Art, Stain Painting.

● *Color and Field 1890–1970* (Buffalo, Albright-Knox Art Gallery, 1970).

● I Sandler 'Color Field painters' – in – *Abstract expressionism: the triumph of American painting* (Pall Mall Press, 1970) 148–57.

● W Domingo 'Color abstraction: a survey of recent American paintings' *Arts Magazine* **45** January 1971 34–40.

● E Henning 'Colour and Field' *Art International* **15** (5) May 20 1971 46–50.

● T Hess *Barnett Newman* (Tate Gallery, 1972).

152 COLOUR SUPPLEMENTS Magazines illustrated with colour photographs introduced by several 'posh' or quality Sunday newspapers in Britain during the 1960s in order to carry features with picture spreads and full-colour advertisements. The first was produced by *The Sunday Times* in 1962 (editor: Mark Boxer), the second was *The Observer* in September 1964 (the *Sunday Telegraph* also started a magazine in 1964 but it was at first published on Fridays). More down-market Sunday newspapers then followed suit. The Colour Sups of the '60s were highly influential in terms of consumerism, fashion, photography, design and lifestyle.

Those of *The Sunday Times* regularly featured profiles of contemporary artists and art movements which helped to popularize pop and op art. Over the decades advertising became more and more dominant with the result that by the 1980s the colour magazine had become, as one writer put it, 'an editorial disaster area'.

● See also Magazine Art, Op Art, Pop Art, Pop Design.

● K Baynes 'The *Sunday Times Magazine:* news and image' *Graphis* **34** (196) 1978–9 98–113.

● 'The *Sunday Times Magazine*' (three articles) *Creative Camera* (211) July–August 1982 616–27.

● C Osman 'The Colour Supplements' *Creative Camera* (231) March 1984 1296–9.

● M Slavin 'Colour supplement living' *Ten 8* (23) 1986 2–25.

153 COMBINE PAINTINGS (Also Stand-up Paintings) Robert Rauschenberg's name for those of his mixed-media works dating from the 1950s combining a painted surface with non-art objects such as Coke bottles, pillows, radios, stuffed birds and rams, tyres.... In the '60s painting was combined more with silk-screened photographic images. John Cage observed that Rauschenberg's three-dimensional collages were as non-relational as the reports in a newspaper. Some Combines were displayed on walls, others rested on the floors of galleries. The works completely transcended the traditional artforms of painting and sculpture.

● See also Assemblage Art, Inter-Media, Junk Culture/Sculpture, Neo-Dada, Tableau.

● *Robert Rauschenberg: paintings, drawings and combines 1949–64* (Whitechapel Art Gallery, 1964).

● A Forge *Robert Rauschenberg* (NY, Abrams, 1969).

154 COMIC ART (Also Strip Language) Arguably, the design and illustration of comics and cartoons is an art in its own right (and a number of books and exhibitions have taken this view), but in this instance the term 'Comic Art' refers to works of fine art based on comics either iconographically or stylistically. The list of modern artists who have represented comic characters, or used the comic's narrative strip format, or imitated the graphic styles favoured by comic draughtsmen, is a long one: Peter Blake, Philip Guston, Roy Lichtenstein, Keith Haring, Philip Pearlstein, Oyvind Fahlstrom, Sigmar Polke, Andy Warhol, Karl Wirsum, David Salle, Michael Sandle, Ronnie Cutrone, Claes Oldenburg, etc. Comics – mainly American ones – have been of most interest to pop artists, New York graffiti writers, Chicago painters of the imagist persuasion, and French painters belonging to the Free Figuration tendency. While the majority of artists who appropriate comic imagery do so in an affectionate, celebratory way, there are some whose purposes are parody, irony and criticism. Amongst art theorists what provokes most discussion about comic-based art is the significance of the transposition of mass culture material into a fine art context. Cartoonists gain their revenge for the pillaging of their work by fine artists by satirizing the pretensions of modern art as the Tate Gallery exhibition of 1973 demonstrated.

In Britain during the 1980s a number of artschool graduates chose to work directly with popular cultural forms – by making and selling their own comics, for instance – rather than becoming painters or sculptors.

● See also Bande Dessinée, Chicago Imagists, Comix, Disneyana, Figuration Libre, Graffiti, Graphic Novels, Narrative Figuration/Painting.

● A Boime 'Roy Lichtenstein and the comic strip' *Art Journal* **28** (2) Winter 1968–9 155–9.

● G Melly & J Glaves-Smith *A child of six could do it! Cartoons about modern art* (Tate Gallery, 1973).

● *The Comic Art show* (NY, Whitney Museum of American Art, 1983).

● D Deitcher 'Comic connoisseurs' *Art in America* **72** (2) February 1984 101–6.

● *Strip Language: an exploration of representation and comment, serial image and text* (Gimpel Fils, 1984) Leaflet.

● S Wagstaff & others *Comic iconoclasm* (London, ICA, 1987).

155 COMIX (Also Alternative Comix, Head Comix, Komix, Underground Comix) A visual expression of the underground or alternative sub-culture of the late 1960s and early '70s. The movement began on the West Coast of the United States with the appearance of comic books such as *Zap Comix* (1967) and *Yellow Dog* (1968). The artists – Robert Crumb, Rick Griffin, Victor Moscoso,

Gilbert Sheldon, Skip Williamson and S. Clay Wilson – transgressed the rules of the Comics Code in order to introduce ideas, themes and images that were more radical and offensive (to conventional taste and to feminists) than those found in mainstream comics. Crumb became internationally famous for his powerful, freaky drawings treating such themes as drugs, sex, obscenity, politics and the frowzy hippy lifestyle, and for his memorable characters Mr Natural, Honeybunch Kaminsky and Fritz the Cat.

Comix were distributed in Europe via Amsterdam and David Zack wrote about them in *Art & Artists.* In 1970 the American Arts Documentation Centre at Exeter University mounted a travelling exhibition devoted to the American underground press. *Cyclops,* the first British Comix appeared in 1970. It introduced the work of Edward Barker, Mal Dean, Malcolm McNeill and Raymond Lowry. Wider circulations were achieved by *Nasty Tales* (1971) and *Cozmic Comics* (1971) which featured strips by Mick Farren, William Rankin, Cap Stelling and Chris Welch alongside reprints of American examples. The demise of *Nasty Tales* around 1974 coincided with the emergence of another strand of the Comix movement, i.e. 'alternative' Comix exemplified by *Class War Comix* drawn by Clifford Harper. In July 1976 the Birmingham Arts Lab hosted the Konvention of Alternative Komix which resulted in the publication of *Streetcomix* No:2, 1976, featuring the work of Brodnax, Hunt Emerson, Bob Gale and Sue Varty. Emerson also produced several issues of *Large Cow Comix* in small quantities that typified the condition of alternative Comix in Britain.

● See also Arts Lab, Bande Dessinée, Comic Art, Graphic Novels, Narrative Figuration/Painting, Underground Art.

◉ D Zack 'Smut for love, art and society' *Art & Artists* **4** (9) December 1969 12–17.

◉ R Lewis 'The American underground press' *Assistant Librarian* **63** (8) August 1970 122–4.

◉ B Abel 'Up from underground: notes on the new Comix' – in – *Mass culture revisited* R Rosenberg & D White (eds) (NY, Van Nostrand Reinhold, 1971) 423–43.

◉ L Daniels *Comix: a history of comic books in America* (NY, Outerbridge, 1971).

◉ M Estren *A history of underground comics* (San Francisco, Straight Arrow, 1974).

◉ 'Underground comics' *Sounds* January 15 1977 16–17.

◉ R Crumb *R Crumb's head Comix: twenty years later* (Plexus, 1991).

156 COMMODITY AESTHETICS

An expression employed by the German Marxist philosopher Wolfgang Fritz Haug from 1970 onwards to refer to the aesthetic innovations capitalist firms regularly make in the appearance of their products in order to achieve new sales. Aesthetic revamping of goods, he argues, is all too often accompanied by a deterioration in their basic use-values. He also employs the expression 'the technocracy of sensuousness' and contends that 'the entire world of useful things is subjugated within its sensuous organization to a permanent revolutionizing which feeds back into the sensuous organization of people themselves'. Haug's critique has also been concerned with the role of advertising and packaging in creating 'imaginary spaces' around commodities. The question of the relationship between design and commodities was of much concern in the 1980s, witness the theme of the opening exhibition of London's Design Museum in 1989: 'Commerce and culture'. The commodity status of art was also of interest in the same decade and a number of artists made works of art which commented on the very issue.

● See also Neo-Geo, Reception Theory/Aesthetics, Styling.

◉ W Haug *Critique of Commodity Aesthetics: appearance, sexuality and advertising in capitalist society* (Cambridge, Polity Press, 1986).

◉ — *Commodity Aesthetics, ideology and culture* (NY, International General, 1987).

◉ J Walker 'Artworks as commodity' *Circa* (Belfast) (32) January–February 1987 26–30.

◉ S Jhally *The codes of advertising* (F Pinter, 1987).

157 COMMON GROUND (CG)

A British ecology/ environment/ heritage group (or 'umbrella' organization since power is decentralized) founded in 1983 for the purpose of promoting the importance of a common cultural heritage: plants, animals, familiar and local places. CG is not an arts organization but it initiates arts projects as one way of achieving its aims. For instance, the 'New Milestones Project' (1985–88) in Dorset encouraged the creation of a new generation of town, village and countryside or 'wayside' sculptures, small-scale works intended to express a sense of history, a love of place and the natural world. Carved sculptures in stone and wood were commissioned by landholders and local communities from such artists as Andy Goldsworthy, Peter Randall Page and Simon Thomas. CG's funding derives from a variety of sources: charitable trusts, individuals, businesses and government agencies (e.g. the Arts Council).

COMMON GROUND PETER RANDALL-PAGE, 'Wayside carving 1' (1986), West Lulworth, Dorset. Commissioned by the Weld Estate with Common Ground. Photo: Rory Coonan/Arts Council.

'Common Ground' was also the title of a 1982 exhibition and publication concerning works by five artists – Hamish Fulton, Helen and Newton Harrison, Michael Singer and Alan Sonfist – who undertook environmental projects in the Florida landscape.

● See also Community Art & Media, Earth & Land Art, Ecological Art, Environmental Art, Heritage Industry, Public Art.

● M Auping *Common Ground: five artists in the Florida landscape* (Sarasota, Florida, John & Mable Ringling Museum of Art, 1982).

● J Morland *New Milestones: sculpture, community and the land* (Common Ground, 1988).

● M Miles & others *Art for public places: critical essays* (Winchester School of Art Press, 1989).

158 COMMUNITY ARCHITECTURE

(Including Activist Tradition, People's Architecture, Progressive Architecture) The term 'Community Architecture' is credited to Charles Knevitt (architectural critic of *The Times*) and dates from 1975 but its origins lay in the previous decade. In the years following 1968 various small groups were formed by politically and socially conscious architects seeking an alternative to commercial/ corporate architecture, the modernism – functionalism paradigm, 'top down' paternalistic planning and the professional organizations and institutions which served the status quo. Examples of these radical groups included: ARSE (Architects for a Really Socialist Environment) founded in 1969; Street Farmer (a co-op consisting of Graham Caine, Peter Crump and Bruce Haggert which opposed mass production and large-scale technology and advocated instead ecology, amateur architecture and community gardening); NAM (New Architecture Movement); ARC (Architects' Revolutionary Council) founded in 1973. ARC published a broadsheet called *Red House* (1976–) in which they attacked the Royal Institute of British Architects (RIBA) and argued for an architecture which served the needs of ordinary people in a given locality or groups with some common interest.

Community Architecture is the consequence of the involvement of ordinary people (generally those in the deprived and run-down areas of inner cities) in the decision-making processes by which buildings come into being. Community architects – many of them women – live and work on-site in order to provide expertise and skills to communities. They act as designers, catalysts, enablers and advocates (see also Advocacy Planning). Local people are consulted at every stage and/or take charge of the overall scheme. This type of architecture is slow to come to fruition because it depends upon the active involvement of tenants in the planning, design and development processes. In the case of new schemes, teams of unemployed people with building skills are recruited so that self-build housing projects can be undertaken. (The book by Wates and Knevitt cited below includes a checklist of characteristics of Community Architecture as against those of conventional architecture.)

In practice Community Architecture often consisted of small-scale projects, in-fill rather than wholesale redevelopment, or the rehabilitation of old housing. In Holland Wiek Röling, chief architect of Haarlem, has engaged in Community Architecture for a number of years. He has argued that architects should take prime responsibility for the design of the exteriors of buildings and tenants for their interiors. In Britain the Byker housing scheme, Newcastle upon Tyne, designed by Ralph Erskine in the 1960s is cited by some writers as an early example of Community Architecture. Other successful projects have been undertaken in provincial towns such as Macclesfield, Liverpool and Leicester.

During the 1970s and '80s Community Architecture proved to be highly controversial. It aroused the contempt of many professional architects and architectural critics who maintained that it could not solve the total housing needs of society nor could it result in masterpieces of modern architecture because public taste was unimaginative and favoured traditional styles. However, in 1976 the RIBA set up a Community Architecture Group (CAG) to encourage further development and to provide a resource centre. That the movement had gained considerable influence in Britain by the mid '80s was signalled by the election of Rod Hackney, a leading advocate, to the presidency of the RIBA and by the fact that the aims of community architects were publicly endorsed by Prince Charles of the British Royal Family.

● See also Advocacy Planning, ARCH, Participatory Design, Radical Design, SAR, Social Architecture/ Design.

● C Jencks 'The activist tradition' – in – *Architecture 2000: predictions and methods* (Studio Vista, 1971) 75–89.

● Street Farmer 'A threatening letter to all architects' *AAQ* **4** (4) October–December 1972 17–20.

● M Pawley 'Fallen arches of the barefoot architect' *Guardian* August 12 1985 9.

● R Hackney, J Lubbock & J Turner 'A design with people in mind' *Guardian* August 26 1985 7.

● M Pawley 'What's wrong with DIY' *Guardian* September 9 1985 11.

● 'The man and the myth of Community Architecture' *Guardian* July 3 1987 21.

● N Wates & C Knevitt *Community Architecture* (Penguin Books, 1987).

● W Röling & R Hackney 'Community Architecture and its role in inner city regeneration' *Royal Society of Arts Journal* **CXXXVII** (5391) February 1989 149–62.

● D Brown & others 'The rise & fall of Community Architecture' *Architectural Design* **60** (1/2) 1990 31–51.

● R Hackney *The good, the bad and the ugly: cities in crisis* (F Muller, 1990).

● E Lozano *Community design and the culture of cities* (Cambridge University Press, 1991).

159 COMMUNITY ART & MEDIA

This form of art emerged during the late 1960s and early '70s in Britain, Australia and the United States as a result of artists' dissatisfaction with the art gallery/museum system serving the middle classes, and with modes of abstract art (e.g. minimalism) which appeared to have no meaning for the mass of the people. Radical artists began to form groups and co-ops, and to establish themselves in particular communities and neighbourhoods, especially inner city areas, and to generate work in dialogue with specific groups such as the residents of a housing estate or the population of a school. Examples of such artist groups and organizations in Britain included: Action Space, Basement Project, Blackfriars Photography Project, Fine Heart Squad, Free Form Arts Trust, Greenwich Mural Workshop, Inter-Change, Paddington Printshop, THAP (Tower Hamlets Arts Project), Welfare State, West London Media Work-

COMMUNITY ART PETER DUNN & LORAINE LEESON, 'Big money is moving in' (1983). Photomural, 18' x 12' from the series 'The Changing Picture of Docklands'. Docklands, London. Photo: Dunn & Leeson.

shop. In the USA: Chicago Mural Group, City Arts Workshop, Graffiti Alternatives Workshop, L A Fine Arts Squad.

Often the artists' motivations were political: they wanted to transform environments, consciousnesses, society, to intervene in local politics and to give a voice to the poor and the powerless. A huge mural in Battersea, London, called 'The good the bad and the ugly' (1979) by Brian Barnes and the Wandsworth Mural Workshop was so critical in its content of local businesses and politicians that it was destroyed by the owners of the wall on which it was painted.

Community artists were willing to employ a range of forms and media: street theatre, mural painting, poster and photography workshops, video recording, television and radio broadcasting, etc. Festivals and events employing traditional popular forms and inflatables, play structures and so forth were also organized in order to make art that was 'live'. Professionally trained artists acted as catalysts, organizers and teachers. They sought to involve local people in the production of art in order to liberate latent creative abilities and to overcome the alienation of the artist from society. And where a community spirit was lacking, they employed art in order to nurture one.

Since process was more important than end-product, high aesthetic quality was not the first consideration. The poor technical and artistic quality of many examples of Community Art resulted in much criticism from the art-world and art dealers had no time for this kind of work because it was not a commodity from which they could profit. Since Community Murals had to compete in the street against the very sophisticated images of advertising, the naivety of their pictorial rhetoric was frequently exposed. Local people also attacked murals for being cosmetic, afterthoughts designed to hide squalor or to compensate for brutal new architecture.

Funding for Community Arts activities derived from a variety of sources: national and local arts councils, private companies, charitable foundations, educational authorities, monies for youth employment, etc. The British Arts Council established a Community Arts working party in 1973 and in 1974 an Association of Community Artists (ACA) was formed to co-ordinate activities nationwide. In the USA a journal entitled *Community Murals* began publication in San Francisco in 1978.

The concept of community is theoretically problematic and it raises questions as to its relation with other issues such as class, gender and race. As sources of funding dwindled in the 1980s and scepticism grew concerning the correctness of the politics of community-based action, more and more artists reverted to the art gallery

system or made contributions via political, feminist and black art; there was also a significant shift of emphasis away from Community Art to public art. Despite the decline of the Community Arts movement, it did mount an effective challenge to traditional conceptions of art and many of its innovations and practices were in fact incorporated into the system as a whole.

● See also APG, Common Ground, Free Form Arts Trust, Inter-Change, Pictorial Rhetoric, Political Art, Public Art, Street Art, Video Art.

● *Community Arts: the report of the Community Arts Working Party* (Arts Council, 1974).

● 'The surge in Community Arts' *Arts in Society* Spring–Summer 1975 (Special issue).

● E Cockcroft & others *Towards a people's art: the contemporary mural movement* (NY, Dutton, 1977).

● S Braden *Artists and people* (Routledge & Kegan Paul, 1978).

P Lewis *Community television and cable in Britain* (BFI, 1978).

● 'Photography in the community' *Camerawork* (13) 1979.

● H Nigg & G Wade *Community Media: community communication in the UK: video, local TV, film and photography* (Zürich, Regenbogen, 1980).

● *Community Arts: principles and practices* (Manchester, Shelton Trust, 1981) Conference proceedings.

● M Pinhorn *Rainbow report* (Greater London Arts Council, 1982).

● A Barnett *Community Murals: the people's art* (Associated Universities Press, 1984).

● D Humphries & R Monk *The mural movement: a guide to Community Murals in Australia* (Sydney, Arts Council of New South Wales, 1984).

● O Kelly *Community, art and the state: storming the citadels* (Comedia, 1984).

● Ray Walker Memorial Committee *Ray Walker* (Royal Festival Hall, 1985).

● S Lobb & C Kenna *Mural Manual* (Greenwich Mural Workshop/Sunderland, AN Publications, 1991).

160 COMPUTER-AIDED DESIGN (Also CAD-CAM meaning Computer-Aided Design – Computer-Aided Manufacture; Computer Graphics) During the 1970s and '80s computers were increasingly employed in the fields of architectural, engineering, industrial and graphic design. Complex, three-dimensional objects such as buildings, oil-rigs, cars and aircraft could be represented by mathematical models stored in the computer's memory. Images of these models could be studied on VDUs (visual display units) from all angles and transformed at will. It was obviously cheaper and quicker to alter computer simulations than real models or products. In industry more and more manufacturers employed computer-controlled machine tools and robots to increase the volume and precision of their output and to reduce their dependence upon human labour. Hence the expressions Flexible Manufacturing Systems (FMS) and Computer-Integrated Manufacturing (CIM). Ultimately, whole factories and warehouses can be automated.

Computers have revolutionized image-based media such as graphics, cartoon animation, sci-fi feature films, video games, television logos and adverts, rock music videos, etc. They have also made an impact on British art and design education. At Middlesex Polytechnic in London a National Centre for Computer-Aided Art & Design was established in 1986. And in the same year a new professional body was founded – ACADE: The Association for Computing in Art & Design Education – to act as a national forum. In the United States a National Computer Graphics Association (NCGA) has existed since the late '70s; it has an art section and holds annual conferences (proceedings are published).

Computers have a short history but even so the rapid pace of technological development in this sphere means that machines and systems rapidly become out of date. It is therefore perhaps not surprising that a museum devoted to computers has already been established (1983) in Boston, Massachusetts.

● See also Architecture Machine, Design Methods, Fractal Geometry, Hyper-Graphics/ Media, Quantel Paintbox, Rock Video, Simulation/ Simulacra/ Hyperreality.

● C Foster *Computer architecture* (NY, Van Nostrand Reinhold, 1970).

● H Hyman *The computer in design* (Studio Vista, 1973).

● M Prueitt *Computer graphics* (NY, Dover, 1975).

● 'Computer-Aided Design' *Design* (336) December 1976 38–47.

● S Bayley & J Woudhuysen *Robots* (Boilerhouse Project/Victoria & Albert Museum, 1984).

● A Jankel & R Morton *Creative computer graphics* (Cambridge University Press, 1984).

● H Franke *Computer graphics – computer art* (Berlin, Springer, 2nd ed 1985).

● J Lewell *Computer graphics* (Orbis, 1985).

● J May *Computer graphics* (Secker & Warburg, 1985).

● R Reynolds *Computing for architects* (Butterworths, 1987).

● P Burger & D Gillies *Interactive computer graphics* (Wokingham, Berks, Addison-Wesley, 1989).

● J Landsdown *Teach yourself computer graphics* (Hodder & Stoughton, 1989).

● A Penman *The CAD systems handbook: new technology for architects and planners* (ADT Press/Longman, 1989).

● 'CAD: a special report' *Design* (500) August 1990 55–72.

(Also Pixel Art, Preformulated Art, Programmed Art) Throughout history artists have used tools to make images and objects. The computer is simply a sophisticated kind of tool, hence Computer Art is more accurately described as 'computer-aided or computer-generated art'. (If machines with independent artificial intelligences could be invented, then a really unique and authentic Computer Art might emerge.) It has been produced internationally since about 1956 by people belonging to a variety of professions – in fact, anyone with access to computer time. Although computers had been used for a number of years to produce concrete poetry and electronic music, their relevance to the visual arts was not recognized until the 'Cybernetic Serendipity' show held at the ICA, London, in 1968 (although a display of Computer graphics had taken place at the Howard Wise Gallery, New York, in 1965). As a result of this exhibition, a Computer Arts Society (CAS) was founded in Britain which from '69 onwards published a bulletin entitled *Page*.

Initially the 'art' produced via computers was mostly drawings and graphics. Computers linked to printers and plotters were programmed to print out specified geometric shapes in random combinations or to transform images by a series of discrete steps, e.g. the image of a man into a bottle and then a map of Africa. However, as Robert Mallary and David Morris demonstrated, sculpture could also be produced with the help of punched tape and milling machines. The British artist William Latham has used computers to generate designs for weird, complex, organic forms which he calls 'computer sculptures' even though they exist only in 2-D form thus far. His Cibachrome prints and animated film were shown at the 'Conquest of form' exhibition at the Arnolfini Gallery,

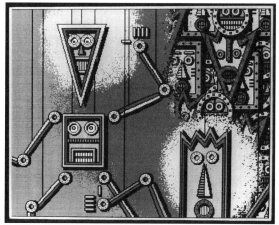

COMPUTER ART ANTHONY LEE, 'Out of control' (1989). Photo: Collins Gallery, Glasgow.

Bristol, in 1988.

Computer Art was similar to photography in the sense that a single program could be used to generate a large number of identical images (hence the potential for a significant democratization of art). But if the program included a random factor then nothing but unique images could be created. Artists devised both figurative and abstract images. Since most artists did not possess programming skills, their interaction with computers was greatly facilitated by the use of cathode ray tubes and light pens. In the 1980s highly expensive and sophisticated computer graphics machines became available which enabled artists to 'paint' directly with light. Colour photography and printing enabled such images to be fixed permanently. Alternatively, video recordings of Computer Art patterns could be replayed on TV monitors. Since many computer images were generated by scientists and commercial designers, the distinction between Computer Graphics and Computer Art was often hard to discern. If the latter served no immediate utilitarian purpose, was aesthetically pleasing, and was exhibited in an art gallery then it counted as art rather than design.

Another key technological development was the advent of cheap home or personal micro-computers, with graphics tablets and dot matrix printers, which made it possible for millions of ordinary people to create computer images if they so desired. Artists contributing to Computer Art shows included: Harold Cohen, Jonathan Inglis, Alyce Kaprow, Scott Daly, Manfred Mohr, Brian Reffin, Barbara Sykes, Brian Smith and John Whitney. Most professional fine artists were not specialists in the medium; in 1988 the American David Em (b. 1949) claimed to be the first full-time computer artist.

Computer conferencing was a form of international communication developed for business and military use but in 1980 the British artist Roy Ascott employed this technique to bring a number of artists located in different countries into contact with each other and a data base in order to exchange ideas and images, to engage in interactive creation.

The data-processing capabilities of computers have prompted some art historians to apply computing techniques to the traditional activities of art history, e.g. stylistic and iconographic analysis.

● See also Architecture Machine, Concrete Poetry, Cybernetic Art, Electronic Art, Fractal Geometry, Information Graphics, Programmed Art, Quantel Paintbox, Technological Art, Telematics, Video Art.

● J Reichardt (ed) *Cybernetic Serendipity: the computer and the arts* (Studio International, 1968).

● —*The computer in art* (Studio Vista, 1971).

● J Lomax (ed) *Computers in the creative arts: a study guide* (National Computing Centre, 1973).

● H Cohen 'On purpose: an enquiry into the possible roles of the computer in art' *Studio International* **187** (962) January 1974 9–16.

● R Leavitt (ed) *Artists and computers* (NY, Crown/Harmony Books, 1976).

● J Deken *Computer images: state of the art* (Thames & Hudson, 1983).

● *Cadre '84: computers in art and design research and education* (California, San Jose State University Art Dept, 1984).

● M Prueitt *Art & the computer* (NY, McGraw Hill, 1984).

● H Franke *Computer graphics – Computer Art* (Berlin, Springer, 2nd ed 1985).

● B Smith *Soft computing: art and design* (Addison Wesley, 1985).

● S Berstein & L McGarry *Making art on your computer* (NY, Watson Guptil, 1986).

● P Hagoort & R Maessen (eds) *Geest, computer, art* (Utrecht, Stichting Grafiet, 1986).

● C Goodman *Digital visions: computers & art* (NY, Abrams, 1987).

● A Mercader (ed) *Pixel art* (Barcelona, Instituto de Estudios NorteAmericanos, 1988).

● D Ross & D Em *The art of David Em: 100 computer paintings* (NY, Abrams, 1988).

● W Vaughan & A Hamber *Computers and art history* (Mansell, 1988).

● R Loveless (ed) *The computer revolution in the arts* (Tampa, Florida, University of South Florida Press, 1989).

● T Gips (ed) 'Computers & art: issues of content' *Art Journal* **49** (3) Fall 1990 (includes chronology, bibliography & glossary).

162 **CONCEPTUAL ARCHITECTURE** (Also Imaginary/ Invisible/ Nowhere/ Paper Architecture) This term became fashionable in architectural circles shortly after conceptual art made its appearance. Plans, drawings and models for buildings and cities which have never been constructed can be regarded as examples of architecture arrested at the conceptual stage of development, hence 'Conceptual Architecture'. In 1970 a special issue of *Design Quarterly,* edited by J. Margolies, was devoted to this theme. Contributors were asked to consider communications/psychological/entertainment environments. In response they devised a number of projects, some serious and some humorous: plans for futuristic cities, a menu for 'eatable architecture', and graphics by those experimental groups specializing in utopian or fantastic schemes. An 'essay' by Peter Eisenman had no text, only footnotes.

Friedrich St Florian has proposed an architecture of synthetic space as an alternative to permanent buildings, to be activated only for specific purposes. Such architecture would consist of space-defining conceptual structures (such as those used in air traffic control). He has also suggested 'simulated architecture', i.e. holographic images of monuments projected into the sky by lasers. A demonstration of his ideas was given at the Moderna Museet, Stockholm, in 1969.

Earlier, in 1960, the architect Werner Ruhnau and the artist Yves Klein forwarded the idea of 'aerial' or 'immaterial' architecture, i.e. a city roofed by moving air with 'walls' of water and fire instead of buildings. Conventional furniture would be replaced by air beds and seats. Bernard Etkin and Peter Goering of the University of Toronto Institute for Aerospace Studies have conducted research into the use of jets of air instead of buildings. Such 'invisible' architecture would represent an expenditure of energy instead of materials and allow for 'instant' structures.

At a conference on Conceptual Architecture held at Art Net, London, in 1975 Will Alsop defined it as: 'a limitless activity devoid of direction or dogma', i.e. pure research of speculation. However, he also claimed that the word 'conceptual' could be applied to: (a) work which was practical but could not be realized for lack of funds; (b) imaginative work that was impractical, done purely for its own sake. According to Alsop, Conceptual Architecture did not preclude building as an activity, but it was the process that counted as architecture, not the end result.

Conceptual Architecture tends to remain on paper, hence the ironic term 'paper' architecture applied to Glenn Small's visionary designs for a 'building' $1^1/_2$ miles high and 50 miles long capable of housing 11 million people called 'Biomorphic Biosphere Megastructure' (BBM). Small previously regarded himself as a 'biological architect'. He was also one of the founders of Sci-Arc, the Southern California Institute of Architecture. Rather than make drawings, Small used fragments of mass-media imagery and a photocopier to generate collages of tall structures he called 'copycat skyscrapers'.

● See also Biotecture, Copy Art, Fantastic Architecture, Megastructures, Process Art, Radical Design, Simulation/Simulcra/Hyperreality, Utopian Architecture, Visionary Architecture.

● 'Imaginary architecture' *Domus* (491) October 1970 48–54.
● 'Conceptual Architecture' *Design Quarterly* (78/79) 1970.
● P Eisenman 'Notes on Conceptual Architecture' *Casabella* (359/360) 1971 49–56.
● G Shane 'Conceptual Architecture: betrayal or breakthrough?' *Architectural Design* **45** (3) March 1975 187–8.
● W Alsop 'Conceptual Architecture: an appraisal within four walls' *Net* (1) 1975.
● Gruppo Cavart 'Impossible architecture: possible answers' *Casabella* (411) March 1976 8–13.
● M Pawley 'California dreamer' (Glenn Small) *Guardian* May 26 1988 26.

163 CONCEPTUAL ART

(Including Analytical Art, Begriff Kunst, Con/ Concept/ Dematerialized/ Head/ Idea/ Impossible/ Project/ Theoretical Art) An international avant garde tendency fashionable in the West during the late 1960s and early '70s. It emerged as a result of a younger generation of artists sensing a crisis in the traditional artforms of painting and sculpture and being influenced by the emphasis placed on decision making – the conceptual phase – in minimal and process art (i.e. rules for the generation of works of art). It also reflected the influence of Marcel Duchamp (his writings and readymades), Yves Klein, Piero Manzoni and Jasper Johns, all of whom raised questions about the ontological status of the art object. Conceptual Art was in part a critique of earlier forms of art and the art market, in part an enquiry into the nature of art, and in part the forwarding of concepts or propositions as art.

Conceptual Art was preceded by 'concept art', a phenomenon of the early 1960s associated with the Fluxus artists Henry Flynt and Yoko Ono. Flynt defined concept art as 'an art of which the material is concepts, as the material of, e.g., music is sound. Since concepts are closely bound up with language, concept art is a kind of art of which the material is language.' Ono's concept art consisted of short sets of instructions for the performance of various actions, some mental, some physical, e.g. 'Painting to be constructed in your head: Observe three paintings carefully. Mix them well in your head' (1962).

The term 'Conceptual Art' derived from Sol Lewitt's 1967 'Paragraphs on Conceptual Art'. As in concept art, language was all-important as a medium of expression but above all it was concepts or ideas that counted. As Lewitt observed, 'an idea is a machine that makes art'. Conceptual artists talked and wrote rather than painted or carved; they displayed texts in galleries and published articles and magazines. Imagery took a back seat though some diagrams, maps, videos and photographs were employed. Since Conceptual artists used language to speak about art and as art, their discourse tended to blur with that of critics, historians, theorists and aestheticians. Charles Harrison, an art historian, was in fact closely associated with certain British Conceptualists.

Conceptual artists tended to despise the art object and the craft skills associated with it. This gave rise to such expressions as 'anti-object art', 'post-object art' and 'the dematerialization of the art object'. Initially, in pursuit of the latter, works were devised that employed inert gases or electromagnetic waves whose existence was only detectable via readings on instruments. The lack of conventional art objects mounted a challenge to the commercial art system but it was not long before collectors began to purchase the texts and visual displays Conceptual artists used to communicate. Even so, the emphasis on texts increased the power of the art magazine at the expense of the gallery.

Amongst leading Conceptual artists were those constituting the Anglo-American grouping Art & Language (chiefly Michael Baldwin, Joseph Kosuth and Mel Ramsden), plus Mel Bochner, Victor Burgin, Douglas Huebler, On Kawara, John Stezaker, Bernar Venet, Lawrence Weiner and Ian Wilson. Conceptual artists, critical of the individualism of earlier art, often collaborated or worked collectively. They were also keen on forming groups and organizations. Besides Art & Language there was, in San Francisco, the 'Museum of Conceptual Art'(MOCA) founded by Tom Marioni in 1970, and in Tokyo the 'Conceptual Art Research Association' (CARA) formed by Tarsua Yamamoto.

Analysis and theory were two key ingredients of Conceptual Art. In fact a sub-category of Conceptualism was called 'analytical art'. The term was devised by Terry Atkinson and served as the title for a British magazine two issues of which appeared in 1971–2. The use of the word 'analytical' reflected the influence of the analytical school of British philosophy. 'Theoretical art' was another sub-category: in New York Ian Burn and Mel Ramsden founded the 'Society for Theoretical Art and Analyses' while in London the artists Stezaker, Jon Bird, Peter Berry, Paul Wood, Kevin Wright and David Holmscroft produced 'theoretical art' via the short-lived magazine *Frameworks Journal* (1973). Stezaker in particular was keen to develop a theory *for* art rather than merely a theory *of* art.

Conceptual Art aroused negative reactions because it lacked the sensory and sensual appeal of paintings and sculptures. It was called 'verbiage', 'gibberish', 'cerebral wanking'. Even its advocates admitted it was intellectually difficult and demanding. Nevertheless, it did perform a useful service in drawing attention to the conceptual dimension of all art and during its Left-wing political phase (mid 1970s) it provided an illuminating critique of the artworld. By the mid '70s the term 'post-conceptual' made an appearance indicating that the movement was past its peak.

For more than a decade Conceptual Art was neglected as a return to painting and sculpture occurred and the vogue for neo-expressionism carried all before it. However, Conceptualism had made a difference and with the advent of neo-geo in the mid 1980s its influence was felt

again and the term 'neo-conceptual' began to be applied to the work of younger painters and sculptors. A renewed historical interest in the movement was also indicated by several exhibitions and the special section of *Flash Art* devoted to Conceptual Art published in the Autumn of 1988.

● See also Art & Language, Collaborations, Meta-Art, Neo-Expressionism, Neo-Geo, Political Art, Post-Object Art.

● S Lewitt 'Paragraphs on Conceptual Art' *Artforum* **5** (10) Summer 1967 79–83.

● *Art in the mind* (Oberlin, Ohio, Allen Memorial Museum, 1970).

● *Conceptual Art & conceptual aspects* (NY, Cultural Center, 1970).

● *Idea structures* (Camden Art Centre, Central Library, 1970).

● Y Ono *Grapefruit* (Peter Owen, 1970).

● K Groh *If I had a mind...Concept Art, Project Art* (Cologne, Dumont, 1971).

● K Friedman 'Notes on Concept Art' *Schmuck* March 1972 6–15; also published in *The aesthetics* (Cullompton, Devon, Beau Geste Press, 1973) 39–48.

● D Brook 'Toward a definition of Conceptual Art' *Leonardo* **5** (1) Winter 1972 49–50.

● U Meyer & others *Conceptual Art* (NY, Dutton, 1972).

● *The new art* (Hayward Gallery, 1972).

● K Honnef *Concept Art* (Cologne, Phaidon, 1973).

● L Lippard *Six years: the dematerialization of the art object from 1966 to 1972...* (Studio Vista, 1973).

● H Flynt *Blueprint for a higher civilization* (Milan, Multhipla Edizioni, 1975).

● S Foley *Space, time, sound: Conceptual Art in the San Francisco Bay Area, the 1970s* (San Francisco Museum of Art, 1981).

● *Art minimal et Conceptuel: une génération autre* (Dunkirk, École de Beaux-Arts, 1986).

● M-A Staniszewski & others 'Conceptual supplement' *Flash Art* (143) November–December 1988 87–107.

● A Meseure & D Elger *In other words: Wort und Schrift in Bildern der Konzeptuellen Kunst* (Stuttgart, Edition Cantz, 1989).

● S Pagé & others *L'Art Conceptuel, une perspective* (Paris, Musée d'Art Moderne de la Ville de Paris, 1989).

● D Ross (ed) *Between spring and summer: Soviet Conceptual Art in the era of late communism* (Cambridge, Mass, MIT Press, 1991).

164 CONCEPTUAL CLOTHING Title of a 1987–8 British touring exhibition curated by Fran Cottell and Marian Schoettle featuring works by a number of visual artists who had employed clothing either as a medium of expression or as subject matter.

Among the artists contributing were Rasheed Araeen, Sokari Douglas Camp, Yves Klein, Rose Garrard, Susan Hiller and Mary Kelly. Conceptual Clothing marked the interface between fine art and fashion: those fashion designers who created extremely experimental and novel clothes approached the condition of fine art, while those artists who depicted clothes undertook a critique of their meaning and significance.

● See also Usable Art.

● T Polhemus & others *Conceptual Clothing* (Birmingham, Ikon Gallery, 1987).

165 CONCEPTUAL DESIGN A description applied by Renny Ramakers to the late 1980s' work of several Dutch designers: Ed Annink, Peer de Bruyn, Jap van Heest, Jeroen Vinken and others. Influenced by the experimental design of the Italians, they produced objects resembling items of furniture, carpets, wall hangings and dishes, but none were made with industrial production in mind. The objects were one-off, or models or even drawings. These designers assumed the freedom of fine artists and rejected the imperatives of utility, durability and truth to materials.

● See also Radical Design.

● R Ramakers 'Between art and function: Conceptual Design' *DA + AT (Dutch Art + Architecture Today)* (21) June 1987 27–31.

166 CONCERNED PHOTOGRAPHY (Including Activist/Committed/Community Photography) A liberal, humanist conception of the role of photography in society: photography conceived 'as a medium for revealing the human condition, commenting on the events of our time and improving understanding among people'. Cornell Capa established an international fund for Concerned Photography in 1966 and an exhibition with the title 'The Concerned Photographer' was mounted at the Riverside Museum, New York, in 1967. Subsequently, versions of this show toured the United States and Europe. Photographers who have been placed in this category include: Werner Bischof, Robert Capa, David Seymour 'Chim', Bruce Davidson, Leonard Freed, Ernst Haas, André Kertész, Donald McCullin, Gordon Parks, Marc Riboud and William Eugene Smith. These photographers acted as witnesses to the twentieth century by documenting scenes of war, death, grief, happiness, slums, minorities and the gamut of relations between humans in groups. Concerned Photography was, therefore, a variety of social documentary photography and/or photojournalism.

In the 1970s Concerned Photography became more committed, practical and specific in the sense that photographers with social consciences began to intervene in local communities with the intention of demystifying the medium, raising ideological awareness and instituting social change (hence, 'community photography'). For instance, in the East End of London the Half Moon Photography Workshop was established. It mounted exhibitions, encouraged laypeople and children to take up photography, and for over a decade it published a low-cost magazine called *Camerawork* in which the ethics and politics of photography were discussed.

Even more political is 'Activist Photography'. This term was proposed by the American photographer Steve Cagan in 1988. He advocated a type of photography capable of documenting reality but also aware of the political issues of representation pointed out by Left-wing critics of the documentary genre. Activist Photography implies 'photography with a clear set of political agendas (including, but not limited to, internal criticism of fields of art and media), which is most comprehensible as a range of practices within a framework provided by political activities, campaigns, or organisations, which is to be judged primarily in terms of their contributions to these movements'.

● See also Community Art & Media, Factography, Photo-Works, Political Art.

● 'The Concerned Photographer' *Camera* May 1969 (special issue).

● C Capa (ed) *The Concerned Photographer* 2 vols (Thames & Hudson, 1972).

● — 'The Concerned Photographers' *Zoom* (16) 1973 78–95. *Camerawork* (1) February 1976 (Magazine of the Half Moon Photography Workshop).

● S Braden *Committing photography* (Pluto, 1983).

● S Cagan 'Speakeasy' *New Art Examiner* **16** (4) December 1988 13–14.

167 CONCRETE ART (In French: Art Concret, in Italian: Arte Concreta, in German: Konkrete Kunst) A type of abstract art, mainly geometric, produced and advocated by a group of artists established in Paris in 1930 led by Theo van Doesburg (1883–1931), who edited one issue of a review/manifesto entitled 'Art Concret'. The word 'concrete' was intended as a replacement for the word 'abstract'; the latter suggested a process of abstraction from nature, whereas Concrete artists saw themselves as operating in parallel to nature: they painted or built new works of art from basic forms, planes, colours and materials. These, they claimed, were 'the concretion of the creative spirit'. Such works were to be conceived in the mind beforehand, executed mechanically, and demonstrate absolute clarity. Some Concrete artists were later to turn to mathematics as a way of deciding questions of structure, proportion and composition. The difference between Concrete Art and constructivism is hard to discern. Indeed, some constructivist anthologies reprint van Doesburg's 1930 manifesto.

Concrete Art became an international movement during the late 1930s and it survived the Second World War because leading practitioners lived in neutral countries such as Switzerland, Sweden, Brazil and Argentina. Major exponents in the post-1945 era were Max Bill, Jean Arp, Richard Lohse, Karl Gerstner and Josef Albers. In the immediate post-war period, major exhibitions of Concrete Art were organized and a number of groups formed. In Italy, for example, the critic Gillo Dorfles, Gianni Monnet, Atanasio Soldati and Bruno Munari founded in Milan in 1948 the 'Movimento per L'Arte Concreta' (MAC). Lucio Fontana and Guiseppe Capogrossi were associated with MAC for a time. The term 'concrete' also gained wider currency when it was adopted by a new generation of artists concerned with concrete poetry.

In 1960 Bill organized a large-scale exhibition of Concrete Art in Zürich surveying 50 years of its development. Since then the mainstream of art has moved away from Concrete Art, even though some artists continue to be inspired by its aesthetic principles.

● See also Astratto-Concreto, Concrete Poetry, Constructionism, Constructivism, Geometric Abstraction, Structurism.

● *Konkrete Kunst* (Basle, Kunsthalle, 1944).

● *Art Concret* (Paris, Galerie Drouin, 1945).

● *Spirale* (Bern, 1953–64), quarterly devoted to Concrete Art.

● *Konkrete Kunst: 50 Jahre entwicklung* (Zürich, Kunstgesellschaft, 1960).

● M Staber *Konkrete Kunst* (St Gallen, 1966).

● P Fossati *Il Movimento Arte Concreta (1948–58): materiali e documenti* (Turin, Martano, 1980).

● L Caramel *M.A.C. Movimento Arte Concreta Vol 1 1948 –52; Vol 2 1953–58* (Modena, Gallarate Civica Galleria d'Arte Moderna, 1984).

168 **CONCRETE POETRY** (Including Audiovisual/ Process/ Visual Texts, Calligrams, Constellations, Evident/ Experimental/ Kinetic/ Machine/ Objective/ Optical/ Semiotic Poetry, Framed & Shaped Writing, Ideograms, Poem-Paintings, Popcrete, Publit, Typewriter/Word Art) Concrete Poetry is a hybrid artform: it combines characteristics of literature and visual art. Typically, the Concrete poet arranges language elements freely across a surface, not just in linear syntax. The aesthetic appeal and meanings of such poems derive not only from the sense of the words but also from the typographic characteristics of the lettering, and the spatial and pictorial characteristics of the work as a whole.

Stéphane Mallarmé's 'Un coup de dés' was an important influence on the emergence of Concrete Poetry, and so were the poetry and manifestos of the dadaists, constructivists and futurists. Carlo Belloli's 'wall text-poems' of 1943 were a direct response to Marinetti's call for 'a poetry of nouns only' standing in their 'naked purity and essential colour'. Another historical precedent were the 'calligrams' of Guillaume Apollinaire (the title of a 1918 book of poems). Calligrams have also been called 'framed' or 'shaped writings'. They are visual puns, poems drawn or printed in such a way as to form a picture or image, e.g. Lewis Carroll's description of a mouse's tail meandering down the page in the shape of a mouse's tail.

In the 1940s the Lettrists employed letter forms in their paintings and in 1953 the Swede Öyvind Fahlström began to use the term 'Concrete Poetry' in order to relate his own poetry to *musique concrète*. The movement took its definitive form in the work of Eugen Gomringer, based in Switzerland, and the Noigandres Group of Brazil. In 1955 when Gomringer and Decio Pignatari, one of the Noigandres, agreed on the name 'Concrete Poetry', they were taking as their model the concrete art of Max Bill. To make a similarly self-sufficient art out of words the poets used the device of self-reference, so that meaning and appearance coincided or strongly interacted. This was achieved by exemplifying in the poem's structure some quality or process, by arranging words to form a shape or image, or by devising word clusters defining limited areas of meaning which then challenged readers to make their own connections. Concrete poets saw their work as a way of improving the efficiency of

silence silence silence
silence silence silence
silence   silence
silence silence silence
silence silence silence

CONCRETE POETRY EUGEN GOMRINGER, 'Silence' (1954).

language and the influence of disciplines such as linguistics and information theory was evident in the repetitions and permutations they used so frequently.

Concrete Poetry was an international movement: it was produced in Germany by Claus Bremer, in Austria by Gerhard Ruhm and Friedrich Achleitner, in Mexico by Mathias Goeritz, in Britain by Edwin Morgan, Ian Hamilton Finlay, John Furnival and Bob Cobbing, in the United States by Emmett Williams and in Czechoslovakia by Zenek Barborka. The latter's 'process texts' expanded the form to book length.

During the '60s 'word art' proliferated in many forms and under many different labels. Artists employed countless variations of layout, paper, typeface and colour. Finlay even used stone, metal and other materials and placed his carved poems in a landscape setting to which the sense of the poem often related. Pignatari specialized in 'semiotic poems' and Augusto de Campos, another of the Noigandres, developed photo-sequences he called 'popcrete'. Meanwhile, Belloli signalled his differences with other Concrete poets by calling his work 'audiovisual texts'. The visual qualities of word and letter forms were explored in Franz Mon's 'poetry of surface', in Ferdinand Kriwet's 'publit' and 'poem-paintings', in Jirí Kolár's 'evident poetry' and in Jirí Valoch's 'optical poetry'.

The pattern-making potential of typewriters was exploited by Dom Sylvester Houédard, a 'kinetic poet' who produced 'typestracts'. Another typewriter poet, Pierre Garnier, called his work 'machine poetry' and published a manifesto in 1963 in which he used 'spatialism' (also used by Fontana in the '40s) to encompass all the then-current trends in word art. Subsequently, all labels fell out of favour apart from 'visual texts' and 'Concrete Poetry'.

● See also Concrete Art, Letraset, Lettrism, Spatialism.

● G Apollinaire *Calligrammes: poèmes de la paix et de la guerre* (Paris, Merecure de France, 1918).

● J Reichardt *Between poetry and painting* (ICA, 1965).

● S Bann (ed) *Concrete Poetry: an international anthology* (London Magazine, 1967).

● E Williams (ed) *An anthology of Concrete Poetry* (NY, Something Else Press, 1967).

● P Mayer 'Framed and shaped writing' *Studio International* **176** (903) September 1968 110–14.

● M Solt (ed) *Concrete Poetry: a world view* (Bloomington, Indiana University Press, 1968).

● S Themerson *Apollinaire's lyrical ideograms* (Gaberbocchus, 1968).

● B Bowler *The word as image* (Studio Vista, 1970).

● R Kostelanetz (ed) *Imaged words and worded images* (NY, Outerbridge & Dienstfrey, 1970).

● E Wildman (ed) *Anthology of Concretism* (Chicago, Swallow Press, 2nd ed 1970).

● *? Concrete Poetry* (Amsterdam, Stedelijk Museum, 1971).

● J Sharkey (ed) *Mindplay: an anthology of British Concrete Poetry* (Lorrimer, 1971).

● *Arkos* **6** (8) March 1972 (Special issue).

● P Finch (ed) *Typewriter poems* (Second Aeon Publications/Something Else Press, 1972).

● A Riddell (ed) *Typewriter Art* (London Magazine, 1975).

● B Cobbing & P Mayer *Concerning Concrete Poetry* (Writers' Forum, 1978).

● D Seaman *Concrete Poetry in France* (Ann Arbor, Michigan, University of Michigan Research Press, 1982).

169 CONRAN FOUNDATION An educational charity established in the late 1970s by the British designer and businessman Sir Terence Conran (founder of Habitat, the Conran Design Group/ Conran Associates) for the purpose of raising the level of public discussion about design. From 1982 to 1986 the Foundation funded a gallery called 'The Boilerhouse Project' situated in the basement of the Victoria & Albert Museum which mounted a series of exhibitions explor-

CONRAN FOUNDATION STUART MOSSCROP/CONRAN ROCHE, The Design Museum, Butler's Wharf, London (1989). Photo: Roderick Coyne.

ing different aspects of design. The director of the Boiler-house was the art and design historian Stephen Bayley. Later he was appointed chief executive of the new Design Museum at Butler's Wharf, London, funded by the Conran Foundation, which opened in 1989. Design journalists perceived the Foundation's promotion of design as a private-enterprise rival to the state-supported Design Council; the Design Museum too was intended to fulfil a role the Victoria & Albert could not afford to perform.

● See also Design Council, Habitat.

● T Conran & Lord Reilly *Conran Associates* (CA, 1979).

● C McDowell 'The Boilerhouse man' *Guardian* August 1 1985 8.

● P Tabor 'Boilerhouse to Bauhaus: the Design Museum' *Architects Journal* August 16 1989 31–47.

● S Bayley & others 'The Design Museum' *Museums Journal* **89** November 1989 23–9.

170 CONSTRUCTIONISM

This term was coined in 1938 by the American artist Charles Biederman to describe his method of working and his colourful, abstract reliefs. The French artist Jean Gorin produced similar works at the same time but the artists were unaware of each other's achievements until the late 1940s. Subsequently, a number of American and European artists adopted the Constructionist mantle – some indiscriminately, because in 1952 Biederman felt constrained to introduce a new term: 'structurism'.

During the '50s a clutch of British artists – John Ernest, Adrian Heath, Anthony Hill, Kenneth and Mary Martin, Victor Pasmore, Peter Stroud and Gillian Wise – were influenced by Biederman's example. Pasmore in particular was deeply impressed by Biederman's monumental history of art as the evolution of visual knowledge, which he read in 1951.

'Constructionism' and 'constructivism' are very similar and this has caused confusion. In 1980 an exhibition selected by the German kinetic artist Gerhard von Graevenitz, devoted to the theme of construction in contemporary art, was held at the Hayward Gallery, London. (It featured works by 56 European and American artists including Anthony Hill, Kenneth Martin, Richard Long, Mario Merz and Carl Andre.) The show's conception was attacked by Stephen Bann, a supporter of constructivist art, on the grounds that it did not do justice to the historical achievements of constructivism. Von Graevenitz replied that the show had 'nothing to do with constructivism or constructive art'. A show about expression in art, he argued, need not necessarily be about expressionism.

● See also Constructivism, Structurism.

◐ C Biederman *Art as the evolution of visual knowledge* (Red Wing, Minnesota, Biederman, 1948).

◐ *Pier & Ocean: Construction in the art of the '70s* (Hayward Gallery, 1980).

◐ S Bann 'Polemics: "Pier and Ocean" – some adverse reflections' *Art Monthly* (37) 1980 24–6.

171 CONSTRUCTIVISM

Art historians generally locate the origins of Constructivism in the work and writings produced by certain Soviet artists in the 1920s (e.g. Naum Gabo, Antoine Pevsner, Vladimir Tatlin, El Lissitzky and others). Yet in spite of its historical, geographical and cultural specificity, writers such as George Rickey, Willy Rotzler and Stephen Bann have extended the label to encompass later movements in Europe and North America. This prompted Ronald Hunt to remark in 1974: 'Constructivism must be just about the most abused term in current art usage'. Historians found it necessary therefore to distinguish between Soviet Constructivism and the later developments of European and International Constructivism. It is impossible here to clarify all the shades of meaning of 'Constructivism'. Crudely, Constructive art is generally abstract, three-dimensional and based on the principle that art is a new, human product – a construction made from real materials – that adds to reality instead of imitating it.

Bann perceived Constructivism as a major tendency of twentieth-century art which now constitutes a tradition within which new generations of artists can work – witness the British Arts Council 1978 touring show he organized entitled 'Constructivist context' featuring works by Chris Watts, Jeffrey Steele, Terry Pope and Kenneth Martin.

Another sign of the continued vitality of International Constructivism was the 1983 gathering of post-1945 Constructivists which took place at Kemi, Finland. A symposium–exhibition on the theme of 'Nature– Structure– Sculpture' was organized by Arbeitskreis, the International Workshop for Systematic Constructive Art. Another sign was the PRO Foundation in Holland. 'Stichting PRO–pro art and architecture' was founded in 1986 by the Dutch artist Fré Ilgen for the purpose of promoting all forms of contemporary Constructivism. (The prefix 'pro' was adopted in the sense of 'for' and 'before' as in 'pro-logue'.) It rapidly became an international network linked by a newsletter. The PRO Foundation, based in Dordrecht, has organized conferences, arranged exhibitions and established an archive and drawings collection. The third international PRO conference held in Rotterdam in 1989 was devoted to the topic of

'Constructivism: man vs environment'. Avoiding any singular or dogmatic definition of Constructivism, Ilgen claimed that it was an approach suited to all forms of art and design committed to improving the conditions of human society. This was to be achieved via a study of man (*sic*) as part of nature in order to arrive at universal principles. Also in 1989 an international conference on 'systematic' and Constructive art (plus an exhibition) was held in Madrid. Speakers included Joost Baljeu, Eli Bornstein, Antonio Carillo and Michael Stephen.

● See also Concrete Art, Constructionism, Structurism, Systems Group.

● G Rickey *Constructivism: origins and evolution* (Studio Vista, 1967).

● R Hunt 'Constructivism mistaken' *Studio International* **188** (971) November 1974 209.

● S Bann (ed) *The tradition of Constructivism* (Thames & Hudson, 1974).

● W Rotzler *Constructive concepts: a history of Constructive art from cubism to the present* (Zürich, ABC Ed, 1977).

● S Winter 'The Constructivist fallacy' *Artscribe* (12) June 1978 46–8.

● S Bann *Constructivist context* (Arts Council, 1978), touring exhibition.

● M Hughes 'Artnotes' *Art Monthly* (70) October 1983 20.

● PRO Foundation *Report on the activities 1988–88* (Dordrecht, Netherlands, Stichting PRO, 1988).

● T Giles 'Systematic and Constructive Art' *Art Monthly* (128) July–August 1989 26–7.

● *Arte Sistematico y Constructivo* (Madrid, Centro Cultural de la Villa, 1989).

● *Constructivism: man versus environment* (Dordrecht, Netherlands, PRO Foundation, 1989).

172 CONSULTANT DESIGN

The kind of design engaged in by independent or freelance designers or teams of designers who are 'consulted' by industry and business. Consultant designers work on particular commissions for limited periods of time, they also work for several clients at once as against 'in-house' designers who are employed by one firm permanently. Two well-known British design consultancies are Pentagram and the Design Research Unit. The design consultancy business has grown enormously in the decades since Frank Mercer's 1947 book on the subject, especially during the '80s, dubbed 'the design decade'.

● See also Corporate Design, Design Research Unit, Pentagram.

● F Mercer *The industrial Design Consultant: who he is and what he does* (Studio, 1947).

● P Sparke *Consultant Design: the history and practice of the designer in industry* (Pembridge Press, 1983).

● B McAlhone *British Design Consultancy, anatomy of a billion-pound business* (Design Council, 1987).

173 CONTEMPORARY ART SOCIETY (CAS)

A British charitable organization founded in 1910 for the purpose of patronage; specifically, the acquisition of works of art from living artists for gift or loan to public collections. Over 4,000 works have been presented to galleries since CAS was established. Funds derive almost entirely from voluntary subscriptions by individual and corporate members, though public galleries also pay an annual fee. Works are selected for purchase by two committee members rotated annually, hence decision by committee is avoided. The Society is based at the Tate Gallery, London. To encourage membership it arranges previews of exhibitions, visits to galleries, studios and private collections, and foreign art tours. Since 1984 it has organized an annual market of contemporary art in London in order to raise money. For further information see the Society's annual reports and the 1985 commemorative book.

● (Special issue on CAS) *Art & Artists* (193) October 1982.

● Judith Bumpus *The Contemporary Art Society 1910–1985* (CAS, 1985).

● A Bowness & others *British contemporary art 1910–90: 80 years of collecting by the Contemporary Art Society* (Herbert Press, 1991).

174 CONTEMPORARY STYLE

During the period 1945 to '56 the word 'contemporary' became fashionable in Britain, e.g. the Institute of Contemporary Art was founded in 1947, Herbert Read's book *Contemporary British art* was published in 1951. The result was that the word came to be identified with a certain style prevalent in the painting, sculpture and design of the '50s: a spiky, spindly look, gaiety, lightness. The style drew upon some features of 'action painting' and 'geometry of fear' type sculpture. In architecture the look derived from the use of lightweight, open metal structures, while in furniture it derived from the use of thin metal rods, pale timber instead of dark, wooden legs that were tapered and splayed out, metal fittings with coloured plastic blobs at their extremities (the latter were derived from scientific models of molecules). Magazine racks were constructed from wire covered with plastic, the gaps between metal supports were bridged by decorative lacing made of plastic; the lacing reflected the influence of certain sculptures by Naum Gabo, Alexander Calder and Barbara Hepworth. Wallpaper and textile design favoured geometric patterns: snow crystals, coffin shapes or elongated hexagons. Peter Cook said of the design of 1952 that it was 'a mixture of post-war spin off (the technology of laminates, alloys and micro-mechanics) and latter-day thirties styling'.

The Contemporary Style was encapsulated and popularized by the 1951 Festival of Britain though this exhibition also gave rise to other terms: 'festival style', 'South Bank style' and 'new English style'. There was much debate amongst design historians as to whether or not there was such a thing as 'festival style' (and whether or not it was 'flimsy and effeminate'). In the context of the exhibition, experiments with new materials and new forms were acceptable, but the mannerisms of 1951 quickly became clichés disfiguring the interior decor of coffee bars and pubs, and such exterior features as street furniture. Many Contemporary Style products, it turned out, were eccentric in design, uncomfortable and poorly made. This did not prevent them from becoming, in later decades, collector's items amongst enthusiasts for everything to do with the 1950s.

● See also Art Ultra, Austerity/Binge, Populuxe.

◉ H Read *Contemporary British art* (Harmondsworth, Penguin, 1951; rev ed 1964).

◉ P Reilly 'Don't be afraid of Contemporary design' *Ideal Home yearbook* (1953).

◉ J Gloag 'Contemporary design' *DIA yearbook* (1957) 18–24.

◉ 'FoB + 10' *Design* (149) May 1961 40–51.

◉ M Frayn 'Festival'– in – *Age of austerity* M Sissons & P French (eds) (Harmondsworth, Penguin, 1964) 330–53.

◉ P Cook *Experimental architecture* (Studio Vista, 1971).

◉ M Banham & B Hillier (eds) *A tonic to the nation: the Festival of Britain 1951* (Thames & Hudson, 1976).

◉ *Artists of the Festival of Britain* (Birmingham City Art Gallery, 1978).

◉ 'Jim Burgess: room of my own' ('50s collector) *Observer Colour Supplement* February 10 1985 40–1.

CONTEMPORARY STYLE Robert Matthew & others, London County Council Architects Dept; Royal Festival Hall, South Bank, London (1951). Photo: Roderick Coyne.

◉ P Powell & L Peel *50s and 60s style* (Apple Press, 1988).

175 CONTEXTUAL ARCHITECTURE

(Also Contextualism) The degree to which new architecture is sensitive to its site and location varies from building to building and place to place. Contextual Architecture takes particular account of what already exists. The term has been used to cover such things as building conservation, alterations, renovations and infill. As an example of the challenge of context one could cite the 1980s commission given to Robert Venturi for a new extension to the National Gallery in Trafalgar Square, London. Earlier designs by other architects had been rejected because they did not meet the twofold demand that the new building relate harmoniously to the National Gallery itself and the Square as a whole.

'Contextualism' is a term employed by such writers as T. Schumaker and G. Shane. It refers to an approach to urban planning which considers the city in its totality, the view that the experience of a city is more than the sum of its parts. According to Graham Shane, architectural design 'must fit with, respond to, mediate its surroundings, perhaps completing a pattern implicit in the street layout or introducing a new one. Crucial to this appreciation of urban patterns is the gestalt double-image of the figure ground'. Shane maintained that 'during the mid-1960s there was a conscious revival of the contextualist approach on both sides of the Atlantic.'

In a 1974 essay Stuart Cohen argued that architects had to take account of two kinds of context: the physical and the cultural.

● See also Collage City, Collective Form, Environmental Design, Townscape, Urbanism.

◉ T Schumaker 'Contextualism: urban ideals and deformations' *Casabella* (359/360) 1971 78–86.

◉ S Cohen 'Physical context/cultural context, including it all' *Oppositions* (2) January 1974 1–40.

◉ G Shane 'Contextualism' *Architectural Design* **46** (11) November 1976 676–9.

◉ K Ray (ed) *Contextual Architecture: responding to existing style* (NY, McGraw-Hill, 1980).

◉ A Tugnutt & M Robertson *Making townscape: a contextual approach to building in an urban setting* (Mitchell, 1987).

176 CONTEXTUAL ART

A term popularized by the Polish art theorist Jan Swidzinski during the mid 1970s and adopted by a number of Polish artists. Swidzinski was critical of the Western vogue for conceptual art on the grounds that it operated in the realm of aesthetics rather than in social reality. His alternative – Contextual Art – was defined as 'a social act performed within the process of reality', it was both 'subjective and objective' and capable of changing reality by 'breaking down old meanings and constructing new ones'. A conference and exhibition with the title 'Art as Contextual Art' was held at Lund University and Malmö, Sweden, in 1976. A debate between Contextual and Conceptual artists was also organized by the Centre for Experimental Art & Communication (CEAC) in Toronto in the same year.

● See also Conceptual Art.

● J Swidzinski 'Art as Contextual Art' *Parachute* (Canada) (5) Winter 1976 22–5.

● *Art as Contextual Art* (Lund, Edition Sellen-GalerieS:t Petn, 1976).

● J Swidzinski *Quotations on Contextual Art* (Eindhoven, Het Appollohuis, 1988).

177 CONTINUITÀ

An Italian group established in Rome in 1961 which included the artists Pietro Consagra, Piero Dorazio, Achille Perilli and Giulio Turcato and the critic Carlo Argan. Lucio Fontana joined later. Some of these artists had previously been members of Forma. The use of the word 'continuity' signalled a desire to connect with the tradition of historic Italian art, to restore a sense of order and structure after the disorder of l'art informel, and to effect a bridge between artworks and their display spaces.

● See also Art Informel, Forma.

178 CONTINUUM

A group formed by four artists – Robert Janz, Dante Leonelli, Liliane Lijn and Michael McKinnon – exhibiting light and motion works at the Axiom Gallery, London, in 1968. When Continuum showed at the Hayward Gallery two years later it consisted of Janz, Leonelli and McKinnon. The name 'Continuum' referred to transformations through time achieved by artworks capable of real change. Although their works resembled kinetics, the members of this group claimed they had more in common with American artists such as Kenneth Noland and George Rickey. Continuum involved close co-operation but not anonymous, collective work. The group employed modern materials such as neon light and plastics and maintained close contact with industry.

● See also Kinetic Art, Light Art, Technological Art, Time-Based Arts.

● Arts Council of Great Britain *Continuum* (Hayward Gallery, 1970).

● C Morgan 'Continuum light and motion systems' *Art & Artists* **5** (3) June 1970 60–3.

● B Denvir 'London Letter: Continuum' *Art International* **14** (7) September 1970 98–100.

179 CONTRACT FURNITURE

Large quantities of furniture supplied as a result of an agreement or contract between an architect or a corporation and a furniture manufacturer or supplier. During the building booms which followed the Second World War, many huge office blocks and other types of buildings were constructed that required complete ranges of furniture to equip them; as a result, Contract Furniture became an important and profitable part of the furnishing trade. Because architects ordered such large quantities of furniture, they were able to demand improvements in design and quality.

● S Southin 'Furniture – subject to contract' *Design* (182) February 1964 22–9.

Contract Furniture 1988 (Design Council, 1988).

180 COOL ART

(Including Cold Art, Cool School, Kalte Kunst, Pittura Fredda) The adjectives 'cool' and 'cold' (in German 'kalte', in Italian 'fredda') have been applied, metaphorically, by various art critics to several different kinds of art manifesting qualities of detachment, severity, impersonality, hermeticism and austerity – the sort of art that appeals to the intellect rather than to the emotions or senses. Geometric, abstract art composed of repetitive structures or units and relying on mathematical system was often considered 'cold'. For instance, the Swiss concrete artist–designer Karl Gerstner produced abstract, programmed works and published a book entitled *Kalte Kunst* (1957/63). However, a figurative artform such as pop was also considered 'cool' because of the impersonal techniques and amoral attitudes adopted by certain leading figures, in particular Andy Warhol. (To be 'cool' – relaxed and in control – was a quality much admired by the young in the '60s.) In 1964 Philip Leider called a group of Los Angeles artists – Robert Irwin, Kenneth Price, Joe Goode, Ed Ruscha, Larry Bell and others – the 'Cool School' because their work manifested 'a hatred of the superfluous, a drive towards compression, a precision of execution ... impeccability of surface' and marked 'a new distance between artist and viewer', i.e. a 'hands-off' quality. Coldness has also been detected in hard-edge painting, fundamental painting and minimal art.

● See also Concrete Art, Finish Fetish, Geometric Abstraction, Pop Art.

● K Gerstner *Kalte Kunst? Zum Standort der heutigen Malerei* (Teufen, Switzerland, A Niggli, 1957;2nd ed 1963).

• P Leider 'The Cool School' *Artforum* **2** (12) Summer 1964 47.

• I Sandler 'The new Cool Art' *Art in America* **53** (1) February 1965 99–101.

• J Wolfram 'Isms Cool or isms isn't?' *Art & Artists* **2** (2) May 1967 12–15.

• J Clay 'The Cool school is not on the rocks' *Realities* (200) July 1967 74–9.

• L Aldrich *Cool Art* (Ridgefield, Connecticut, Aldrich Museum of Contemporary Art, 1968).

• H Coulonges 'The new Cool School' *Realities* (253) December 1971 50–7.

• G Celant 'American "Cool" painting' *Domus* (523) June 1973 49–51.

• — 'La "Pittura Fredda" Europea' *Domus* (527) October 1973 52–4.

181 **COOP HIMMELBLAU** (Sky Blue Co-operative) A Viennese, experimental architecture and design team founded by Wolf Prix and Helmut Swiczinsky in the late 1960s. At first Coop. Himmelblau took part in happenings and exhibitions to promote their conception of architecture as 'active, open, wild, mobile' and as a form of environmental art. They designed inflatable pods or living environments and mobile playgrounds with titles like 'Cloud 1' and 'Astro balloon II'. The structures they conceived were space-age, futuristic and fantastic, with various forms of feedback systems to stimulate or relax their users. Then in the '70s the team designed interiors for bars, apartments, shops and offices in various cities. In the '80s they obtained more complex commissions such as the design for a new town at Melun-Seuart near Paris.

● See also Arthropods, Environmental Art/Design, Pneumatic Architecture, Radical Design.

• Coop. Himmelblau *Coop. Himmelblau: architecture is now: projects ...1968–83* (NY, Rizzoli, 1983/London, Thames & Hudson, 1984).

• D Jones-Evans 'Coop. Himmelblau: art of architecture' *Tension* (Australia) (13) 1988 16–19.

• M Sorkin & others *Coop. Himmelblau: Blaubox* (Architectural Association, 1988).

• P Cook 'Spreadeagled' (Offices, Vienna) *Architectural Review* **186** (1112) October 1989 76–80.

182 **COPY ART** (Also Copier Art, Copygraphy, Electroworks, Photocopy Art, Xerography) A form of two-dimensional art produced with the aid of Xerox or photocopying machines. The electrostatic copying process was invented by Chester Carlson in 1938 but the vogue for Copy Art dates from the mid 1970s. Since then exhibitions of Copy Art have been held around the world at art fairs, in private galleries and in community art centres. The first major survey of Copy Art – Electroworks – took place at George Eastman House, Rochester, New York, in 1979. A year later in San Francisco Ginny Lloyd opened an 'electro arts' gallery in order to show local xerox artists, while in New York an International Society of Copier Artists was founded in 1982 by Louise Neaderland to promote the activity. Members keep in touch via a quarterly magazine which often consists of anthologies of Copy Art.

During the '80s Valencia in Spain became a key centre for Copy Art: in 1983 José Alcalá and Fernando Canales of the Faculty of Fine Art teamed up (Alcalacanales) to explore the implications for art of copiers; in 1985 they instituted an International Copy Art Biennale and they have since issued several glossy catalogues documenting the growth of the movement. In Germany Klaus Urbons founded a Museum für Fotokopie in Mülheim while in London the artist–teacher Simon Lewandowski tirelessly supported the medium: in 1989 he curated a Copy Art show at the International Contemporary Art Fair at Olympia; he is the author of several articles on the subject.

Using copiers artists and designers can reproduce simply and cheaply existing images (or details of them) selected from the cornucopia of pictures supplied by the mass media , but exact duplication is rarely their aim. What interests them more are the opportunities for montage, distortion and transformation. In this respect any degradation of the image during copying or re-copying is an advantage, not a disadvantage. Artists can reduce or enlarge images and modulate their original colour schemes by changing the hue and tone settings on the machine. (Colour photocopiers date from the late '60s but became generally available in the mid 1970s.) Variations of colour and texture can be achieved simply by inserting different kinds of paper into the machine. By copying onto special materials, image-transfers to fabric or T-shirts are possible. By moving the original during scanning, blurs and smears can be generated. Images can also be reworked by hand and then copied again. Superimposition or layers of images result from copying onto already printed sheets of paper. The same image can be repeated over and over again and then assembled into larger patterns, Warhol fashion. Alternatively, different images can be collaged together to produce complex billboard-size murals or room-sized installations. Artists can also place their bodies on the machine and copy parts of them. Three-dimensional objects placed on the document glass of the machine are reproduced in a distorted fashion because of the machine's shallow depth of field.

COPY ART ALISON MARCHANT, 'Wallpaper history/reprinted pages' (1989). Detail of laser photocopy 6' x 6'. Installation at the Tom Allen Community Centre, London. Photo: Marchant.

In short, the artistic potential of the technology depends upon ways of exploiting it that tend to stretch its normal operations and commercial functions.

Because this form of art is based on mechanical reproduction and the machines are widely distributed, it has a high democratic potential in the sense that people without artistic training can make examples for small sums of money. This point was made by the Italian artist–designer Bruno Munari as early as 1970 when he installed a Rank Xerox machine at the 35th Venice Biennale for the use of visitors. Copy artists exhibit in galleries but they also make use of the international mail art network in order to circulate and distribute their work: they make postcards or publish collections in book or magazine form. Size of edition tends to be small but additional copies can, of course, easily be generated via the photocopier. Mail art can be interactive in the sense that artists can add to what they receive and post it out again. Even faster than the mail is the fax system; Copy artists can annihilate space and time by faxing their images across the globe in moments.

Photocopiers can also make works of art by professional artists available to large numbers of people at low prices – hence the proposal for 'throwaway art' – even though when this happens it challenges the rarity value of art and the financial basis of the gallery–dealer system. It seems therefore a negation of this democratic potential when Copy Art murals are offered for sale in community centres at high prices. However, it should be recognized that many artists argue that what appeals to them about xeroxing is not its capacity to generate masses of identical images but rather its capacity to generate an endless series of unique, original images. The latter can then, if desired, serve as 'sketches' in the creation of larger-scale, more permanent silk-screened canvases (as in art of John

Stezaker). For some artists copying is just one facet of their work but others specialize in Copy Art.

The fact that Copy artists depend upon the same machines does not mean that they share a common style or aesthetic. Artists as various as Ian Burn (a conceptual/process artist who made 'Xerox Book' in 1968), Laurie Rae Chamberlain (a punk-inspired colour xeroxer exhibiting in the mid 1970s) and Helen Chadwick (a feminist artist using her own body as subject matter in the 1980s) have employed photocopiers for very different purposes.

Other artists who have made significant use of the machines include: Tim Head, Ginny Lloyd, Sonia Sheridan, Tom Norton, David Hockney, Russell Mills, Carol Key, Sarah Willis, Graham Harwood, Alison Marchant, and the Copyart Collective of Camden.

Manufacturers of the machines are an obvious source of funding for artistic experimentation with copiers and such companies as Rank Xerox, Canon and Selex have been willing to lend machines, sponsor shows and pay for artists-in-residence schemes.

● See also Book Art, Generative Systems, Media Art, Multiples, Photo-Montage, Plagiarists, Silk- Screenprinting, Simulation/Simulcra/Hyperreality.

● I Burn *Xerox book* (NY, Ian Burn, 1968).

● P Firpo & others *Copy Art: the first complete guide to the copy machine* (NY, Richard Marek, 1978).

● M McCray *Electroworks* (Rochester, NY, International Museum of Photography, George Eastman House, 1979).

● B Cushman 'Copy Art: San Francisco revolution' *Umbrella* **3** (5) September 1980 97.

● C Rigal *L'artiste et le photocopie* (Paris, Édition Galerie Trans/form, 1981).

● J Alcalá Mellado & J Canales *Copy Art: la fotocopia como soporte expresivo* (Alicante, Centro Eusebio Sempere de Arte y Comunicación Visual, 1986).

● G Harwood *John & other stories* (Working Press, 1987).

● G Muhleck & M Brunet-Weinmann *Medium: Photocopy, Canadian & German Copygraphy* (Montréal, Centre Saidye Bronfman, 1987).

● J Alcalá Mellado & J Canales *Los seminarios de electrografia* (València, Universidad Politécnica de València, 1988).

● *2 Bienal Internacional Electrografia y Copy Art* (València, Ajuntament de València, 1988).

● M Klotz & others (eds) *50 Jahr Xerografie, Fotokopie in der Kunst* (NY, Astoria, 1988).

● B Sanjuan *Elektrografien Alcalacanales* (Mülheim an der Ruhr, Museum für Fotokopie, 1988).

● S Lewandowski 'Copyart' *Artists Newsletter* August 1988 23–5.

● — 'Copygraphy – Photocopy Art' *Alba* (11) Spring 1989 65–7.

(Also Company Handwriting, Corporate Image, Corporate or Group Identity, House Style) Large commercial companies, businesses, airlines and public utilities with many sub-divisions can suffer from problems of public image and communication because of a lack of unity and impact in their outward appearance. To remedy this they often commission designers to ensure that the design of their logo, packaging, letterheads, signs, etc., conforms to a master pattern. (For the Bovis group of companies, the design consultants Wolff Olins employed the image of a hovering humming-bird as a logo.) The aim of Corporate Design is to achieve a visual projection of the company and its activities as a whole. In the first instance it is normally important to create a sense of identity and common purpose within the organizations concerned and this may involve more than a visual re-styling, it may involve a re-design of the internal structures. In the case of conglomerates offering a variety of products and services, television advertising is increasingly being used to convey to the public a positive impression of the organization concerned.

● See also Consultant Design, Design Research Unit, Pentagram, Styling.

● F Henrion & A Parkin *Design coordination and corporate*

Press reproduction guide for the new Akzo corporate mark

All versions to print positive as shown, on a white background.

Non-repro blue not to print

AKZO

For 4 colour halftone process   For 2 colour line   For single colour black only

AKZO   **AKZO**   **AKZO**

To achieve Akzo colours, print percentage tints of process colours as follows

Blue — Pantone process blue
Grey — Pantone cool grey 9

Blue   Grey
100% Cyan   70% Black

CORPORATE DESIGN WOLFF OLINS, 'Corporate mark for AKZO, a Dutch chemical company' (1988). Illus. courtesy of Wolff Olins.

image (Studio Vista, 1967).

● W Olins *The corporate personality: an inquiry into the nature of corporate identity* (Design Council, 1978).

● V Brooks 'Triumph of the corporate style: communications design in the 1970s' *Print* **34** (1) January–February 1980 25–31.

● R Yee & K Gustafson *Corporate design: the interior design and architecture of corporate America* (Thames & Hudson, 1983).

● D Carter *American corporate identity: the state of the art in the '80s* (NY, Art Direction Books, 1986).

● D Nye *Image worlds: corporate identities at General Electric* (Cambridge, Mass, MIT Press, 1986).

● P Gorb & E Schneider (eds) *Design talks!* (Design Council, 1988).

● V Napoles *Corporate identity design* (NY, Van Nostrand Reinhold, 1988).

● E Booth-Clibborn (ed) *The best of British Corporate Design* (Internos Books, 1989).

● W Olins *Corporate identity: making business strategy visible through design* (Thames & Hudson, 1989).

● M Pedersen (ed) *Graphis Corporate Identity 1* (Zürich, Graphis Press, 1990).

(Also Co-realism) A term devised by Frederick J Kiesler (1896–1965), an American of Austrian origin, skilled in a number of arts – painting, sculpture, architecture, theatre and interior design – and who was associated with several modern movements including de Stijl and surrealism. He was also dubbed 'the father of happenings'. In an article published in 1939 Kiesler argued that forms are 'the visible trading posts of visible and invisible forces'; that what we call reality consists of these two categories of forces continually interacting. The exchange of forces he called 'co-reality' and the science of its relationships 'Correalism'. The term was also intended to signify the continuity of space and time and the correlation between human beings and their environment, sculptures and their contexts. During his career Kiesler proposed various kinds of visionary architecture – endless (the Endless House, 1923, 1960)...spiral... magical – all of which were opposed to the functionalism he regarded as 'the mysticism of hygiene'.

● See also Contextual Architecture, Environmental Art, Happenings, Visionary Architecture.

● F Kiesler 'On Correalism and biotechnique' *Architectural Record* **86** September 1939 60–75.

● *Frederick Kiesler: environmental sculpture* (NY, Guggenheim Museum, 1964).

● F Kiesler 'Second manifesto of co-realism' *Art International* **9** (2) March 1965 16–19.

● —*Inside the endless house* (NY, Simon & Schuster, 1966).

● V Conrads (ed) *Programmes and manifestos on 20th-century architecture* (Lund Humphries, 1970) 150–1.

● L Phillips *Frederick Kiesler* (NY, Whitney Museum of American Art/Norton, 1989).

185 COSMIC ARCHITECTURE

A term used by the Japanese architect Monta Mozuna about his own designs and buildings from 1970 onwards (e.g. the Zen Temple, Tokyo (1979)), inspired by cosmological and esoteric ideas. Cosmic Architecture attempted to find physical forms capable of embodying the energies, laws and structures of the universe. It also used light to generate magical effects. Mozuna invoked the past to justify his practice: he claimed that much ancient architecture built by many different cultures was based on cosmology. He also generated several other terms: 'twin architecture', 'architecture in architecture' and 'anti-dwelling house'.

● M Mozuna 'Theory of Cosmic Architecture' *A new wave of Japanese architecture* introd K Frampton (NY, IAUS: Institute for Architecture & Urban Studies, 1978), catalogue 10, 80–5.

● P Portoghesi *Postmodern: the architecture of the postindustrial society* (NY, Rizzoli, 1983) 152–4.

● B Bognar *Contemporary Japanese architecture: its development and challenge* (NY, Van Nostrand Reinhold, 1985) 265–76.

186 COSMIC ART

(Also Metaphysical Art, Synthetic Art) A term used by the American professor of philosophy Raymond Piper (1888–1961) to characterize the works of art he studied from around the world. (Piper's research collection consisted of 2,500 reproductions and interviews with over 2,000 artists from 64 countries.) The works included paintings, drawings and sculptures. In terms of content, what they had in common was a preoccupation with ultimate issues: the nature of the universe, soul and spirit, humankind's relation to God, death, transcendence, psychic and mystical experiences. Mandala forms were often featured and also images of flames, radiance or glories of light. Aside from Max Bill and Morris Graves, most of the artists Piper admired were little known to the artworld. Much of the art was bathetic and verged on kitsch. John Latham, a British avant garde artist whose work since 1954 has been concerned with cosmological themes from a scientific rather than a mystical perspective, was not represented in Piper's posthumous book.

● See also Psychedelic Art, Tantra Art, Visionary Art.

● I Swann 'Cosmic Art' *Psychic* **4** (49) February 1973.

● R & L Piper *Cosmic Art* (ed) I Swann (NY, Hawthorn Books, 1975).

187 COVENTRY CATHEDRAL

In 1940, during the bombing of the Second World War, the ancient Gothic cathedral of the British industrial town of Coventry was reduced to an empty shell. A new building designed by the modern architect Basil Spence was constructed between 1952 and '62 and became emblematic of the period of post-war reconstruction and of twentieth-century Christian art. The building was notable for the diverse contributions made by British artists: an external sculpture of St Michael by Jacob Epstein, stained glass windows by John Piper and Patrick Reyntiens, a lectern eagle sculpture by Elizabeth Frink, glass engravings by John Hutton, a high altar cross in silver and gold by Geoffrey Clarke, and a huge tapestry depicting Christ in glory based on a painting by Graham Sutherland. Coventry Cathedral proved to be extremely popular in terms of attracting visitors and has been described by later writers as 'a '50s time capsule'. An art-historical exhibition entitled 'To build a Cathedral' was held at the Mead Gallery, Warwick University, in 1987.

● (Coventry Cathedral issue) *Sunday Times Colour Section* May 20 1962.

● R Furneaux Jordan 'Coventry Cathedral' *The Studio* **164** (832) August 1962 54–7.

COVENTRY CATHEDRAL SIR BASIL SPENCE, architect. The eastern side of the new Coventry Cathedral (1951-62) showing porch and Jacob Epstein's bronze sculpture 'St Michael & The devil'. Photo: Harland Walshaw.

● R Howard *Ruined and rebuilt: the story of Coventry Cathedral 1939–62* (Coventry Cathedral Council, 1962).

● B Spence *Phoenix at Coventry: the building of a cathedral* (Geoffrey Bles, 1962).

● — & H Snoek *Out of the ashes: a progress through Coventry Cathedral* (Geoffrey Bles, 1963).

● A Revai (ed) *Christ in glory in the tetramorph: the genesis of the great tapestry* (Pallas Gallery/Zwemmer, 1964).

● H Williams *Coventry Cathedral: a guide...* (Hodder & Stoughton, 1966).

● M Pawley 'Building revisits 1' *Architects Journal* May 9 1984 47–53.

● J Thomas *Coventry Cathedral* (Unwin Hyman, 1987), The New Bell's Cathedral Guides.

188 COWBOY ART (Also Western Art) In the nineteenth century, during the era of the Wild West, a number of artists anticipated the film genre of the Western by depicting the American Indians and the pioneers, plus scenes of buffalo hunting, cattle herding, gunfights, cowboys on horseback, and so on. The best known of these artists were George Catlin, Frederic Remington and Charles M. Russell.

Today, in the Western states of the USA, several groups of artists exist – some of whom have worked as cowboys and some of whom have been successful in the field of commercial art – who continue the tradition established by Remington *et al.* by making sculptures and paintings of Wild West subjects. Five such artists – George Phippen, Charlie Dye, Joe Beeler, John Hampton and Fred Harmon – founded in 1965 the Cowboy Artists of America (CAA) which organizes annual shows/sales with published catalogues. Another association with an annual show is the National Academy of Western Art (NAWA) established by Dean Krakel in 1973. Other respected Cowboy artists are: Frank Polk, Jim Boren, Bill Nebeker, William Bent, Bill Owen and Gordon Snidow. A special museum devoted to Cowboy Art has been proposed for Corville, Texas. (A Cowboy Hall of Fame exists in Tulsa, Oklahoma.)

Cowboy Art was and is academic and illustrative in character, consequently it is ignored by histories of modern American art. The contemporary variety of Cowboy Art is also historicist and nostalgic (J. Gray Sweeney of Arizona State University describes it as a regional art with a machismo value structure that provides an anachronistic vision of national identity); nevertheless it is popular and sells for high prices.

● H McCracken *Frederic Remington: artist of the old West* (Philadelphia, Lippincott, 1947).

● P Rossi & D Hunt *The art of the old West from the collection of the Gilcrease Institute (Tulsa, Oklahoma)* (NY, Knopf, 1971).

● *The American West: painters from Catlin to Russell* (Los Angeles, County Museum of Art/NY, Viking Press/London, Studio Vista, 1972).

● B Helberg 'Cowboy artists of America' *South Western Art* **5** (4) Winter 1976–7 46–9.

● H Fenwick 'Paint 'em cowboy' *Observer colour Supplement* March 15 1981 42–7.

● M Carroll *Masters of Western art* (NY, Watson-Guptil, 1982).

● C Bruce (ed) *Myth of the West* (Seattle, Henry Art Gallery/NY, Rizzoli, 1990).

● W Truettner (ed) *The West as America : reinterpreting images of the frontier* (Blue Ridge Summit, Penn, Smithsonian Institution Press/ Washington, National Museum of American Art, 1991).

189 CRANBROOK The Cranbrook Academy of Art, Bloomfield Hills, Michigan, is a famous American educational institution. It was founded in the 1920s by George Booth, a wealthy newspaper magnate whose taste and ideas were influenced by the arts and crafts movement of the nineteenth century. Buildings for the Academy's campus were designed by the Finnish architect Eliel Saarinen (1873–1950) and his son Eero (1910–61). They include a museum. Studios of architecture, sculpture, painting, metalwork, bookbinding and ceramics were established and headed by practitioners. The aim was to create a community of artists, designers and students. Well-known designers associated with Cranbrook include Charles and Ray Eames and Florence Knoll. An exhibition celebrating the achievements of the Academy up to 1950 was held in Detroit and New York in 1983.

● See also Art Schools.

● R Judson Clark & others *Design in America: the Cranbrook vision 1925–50* (Detroit Institute of Arts/NY, Metropolitan Museum/Abrams, 1983).

● H Aldersey-Williams & others *New Cranbrook design* (NY, Rizzoli, 1990).

190 CREATIVE SALVAGE (Also Post-Holocaust Design, Punk Design, Salvage Aesthetic/ Art, Trans High Tech) A term coined by the British designer Tom Dixon in the mid 1980s to describe eccentric, anti-good taste furniture by himself, Ron Arad and others, made from discarded metal, concrete and junk. Simon Cox, a jewellery designer, made macabre pieces from scrap metal and the small bones of dead birds and fishes. Robin Cooke created a cocktail cabinet from the front part of a Mercedes car. This type of

CREATIVE SALVAGE SIMON COSTIN, 'A weasel in high heels attempts the dissection of a painted finch' (1989). Mixed-media assemblage. Photo: courtesy of Rebecca Hossack Gallery, London.

work marked a reaction against the fashion for high tech (hence the term 'Trans High Tech') and it blurred the difference between fine art and design. To some critics the work looked like the kind of art and design that might follow a nuclear disaster (hence 'Post-Holocaust Design'). Meanwhile, fine artists like Bill Woodrow and Tony Cragg made sculptures from waste materials, and Julian Opie and Robert Gober constructed art objects resembling household fittings.

Since examples of Creative Salvage tended to be handmade and one-off, they were expensive to buy. A London gallery/shop selling and promoting this type of work was 'Crucial', Notting Hill Gate, founded in 1985 by Joshua and Kitty Bowler. A show entitled the 'Creative Salvage Ideal Home Exhibition' was held at the Cuts Gallery and One Off, London, in August 1985.

● See also Assemblage Art, High-Tech, High-Touch, Junk Culture/Sculpture, Low-Tech, Mutoid Waste Co, Neo-Geo, New British Sculpture, Punk, Reactivart.

● G Howell 'Britain's answer to the armchair critics' *Sunday Times Magazine* November 10 1985 56–61.

● D Sudjic *Ron Arad: restless furniture* (Fourth Estate/Wordsearch, 1989).

● J Wilde 'St Valentine's day masochist' (Simon Costin)

191 CRITICAL REALISM

(Also Ugly Realism) This term was employed by Russian literary critics for many years to refer to writings which accurately described the negative aspects of bourgeois society and which, therefore, were looked upon with favour by socialists. For a Marxist critic such as the Hungarian György Lukács, Critical Realism was the appropriate mode for a socially conscious artist in a pre-revolutionary, bourgeois society; after a Left-wing revolution socialist realism would replace Critical Realism. Lukács wrote extensively about bourgeois and Critical Realism in literature and emphasized the importance of the typical in the latter.

In the visual arts 'Kritischer Realismus' was a term adopted by the Aspekt group of German artists – Hans-Jürgen Diehl, Wolfgang Petrick, Peter Sorge, Klaus Vogelgensang and Bettina Von Arnim – who made photo-montages, drawings and paintings attacking contemporary German society in the early 1970s. Their work was included in a 1978 exhibition held at the ICA, London, organized by Sarah Kent. This show juxtaposed works from the 1920s (by Otto Dix, George Grosz, Rudolf Schlichter, John Heartfield and others) and the 1970s in order to demonstrate certain connections between past and present. Because the images and films on display considered life in Berlin to be harsh and brutal, Kent described them as 'ugly realism'. Most of the artists concerned favoured a highly detailed, quasi-photographic, impersonal mode of representation – hence the recurrence of 'realism'.

Also in the '70s, the Swedish artist Peter Dahl employed the term 'Critical Realism' in relation to his own paintings, in particular to a series of 20 works entitled 'Dreams from the corner of the sofa' which caused a scandal because they depicted a sexual fantasy involving a member of the Swedish Royal Family.

In 1987 'Critical Realism' was chosen as the title of a British touring exhibition curated by the art historian Brandon Taylor, an admirer of Lukács' writings. The show included paintings, photo-montages, photographs, sculptures and cartoons by such artists as Steve Bell, Stuart Brisley, Sue Coe, Joan Dawson, Ken Currie, Jo Spence and John Yeadon. According to Taylor, this work examined the realities of Britain in the 1980s 'in as direct and truthful a manner as possible'. It was critical because it commented upon such issues as unemployment, widening divisions between rich and poor, and so on. Taylor perceived precedents for this form of realism in the earlier satirical images of Gillray, Rowlandson and Hogarth.

CRITICAL REALISM JOAN DAWSON, 'Heroes' (1982). Oil on canvas, 5' x 5'. Included in Brandon Taylor's Critical Realism exhibition. Photo: Dawson.

● See also Aspekt Group, Capitalist Realism.

● G Lukács *The meaning of contemporary realism* (Merlin Press, 1963).

● I Deutscher 'Georg Lukács and "Critical Realism"' *The Listener* 3 September 1966.

● M Wadell 'Critical Realism: a case study' *ARIS* 1974 1–114.

● S Kent & others *Berlin, a critical view: Ugly Realism '20s–'70s* (ICA, 1978).

● B Taylor & J Steyn *Critical Realism: Britain in the 1980s through the work of 28 artists* (Nottingham Castle Museum, 1987).

● M Gibbs 'Critical Realism' (12 American photographers) *Perspektif* (Rotterdam) (39) 1990 38–58.

192 CRITICAL REGIONALISM

A term coined by Alex Tzonis and Liliane Lefaivre in 1981 and adopted by the architectural critic and historian Kenneth Frampton. He considered it a strategy for achieving a more human kind of architecture. Regionalism, according to Tzonis and Lefaivre, 'upholds individual and local architectonic features against more universal and abstract ones'. Frampton argued that modern architecture should encourage regional variation rather than continue in the direction of global uniformity and mediocrity. However, he did not favour a return to vernacular styles or nostalgic historicist solutions involving a rejection of modern technology. The modern architect's task was to 'mediate the impact of universal civilisation with elements derived *indirectly* from the peculiarities of a particular place'. He retained the word 'critical' because architects had to be aware of the negative consequences of technology and industrialization, hence he sought a type of modern architecture that was critical of modernism and regionalism but which found new solutions in relation to both universal and local cultures. Frampton cited buildings by Jorn Utzon and Alvar Aalto as good examples of Critical Regionalism.

● See also Abstract Representation, Provincialism Problem.

● K Frampton 'Toward a Critical Regionalism: six points for an architecture of resistance' – in – *The anti-aesthetic* H Foster (ed) (Port Townsend, Washington, Bay Press, 1983) 16–30.

193 CROSS-OVERS

This term has been used in the American popular music business for decades to refer to records by black singers and groups that overcome racial divisions by becoming popular with whites, i.e. they 'cross-over' from black to white charts. In the 1980s the term was adopted by art critics to refer to artists who move from one relatively autonomous realm to another, e.g. a graffiti writer who leaves the streets and subway for the art gallery system. The paradigmatic instance of Cross-Over was Laurie Anderson. In the 1970s she was a little-known performance and video artist appearing in the lofts and galleries of New York, but as a result of her 1981 hit record 'O Superman' she made the transition from the artworld to the realms of pop music, television and the concert circuit, i.e. from a minority culture to a mass culture. Cross-Overs can occur 'horizontally' – e.g. when a painter becomes a designer – and 'vertically' – when someone ascends from 'low' to 'high' culture.

● See also Art Schools, Graffiti, Rock Art/Design/Fashion, Rock Video.

● J Walker *Cross-Overs: art into pop, pop into art* (Comedia/Methuen, 1987).

194 CULT OBJECTS

Following their invention and manufacture, certain designed products acquire for particular groups of consumers a special status or aura. A Cult Object, according to Deyan Sudjic, is 'a class of artefact which exercises a powerful, but mysterious fascination'. He adds: 'by definition a cult depends upon a group of insiders, tightly knit and linked by secret signs recognizable only to initiates'. Amongst the Cult Objects celebrated in his books are jeeps, Zippo lighters, Aga cookers, Braun shavers, Burberry trenchcoats, Mini cars, Newcastle Brown Ale, Coca-Cola bottles, Lucky Strike cigarettes, Filofaxes, and 501 jeans. Cult Objects appear to be the consumer society equivalent of the fetishes and ritual objects which played such an important part in tribal societies and in religions.

● See also Braun, Coca-Cola Collectibles/Design, Filofax.

○ D Sudjic *Cult Objects: the complete guide to having it all* (Paladin/Granada, 1985).

195 CULTURED PAINTING

(La Pittura Colta. Also Anacronismo, Art on Art, Ipermanierismo, Hyper- or Neo-Mannerism, New Metaphysical Painting) Art can be about nature or about art itself (or both). 'Cultured' or 'Cultivated' painting was an intellectual form of art reflecting on the past of art, in particular the styles of classicism, neo-classicism and mannerism. Various exhibitions of Cultured Painting took place in Europe during the early 1980s and it made a significant showing in the 'Art as a mirror' section of the 1984 Venice Biennale. Most of the artists associated with the tendency were Italian – Carlo Bertocci, Carlo Maria Mariani, Alberto Abate, Lorenzo Bonechi, Franco Piruca, Ubaldo Bartolini, Bruno d'Arcevia, Omar Galliani and Stefano di Stasio – though some shows also featured the work of the Britishers Stephen McKenna and Christopher Lebrun and the Frenchman Gerard Garouste.

In Italy the critic Italo Mussa employed the term 'La Pittura Colta' while Maurizio Calvesi preferred 'Anachronisti', and Italo Tomassoni favoured 'Hyper-mannerism'. Some Cultured paintings simulated both the subjects and styles of the past, while others featured modern subjects (e.g. a portrait of Warhol) executed in a classical, old master style. (The precise, traditional methods employed by the artists were clearly intended as a complete contrast to the crude violence of neo-expressionist painting.) This kind of work, although apparently post-modernist in its return to pre-modern models, was said to have emerged in part from conceptual art and to reflect the influence of the metaphysical painter Giorgio de Chirico. In fact, the term 'New Metaphysical Painting' was used by critics in different countries to describe the late 1980s' work of two groups of artists, one German and one Italian. Bernard Schulz used it in reference to the Berlin painters Hermann Albert and his students Peter Schindler, Andreas Weishaupt and Stephanus Heidacker while Italo Mussa and Hugh Cumming used it in reference to Alberto Abate, Aulo, Carlo Bertocci, Renato Bianchini, Luigi Campanelli, Walter Gatti and Massimo Livadiotti. These artists were associated with the Centro di Cultura Ausoni in Rome and the Jack Shainman Gallery in New York.

Regarded by some critics as the epitome of reaction and nostalgia, the anachronisms and academicism of Cultured Painting were quite deliberate and ironic.

CULTURED PAINTING WALTER GATTI, 'Paradiso terrestre' (1986). Oil on canvas, 59" x 59". Photo: Jack Shainman Gallery, New York.

● See also Arcadian Painting, Conceptual Art, Neo-Expressionism, Post-Modernism, Retro, Simulation / Simulcra / Hyperreality.

○ I Mussa *Carlo Maria Mariani* (Rome, De Luca Editore, 1980).

○ — *La Pittura Colta* (Rome, Galleria Monti, 1983).

○ M Calvesi & I Tomassoni *Anacronismo, Ipermanierismo* (Venice, Biennale Internazionale d'Arte di Venezia, 1984). *La Pittura Colta* (Edward Totah Gallery, 1984).

○ I Tomassoni *Hypermannerism* (Milan, Giancarlo Politi Editore, 1985)

○ B Schulz 'The return of things' *Flash Art* (128) May–June 1986.

○ I Mussa *The New Metaphysical dream* (NY/Washington, Jack Shainman Gallery/Rome, De Luca Editore, 1986).

○ H Cumming 'New Metaphysical Painting' *Art & Design* **4** (7/8) 1988 76–80.

196 CURWEN STUDIO

A London printmaking studio noted for the high quality of its lithographs produced in association with such leading British artists as Alan Davie, Ceri Richards, John Piper and Henry Moore. The Curwen Press dated from the nineteenth century. Under Harold Curwen (printer) and Oliver Simon (typographer), in the period between the two world wars, it became famous for its book illustration and typography. The Curwen Studio was established by Timothy Simon in Plaistow, East London, in 1958 as a separate facility for making original lithographs by fine artists. Its lithographic manager was Stanley Jones. A gift of the Studio's lithographs was made to the Print Collection of the Tate Gallery, London, in the 1970s.

● See also Atelier 17, Collaborations, Kelpra Studio, Tamarind Lithography Workshop, Tyler Graphics.

● P Gilmour *Lithographs from the Curwen Studio: a retrospective of fifteen years* (Camden Art Centre, 1973).

● —*Artists at Curwen: a celebration of the gift of artists' prints from the Curwen Studio* (Tate Gallery, 1977).

197 CUSTOMIZING & CUSTOM PAINTING

The mass-production methods of modern industry have tended to result in goods that are highly uniform, hence the practice of 'customizing', i.e. changing a standard product by decorating it with paint or by adding accessories in order to tailor it to the customer, in order to individualize or personalize it. In Southern California this practice has been applied to motor cars and cycles since the late 1940s. Its originator is thought to have been Van Dutch Holland. The opposite to a mass-produced model is the 'custom-built' car. The so-called 'kustom car cult' involved the total fabrication of unique vehicles from new parts or from a mixture of old and new parts. Customizing can be undertaken, therefore, by ordinary consumers or by small firms specializing in the practice.

During the early 1960s the concept of Customizing influenced a number of British artists. The term 'Custom Painting' was used by the pop artist Peter Phillips to describe a series of his own works. He selected motifs and emblems from particular subcultures, such as that of the leather-jacketed rockers, as a step towards a custommade art. While Phillips and Gerald Laing were living in New York in 1964–5, they devised a market research project called 'Hybrid Enterprises'. Kits of materials consisting of colour samples, optical patterns, choice of forms and statistical sheets were compiled and issued to people in the artworld for their reactions. When the data was returned, it was processed by computer and then three-dimensional art objects were made from glamorous materials such as aluminium and perspex in accordance with the preferences revealed by the survey. At the same time in London a group of ex-Slade students calling themselves 'Fine Artz Associates' (Terry Atkinson, John Bowstead, Roger Jeffs and Bernard Jennings) advocated a new role for art in a consumer/leisure society. They operated as a team and tried to emulate the Customizing approach typical of teenage subcultures, and to imitate business methods such as motivation research and devices such as styling.

● See also Car Culture, Pop Art, Reception Theory/Aesthetics, Styling, Subculture.

● Fine Artz Associates 'Visualizing...' *Ark* (35) Spring 1964 38–41.

CUSTOMIZING & CUSTOM PAINTING Customized scooter. Mid 1960s.

● — 'A Fine Artz view of teenage cults' *Ark* (36) Summer 1964 39–48.

● 'Hybrid Consumer Research Project' *ICA Bulletin* (151) October 1965 17–18.

● T Wolfe *The kandy kolored tangerine flake streamlined baby* (J Cape, 1966) 76–107.

● C Card 'Custom Painting' (letter) *Studio International* 174 (891) July–August 1967 7.

● F Schulke 'Portrait of the artist as an easy rider' *Sunday Times Magazine* September 2 1973 44–5.

● G Laing 'Hybrid' *Control Magazine* (8) August 1974 15.

● M Beedie *Customizing vans* (Godfrey Cave Associates, 1978).

● C Burnham *Customizing cars* (Godfrey Cave Associates, 1980).

● R Nichols & J Basten *Custom cars* (Star/W H Allen, 1981).

● J-R Piccard *Dream cars* (Orbis, 1981).

● F Basham, B Ugetti & P Rambali *Car culture* (Plexus, 1982).

● *Peter Phillips* (Liverpool, Walker Art Gallery, 1982).

198 CYBERNETIC ART

(Also Cyberart, Cyborg Art, Post-Kinetic Art) Norbert Weiner, the principal founder of the scientific theory of cybernetics, defined it as 'control and communication in the animal and in the machine', and also as the study of messages as a means of controlling machinery and society. Fundamental to cybernetics is the concept of feedback, i.e. the return of part of the energy output of a system, in the form of information, for correcting or controlling the future behaviour of the system. During the 1960s a number of artists, predominantly European kineticists, began to apply these ideas in their work. Cybernetics seemed to provide a means of overcoming the limitations of kinetic art in respect of spectator participation. Several Cybernetic sculptures were built which were capable of responding to environmental stimuli, including the proximity of spectators or any sounds they might make. Nicolas Schöffer created such a work as early as 1954. Other artists who produced similar sculptures or environments were Enrique Castro-Cid, Nam June Paik, Charles Mattox, Robert Breer and the American art and technology group called PULSA. Jack Burnham believed that the aim of 'Cyborg Art' – the cybernetic organism as an artform – was to achieve the same degree of communicative interaction as two people conversing. Such art attempted to simulate the structure of life rather than imitating its surface appearance. Its ultimate goal was total integration with intelligent life forms; at this level artefacts would be replaced by systems and Cybernetic Art would be superseded by systems art.

Roy Ascott, a British artist and educator, made use of cybernetics in his work and theories during the '60s. A trend towards a fusion of the arts, he considered, could be accounted for by a 'cybernetic vision' in which art was regarded as a behaviour within society. Several other British artists who were cybernetic-orientated contributed to *Control Magazine* edited by Stephen Willats. Cybernetics and computers were closely linked, consequently some critics used the terms 'Cybernetic Art' and 'computer art' interchangeably; however, the two are not identical.

● See also Behavioural Art, Computer Art, Kinetic Art, PULSA, Systems Art, Telematics.

R Ascott 'Behaviourist art and the cybernetic vision' part 1 *Cybernetica* **9** (4) 1966 247–64; part 2 *Cybernetica* **10** (1) 1967 25–56.

— 'The cybernetic stance: my process and purpose' *Leonardo* **1** (2) April 1968 105–12.

CYBERNETIC ART NICOLAS SCHÖFFER 'Design for a Light Tower'. Source of illustration J. Reichardt (ed) *Cybernetic Serendipity* (Studio International, 1968).

J Burnham 'Robot & Cyborg Art' – in – *Beyond modern sculpture...* (Allen Lane, Penguin Press, 1968) 312– 76.

J Reichardt (ed) *Cybernetic Serendipity: the computer and the arts* (Studio International, 1968).

M Apter 'Cybernetics and art' *Leonardo* **2** (3) July 1969 257–65.

M Rosenberg *The cybernetics of art: reason and the rainbow* (NY, Gordon & Breach, 1983).

V Bonacic 'A transcendental concept for Cybernetic Art in the 21st century' *Leonardo* **22** (1) 1989 109–11.

199 DAU AL SET

A Spanish, avant garde group of poets and artists active in Barcelona from 1948 to '53. The group also published a magazine with the title 'Dau Al Set' which means 'die or dice with seven'. Since dice have only six as a maximum the expression implied going beyond normal limits. The best-known visual artists of the group were Antonio Tàpies, Juan-José Tharrats and Modesto Cuixart. At first they supported surrealism but later their work became more abstract and they contributed to the European tendencies called l'art informel and matter art. Examples of the art of Dau Al Set are preserved in the Museum of Abstract Art in Cuenca, Spain.

● See also Art Informel, El Paso, Matter Art.

○ *Aspectos de una decada: pintura Española 1955–65* (Madrid, Sala de Exposiciones de la Fundacion Caja de Pensiones, 1988).

200 DECONSTRUCTION

A philosophical and literary term associated with the post-structuralist writings of the French scholars Jacques Derrida, Jean-Francois Lyotard and their followers. With doubtful justification it was applied to the visual arts – especially architecture – during the late 1980s. (Derrida himself has elaborated upon writings on the visual arts in his book *The truth in painting*). Deconstructionists are extreme sceptics who reject the truth and knowledge claims made by existing philosophical systems. They undertake 'readings' of texts in order to show that they are ultimately illogical and self-contradictory. (They also produce texts which are as much literature as philosophy.) The binary oppositions – e.g. nature/culture – favoured by structuralists are attacked to release what they repress. Deconstruction is not a dismantling of a system but a demonstration of the fact that it has already dismantled itself. Literary texts are said to undermine their own claims to have determinate meanings – texts always have a surplus of meaning and they resist attempts to pin meaning down. Deconstruction, it is said, is not a method, critique, analysis, theory, or practice. Like anti-art art, it appears to be a type of philosophizing continually at war with the very possibility of philosophy.

During June–August 1988 an exhibition of 'Deconstructivist' architecture was held at MoMA in New York which featured the work of Peter Eisenman, Bernard Tschmumi, Zaha Hadid, Coop. Himmelblau, Frank Gehry, Rem Koolhaas and Daniel Libeskind. (The show's title involved a play on the words 'deconstruction' and 'constructivism'.) An international symposium on Deconstruction and architecture also took place at the Tate Gallery in March 1988. Deconstructivist architects were said to use the critical tactics of Deconstruction in order to question accepted architectural notions of form, function, permanence, harmony, order, meaning and beauty. For example, the modernist dictum 'form follows function' became 'function follows deformation'. Their post-modern architecture was thus a violation of existing conceptions of architecture. The results were described as 'heterogeneous ideas yoked together by violence'. There was a willingness to exploit superimposition, fragmentation, discord, discontinuity and distortions, to 'make the repressed structural', to design buildings – 'follies' – with no pre-determined purpose, to disturb the relationship between the inside and the outside, and to displace and destabilize context through 'estrangement'. However, it was emphatically denied that Deconstructivist architecture was a new 'ism' or style. Douglas Davis judged that it was nostalgic, 'neomodernity dressed in postmodern drag'.

In regard to visual artists other than architects, two categories can be identified: those whose artistic project parallels philosophical Deconstruction unknowingly and those who have read Derrida *et al.* and been influenced by their ideas. Amongst the artists who have been claimed for Deconstruction are Francis Bacon, Marcel Duchamp, Jasper Johns, Valerio Adami and Dan Graham. The full list is in fact so extensive and disparate that it is hard to perceive any common denominator and hence it would appear Deconstructive art is anything critics care to label as such. Indeed, it would seem that all art is 'already deconstructive' because all art 'exceeds its concepts'.

Deconstruction has many critics on the Left who regard it as an empty, negative school of thought which evades social and political responsibilities. The architecture associated with it has also been attacked for being élitist, self-indulgent, arrogant and uninhabitable.

● See also Post-Modernism, Structuralism & Art/Design.

◉ C Norris *Deconstruction: theory and practice* (Methuen, 1982).

◉ J Derrida *The truth in painting* (Chicago, University of Chicago Press, 1987).

◉ D Lodge 'Deconstruction' *Guardian* April 8 1988 25.

◉ 'The new modernism: Deconstructionist tendencies in art' *Art & Design* **4** (3/4) April 1988.

◉ D Petherbridge 'Da da Deconstruction lives' *Art Monthly* (117) June 1988 8–11.

◉ 'Deconstruction in architecture and urbanism' *Architectural Design* **58** (3/4) 1988.

◉ P Johnson & M Wigley *Deconstructivist architecture* (NY, MoMA, 1988).

◉ C Norris & A Benjamin *What is Deconstruction?* (Academy Editions, 1988).

◉ D Davis 'Slaying the neo-modern dragon' *Art in America* **77** (1) January 1989 43–9.

◉ 'Deconstruction II' *Architectural Design* **58** (1/2) 1989.

◉ *Deconstruction: omnibus volume* (Academy Editions, 1989).

◉ G Broadbent *Deconstruction: a student guide* (Academy Editions, 1991).

201 DEFENSIVE ARCHITECTURE

This term obviously describes military forts and bunkers but it has also been applied to certain Japanese houses built in the 1970s. Because the urban environment was a source of pollution, noise, stress and potential violence, architects such as Tadao Ando and Mayumi Miyawaki responded by designing houses that looked inwards and whose outer shells provided a sense of protection for their inhabitants. The houses tended to consist of basic geometric forms – cubes, cylinders and so forth – (hence the additional label 'primary architecture') with outer walls made from thick concrete, and small internal gardens or patios. Oscar Newman's well-known book about 'defensible space' discusses this important human need.

● See also Hard Architecture.

◉ O Newman *Defensible space: people and design in the violent city* (NY, MacMillan, 1972).

◉ B Bognar *Contemporary Japanese architecture: its development and challenge* (NY, Van Nostrand Reinhold, 1985) 276–85.

202 DEMOCRATIC ART

Arguably, in the past the fine arts were the preserve of wealthy élites, the ruling groups of hierarchical societies. Since the word 'democracy' stems from the Greek 'demos' (people) and 'kratos' (rule), Democratic Art would be any form of culture appealing to, serving the needs of, and available to the majority of the population. The expression 'the democratization of art' normally means something different, i.e. making the traditional high arts more widely available via such means as education, public museums or TV arts programmes. (Another meaning of 'Democratic Art' would be the art of Western democracies as against the art of despotic or totalitarian regimes.)

The label 'Democratic Art' is sometimes used in relation to certain kinds of civic or municipal architecture, but more commonly it is applied to those forms of communication which utilize mass production and mechanical reproduction techniques in order to reach huge audiences, e.g. books, prints and films. (Some observers, however, regard commercial forms of mass culture as 'undemocratic'.) The terms 'Democratic Art' and 'popular art' are virtually synonymous but some critics distinguish between them; e.g. Andrew Brighton once remarked: 'I wasn't calling for a popular, a democratized art, but a democratic art. By which I meant an art that enables people to recognize themselves and to create themselves in the world.'

Rainer Gross (b. 1951), a German artist resident in New York, was said in the 1980s to produce 'Democratic paintings' because they involved a 'levelling' process, i.e. his pictures combined motifs from high art and images from department store kitsch.

● See also Carnival, Community Art & Media, Kitsch, Mass Art, Multiples, Political Art, Popular Art, Totalitarian Art.

◉ G Jowitt *Film: the Democratic Art* (Boston, Little Brown, 1976).

◉ A Brighton (debate contribution) 'The state of British art' *Studio International* **194** (989) 1978 119.

◉ P Marzio *The Democratic Art: chromolithography 1840–1900, pictures for a nineteenth-century America* (Scolar Press, 1980).

◉ C Jencks (ed) *The architecture of democracy* (Art & Design Profile, 1987); proposals for Phoenix Municipal Government Center design competition.

203 DEMONTAGE

A German word meaning 'to dismantle'. It formed half the title of a 1988 exhibition devised by Uli Bohnen and held at Neue Galerie, Ludwig collection, Aachen (plus four other venues). The show featured paintings, constructions and photographs dating from the 1980s by artists from several continents, e.g. Mike Bidlo, Komar & Melamid, Milan Kunc, Sherrie Levine, Ronnie Cutrone, Errò, and others. What these artists had in common was the fact that they made art about art. By mimicking the art of the past they paid homage to it but simultaneously they 'dismantled' or transgressed it in various ways. Some of these artists quoted past works and combined them ironically, some re-staged famous photographs, some displaced historical meanings by irreverent treatments of political symbols, while others replicated the works of modern masters in order to raise questions about originality in art and the relationship between originals and reproductions.

Art based on other images has tended to be called in the United States 'appropriation art'.

● See also Copy Art, Komar & Melamid, Media Art, Meta -Art, Plagiarists, Simulation/Simulacra/Hyperreality, Staged Photography.

○ *The art of appropriation* (NY, Alternative Museum, 1985).

○ U Bohnen (ed) *Hommage Demontage* (Cologne, Druck & Verlagshaus Wienand, 1988).

204 DESIGN COUNCIL

A British organization established by the Board of Trade in 1944 and known until 1972 as the 'Council of Industrial Design' (CoID). One purpose was to promote the improvement of design in the products of British industry by encouraging industry and business to employ designers. Another was to raise the standard of public taste. These aims were to be achieved by approving goods, giving awards and publicity, and by organizing conferences and mounting exhibitions. In 1949 the Council began publication of *Design* magazine and in 1956 a permanent display space – the Design Centre – located in the Haymarket, London, was opened to the public. Detailed information on the activities of the Council can be found in its annual reports. The director of the CoID from 1947 to '59 was the furniture designer Gordon Russell. His successors have included Paul Reilly, Keith Grant and Ivor Owen. In the 1980s the Design Centre/Council was criticized for being 'faceless, bland, and parochial'.

● See also Britain Can Make It, Conran Foundation, 'Good Design'.

○ 'The Design Centre: a special issue' *Design* (89) May 1956.

○ M Farr *The Council of Industrial Design* (Milan, La Rinascentre, 1963).

○ F MacCarthy *All things bright and beautiful: design in Britain 1830 to today* (Allen & Unwin, 1972).

○ D Johnston 'Design Council and the Design Centre' *Museums Journal* **74** December 1974 118–21.

○ J Blake 'Design Centre story, London' *Design* (341) May 1977 26–7.

○ 'The Design Council: dead as a dodo?' *Vogue* (UK) **144** (2277) February 1987 166–7, + 187 (Lord Snowdon interviews Simon Hornby).

205 DESIGN HISTORY SOCIETY (DHS)

An academic organization established in 1977 by British art and design historians and museum curators, many of whom were members of the Association of Art Historians. The aim of DHS is to further the study of the history of design – particularly the industrial design of the nineteenth and twentieth centuries – and to communicate research findings to a wider public. Study days and visits have been arranged and annual conferences have been held and their proceedings have been published in book form by the Design Council. For several years the Society issued a newsletter and in 1988 it began publication of *The Journal of Design History*.

Membership of the DHS is international but the presence and status of Design History naturally varies from country to country. In the United States a Design History Forum was established at the College Art Association annual meeting in 1983. The University of Illinois also publishes a relevant serial: *Design Issues: a journal of History, Theory, and Criticism* (1984–).

Confusion as to the meaning of the words 'Design History' can arise because they are often used to refer to both the intellectual discipline and the object of study. Clarity can be maintained by using 'Design History' for the former and 'History of Design' for the latter.

● See also Association of Art Historians, Design Council, New Art History.

○ H Conway (ed) *Design History: a students' handbook* (Allen & Unwin, 1987).

○ V Margolin 'A decade of Design History in the United States 1977–87' *Journal of Design History* **1** (1) 1988 51–72.

○ J Walker *Design History and the history of design* (Pluto Press, 1989).

206 DESIGN METHODS

Following the success of the scientific methods of objective logical analysis, research and experiment in solving problems during the Second World War, many engineers, designers and architects came to believe that the application of rational, systematic methods of analysis and procedure could be equally effective in the field of design decision-making. A Design Methods Group (DMG) was founded at the Department of Architecture, University of California and it began a series of publications in 1966 which became ten years later the journal *Design Methods & Theories*. In Britain members of the Design Research Society (DRS), founded in 1967, also showed a keen interest in the question of methodology. The Design Methods movement gathered strength in the mid 1960s but then suffered a decline in the '70s as leading advocates such as Christopher Jones and Christopher

Alexander became disillusioned with them and reacted against their 'machine language and behaviourism'.

● See also Computer-Aided Design, Design Research Society.

● C Jones & D Thorley (eds) *Papers presented at the conference on systematic and intuitive methods in engineering, industrial design, architecture* (Oxford, Pergamon, 1963).

● L Archer *Systematic methods for designers* (Council of Industrial Design, 1965).

● S Gregory (ed) *The Design Method* (Butterworth, 1966).

● C Jones *Design Methods: seeds of human futures* (Wiley–Interscience, 1970).

● L Archer 'What ever became of design methodology?' *Design Studies* **1** (1) 1979 17–18.

● G Broadbent 'The development of Design Methods' *Design Methods & Theories* **13** (1) 1979 41–5.

● R Jacques & J Powell (eds) *Design: science: method* (Guildford, Surrey, IPC Press, 1981), proceedings of DRS conference Portsmouth December 1980.

207 DESIGN RESEARCH SOCIETY (DRS)

An organization founded in Britain in 1967 as a consequence of a conference on design methods held in London in 1962. Its international membership includes architects, designers and academics. The DRS is concerned with theoretical deliberations about design and is interdisciplinary in character. Its aims are to develop knowledge about design, to serve as a forum for communication, and to promote the improvement of design performance. It has organized many international conferences on such themes as design participation, design science/method and urban renewal; conference proceedings have been published. The DRS publishes the quarterly journal *Design Studies* and the newsletter *Design Research*. Since 1989 the DRS has been affiliated with the Chartered Society of Designers.

● See also Design Methods, Participatory Design.

208 DESIGN RESEARCH UNIT (DRU)

A British design office established in 1943 when its founding partners were in the Ministry of Information. The idea for DRU was originated by Marcus Brumwell, Milner Gray, Misha Black and Herbert Read; the last mentioned became its first director. DRU's function was to provide a practical service to industry in the form of advice, research and consultancy. The aim was to improve the quality of design in British products so that they could compete in the post-1945 world markets. Over the years the scope of its work has widened to include architecture, interior design, graphics, exhibitions and design for transport. DRU has undertaken projects in many parts of the world and its present directors continue to maintain the ideals of its founders in providing quality of service and excellence in design. Sir Misha Black died in 1977; an archive of his work is held by the Victoria & Albert Museum.

● See also Consultant Design, Corporate Design.

● J & A Blake *The practical idealists: twenty-five years of designing for industry* (Lund Humphries, 1969).

● A Blake *Misha Black* (Design Council, 1984).

● —*Milner Gray* (Design Council, 1986).

209 DESIGNERS & ART DIRECTORS ASSOCIATION (D&AD)

A London-based organization established in 1962 in order to promote creativity in the fields of advertising and graphic design by giving awards to the best work. D&AD organizes exhibitions and issues an annual volume reproducing the finest examples. Membership of the Association is restricted to those that have won awards and juries are dominated by D&AD members; as a consequence, the organization was accused in 1989 of being self-perpetuating, conservative in its taste, and neglectful of the work of young, radical designers.

● S Moss 'Style guru...' *Guardian* October 2 1989 21.

210 DESTRUCTIVE ART

(Also Auto-Creative and Destructive Art, DIAS) A variety of avant garde art which first appeared in Britain in the late 1950s. Then during the '60s it was manifested in both Europe and the United States. As its name suggests, this form of art was concerned with the issues of human destruction and violence: it took the issues as subject matter but it also employed destruction as an artistic technique in order to exemplify literally the point being made. The main artists involved were Tosun Bayrak, Günter Brus, John Latham, Gustav Metzger, Otto Mühl, Ralph Ortiz, Werner Schreib, Jean Tinguely, Jean Toche, Wolf Vostell. Some of these artists were concerned about the stockpiling of nuclear weapons, the ever-escalating violence of wars; they wanted to protest against these developments in a way that would shock, provoke debate, and challenge the affirmative, ornamental conception of art.

Tinguely specialized in self-destroying kinetic machines; Metzger, the author of a manifesto on 'Auto-Destructive Art' (1959), liked to spray acid on to sheets of nylon so that the work was simultaneously creative and destructive; Schreib drew images with fire ('pyrogravure'); Toche smashed typewriters; Latham built and then burnt/exploded 'skoob towers' ('skoob' equals 'books' spelt backwards); Bayrak staged events in the street involving blood and animal corpses. Most

DESTRUCTIVE ART Gustav Metzger 'Demonstration' (1961). London, South Bank. Photo: courtesy of the artist.

Destructive Art was time-based because witnessing the process of destruction was vital, and most of it took place in public so as to reach a wide audience. In fact, most actions and happenings of the '50s and '60s – especially the 'direct art' of the Austrians – contained a high proportion of aggression and destructive activity.

In 1966 Metzger and John Sharkey organized in London an international gathering of Destructive artists called 'The Destruction in Art Symposium' (DIAS). More than twenty artists from ten countries attended and the events they mounted created a furore in the press and led to prosecutions for 'indecent exhibitions'. The artists claimed that human aggression could be sublimated through Destructive Art. Critics did not agree. In their opinion the DIAS was 'perverse, ugly and anti-social'. A second DIAS was held in the United States in 1968. Although Destructive Art was necessarily short-lived and failed to achieve its political goals, it did influence artists of succeeding generations and destruction was incorporated into the repertoire of visual arts and rock music groups specializing in public performances.

● See also Actions, Direct Art, Happenings, Affiches Lacérées, Street Art, Time-Based Arts.

◌ G Metzger 'Machine, Auto-Creative and Auto-Destructive Art' *Ark* (32) Summer 1962 7–8.

◌ —*Auto-Destructive Art* (Destruction/Creation, 1965).

◌ (Issues on violence and destruction in art) *Art & Artists* **1** (5) August 1966; *Art & Artists* **1** (7) October 1966.

◌ 'Excerpts from selected papers presented at the 1966 Destruction in Art Symposium' *Studio International* **172** (884) December 1966 282–3.

◌ *Destruction in art: destroy to create* (NY, Finch College of Art, 1968).

◌ H McLaren 'Notes on discord: Einsturzende Neubaten and the destruction of structures' *Variant* (Glasgow) (4) Winter–Spring 1987-88 24–5.

DIA ART FOUNDATION

An American, non-profit-making organization founded by the art dealer Heiner Friedrich in 1974 (he resigned as vice-president in the mid '80s) for the purpose of promoting and exhibiting works of art that could not obtain sponsorship by virtue of their size or nature, e.g. very large sculptures, site-specific works and installations.

'Dia' is a Greek word signifying transition. Initially, financial support was provided by stock owned by Phillipa de Menil Pellizi. A collection of over 900 works was established and Dia acquired several premises in New York and elsewhere for administration, exhibitions and for the long-term display of installations by, for instance, Walter de Maria, Dan Flavin and John Chamberlain. Dia also funded a series of monuments in the desert of West Texas – the so-called 'Marfa Project' (350 acres, the Chinati Foundation, Marfa, 1988) – conceived and begun by the minimalist Donald Judd. After a financial and organizational crisis in the mid '80s Dia was reconstituted. Subsequently it supported a series of forums – 'Discussions in contemporary culture' – whose proceedings have been published.

● See also Earth & Land Art, Installation, Minimal Art, Site-Specific Art.

● P Hoban 'Medicis for a moment: the collapse of the DIA dream' *New York* November 25 1985 52–8.

● M Woodruff 'A DIA whose time has come' *New Art Examiner* **15** (4) December 1987 40–3.

DIAGRAMS

The word 'diagram' derives from a Greek term meaning 'to mark out in lines'. Diagrams are, therefore, linear devices which provide an outline or general scheme of an object, situation or process so as to exhibit selected relationships without depicting every surface detail. Fine distinctions can be made between charts, graphs, plans, tables, maps and Diagrams, but the latter word is often used as a blanket term; alternatively, some writers have proposed 'paragrams'.

Although Diagrams are chiefly employed by scientists, logicians and statisticians, they are also used by art and design historians, art critics, art educators, philosophers and psychologists of art, and by artists, architects and designers. During the late 1960s and '70s a significant increase took place in the use of Diagrams or diagrammatic graphic layouts by artists, particularly those associated with conceptual and behavioural art. This was probably due to the influence of such disciplines as cybernetics, linguistics and structuralism. Artists who have used Diagrams in various ways include: Joseph

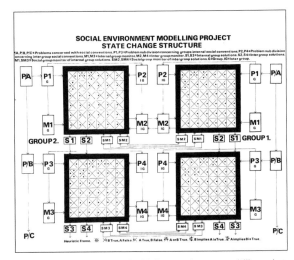

DIAGRAMS STEPHEN WILLATS, 'Social change environment modelling project, state change structure' (1973). 20" x 30". Photo: Willats.

Beuys, Daniel Buren, Victor Burgin, Lawrence Burt, John Hilliard, Joseph Kosuth, Ad Reinhardt, John Stezaker, Bernar Venet and Stephen Willats. One can also cite the use of diagrammatic layouts in tantra and yoga art, and in concrete poetry. An exhibition about the role of Diagrams in the discourse of art and art history, in tape-slide form, was presented by John A. Walker at The Gallery, London, in 1975.

Since most Diagrams contained a range of coding devices, including pictorial and linguistic ones, they were of particular interest to those artists who wanted to combine language and visual representation. By demonstrating the value of multiple coding systems, Diagrams were exemplary; they contradicted the formalist/modernist painting idea that each medium should strive for absolute purity. Diagrams perform utilitarian functions so effectively that their aesthetic quality and role in communication can easily be overlooked. A famous example of such a diagram is that for the London Underground system originally designed by Henry C. Beck in 1931.

● See also Behavioural Art, Conceptual Art, Formalism & Formalist Criticism, Information Graphics, Modernist Painting, Tantra Art.

● K Garland 'The design of the London Underground Diagram' *Penrose Annual* **62** 1969 68–82.

● A Lockwood *Diagrams: a visual survey of graphs, maps, charts and Diagrams for the graphic designer* (Studio Vista, 1969).

● J Bertin & others *La sémiologie graphique: les Diagrammes, les reseaux, les cartes* (The Hague/Paris, Mouton, 2nd ed 1973).

● W Herdeg *Graphis Diagrams: the graphic visualization of abstract data* (Zürich, Graphis Press, 1974).

● J Walker 'Diagrams: their relevance to art' *Control Magazine* (9) December 1975 18–20.

● K Albarn & J Smith *Diagram: the instrument of thought* (Thames & Hudson, 1977).

● J Walker 'The London Underground Diagram' *Icographic* (14/15) 1979 2–4.

213 DIASPORIST PAINTING

A term invented by the painter R. B. Kitaj to characterize his own work and that of any other 'displaced' artists whose art reflects the experience of living in 'exile' from their homelands. ('Diaspora' is a Greek word meaning 'scattering' or 'dispersion'; it has been applied particularly to the fate of the Jewish people.) Kitaj is a Jewish-American resident in London.

● R Kitaj *First Diasporist manifesto* (Thames & Hudson, 1989).

214 DIRECT ART

(Also Viennese Actionism) A group of Austrian artists – Otto Mühl, Hermann Nitsch and Günter Brus – called themselves at one point the 'Vienna Institute for Direct Art'. At first these artists produced violent action paintings and crude assemblages but they became dissatisfied with the secondary nature of painting and sculpture: they sought a form of expression that was more immediate and direct.

During the early 1960s they organized a series of 'actions' similar to the 'happenings' of New York that became notorious because of their brutal, sado-masochistic content involving nakedness, blood, and the destruction of animal corpses. The movement was also known as 'Wiener Aktionismus', the central idea of which was 'material action', i.e. the insistence that rituals and ceremonies be real – direct, literal events – not pretended events as in conventional drama. Nitsch's events took place under the rubric of 'Orgy Mystery Theatre' (O-M Theatre). The Italian critic Lea Vergine called their work 'Irritart' because it functioned as a social irritant.

Other artists who engaged in similar activities in the '60s were Alfons Schilling, Adolf Frohner, Rudolf Schwarzkogler (1940–69), Otmar Bauer, Arnulf Rainer (advocate of 'catatonic art') and Kurt Kren, an Austrian film-maker who documented the rituals of Brus and co. A retrospective exhibition of Actionism was held in Germany and Austria in 1988. It was also due to be shown in Edinburgh but was cancelled because, some suspected, it was considered too shocking for the people of Scotland.

● See also Actions, Body Art, Happenings, Performance Art.

● O Mühl *Mama & papa – materialaktion 63–69* (Frankfurt, Kohlkunst-Verlag, 1969).

DIRECT ART HERMANN NITSCH, 'Action 48' (1975). Photo: André Morain/ Galerie Stadler, Paris.

● H Nitsch *Orgien, mysterien theater* (Darmstadt, Maerz Verlag, 1969).

● G Brus (ed) *Die Schastromel nr 3* (Cologne, Interfunctionen, 1970).

● *Wien: bildkompendium Wiener Aktionismus und film* (Frankfurt, Kohlkunst-Verlag, 1970).

● P Weiermair 'New tendencies in Austrian art' *Studio International* **183** (944) May 1972 207–9.

● K Tsiakma 'Hermann Nitsch: a modern ritual' *Studio International* **192** (928) July–August 1976 13–15.

● D Schwarz & V Loers (eds) *Von der Aktionsmalerei zum Aktionismus Wien 1960–65, 1960–71* 2 vols (Klagenfurt, Ritter Verlag, 1988–89).

215 DISINFORMATION

'A technique of half-truths, bias editorialism and the deletion of pertinent information used by the printed and electronic media of Western democracies in order to create national opinion and consent' (Geno Rodriguez). Theme of an exhibition organized by Rodriguez held in New York in 1985 featuring works in a variety of media by Rudolf Baranik, Michael Corris, May Stevens, Leon Golub, Jerry Kearns and others designed 'to unmask the extent of Disinformation largely through satire and documentary exposure'(Baranik).

● See also Information, Political Art.

● *Disinformation: the manufacture of consent* (NY, Alternative Museum, 1985).

216 DISNEYANA

Walt Disney (1901–66) was, in the words of David Kunzle, 'the century's most important figure in bourgeois popular culture'. And although Disney is dead his empire persists via Walt Disney Productions, a multinational, multi-million dollar corporation, promoting Disney products and fantasy amusement parks throughout the world. Disney's cute anthropomorphized animal characters – Mickey Mouse, Donald Duck, Goofy, Pluto, etc. – live on in a variety of forms and media: comic strips, animated cartoons and feature films, TV programmes, collectibles of all kinds. A secondary income is derived from these animals via the licensing method known as 'character merchandising'.

Writings on the Disney phenomenon fall into three types: (1) uncritical celebrations of the man and his artistic achievements as head of a team of brilliant animators and as the visionary architect of artificial worlds like Epcot; (2) those taking a camp and connoisseurial interest in Disney products; (3) critical texts seeking to analyse and demystify the Disney myth and to expose the ideological/political role played by Disney products, particularly in developing countries.

A number of fine artists have made use of Disney characters in a critical manner. For instance, the British anti-war sculptor Michael Sandle employed the head of Mickey Mouse as an emblem of propaganda and dictatorship in several of his 1980s bronze pieces. Other artists have depicted Disney's cartoon creatures in a celebratory or satirical manner, e.g. Roy Lichtenstein, Claes Oldenburg, Andy Warhol, Colin Self, Markus Raetz, Keith Haring and Paul Blanca.

● See also Comic Art, Globalization, Kitsch, Popular Art.

● R Field *The art of Walt Disney* (Collins, 1944).

● D Miller *The story of Walt Disney* (NY, Holt, 1957).

● R Schickel *Walt Disney* (Weidenfeld & Nicolson, 1968).

● L Maltin *The Disney films* (NY, Crown, 1973).

● C Munsey *Disneyana: Walt Disney collectibles* (NY, Hawthorn Books, 1974).

● A Dorfman & A Mattelart *How to read Donald Duck: imperialist ideology in the Disney comic* (NY, International General, 1975).

● C Finch *The art of Walt Disney: from Mickey Mouse to the magic kingdoms* (NY, Abrams, 1975).

● B Thomas *The Walt Disney biography* (NEL/Times Mirror, 1977).

● D Walker (ed) 'Animated architecture' *Architectural Design* **52** (9/10) October 1982.

● A Bailey *Walt Disney, world of fantasy* (Dragons World, 1982).

● *Walt Disney's Epcot* (NY, Abrams, 1982).

● J Taylor *Storming the magic kingdom* (NY, Viking, 1988).

● R Hollis & B Sibley *The Disney Studio story* (Octopus, 1989).

● R Grover *The Disney Touch* (Business One Irwin, 1991).

217 DISSIDENTS

Name given by Gaston Diehl to a group of Venezuelan artists whose abstractions provoked a scandal in Caracas in 1949. The best-known member of the Dissidents was the painter and sculptor Alejandro Otero who had visited Paris in 1945. When Otero returned to Paris in 1949 he and others began publication of a magazine – *Revista Los Disidentes* (5 issues, 1950) – attacking the conservativism of Venezuelan culture.

● See also Latin American Art.

● *Alejandro Otero: a retrospective exhibition* (Austin, University of Texas, 1975).

218 DIY

(Do-It-Yourself) A form of popular or anonymous design and craft. Although DIY occurred before 1945, a massive expansion took place in the activities of home decorating, repairs, alterations and conversions during the affluent years of the late 1950s and '60s. Such tasks were undertaken, for reasons of cheapness and pleasure, by ordinary householders rather than by professional tradesmen.

To cater for the increase in demand for tools (especially folding work-benches, blowtorches, electric power drills, saws and sanders) and materials (especially plywood, ceramic tiles, emulsion paints, and plastics) a multi-million-pound manufacturing and retail trade developed which now takes the form of huge self-service superstores. Since DIY enthusiasts also required technical advice, there was a comparable growth in DIY magazines, exhibitions and TV programmes. David Johnson launched *Do-It-Yourself* magazine in Britain in March 1957.

DIY even extends to architecture: some extremely ambitious DIY enthusiasts – individuals and co-operatives – have built their own homes.

● See also Anonymous Design, Hobby Art, Popular Art.

● D Johnson 'The history and development of Do-It-Yourself'

– in – *Leisure in the twentieth century* (Design Council, 1977) 68–71 (Proceedings of the 1976 Design History Society Conference); see also C Brooks 'The amateur mechanic and the modern movement' 24–31.

● S Wood 'Hand-built homes' *Sunday Times Magazine* October 23 1983 120–4.

219 DOCKLANDS

A huge area of land east of Tower Bridge adjoining the River Thames and encompassing the old docks, quays and warehouses of the Port of London. For decades this zone near the City of London (an international financial centre) declined due to the containerization of shipping and the lack of finance for new industry and housing available to local government authorities. Then, in 1981, the Conservative Government under Mrs Thatcher declared Docklands an enterprise zone and suspended normal planning regulations. The London Docklands Development Corporation (LDDC) was formed to revamp the area. A frenzy of new construction ensued: a light railway and an airport were built, Victorian warehouses were converted into shops, flats and a Design Museum, and a plethora of new offices, shops, hotels, houses and factories were started. One new development – Canary Wharf, Isle of Dogs – has been described as the largest commercial building scheme in Europe; the architect of the monumental complex of buildings (which includes a tower block 800ft high) was the American Cesar Pelli. Jonathan Glancey summed up the look of this project as: 'a mini-Manhattan or Chicago skyline characterized by weighty neo-Edwardian and Art Deco style palazzi'.

Since the buildings of the area were by different architects who employed a variety of styles, materials, shapes and sizes, Docklands rapidly became a post-modernist jumble. In the view of many, the design of some buildings was execrable ('disposable architecture'); however, two examples were highly rated by architectural critics: John Outram's colourful, ornamental, post-modern style Pumping Station, Blackwall (1988) and Nicholas Grimshaw's high-tech, metal-and-glass, *Financial Times*' Printing Works, Isle of Dogs (1988).

Given the private property free-for-all, Docklands as a whole lacked a sense of coherence; it was also without an adequate road and public transport network; as a result, many observers considered it to be a planning and architectural disaster. Local people too were resentful because the commercial developments provided little in the way of jobs and housing for them. Even Prince Charles thought the new Docklands a 'triumph of commercial expediency over civic values'.

From 1982 the community artists Peter Dunn and Loraine Leeson were involved in a billboard campaign of criticism known as the Docklands Community Poster Project.

● See also Billboard Art, Community Art & Media, English Extremists, High-Tech, Post-Modern Architecture.

● P Burton 'LDDC – a new broom' *Town & Country Planning* **51** May 1982 124–6.

● N Broackes 'The regeneration of London's Docklands' *Royal Society of Arts Journal* **132** January 1984 105–17.

● 'London Docklands: a special report' *The Times* April 19 1985 15–20; November 18 1986 16–21.

● 'Docklands in the dock' (special issue) *Architects Journal* September 25 1985.

● R Foss 'Docklands: the art of struggle' *Fires* (3) 1987 35–8.

● *Docklands heritage: conservation and regeneration in London's Docklands* (LDDC, 1987).

● A Derbyshire 'Entering the enterprise zone' *RIBA Journal* March 1989 38–41.

● 'Docklands developments' *Architectural Review* **185** (1106) April 1989, thematic issue.

● J Glancey *New British architecture* (Thames & Hudson, 1989).

● J Bird 'Report from London: Dystopia on the Thames' *Art in America* **78** (7) July 1990 89–97.

● S Al Naib *London Docklands: past, present & future* (Polytechnic of East London, 1990).

220 DOCUMENTA

Title of a mammoth, international exhibition 'documenting' a cross-section of contemporary avant garde art held every four to five years in the summer months at Kassel, Germany, since 1955. Professor Arnold Bode was the 'father' of the idea and the exhibition was instituted by the Gesellschaft für Abendlandsische Kunst (Society for Western Art). Documenta exhibitions have often been organized on a thematic basis, for example, in 1972 the theme was 'questioning reality', in 1977 'art and media', and in 1987 'art and society'. Each exhibition is normally accompanied by a massive catalogue and is reviewed in detail by leading art magazines. Not everyone is convinced that such a huge exhibition is good for art.

In a critical article René Denizot claimed that Documenta 5 was exemplary because it revealed 'the supremacy of the gallery as an institution, an iron collar from which art could never be set free'.

● R Denizot 'Exposition of an exhibition: a backward look at Documenta 5' *Studio International* **185** (953) March 1973 98–9.

● R Cork 'What does Documenta document?' *Studio Interna-*

DOCUMENTA A view of the Fridericianum, Kassel, with STEPHEN ANTONAKOS's 'Incomplete Square' on the corner of the building (l) and RICHARD SERRA's steel sculpture (r), Documenta VI (1977).

tional **194** (988) January 1978 37–47.

● *Documenta 8* (3 vols) (Kassel, Weber & Weidmeyer, 1987).

● I Rogoff 'Barricades into blockades: Documenta 8 and the spirit of '68' *Art History* **12** (2) June 1989 240–6.

221 DRIFTWOOD AESTHETIC/ SCULPTURE

During the 1950s a vogue developed for collecting driftwood and other found objects from the beach. The suggestive forms, textures and colours of such weathered objects have stimulated the imaginations of many modern artists. Margaret Mellis (b 1914), a distinguished British artist, has specialized in constructing reliefs from driftwood found on the beaches of Suffolk since the mid 1970s. Making sculptures from driftwood is also an amateur craft.

● See also Assemblage Art.

● D Bourdon 'The Driftwood Aesthetic' *Art Journal* **25** (1) Fall 1965 26–32.

● R Lumb *The magic and making of Driftwood Sculptures* (Tunbridge Wells, Kent, Midas Books, 1983).

● J Spalding *Margaret Mellis retrospective 1940-87* (Redfern Gallery, 1987).

● E Kendall 'Room of my own: Margaret Mellis' *Observer Magazine* June 9 1991 62-3.

222 DRIP PAINTING

Although several artists have been credited with the invention of this technique, it is primarily associated with the late 1940s and early '50s work of the American abstract expressionist Jackson Pollock. (In 1956 *Time* magazine dubbed him 'Jack the dripper'.) Unstretched canvas was laid on the floor of his barn studio. Pollock then worked around it pouring and flinging skeins of liquid oil and household paints from cans with the aid of brushes and sticks. Some cans had holes in them so that paint could dribble out. Drawing and painting, line and colour, were thus compressed into a single action. Critics used the phrase 'energy made visible'. Pollock's method of painting was made famous by the photographs and films Hans Namuth made in the '50s. Such images foregrounded the performance and processes of the artist and hence were influential in terms of performance and process art. The scholar Francis O'Connor has argued that close analysis of the photos and films shows that the word 'dripping' is an inaccurate description of Pollock's technique; O'Connor prefers 'pouring'.

● See also Abstract Expressionism, Action Painting, Performance Art, Process Art, Stain Painting, Tachisme.

● R Goodnough 'Pollock paints a picture' *Art News* (3) May 1951 38–41.

● F O'Connor 'Hans Namuth's photographs of Jackson Pollock as art historical documentation' *Art Journal* **39** (1) Fall

1979 48–9.

D Elliott & B Rose *Jackson Pollock: drawing into painting* (Oxford, MoMA, 1979).

H Namuth *Pollock painting* B Rose (ed) (NY, Agrinde Publications, 1980).

223 DÜSSELDORF SCHOOL

After 1960 Düsseldorf became an important international art centre where German and other European artists continued the tradition of experimentation established by Group Zero. The best known of these artists were Dieter Rot and Joseph Beuys (1921–86). During the '60s Beuys taught at the Düsseldorf KunstAkademie where his radical education policies eventually resulted in a confrontation with the authorities. Richard Demarco organized a large-scale exhibition of the Düsseldorf School in Edinburgh in 1970 and its history was reviewed again in a show held in Düsseldorf itself in 1987. By the end of the '80s some critics considered that Cologne had replaced Düsseldorf as Europe's art capital.

● See also Zero.

Strategy: get arts (Edinburgh, Richard Demarco Gallery/Edinburgh School of Art, 1970).

Brennpunkt Düsseldorf 1962–87 (Düsseldorf, Kunstmuseum, 1987).

224 DUTCH STRUCTURALISTS

(Also Dutch School) A description applied by architectural critics to several Dutch architects, most notably Aldo van Eyck, Piet Blom and Herman Hertzberger (the latter's work has also been called 'musical architecture' because he designed buildings as instruments for users to play). Their architecture of the 1960s and '70s was related in part to the de Stijl movement of the 1920s. The use of the word 'structuralism' reflected the influence of the anthropological theories of Claude Lévi-Strauss and referred to the expression of space and structure together. In practice these architects rejected the massive, monolithic blocks typical of so much modern architecture and designed instead areas of housing, shops and offices consisting of labyrinths of small space cells, or autonomous but related units that added up to complex wholes. Hertzberger also advocated co-determination in architecture, i.e. inhabitants were encouraged to complete his buildings' interiors. The theories of the Dutch Structuralists were made public via the magazine *Forum* issued by van Eyck.

● See also Participatory Design, Structuralism & Art/Design.

'Herman Hertzberger: musical architecture' *Architects Journal* **163** (14) April 7 1976 67–78.

A Luchinger 'Dutch Structuralism' *A & U (Architecture and Urbanism, Tokyo*) (75) March 1977 47–65.

'*Forum* fellowship' *Architectural Review* **187** January 1990 30–97.

225 DVIZHENIE

(Also Group Dvizhenie, Moscow Kineticists) The name of a group of Soviet experimental, constructivist and kinetic artists led by Lev Nusberg founded in 1962. In Russian the word 'Dvizhenie' (which is spelled a dozen different ways in the West) means 'movement'. The group numbered around 20 people (who came from various disciplines) and undertook a number of public commissions in the USSR including a kinetic wall structure and ceiling for a stadium in Leningrad and multimedia performances involving projected light, music and film images. Their work was one of the few manifestations of contemporary Soviet art which received attention in the West during the 1960s and '70s.

● See also Constructivism, Experimental Art, Kinetic Art, Technological Art, Unofficial Soviet Art.

D Konecny 'Moscow Kineticists' *Studio International* **172** (880) August 1966 90–2.

L Nusberg 'What is kineticism?' *Form* (UK) (4) April 15 1967 19–22.

'A kinetic performance in Leningrad' *Studio International* **174** (895) December 1967 287.

Dvijenie catalogue (Nurenberg Biennale, 1969).

A Pohribny 'Art and artists of the underground' *Problems of Communism* (19) March–April 1970 26–34.

P Restany 'L'humanisme technologique en USSR: Lev Nusberg et le Groupe Dvizhenie' *Domus* (524) July 1973 52–4.

226 DYMAXION

This word is a combination of 'dynamism', 'maximum' and 'ion'. It was coined in 1929 by two public relations men working for Marshal Fields, the Chicago department store, to describe a futuristic house, created by the visionary designer R Buckminster Fuller (1895–1983), displayed in the store as a setting for new furniture. They invented the word after a close study of Fuller's writings and vocabulary. Subsequently, Fuller often employed the word: Dymaxion car, Dymaxion bathroom, Dymaxion chronofile, etc. He meant by it: maximum efficiency and performance in terms of available technology.

● See also Synergetics.

R Marks *The Dymaxion world of Buckminster Fuller* (Carbondale & Edwardsville, Southern Illinois University Press, 1960).

227   **EARTH &**
EARTHWORK
ARCHITECTURE

(Also Mud Architecture)
Many tribal peoples con-
struct dwellings from earth
or mud. In the late 1960s the
German architect Engelbert Kremser proposed to make
buildings by applying concrete to mounds of soil serving
as formworks. Once the concrete had set, the earth could
be removed leaving cave-like structures which would,
according to Kremser, 'reinstate the almost forgotten
relationship between architecture and sculpture'.

● See also Utopian Architecture.

◉ 'Earthwork Architecture' *Architectural Review* **145** (866)
April 1969 241–3.

◉ R Hobbs (ed) 'Earthworks: past and present' *Art Journal* **42**
(3) Fall 1982, thematic issue.

◉ J Dethier *Down to earth: Mud Architecture* (Thames & Hudson, 1983).

228   **EARTH &**
LAND ART

(Also Dirt Art, Earthworks,
Field Art, Site Art, Terrestrial Art, Topological Art) An
international tendency with-
in Western avant garde art dating from the mid 1960s,
developing out of minimal art and having close relations
with arte povera and conceptual art. Artists associated
with this tendency included Carl Andre, Walter de
Maria, Jan Dibbets, Hamish Fulton, Michael Heizer, Sol
Lewitt, Robert Morris, Neil Jenny, Richard Long, Dennis Oppenheim and Robert Smithson. Earth artists left
the urban environment and went into the countryside,
deserts and wild regions of the world. They rejected the
conventional materials and methods of sculpture in
favour of natural materials such as rocks, soil, branches,
turf and snow. They began by dumping quantities of
these materials on to the floors of galleries, then they dug
into the earth's crust creating holes and trenches which

EARTH & LAND ART RICHARD LONG, 'England' (1968). Photo: Long.

Andre called 'negative sculptures'. Later on, earth-moving equipment and dynamite were used to construct grandiose monuments reminiscent of prehistoric earthworks. Earth and Land artists shared an interest with members of the underground subculture of the '60s in ancient barrows, Stonehenge, ley lines, and the mysterious Nazca lines of the Peruvian desert. Earth Art was also called 'the new picturesque' because of its affinities with the eighteenth-century vogue for landscape gardening.

The introduction of the term 'Land Art' indicated a shift away from the sculptural emphasis on materials, toward a more pictorial attitude, i.e. simple patterns and motifs such as crosses were 'drawn' on the ground by walking through grass or scraping away snow. Some works could only be seen to best advantage from an aircraft. The term 'Field Art' applied to works situated in farming areas where an artist had directed the harvesting of crops or controlled the layout of crop seeding. In the case of Long and Fulton, there was a performance element in the sense that long walks and cycle rides were undertaken and these were recorded photographically. In Dibbets' case the role of photography was even more vital because the shapes he cut in grass revealed peculiar optical illusions when photographed from specific viewpoints. Sets of photographs were published in book form or displayed in galleries and offered for sale. As in conceptual art, documentation became crucial because so many examples of Earth and Land Art were executed in remote places far from urban centres. This kind of art did not, however, escape the city and the art system altogether – the artists were still dependent on the artworld, dealers and patrons. Even so, a dialectic was established between town and country, culture and nature.

● See also Arte Povera, Conceptual Art, Ecological Art, Environmental Art, Performance Art, SITE, Site-Specific Art.

● P Hutchinson 'Earth in upheaval: Earthworks and landscapes' *Arts Magazine* **43** (2) November 1968 19–21.

● S Tillim 'Earthworks and the new picturesque' *Artforum* **7** (4) December 1968 42–5.

● M Reiche *Mystery of the desert* (Stuttgart, Vaihinger, 1968).

● *Earth Art* (Ithaca, Andrew Dickson White Museum, 1969).

● (Land Art: several photo essays) *Avalanche* (1) Fall 1970.

● 'Land Art/Earthworks' *Interfunctionen* (7) September 1971 46–59.

● D Hickey 'Earthscapes, landworks and Oz' *Art in America* **59** (5) September–October 1971 40–9.

● R Morris 'Aligned with Nazca' *Artforum* **14** (2) October 1975 26–39.

● E Baker 'Artworks on the land' *Art in America* **64** (1) January–February 1976 92–6.

● *Probing the earth: contemporary land projects* (Washington, Hirshhorn Museum & Sculpture Garden, 1977).

● R Smithson *The writings of Robert Smithson* N Holt (ed) (NY, New York University Press, 1979).

● R Hobbs (ed) 'Earthworks: past and present' *Art Journal* **42** (3) Fall 1982, thematic issue.

● R Hobbs & others *Robert Smithson: sculpture* (Ithaca & London, Cornell University Press, 1982).

● R Araeen 'Long walks around the world' *Art Monthly* (69) September 1983 25–6.

● L Lippard *Overlay: contemporary art and the art of prehistory* (NY, Pantheon Books, 1983).

● A Sonfist (ed) *Art in the land. A critical anthology of environmental art* (NY, Dutton, 1983).

● P Harlice *Earth-scale art: a bibliography, directory of artists & index of reproductions* (Jefferson, North Carolina/London, McFarland & Co, 1984).

● R Fuchs *Richard Long* (NY, Guggenheim Museum/London, Thames & Hudson, 1986).

229 EAST VILLAGE ART

The East Village is a district of Manhattan, New York City which was once poverty stricken and run-down but which was subject to gentrification in the early 1980s, partly as a consequence of artists and art galleries moving in. (Art and artists often function as a kind of unwitting advance guard of property redevelopment and urban renewal but by the end of the process poor people have been displaced, artists find they cannot afford the higher rents and the original 'bohemian' atmosphere of the district has been destroyed.) The expression 'East Village Art' has been used to describe the kind of work produced by artists exhibiting in the 30 or more East Village galleries or stores. Some of the best known were: Fun Gallery, Deborah Sharpe, Pat Hearn, Civilian Warfare, Virtual Garrison, and PPOW.

In 1981 the East Village became fashionable as a result of a vogue for graffiti art: Jean-Michel Basquiat, Futura 2000, Keith Haring, Kenny Scharf and others. As more art stores opened, works by a younger generation of artists made reference to pop, surrealism and German expressionism. The art was typified by energy, primitivism, wit, parody and, in the eyes of some critics, extremely poor quality. While the aim of the East Village scene was to market art, the commercial process was often mocked in the process.

● See also Alternative Spaces, Graffiti, New York School, SoHo.

● R Hughes 'Careerism and hype amidst the image haze' *Time* June 17 1985 46–51.

● C Roberts 'East Village Art/East Village artstores' *Artscribe* (54) September–October 1985 51–5.

● *The East Village scene* (Philadelphia, ICA, Pennsylvania University, 1985).

Neo-New York (Santa Barbara, California, University Art Museum, 1985).

R Deutsche & C Ryan 'The fine art of gentrification' – in – *October: the first decade 1976–86* A Michelson & others (eds)(Cambridge, Mass, MIT Press, 1987) 151–71.

230 EAT

(Experiments in Art & Technology) In the autumn of 1966 a festival of art and technology entitled 'Nine evenings: theatre and engineering' was held in New York as a result of which the organization EAT was founded in January 1967. Its director was Billy Kluver (of Bell Telephone Laboratories) and its members included Robert Rauschenberg, Gyorgy Kepes, John Cage and R. Buckminster Fuller. EAT's aim was to foster co-operation between artists and technologists by matching their interests and specialities. An exhibition of works by members of EAT called 'Some more beginnings' was held at the Brooklyn Museum in 1969. It included computer-generated films, kinetic art, 'liquid' sculpture and psychedelic environments.

● See also Kinetic Art, Psychedelic Art, Technological Art.

EAT News **1** (1) 1967.

J Reichardt 'EAT and after' *Studio International* **175** (900) May 1968 236–7.

B Kluver 'EAT' *Metro* (14) June 1968 55–8.

'Experiments in Art & Technology (EAT), New York' *Leonardo* **1** (4) October 1968 487–8.

A Herve 'Eating into art' *Réalités* (225) August 1969 52–5.

G Youngblood 'The open empire' *Studio International* **179** (921) April 1970 177–8.

EAT *Pavilions* (NY, Dutton, 1973).

231 ECOLOGICAL ARCHITECTURE

In response to the problems of expensive fuels and dwindling world energy resources various research projects have been undertaken since 1970, in Europe and North America, to construct self-sufficient, self-servicing houses. The aim has been to design a house largely, but not totally, independent of public mains supplies by exploiting ambient energy sources – solar radiation, wind power – and by recycling techniques – using rainwater, human waste to produce gas for cooking or as a fertilizer. The projects included Graham Caine's 'Ecological house' which he built in South London, the 'Autonomous house' built by Jaap t'Hooft at De Kleine Aarde in Holland, and the 'Autarchic house' research project undertaken at Cambridge by Alexander Pike. The latter concentrated on theoretical problems in order to establish principles for realistic production techniques.

● See also Arcology, Green Design.

G Leach 'Living off the sun in South London' *Observer* August 27 1972 1–2.

G Caine 'A revolutionary structure' *Oz* (45) November 1972 12–13.

A Pike 'Autonomous house' *Architectural Design* **44** (11) 1974 681–9.

T Osman 'Dome sweet dome' *Sunday Times Magazine* November 30 1975 68–75.

A Tucker 'Brave new Autarchic house' *Guardian* December 30 1975 6.

A Pike 'The Cambridge Autarchic house' – in – *Architecture: opportunities, achievements* B Goldstein (ed) (RIBA, 1977) 49–52.

232 ECOLOGICAL ART

(Also Bio-Kinetic Art, Eco Art, Ecologic Art, Environmental Art, Systems Art, Thermostat Art) The health of the world's ecological system became a matter of concern during the 1960s with the result that late in the decade a number of artists began to produce work with an ecological dimension, e.g. Luis F. Benedit, Hans Haacke, Peter Hutchinson, Robert Irwin, David Medalla, Newton Harrison, Dennis Oppenheim, Charles Ross, Alan Sonfist, Takis and John van Saun. (The first use of the term 'Ecological Art' was by the critic Herb Aach in 1968.) Precedents for it were found in certain works by Marcel Duchamp and Yves Klein, i.e. those employing the weather as a means of creation.

This kind of art made use of natural forces and chemical or biological, cyclical processes. It involved such disparate elements as fire, the wind, water, crystals, worms, locusts, bees, snails, fungus and such activities as planting crops and farming fish. Eco Art 'worked' in a literal way because artists created open systems that interacted with nature. Some artists created works in unusual environments, e.g. in 1969 Hutchinson and Oppenheim devised works in the sea off the coast of Tobago in the West Indies. Art magazines labelled them 'oceanographic art', and 'underwater' or 'scuba sculpture'. When artists used the four elements of nature, a link with alchemy was implied. Alchemy and the occult also became fashionable in the '60s. Historians discovered the extent of Duchamp's and Klein's interest in alchemy and the artists Haacke, van Saun, Takis and Ross were dubbed 'the new alchemists' because they isolated and made visible 'the elements, systems and forces around which the phenomenal world coheres'.

Ecological artists wanted to raise the public's awareness of ecological issues by displaying microcosmic models of macrocosmic phenomena. However, this strategy sometimes backfired: protests were mounted at

the Hayward Gallery in 1971 when it was proposed to kill and eat catfish grown in a fish farm being presented as a work of art by the American artist Newton Harrison.
● See also Air Art, Environmental Art, Green Design, Robot Art, Systems Art.

● *Ecologic Art* (NY, John Gibson Gallery, 1969).
● A Robbin 'Peter Hutchinson's Ecological Art' *Art International* **14** (2) February 1970 52–5.
● 'Art & ecology' *ArtsCanada* **27** (4) August 1970, special issue.
● *Earth, air, fire, water: elements of art* 2 vols (Boston, Museum of Fine Arts, 1971).
● D Young 'The new alchemists' *Art & Artists* **5** (11) February 1971 46–9.
● C Nemser 'The alchemist and the phenomenologist' *Art in America* **59** (2) March–April 1971 100–3.
● F Arnold 'Art: Alan Sonfist' *New Scientist* August 5 1971 336–7.
● J Benthall 'Sonfist's art' (letter) *New Scientist* August 12 1971 389.
● —'Art & ecology'– in – *Science & technology in art today* (Thames & Hudson, 1972) 126–41.
● G Kepes (ed) *Arts of the environment* (Aiden Ellis, 1972).
● *Écologie Écologisme* (Lausanne, Institut d'Étude et de Recherche en Information Visuelle, 1975).
● E Fry *Projects in nature* (Far Hill, New Jersey, Merriewold West Inc, 1975).
● E Heartney 'Eco-logic' *Sculpture* **9** (2) March–April 1990 36–41.
● R Cembalest 'The Ecological Art explosion' *Art News* 90 (6) Summer 1991 96-105.

233 EKISTICS A neologism coined from several Greek words meaning 'home', 'settlement' and 'settling down'. It was devised by the Greek architect and planner Constantinos A. Doxiadis (1913–75) towards the end of the Second World War, to designate a new field of knowledge: the science of human settlements. Ekistics collates information from many different disciplines, e.g. economics, social sciences, history, anthropology, technology, city and regional planning. It also seeks to employ systematic, mathematical and scientific techniques in applying this knowledge. Doxiadis became president of the Athens Centre for Ekistics founded in 1963; it began publication of a journal *Ekistics*. A World Society for Ekistics was established in London in 1965.
● See also Design Methods, Environmental Design, Urbanism.

● C Doxiadis *Ekistics: an introduction to the science of human settlements* (Hutchinson, 1968).
● J Papaioannou 'C A Doxiadis' early career and the birth of Ekistics' *Ekistics* **41** June 1976 313–19.
● C Doxiadis *Ecology and Ekistics* (Paul Elek, 1977).

234 EL PASO (The Step or Passage) A Spanish association of writers and visual artists active in Madrid between 1957 and '60. The best- known artist-members were Rafael Canogar, Luis Feitó, Manuel Millares and Antonio Saura. After being influenced by surrealism these artists began to produce paintings that were abstract or semi-abstract, executed with thick impasto and expressionistic gestures. The work contributed to the international tendencies called l'art informel and tachisme. Examples are preserved in the Museum of Abstract Art, Cuenca, Spain.
● See also Art Informel, Dau Al Set, Tachisme.

● *Grupo El Paso* (Madrid, Libreria Buchholz, 1957).
● F O'Hara *New Spanish painting and sculpture* (NY, MoMA, 1960).
● *Aspectos de una decada: pintura Española 1955–65* (Madrid, Sala de Exposiciónes de la Fundación Caja de Pensiónes, 1988).

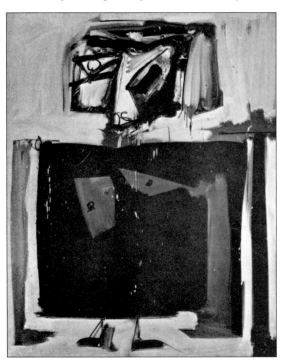

EL PASO Antonio Saura, 'The clergyman' (1960). Oil on canvas. 64" x 51". Photo: Marlborough Gallery, London.

235 ELECTROGRAPHIC ARCHITECTURE (Also Electric Art, Electronic Signage, Illuminations, Neon Signs) An expression devised by the American writer Tom Wolfe to describe the large-scale, electric light advertising signs found in the United States, especially in places like Las Vegas and Los Angeles. Electrographics were not simply lettering but pictures or representational sculptures; they were programmed to change over time and so presented a pulsating, colourful, hypnotic visual spectacle. In some instances they were designed to be 'read' from moving automobiles. According to Wolfe, the creations of anonymous commercial artists were 'wild, baroque' and expressed a 'new age of motion and mass wealth'. In Britain a similar popular culture phenomenon are the 'Illuminations' which seaside resorts such as Blackpool organize in order to attract visitors out of season.

Fine artists are increasingly using electronic signs as a form of public art. The American artist Jenny Holzer, for instance, employs Spectacolor (commercial advertising) screens to display a stream of bizarre slogans and messages. A major presentation of her work was one of the highlights of the 1990 Venice Biennale.

● See also Billboard Art, Electronic Art, Hi-Way Culture, Light Art, Public Art.

▨ T Wolfe 'Electrographic Architecture' *Architectural Design* **39** (7) July 1969 379–82.

▨ M Proulx *Electric Art* (NY, Rizzoli, 1977).

▨ J Simon *Jenny Holzer: Signs* (Iowa, Des Moines Arts Center, 1986).

▨ R Stern *The new Let there be Neon* (NY, Abrams, rev ed 1988).

▨ F Sweet 'Bright lights, big city' *Design* (499) July 1990 15–18.

236 ELECTRONIC ART (Also Arts Électroniques, Ars Electronica) A variety of kinetic art. An electron is an elementary particle which is a constituent of all atoms. Oscilloscopes contain electron guns which fire streams of electrons at screens coated with fluorescent material which glow when struck. In this way visual patterns can be produced and these in turn can be recorded on film or videotape. The term 'Electronic Art' has been applied to works produced by artists using such technology. Ben F. Laposky, for instance, worked with such devices from 1950 and called his pieces 'oscillons' or 'electronic abstractions'. Since television pictures are produced via electrons, the term has also been applied to artists such as Nam June Paik who employ multiple TV sets.

Any artwork making use of electricity, such as neon sculpture, tends to be designated 'Electric Art' and grouped together with 'Electronic Art' for the purposes of museum display.

Ronald Pellegrino, director of Electronic Arts Productions and author of a book on the Electronic Arts of sound and light, includes in this category electronic music, computer graphics, videographics, lasergraphics, electronically generated film graphics and laser light forms. A list of separate types does not do justice to this kind of work because it is generally multi-media in character, i.e. it combines sounds and light, music and images. Electronic artists experiment with advanced technology. They generate works which are dynamic rather than static – real-time, ephemeral pieces based on energy and wave forms. Such displays are often environmental and interactive; they involve collaborative production and audience participation.

Festivals of Electronic Art have become increasingly popular in recent years; for instance, they have been held in Rennes (France), Linz (Austria) and Montreal (Canada). In Holland an International Symposium on Electronic Art has been organized by the Groningen Polytechnic and the National Institute for Computer Animation. The second such symposium – SISEA – took place in November 1990.

● See also Computer Art, Expanded Cinema, Kinetic Art, Laser Art, Light Art, Participatory Art, Sound Art, Technological Art, Telematics, USCO, Video Art.

▨ *Electric art* (Los Angeles, California University, 1969).

▨ *Electronic Art: elektronische und elektrische Objekte und Environments, neon Objekte* (Düsseldorf, Verlag Kalender, 1969).

▨ R Pellegrino *The Electronic Arts of sound and light* (NY, Van Nostrand Reinhold, 1983).

▨ (Special issue on Electronic Arts) *Leonardo* **21** (4) September 1988.

▨ C Delalande (ed) *Festival des Arts Électroniques* (Rennes, Le Grand Huit, 1988).

▨ G Hattinger & P Weibel (eds) *Ars Électronica: the merging of different artistic disciplines related to the scene* (Linz, Brucknerhaus, 1988).

▨ M Eisenbeis & H Hagebölling (eds) *Synthesis: visual arts in the electronic culture* (Offenbach am Main, Hochschule für Gestaltung, 1989).

237 ENGLISH EXTREMISTS A term applied to a team of English post-modern architects exhibiting plans and photographs at the Heinz Gallery, Royal Institute of British Architects in 1988. The group – CZWG (Nick Campbell, Roger Zoglovitch, Rex Wilkinson and Piers Gough) – were extreme in their historical appropriations and references, and in their extravagant mix of styles. They trained at the Architectural Association in the 1960s and undertook boutique commissions late in the decade. Their practice – CZWG – was formed officially in 1977. (It employs over 30 workers; Zoglovitch has now left the team.) One of their

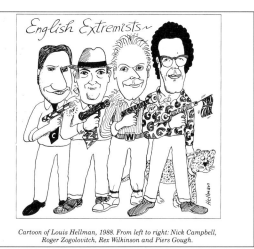

Cartoon of Louis Hellman, 1988. From left to right: Nick Campbell,
Roger Zogolovitch, Rex Wilkinson and Piers Gough.

ENGLISH EXTREMISTS Louis Hellman, 'Cartoon of the English Extremists'
(1988). From left to right: Nick Campbell, Roger Zogolovitch, Rex Wilkinson
and Piers Gough.

best-known achievements is the house of the TV personality Janet Street-Porter. Some newspaper critics disliked
the irreverence and wit of their designs and described one
of their developments – 'Cascades', a tower-block in
London's Docklands – as 'visual chaos...crazy jumble...grotesque and shapeless...Pop Art building'. Gough

ENGLISH EXTREMISTS CZWG 'Cascades' (1988). Docklands, London.
Photo: Roderick Coyne.

himself characterized some of their output as 'B-movie
architecture'.

● See also Pop Architecture, Post-Modern Architecture.

◉ D Sudjic, J Meade & P Cook *English Extremists: the architecture of Campbell, Zoglovitch, Wilkinson and Gough*
(Blueprint/Fourth Estate, 1988).

◉ K Wright 'Architecture: English eclecticism' *Modern
Painters* **2** (4) Winter 1989–90 56–61.

238 ENGLISH STYLE Title of a book with photographs by Ken Kirkwood
about examples of interior
design and decoration in
England and North America purporting to share certain
national characteristics. Although the term was singular,
English Style was said to be diverse. It was also said to be
a synthesis of the old and new, a mix of the comfortable
and the eccentric, understated, liveable, emphasizing
permanence and quality. Apparently, English Style
(which is not, one presumes, the same as British style)
was to be found in thatched cottages as well as in country
houses. And since examples occurred in the United
States it was also an exportable style.

A sub-genre of English Style is the English Country
Style. This is a style particularly associated with the work
of the firm Colefax & Fowler.

◉ S Slesin & S Cliff *English Style* (Thames & Hudson, 1984).

◉ E Dickson *Colefax & Fowler: the best in English interior
decoration* (Barrie & Jenkins, 1989).

239 ENTROPY & ART Entropy is a controversial
and puzzling scientific con-
cept dating from the nineteenth century. It is generally
defined as a quantitative measure of the degree of disorder in a system. Given that in natural processes an
increase in entropy occurs, it has seemed to some
observers that the universe is progressively tending
towards a state of disorder known as maximum entropy.
In 1971 the psychologist and aesthetician Rudolf Arnheim examined the discrepancy between nature's
alleged drive towards chaos and the artist's drive towards
order. His book provoked a series of articles in *Leonardo*
in 1973 by both artists and scientists in which Arnheim
was accused of misapplying the concept. The American
sculptor Robert Smithson also made use of the term
'entropy' in his writings. In 1966 he claimed that minimal sculptors and painters 'provided a visual analog of
the second law of thermodynamics' by destroying classical notions of time and space.

◉ R Arnheim *Entropy and Art: an essay on disorder and order*
(Berkeley & Los Angeles, University of California Press,
1971).

R Smithson *The writings of Robert Smithson* N Holt (ed) (NY, New York University Press, 1979).

240 ENVIRONMENTAL AESTHETICS

A somewhat amorphous field of research concerned with the visual quality of the physical environment, both man-made and natural. This type of research is interdisciplinary in character and involves artists, architects, designers, geographers, planners and social scientists.

B Sadler & A Carlson (eds) *Environmental Aesthetics: essays in interpretation* (Victoria, British Columbia, University of Victoria, 1982).

J Nasar (ed) *Environmental Aesthetics* (Cambridge University Press, 1988).

241 ENVIRONMENTAL ART

(Also Arte Ambiental, Art Spaces) The word 'environment' is ambiguous: it can mean a small interior space, or the urban context, or the whole ecosphere of the planet Earth. One can also speak of 'social' and 'media environments'. In the discourse of art criticism, 'environment' normally signifies works involving interior spaces (for art dealing with the ecosphere the term 'ecological' is used; public art and community art are two kinds of practice intended to change the external, urban environment). Such art is deemed 'environmental' when the construction the artist provides is large enough to enclose the spectator so that he or she can move about within it or through it. When artists create environments they are, of course, competing with architects, interior designers, museum and display designers and the creators of booths at funfairs.

Artists' environments cannot be characterized according to a common aesthetic or style because they have been generated by artists loyal to very different movements, from dada to minimalism. Environmental Art can be very crowded, cluttered and messy or extremely sparse and abstract. Key precedents before 1945 were Kurt Schwitters' 'Merzbauten' and the major surrealist exhibitions with their elaborate decor. Even some painters had environmental ambitions: witness the huge colour-field canvases of Barnett Newman intended to overwhelm the spectator's field of vision.

The growing popularity of Environmental Art in the post 1945 era reflected the desire on the part of many artists to escape the limitations of the single art object and to resist the commodification associated with such objects. By designing a whole space, or series of spaces, artists could provide a much more intense and comprehensive sensory experience for visitors. Not only could light levels, sounds and movement be controlled but space itself could be literally articulated by means of screens, passageways, tunnels and so forth. Later on, artists discovered that Environmental Art did not need to rely upon solid materials because spatial experience could be modulated by means of light beams and sound waves (see Laser Art and PULSA).

A whole book would be required to supply a history of Environmental Art; consequently the following list is simply intended to indicate the variety of environments created since 1945. In the pop art idiom: Claes Oldenburg's 'The Store' (1965). In the collage/assemblage idiom: Ed Kienholz's replica brothel 'Roxy's' (1961) and bar 'The Beanery' (1965). In the minimalist idiom: at the Tate Gallery in 1970 three Los Angeles artists – Larry Bell, Robert Irwin and Doug Wheeler – devised three austere environments designed to control the spectator's perceptual experience. In the situationist idiom: Giuseppe Pinot-Gallizio's 'Grotto of anti-matter' (1959). In the constructivist idiom: Victor Pasmore's two environments of 1957 and '59 called 'Exhibit I & II'. In a light art idiom: Lucas Samaras' 'Room 2' made entirely from mirrors and lights. In the psychedelic idiom: Allen Atwell's 1964 'Psychedelic Temple', a room with all its surfaces covered with painted imagery. Various styles: in 1970 ten young artists created fanciful domestic interiors based on the theme of 'the sitting-room' at the ICA, London.

A historical and contemporary survey of Environmental Art was provided at the 1976 Venice Biennale when the Italian critic Germano Celant organized a show entitled 'ambient art'. Often the artists who made environments did so as part of a broader range of concerns. A case in point was the British group Space Structure Workshop (SSW) founded in 1968 as the culmination of ideas that had been developing from the early 1960s. Members included Maurice Agis, Peter Jones and Terry Scales. SSW was concerned with collaborations with industry, staging public events and providing environments using air structures with the aim of integrating space, colour and sound. By providing alternative aesthetic experiences, SSW hoped to liberate the senses of the public, to heighten their awareness of a dehumanized urban environment and thus stimulate social and political change. SSW was active in Britain and Holland during the late '60s and early '70s.

● See also Air Art, Community Art, Earth & Land Art, Ecological Art, Free Form Arts Trust, Installation, Participatory Art, Public Art, Total Art/Design.

Environments, situations, spaces (NY, Martha Jackson Gallery, 1961).

S Bann 'Environmental Art' *Studio International* **173** (886) February 1967 78–82.

N Piene 'Environments and performances' *Art in America*

55 (3) May–June 1967 39–47.

● C Oldenburg *Store days* (NY, Something Else Press, 1967).

● J Lipman 'Period rooms the sixties and the seventies' *Art in America* 58 (6) November–December 1970 126–9.

● H Rosenberg 'Light! Lights!' – in – *Artworks and packages* (NY, Dell, 1971) 132–43.

● 'Spaceplace: selections from the notes of Agis, Jones, Marigold and Pitt' *Studio International* 183 (940) January 1972 34–7.

● A Henri *Environments and happenings* (Thames & Hudson, 1974).

● C Celant 'Artspaces' *Studio International* 190 (977) September–October 1975 114–23.

● G Stevens *Nothing: a paradigm for 1984* (Airworks/Seven Dials Gallery, 1984).

242 ENVIRONMENTAL DESIGN

An interdisciplinary field of study/ research that became fashionable in the 1960s. It was defined by Maurice Jay as 'the scientific design and control of the man-made environment'. In a narrow sense the expression meant the design of interior spaces; in a broader sense, the design of the whole external physical environment in cities and in the countryside. Such a project necessarily required the co-operation of many different disciplines: architecture, urban planning, landscape gardening, civil engineering, acoustics, ergonomics, etc. In 1968 the first meeting of EDRA – the Environmental Design Research Association – was held in North Carolina. It proposed to undertake research into those aspects of the social and behavioural sciences of relevance to Environmental Design. Three journals were connected with EDRA: *Environment & Behaviour, Man Environment Systems,* and *Design Methods Group Newsletter.* The Association also published the proceedings of its annual conferences.

● See also Centre de Recherche d'Ambiances, Design Methods, Environmental Aesthetics, Green Design, Supergraphics, Townscape.

● M Jay 'Environmental Design: an introduction' *Design* (218) February 1967 44–9 (first of a series of articles).

● R Dober *Environmental Design* (NY, Van Nostrand Reinhold, 1969).

● T Crosby *How to play the environment game* (Harmondsworth, Penguin/Arts Council of Great Britain, 1973).

● L Krasner (ed) *Environmental Design and human behaviour* (NY, Pergamon, 1980).

● *Environmental Design: best selection 2* (Tokyo, 1987).

243 EQUIPO CRÓNICA

(Chronicle Group) Name adopted by two Spanish, politically committed painters in 1964. Rafael Solbés (1943–81) and Manuel Valdés came from Valencia and set themselves the task of producing critical, ironic chronicles of everyday life in societies controlled by big business and the military. (Joan Antoni Toledo also participated for a time.) Their figurative paintings (and some sculptures) were executed in an impersonal, simplified, poster-like style which owed something to Spanish folk art and something to pop art. Images quoted from the history of art and from the mass media were juxtaposed in order to point to the continuation of ancient power structures into modern times. Themes such as 'politics and culture' (1971) were explored via a series of canvases. Individual pieces often consisted of several separate images arranged in a logical sequence. Indeed, small, portable canvases were used so that exhibitions could be easily mounted in non-art venues; the latter were favoured in order to avoid the attentions of the censor. Art critics characterized their work as 'seditious figuration', i.e. a Spanish variant of the European tendency called 'narrative figuration', and 'dialectical realism'. Equipo Crónica received considerable recognition in the European artworld of the late '60s and early '70s. The partnership ended in 1981 with the death of Solbés. A retrospective exhibition of Equipo Crónica's work toured Spain in 1989.

● See also Collaborations, Narrative Figuration/Painting, Political Art.

● T Llorens *Equipo Crónica* (Barcelona, Gustavo Gili, 1972).

● —'Equipo Crónica' *Opus International* (50) May 1974 78–89.

● D Giralt-Miracle 'Recording reality' *Art & Artists* 12 (3) June 1977 30–5.

● D Cameron 'Contents under pressure: Equipo Crónica' *Artforum* 28 (3) November 1989 124–30.

● *Equipo Crónica 1965–81* (Madrid, Ministerio de Cultura, 1989).

244 EQUIPO 57

(Team 57) An association of Spanish artists inspired by the constructivist work of Gabo and Pevsner and opposed to the gestural expressions of l'art informel. They favoured rational, systematic abstraction and collective, anonymous production. The group was founded in 1957 after a split in the earlier Grupo Espacio. Its members came from Córdoba and they included: José Durarte, Juan Serrano, Angel Duart, Augustin Ibarola and Juan Cuenca. The Italian-born painter Marino di Teana subsequently participated. A manifesto was pub-

EQUIPO 57 'C.15' (1961). Oil on canvas 121cm x 121 cm. Photo: Galerie Suzanne, Bollag.

lished in French in 1957 and the group contributed to many exhibitions of the nouvelle tendance and op art in Europe and the United States in the early '60s. Equipo 57 finally disbanded in 1966.
● See also Constructivism, Nouvelle Tendance, Op Art.
● Equipo 57 *Interactivité de l' espace plastique* (Madrid, Gráficos Reunidas, 1957).
● J Moreno Galvan *Equipo 57: pintura, escultura, estructuras espaciales* (Madrid, Darro Gallery, 1960).
● *Equipo 57* (Geneva, Galerie d'Art Actual, 1966).

245 EQUIPO REALIDAD A Spanish team active in the mid 1960s consisting of two painters, Juan Cardella and Jorge Ballester, formed in Valencia. Their work was somewhat similar to that of Equipo Crónica: a simplified, poster-like style of 'narrative figuration'; multi-part canvases generating comments critical of society via a montage of images quoted from the history of art and from contemporary documentary photography.
● See also Equipo Crónica, Narrative Figuration/Painting.

246 ERGONOMICS (Also Human Engineering, Human Factors Engineering, Natural Design) This word, invented by Hywel Murrell, derives from the Greek 'ergon' meaning 'work' and 'nomos' meaning 'law'. It refers to an interdisciplinary science dating from the military research undertaken during the Second World War which is of vital importance to designers. Ergonomics' prime concern is the usability of designed products (as against their function and appearance), and the relation between human beings and machines: for example, finding out by empirical research and measurement what is the most efficient layout for a panel of instruments or what is the most suitable seat for driving a car. This involves studying the bodily capabilities and limitations of human beings when at work, when interacting with tools, machines or environments. (Anthropometrics is the name of the science of measuring the size and proportions of the human body.) The statistical data collected by ergonomic researchers is clearly of value to all engineers and designers. An Ergonomics Research Society (ERS) was established in Cambridge in 1950 and an International Ergonomics Association (IEA) in Leiden in 1957. The journal *Ergonomics* was founded in 1958 and *Applied Ergonomics* in 1970. In Sweden in 1979 the Ergonomi Design Gruppen was founded as a co-operative by 14 designers. As its name indicated, the consultancy was particularly concerned with the ergonomic aspects of design especially in relation to the needs of disabled people.
● See also Environmental Design.
● C Morgan & others (eds) *Human Engineering guide to equipment design* (NY, McGraw-Hill, 1963).
● K Murrell *Ergonomics: man in his working environment* (Chapman & Hall, 1965).
● A Damon & others *The human body in equipment design* (Cambridge, Mass, Harvard University Press, 1966).
● J Croney *Anthropometrics for designers* (Batsford, 1971).
● E McCormick *Human Factors Engineering* (NY, McGraw-Hill, 5th ed 1972).
● O Edholm & H Murrell *History of the Ergonomics Research Society...* (Taylor & Francis, 1974).
● D McFadden (ed) *Scandinavian modern design 1880–1980* (NY, Abrams, 1982).
● S Bayley *Natural Design: the search for comfort and efficiency* (Boilerhouse Project/Victoria & Albert Museum, 1985).
● H Murrell 'How Ergonomics became part of design' – in – *From Spitfire to microchip: studies in the history of design from 1945* N Hamilton (ed) (Design Council, 1985) 72–5.
● J Wilson & others (eds) *New methods in applied Ergonomics* (Taylor & Francis, 1987).
● E Megaw (ed) *Contemporary Ergonomics* (Taylor & Francis, 1989).
● E Lovesey (ed) *Contemporary Ergonomics 1991: Ergonomics - design for performance* (Taylor & Francis, 1991).

Although Erotic Art is not specific to the post-1945 era, it was only in the 1960s that, as a result of social changes in the Western world, Erotic Art became respectable in academic circles. A course about Erotic Art was introduced into British art colleges by the art historian Peter Webb in 1968. It also became a subject suitable for popular consumption via books and exhibitions. Drs Phyllis and Eberhard Kronhausen organized large-scale, international exhibitions of Erotic Art in Denmark and Sweden in 1968–9 that attracted over a quarter of a million visitors.

Erotic Art has been defined as 'art that arouses sexual sensations in body or mind'. It is assumed, somewhat naively, that what arouses these sensations are depictions of sexual intercourse or related behaviour. Most surveys of Erotic Art consist therefore of reproductions of drawings, paintings and sculptures depicting sexual behaviour of various kinds. However, depending on how that behaviour is depicted, the images may be considered erotic or un-erotic. (Toulouse-Lautrec's paintings of brothels and prostitutes are surely too harshly realistic to be thought erotic.) Responses will also vary from person to person. While sexual behaviour may be universal as far as humans are concerned, 'the erotic' is surely a cultural matter which varies from age to age, society to society. If 'the erotic' is considered a feeling of sensuality or sensuousness, then some people may well find paintings of fruit or landscapes erotic. Since the visual arts are by definition dependent upon the sense of sight, then the issues of voyeurism and scopophilia are crucial to any account of Erotic Art.

Erotic Art and pornography are generally considered mutually exclusive even though both depict sex. (The distinction is maintained by stressing the importance of skill and the aesthetic quality of art, even though, arguably, some degree of aesthetic appeal is also typical of certain kinds of pornography.) This often results in a double standard, i.e. one sort of morality is applied to art, and another to pornography.

Artists noted for their contributions to the category of Erotic Art in the decades since 1945 include: Vito Acconci, Francis Bacon, Balthus, Hans Bellmer, Barry Burman, Judy Chicago (her vaginal imagery pictures), Robert Crumb, Leonor Fini, David Hockney, Allen Jones, Pierre Klossowski, Richard Lindner, Pablo Picasso, Rebecca Scott, Sylvia Sleigh and Andy Warhol (films).

● See also Gay Art, Pin-Ups, Scopophilia.

● P & E Kronhausen *Erotic Art, a survey of erotic fact and fancy in fine arts* 2 vols (NY, Grove Press, 1968–70).

● (Erotic Art issue) *Art & Artists* **5** (5) August 1970.

● P Gerhard *Pornography or art?* (Words & Pictures, 1971).

● M Peckham *Art and pornography* (NY, Harper & Row, 1971).

● V Kahmen *Eroticism in contemporary art* (Studio Vista, 1972).

● E Lucie-Smith *Eroticism in Western art* (Thames & Hudson, 1972).

● E Phillips (ed) *The Left and the erotic* (Lawrence & Wishart, 1983).

● P Webb (& others) *The Erotic Arts* (Secker & Warburg, 2nd ed 1983), this text contains a detailed bibliography.

● S Kappeler *The pornography of representation* (Oxford, Polity Press, 1986).

● T Gracyk 'Pornographic representations: aesthetic considerations' *Journal of Aesthetic Education* **21** (4) Winter 1987 103–21.

● E Burt *Erotic Art: an annotated bibliography with essays* (Boston, Mass, G K Hall, 1989).

● E Lucie-Smith *Sexuality in Western art* (Thames & Hudson, 1991).

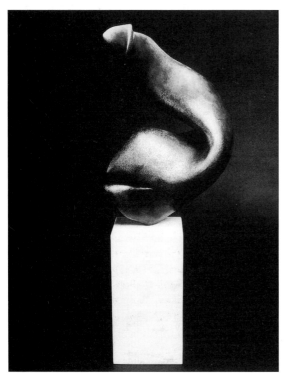

EROTIC ART MARILYN TABATZNIK, 'Arrogance' (1989). Ceramic & marble, height: 70 cm. Photo: Brian E. Rybolt, courtesy of Michaelson & Orient, twentieth century ceramics, London.

'Ersatz' is a German word meaning 'substitute', 'replacement' or, pejoratively, 'a phoney'. Charles Jencks employed the term to describe architecture with forms borrowed indiscriminately from several sources. He identified many subdivisions within the category, e. g. synthetic, trompe l'oeil counterfeit, eclectic, delirious trademark, iconic advertisement, etc. Ersatz Architecture was to be found on both sides of the Atlantic, but it was most virulent in Los Angeles. Jencks regarded it as the authentic culture of the masses and claimed that new principles of mediocrity were needed to evaluate it. This kind of architecture was partly the result of modern technology because it enabled any known style to be imitated. However, exact copies were not necessary; pastiches could also capture the essence of the original, e.g. Grauman's Chinese Theatre, the structures inside Walt Disney World, Orlando, Florida. Alistair Best preferred the term 'kitsch architecture' to describe buildings that provided 'exotic substitutes', 'skin-deep' or 'instant' environments. He cited as examples Disney World and the Watney Mann Schooner Inns; he also considered them examples of 'escapist design'.

● See also Camp, Kitsch, Pop Architecture.

● A Best 'Flight of fancy' *Design* (293) May 1973 60–5.

● C Jencks 'Ersatz in LA' *Architectural Design* **43** (9) September 1973 596–601.

● — 'Trompe l'oeil counterfeit' *Studio International* **190** (977) September–October 1975 108–14.

This expression began to be used in art circles in the late 1960s to refer to art produced by people who share a common culture by virtue of inheriting social customs, speaking the same language and belonging to a particular tribe, nation, race, e.g. Eskimos, Puerto Ricans, Afro-Americans and Chicanos (in 1975 an organization called 'MARCH' – Movimento ARistico CHicano – based in Chicago was founded to promote Chicano art; in New York a Museum of Contemporary Hispanic Art (MOCHA) has been established). Fashion journalists and museum curators also began to refer to beads and necklaces from Africa as 'Ethnic jewellery'.

A 1976 survey of the cultural activities of ethnic minorities in Britain (hence 'minority arts') – West Indians, Asians, Poles, Ukrainians, Cypriots, Chinese – conducted by Naseem Khan revealed that little financial support or encouragement was forthcoming from official bodies and the broadcasting media. In Khan's view, Ethnic Arts brought a new stimulus and variety to British society. The latter was quite clearly a multi-cultural society. Following Khan's report the situation improved somewhat. A Minorities Arts Advisory Service (MAAS) was established in London and it published the magazine *Artrage* (which described itself as an 'inter-cultural' magazine).

Most of the literature on Ethnic Arts has been produced by anthropologists. Nelson Graburn has discussed them in conjunction with Tourist Arts, i.e. the kind of exotic artefacts purporting to be expressions of local cultures sold at airports as souvenirs (hence 'airport art'). He has also employed the term 'Fourth World arts' as a collective name for the artistic production of 'all aboriginal or native peoples whose lands fall within the national boundaries and techno-bureaucratic administrations of the countries of the First, Second and Third worlds'; hence the expression is an alternative to 'minority arts'. Once pluralism became typical of the artworld, displays of Ethnic Art could be routinely incorporated into international survey exhibitions such as the biennale held in Sydney in 1986.

Some British artists who derive from ethnic minorities object to the concept of 'Ethnic Art' because they consider it degrading and patronizing and because it presumes they will produce work in an idiom different from the majority culture, whereas some of these artists are modernists working in an international style. Still others seek to come to terms with two worlds by creating art that fuses majority and minority cultures.

● See also Black Art, Carnival, Inuit Art, OBAALA, Orature, Pluralism, Popular Art, Township Art.

● N Graburn *Ethnic and tourist arts: cultural expressions from the Fourth World* (Berkeley, University of California Press, 1976).

● N Khan *The arts Britain ignores* (Community Relations Commission, 1976).

● J Grigsby *Art and ethnics: background for teaching youth in a pluralistic society* (Dubuque, Iowa, W C Brown, 1977).

● P Henley 'The economic and aesthetic value of Ethnic Art' *New Society* **898** (99) December 1979 639–41.

● A Smith *The ethnic revival in the modern world* (Cambridge University Press, 1981).

● *Tribal and Ethnic Art* (Oxford, Clio Press, 1982), Modern Art Bibliographies series no 1.

● M McLeod & J Mack *Ethnic sculpture* (British Museum, 1985).

● *From two worlds* (Whitechapel Art Gallery, 1986).

● S Nairne, G Dunlop & J Wyver 'Identity, culture and power'– in –*State of the arts: ideas & images in the 1980s* (Chatto & Windus/Channel 4 TV, 1987) 205–46.

● J Mack (ed) *Ethnic jewellery* (British Museum, 1988).

● E Burt *Ethnoart: Africa, Oceania, and the Americas: a bibliography of theses and dissertations* (NY, Garland Publishing, 1989).

Ethology is a science concerned with the function and evolution of animal behaviour patterns. Ethological theory, when applied to art, suggests that people have built-in species reactions to certain combinations of forms, colours, etc., in the same way that animals instinctively respond to danger signals peculiar to their species. If these triggers could be identified then artists could manipulate them in a conscious manner to produce predetermined effects. R. Coss cites Klee and Miró as examples of artists who used 'emotional releasers'. The argument that all people react in much the same way to an image of an eye, or to a many-legged insect, is disputed by phenomenologists and existentialists who stress the individuality of each person's circumstances and learned responses.

● See also Experimental Aesthetics.

● D Sandle 'The science of art' *Science Journal* March 1967 2–7.

● R Coss 'The ethological command in art' *Leonardo* **1** (3) July 1968 273–87.

● G Rump 'The possible impact of comparative ethology on the analysis of works of art' *Leonardo* **11** (1) Winter 1978 63–7.

● E Dissanayake *What is art for?* (University of Washington Press, 1989).

251 EVENTSTRUCTURE A theoretical notion propounded by the British artist John Latham in the years since 1954. Latham's assumption was that time is all-important, hence Eventstructure encapsulated the idea of structure in events or through time, rather than structure in space. Processes became more important than products. In 1967 Latham's ideas were adopted by three artists – Theo Botschiver, Jeffrey Shaw and Sean Wellesley-Miller – who formed, in Amsterdam, the 'Eventstructure Research Group' (ERG). The purpose of ERG was to devise an alternative to 'museum art' by staging events in the street and at public festivals. They encouraged audience participation and adult play by providing PVC inflatables, some in the form of tubes floating on water. Their work was described as 'operational art' and vaunted as 'an art of real consequences'.

● See also Air Art, Participatory Art, Public Art, Street Art.

● J Latham 'Eventstructure' *Studio International* **174** (892) September 1967 82.

● 'Concepts for an operational art...' *Art & Artists* **3** (10) January 1969 46–9.

● T Smith 'Eventstructure Research Group in Australia' *Studio International* **184** (948) October 1972 149–50.

● J Shaw 'Eventstructure Research Group' *Mewspaper* (Royal College of Art) (22) April–May 1974 3–4.

EVENTSTRUCTURE EVENTSTRUCTURE RESEARCH GROUP, 'Plastic tube for pedestrians over the Maschsee, Hanover' (1970). Photo: ERG.

252 EXHIBIT I&II Two abstract, environmental constructions devised by Victor Pasmore and Richard Hamilton. Exhibit I was shown at the ICA, London and at Newcastle upon Tyne in 1957, and Exhibit II at Newcastle in 1959. Variously coloured acrylic sheets, with differing degrees of transparency, were placed at right angles to each other in metal frameworks or hung from the ceiling. The result was a maze-like spatial structure within which spectators could move, though this was not encouraged in the case of Exhibit II, where variations of transparency alone created an impression of penetration.

● See also Constructionism, Constructivism, Environmental Art, Installation.

● L Alloway 'An exhibit' *Architectural Design* August 1957 238–9.

● — *An exhibit* (Newcastle upon Tyne, Hatton Gallery/London, ICA, 1957).

● R Hamilton *Collected words 1953–82* (Thames & Hudson, 1982).

253 EXISTENTIALISM & ART There is a twofold relation between existentialism and art: (1) the interest existentialist philosophers have shown in aesthetic theory; and (2) the influence of the philosophy of existentialism – often misrepresented and popularized – on artistic practice. To existentialist philosophers – given their view of human life as a continual process of choice and their stress on subjectivity and individualism – the artist at work often serves, in their writings, as the paradigm of authentic human existence. Although Sartre's theory of committed or 'engaged' art refers to literature, the idea that artists must accept responsibility for the effect of what they produce, despite the unpredictable nature of an absurd world, can obviously be extended to all creative media. However, it is not possible to identify a specifically existentialist aesthetic because different existentialist writers draw variously on Marxist, Freudian, Jungian and sundry other explanations of the phenomenon of art.

Existentialism was a fashionable philosophy in the immediate post-1945 years and it was then that its influence on art – action painting, tachisme, geometry of fear, Giacometti and Francis Bacon – was at its height. While this influence was more an emotional identification with existentialism rather than a technical understanding of its theory, it is clear that the emphasis in action painting on the unpremeditated creative act, and the high moral commitment of the artist, was akin to the existentialist's view of humans as isolated, alienated beings, facing tragic/absurd choices which are only resolved through action. Sartre's view that 'there are no aesthetic values a priori but there are values which appear in due course in the coherence of the picture' seems particularly close to the aesthetic of action painting.

Often the term 'existentialist' was used loosely to refer to the experience of anxiety, anomie, alienation and meaninglessness common to life in modern cities. By extension, there was a tendency for any art portraying disturbed or tortured people to be described as 'existentialist'. For instance, Barry Schwartz in his book *The new humanism* included in his category 'existential humanism' works depicting 'the betrayal of human potential and the anguish of diminished men' (e.g. paintings by F. Bacon). Similarly, Donald Kuspit in his book about Leon Golub – an American artist who has relentlessly represented human conflict, oppression and torture – characterized him as an 'existentialist/activist painter'.

● See also Action Painting, Geometry of Fear, Humanist Art, Political Art, Tachisme.

● V Ames 'Existentialism and the arts' *Journal of Aesthetics & Art Criticism* **9** (3) March 1951 252–6.

● D Ashton *The unknown shore: a view of contemporary art* (Studio Vista, 1962).

● A Fallico *Art and Existentialism* (Englewood Cliffs, New Jersey, Prentice Hall, 1962).

● E Kaelin *An Existentialist aesthetic: the theories of Sartre and Merleau-Ponty* (Madison, Milwaukee, University of Wisconsin Press, 1962).

● G Bauer *Sartre and the artist* (Chicago, University of Chicago Press, 1969).

● M Rowell *La peinture, le geste, l'action: l'Existentialisme en peinture* (Paris, Éditions Klincksieck, 1972).

● B Schwartz *The new humanism: art in a time of change* (David & Charles, 1974).

● D Kuspit *Leon Golub: Existentialist/activist painter* (New Brunswick, New Jersey, Rutgers University Press, 1985).

254 EXPANDED CINEMA

(Also Expanded Media) This term appears to date from the mid 1960s. It was used in avant garde and underground film circles in the United States to describe film showings that went beyond conventional presentations. The term gained wider currency mainly as a result of a 1970 text by the American film critic Gene Youngblood in which he enthusiastically documented the advances in audio-visual media in the United States during the 1960s, e.g. synaesthetic/ cybernetic/ holographic cinema, computer-generated films, multi-projection environments, intermedia theatre, and so on. However, according to Youngblood, Expanded Cinema was not simply a question of technological developments. He remarked: 'When we say expanded cinema we actually mean expanded consciousness...the intermedia network of cinema and television...now functions as nothing less than the nervous system of mankind.' The term proved a useful one and it was widely adopted, particularly in Britain.

A festival of Expanded Cinema featuring the work of over 30 film-makers took place at the ICA, London in 1976. It included multi-screen projections, films plus live performances, and 'film-sculpture'. According to Deke Dusinberre, the British version of Expanded Cinema did not depend on expanded technology to achieve expanded perception, rather it extended the possibilities of old technology. By 'dwelling on the techniques of cinematic presentation', it recruited the 'spectator into active participation in the aesthetic discourse'. From 1979 onwards an annual festival of films, video, photography, sound and performance by artists and art students called 'The Expanded Media Show' was held at various galleries in Sheffield, Yorkshire.

● See also Computer Art, Holographic Art, Inter-Media, Laser Art, Media Art, Projected Art, Structural/ Materialist Film, Underground Film, Video Art.

● S Renan 'Expanded Cinema' – in – *The underground film: an introduction to its development in America* (Studio Vista, 1968) 227–57.

● G Youngblood *Expanded Cinema* (NY, Dutton, 1970).

● D Dusinberre 'On Expanding Cinema' *Studio International* **190** (978) November–December 1975 220–4.

● D Curtis 'The festival of Expanded Cinema' *Studio International* **191** (980) March–April 1976 209–12.

● R Wilson 'The Expanded Media Show' *Aspects* (26) Spring 1984 14.

255 EXPENDABILITY IN DESIGN

(Also Planned or Style Obsolescence, Throw-Away Aesthetic) All designed goods break down or wear out eventually, consequently every product has a presumed lifespan built in at the design stage. In previous centuries goods were generally designed to be durable but in the twentieth century, especially during the 1950s and '60s, the idea that goods could be thrown away and replaced rather than repaired, that goods might be intended to last a very short time (e.g. paper cups), gained wide public acceptance in the affluent societies of the West. (Arguably, ever-expanding production and consumption, plus an ever-accelerating rate of turnover of goods, are the inevitable characteristics of the dynamic of a capitalist economy.) More recently an awareness of ecological problems has led to a change in attitude and the profligate use of the Earth's resources is now frowned upon.

Designers can plan for a product's breakdown or obsolescence in three ways: (1) they can design goods with poor-quality materials so that they last only a short time; (2) they can use new styles to outmode existing products thereby encouraging consumers to buy new models even before their old ones have worn out (the latter tactic is endemic in the fashion industry and was imitated by American car manufacturers such as General Motors (see Styling)); (3) they can invent or design products with new or improved functions so that people are stimulated to acquire 'state-of-the-art' technology (e.g. replacing an electric typewriter with a word-processor).

● See also Ecological Architecture, Pop Design.

● G Nelson 'Obsolescence' *Industrial Design* (6) 1956.

● V Packard *The waste makers* (NY, McKay/London, Longman, 1960).

● R Banham 'A Throw-away Aesthetic' – in – *Design by choice* P Sparke (ed) (Academy Editions, 1981) 90–3.

● N Whiteley 'Toward a throw-away culture: consumerism, "Style Obsolescence" and cultural theory in the 1950s and '60s' *Oxford Art Journal* **10** (2) 1987 3–27.

256 EXPENDABLE ART

(Also Disposable Art, Ephemeral Art, Perishable Art, Throw-Away Art, Transient Art) Contrary to received opinion no work of art is 'timeless'. Over time, all works of art age, are subject to decay or mutilation and destruction. In the past artists tried to resist dissolution by the use of durable materials and careful craftsmanship; in contrast, many modern artists have been indifferent to permanence and perpetuity. While there was no school of 'Expendable Art', the notion of expendability did permeate much art activity in the decades since the end of the Second World War, especially the 1960s. It was manifested in various ways: (1) the use by action painters of cheap household paints instead of good-quality oil pigments; the use by assemblage artists of all kinds of disparate materials and junk crudely collaged together

meant that the lifespan of the artefacts was likely to be short – at the very least, they posed great problems to museum conservationists; (2) the use by certain minimalist and arte povera artists of materials on a once-only basis (e.g. Carl Andre's sculptures made from bricks – after an exhibition the bricks were returned to the brickyard) – if the artist needed to reconstitute the work then new materials could be obtained or the old ones recycled; (3) the development of forms of art in which expendability was crucial to their aesthetic, e.g. destructive art, food art and process art; (4) the increased popularity amongst artists of time-based arts such as actions, happenings, installations and performance; these were temporary, ephemeral or transient by their very nature and no end-products were envisaged.

The expression 'the life of a work of art' can refer to either its physical lifespan or its cultural lifespan. These usually function at different rates: art objects can continue to exist physically long after they have ceased to play any role in cultural life. Expendability was one of the characteristics of popular culture Richard Hamilton identified in a famous letter, though it was not one he emulated in his own pop art. The enormous quantity of new mass-media images means that there is a rapid turnover; the cultural currency of images is thus very short. Some pop art shared this characteristic. Indeed, one description of pop was 'one-shot art': it made a brief impact, was exhausted of meaning and was then forgotten.

● See also Pop Art, Time-based Arts.

● J Reichardt 'Expendable Art' *Architectural Design* **30** (10) October 1960 421–2.

● H Rosenberg 'The art object and the aesthetics of impermanence' – in – *The anxious object: art today and its audience* (Thames & Hudson, 1965) 88–96.

● D Bourdon 'Disposable Art – plastic man' *Life* August 22 1969 62–7.

● J Guilfoyle 'Now you see it...' *Industrial Design* **20** (5) June 1973 42–5.

257 EXPERIMENTAL AESTHETICS

A branch of psychology originating in the 1870s with Gustav Fechner's studies of aesthetic preference (*Vorschule der Aesthetic,* Leipzig, 1876). Its purpose is to find experimentally validated 'truths' about the power and appeal of art and its elements (e.g. colours), cross-culturally as well as in particular communities. The first International Colloquium on Experimental Aesthetics was held in Paris in June 1965. From this period too a group in Toronto under Professor D. Berlyne undertook research in this field.

● See also Artology.

● N Kiell *Psychiatry and psychology in the visual arts and aesthetics: a bibliography* (Madison & Milwaukee, University of Wisconsin Press, 1965).

● J Hogg (ed) *Psychology and the visual arts: selected readings* (Harmondsworth, Penguin Books, 1969).

● R Pickford *Psychology and visual aesthetics* (Hutchinson Educational, 1972).

● F Molnar 'Experimental Aesthetics or the science of art' *Leonardo* **7** (1) Winter 1974 23–6.

● D Berlyne (ed) *Studies in the new Experimental Aesthetics: steps towards an objective psychology of aesthetic experience* (NY, John Wiley, 1974).

258 EXPERIMENTAL ARCHITECTURE

Title of a 1970 book by Peter Cook surveying the structures and designs of individuals and groups from a variety of countries committed to invention and experimentation in terms of forms, materials, technology, construction methods and social engineering. Individuals discussed included Alison & Peter Smithson, Paolo Soleri, Michael Webb, Kenzo Tange, Yona Friedman, Bruce Goff, Frei Otto and Cedric Price. Groups discussed included Archigram, Haus-Rucker Co., NER Group, Metabolist Group and Utopie Group. Experimental Architecture often involved a challenge to existing limits and concepts of architecture and environmental design. Cook noted that his survey might prompt a redefinition of experiment in architecture: 'to experiment out of architecture'. Experimental architects are orientated towards the future, consequently there is an overlap with utopian or visionary architecture.

● See also Conceptual Architecture, Fantastic Architecture, Utopian Architecture, Visionary Architecture.

● P Cook *Experimental Architecture* (Studio Vista, 1970).

259 EXPERIMENTAL ART

In the literature of twentieth-century art, the word 'experimental' meaning 'novel', 'daring', 'outlandish', 'provocative' is virtually synonymous with 'avant garde'. Paradoxically, it is a word with both positive and negative associations: positive in the sense of artists being open to new experiences, adopting chance procedures and new techniques, and playing with their materials in order to see what will happen; negative in the sense of 'a trial run, something transitional – not a fully mature and complete work'. Ernst Gombrich, an art historian unsympathetic to modern art, subsumed all twentieth-century art (the final chapter of *The story of art*) under the rubric 'experimental' with the implication that it was tentative and provisional.

It was modern science, of course, which made the experimental method so important. John Constable, the British landscape painter, believed that experiments in art were directly analogous to those of science: 'painting is a science, and should be pursued as an inquiry into the laws of nature. Why, then, may not landscape be considered as a branch of natural philosophy, of which the pictures are but experiments?' Similarly, Stephen Bann defined an experimental artist as one 'committed to a particular path of controlled activity, of which the works he produces remain as evidence'. Picasso was fond of describing his artistic activities as 'research' and said his objective was to find things, to make new discoveries. Such discoveries are normally made by those with prepared minds, by the theoretically informed, by those actively seeking to solve certain problems. (Also, posterity is only interested in those who succeed in making striking discoveries, not those who search randomly and find nothing.)

The value of the scientific metaphor in art has its limitations because of significant differences between the two realms, e.g. in science, discoveries made by chance are not so highly thought of as those confirmed in experiments which were predicted in theories. Michael Chanan has argued that art is like science in that it is a problem-solving activity but unlike science because its results are unpredictable and unmeasurable. Another difference is that in science experiments are a means to an end, whereas in art the 'experiments' are prized in their own right.

'Experimental' was a vogue word in the 1960s when many artists flirted with science and technology. Subsequently, it fell out of favour. However, in London during the autumn of 1988 an international festival of Experimental Art called 'Edge 88' was held at the AIR Gallery and several other spaces.

● See also Avant Garde Art, EAT, Technological Art.

● R Wedewer 'Experimental painting' *Cimaise* (53) May–June 1961 28–43.

● F Malina 'Some reflections on the differences between science and art' – in – *Data: directions in art, theory and aesthetics;* A Hill (ed)(Faber & Faber, 1968) 134–45.

● S Bann *Experimental painting...* (Studio Vista, 1970).

● M Chanan 'Art as experiment' *British Journal of Aesthetics* **12** (2) Spring 1972 133–47.

● E Gombrich 'Experimental Art' – in – *The story of art* (Phaidon, 12th ed 1972) 442–75.

● *Edge 88* (Festival guide, special issue of *Performance Art* magazine, 1988).

● M Dickson 'Edge 88 Festival, thoughts of an outsider' *Variant* (Glasgow) (6) 1989 36–7.

260 **EXPERIMENTAL ART FOUNDATION (EAF)** An influential organization and exhibition space in Adelaide, capital of South Australia. EAF was established in 1974 in order to promote contemporary experimental art, in particular inter-media, post-object, conceptual and performance art. Various individuals contributed to its formation but the main protagonist was the art theorist Dr Donald Brook who perceived the need for a centre that would mount a critical challenge to existing concepts of art and conventional ideas about art's social function. Over the years EAF has mounted many exhibitions of work by Australian and foreign artists, organized touring exhibitions, arranged lecture series, maintained a bookshop and publishing programme, supported an artist-in-residence scheme, housed the Australian Network for Art and Technology, and built up a library and visual archive. EAF was financed via membership fees and by grants from arts funding bodies. A council elected from the membership determined EAF's policy.

● See also Post-Object Art.

◉ S Britton (ed) *A decade at the EAF: a history of the Experimental Art Foundation 1974–84* (Adelaide, Australia, EAF, 1984).

261 **EXPERIMENTAL GROUP** An artists' group founded in 1948 in Holland by Karel Appel, Corneille, Constant, Anton Rooskens, Eugene Brands and Theo Wolvecamp. They produced figurative paintings influenced by child and 'primitive' art executed in a loose, improvised style. They also published a review *Reflex*, two issues of which appeared in 1948 and '49. The Experimental Group did not exist for very long, but its ideas were continued in the broader, international organization called CoBrA.

● See also Art Informel, CoBrA.

◉ Constant 'Les neuf points du Groupe Expérimental Hollandais' *Le Petit CoBrA* (Brussels) (1) February 1949.

◉ —'De Experimentele Groep' *Kunst en Kultur* (Amsterdam) **10** (11) November 1949.

◉ A van Eyck *Een appèl aan de verbeelding* (Amsterdam, CoBrA, 1950) (pamphlet, Dutch Experimental Group).

◉ B Schierbeek *De Experimentelen* (Amsterdam, Meulenhoff, 1963).

F

262 FACE, THE

According to its editor, *The Face* is 'the world's best dressed magazine'. A highly successful, post-modernist, glossy, British style magazine. Published monthly, it features all that is new in rock and pop music, fashion, films, books, subcultures, art and design. It was founded by the music paper journalist Nick Logan in May 1980 and rapidly came to epitomize the *Zeitgeist* of the decade with its obsession with style and design. *The Face* is notable for the priority given to photographs, layout and experimental typography. Its distinctive look was primarily due to its designer (from 1981–6) Neville Brody (ex-London College of Printing). The magazine's influence on other journals and advertisements was immense. An exhibition celebrating *The Face* was held at the Photographers' Gallery in London in 1985.

● See also Magazine Art, Zeitgeist.

D Hebdige 'The bottom line on planet one: squaring up to *The Face*' *Ten 8* (19) September 1985 40–9.

'The magazine of the decade: 100 issues' *The Face* (100) September 1988.

J Wozencroft *The graphic language of Neville Brody* (Thames & Hudson, 1988).

263 FACTOGRAPHY

Revival of a term originally used in the 1920s to describe the 'dialectical documentary' work of such artists as Mayakovsky, Tretyakov, Rodchenko (of the *Novy Lef* group), Klutsis, Vertov, Shub, etc. Factography as a technique was discussed by Chuzak (of *Novy Lef*) and by Walter Benjamin in his essay 'The author as producer' (though he did not use the term). Ronald Hunt explains: 'The factograph documents, but does not leave that document as simple experience...the document must be set in context by a dialectical, revealing addition, and this may be, depending on the situation, a pictorial addition, a juxtaposed shot, etc.' Two artists working in the 1970s whom Hunt regarded as factographers were Conrad Atkinson and Hans Haacke. Both produced factual photo-text works, based on research, addressing politically loaded issues such as labour disputes and the ownership of slum houses.

● See also Photo-montage, Photo-works, Political Art.

R Hunt 'For Factography!' *Studio International* **191** (980) March–April 1976 96–9.

B Buchloh 'From faktura to Factography' *October* (30) Fall 1984 82–119.

264 FAIRGROUND ART

A form of popular art that has been extensively documented in recent decades. The mechanization of fairground 'rides' by steam power took place in the late nineteenth century and their elaborate painted decoration dates from the same period. Originally, the power source was in the centre of each ride and this was heavily ornamented, as were the proscenium arches, with cut-glass mirrors, gilding, figurines, battle scenes, peacocks, jungle scenes and so forth. The style was also found in music

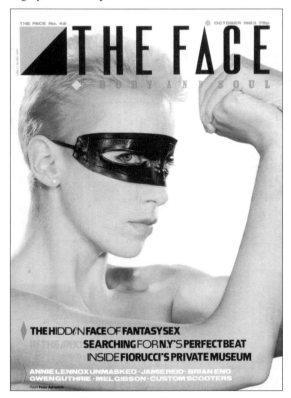

FACE, THE Cover of issue (42) October 1983. Photo: courtesy of Nick Logan.

halls and public houses at the turn of the century. In the 1920s electrification reduced the importance of the centre but arches were still colourfully adorned. Dodgems and the waltzer were added in the '20s and the imagery changed to represent speed and winged figures; even art deco and abstract motifs became popular. Subsequently, the original fairground baroque lost ground as Disney characters, film stars, war heroes and politicians crowded amongst the jungle scenes and heraldic figures. The existence of itinerant fairs has been threatened by economic problems and skilled decorators are now in short supply. One active in the 1970s with a workshop in South London was Fred Fowle.

● See also Carnival, Popular Art.

F Fried *A pictorial history of the carousel* (NY, A S Barnes, 1964).

● D Braithwaite *Fairground architecture* (Hugh Evelyn, 1968).

● G Weedon & J Gorman 'English fairground decoration' – in – *The Penrose graphic arts international annual* **66** (Lund Humphries, 1973) 33–48.

● D Scott-Stewart & M Williams *Fairground snaps* (Idea Books, 1974).

● G Weedon & R Ward *Fairground Art* (White Mouse Editions, 1982).

● C Dinger *Art of the carousel* (NJ, Green Village, 1984).

265 FANTASTIC ARCHITECTURE

A broad category encompassing buildings and designs that depart from the norms of architecture by being extraordinarily imaginative, eccentric or fantastical. Examples include structures by professionals such as the art nouveau Spanish architect Antonio Gaudi (his cathedral in Barcelona) and by obsessive outsiders such as Simon Rodia who built the Watts Towers in Los Angeles. Often, Fantastic Architecture is excessively ornamented, employs many disparate materials, and is 'irrational' in its form compared to the 'rational' architecture of the modernists. Surveys of Fantastic Architecture have provided a corrective to the partial view of modern architecture as a logical and functional development by citing the expressionistic designs of architects like Bruno Taut, Hermann Finsterlin and Paul Scheerbart. The adjective 'fantastic' has also been applied to designs for futuristic, high-technology megastructures. Technological progress has often meant that schemes which seem fantastic when they are first proposed, become everyday reality within a few years.

● See also Conceptual Architecture, Experimental Architecture, Megastructures, Pop Architecture, Rational Architecture, Utopian Architecture, Visionary Architecture.

● 'Architectures Fantastiques' *L'Architecture d'Aujourd'hui* **33** (102) June–July 1962, thematic issue.

● U Conrads & H Sperlich *The architecture of fantasy: utopian building and planning in modern times* (NY, Praeger, 1962).

● W Vostell & D Higgins *Fantastic Architecture* (NY, Something Else Press, 1969).

● M Schuyt & J Elffers *Fantastic Architecture: personal and eccentric visions* (NY, Abrams/London, Thames & Hudson, 1980).

266 FANTASTIC ART

(Also Fantasy Art, Art of the Fantastic) A very broad category encompassing any art or illustration depicting dreams, visions of the future, or imaginary, grotesque, irrational, fanciful, strange and unreal events. From an atheist's standpoint, all images of Greek and Roman myths and all images depicting Christian miracles could be regarded as examples of Fantastic Art. However, in the twentieth century the term is normally used in respect of surrealist works, science fiction and horror comics, films, etc. In 1936 Alfred Barr organized an exhibition at MoMA in New York which employed the term in its title.

● See also Sci-Fi Art.

● A Barr *Fantastic Art, dada, surrealism* (NY, MoMA, 1936).

● K Hume *Fantasy and mimesis* (Methuen, 1984).

● V Burgin & others (eds) *Formations of fantasy* (Methuen, 1986).

● D Palumbo (ed) *Eros in the mind's eye: sexuality and the fantastic in art and film* (Westport, Connecticut, Greenwood Books, 1986).

● D Morse *The fantastic in world literature and the arts: selected essays from the fifth international conference on the fantastic in the arts* (Westport, Connecticut, Greenwood Books, 1987).

● H Day & H Sturges *Art of the fantastic: Latin America 1920–87* (Bloomington, Indiana University Press, 1988).

● C Evans (text), M Dean (ed) *Dream makers: six Fantasy artists at work* (Limpsfield, Surrey, Paper Tiger/Dragon's World, 1988).

● D Palumbo (ed) *Spectrum of the fantastic: selected essays from the sixth international conference on the fantastic in the arts* (Westport, Connecticut, Greenwood Books, 1988).

267 FANTASTIC REALISM

(Or Phantastischen Realismus) An aspect of Austrian art in the immediate post-1945 period. The painters Ernst Fuchs, Erich Brauer, Rudolf Hausner, Wolfgang Hutter and Anton Lehmdem became known collectively as the 'Vienna School of Fantastic Realists'. They were mostly ex-students of A Gütersloh, a teacher at the Vienna Academy, whose classes they attended in the late 1940s. They also studied paintings by the mannerists and such old masters as Breughel and Van Eyck in the collection of the Museum of the History of Art, Vienna. The Fantastic Realists shared a taste for literary and visionary content, and academic techniques. Their work, in its combination of fantastic images and minute detail, also had affinities with pre-war surrealism. These artists achieved popular and official recognition but their art has been criticized by Peter Weiermair on the grounds of 'bland virtuosity' and 'erotic voyeurism'.

● See also Erotic Art.

◉ W Schmied *Malerei des Phantastischen Realismus – die Wiener Schule* (Vienna, Forum Verlag, 1964).

◉ —'The imaginary and the fantastic' – in – *Figurative art since 1945* J Hodin & others (Thames & Hudson, 1971) 123–47.

◉ *Phantastischer Realismus: Malerei und Graphik aus dem Besitz der Stadt Wien* (Innsbruck, Tiroler Landesmuseum Ferdinandeum, 1972).

◉ W Schmied *Zweihundert jahre Phantastische Malerei* (Berlin, Rembrandt Verlag, 1973).

◉ J Muschik *Die Wiener Schule des Phantastischen Realismus* (Munich, Bertelsmann/Vienna, Gütersloh, 1974).

---

268 FAST TRACK CONSTRUCTION

This expression became fashionable in architectural circles during the 1980s. It refers to a building method, i.e. construction begins even before all the design work has been completed and all the finance raised. The aim is to erect buildings as rapidly as possible. However, changes of mind about materials and design features during the course of building can delay completion and cause costs to exceed their budget. A New York skyscraper built according to this method was 'Worldwide Plaza' (1986–9), an office block designed by David Childs of Skidmore, Owings & Merrill (SOM). Karl Sabbagh made a series of TV films and wrote a book about it. A reviewer – Hugh Aldersey-Williams – declared Sabbagh's book revealed 'the chaos of "fast track" construction in the hands of mediocre architects, grasping developers and craven city authorities'.

◉ K Sabbagh *Skyscraper: the making of a building* (Macmillan/ Channel 4 TV, 1989).

◉ —'Tall storeys' *Listener* **122** (3141) November 23 14–15.

◉ H Aldersey-Williams 'Brute force and ignorance' *Blueprint* (64) February 1990 51.

269 FEMINIST ARCHITECTURE & DESIGN

Feminists argue that we live in a *man-made* world which results, therefore, in buildings, cities, cars and appliances which fail to take into account the needs, values and safety of women and mothers with children. Male-dominated industry does, of course, design new products with women in mind – e.g. labour- saving devices such as washing machines – which may be of some value to women but they do not usually challenge the division of labour by gender – it is still women who are expected to do the washing. The gendering of products indeed – scooters = feminine, motor-bikes = masculine – is one of the issues Feminist designers wish to address.

Feminist Design is design for women by women conscious of the long-term goals of the women's liberation movement, or design by men sympathetic to those goals. (There are many women designers who are not feminists.) In Britain in 1978 a Feminist Design Collective was established. Two years later this split and the group Matrix was formed. Matrix was an architectural team consisting of seven women architects, designers and builders. These collectives designed houses, health and children's centres in close association with the women's groups who were the clients.

◉ 'Women and architecture, special issue' *Architectural Design* **45** (8) August 1975.

◉ S Torre (ed) *Women in American architecture* (NY, Whitney Library of Design, 1977).

◉ D Hayden *The grand domestic revolution: a history of Feminist Designs for American homes, neighborhoods and cities* (Cambridge, Mass, MIT Press, 1979).

◉ S de Brettville 'Feminist Design...' *Design and society 1* (Design Council, 1984) (conference proceedings).

◉ Matrix *Making space: women and the man-made environment* (Pluto Press, 1984).

◉ 'Feminism & design, special issue' *FAN (Feminist Art News)* **2** (3) December 1985.

◉ C Erlemann 'What is Feminist Architecture?' – in – *Feminist aesthetics* G Ecker (ed) (Women's Press, 1985) 125–34.

◉ J Attfield & P Kirkham (eds) *A view from the interior: feminism, women and design* (Women's Press, 1989).

◉ C Buckley *Women designers in the pottery industry 1870–1955* (Women's Press, 1989).

◉ P Frank & others *Women in design: careers and life histories since 1900* 2 vols (Stuttgart, Design Centre, 1989).

◉ C Lorenz *Women in architecture* (Trefoil, 1989).

270 FEMINIST ART

(Also Post-Masculine Art) Works of visual art produced in the West since the late 1960s by women motivated by the aims and concerns of the women's movement – essentially an extension into the cultural realm of the aim of the earlier suffragette movement, i.e. the political emancipation of women. In parallel with the emergence of Feminist Art, there was also a development of

FEMINIST ART MAY STEVENS, 'Ordinary/extraordinary: Alice Stevens & Rosa Luxemburg' (1986?). Lithograph based on a 1978 collage, 18" x 24". Collection: J Walker, London.

art criticism and art history. Theory informed practice and vice versa. Of crucial importance to both artists and theorists was the issue of the role of sexual difference/gender in relation to art. Most of the art of the past, it was argued, had not been gender-neutral, it had been 'male art'.

In the decades following World War II many more women than ever before were trained as artists and succeeded in the artworld (e.g. Laurie Anderson, Gillian Ayres, Lee Bontecou, Louise Bourgeois, Hannah Darboven, Rita Donagh, Elizabeth Frink, Grace Hartigan, Jann Haworth, Eva Hesse, Tess Jaray, Lee Krasner, Liliane Lijn, Agnes Martin, Joan Mitchell, Marisol, Alice Neel, Bridget Riley), but this did not mean that all these women were feminists; much contemporary art by women has been very similar in terms of content and style to that of men. Nor did it mean that the discrimination against women within the artworld (e.g. in terms of representation in mixed and open exhibitions) had been overcome. Battles had to be fought to gain greater equality, and an improvement was achieved; even so, many feminists felt compelled to set up a parallel network to the male-dominated artworld: i.e. Feminist artists' organizations and workshops (e.g. WAR – Women Artists in Revolution, New York, 1969; AIR – Artists in Residence, a New York co-operative founded in 1972; Women Artists Slide Library), Feminist Art magazines (e.g. *Women & Art* (1971), *Feminist Art Journal* (1972)), art galleries, exhibitions, museums (e.g. National Museum of Women in the Arts). The separatist strategy had some obvious short-term advantages, but also some long-term disadvantages.

Feminist artists are distinguished from other female artists by being self-consciously feminist, by addressing feminist issues in the content and form of their work: for instance, the craft/fine art issue. Some Feminist artists have deliberately adopted craft techniques historically associated with women's work in order to re-evaluate that tradition and to undermine the category of 'fine art'. Another pressing issue has been 'images of women'; how should women be represented in art given the long history of erotic female nudes painted by men for men? Some feminists have turned the tables by taking men as their subject matter, while others have explored the questions of subjectivity and self-identity via a reworking of mass-media stereotypes. Eroticism and sexuality have been favourite themes because the women's movement encouraged women to explore and enjoy their sexuality and to analyse the ways it is used socially and exploited commercially. In fact, the subject matter of Feminist Art has ranged from the routine, domestic chores of housework and caring for children – 'maintenance art' – to the 'cosmic mother' associated with the archetypes and myths of ancient matriarchies. Many topics in Feminist Art derive from the specific experience of women in a patriarchal/violent male society: e.g. rape (Margaret Harrison's 1978 painting 'Rape'; Lisa Pattenden's 'Marks that fade scars that don't' (1987), a photo-documentary work about the artist's own experience of being raped).

Of particular concern to Feminist artists and art historians has been the issue of 'hidden from history'. Judy Chicago's and others' massive project 'The dinner party' (1979) was designed to celebrate the achievements of hundreds of women neglected by historians. Feminist art historians meanwhile laboured to recover the names of female artists of the past unfairly excluded from the standard histories of art, and to find an answer to the question 'why have there been no great women artists?'.

Artists noted for their contributions to Feminist Art include: Helen Chadwick, Judy Chicago, Rose Finn-Kelcey (a performance artist), Margaret Harrison, Alexis Hunter, Mary Kelly, Barbara Kruger, Yve Lomax, Yoko Ono, Adrian Piper, Yvonne Rainier (a film-maker), Martha Rosler (a video artist), Cindy Sherman, Miriam Shapiro, Monica Sjöö, Sylvia Sleigh, Jo Spence (a photographer), Nancy Spero, May Stevens and Kate Walker. Their works encompass a tremendous variety of forms, media and styles.

Within the complex and demanding theoretical debate associated with Feminist Art, certain issues and questions remain contentious: how to evolve standards of judgement as alternatives to those of men which have been largely rejected; how to present a new content and remain comprehensible while at the same time contending with the dominant male artistic 'languages'; is there, or ought there to be, a specifically feminist or matriarchal aesthetic? Can Feminist Art escape the fate of being merely an additional category within pluralism? Can it achieve its goal of radically transforming both art and society?

● See also Erotic Art, Hobby Art, National Museum of Women in the Arts, Pluralism, Post-Feminist Art, Women Artists Slide Library.

● A Krasilovsky 'Feminism in the arts: an interim bibliography' *Artforum* **10** (10) June 1972 72–5.

● T Hess & E Baker (eds) *Art & sexual politics* (Collier-MacMillan, 1973).

● T Hess & L Nochlin *Woman as sex object...* (Allen Lane, 1973).

● M Sjöö (ed) *Some thoughts on Feminist Art* (Bristol Women's Centre, 1974).

● J Chicago *Through the flower...* (NY, Doubleday, 1975).

● C Nemser *Art talk: conversations with twelve women artists* (NY, Scribners, 1975).

● L Alloway 'Women's art in the '70s' *Art in America* **64** (3) May–June 1976 64–72.

● L Lippard *From the center: feminist essays on women's art* (NY, Dutton, 1976).

● *Women artists: 1550–1950* (Los Angeles County Museum of Art, 1976).

● 'Women's art' (special issue) *Studio International* **193** (987) March 1977.

● L Tickner 'The body politic: female sexuality and women artists since 1970' *Art History* **1** (2) June 1978 236–47.

● G Greer *The obstacle race* (Secker & Warburg, 1979).

● J Chicago *The Dinner Party needlework: embroidering our heritage* (Garden City, New York, Anchor Books/Doubleday, 1980).

● *Issue: social strategies by women artists* (ICA, 1980).

● *Women's images of men* (ICA, 1980).

● R Parker & G Pollock *Old mistresses: women, art and ideology* (Routledge & Kegan Paul, 1981).

● *Sense and sensibility in Feminist Art practice* (Nottingham, Midland Group, 1982).

● R Parker *The subversive stitch: embroidery and the making of the feminine* (Women's Press, 1984).

● *Difference: on representation and sexuality* (NY, New Museum of Contemporary Art, 1984/London, ICA, 1985).

● G Ecker (ed) *Feminist aesthetics* (Women's Press, 1985).

● R Parker & G Pollock (eds) *Framing feminism: art and the women's movement 1970–85* (Routledge & Kegan Paul, 1987).

● H Robinson (ed) *Visibly female: feminism and art today* (Camden Press, 1987).

● R Betterton (ed) *Looking on: images of femininity in the visual arts and media* (Pandora, 1987).

● W Beckett *Contemporary women artists* (Oxford, Phaidon, 1988).

● G Pollock *Vision and difference: femininity, feminism and histories of art* (Methuen, 1988).

● L Tickner *The spectacle of women: imagery of the suffrage campaign 1907–14* (Chatto & Windus, 1988).

● J Wolff *The art of women* (MacMillan, 1988).

● *Along the lines of resistance: an exhibition of contemporary Feminist Art* (Barnsley, Cooper Gallery, 1988–9).

● W Chadwick *Women, art, and society* (Thames & Hudson, 1990).

271 FIGURATION LIBRE (Free Figuration) A term invented by the French artist Ben Vautier in 1981 to characterize the paintings of a group of four young artists: Robert Combas, Hervé Di Rosa, Rémy Blanchard and François Boisrond. According to Combas, la Figuration Libre 'is to do what one likes as much as possible...to amuse oneself, to be cool...to have fun'. The results, in his case, were crude pictures in vivid colours, crowded with figures and incident, drawn and painted in a style derived from comic strips. His subjects were those of popular culture: violence, war, sex and rock 'n' roll. The other members of the group painted in a more expressionist or slapdash way, with child-like directness, but also drew inspiration from popular sources like TV, the cinema, graffiti, advertising and kitsch. Their pictures were imbued with tremendous energy and sardonic humour. They were hailed as the first new movement in French art for years. An exhibition celebrating the work was held in Paris in 1985. It signalled the extension of the label to certain American artists deemed to be working in a similar way, e.g. Jean-Michel Basquiat, Keith Haring and Kenny Scharf. Critics surveying the new painting of the 1980s frequently cited Figuration Libre as the French contribution to the broader categories of new image painting or trans-avant garde.

● See also Comic Art, Figurative Art, New Image Painting, Trans-Avant Garde.

● A Berthon 'Back to painting' *The Face* (32) December 1982 47–51.

● *Figuration Libre* (Paris, ARC Musée d'Art Moderne de la Ville de Paris, 1985).

FIGURATIVE ARCHITECTURE

This expression was used by the Italian architect and critic Paolo Portoghesi about the late 1970s/early 1980s work of the American architect Michael Graves. According to Portoghesi, figuration in architecture concerned 'not the direct imitation of nature, but rather the reproduction of a series of conventional archetypes like the hut, the wall, the column, the door, the pediment and so on'. (It was a sign of post-modernism, an architectural equivalent of the return to figuration in painting in reaction to the dominance of abstraction.) The traditional principles of order in architecture, it was considered, derived in large part from the human body. Graves himself remarked that architecture should be concerned with 'the metaphorical representation of man and the landscape'. Figurative Architecture was therefore an attempt to restore the conventional and linguistic character of the art of architecture, to re-establish the continuity with the past ruptured by the advent of modernism.

'Figurative Architecture' was also the title given to an exhibition of designs and documentation of the work of five young Irish architects – Paul Keogh, Sheila O'Donnell, Derek Tynan, John Tuomey and Rachael Chidlow – all of whom (except Chidlow) studied at University College, Dublin. The architecture of Aldo Rossi was an important influence upon their work.

● See also Abstract Representation, Analogical Architecture, Post-Modern Architecture, Symbolic Architecture.

● M Graves 'A case for Figurative Architecture' *Architectural Design* **53** (7/8) 1983 98–9.

● P Portoghesi *Postmodern: the architecture of the postindustrial society* (NY, Rizzoli, 1983) 90–1.

● C MacDonald & others *Figurative Architecture: the work of five Dublin architects* (Architectural Association, 1986).

273 FIGURATIVE ART

Before the advent of modern art, this term was unnecessary because most European art depicted the human figure. Figuration only took on a special significance once abstraction became an important idiom. Periodically, in the post-1945 era artists have sought to revive figuration and this has given rise to a series of art labels including the word, e.g. Bay Area figuration, new Spanish figuration, figurative expressionism. (See under 'Figurative art/Painting' in the index.) Curators too have been fond of organizing mixed shows of artists reworking the image of the human body, hence the frequent announcements of 'a return to figuration'. Some critics have considered that abstraction was the consequence of an inner historical logic associated with modern art, but this has

not prevented artists such as Ron Kitaj, David Hockney, Francis Bacon, Henry Moore and Leon Golub from successfully combining figuration and modernist devices. Also, many painters thought of as completely abstract – e.g. Jackson Pollock – have permitted figurative elements to surface in their work.

● See also Bay Area Figuration, Critical Realism, Humanist Art, Neo-Expressionism, New Image Painting, Photo-Realism, School of London, Superhumanism, Verist Sculpture.

● P Selz *New images of Man* (NY, MoMA, 1959).

● H Hodgkin & others 'On figuration and the narrative in art' *Studio International* **172** (881) September 1966 140–4.

● J Hodin & others *Figurative Art since 1945* (Thames & Hudson, 1971).

● R Kitaj *The human clay* (Hayward Gallery/Arts Council of Great Britain, 1976).

● L Gowing *Eight figurative painters* (New Haven, Connecticut, Yale Center for British Art, 1981).

● *New Spanish figuration* (ICA, 1982).

● G Nordland & others *New figuration in America* (Milwaukee, Art Museum, 1982).

● N Lynton *Human interest: 50 years of British art about people* (Manchester, Cornerhouse, 1985).

● H Cumming 'New Figurative Art: a survey' *Art & Design* **4** (9/10) 1988 45–59.

● T Krens (ed) *Refigured painting: the German image 1960–88* (Munich, Prestel Verlag, 1988).

● P Schimmel & J Stein *The figurative fifties: New York figurative expressionism* (Newport Beach, California, Newport Harbor Art Museum, 1988).

● N Lynton *Picturing people: British Figurative Art since 1945* (British Council, 1990).

● R Paulson *Figure & abstraction in contemporary painting* (New Brunswick, NJ, Rutgers University Press, 1990).

274 FILOFAX

A loose-leaf diary / address/ note book or 'personal organizer' which was originally an American invention for holding technical information dating from the 1910s. For many years Filofaxes were used just by the clergy and the military but then in Britain during the early and mid 1980s expensive, leather-bound Filofaxes became extremely fashionable accessories amongst business executives and media folk, so much so that they became symbols of the Yuppie lifestyle. Filofaxes were produced by Norman & Hill of Ilford. The rapid success of this company was halted in 1988 as a result of Japanese firms copying their products.

● See also Cult Objects, Lifestyle.

● P Silverton 'Filohacks in a frenzy of style' *Observer* October 27 1985 51.

● D Sudjic, *Cult objects* (Paladin, 1985).
● B Campbell & W Wheeler 'Filofaxions' *Marxism Today* December 1988 32–3.
● I Sinclair *Filofax facts* (David Fulton, 1988).

275 FINISH FETISH

(Also California Finish Fetish, LA Look, Venice Surface) During the 1960s some American artists, in particular those based in Los Angeles – Larry Bell, John McCracken, John Eversley and Ed Ruscha – were fanatically concerned to endow their paintings, sculptures and environmental constructions with a smooth, high-gloss surface equal to those found on highly polished automobiles. Peter Plagens described Finish Fetish as 'extra spit and polish in pop and minimal art plus space age materials'. Complicated procedures and expensive technology were often required to produce a perfect sheen. The cult of impeccable finish was part of a wider Los Angeles aesthetic shared by craftspersons such as those who made surfboards. It also reflected the influence of Hollywood and its emphasis on the surface of things, the façade.

● P Plagens 'The LA Look' – in – *Sunshine muse: contemporary art on the West Coast* (NY, Praeger, 1974).

276 FITZROVIANS

British artists, writers and Bohemians associated with the area of central London called 'Fitzrovia' which takes its name from the Fitzroy Tavern near Tottenham Court Road. The term 'Fitzrovia' was first used in a *Times Literary Supplement* book review in 1958. Hugh David argues that the Bohemian milieu existed from 1900 to 1955. Amongst those who worked, ate and drank in Fitzrovia were Augustus John, Walter Sickert, W. B. Yeats, Michael Arlen, Julian Maclaren-Ross, Dylan Thomas, John Minton and Keith Vaughan.

● H David *The Fitzrovians: a portrait of a Bohemian society 1900–55* (Michael Joseph, 1988).

277 FLUXUS

An international avant garde movement born officially in 1962 and active throughout the '60s and early '70s. The word 'fluxus' is Latin for 'flowing'; in English 'flux' means a 'gushing forth, an abnormal discharge, a fusion, a state of continuous change'; all these shades of meaning applied to the art or anti-art tendency Fluxus. According to a Fluxus manifesto, its aim was to 'purge the world of bourgeois sickness, "intellectual", professional and commercialized culture, purge the world of dead art', to generate 'a revolutionary flood and tide in art, promote living art, anti-art, promote non-art reality...' and to fuse 'the cadres of cultural, social and political revolutionaries into united front and action'. Fluxus spanned the Atlantic: activities took place primarily in Germany and New York, but Fluxus 'festivals' were also held in Paris, London, Amsterdam and Copenhagen. Fluxus artists delighted in organizing entertaining events, concerts of electronic music, anti-theatre and street art, which were similar in some respects to the happenings of the 1950s and the actions of European artists and also to amateur theatricals. One of the most striking features of Fluxus was its multi-media/ inter-media character: works in several media were often presented during the same evening and Fluxus artists mingled media with no regard for the purity of medium aesthetic. They tended to despise the professional artworld and avoided producing paintings and sculptures for the art market; though they did generate an enormous number of visual and literary products: books, pamphlets, posters, diagrams, musical scores, films, multiples, etc.

The roll-call of participants in Fluxus includes almost every major avant garde artist of the 1960s: Beuys, George Brecht, Robert Filliou, Henry Flynt, Dick Higgins, George Maciunas, Yoko Ono, Ben Vautier, Wolf Vostell, Robert Watts, Emmett Williams, La Monte Young and others too numerous to mention. The movement was co-ordinated, and its myriad publications edited, by Maciunas (he also invented the name). Fluxus is said to have ended in 1978 with the death of Maciunas. Filliou described Fluxus as a 'non-group' because it was composed of individualists with different ideas and aesthetic principles. This was true but the artists did share an iconoclastic, dada-like spirit, a desire to introduce spontaneity, joy and humour into art while avoiding at all costs any limiting theory or programme. Writing in 1972, Ken Friedman claimed that Fluxus originated the notion of 'concept art'. Despite the radical, experimental nature of Fluxus and its vaunting of the ephemeral, it now occupies a place in the histories of art and in the private collections and museums of modern art.

● See also Actions, Affiches Lacérées, Conceptual Art, Destructive Art, Happenings, Inter-Media, Political Art.

● *Fluxus cc V TRE* (Fluxus newspaper, 9 issues 1964–70).
● *Happening & Fluxus* (Cologne, Kolnischer Kunstverein, 1970).
● K Friedman 'Notes on concept art' *Schmuck* March 1972 6–16.
● 'Free Fluxus now' *Art & Artists* **7** (7) October 1972, special issue.
● *Fluxshoe* (Cullompton, Devon, Beau Geste Press, 1972).
● (Fluxus special issue) *Flash Art* (84/85) October– November 1978.
● H Martin *An introduction to George Brecht's book of the*

tumbler on fire (Milan, Multhipla Edizioni, 1978).

⬤ H Ruhé *Fluxus: the most radical and experimental art movement of the sixties* (Amsterdam, Gallery A, 1979).

⬤ J Hendricks *Fluxus codex* (Detroit, Michigan, Gilbert & Lila Silvermann Fluxus Collection/NY, Abrams, 1988).

⬤ C Phillpot & J Hendricks *Fluxus: selections from the Gilbert and Lila Silvermann Collection* (NY, MoMA, 1988).

FOOD ART

(Also Eat/Gourmet/Gustatory Art & Gourmandism) Cooking and baking have long been described as 'arts' and the decoration of food, especially the icing of cakes, is a minor popular art in its own right. However, the label 'Food Art' that emerged in the 1970s did not refer to these everyday arts but to three kinds of work produced by fine artists, i.e:

(1) Alterations to the shape and colour of existing foodstuffs and the creation of new objects composed of edible materials: Daniel Spoerri, a Swiss artist, ran a restaurant/gallery in Düsseldorf for a number of years called 'Eat Art' where invited artists exploited different foodstuffs; the American painter Richard Lindner issued a series of gingerbread multiples; the German artist Tim Schroder altered the shape of food and gave it bizarre colours by adding vegetable dyes; food thus treated was often served during festivals: two Paris-based artists – Antoni Miralda and Dorothée Selz – organized such events.

(2) Paintings and sculptures depicting food: Wayne Thiebaud, the American West Coast artist, delighted in painting items of food, such as fancy cakes, which he rendered in thick succulent impasto in order to simulate the actual quality of cream and icing sugar; another American pop artist – Claes Oldenburg – often employed food as subject matter, e.g. his sculptural versions of hamburgers and ice-cream cones greatly enlarged and composed of incongruous materials; in 1964 a show called 'The Supermarket' was held at the Bianchini Gallery, New York in which pop artists displayed images and three-dimensional replicas of vegetables, fruit and canned goods arranged and signposted in faithful imitation of a real supermarket.

(3) Artworks composed of edible materials depicting food: Peter Kuttner, an artist fond of colouring food, once submitted to a Royal Academy summer exhibition a 'painting' of a cake made of edible matter entitled 'Something for the critic to get his teeth into'.

Readers may feel that Food Art lacks significance; however, it is possible for this type of art to make serious points, e.g. in 1973 Carl Andre made a sculpture called 'American decay' from large quantities of cottage cheese and tomato ketchup – the ingredients of President

FOOD ART PETER KUTTNER with 'Something for the critics to get their teeth into' (1975). Made from icing. Photo: Kuttner.

Richard Nixon's favourite snacks – and then left it to putrefy. Another significant feminist work about a symbolic meal was 'The Dinner Party' by Judy Chicago, Susan Hill and a large team of helpers. This 1979 work paid homage to hundreds of women important in different fields throughout history; in effect it was 'a Last Supper for those who did the cooking'.

Academics have also paid serious attention to food as an artform: the British anthropologist Mary Douglas has examined the aesthetic appeal of food and the formal rules governing the combination of dishes, the structure of courses, which make up the 'events' we call 'meals'.

⬤ See also Feminist Art, Pop Art, Popular Art.

⬤ 'Artefacts for eating: the confectioner's plastic art, Eat Art' *Die Kunst und das schöne Heim* **82** (12) December 1970 769–73.

⬤ 'Events by Miralda and Selz' *Studio International* **181** (932) April 1972 167.

⬤ P Kuttner 'Coloured food' *Studio International* **181** (932) April 1972 166.

⬤ M Deserti 'Cucina: a tavola con l'arte' *Casa Vogue* (14) May–June 1972 126–9.

⬤ *Eats, an exhibition of food in art* (Hempstead, New York, Hofstra University, Emily Lowe Gallery, 1972).

⬤ M Douglas 'Food as an artform' *Studio International* **188** (969) September 1974 83–8.

⬤ J Chicago *The Dinner Party needlework: embroidering our*

heritage (Garden City, New York, Anchor Books /Doubleday, 1980).

● M Quinet 'Food as art: the problem of function' *British Journal of Aesthetics* **21** (2) Spring 1981 159–71.

● M Bellini (ed) *Eating by design* (Milan, Electa, 1981).

279 FOOL, THE

A late 1960s design group with three Dutch members – Seemon Posthuma a painter, Marijke Koger a commercial artist, Josje Leeger a fashion designer – and one English member – Barrie Finch a theatre publicist. The Fool was formed in London in 1967 and was soon designing posters, record covers, costumes and stage sets for such rock bands as Cream, the Hollies, Procul Harum and the Beatles. When the latter established their record label and philanthropic venture Apple, The Fool became heavily involved. During Apple's short life – December 1967 to July 1968 – the boutique at 94 Baker Street sold various products including painted furniture and clothes designed by the group. They also painted a brightly coloured mural on the exterior of the building. Later on they designed sets, costumes, a title sequence and a dance number for a movie with music by George Harrison. The Fool delighted in romantic hippie clothing with rainbow colours made from sumptuous materials. Adopting a multi-cultural perspective, they borrowed liberally from the arts and crafts of India, Russia, Turkey and North Africa. An excess of colour, pattern and richness characterized their work. Historians of the Beatles tend to blame them for much of the profligate expenditure which eventually ruined Apple.

Not content with designing, The Fool tried their hand at performing music and recording: in 1968 Mercury released a psychedelic LP entitled 'The Fool' and in 1969 they toured the United States. A year later they disbanded. The design style of The Fool marked the point at which acid and flower power became kitsch; however, in the 1980s their products began to surface in auctions of '60s memorabilia. What was significant about The Fool in terms of future trends, was their eclecticism, their willingness to design in many fields, and to fuse art, design and music.

● See also Pop Design, Psychedelic Art, Rock Art/ Design/ Fashion.

● M Green 'The Fool's paradise' *Observer Colour Supplement* December 3 1967 42–7.

● V Joynson *The acid trip: a complete guide to psychedelic music* (Todmorden, Lancs, Babylon Books, 1984).

280 FORMA

A group of Italian artists established in Rome in 1947. They were committed to abstraction rather than to the then fashionable social realism. Members included Achille Perilli, Piero Dorazio, Giulio Turcato, Pietro Consagra, Carla Accardi and Antonio Sanfilippo. They exhibited at the Venice Biennale in 1948 and issued a monthly review entitled *Forma I;* they proclaimed in a manifesto that they were both formalists and Marxists.

● See also Continuità.

● *Forma I* (Rome) April 1947.

● M Fagiolo dell'Arco *Forma I* (Rome, Galleria Arco D'Aliberti, 1966).

281 FORMALISM & FORMALIST CRITICISM

Formalism is a tendency within the practice and theory of art to assign priority to the form of an artwork at the expense of all other characteristics. For those critical of this tendency, the term 'Formalist' is one of abuse. All works of art involve forms – shapes, colours, structures, patterns, compositional relationships – but traditionally they have also involved content – subject matter, the representation of an external reality, symbolism, narration and so forth. However, with the advent of modern abstract art, paintings began to appear which consisted of nothing but forms, shapes, colours, etc. Some abstract artists have in fact intended their forms to be symbolic, e.g. the abstract expressionists, but others have rigorously excluded all illusions and all allusions, e.g. the minimalists of the '60s. The paintings of Frank Stella can be taken as paradigmatic of Formalist abstraction. Leftwing critics tend to object to this type of art because it has no social content. Presumably, the opposite of Formalism would be 'contentism' – priority given to content at the expense of form – the kind of thing typical of socialist realism.

Formalist Criticism is a type of criticism which concentrates on the form of works of art at the expense of their content and social, historical context. Two British Formalist critics were Clive Bell and Roger Fry who wrote in the 1910s and '20s. When they were confronted by a range of visual artefacts from many periods, cultures and places and asked 'what do they all have in common?', the answer was 'significant form'. Thus form came to be seen as essential and everything else as inessential. A school of Formalist Criticism also developed in Russia in the 1910s and '20s: Russian Formalism. Mostly the critics concerned theorized about poetry and literature, i.e. Viktor Shklovsky, Boris Tomashevsky, Boris Eichenbaum and Roman Jakobson. These critics were influenced by linguistics and were particularly interested in the formal devices used by revolutionary avant garde artists. It has been claimed that the Soviet critics were concerned with all aspects of art, even content.

In the United States from 1960 onwards the Formalist tradition of art criticism received new impetus under the influence of Clement Greenberg and British linguistic philosophy. Greenberg, the leading Formalist critic, promoted theories of media purity and autonomy. His followers – writers like Michael Fried, Rosalind Krauss, Sidney Tillim and others – were mostly associated with *Artforum* magazine. They rejected lyrical descriptions and literary interpretations in favour of close, formal analysis. The kind of art they tended to support was abstract because content, symbolism, etc., were all regarded as 'extraneous'. The intentions, opinions and beliefs of the artist were also considered irrelevant. Leo Steinberg said their attitude was interdictory (telling artists what they must and must not do) and this is why he called it 'preventive aesthetics'.

During the 1970s British artists associated with conceptual art and political art debated the issue of Formalism in art and criticism at great length. Seeking an alternative to the American tradition of Formalism represented by artists like Stella and critics like Greenberg, they looked to the Soviet tradition in the hope of developing an alternative, what Victor Burgin called 'Socialist Formalism'.

● See also Modernist Painting, Objecthood, Presence.

◉ C Bell *Art* (1914) (Arrow Books, 1961).

◉ V Erlich *Russian Formalism* (The Hague, Mouton, 1955).

◉ B Reise 'Greenberg and the group: a retrospective view' Part 1 *Studio International* **175** (900) May 1968 254–6; Part 2 *Studio International* **175** (901) June 1968 314–16.

◉ R Ekman 'Paradoxes of Formalism' *British Journal of Aesthetics* **10** (4) October 1970 350–8.

◉ L Steinberg 'Reflections on the state of criticism' *Artforum* **10** (7) March 1972 37–49.

◉ C Greenberg 'The necessity of "Formalism"' *Art International* **16** (8) October 1972 105–6.

◉ S Foster 'Clement Greenberg: Formalism in the '40s and '50s' *Art Journal* **35** (1) Fall 1975 20–4.

◉ V Burgin 'Socialist Formalism' *Studio International* **191** (980) March–April 1976 148–54.

◉ P Medvedev & M Bakhtin *The formal method in literary scholarship...* (Baltimore, Johns Hopkins University Press, 1978).

◉ T Bennett *Formalism and Marxism* (Methuen, 1979).

◉ D Kuspit *Clement Greenberg, art critic* (Madison, Wisconsin, University of Wisconsin Press, 1979).

◉ D Curtin 'Varieties of aesthetic Formalism' *Journal of Aesthetics & Art Criticism* **40** (3) Spring 1982 315–26.

◉ F Frascina (ed) *Pollock and after: the critical debate* (Harper & Row, 1985).

◉ C Greenberg *Collected essays* 2 vols (Chicago, University of Chicago Press, 1986).

A new branch of mathematics concerned with the morphology of the amorphous or the chaotic which excited the interest of many scientists, artists and critics in the 1980s. The name was devised in the 1970s by Benoit Mandelbrot, a professor of mathematics and discoverer of the Mandelbrot set (1980). Fractal Geometry is concerned with shapes in nature which are, for practical purposes, infinitely complicated (e.g. coastlines, clouds, tree bark, mountains). Many Fractals are self-similar structures, that is structures composed of parts which are themselves of the same structure (e.g. zig-zags composed of smaller zig-zags). Mandelbrot used a computer plus cathode ray tube and printer to generate images of his mathematical equations.

A number of mathematicians and physicists at the University of Bremen held a workshop called 'Chaotic Dynamics' in 1981 and then formed the 'Complex Dynamics Research Group' to study Fractals in a computer graphics laboratory. These scientists use the term 'map art' to describe the colour photographs of Fractals generated via iteration procedures on computers. The lat-

FRACTAL GEOMETRY Image from H-O PEITGEN & P H RICHTER'S *The beauty of fractals* (1986). Copyright the authors & Springer Verlag.

ter were exhibited worldwide in a show called 'Frontiers of chaos' organized in 1985 by the Group with the aid of the Goethe Institute of Munich. Fractal images attracted the attention of the artworld because of their strange beauty (they resembled psychedelic imagery).

● See also Computer Art, Psychedelic Art.

● B Mandelbrot *The Fractal Geometry of nature* (San Francisco, Freeman, 1982).

● A Jankel & R Morton *Creative computer graphics* (Cambridge University Press, 1984).

● H-0 Peitgen & P Richter/Complex Dynamics Research Group, University of Bremen *Frontiers of chaos: computer graphics face complex dynamics* (Bremen, Map Art/Munich, Goethe Institute, 1985).

● —*The beauty of Fractals: images of complex dynamical systems* (Berlin, Springer-Verlag, 1986).

● P Coates & M Reidelbachz 'Frontiers of chaos: computer graphics of Fractal boundaries' *Real Life* (17/18) Winter 1987–8 12–15.

● P Atkins 'The rose, the lion, and the ultimate oyster' *Modern Painters* **2** (4) Winter 1989–90 50–5.

283 | **FRANKFURT SCHOOL AESTHETICS** (Also Critical Theory) The term 'Frankfurt School' refers to a specific approach to philosophy and to a group of neo-Marxist philosophers and social theorists who were members of, or were associated with, the Institut für Sozialforschung (Institute for Social Research) operative in Frankfurt from 1923 to '33 and from 1950 onwards. The best known of these theorists were Theodor Adorno, Walter Benjamin, Erich Fromm, Jürgen Habermas, Max Horkheimer, Leo Lowenthal, Herbert Marcuse and Franz Neumann. In the 1930s Jewish/Marxist intellectuals had to flee Europe to escape the Nazis and for a period the Frankfurt School was located in the United States. During the '60s the ideas of the Frankfurt School became fashionable amongst the New Left and the student activists in Europe. Through the writings of Marcuse, they also influenced a generation of protesting American students.

Frankfurt School philosophy has been summed up by the term 'Critical Theory' (essentially a euphemism for Marxism), i.e. an open- ended search accompanied by an aversion to closed philosophical systems; analysis allied to empirical research; a synoptic interdisciplinary approach; a dialectical critique of other thinkers; a negative, critical attitude towards fascism and bourgeois society; theory for revolutionary praxis rather than for its own sake (however, agitprop art was not welcomed); pessimism. Aesthetics, art, music and mass culture were topics of particular interest to the Frankfurt School: Adorno wrote on modern music, aesthetics and radio;

Horkheimer, Adorno and Marcuse wrote hostile critiques of mass culture and its relation to art; Marcuse also wrote on the aesthetic dimension; Benjamin wrote on poetry, theatre, photography and mechanical reproduction and its implications for art; Lowenthal focused on literature. They regarded art, variously, as a code which when deciphered revealed the hidden processes of society; as a negating force which by its very existence opposed the domination of the mass culture industry; as a foretaste of a future society radically different from existing ones.

Notwithstanding the insights of Critical Theory, there was little in the writings of the Frankfurt School philosophers (apart from Benjamin) that was of immediate value to practising Left-wing artists. The latter found Brecht's writings more useful because he combined theory and practice.

● See also Marxist Aesthetics, Political Art.

● M Horkheimer 'Art and mass culture' *Studies in Philosophy and Social Science* **9** (2) 1941.

● W Benjamin *Illuminations* (J Cape, 1970).

● M Jay *The dialectical imagination: a history of the Frankfurt School* (Heinemann, 1973).

● P Slater 'The aesthetic theory of the Frankfurt School' *Working Papers in Cultural Studies* (6) Autumn 1974 172–211.

● H Paetzold *Neo-Marxistische Asthetik* 2 vols (Düsseldorf, Schwann Verlag, 1974).

● H Marcuse *The aesthetic dimension* (MacMillan, 1979).

● T Adorno *Aesthetic theory* (Routledge & Kegan Paul, 1984).

284 | **FREE ABSTRACTION** A style of drawing associated with works dating mainly from the 1950s by certain German artists. The artists in question were Peter Brüning, Bernard Schultze, Emil Schumacher, K. R. H. Sonderborg and Hann Trier. Their art tended towards the abstract but it rejected geometric forms. It was 'free' as in 'free-hand' and 'free-flowing': characterized by rapid, intuitive scribbles and calligraphic brushmarks. Essentially this kind of work was a sub-genre of European l'art informel or tachisme.

● See also Art Informel, Lyrical Abstraction, Tachisme.

● G Aust *The art of German drawing VII: Free Abstraction* (Goethe-Institut London, 1990).

285 | **FREE FORM ARTS TRUST** A charitable organization founded in 1969 by a group of British artists who wanted to work on environmental projects outside the gallery system and to involve members of the community living in run-down inner city areas. Martin Goodrich, who trained as a painter at the Royal College of Art, was one of the main founders.

Eventually, a core of 25 people plus consultants ran Free Form. They included fine artists, architects and landscape designers. A technical centre for local people was set up in Hackney, London, and a regional office was opened in North Shields, Tyneside. Funding was supplied by the Arts Council, local councils and the Department of the Environment. Successful projects have included: an exotic garden for the disabled; a mixed-media mural for a housing estate; the decoration of large-scale hoardings around building sites with colourful, trompe l'oeil imagery.

In 1989 Free Form established Artworks as a separate profit-making company whose aim was to provide paintings and decoration for building site hoardings. The intention was to improve the urban environment and to demonstrate that art need not be confined to galleries. By earning money from such commercial commissions, Free Form also hoped to subsidize their other non-commercial activities. Dedicated to urban regeneration, the Trust also sought to create work for local craftspeople and to establish studios for the production of ceramics, mosaics and stained glass. Increasingly Free Form finds itself becoming involved in the community architecture movement. Free Form activities are a blend of community, environmental and public art.

● See also Billboard Art, Community Architecture, Community Art & Media, Environmental Art, Public Art, Street Art.

L Relph-Knight 'The bright rise of Free Form' *Building suppt* April 8 1988 26–7.

C Melhuish 'Street values' *Building Design* May 19 1989.

286 FREE FORMS

Organic, biomorphic forms or shapes produced by freehand drawing, as opposed to rectangular or circular shapes produced by rulers and compasses. This term was applied to the kind of forms found in paintings by Arshile Gorky, William Baziotes and Mark Rothko created in the 1940s; these artists had been influenced by the work of the dada sculptor Hans Arp and by the surrealist painter Joan Miró. In the following decade Free Forms, or 'quartics' as they were called in coordinate geometry, became popular in the applied arts, e.g. kidney, boomerang, egg shapes and rounded squares appeared in the design of furniture, fabrics and tableware.

J Wedd 'Quartics' *Design* (49) January 1953 15–17.

—'Two familiar quartics' *Design* (59) November 1953 25–7.

L Alloway 'The biomorphic forties' *Artforum* **4** (1) September 1965 18–22.

J Manser 'Free Form furniture' *Design* (240) December 1968 28–33.

R Metzger *Biomorphism in American painting* (UCLA, 1973), *Dissertation Abstracts International* **36** (4) December 1973 3264 A (73–28735).

287 FREESTYLE

(Also 'No Rules' Architecture) A term employed by the writer-photographer Tim Street-Porter to characterize the 'new wave' of architecture and interior design appearing in Los Angeles between 1978 and '86. The architects and designers concerned were Frank Gehry, Eric Moss, Frederick Fisher, Brian Murphy, Peter Shine and Morphosis (i.e. the architectural team of Thom Mayne & Michael Rotunda). Most of the architecture built was low-rise, small-scale residential and commercial properties. According to Street-Porter, Freestyle began with the provocative 'Gehry House', Santa Monica (1978), by Frank Gehry, which involved the preservation of a conventional house inside a strange shell made from chain link, wired glass and corrugated metal. The colourful 'Petal House' (1982) by Moss was equally odd: it had roof elements resembling the unfolding petals of a flower. In terms of furniture and interiors, no single style prevailed but the work was often highly original, humorous and pastel coloured.

Freestyle designers drew their inspiration from the physical and cultural environments of Los Angeles and Hollywood; they were also influenced by contemporary art and by California new wave graphics; they were 'free-spirited' in the sense that they felt able to break the rules and norms of conventional design and to make architecture that was 'fundamentally sensual'.

● See also Finish Fetish.

T Street-Porter *Freestyle: the new architecture and interior design from Los Angeles* (NY, Stewart, Tabori & Chang, 1986).

P Cook & A Colquhoun *Morphosis: buildings and projects* (NY, Rizzoli, 1989).

288 FREUDIAN AESTHETICS

Sigmund Freud's revolutionary theory of the unconscious and his psychoanalytic method inspired many later writers to apply his ideas to the phenomenon of art. (Freud himself wrote essays on Leonardo, Michelangelo and Dostoevsky.) Those whom Freud influenced include: Anton Ehrenzweig, Peter Fuller, Ernst Kris, Marion Milner, Victor Lowenfeld and Adrian Stokes. The problematic of Freudian aesthetics encompassed: the role of the unconscious in the production and appreciation of art; the relation between dreams, fantasies and art/creativity; the relation between art and neurosis, and the value of art as therapy; the function of art to the psyche; the relevance of psychoanalytic findings concerning an artist's personality and childhood to his or her art. Freudian theory has also inspired the imaginations of numerous artists, most notably the surrealists.

In France Freud's legacy was re-interpreted and extended by Jacques Lacan. His complex theories, in particular the idea of the mirror-phase in child development, was influential amongst film- and video-makers/theorists in the 1970s (see, for example, the magazine *Screen* **16** (2) Summer 1975). Lacan's ideas were also vital to Mary Kelly and her ambitious work about the growth of her son 'Post-Partum document' (1973–9).

● See also Art Therapy, Jungian Aesthetics.

◉ A Ehrenzweig *The psychoanalysis of artistic vision and hearing* (Routledge & Kegan Paul, 1953).

◉ E Kris *Psychoanalytic explorations in art* (Allen & Unwin, 1953).

◉ N Keill *Psychiatry and psychology in the visual arts and aesthetics: a bibliography* (Madison & Milwaukee, University of Wisconsin, 1965).

◉ A Ehrenzweig *The hidden order of art* (Weidenfeld & Nicolson, 1967).

◉ A Stokes *The image in form: selected writings of Adrian Stokes* R Wollheim (ed) (Harmondsworth, Penguin Books, 1972).

◉ J Spector *The aesthetics of Freud: a study in psychoanalysis and art* (Allen Lane, 1973).

◉ S Marshall 'Video art, the imaginary and the parole vide' *Studio International* **191** (981) May–June 1976 243–7.

◉ P Fuller *Art & psychoanalysis* (Writers & Readers, 1980).

◉ J Walker 'Dream-work and artwork' *Leonardo* **16** (2) 1983 109–14.

◉ M Kelly *Post-Partum document* (Routledge & Kegan Paul, 1983).

◉ M Gedo (ed) *Psychoanalytic perspectives on art* (NY, Analytic Press, 1985).

289 FRONTE NUOVO DELLA ARTI (New Front of the Arts) In Italy in the immediate post-1945 period the spirit of co-operation and unity typical of the wartime resistance encouraged avant garde artists who worked in different styles and subscribed to different aesthetic and political programmes to join together in common organizations and exhibitions. One such manifestation was Nuova Secessione Artistica Italiana founded in September 1945. New Front of the Arts was another formed by 12 artists in 1947. It was sponsored by the critic Guiseppe Marchiori and had its first exhibition in Milan in 1947. The best-known artists associated with it were Renato Birolli, Renato Guttuso, Guiseppe Santomaso, Emilio Vedova and Ennio Morlotti.

◉ *Prima Mostra del 'Fronte Nuovo delle Arti'* (Milan, Galleria della Spiga, 1947).

◉ G Marchiori *Il Fronte Nuovo delle Arti* (Venice, Biennale Internazionale d'Arte di Venezia, 1948).

290 FUNDAMENTAL PAINTING (Including Absolute/ Analytische/Essential/ Geplante (planned) / Introspective/ Opaque/ Post-Conceptual/ Post-Minimal/ Pure/ Reductivist/ Silent Painting and Nouvelle Peinture) A term coined by E. de Wilde to characterize austere abstract paintings produced from about 1960 onwards by such European and American artists as Jake Berthot, Louis Cane, Alan Charlton, Robert Mangold, Brice Marden, Agnes Martin, Edda Renouf, Gerhard Richter and Robert Ryman. 'Fundamental Painting' was devised as the title of an exhibition of such paintings held at the Stedelijk Museum, Amsterdam in 1975.

This show was the culmination of a series of exhibitions which had given rise to the plethora of alternative terms listed above. The shows were evidence of an attempt on the part of curators and dealers to reinstate painting as the leading form of art in the aftermath of conceptualism. Since Fundamental Painting was, in the words of de Wilde, 'a reflection on the foundations of painting', it continued the self-critical tendency which Greenberg identified as the essence of modernism but in its emphasis on process and the literal, physical character of its materials, it also incorporated certain notions derived from minimalism.

FUNDAMENTAL PAINTING ROBERT RYMAN, 'Untitled' (1970). Oil on fibreglass with paper frame, 6" x 6".

Arguably, the attempts to reduce painting to an essence, to define it in terms of means rather than ends or functions, and to make it autonomous were misguided and anti-social. By 1980 many painters had moved in quite another direction, i.e. towards neo-expressionist figuration.

● See also Conceptual Art, Minimal Art, Modernist Painting, Neo-Expressionism.

● C Ratcliff 'Once more with feeling' *Art News* **71** (4) Summer 1972 34–7, 67–9.

● *Arte come Arte* (Milan, Centro Communitario di Brera, 1973).

● R Brooks 'An international exhibition of post-minimal painting' *Studio International* **188** (972) December 1974 11–12 (review section).

● *Nouvelle Peinture en France: pratiques/theories* (Saint Etienne, Musée d'Art et d'Industrie, 1974).

● C Blok 'Holland' *Studio International* **190** (976) July–August 1975 74–5.

● *Fundamental Painting* (Amsterdam, Stedelijk Museum, 1975).

● J Walker 'John Hoyland and Bob Law' *Studio International* **191** (979) January–February 1976 79–81.

FUNK ART DAVID GILHOOLY, 'Elephant Ottoman No 2' (1966). White earthenware, vinyl, plywood. 8" x 21". Collection Miss Brenda Richardson, Berkeley, California.

291 FUNK ART

(Also Funck, Phunck & Grotesque / Sick Art) The adjective 'funky' was first applied to visual works of art by artists living in the Bay Area of San Francisco in the late 1950s. The word was borrowed from blues or jazz terminology where it meant a heavy beat, an earthy, sensual sound. It also had sexual connotations: one artist's work was described as 'funky as a whore's drawers'. In 1967 'funky' was shortened to 'funk' when an exhibition with this title was held at the University of California. Artists associated with the tendency included Robert Arneson, Clayton Bailey, Bruce Connor, David Gilhooly, Mel Henderson, Robert Hudson, Kenneth Price, Joseph Pugliese, Richard Shaw, Chris Unterscher, Peter Vandenberge and Peter Voulkos.

Funk Art was usually three-dimensional but it did not resemble traditional sculpture. Rather it was an uneasy hybrid of painting and sculpture. Materials such as leather, clay, steel, fibre-glass, nylon, vinyl and fur were employed in bizarre combinations. Many Funk artists were ceramicists (their work was also called 'pop ceramics') and clay seemed a medium peculiarly appropriate to their needs. The resulting objects were eccentric in appearance and their imagery was often visceral, organic or biomorphic with ribald sexual or scatological connotations. Funk artists drew their inspiration from the vulgar world around them rather than from fine art. Their aesthetic was anti-functional, anti-Bauhaus, anti-intellectual and anti-formal; in one writer's view 'an aesthetic of obscenity'. Precedents for Funk were found in the sculptures of Joan Miró, Marcel Duchamp's readymades, the architecture of Antonio Gaudi and in the pop objects of Claes Oldenburg.

● See also Kitsch, Pop Art.

● H Paris 'Sweet land of Funk' *Art in America* **55** March 1967 94–8.

● J Monte '"Making it" with Funk' *Artforum* **5** (10) Summer 1967 56–9.

● P Selz *Funk* (Berkeley, University of California, 1967).

● D Zack 'Funk Art' *Art & Artists* **2** (1) April 1967 36– 9.

● — 'Funk 2: the grotesque show at Berkeley' *Art & Artists* **2** (7) October 1967 20–1.

● —'California myth making' *Art & Artists* **4** (4) July 1969 26–31.

● J Pierre 'Funk Art' *L'Oeil* (190) October 1970 18–27, + 68.

● J Jacopetti & J Wainwright *Native Funk and flash* (San Francisco, Scrimshaw Press, 1974).

292 FUTURE SYSTEMS

A small Anglo-American architectural design consultancy founded by Jan Kaplicky and David Nixon in 1979 for the purpose of achieving a synthesis of technology, ecology and popular architecture. From 1989 the partners of the London-based consultancy were Kaplicky (b Prague 1937) and Amanda Levete (b London 1955).

Few of their schemes were built and so Future Systems produced drawings and photo-montages of their carefully researched projects, e.g. a low cost shelter for use in disasters; a lightweight, high-tech, mobile home that could be moved from place to place by helicopter; a 'green' office building; a 480m tower for Hyde Park. In the mid 1980s Future Systems received commissions from NASA, the American Space Agency, to design

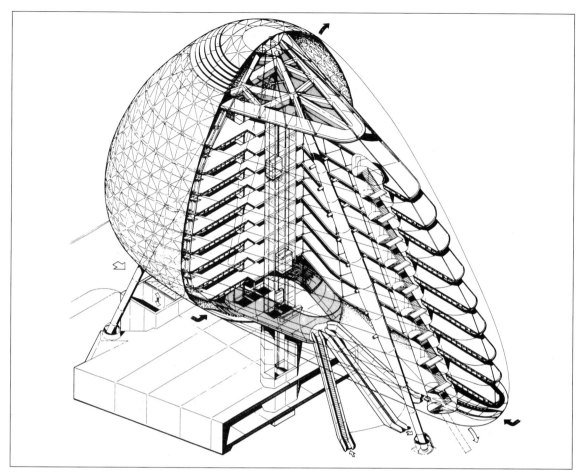

FUTURE SYSTEMS Design for a green office building in the City of London. An Ove Arup-inspired research project. (1990).

platforms and crew quarters for space stations, and also from Harrods' London store to redesign the 'Way In' boutique. In 1990 they were commissioned to design a gateway for Chiswick Business Park.

Exhibitions of the work of Future Systems were held at the Royal Institute of British Architects, London in October 1982 and March 1991.

● See also Conceptual Architecture, Green Design, High-Tech, Utopian Architecture.

◉ P Rambali 'Mobile homes' *The Face* (36) April 1983 56–7.
◉ L Relph-Knight 'Flexible futures' *Building Design* (674) January 27 1984 15–17.
◉ M Pawley 'The shape for things to come' *Guardian* May 6 1985 7.
◉ J Welsh & C Davies 'Future Systems' *Building Design* March 1 1991 17–24.

293 **G PLAN FURNITURE**

A brand of contemporary-style domestic furniture popular in Britain during the 1950s and '60s. It was introduced by Leslie Gomme of the High Wycombe company E. Gomme & Sons, established by Ebenezer Gomme in 1898 (the firm became G Plan Ltd in 1987). The original G Plan range was launched in 1953. Its durability and lack of fussy ornament recalled the standards set by wartime utility furniture. Rounded corners and tapered legs were common features of chairs and tables. Good-quality woods like oak and teak were used and there was a high standard of craftsmanship in both finish and upholstery. Because the various units were co-ordinated, it was possible to build up a unified interior gradually. In the 1980s new G Plan ranges are still being made and bought. Stylistically they tend to be unadventurous, appealing to a middle-class public with middle-of-the-road tastes.

● See also Contemporary Style, Utility.

294 **GAME ART**

(Also Ludic/Play/Toy Art) Games, toys and playthings devised by fine artists. An exhibition of such works entitled 'Play Orbit' was held at the ICA, London in 1969. In France David Roditi, Simon Koszel and Xavier de la Salle established, in the late 1960s, 'Group Ludic' ('ludic' is Latin for 'play') for the purpose of designing play structures for children in parks and other public places. During the '60s Game Art was directed towards children but also towards adults because artists became convinced of the need for greater public participation in art and the need for adults to play. A British group promoting the latter was GASP (Games of Art for Spectator Participation), founded in 1970 by Rob Cob, Julian Dunn and Harry Henderson. During the '70s Don Pavey devised a series of art-based games for use in education.

In the period following the Second World War, games were taken seriously by scientists, economists and military strategists, e.g. the theory of games and war games. The Swedish artist Öyvind Fahlström (1928–76) made certain works about war games in the early '60s; his constructions had movable parts so that viewers could alter their configurations.

Ludwig Wittgenstein once used the analogy of the game in his linguistic philosophy and on occasion art critics apply the same analogy to art. There is certainly an element of play in art of the experimental kind and there is also an art in playing games. The key difference between them seems to be that in games rules are enforced, whereas in art they are often broken. Marcel Duchamp was an artist whose *oeuvre* included many playful, game-like activities; legend also had it that he gave up art for chess.

● See also Cybernetic Art, Participatory Art.

J von Neumann & O Morgenstern *Theory of games and economic behaviour* (Princeton University Press, 1944; Oxford University Press, 1953).

J Huizinga *Homo Ludens: a study of the play element in culture* (Routledge, 1949; Paladin, 1970).

'Games & Toys' *Encyclopedia of World Art* vol 6 (NY, McGraw-Hill, 1962) cols 1–18.

'Fun & games' *Art & Artists* **2** (9) December 1967, special issue.

F Popper 'Le Group Ludic' *Prisme International* (6) May–June 1969 50–9.

G Ortman 'Artists' games' *Art in America* **57** (6) November–December 1969 67–77.

J Reichardt (ed) *Play Orbit* (Studio International, 1969).

N Calas 'Games' – in – *Icons and images of the sixties* by N & E Calas (NY, Dutton, 1971) 316–23.

A Everitt 'Four exhibitions in the Midlands' *Studio International* **183** (941) February 1972 76–8.

Games that artists play (Camden Arts Centre, 1972).

B Tilghman 'Wittgenstein, games and art' *Journal of Aesthetics & Art Criticism* **31** (4) Summer 1973 517–24.

(Art & sport, special issue on) *Du* (425) 1976.

D Pavey *Art-based games* (Methuen, 1979).

M Thomas 'The game-as-art form: historic roots and recent trends' *Leonardo* **21** (4) 1988 421–3.

295 **GARBAGE HOUSING**

Dwellings made from waste products such as empty bottles and cans which have themselves been designed with this secondary use in mind. In this sense Garbage Housing is different from the one-off use of waste products as building materials. The concept owed much to Martin Pawley, an American architect, who developed his ideas while working on emergency housing problems in Chile in 1972–3. The design for re-use concept was pioneered by the 'WoBo', a bottle which could serve as a brick when empty, designed by John Habraken for Heineken Breweries, Netherlands in 1962.

● See also Ecological Architecture.

● M Pawley 'Garbage Housing' *Architectural Design* **43** (12) December 1973 764–84.

● —*Garbage Housing* (Architectural Press, 1975).

● R van der Berg 'About re-use' *Domus* (562) September 1976 18–26.

296   GAY ART

(Also Homo-erotic Art) As the song 'Glad to be gay' indicates, there are some cultural expressions which openly celebrate homosexuality. (The use of the word 'gay' to mean 'homosexual' is fairly recent and has been popularized by the Gay Liberation Movement.) 'Gay Art', then, refers to those works that articulate aspects of the sexual and emotional experiences of male and female homosexual artists. Some critics have argued that Gay Art is made by gays, about gays, for gays and hence is inseparable from gay subculture.

It has long been known that many famous artists of the past were homosexuals (or bisexuals) – Donatello, Michelangelo, Leonardo, Caravaggio, Rosa Bonheur, Oscar Wilde, etc. – but it was only with the advent of a more liberal social climate during the 1960s that explicitly homosexual art could be openly exhibited and discussed. The charm and frankness of David Hockney's images and his popular success in the '60s made Gay Art fashionable in Britain, while in New York the influence of Warhol's 'Factory' scene and films was crucial. Since that time many gay artists have used their art defiantly to assert the value of the homosexual experience and lifestyle. Amongst the modern artists, film-makers and photographers cited in the literature on the subject are: Hockney, Warhol, Keith Vaughan, John Minton, Robert Colquhoun, Robert McBryde, Edward Burra, Francis Bacon, John Yeadon, Paul Cadmus, Gilbert & George, Mario Dubsky, Derek Jarman, Robert Mapplethorpe, Jean-Marc Prouveur, Tom of Finland, Delmas Howe, Philip Core, Rainer Fetting, Tony Benn, Yve Lomax, Tamara de Lempicka, Leonor Fini, Marie Laurencin, Monica Sjöö and June Redfern. Reviews of Gay Art exhibitions appear to some extent in mainstream art magazines but interested readers would also need to refer to articles in more specialist publications such as *Gay News, The Ladder, The Advocate,* and *Heresies.*

Paintings and sculptures depicting female nudes, or

GAY ART PHILIP CORE, 'Wooden sculptures, Claustrophobia exhibition' (1988). Photo: Watermans Art Centre, Brentford.

male nudes, or acts of love-making by individuals of the same sex can obviously be regarded as having a 'gay' content, but the presence of homosexuality in the works of artists like Jasper Johns and Robert Rauschenberg is much more problematical. (Can a gay sensibility be detected in an abstract painting, one wonders?) Furthermore, it is presumably possible for a heterosexual artist to tackle a homo-erotic theme. The question 'what constitutes a "gay aesthetic"?' is thus of comparable difficulty to the question 'what constitutes a "feminist aesthetic"?'.

● See also Art Against Aids, Camp, Erotic Art, Feminist Art.

● S Marone 'Homosexuality and art' *International Journal of Sociology* **7** (4) May 1954.

● 'Lesbian art and artists' *Heresies* **1** (3) Fall 1977 (special issue; bibliography).

● M Walters *The nude male: a new perspective* (Paddington Press, 1978).

● E Lucie-Smith 'The Gay seventies?' *Art & Artists* **14** (8) December 1979 4–11.

● D Ireland & J Weinstein (eds) 'Is there a Gay culture?' *SoHo News* (supplement) June 25 1980.

● A Ellenzweig 'The homosexual aesthetic' *American Photography* August 1980 60–3.

● J Perreault 'I'm asking – does it exist? What is it? Whom is it for?' *Artforum* **19** (3) November 1980 74–5.

● V Russo *The celluloid closet: homosexuality in the movies* (NY, Harper & Row, 1981).

● N Moufarrege 'Lavender: on homosexuality and art' *Arts Magazine* **57** (2) October 1982 78–81.

● D Cameron *Extended sensibilities: homosexual presence in contemporary art* (NY, New Museum, 1982).

● E Cooper *The sexual perspective: homosexuality and art in the last 100 years in the West* (Routledge & Kegan Paul, 1986).

● J Saslow *Ganymede in the Renaissance: homosexuality in art and society* (Yale University Press, 1986).

● N Stanley *Out in art* (Gay Men's Press, 1986).

297 GEAM (Groupe d'Étude d'Architecture Mobile) A group formed by the architects Yona Friedman, Paul May-mont, Frei Otto, Eckhard Schultze-Fielitz, Werner Ruh-nau and D. G. Emmerich in 1957. Its purpose was to explore the implications of the crisis in architecture brought about by accelerated demographic, social and technological change. A more flexible and mobile kind of architecture was envisaged as a solution. GEAM evolved into GIAP (Groupe International d'Architecture Prospective), a group led by Michel Ragon which met from 1965 onwards to discuss visionary and futuristic concepts of architecture and town planning.

● See also Conceptual Architecture, Mobile Architecture, Utopian Architecture.

● M Ragon 'Le Groupe International d'Architecture Prospective' *Cimaise* (79) January–March 1967 42–51.

298 GENERAL IDEA A Canadian group of experimental and iconoclastic artists formed 'accidentally' in Toronto in 1968 by the trio A. A. Bronson, Felix Partz and Jorge Zontal. Partz trained at art school while the other two studied architecture. At first GI created fake storefronts and window displays. They then engaged in an ironic enterprise of self-promotion and self-packaging. They also joined the mail art network. During the '70s and '80s they exhibited internationally, producing work in a variety of forms and media: collages published in magazines (particularly in their own magazine *FILE* founded in 1972), books, paintings, photographs, films, videotapes, gallery installations, performances. Most of the output of GI was dadaist in character and satirized contemporary art, myths and mass culture (e.g. *FILE* was a zany version of *Life* magazine). The collaborative and mixed-media activities of GI have proved difficult for the commercial gallery system to assimilate.

● See also Magazine Art, Mail Art, Media Art, Performance Art, Video Art.

○ *Ménage à trois: General Idea* (Toronto, Art Metropole, 1978).

○ J Annear 'An interview with General Idea' *Art & Text* (8) Summer 1982–3 49–56.

○ C Hume 'General Idea' *Art Magazine* (Canada) **14** (634) June–August 1983 38–9.

○ J Mays 'Must we burn General Idea?' *Vanguard* (Canada) **13** (9) November 1984 10–15.

○ *General Idea 1968–84* (Montreal, Musée d'Art Contemporain, 1984).

○ L Touraine 'General Idea..' *Vie des Arts* (Canada) **30** (120) September 1985 32–3.

○ *The armory of the 1984 Miss General Idea Pavilion* (Buffalo, NY, Albright Knox Gallery, 1986).

299 GENERATIVE ART A type of geometric abstract art in which simple forms were repeated or developed in various ways in order to 'generate' a more complex design. This sort of work was produced by the Argentine artists Eduardo McEntyre and Miguel Vidal in the late 1960s. The term 'Generative Art' has also been employed by Paul Neagu (b. 1938), a Rumanian-born artist resident in Britain. In 1972 the Generative Art Group (GAG) was founded. It consisted of the painters Husny Belmood and Edward Larsocchi, the designer Philip Honeysuckle and the poet Anton Paidola. In fact the members of GAG were fictional beings, the multiple personae of Neagu, an artist noted for the diversity of his output: paintings, drawings, tactile objects, performances and publications. He has also written a manifesto on 'palpable art'.

● See also Geometric Abstraction.

○ A MacKintosh 'Paul Neagu' *Art & Artists* **6** (5) September 1971 52–3.

○ P Neagu *Generative Art Group* (Neagu, 1972).

○ *Gradually going tornado...* (Sunderland, Coelfrith Press, 1976).

300 GENERATIVE SYSTEMS The name of an art–science research programme established by the School of the Art Institute of Chicago (SAIC) in 1970 in response to social change caused in part by the computer–robot communications revolution. The term itself had been employed by scientists but was re-invented by Ian Robertson and Sonia Sheridan. The word 'generative' signified both creation and evolution. With the help of industry, the programme explored the potential for art of new electronic imaging machines and video, sound, computer systems. One aim of the programme was to democratize art by developing systems simple enough to be used by the general public. Initially work was undertaken with copying machines and this led to a limited conception of the aim of the programme. According to Sheridan, 'copy art' was a commercial spin-off from Generative Systems and much less significant

● See also Computer Art, Copy Art, Systems Art, Telematics.

● S Sheridan 'Generative Systems' *Afterimage* (Rochester, NY, Visual Workshop) April 1972 1–4.

● — 'Generative Systems: six years later' *Afterimage* March 1975 6–10.

● — 'Generative Systems versus copy art: a clarification of terms' *Leonardo* **16** (2) Spring 1983 103–8.

301 GEOMETRIC ABSTRACTION

A subcategory of modern abstract art, encompassing both sculpture and painting, which finds in geometric forms – circles, spheres, rectangles, cubes, triangles, pyramids, etc. – universal symbols for rational, idealist concepts. Typically, Geometric Abstract painters employ primary colours which are painted in a flat, impersonal manner to generate shapes with hard edges, e.g. Kasimir Malevich, Piet Mondrian, Theo van Doesburg, Max Bill, Alexander Liberman, Burgoyne Diller, Ellsworth Kelly, Frank Stella. Because of its cool rationality, this kind of work has also been called 'cold abstraction' and described as 'hygienic'. This kind of art developed largely in Europe in the years between the two World Wars and was associated with the Bauhaus, concrete art, de Stijl and international constructivism. In the 1940s and '50s abstract art went through an anti-geometric phase as most painters favoured a gestural, intuitive approach. However, by the early '60s geometry had made a come-back with such movements as hard-edge painting, op and minimal art.

● See also Cool Art, Formalism & Formalist Criticism , Generative Art.

● *Geometric Abstraction in America* (NY, Whitney Museum of American Art, 1962).

● H Jaffe 'Geometrical Abstraction: its origins, principles and evolution' – in – *Abstract art since 1945* by W Haftmann & others (Thames & Hudson, 1971) 163–90.

● *Geometric Abstraction* (Omaha, University of Nebraska, 1974).

● M Dabrowski *Contrasts of form: Geometric Abstract art 1910–80...* (NY, MoMA/London, Thames & Hudson, 1985).

302 GEOMETRY OF FEAR

A memorable phrase invented by Herbert Read to characterize the work of a number of British sculptors – Kenneth Armitage, Reg Butler, Lynn Chadwick, Bernard Meadows and F. E. MacWilliam – exhibiting at the Venice Biennale of 1952. Their sculpture reflected the influence of Alberto Giacometti and Germaine Richier; it had an angst-ridden look typical of the postwar mood of tension and uncertainty. The work was figurative but it often combined human and animal forms. Welded metal rods were used to construct cage-like structures enclosing or piercing modelled forms with 'tortured' surface textures.

● H Read *New aspects of British sculpture* (Venice Biennale, 1952).

303 GEOMETRY OF RAGE

Title of an exhibition conceived by Lewis Biggs and Jeremy Rees held in Bristol and Glasgow in 1984. It featured works by Denis Masi, Deanna Petherbridge and Michael Sandle, three artists who employed different media and iconographies. The show's title was clearly a play on Herbert Read's phrase 'geometry of fear'. What the artists had in common were: (a) feelings of anger, bitterness and cynicism at the continuing threat of war, at

GEOMETRY OF RAGE DEANNA PETHERBRIDGE, 'Debris of war' (1984). Drawing, pen & ink on paper 60" x 48". Collection: Imperial War Museum, London. Photo: Petherbridge.

political hypocrisy, at the society of misinformation and surveillance they perceived around them; and (b) a conviction that these strong feelings were best represented in a cool, precise, disciplined manner as against an expressionist mode of representation; hence 'Geometry of Rage'.

● L Biggs & others *Geometry of Rage* (Bristol, Arnolfini Gallery, 1984).

304 GILBERT & GEORGE

A deadpan double-act by two London-based artists who renounced the use of their surnames and blended their separate identities into a composite 'living sculpture'. G & G studied sculpture at St Martin's School of Art, London, in the mid '60s but diverged from the Caro-inspired metal and colour sculpture of their predecessors by devising performances and a populist aesthetic they called 'Art for All'. Their best-known performance 'Underneath the arches' (1969–70) consisted of the pair standing on a table dressed in conservative suits but with gold faces repeating a series of robot-like movements to the tune of the pre-war musical hall song which supplied the title of the piece. Subsequently, G & G produced landscape paintings, videotapes, films, books, magazine features and multi-part photo-murals. Perversely, most of this disparate output was called 'sculpture'. Like the superstars of the cinema and pop music, G & G made their whole public lives into art. In return for fame they offered their audiences wit, nostalgia, a parody of Englishness, and a satire of the artistic life and the art-world which they simultaneously sent up and milked. During the '80s G & G received worldwide acclaim and official honours. However, they were also subject to much criticism on the grounds that their huge photo-murals were bad art, and also that their works concerning contemporary Britain were obscene and racist.

● See also Body Art, Conceptual Art, Living Sculpture, Performance Art, Photo-Works.

● G & G *Side by side* (Art for All, 1972).

● — *Oh the grand old Duke of York* (Lucerne, Kunstmuseum, 1972).

● — *Dark shadow* (Nigel Greenwood, 1976).

● — *The world of Gilbert & George* (Film, 1981).

● R Brooks 'Shake hands with the devil' *Artforum* **22** (10) Summer 1984 56–60.

● *Gilbert & George* (Baltimore Museum, 1984).

● G & G *The paintings* (Edinburgh, Fruitmarket Gallery, 1986).

● C Ratcliff *Gilbert & George: the complete pictures 1971–85* (Thames & Hudson, 1986).

● W Jahn *The art of Gilbert & George* (Thames & Hudson, 1989).

305 GLOBAL OR WORLD ART

During the 1980s an increased consciousness developed amongst artists, art theorists, curators and consumers based in the major metropolitan centres concerning the global context of art. The expansion of worldwide communication systems and increased travel led to a heightened awareness of the musical and visual cultures of small, poor and developing nations. But this awareness also applied to the metropolitan centres themselves since most of them contained minorities who originated in the peripheries. In popular music circles the term 'world music' became fashionable as recordings by groups from Africa and other areas became successful in Europe and North America. Record stores, to avoid scattering, grouped records from many places under the easy-to-find category 'world music' despite the impression of uniformity this implied and despite the implication that Euro-American music was not part of world music.

In terms of the visual arts it was significant that the 26th International Congress of the History of Art held in Washington D C in 1986 was devoted to the theme of World Art. Stuart Hall's keynote address to the annual conference of the Association of Art Historians held in London in 1989 was about globalization and its impact on culture. Also in 1989, the journal *Art in America* published a special issue entitled 'The global issue'. Much critical attention was focused on the massive French exhibition 'Magiciens de la Terre' held at the Pompidou Centre, Paris and the Grand Hall at La Villette. The show, organized by Jean-Hubert Martin assisted by a team of international advisers, attempted a global coverage. Artefacts, installations, ritual and holy objects made by Australian Aborigines, Buddhist monks, and other creators unknown to the Western art markets were exhibited alongside works by established professional artists from the developed world (e.g. Richard Long, Anselm

GLOBAL ART JOSÉ BÉDIA, 'Vive en la linea (Il vit sur le rail)' (1989). Detail of a mixed-media installation, 6m x 8m x 2m. Magiciens de la Terre exhibition, La Grande Halle, La Villette. Photo courtesy of Anita Doornheim.

Kiefer, Sigmar Polke, Barbara Kruger) and by lesser-known artists from the ethnic minorities within metropolitan centres (e.g. Rasheed Araeen). According to Eleanor Heartney, the organizers 'emphasized societies in transition' and featured artists who represented 'an exchange of influences between their respective cultures'. Many of the 'third world' creators who participated revealed 'a self-conscious interface with Western culture, modern technology or the world art market'.

Global Art – in the sense of works of art created via the interaction of artists located in different parts of the world – was also made possible by technological means, e.g. the use of international communication systems such as telefax machines for transmitting images back and forth.

● See also Ethnic Art, Hybrid Culture, Provincialism Problem, Telematics.

● *Beuys, Warhol, Higashiyama: Global-Art-Fusion* (Bern, Art-Fusion-Edition, 1986).

● I Lavin (ed) *World Art: themes of unity in diversity* 3 vols (Pennsylvania & London, Penn State University Press, 1988).

● 'The global issue' *Art in America* **77** (7) July 1989.

● J-H Hubert & others *Magiciens de la Terre* (Paris, Éditions du Centre Pompidou, 1989).

306 GLOBALIZATION

A term used in business and design circles during the 1980s referring to the necessity for industry and commerce to think of their market as the whole world. This idea was popularized by Theodore Levitt in an article in the *Harvard Business Review*. The advertising firm of Saatchi & Saatchi expanded to become the largest in the world with a view to offering their clients global coverage. Globalization implies ever-increasing homogenization until a single world culture is achieved. In reaction to the latter prospect, many firms and designers have emphasized national differences in design and promoted the idea of 'niche marketing', i.e. making, designing and selling goods for particular, specialist sectors.

● See also Saatchi Collection.

● T Levitt, 'The globalization of markets' *Harvard Business Review* (3) May–June 1983 92–102.

● M Featherstone (ed) *Global culture: nationalism, Globalization and modernity* (Sage Publications, 1990).

● A King (ed) *Culture Globalization and the world system* (Macmillan, 1991).

307 GOLDSMITHS

An art college which is part of London University situated in New Cross, South London. During the 1980s Goldsmiths became the most fashionable institution at which to study fine art in Britain. This was mainly due to

a part-time MA course taught by Gerard Hemsworth and Nick de Ville. Michael Craig-Martin was also an influential tutor. The painting and sculpture produced tended towards the post-minimalist and post-conceptual. 'Slick conceptualism' and 'cool school' were two critical assessments. Students at the college organized their own exhibitions (notably the 'Freeze' shows held in London's Docklands in 1989) and publicity; they succeeded in attracting the attention of dealers and collectors. Marketing art became as important as making it. The survey exhibition 'The British Art Show' held at Glasgow, Leeds and London in 1990 included a strong contingent of artists who had trained at Goldsmiths. Ex-students include Ian Davenport, Grenville Davey, Gary Hume, Simon Linke, Lisa Milroy, Julian Opie and Caroline Russell.

● See also Art Schools.

M Currah 'The gold rush' *City Limits* November 23–30 1989 14–15.

● A Graham-Dixon 'Pupils of the cool school' *Independent* January 30 1990 14.

308 'GOOD DESIGN'

In the 1940s and '50s well-intentioned designers and officials attached to such institutions as the Design Council in London and the Museum of Modern Art in New York espoused the cause of modern design in articles, lectures and exhibitions, and also by means of design awards and seals of approval given to selected products. Their aim was to raise the standards of design in manufacturing and to wean the mass of the public away from kitsch. Modern design was said be honest, functional, to have integrity, to exemplify truth to materials. It was praised as decent, modest and wholesome. Good Design thus came to be regarded as good in a moral as well as an aesthetic sense. Radical modernism was watered down until eventually a middle-brow standard emerged with the result that Good Design became a cliché and acquired its disparaging inverted commas. It was, remarked Christopher Cornford, 'like cold rice pud: plain, nutritious, high minded and off-white'. In the late '50s and in the '60s such design came to seem dowdy and boring in comparison to certain products imported from Italy and the new pop design of Carnaby Street.

● See also Carnaby Street, Design Council, Italian Craze, Kitsch, Machine Aesthetic/Art, Pop Design, Post-Modern Design.

● E Wilkes 'The fundamentals of Good Design' *Art & Industry* May 1948 184–9.

● G Russell 'What we mean by Good Design' *Architects Journal* July 15 1948 66–7.

● — 'Good Design is not a luxury' *Design* (1) 1949 2–6.

L Archer 'What is Good Design?' Part 1 *Design* (137) May 1960 28–33; Part 2 *Design* (140) August 1960 26–31.

C Cornford 'Cold rice pudding and revisionism' *Design* (231) March 1968 46–8.

F MacCarthy *All things bright and beautiful...* (Allen & Unwin, 1972).

J Pile 'What is Good Design?' *Art News* **80** (2) February 1981 87–92.

P Sparke *Whatever happened to 'Good Design'? A simple guide to the new directions* (Heal & Son, 1983).

309 GRAFFITI

(Also Frontier/ Spraycan/ Subway Art) Originally, Graffiti were crude drawings, caricatures or writings scratched into the surface of walls ('graffio' is Italian for 'scratch'), but today they are almost invariably painted or written marks executed with cans of spray paint or with felt-tipped pens and magic markers. Graffiti have constituted a kind of subversive folk art since the days of ancient Egypt but only in the twentieth century, as a result of modernism's cult of the primitive, have they been taken seriously as a form of popular culture, influenced professional artists and attained the status of art in their own right. Amongst painters whose work shows signs of the influence of Graffiti are Jean Dubuffet, David Hockney, Antonio Tàpies and Cy Twombly.

A striking outbreak of popular Graffiti occurred in New York during the 1970s when subway trains were 'bombed', i.e. covered with polychromatic 'name writings' and 'tags' (invented names, stylized signatures). Later on, much more ambitious designs were created which involved elaborate interlocking letters, figures and imagery quoted from fine art and the mass-media sources. (This type of work was labelled 'Subway Art', 'Spraycan Art', 'Frontier Art'.) While the transit authorities viewed the Graffiti as crime/vandalism and tried to eliminate them, others regarded them as an authentic expression of grassroots culture manifesting, in many cases, considerable energy, creativity and skill. On investigation it turned out that they were the work of various groups of 'deprived' teenagers. Each 'crew' had their own techniques, rules, vocabulary, stylistic mannerisms (e.g. 'wild style') and even martyrs (by electrocution). The process of social assimilation was rapid. Graffiti writers were encouraged to paint public or community murals on approved walls and private murals in hotels, shops, and nightclubs as an alternative to defacing trains and other property. They also contributed to the black hip hop breakdancing, rapping and scratch music scene of New York by providing backdrops for record covers and rock videos.

A number of New York art galleries opened in order to exhibit and sell Graffiti executed on canvas or wooden supports, e.g. Razor, P.S.1., Shafrazi, Fashion Moda. This development gave rise to the expression 'post-Graffiti art'. As a result of the artworld vogue for Graffiti in the 1980s, a number of writers 'crossed over' from the subway to the gallery context and became successful professional artists, e.g. Jean-Michel Basquiat (1960–88), Lenny McGurr, Fred Braithwaite, Lee Quinones. Also, artschool-trained individuals such as Keith Haring (1958-90) developed a primitivistic style strongly influenced by Graffiti. Haring moved back and forth from the subway/street to the art and design worlds. In June 1989 a Museum of American Graffiti was opened in New York City.

Following books, exhibitions, films and TV programmes about New York's subway writers, the habit spread to many cities throughout the world. In London sophisticated examples appeared in the Notting Hill area. Other British examples were generated by feminists making critical attacks upon sexist advertising. Not all Graffiti were what they seemed: record companies employed people to spray slogans and the names of bands as a form of publicity. So, the graphic spontaneity, vulgarity and subversion of Graffiti quickly became part of the repertoire of the manipulative devices of the advertising industry. In 1990 London-based groups of so-called 'graff-ites' toured Europe giving performances in the manner of rock bands. At home they also staged events mixing music, dance and spraycan style called 'West London Pressure'.

● See also Art Brut, Cross-overs, East Village Art, Matter Art, Popular Art, Rock Video.

R Freeman *Graffiti* (Hutchinson, 1966).

M Kurlansky *The faith of Graffiti* (NY, Praeger, 1974); English edition: *Watching my name go by* (Mathews Miller Dunbar, 1974).

R Reisner *Graffiti: two thousand years of wall writing* (Muller, 1974).

GRAFFITI 'Crime' (1980s). Spraycan paint on flyover near Portobello Rd., London. Photo: Anna Groom.

● *United Graffiti Artists* (NY, Artists' Space, 1975).

● R Perry & G Melly *The writing on the wall* (H Hamilton, 1976).

● N Rees *Graffiti lives OK* (Unwin Paperbacks, 1979); *Graffiti (2)* (Unwin Paperbacks, 1980).

● J Charoux (photographer) *London Graffiti* (W H Allen, 1980).

● J Posener *Spray it loud* (Routledge & Kegan Paul, 1982).

● R Castleman *Getting up* (Cambridge, Mass, MIT Press, 1983).

● P Bianchi *Graffiti* (Basel, Birkhauser, 1984).

● M Cooper & H Chalfont *Subway Art* (Thames & Hudson, 1984).

● *Frontier Art: New York Graffiti* (Bologna, Museum of Modern Art, 1984).

● H Geldzahler *Art in transit* (NY, Crown, 1984).

● *Jean-Michel Basquiat* (ICA, 1984).

● *USA Graffiti artists* (Rotterdam, Museum Van Boymans, 1984).

● *Lee Quinones: new horizons* (Riverside Studios, 1985).

● J-C Bailly & J Huber (photographer) *Paris Graffiti* (Thames & Hudson, 1986).

● J Posener *Louder than words* (Pandora Press, 1986).

● H Chalfont & J Prigoff *Spraycan Art* (Thames & Hudson, 1987).

● C Rose 'A hard graff for a piece of the action' *Observer* April 22 1990 49.

● J Bushnell *Moscow Graffiti: language and subculture* (Unwin Hyman, 1990).

GRAPHIC NOVELS WILL EISNER, drawing from *A contract with God and other tenement stories* (1978, 1985). Illus courtesy of Titan Books, London.

310 GRAPHIC NOVELS

(Also Designer/ New Wave Comics, Graphic Docudramas) In Britain and the USA during the 1980s a comics boom occurred as comic books began to be taken seriously by adult readers and by mainstream publishers. One sign of this was the appearance of expensive, lengthy, trade-size paperbacks with high production values in terms of paper quality, printing and colour reproduction. These 'Graphic Novels' were also unusual in tackling complex issues and serious historical subjects such as the Holocaust, in humanizing the superheroes of earlier juvenile comics, and in depicting contemporary urban society with harsh realism. Normally these books were the result of collaborations between writers and illustrators. Many of these writers and artists became celebrities and, unlike earlier generations of comic artists, they received royalty payments from publishers. Often, the imagery was more realistic in style, more akin to traditional paintings, than the general run of comics and cartoons with their schematic, linear designs. The first Graphic Novel is deemed to have been Will Eisner's *A contract with God* (1978); other notable examples were: Frank Miller and Klaus Janson's *Batman: the Dark Knight returns* (1986); Alan Moore's and Dave Gibbons' *Watchmen* (1987); Dean Motter and Gilbert and Jaime Hernandez's *The return of Mister X* (1987); Art Spielgelman's *Maus* (1989); Keiji Nakazawa's *Barefoot Gen* (1989); Grant Morrison and Dave McKean's *Arkham Asylum* (1989); Alan Moore and Bill Sienkiewicz's *Brought to light* (1989). Publishers of Graphic Novels included Penguin and Titan Books.

● See also Bande Dessinée, Collaborations, Comic Art, Comix, Narrative Figuration.

● M Gilmore 'Hot comic books' *Rolling Stone* (578) May 17 1990 57–65.

311 GRAPUS

A French graphic design team founded in Paris in 1970 by Pierre Bernard, Gérard Paris-Clavel and François Miehe. The founders studied at the École Nationale Supérieure des Arts Décoratifs in Paris and two of them also studied poster design in Poland under

Henryk Tomaszewski. (Others have since participated and the size of the group has fluctuated.) All three were committed to communism, hence they functioned as a collective and placed their design skills in the service of Left-wing political parties, causes and issues, and in the service of trade unions and arts institutions, rather than in the service of commerce or the mass media. However, they considered themselves to be creators rather than mere technicians. During the 1970s Grapus became particularly noted for their incisive and thought-provoking posters, though they also designed stickers, buttons, three-dimensional figures for use on street corners, theatre programmes, stage sets, magazines, exhibitions, audio-visual displays and so on. The expressions 'graphic resistance' and 'poster guerrillas' have been used about Grapus.

● See also Atelier Populaire, Political Art, Prop Art.

● A Alexandre 'Ateliers: Grapus' *Novum Gebrauchsgraphik* **50** August 1979 3–10..

● G Mermoz 'Grapus, the floating image' *Idea* (166) May 1981 100–13.

● F Barré 'Grapus' *Graphis* **37** (213) 1981 58–63.

● *Grapus* (Paris, Musée de l'Affiche, 1982).

312 GRAV

(Groupe de Recherche d'Art Visuel) An important artists' group founded in Paris in 1960 for the purpose of undertaking research into light, illusion, movement and visual perception. Its membership of 11 included François Morellet, Julio Le Parc and Yvaral. They were inspired by the work and theories of Victor Vasarely and were closely associated with the Nouvelle Tendance in Europe and the Denise René Gallery in Paris. GRAV opposed the personal expression type of improvised abstract painting fashionable in the '50s by instituting a quasi-scientific programme of research and by adopting a collective approach to artistic production. They sought to increase spectator involvement by designing multimedia environments and participatory works, some involving games. They also sought to reach a wider audience via the manufacture of multiples. Much of the work of GRAV has been categorized as 'kinetic' and 'op art'. The group became defunct in 1969 because its members, having developed in different directions, could no longer agree on a common policy.

● See also Collaborations, Environmental Art, Game Art, Kinetic Art, Multiples, Nouvelle Tendance, Op Art, Participatory Art, Technological Art.

● C Barrett 'Mystification and the Groupe de Recherche' *Studio International* **172** (880) August 1966 93–5.

● 'Texts of the Groupe de Recherche d'Art Visuel 1960–5' *Image* Winter 1966 13–30.

● *Groupe de Recherche d'Art Visuel* (Dortmund, Museum am Ostwall, 1968).

● J Stein 'Dissolution of GRAV' *Leonardo* **2** (3) 1969 295–6.

● S Bann 'Groupe de Recherche d'Art Visuel: Yvaral' – in – *Experimental painting* (Studio Vista, 1970) 41–6.

313 GREEN ARCHITECTURE

A term employed by Barbara Solomon in 1988 as the title of a text about formal, picturesque and agrarian gardens and their relationship to buildings. Green Architecture occurs, she says, 'where landscape and architecture overlap'. Another meaning of 'Green Architecture' is: buildings constructed according to the principles and aims of the 'green' or environmental movement, e.g. superinsulated buildings designed to limit the use of energy.

● See also Ecological Architecture, Green Design.

● B Solomon *Green Architecture and the agrarian garden* (NY, Rizzoli, 1988).

● B Evans 'Build it green: superinsulation' *Architects Journal* **191** (10) March 7 1990 65–8.

● 'Green Architecture' *Architectural Review* **CLXXXVII** (1123) September 1990. (thematic issue).

● B & R Vale *Towards a Green Architecture* (RIBA, 1991).

314 GREEN DESIGN

(Also Eco-Design) Concern for the future of the planet Earth increased significantly in the 1980s. Campaigning groups and political parties committed to ending the pollution of the environment and the destruction of natural resources were called 'Green parties' or 'the Greens'. The implications of the Greens' critique of the present system for the redesign of the power industries, heavy and light industry, the agribusiness, waste disposal, transport, consumer goods, packaging, lifestyles, etc., were immense. Green Design, therefore, is any design taking account of such ecological principles as reduction of pollution, sustainable growth, recycling, energy efficiency, conservation of scarce resources, environment-friendly materials, products that are cleaner, quieter and more durable.

Consumer boycotts of certain harmful products persuaded manufacturers to alter their design. In the late '80s many businesses responded to public concern by producing so-called 'Green products', e.g. Ecover, phosphate-free soap powders from Belgium. The Green consumerism which followed was regarded with scepticism by 'dark greens' (i.e. fundamentalists) because they want to see reductions in consumption. Earlier, in 1986, the Design Council in London mounted an exhibition called 'The Green Designer'; another entitled 'More

GREEN DESIGN Ecover washing powder & bleach (1990). Photo: Ecover, Steyning, West Sussex.

from less' took place in the Winter of 1990-91 . Seminars and day schools on Green Design were organized in many art colleges and in May 1990 the Design Museum in London organized a conference on the topic. Green Design consultancies were established in Britain, plus an Ecological Design Association.

In terms of transportation, Green Design ranged from changes in the engines of conventional cars to take unleaded petrol and to reduce fuel consumption, to Anthony Howard's 'Africar' (a cheap, wooden vehicle designed for Africa). Volvo in Sweden renewed its commitment to making 'environmentally friendly' cars and buses, while Renault in France designed an electric car. (Some Greens advocate a switch from private cars to public transport, or the use of bicycles instead of cars.) Fashion also witnessed changes: during the '80s Anita Roddick's chain of Body Shops was highly successful in selling natural cosmetics; campaigns against the use of animal furs for clothes cut the trade in pelts; in 1989 Friends of the Earth commissioned a range of clothes made of biodegradable materials while the British group Reactivart re-used old clothes. Green furniture too was produced by the firm of Chapel & Mills, West Yorkshire: it was 'green' because it was simple, practical and built to last, it made use of reclaimed timbers and organic oils, waxes and varnish, it did not use tropical hardwoods, etc.

● See also Ecological Architecture/Art, Information Graphics, Low-Tech, Reactivart.

● E Schumacher *Small is beautiful: a study of economics as if people mattered* (Blond & Briggs, 1973).

● V Papanek *Seeing the world whole: interaction between ecology and design* (Lawrence, Kansas, University of Kansas Press, 1982).

● J Elkington Associates & others *The Green designer* (Design Council, 1986).

● J Elkington & T Burke *The Green capitalists: industry's search for environmental excellence* (Gollancz, 1987).

● M Henstock *Design for recyclability* (Institute of Metals, 1988).

● J Hailes & J Elkington *The Green consumer guide* (Victor Gollancz, 1988).

● *Green Magazine* **1** (1) October 1989.

● A de Forest & T Viemeister 'Waste not, want not' *ID (Magazine of International Design)* November–December 1989 64–7.

● A Fox & R Murrell *Green Design: a guide to the environmental impact of materials* (ADT/Longman, 1989).

● 'Shopping for the planet: Green consumerism' *New Internationalist* (203) January 1990.

● *More from less* (Design Council/British Gas, 1990), 24pp brochure.

● P Burall *Green Design* (Design Council, 1991).

● D MacKenzie *Green Design: design for the environment* (Laurence King, 1991).

● V Papanek 'Industrial design, ecology and the environment' *Design World* (Australia) (20) 1991 2–7.

315 **GREY ORGANIZATION (GO)** Group name adopted in the mid 1980s by three young, London-based artists – Daniel Clegg, Toby Mott and Paul Spencer – who followed in the footsteps of

The Grey Boys
A revolt into Fashion?

Picture: Dick Scott-Stewart

GREY ORGANIZATION THE GREY ORGANIZATION in *Artline* (1985). Photo: Dick Scott-Stewart.

Gilbert & George and Andy Warhol's business art. GO presented a uniform image: their hair was closely cropped and they wore grey business suits. Grey was selected because it was 'a neutral zone in which anything could occur', e.g. paintings, videos, prints, T-shirts, provocative demonstrations. Like a commercial firm, the artists believed in organization and business with art as their product. They also attempted to found a kind of sub-culture or movement – in 1984 the membership of the organization was claimed to be over 100. Their biggest splash in Britain occurred when they flung grey paint over the windows of prestigious West End galleries in Cork Street as a protest against 'the boring and lifeless art establishment'. Subsequently GO moved to New York where they designed album covers, directed TV pro-grammes and mounted art exhibitions.

● See also Business Art, Gilbert & George.

◉ M Snow 'Glad to be Grey!' *New Musical Express* Septem-ber 15 1984 -8.

◉ 'The Grey Organization' *Art & Design* **1** (8) September 1985 36–7.

◉ 'The Grey boys: a revolt into fashion?' *Artline* **2** (9) 1985 14–15.

316 GRIDNIKS

Peter York's humorous name for designers, particu-larly graphic designers. According to York, this pro-fession achieved a new power and status in the 1970s and '80s. He called them 'Gridniks' because of their fond-ness for grids of all kinds: 'men and women educated on graph paper to think in squares...the world of the design solution – modular, conceptual, systematic...'. For a seri-ous study of the history and use of grids in design see the article by Jack H. Williamson listed below.

◉ P York 'Chic graphique' *Modern times: everybody wants everything* (Heinemann, 1984) 26–37.

◉ J Williamson 'The grid: history, use, and meaning' *Design Issues* **3** (2) Fall 1986 15–30.

317 GRIDS

Formal devices popular with many American abstract painters and minimal sculp-tors in the 1960s and '70s, e.g. Eva Hesse, Ellsworth Kelly, Sol Lewitt, Agnes Martin, Larry Poons and Alan Shields. Grids – which painters had traditionally used to square-up canvases – served as neutral armatures for artists to work with or against. As Sol Lewitt once noted, 'a grid is a conve-nience. It stabilizes the measurements and neutralizes space by treating it all equally.' The fact that exhibi-tions of Grid-based art could be organized in the '70s was an indication of how rapidly the device had become

a cliché.

● See also Formalism & Formalist Criticism, Minimal Art, Modular Art, Serial Art.

◉ J Elderfield 'Grids' *Artforum* **10** (9) May 1972 52–9.

Grids, Grids... (Philadelphia, University of Pennsylvania / ICA, 1972).

◉ A Goldin 'Patterns,Grids and painting' *Artforum* **14** (1) September 1975 50–4.

◉ R Krauss 'Grids' *October* (9) Summer 1979 50–64.

◉ — *Grids, formats and image in twentieth- century art* (NY, Pace Gallery, 1979).

318 GROUNDSCRAPERS

According to the British TV arts programme *Signals* (Channel 4, December 7 1988), a term used in the late 1980s by architects and developers to describe a new type of office block being constructed in the City of Lon-don and in the Docklands area. Unlike the skyscraper offices of the past – which extended vertically – Ground-scrapers extend horizontally; they provide huge areas of space but are only a few storeys high. The reason for this change of design was not primarily stylistic, it was rather a response to new commercial needs and new technolo-gies, i.e. the new electronic equipment needed for inter-national business required horizontal spaces with raised floors so that cabling could run underneath; also, the growing number of commodity markets required long, open spaces uninterrupted by columns.

Reyner Banham discussed the concept of Ground-scrapers in a 1976 review of the Free University of Berlin building (1962–3) designed by the multi-national Paris partnership of Josic/Candilis/Woods. According to Ban-ham, a Groundscraper 'must appear to crawl on its belly, like a snake in Eden'.

● See also Docklands.

◉ R Banham 'Ground scraping' *New Society* **37** (723) August 12 1976 352–3.

319 GROUP MATERIAL (GM)

A loose association of femi-nist and Left-wing Ameri-can artists (including Tim Rollins, Mundy McLaugh-lin, Julie Ault and Doug Ashford) and others, founded in New York in 1979. GM organized numerous discus-sions, workshops, projects and exhibitions with the aim of providing structures within which hundreds could par-ticipate. They argued that a radical, community-based art practice was one that helped to organize people so that they could speak for themselves. Shows of posters were put on in the subway and in the street; however, GM also exhibited in their own gallery and in public museums. Displays tended to be thematic – tackling issues of race, gender, consumption, imperialism, anti-Baudrillard, democracy – and were conceived as collective, unified presentations. The question of art's relation to context – physical and social – was important, as was the development of a method embracing 'a social means of production and distribution'.

● See also Alternative Spaces, Collaborations, Community Art, KOS, Political Art.

● P Hall 'Group Material, an interview' *Real Life* (11/12) Winter 1983 2–9.

● W Olander 'Material world' *Art in America* **77** (1) January 1989 122–8, + 167.

● B Wallis (ed) *Democracy: a project by Group Material* (NY, Dia Art Foundation/Bay Press, 1990).

320 GROUPE ESPACE, LE

An association of geometric abstract artists, architects and builders founded in Paris in October 1951 by André Bloc and Del Marle. (Earlier, in 1949, Bloc had formed, with Le Corbusier, 'L'Association pour une Synthèse des Arts Plastique'.) Its membership eventually grew to over 100 and included Arno Jacobsen, Richard Neutra, Nicolas Schöffer, Edgard Pillet, Jean Gorin and Victor Vasarely. A manifesto was issued in 1953. The work of Le Groupe Espace was influenced by the pre-1945 movements constructivism and neo-plasticism, and it overlapped with the kinetic art of the '50s. As the name of the group indicated, these artists were concerned with space in art, architecture and town planning. They sought the closest possible collaboration between art, architecture and the crafts. Their conception of art was anti-individualist in the sense that they aimed for forms of expression that were social, public and collective in character. Their work and ideas were publicized in *Art d'Aujourd'hui* (1949–54) which was launched as a journal devoted to abstraction. The French-British painter Paule Vézelay was president of a British branch of Le Groupe Espace.

● See also Constructivism, Kinetic Art, Spatio-Dynamism, This is Tomorrow.

● A Bloc *Exposition Espace: architecture, formes, couleur* (Biot, Groupe Espace, 1954).

● R Diamant-Berger 'De l'union pour l'art...' *Aujourd'hui: art et architecture* **10** December 1967 54–7.

321 GRUPPO N

A group of Italian experimental artists founded in Padua in 1959. Members included: Alberto Biasi, Ennio Chiggio, Giovanni Costa, Edoardo Landi and Manfredo Massironi. Gruppo N promoted kinetic, light, op, environmental and participatory art. The group also took part in exhibitions of programmed art and in those of the Nouvelle Tendance. Biasi, an artist employing light refracted through prisms, had previously been a member of Gruppo 58 and later, when he moved to Paris, he contributed to the phases movement.

● See also Phases Movement

C Tisdall 'Two Italian kinetic groups' *Studio International* **180** (926) October 1970 132–5.

322 GRUPPO T

A group of Italian experimental artists formed in Milan in 1959 and active during the early '60s. Members included: Giovanni Anceschi, Davide Boriani, Gianni Colombo, Gabriele de Vecchi, Grazio Varisco. Like Gruppo N, these artists were interested in developing forms of kinetic and light art, in constructing environments which involved the participation of the spectator and transcended the art object.

● See also Programmed Art.

● C Tisdall 'Two Italian kinetic groups' *Studio International* **180** (926) October 1970 132–5.

323 GUERRILLA ART ACTION GROUP (GAAG)

A New York art and politics group (or concept – anyone could use its name or ideas) active in the 1970s. Its chief members were Jean Toche and Jon Hendricks. Described as 'the conscience of the artworld', GAAG were critical of contemporary art on the grounds that it was mainly a capitalist commodity, and museums and artists on the grounds that they were adjuncts to fascism. In order to challenge the status quo, GAAG performed a number of 'actions' in public places such as the Museum of Modern Art. They had some success in provoking the authorities since they were arrested several times.

● See also Actions, Art Workers' Coalition, Political Art.

● G Battcock 'Guerrilla Art Action' *Art & Artists* **6** (11) February 1972 22–5.

● 'Art Workers' Coalition, New York (Guerrilla Art Action)' *Die Flug/FluxBlattzeitung* (12) n d (Stuttgart, Albrecht D).

● GAAG 'Letter...' *Left Curve* (1) Spring 1974 4–15.

● *Guerrilla Art Action Group* (NY, Printed Matter, 1979).

324 GUERRILLA GIRLS

(Also G. Girls) A New York group of women artists and activists formed in 1985 for the purpose of combating sexism and racism in the artworld. GG also describe themselves as 'anonymous art agitators' and 'the conscience of the artworld'. They have produced humorous and factual posters, placards and magazine statements, made videos, mounted exhibitions, given lectures and

Dearest Art Collector,
It has come to our
attention that your
collection, like most,
does not contain
enough art by women.
We know that you
feel terrible about this
and will rectify the
situation immediately.
All our love,
Guerrilla Girls

BOX 1056 COOPER STA., NY NY 10276

GUERRILLA GIRLS 'Letter to art collectors'. n. d.

staged public demonstrations, all of which were critical of the white, male domination of the artworld and of the myths sustaining contemporary art. They have also issued bad report cards on 'boy crazy' dealers and critics. Punning on their name, GG wear gorilla masks and costumes during their public appearances. Their activities are funded by private donations.

● See also Feminist Art, Political Art, Prop Art.

◦ G Trebay 'Guerrilla's night out' *Village Voice* October 29 1985 71.

◦ P Taylor 'Where the girls are' *Manhattan Inc* April 1987 178.

◦ M Woodruff 'Monkey business' *Taxi* April 1989 44–7.

◦ M Schor 'Girls will be girls' *Artforum* **19** (1) September 1990 124–9.

325 **GUTAI GROUP**
An association of around 20 Japanese artists devoted to the cause of experimental art founded in Osaka in 1954. The word 'gutai' approximates to the German word 'gestalt'. The original members of Gutai were young artists influenced by the master Jiro Yoshihara (1905–72). They included Sadamasa Motonaga, Kazuo Shiraga, Atsuko Tanaka and Minoru Yoshida. In the West the Gutai Group were particularly noted for their dada-like, mixed-media theatrical events or open-air spectacles which pre-dated the happenings of New York. In 1957 contacts were established between the Group and l'art informel of Europe via Michel Tapié who visited Japan in that year. Following the death of Yoshihara in 1972, the Gutai Group disbanded.

● See also Art Informel, Experimental Art, Happenings.

◦ J Langsner 'Gutai: an on the spot report' *Art International* **9** (3) April 1965 18–24.

◦ M Cohen 'Japan's Gutai Group' *Art in America* **56** (6) November–December 1968 86–9.

◦ J Love 'The group in contemporary Japanese art: Gutai and Jiro Yoshihara' *Art International* **16** (6/7) Summer 1972 123–7, + 143.

◦ Y Inui 'The Gutai Group and sky art' *Sky Art Conference '83* (Cambridge, Mass, MIT/Centre for Advanced Visual Studies, 1983) 8–9, text in German.

◦ *Grupo Gutai* (Madrid, Español de Arte Contemporáneo, 1985).

◦ A Saura 'Espace et geste de Gutai' *Art Press* (109) December 1986 16–19.

H

326 HABITAT

A vogue word among architects and designers in the 1950s and '60s. It means 'a natural environment in which plants and animals develop', hence 'place of abode'. For most humans 'habitats' are artificial environments designed by architects, e.g. Le Corbusier's famous vertical village: 'Unité d'Habitation', Marseilles (1945–52). In 1967, for the Expo at Montreal, the Israeli architect Moshte Safte designed a cliff-like structure using mass-production methods to create modular housing units which were then stacked in various ways. The structure, called 'Habitat', accommodated a large population in a limited space without restricting human needs for privacy and comfort.

The ninth assembly of CIAM (Congrès Internationaux d'Architecture Moderne), held in Aix en Provence in 1954, made Habitat its theme. It was also chosen as the name of a large international conference on the crisis in human settlements, organized by the United Nations, held in Vancouver in 1976.

Terence Conran, the British designer and businessman, opened his first furniture shop called 'Habitat' in London's Fulham Road in 1964. By 1976 he had established an empire of 30 stores (five in Europe) selling simple, well-designed modern furniture and household goods at reasonable prices to young consumers. The Habitat aesthetic was characterized by one writer as 'a mixture of good design basics, like Bentwood, Bauhaus and butcher's block'.

● See also Conran Foundation, 'Good Design'.

M Bateman 'A master of interior design' *Sunday Times Magazine* September 12 1976 22–3.

'Habitat reconsidered' *Architectural Design* **46** (10) October 1976.

B Phillips *The Habitat story* (Weidenfeld & Nicolson, 1984).

327 HAPPENINGS

(Also called Action Theatre, Be-Ins, Event Art, Painters' Theatre, Theatre of Mixed Means, Total Art/Theatre) The term 'Happenings' derived from Allan Kaprow's earliest public work '18 Happenings in 6 parts' performed in New York in 1959. Happenings exploited several media; they were a cross between an art exhibition and a theatrical performance. Since they were developed by painters and sculptors, they foregrounded visual, tactile and olfactory qualities rather than literary or verbal ones. Generally they avoided such features of the traditional theatre as plot, characters, actors and repetition of performance, but they did make use of scripts, specific subjects (e.g. a car crash) and rehearsals, i.e. they were not simply events improvised on the spur of the moment. Happenings were flexible as to time – their duration tended to be uncertain – and place – they could occur in galleries, homes, backyards or in the countryside. Great stress was laid on materials and participants were often made up to look like objects. Cluttered environments, destruction and impermanence were key features of Happenings and since audiences were also expected to take part those who attended had to be prepared to endure physical discomfort and possible abuse.

Precedents for Happenings could be found in dada's Cabaret Voltaire and in the scams of the futurists and surrealists. The collage principle dating back to cubism was obviously also important, as was the emphasis on the artist's process of creation in action painting. In America John Cage and the Black Mountain College were significant influences upon several artists involved in Happenings. The major centre for this kind of art was New York in the late '50s and early '60s. Besides Kaprow there was Jim Dine, Red Grooms, Al Hansen, Claes Oldenburg, George Segal, Robert Whitman, Yoko Ono and George Brecht. Similar activities also took place in cities throughout Europe and in Japan.

● See also Action Painting, Actions, Assemblage Art, Destructive Art, Direct Art, Environmental Art, Fluxus, Gutai Group, Performance Art, Process Art.

J Becker & W Vostell *Happenings* (Hamburg, Rowohlt, 1965).

A Hansen *Primer of Happenings and time/space art* (NY, Something Else Press, 1965).

A Kaprow *Assemblage, environments and Happenings* (NY, Abrams, 1965).

A Kaprow 'The Happenings are dead...long live the Happenings' *Artforum* **4** (7) March 1966 36–9.

M Kirby *Happenings: an illustrated anthology* (NY, Dutton, 1966).

● J-J Lebel *Le Happening* (Paris, Denoel, 1966).

● *Happenings & Fluxus* (Cologne, Kolnischer Kunstverein, 1970).

● R Kostelanetz *The Theatre of Mixed Means* (Pitman, 1970).

● U Kultermann *Art-events and Happenings* (Mathew Miller Dunbar, 1971).

● C Oldenburg *Raw notes* (Halifax, Nova Scotia, Press of the Nova Scotia College of Art & Design, 1973).

● A Henri *Environments and Happenings* (Thames & Hudson, 1974).

● A Kaprow *2 measures* (Torino, Martano Editore, 1976).

328 HAPSHASH AND THE COLOURED COAT

A noted British pop/psychedelic design partnership of the late 1960s. Hapshash was founded in 1967 by two musicians and designers: Michael English (ex-Ealing College of Art) and Nigel Waymouth (economics graduate and part-owner of Granny Takes a Trip, a King's Road boutique selling 'camp' merchandise to pop music stars). They designed colourful, art nouveau-influenced posters for the UFO Club, London, for rock groups like the Incredible String Band, for events like the 'Legalize Pot Rally', plus various images including a Red Indian warrior for the front of the King's Road shop. They also did design work for the underground magazine *International Times*. Hapshash shared the ideals of the hippie subculture it served: it was committed to mind expansion, hallucination and 'turning on' the world.

● See also Camp, The Fool, Pop Art, Psychedelic Art, Underground Art.

● G Melly *Revolt into style: the pop arts in Britain* (Allen Lane, The Penguin Press, 1970).

329 HARD ARCHITECTURE

In his 1974 book *Tight spaces* Robert Sommer argued that American prisons, mental hospitals and other public buildings were increasingly being designed to resist the human imprint: they were impervious, impersonal, inorganic, windowless buildings with rough wall surfaces to discourage graffiti. He maintained that such 'hard', sterile architecture exacerbated alienation and isolation; it was symptomatic of a security state of mind.

● See also Defensive Architecture, Environmental Design, Soft Architecture.

● R Sommer *Tight spaces: Hard Architecture and how to humanize it* (Englewood Cliffs, New Jersey, Prentice Hall, 1974).

330 HARD-EDGE PAINTING

(Also Abstract Classicism) This label was first used by the Californian critic Jules Langsner in 1959 to characterize the abstract paintings of four West Coast artists: Karl Benjamin, Lorser Feitelson, Frederick Hammersley and John McLaughlin. Their work signalled a reaction against the gestural, improvised style of action painting and tachisme fashionable in the 1940s and '50s. According to Lawrence Alloway, a critic who extended the Hard-Edge concept, this type of painting treated the whole picture surface as one unit: forms extended across the canvas from edge to edge so that there were no 'figures on the field' or other depth effects. Paint was applied evenly to produce an immaculate finish, colours were restricted to two or three saturated hues and delineations between areas of colour were abrupt (hence 'Hard-Edge'); often an optical shimmer resulted from the contrast of complementary hues. (If 'Hard-Edge' merely means a technique of painting with sharp rather than fuzzy edges – some writers use the term in this way – then it would be equally applicable to pop art.)

Aside from the artists listed above, the main exponents of the Hard-Edge idiom were Ellsworth Kelly, Alexander Liberman, Al Held and Jack Youngerman. Their precursors were Josef Albers, Ad Reinhardt and Barnett Newman. At first sight this kind of art appeared to continue the European tradition of geometric abstraction, but

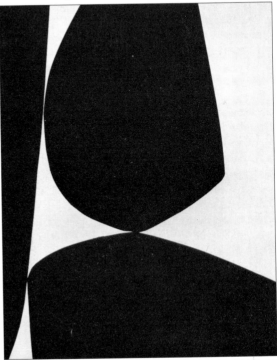

HARD-EDGE PAINTING LORSER FEITELSON, 'Magical space forms' (1962). Oil on canvas, 60" x 50". Photo: Ankrum Gallery.

in most instances the relation was to preceding American painting rather than to the European tradition. Many painters and sculptors outside the United States were influenced by Hard-Edge or arrived at a comparable style independently, especially in Britain (e.g. the situation painters).

● See also Colour-Field Painting, Formalism & Formalist Criticism, Geometric Abstraction, Situation.

● L Alloway 'On the edge' *Architectural Design* **30** (4) April 1960 164–5.

●—'Classicism or Hard-Edge?' *Art International* **4** (2/3) 1960 60–2.

● J Langsner *West Coast Hard-Edge* (ICA, 1960).

● J Coplans 'John McLaughlin, Hard-Edge and American painting' *Artforum* **2** (7) January 1964 28–31.

● J Langsner *California Hard-Edge Painting* (Balboa, California, Pavilion Gallery, 1964).

● M Baigell 'American abstract expressionism and Hard-Edge: some comparisons' *Studio International* **171** (873) January 1966 10–15.

331 HARVARD ARCHITECTURE

A label applied by Klaus Herdeg to the work of a number of architects – Edward Larabee Barnes, John Johansen, Philip Johnson, I. M. Pei, Paul Rudolph and others – who emerged from Harvard University's Graduate School of Design in the 1940s and '50s. At Harvard they were taught by Walter Gropius and Marcel Breuer according to principles first formulated at the Bauhaus in Germany. Herdeg maintained that Barnes *et al.* made contemporary architecture fashionable in the United States. He saw this as a negative development because he was critical of the course at Harvard on the grounds that it involved dichotomies between intellectual and artistic values, verbal and visual truth, plan and appearance. The Bauhaus/Harvard ethos of Gropius and Breuer, in the hands of their students, resulted in 'decorated diagrams', passionless, formalist architecture.

● See also TAC.

● K Herdeg *The decorated diagram: Harvard Architecture and the failure of the Bauhaus legacy* (Cambridge, Mass, MIT Press, 1985).

332 HAUS-RUCKER-CO

(House-Mover-Company) An experimental architecture and design group formed in Austria in 1967 by two architects – Laurids Ortner and Zamp (Gunter Kelp) – and a painter–designer – Klaus Pinter. They were also assisted by a staff of five with other skills. The particular speciality of the Haus-Rucker-Co was plastics (hence they were dubbed 'the plastics people'), pneumatic structures, air mattresses and life-support systems.

● See also Plastics, Pneumatic Architecture.

● 'Haus-Rucker-Co-Live!' *Craft Horizons* **30** (4) August 1970 30–3.

● 'Conceptual architecture' *Design Quarterly* (78/79) 1970 29–33.

● J Burns *Arthropods; new design futures* (NY, Praeger, 1972) 64–71.

● *Haus-Rucker-Co 1967 bis 1983* (Brauschweig, Friedr Vieweg & Sohn, 1984).

333 HERITAGE INDUSTRY

An expression used by the cultural critic / historian Robert Hewison and others in the mid 1980s to describe a movement associated with the decline of British manufacturing industry: instead of goods Britain produced a commodity called 'heritage'. Conservation, preservation and heritage organizations flourished; more and more museums were opened; Britain was in danger of becoming a vast, open-air museum; a false image of the past was retailed for the benefit of citizens and tourists. Hewison argued for a critical culture instead of a closed culture, history instead of heritage, a spirit of renewal instead of nostalgia for a non-existent past.

● See also Retro.

● P Wright *On living in an old country: the national past in contemporary Britain* (Verso, 1985).

● R Hewison *The Heritage Industry: Britain in a climate of decline* (Methuen, 1987).

334 HI-WAY CULTURE

Lawrence Alloway's 1967 term for the icons and hardware associated with the motor car, trucks and highways of the United States. Roadside structures such as gas stations, motels, fast-food restaurants, used-car lots, traffic signs and advertising billboards can all be regarded as examples of American material culture in their own right, but they have also served as motifs in high culture, e.g. in the work of such pop artists as Claes Oldenburg, George Segal, Allan D'Arcangelo and Ed Ruscha.

● See also Billboard Art, Car Culture, Electrographic Architecture, Pop Architecture, Pop Art.

● L Alloway 'HiWay Culture' *Arts Magazine* **41** (4) February 1967 28–33.

● N Calas 'Allan D'Arcangelo' *Art in the age of risk and other essays* (NY, Dutton, 1968) 201–7.

● B O'Doherty 'Highway to Las Vegas' *Art in America* **60** (1) January–February 1972 80–9.

● J Andrews *The well built -elephant and other roadside attractions* (NY, Congdon & Weed, 1985).

335 HIGH STYLES

Title of a major exhibition of twentieth-century American design held in New York in 1985. Like 'high art/culture', the term 'High Styles' was indicative of qualitative and wealth or class differences (styles were 'high' in contrast to 'low' culture, vernacular or mass-produced design). Lisa Phillips: '"High Style"... is reserved for the superlative – for the most important, the ultra fashionable, the unusually dramatic. In America, High Style, with its attendant associations of wealth, status, and power has been a potent signifier of our aspirations and desired identity.'

● See also Pop Design, Popular Art.

◖ L Phillips & others *High Styles: twentieth-century American design* (NY, Whitney Museum of American Art/Summit Books, 1985).

336 HIGH-TECH

(Also Hi-Tech, Industrial Style / Aesthetic, Work Aesthetic) This term has been applied to both interior design and architecture. A High-Tech style of interior design was popular in Europe and North America in the 1970s. It was based upon the re-utilization of industrial materials, equipment and products, i.e. those made for factories, offices, hospitals, restaurants, battleships, etc., as home furnishings. For instance, using builder's scaffolding to make a raised bed or study area within a room, using industrial overalls as everyday wear. The term 'High-Tech' derived from the conjunction of 'high style' and 'technology'. (The opposite of High-Tech was, of course, Low-Tech.) Many people were attracted by the cheapness, no-nonsense design and functionalism of industrial products. Some critics ascribed the vogue for High-Tech to the nostalgia of a post-industrial society for the industrial society.

'High-Tech' was also used to characterize modern architecture constructed from space age materials and pre-fabricated parts, designed by architects who delighted in the look and efficiency of the latest technology. Key examples were: the Sainsbury Centre in Norwich designed by Norman Foster Associates; the Pompidou Centre in Paris designed by Renzo Piano and Richard Rogers; the Lloyd's building in London designed by Richard Rogers Partnership; Nicholas Grimshaw's *Financial Times* Printing Works, Isle of Dogs, London; Michael Hopkins' Schlumberger Research Laboratories, Cambridge and the Mound Stand, Lord's Cricket Ground, London; and the Haj Terminal, Saudi Arabia – a Teflon-coated glass-fibre canopy designed to shelter 80,000 pilgrims – designed by Skidmore, Owings, Merrill (SOM).

HIGH-TECH RICHARD ROGERS PARTNERSHIP, Exterior detail of the Lloyd's building (1979-86), City of London. Photo: Roderick Coyne.

Charles Jencks has also used the term 'slick-tech' (invented in 1977 and defined as 'an exaggeration of a technological image toward the glossy and ultra-smooth') to describe buildings such as Hans Hollein's 'Retti Candle shop', Vienna (1965) and John Portman's American hotels of the '60s and '70s. Sheet metal, polished aluminium and mirror glass were some of the materials slick-tech architects used in pursuit of 'the rhetoric of corporate proficiency'.

● See also High Styles, Low-Tech, Machine Aesthetic/Art, Minimalist Design/Style, Pompidou Centre, Sainsbury Centre, Soft Design/Tech.

◖ J Kron & S Slesin *High-Tech: the industrial style and source book for the home* (Allen Lane, Penguin Press, 1979).

◖ P Buchanan 'A nostalgic utopia or why the British excel at High-Tech' *Items* (15) 1985 4–11.

◖ T Forester *High-Tech society* (Oxford, Blackwell, 1987).

◖ C Davies *High-Tech architecture* (Thames & Hudson, 1988).

◖ C Jencks 'Slick-tech...' *Architecture today* (Academy Editions, 1988) 50–73.

337 HIGH TOUCH

In 1982 John Naisbitt claimed that 'whenever new technology is introduced into society there must be a counterbalancing human response'. He called the latter 'High-Touch': 'the more high-tech, the more High-Touch'. In terms of 1980s interior design, this human response took the form of furnishings in which the specific qualities and textures of a wide range of materials were foregrounded in order to stimulate tactile and visual senses. It also took the form of one-off or limited-edition items made by artist–designers whose bizarre, frequently non-functional designs were intended to counteract the standardized look of mass-produced goods. Robert Janjigian, an American design journalist, borrowed the term from Naisbitt. He identified a 'High-Touch design movement' which was also called 'new materialism' and 'post-modern industrial posh'.

● See also Creative Salvage, High-Tech, New Materialism.

J Naisbitt *Megatrends: ten new directions transforming our lives* (NY, Warner Books, 1982).

R Janjigian *High-Touch: the new materialism in design* (Columbus Books, 1987).

338 HIPGNOSIS

A neologism combining 'hip' (new, groovy) and 'gnosis' (mystical knowledge); also a pun on 'hypnosis'. The name of an exceptionally creative British graphic design team founded in London in 1968 by Storm Thorgerson (MA, Royal College of Art, film and TV) and Aubrey 'Po' Powell while they were still students. The photographer Peter Christopherson joined in 1974. Hipgnosis designed book and magazine covers, advertisements, posters, logos, etc., but became best known for their surreal album covers for the rock group Pink Floyd and many other bands. Their mainly photo-based designs (using staged scenes, montage and airbrush retouching) of the 1970s also became widely known via the lavishly illustrated books they published about their own work and their surveys of album cover imagery.

● See also Rock Art/Design/Fashion, Staged Photography.

Hipgnosis & G Hardie (compilers), S Thorgerson (text) *An ABC of the works of Hipgnosis: Walk away René* (Limpsfield, Surrey, Paper Tiger/Dragon's World, 1978).

S Thorgerson *The photodesigns of Hipgnosis: the goodbye look* (Limpsfield, Surrey, Paper Tiger/Dragon's World, 1982).

339 HISTORICISM

A term employed with different inflections of meaning by scholars belonging to several different disciplines. Nikolaus Pevsner, the architectural historian, used it to characterize a post-modern, anti-rational tendency in twentieth-century architecture and design which was dependent on historical precedents as a source of inspiration. In his view, Historicism marked an unfortunate retreat to those nineteenth-century values modern architects had striven to replace. As examples of stylistic revivals Pevsner listed neo-accommodating, neo-liberty, neo-German expressionism, neo-Perret, neo-de Stijl, neo-art nouveau and neo-school of Amsterdam. Historicism was also a common characteristic of post-modernist painting and sculpture in the 1980s.

● See also Post-Modernism, Retro.

P Collins 'Historicism' *Architectural Review* **127** (762) August 1960 101–3.

N Pevsner 'The return of Historicism' *Studies in art, architecture and design vol 2: Victorian and after* (Thames & Hudson, 1968) 242–59.

340 HOBBY ART

(Related terms: Closet Art, Family Art, Home-made Art, Kit Art, Maintenance Art, Mother Art, Private Art) A term used by the American art critic Lucy Lippard to describe decorative artefacts produced mainly by women in their homes as a pastime. As Lippard observes, amateur hobbies and crafts have a low cultural and artworld status despite the fact that skills and creativity are involved and many books are published which encourage such activities. For some forms of craftwork readymade kits of materials are available, hence the label 'kit art'. Because these artefacts were not normally made for public consumption, Lippard called them 'private' or 'closet art'.

A re-evaluation of craftwork by women was undertaken in the 1970s as a result of the influence of feminism and some women artists, e.g. Kate Walker, Monica Ross and Sue Richardson, began to produce objects in conscious awareness of 'non-prestigious folk traditions'. They organized the British postal event 'Portrait of the artist as a housewife' and also mounted an installation at the ICA, London, in 1977 entitled 'Feministo, a portrait of the artist as a young housewife'.

Work undertaken by women in the home and in paid employment has largely been concerned with the maintenance of existing systems (caring for children, housework, cleaning, etc.). Realising this, the American artist Mierle Laderman Ukeles decided to validate such labour as art by performing cleaning rituals in public museums.

Naturally enough she called these performances 'maintenance art'. As Ukeles pointed out in a 1969 proposal for 'Care – an exhibition of maintenance art', avant garde art is premised on revolution, development and change and consequently its (male?) values are antipathetic to those of women and maintenance art.

In a 1989 book Philip Pacey introduced the term 'family art' to encompass the contributions made by all members of a successful family to their home life. His term included portraits, photographs, children's drawings, hand-painted furniture, embroidered samplers, patchwork quilts, etc. Items such as Christmas decorations and birthday cakes indicated the close connection between visual artefacts and cyclical rituals or social customs. Pacey paid particular attention to the home life of the Swedish painter and farmer Karl Larsson.The home is, of course, a cultural concept not just a place or a building. As Witold Rybczynski has shown, this concept has a history.

● See also DIY, Feminist Art, Mail Art, Naive Art, Popular Art, Suburban Art.

◑ J Burnham 'Problems of criticism 9' *Artforum* **9** (5) January 1971 40–5.

◑ *Issue: social strategies by women artists* (London, ICA, 1980).

◑ H Hammond & C Stallone *Home work: the domestic environment reflected in work by contemporary women artists* (Seneca Falls, NY, National Women's Hall of Fame, n d).

◑ L Lippard 'Making something for nothing (toward a definition of women's "Hobby Art")' *Get the message: a decade of art for social change* (NY, Dutton, 1984) 97–105.

◑ W Rybczynski *Home: short history of an idea* (Heinemann, 1988).

◑ P Pacey *Family Art* (Cambridge, Polity Press, 1989).

341 HOLOCAUST ART

(Also Concentration Camp Art) Many professional artists of Jewish and other races were imprisoned and died in the ghettos, transit and extermination camps established by the Nazis during the Second World War. Perhaps the best known were the Italian-Austrian artist Zoran Music and the Frenchman Boris Taslitzky. In spite of the horrific conditions, constant danger and shortage of materials, drawings, paintings and some carvings were produced within the ghettos and camps. Some in fact were made at the order of the Nazis – as propaganda or for their personal use – others were a form of spiritual resistance and historical witnessing. After the war surviving images were recovered, assembled in archives and presented in exhibitions and publications, generally under the rubric 'art of the holocaust'. Scholars make a distinction between the latter and 'the holocaust in art',

i.e. any works depicting the camps by artists who were not victims.

Since many of the artists concerned had been social realists or expressionists before their imprisonment, these styles continued to be employed in the camps. The horrendous subject matter of the Nazi death camps confronted the artists with an almost impossible task of representation. Art implies aesthetic pleasure but the idea that such scenes of brutality, torture and suffering should give pleasure to the viewer is highly disturbing.

● See also Nazi Art, Prison Art.

◑ G Green *The artists of Terezin* (NY, Hawthorn, 1969).

◑ N Toll *Without surrender: art of the holocaust* (Philadelphia, Running Press, 1978).

◑ Union of American Hebrew Congregations *Spiritual resistance: art from concentration camps 1940–45* (NY, Jewish Museum, 1978).

◑ J Blatter & S Milton *Art of the holocaust* (NY, Rutledge Press, 1981; London, Orbis (& Pan), 1982).

342 HOLOGRAPHIC ART

Examples of fine art executed in the modern, expensive and technically complex medium of holography. Dr Dennis Gabor has been called the 'father of holography' because he developed the theory of holograms in 1947. However, it was not possible to produce holographic images until the invention of lasers in the 1960s. The word derives from the Greek 'holos' meaning 'whole'. A hologram is a recording in emulsion on a photographic glass plate of the wave interference pattern produced by two beams of light when directed at an object. When a beam of laser light is passed through the hologram, a three-dimensional image is generated behind the glass plate and when the viewer changes viewpoint new aspects of a depicted object can be seen just as in reality.

The British artist Margaret Benyon was a pioneer of Holographic Art, making what were called 'holographs' or 'stereo-paintings' from 1968 onwards. Other artists who have worked with the medium include Paul Walton, Martin Richardson, Graham Tunnadine, Claudius Modebe, Paul Newman, Mathew Andrews, Dieter Jung, Harriet Casdin-Silver, Andrew Logan, Michael Wenyon and Susan Gamble. Holography has also been used as a design tool by architects. Clearly, three dimensional-images of future buildings are of value to architects.

Since 1970 a series of exhibitions has taken place of holography and art, e.g.: 'N dimensional Space' (Finch College Museum, 1970); 'Holography and lasers' (London, Royal Academy, 1977); 'Canadian Holography now' (London, Canada House Gallery, 1984); 'The holographic image' (Lisbon, Gulbenkian Foundation, 1985); 'Art by laser' (Salisbury City Library, 1986);

HOLOGRAPHIC ART MARTIN RICHARDSON, 'Mathematical chef' (1986). Pulsed laser hologram. Photo: Richardson.

'Holograms by seven young artists' (Bath National Centre of Photography 1988). A Museum of Holography was also established in New York in 1976 and the Royal College of Art, London, founded a Holography unit in 1985. Several other British art colleges and schools of architecture now have such units.

Holographic images excite a sense of wonder and delight but the question 'in what way can such images count as art?' has exercised several critics. In 1986 Gamble and Wenyon displayed a series of works in opal perspex frames on handpainted easels. They consisted of large-scale holograms which, according to *The Face*, 'placed simple objects in a vivid, shimmering surround of changing light and hues created by an original method known as "laser speckle". The effect was like being immersed in a pool of hallucinatory electric colour.'

● See also Conceptual Architecture, Laser Art.

● H Wilhelmsson 'Holography: a new scientific technique of possible use to artists' *Leonardo* **1** (2) April 1969 161–9.

● D Dickson 'Art: holographs by Margaret Benyon' *New Scientist* May 20 1971 480.

● L Fader & C Leonard 'Holography: a design process aid' *Progressive Architecture* **52** (6) June 1971 92–4.

● *Margaret Benyon* (Nottingham University Gallery, 1971).

● J Benthall 'Laser holography and interference patterning' – in – *Science and technology in art today* (Thames & Hudson, 1972) 85–98.

● M Benyon 'Holography as an art medium' *Leonardo* **6** 1973 1–9.

● M Wenyon *Understanding holography* (David & Charles, 1978).

● P Walton *Space-light: a holography and laser spectacular* (Routledge & Kegan Paul, 1982).

● 'Laser days' *The Face* (77) September 1986 28.

● S Gamble & M Wenyon *The holographic image: eight artists in the age of the laser* (Lisbon, Calouste Gulbenkian Foundation, 1986).

● B Burgmer *Holographic Art: perception, evolution, future* (La Coruna, Daniel Weiss, 1987).

● *Holographics International* (1987–).

● P Zec *Holographie: Geschichte, Technik, Kunst* (Cologne, Dumont, 1987).

● A Pepper 'Holography, visual medium or cheap trick?' *Art Monthly* (122) December–January 1988–9 9–13.

● M Brill (ed) 'Holography as an art medium' *Leonardo* **22** (3/4) 1989, thematic issue.

343 **HOMME-TÉMOIN**

(Man as witness) A group of young French painters including Bernard Buffet, Paul Rebeyrolle, André Minaux and Bernard Lorjou exhibiting in the Gallery Du Bac, Paris, in 1948 whose work became fashionable in the late 1940s. These artists were opposed to abstraction and argued that art should bear witness to the condition of the world. Their still-life paintings and portraits were called 'social realist' and 'expressive realism'. (The latter term is more appropriate than the former.) L'Homme-Témoin produced grey, gloomy, pessimistic, highly stylized images with spiky forms and harsh black outlines which some critics interpreted as a visual equivalent to Jean-Paul Sartre's philosophy existentialism. Buffet's work in particular caught the public imagination and the post-war mood of austerity; as a result he achieved rapid commercial success. Other critics considered his style shallow and mannerist; they called it 'dehydrated art'.

344 **HOSPITAL ARTS**

(Also Health Care Arts, Hospice Arts) Essentially a sub-category of public art. In 1987 it was estimated that 100 of Britain's 350 hospitals provided patients with some kind of artistic experience, ranging from semi-permanent static works such as tile murals and prints to live entertainments such as musical performances and puppet shows. Hospital Arts have gathered force since the mid 1970s when the Manchester Hospitals Arts Project was undertaken. Dr Linda Moss has argued that exposure to art assists the healing process. It also enhances the quality of life for patients and staff, and humanizes the frequently drab or stark interiors and exteriors of hospital buildings. (Of course, the presence of art in hospitals is not unique to the twentieth century: Hogarth painted murals for St Bartholomew's in the 1730s, and nineteenth-century hospital buildings often included murals and stained glass windows.) Some hospitals have employed artists and poets as artists-in-residence and an arts consultant has also overseen the development of the new, low-energy hospital on the Isle of Wight: it has been designed to include works of art and craft. Artists have also been involved in landscaping, e.g. the West Dorset Hospital. Hospices and health centres are other places which increasingly seek arts provision.

In recent years there has been an increase in arts for the disabled (though a distinction is drawn between the disabled and the ill). In 1976 Gina Levete, a former dancer, founded 'Shape', a network offering performance and participatory arts to patients. Later, to facilitate international contacts, she established 'Interlink', an information and advice agency concerned with the promotion of art for the sick and disabled. Levete feared the over-professionalization of art and thought everyone could benefit from taking part in creative activities.

In 1989 the British Health Care Arts Centre, directed by Malcolm Miles, was established at Duncan of Jordanstone College of Art, Dundee for the purposes of undertaking research and development on art in health buildings, providing a national service of advice,

documentation and publishing, and encouraging collaboration between architects and artists in health care buildings.

● See also Art Therapy, Participatory Art, Public Art.

◉ P Coles *Manchester Hospitals Art Project* (Gulbenkian Foundation, 1981).

◉ — *Art in the National Health Service* (Cleveland, Dept of Health & Social Security, 1983).

◉ — *The arts in a health district* (Cleveland, Dept of Health & Social Security, 1985).

◉ E Clouston 'It's the least that Van Gogh could expect' *Guardian* August 12 1987 13.

◉ J Greene *Brightening the long days: hospital tile murals* (Tiles & Architectural Ceramics Society, 1987).

◉ G Levete *The creative tree* (Salisbury, Michael Russell Publishing, 1987).

◉ L Moss *Art for health's sake* (Manchester, Dept of Architecture, Manchester Polytechnic, 1987).

◉ — *Art and health care* (Cleveland, Dept of Health & Social Security, 1988).

◉ M Miles 'Platform – an environment for healing' *Alba* (12) Summer 1989 47.

◉ R Cork 'For the needs of their own spirit: art in hospitals' – in – *Art for public places* M Miles & others (Winchester School of Art Press, 1989) 187–96.

◉ L Greene *Art in hospitals: a guide* (King's Fund/ Greater London Arts, 1989).

HUMANIST ART TAIR SALAKHOV, 'Portrait of the composer Kara Karayev' oil painting (1951).

345 HUMANIST ART

'Humanism', of course, is a word strongly associated with the Italian Renaissance and the figurative art of that period which looked back to classical Greece and Rome for inspiration. In the post–1945 era, however, the expression 'Humanist Art' has been employed by writers in both the West and the East in a somewhat different way. Barry Schwartz, an American advocate of 'Humanist Art', has argued that there is an irreconcilable opposition between technology and humanity. He therefore divided all art into 'humanist' or 'non-humanist' according to whether or not it aligned itself with the increasing technocratization of human existence and the environment. (Humanist Art opposed technology.) He then identified four varieties of Humanist Art: metaphysical, existential, absurdist and political. 'The metaphysical humanist creates work that is active symbolically...he engages the viewer in the interpretation of the work' (e.g. Leonard Baskin, Philip Evergood, George Segal). 'The existential humanist creates images that confront the viewer by provoking a response' (e.g. Duane Hanson, Francis Bacon, John Bratby). 'The absurdists employ a repulsion–curiosity mechanism' (e.g. Robert Crumb, Jim Nutt, Gladys Nilsson). 'The political humanist wants to contact the viewer's feelings of oppression and struggle' (e.g. Ben Shahn, Duane Hanson, Edward Kienholz, May Stevens). Although not all figurative art is humanist, all Humanist Art is figurative as opposed to abstract.

In the USSR where technology was generally regarded as a positive force, the apostle of humanism in art in the 1970s was Vladislav Zimenko. He asserted: 'art at its best has always glorified Man, poeticized his wisdom, strength and beauty and has always been an active means of affirming humanistic ideas...'. Predictably, the humanistic essence of art was equated with Soviet socialist realism. Amongst the artists he praised were: A. Deyneka, A. Plastov, B. Ioganson, V. Ivanov, D. Zhilinsky, and G. Korzhev. Zimenko ignored examples of American Humanist Art (and Chinese peasant painting) and condemned as 'anti-humanist' Western avant garde art movements such as minimalism.

● See also Superhumanism, Unofficial Soviet Art.

● J Alford 'Problems of a humanistic art in a mechanistic culture' *Journal of Aesthetics & Art Criticism* **20** (1) Fall 1961 37–47.

● B Schwartz *The new humanism: art in a time of change* (David & Charles, 1974).

● V Zimenko *The humanism of art* (Moscow, Progress Publishers, 1976).

346 HYBRID CULTURE

(Also Cross-Culture, Cultural Fusion, Intercultural, Syncretism) Any culture (or art, or style) derived from heterogeneous sources, or composed of elements of different or incongruous kinds. Dora Ashton has argued that a breakdown of categories was characteristic of much modern art. The breakdown began before 1914 and resulted in a 'hybrid reformation of new entities'. Modern Japanese culture has also been regarded as 'hybrid' because it is a mixture of Eastern and Western influences. (However, since all human cultures tend to be the result of a mix of elements, the term is not that useful or informative.) The word 'hybrid' has negative connotations – implying an uneasy or unsuccessful conjunction of disparate elements – whereas 'cultural fusion' suggests successful integration. Roger Tredre has employed the term 'cross-culture' to characterize '90s fashion design: 'a deliberate fusion of styles, a patchwork of multi-ethnic images...the melting point of cultures and races'.

A similar concept is Syncretism. In ordinary language it means 'an attempt to combine or reconcile different or opposing principles'. Modern culture, according to the American scholar Daniel Bell, is defined by an 'extraordinary freedom to ransack the world storehouse and to engorge any and every style it comes upon'; therefore, 'Syncretism is the jumbling of styles in modern art, which absorbs African masks or Japanese prints into its modes of depicting spatial perceptions'. Arguably, the hybrid/syncretic tendency is even more evident in postmodern art and design than in modern art.

Appropriating images and styles from foreign cultures can be undertaken by artists and designers in a shallow, exploitative way or in a more profound, respectful way. Mutual borrowing between cultures of equal status should perhaps be distinguished from hierarchical situations in which one culture dominates another (e.g. majority versus minority). Artists who are virtually compelled to reconcile alien cultures are those that move from one country, say Vietnam, to take up residence in another, say the United States, or who are the first-generation children of immigrants. These issues were explored in Britain – an increasingly multi-racial/cultural society – via three exhibitions held in London: 'From two worlds' (Whitechapel Art Gallery, 1986), 'The other story' (Hayward Gallery, 1989), and 'Diverse cultures' (Crafts Council, 1990).

● See also Black Art, Cross-Overs, Diasporist Painting, Ethnic Art, Global or World Art, Japanese Design/Style, Plagiarists, Post-Modern Architecture/Art/Design.

● D Ashton 'The breakdown of categories: hybrid art' *A reading of modern art* (Cleveland, Press of Case Western Reserve

University, 1969) 177–86.

● D Bell *The cultural contradictions of capitalism* (Heinemann, 1976) 13.

● C Abel 'Living in a hybrid world' *Design Studies* **3** (3) July 1982 127–32.

● Y Mitsukumi & others (eds) *The Hybrid Culture: what happened when East and West met* (Tokyo, Mazda, 1984).

● N Serota, G Jantjes & A Solanke *From two worlds* (Whitechapel Art Gallery, 1986).

● R Araeen & others *The other story: Afro-Asian artists in postwar Britain* (South Bank Centre/Hayward Gallery, 1989).

● R Tredre 'Crossing the cultural barriers' *Independent* April 7 1990 35.

● K Kurokawa *Intercultural architecture: the philosophy of symbiosis* (Academy, 1990).

347 HYPER-GRAPHICS/MEDIA

The term 'Hyper-text' was coined by Ted Nelson (based on a 1945 article by Vanavar Bush) to describe an environment where information can be linked freely across subject boundaries. Users are enabled to reorganize the information provided in ways that suit them. During the 1970s and '80s 'Hyper-graphics' was employed to describe four-dimensional figures on computer screens and 'Hyper-media' to describe new interactive digital video displays. The latter were dependent upon computers and sound–image information stored on compact discs (CD-ROM: Compact Disc–Read Only Memory). These systems have been developed by Philips, Sony and the Intel Corporation. To cite two applications: Hyper-media make excellent learning tools; students use a joystick to control continuous full-motion video which enables them to 'travel' and 'look around' a simulated world of an ancient culture, and to follow different pathways through the stored images and sound commentaries. Hyper-graphics can also be of value to designers: a simulated interior can be furnished and decorated in many different ways by drawing upon an image bank of styles and objects stored on the compact disc.

Matt Mullican, an American artist, devised a whole fictional city on a computer database which viewers could explore street by street via a laser disc. The work was sponsored by New York Telephone and technically assisted by Optomystic of Los Angeles. When it was exhibited at MoMA, New York, one critic called it 'techno-art'.

● See also Computer-Aided Design, Computer Art, Quantel Paintbox, Simulation/Simulacra/Hyperreality, Technological Art.

● D Brisson (ed) *Hypergraphics: visualizing complex relationships in art, science and technology* (Boulder, Westview Press, 1978, Bowker, 1979) (symposium sponsored by the American Association for the Advancement of Science).

● M Krueger *Artificial reality* (Reading, Mass, Addison-Wesley, 1983).

● E Barrett *The society of text: hypertext, hypermedia, and the social construction of information* (Cambridge, Mass, MIT Press, 1989).

● P Kunkel 'Hyper media' *ID (Magazine of International Design)* March–April 1989 40–3.

● D Shottenkirk 'Matt Mullican' *Artforum* **28** (5) January 1990 141–2.

● M Pye 'Polygons and pixels: the city as techno-art' *Independent on Sunday* February 11 1990 31.

● N Woodhead *Hypertext & Hypermedia* (Wokingham, Addison-Wesley, 1990).

● H Rheingold *Virtual reality* (Secker & Warburg, 1991).

348 ICA (Institute of Contemporary Arts, London) An important British cultural institution founded in 1947 by Herbert Read and Roland Penrose for the purpose of fostering new developments in the arts. Its programmes of events have included art exhibitions, films, videos, drama, poetry readings, lectures, discussions, concerts and rock music performances. Many leading British artists have been members of the ICA and have formed fruitful associations as a result (e.g. the Independent Group). For many years the ICA was located in Dover Street but it moved to more spacious premises in Nash House, The Mall, in 1967. Several magazines have been published by it: *ICA Bulletin* (1953–68), *ICA Quarterly* (1975) and *Living Arts* (1963–4).

The ICA is an organization which in the past has had a rapid turnover of directors and it has also suffered periodic financial crises (it receives funds from the Arts Council and from entrance charges); nevertheless, it is a multimedia arts centre which has played a vital role in the development of British art since the 1940s. Especially significant has been the ICA's programme of international exhibitions. Many cities in the developed countries of the world now have a comparable institution.

● See also Alternative Spaces, Contemporary Style, Independent Group.

● A Bruce *Art and audience at the ICA* (Arts Council of Great Britain, 1981).

● M Spens 'Winning against the odds' (interview with ICA director Bill McAlister) *Studio International* **196** (1001) August 1983 20–1.

349 ICOGRADA Acronym for 'International Council of Graphic Design Associations', a body founded in 1963. Three years later an audio-visual archive and library service of slides, films and slide-tape lectures relating to graphic design was established and located at the Bolton College of Art & Design, Lancashire.

● S Adshead 'The ICOGRADA audio-visual archive' *Art Libraries Journal* **1** (3) Autumn 1976 18–20.

350 ICP (Institute of Contemporary Prints) A British national graphic archive established in 1973 with the financial aid of the Sir Robert McAlpine Foundation. Stewart Mason, the curator of ICP, persuaded most British publishers of prints to participate in a voluntary deposit scheme. He also acquired Henry Moore's complete graphic archive. During the 1970s the print department of the Tate Gallery took over the work of the ICP.

● 'The National Archive of Graphic Arts' *Arts Review* **28** (1) January 9 1976 6.

351 IMITATION REALISTS Name of a group of Annandale (Australia) artists exhibiting at the Museum of Modern Art in Melbourne in 1962. The artists concerned were Michael Brown, Ross Crothall and Colin Lanceley. They produced figurative paintings that were highly complicated in their compositions and iconographies. Pigment was combined with waste materials/objects because garbage fascinated them. Sometimes the artists worked collaboratively on a single work. Influences included the l'art brut of Jean Dubuffet, assemblage, child art and Sepik, tribal artefacts. The term 'Imitation Realists' indicated 'a figurative art based on substitution' (Maloon); it derived from the fact that pictorial signs could be twice removed from their referents, e.g. in modern tribal art bottle tops replaced the traditional cowrie shells representing eyes. The content of Brown's work, critical of the establishment, provoked charges of obscenity.

● See also Art Brut, Assemblage Art, Collaborations.

● G Catalano *The years of hope* (Melbourne, Oxford University Press, 1981).

● R Hughes *The art of Australia* (Penguin, 1986).

● —*Colin Lanceley* (Sydney, Craftsman's Press, 1987).

● T Maloon 'Colin Lanceley: the man on the dump; sophisticated Lanceley' *Art & Australia* **25** (1) 1987 65–71.

352 INDEPENDENT GROUP (IG) (Also Young Group) The name of an informal think-tank formed by younger members of the ICA, London, which met intermittently between 1952 and '55. The word 'independent' was intended to signify a degree of autonomy from the mother institution, in particular a distance from the aesthetic tastes of Herbert Read and Roland Penrose. But it also signified that the members of the group were highly individualistic. Participants included Lawrence Alloway, Reyner Banham, Magda and Frank Cordell, Toni del Renzio, Richard Hamilton, Nigel Henderson, John McHale, Eduardo Paolozzi, Colin St John Wilson, Alison and Peter Smithson, and William Turnbull. Thus the IG represented a wide cross-section of the visual arts and criticism. The aim of IG was to consider the implications for art and society of science, technology and the mass media at the midpoint of the twentieth century. Topics discussed included: the machine aesthetic, action painting, car styling, consumer goods, fashion and communication theory. Images from American mass-circulation magazines, advertising, the cinema and science fiction were viewed and the term 'pop art' was used to refer to contemporary popular or mass culture. It was only later that Hamilton and Paolozzi began to make pop art from the raw material of popular culture. The deliberations of the IG were known to only a few at the time but they did reach a wider audience via various exhibitions members of the IG were involved in mounting at the ICA and the Whitechapel Gallery in the '50s, e.g. 'Parallel of art and life' (ICA, 1953) and 'This is Tomorrow' (Whitechapel, 1956). In later years some critics made the controversial claim that the IG were the 'fathers' of British pop art. During the period 1985–91 design historians re-examined the history of IG in great detail and exhibitions devoted to it were held in the United States and in Britain.

● See also ICA, Machine Aesthetic/Art, Pop Art, Styling, This is Tomorrow.

◉ L Alloway 'The development of British Pop' –in– *Pop art* by L Lippard & others (Thames & Hudson, 1966) 27–67.

◉ F Whitford 'Paolozzi and the Independent Group' –in– *Eduardo Paolozzi* (Tate Gallery, 1971) 44–8.

◉ R Banham *'Fathers of pop'* (film) (Arts Council, 1979).

A Massey & P Sparke 'The myth of the Independent Group' *Block* (10) 1985 48–56.

◉ A Massey 'The Independent Group' *Burlington Magazine* **129** (1009) April 1987 232–42.

◉ L Alloway & others *Modern dreams: the rise and fall and rise of pop* (Cambridge, Mass, MIT Press, 1988).

◉ D Robbins (ed) *The Independent Group: postwar Britain and the aesthetics of plenty* (Cambridge, Mass, MIT Press, 1990).

INDEPENDENT GROUP EDUARDO PAOLOZZI, 'I was a rich man's plaything' (1947). Collage (from 'Bunk'), 14" x 9". Tate Gallery Collection. Photo: ICA, 1990.

353 INDIGENISMO

An aspect of the arts in Mexico and South America dating from the 1920s and '30s. 'Indigenism' means praising and fostering native values (i.e. the Indian heritage as against foreign/colonial values), re-evaluating indigenous cultures and traditions, and also employing Indian themes in literature and the visual arts.

● See also Latin American Art.

◉ 'Indigenism and social realism' –in– *Art in Latin America* by D Ades & others (Hayward Gallery/South Bank Centre, 1989) 195–213.

354 INFORMATION

Title of a major exhibition held at the Museum of Modern Art, New York, in 1970 curated by Kynaston McShine. The show presented a report, international in scope, on the activities of younger artists and groups working with photographs, films, documents, concepts and language rather than with paint or clay. The choice of the word 'information' as the title reflected the consciousness of the artists of the age of information and mass-communication systems, and also the fact that documentation was itself the means by which the artists presented their ideas.

- See also Conceptual Art, Disinformation, Photoworks.
- K McShine (ed) *Information* (NY, MoMA, 1970).
- G Battcock 'Informative exhibition...' *Arts Magazine* **44** (8) Summer 1970 24–7.

355 INFORMATION FICTION PUBLICITÉ (IFP) A Paris-based art organization founded in 1983–4 by Jean-François Brun and Dominique Pasqualini. IFP does not produce traditional paintings or sculptures; rather it operates between art and philosophy, art and industrial design, fiction and reality, working in response to the contemporary context of the information society, mass-media images and corporate design. During the '80s IFP mounted fashion shows, sales of products and gallery installations consisting of lightboxes showing images of the sky, silent video monitors, re-presentations of billboard advertisements, etc.

- See also Corporate Design, Installation, Media Art.
- G Meyerink 'God, IBM and IFP' *Mediamatic* **3** (1) September 1988 6–8.
- J Sans *Des emblèmes comme attitudes* (Tourcoing, École Régional Supérieure d'Expressions Plastiques, 1988).

356 INFORMATION GRAPHICS A broad term encompassing the design of forms, timetables, diagrams, pictograms, maps, signs, graphics for electronic display systems and the presentation of statistics via print and television. In short, any graphic design concerned with 'conveying essential information to the user with the least distraction and ambiguity' (Wildbur). Information Graphics has been called the 'green' area of design because it presents information in a way which is not so dependent upon the persuasive rhetoric of commercial advertising. In Britain in 1979 a periodical entitled *Information Design Journal* was founded, with the aid of a grant from the Open University, Milton Keynes, to act as a forum for discussion. Designers and researchers associated with the journal have also organized a series of conferences.

- See also Computer Art, Diagrams, Green Design, Isotype, Pictorial Rhetoric, Visual Communication.
- B Purves *Information Graphics* (Thames & Hudson, 1987).
- P Wildbur *Information Graphics: a survey of typographic, diagrammatic and cartographic communication* (Trefoil, 1989).

357 INSTALLATION When paintings and sculptures are exhibited in galleries they can be arranged in a variety of configurations. The particular way in which they are finally disposed is commonly referred to by artists and critics as the 'Installation'. Arranging an exhibition can itself be regarded as a creative task engaged in by artists, dealers and curators. A number of contemporary artists have also conceived and designed thematic exhibitions, e.g. Richard Hamilton, Eduardo Paolozzi, Andy Warhol, and Group Material.

Furthermore, the nature of the display context has been an important factor in the appreciation and reception of modern art (see Brian O'Doherty's account of the 'white cube' – the ideal space of modernism– listed below). In the case of the minimal art exhibitions of the 1960s, the relation between the art objects and the gallery context became as important as the qualities of the objects themselves. Indeed much post-1945 art has sought to transcend the limits of discrete, portable objects: artists have created whole assemblages and mixed-media environments within galleries. As a result, the word 'Installation' has taken on a stronger meaning, i.e. a one-off exhibit fabricated in relation to the specific characteristics of a gallery space. Many contemporary artists have produced Installations. To cite just one example: in 1987 the British artist Richard Wilson half-filled Matt's Gallery in East London with black sump oil. It might seem that such a show could not become a commodity, but in fact this work was bought by the Saatchis. In the late 1980s some artists began to specialize in constructing Installations with the result that a specific genre –'Installation Art' – came into being. One such group working anonymously in Britain constructed critical, mixed-media installations in art centres and non-art spaces in order to challenge orthodox notions of art as discrete objects, the idea that art is only produced by exceptional individuals called 'artists', and in order to involve visitors in the completion of the work. In November 1990 a 'Museum of Installation' (MoI) was established in Great Sutton Street, London.

In the United States the DIA Art Foundation has funded many long-term Installations in cities and rural sites across the country. In Pittsburgh the 'Mattress Factory' (an old warehouse) was established in 1977 by the sculptor Barbara Luderowski specifically for Installations and performance pieces. Funding derives from various sources both public and private. Artists who have constructed Installations in Pittsburgh include Barbara Ess, James Turrell and Bill Woodrow.

- See also Art in Ruins, Assemblage Art, DIA Art Foundation, Environmental Art, Exhibit I & II, Group Material, Happenings, Minimal Art, Site-Specific Art, Video Art.
- G Celant 'Artspaces' *Studio International* **190** (977) September–October 1977 114–23.

INSTALLATION RICHARD WILSON, '20:50' (1987). Used sump oil, steel & wood. Photo: Edward Woodman/Matt's Gallery, London.

● I Wiegand 'Videospace: varieties of the video Installation' –in– *New artists' video: a critical anthology* G Battcock (ed) (NY, Dutton, 1978) 181–91.

● B O'Doherty *Inside the white cube: the ideology of the gallery space* (San Francisco, Lapis Press, 1986).

● C Arthus-Bertrand (curator) *European Installation Art: Felice Varini, Michel Verjux* (Australia, New South Wales, Artspace, 1988).

● E King 'Installation haven: Mattress Factory' *Sculpture* **8** (6) November–December 1989 36–7, + 59.

● *Anon* (Luton, 33 Arts Centre, 1989) 28-page booklet.

● 'Special Installation issue' *Sculpture* **9** (2) March–April 1990.

358 INTER-CHANGE One of the more durable manifestations of 1960s counter-culture or alternative society. A community arts association/charitable trust located in Kentish Town, London, established in 1968. Inter-Action (as it was first called) was directed by the American-born animateur Ed Berman and by the late '70s it had 60 full-time members. Its aim was to involve local people in arts activities in order to nurture a sense of community and to stimulate the creativity latent in everyone. Entertainments and spectacles were provided for children in the hope that adults would join in. Methods employed included: street theatre, a 'fun art' bus, games, and a media van (designed by Pentagram). Inter-Change also ran the Almost Free Theatre and produced films (via In-Films). Their community centre had video and photographic studios, a playground and an urban farm. Flexible buildings designed by Cedric Price were opened in 1977.

● See also Actions, Community Art & Media, Media Art, Street Art.

● P Murray (ed) 'Invisible London' (insert) *Time Out* (116) May 5–11 1972; also published in *Architectural Design* May 1972.

● J Wintle 'A media van' *New Society* April 12 1973.

● P Harrison 'Art and community' *New Society* **27** (590) January 24 1974 202–3.

● S Lyall 'Fun palace mark 2' *Building Design* April 22 1977

12–13.

● R Miller 'Change of art' *Sunday Times Magazine* April 24 1977 84–6.

● G Nicolson 'Inter-Action man' *Observer Magazine* June 24 1979 80–1.

359 INTER-MEDIA

(Also Mixed/ Multi-Media) Three terms art critics use more or less synonymously. They all reflect a significant trend in the art of the modern era and especially the period since 1955: the combination of different materials, artforms and media. Jasper Johns' 1950s neo-dada target paintings with their conjunctions of painting and sculptured objects can be cited as an example; also relevant are Robert Rauschenberg's combine paintings. Andy Warhol is a well-known example of an artist who worked in many media during his career – drawing, painting, photography, film, video, publishing – but who also combined media, e.g. his silkscreened paintings of the 1960s were a synthesis of photography, printing and painting. Mixtures of materials and media often occur when artists from different fields collaborate on theatrical productions, e.g. painters, musicians and dance companies. Such mixtures are also a common characteristic of actions, happenings and performances.

Dick Higgins, a participant in the Fluxus movement, popularized the term 'Inter-Media' which he defined gnomically as 'media between media'. Higgins was the proprietor of 'Something Else Press', a publishing concern which promoted all forms of Inter-Media art. An Inter-Media 'revolution' was said to have taken place whose prophet was the avant garde composer John Cage. Parallels were also drawn with the emergence of interdisciplinary sciences such as cybernetics.

During the '60s various festivals and exhibitions took place dedicated to Inter-Media: 'Inter-media '68' held in New York, and 'Inter-media '69' held in Heidelberg. In the same decade several groups were also formed: 'Art Inter-media', Vienna, founded by Otto Beckmann in 1965, 'Inter-media', Vancouver, founded by Joe Kyle in 1968, 'Inter-media Systems Corporation' established by the American collective known as USCO.

Some writers regarded the Inter/Mixed/Multi-Media trend as indicating the ultimate disintegration of the traditional artforms and announced 'the death of painting'. However, while there are always radical artists who seek to break down the barriers between media, there are always others who like to specialize in just one and who strive to isolate the essential characteristics of their chosen artform (see, for example, Fundamental Painting, Modernist Painting).

● See also Assemblage Art, Combine Paintings, Environmental Art, Expanded Cinema, Fluxus, Happenings, Media Art, Neo-Dada, USCO.

● *Inter-media '69* (Heidelberg, Édition Tangente, 1969).

● L Warshaw 'Inter-media workshop' *Arts in Society* (6) Fall–Winter 1969 448–51.

● D Palazzoli 'Des Intermédia aux extra média' *Opus International* **16** March 1970 18–33.

● U Kultermann *Leben und Kunst: zur Funktion der Intermedia* (Tubingen, Wasmuth, 1970).

● G Youngblood *Expanded cinema* (NY, Dutton, 1971) 345–98.

● S Kranz 'The forms of Inter-media' –in– *Science and technology in the arts* (NY, Van Nostrand Reinhold, 1974) 209–87.

● Experimental Art Foundation & CAYC *Theoretical analysis of the Inter-media artform* (NY, Guggenheim Museum, 1980).

360 INTERNATIONAL ARTISTS' ASSOCIATION (IAA)

An organization of professional artists founded in 1953 as a consequence of the internationalist spirit of the post-war era and the example of the pre-war, anti-fascist Artists' International Association. IAA is affiliated to and subsidized by UNESCO. Its aims are to serve as a forum for artists of all countries (there are 80 national committees), to improve the economic, social and moral conditions of artists and to hold regular assemblies and congresses.

● See also Artists' International, Artists' Unions, National Artists Association.

● R Coward & S Swale 'Imperfect present: IAA' *AND Journal of Art & Art Education* (11/12) 1987 18–21.

361 INTERNATIONAL TYPOGRAPHIC STYLE

(Also Swiss Design) During the 1950s Swiss graphic designers such as Richard Lohse, Josef Müller-Brockmann, Hans Neuburg and Carlo Vivarelli became noted for a distinctive kind of layout and typography which came to be called the 'International Typographic Style'. According to Philip Meggs, the style was characterized by 'a visual unity of design achieved by asymmetrical organization of the elements of the design on a mathematically drawn grid...the use of sans-serif type (particularly Helvetica, 1957–) ...typography set in a flush-left and ragged-right margin configuration...objective photography...'. Clarity, order and social utility were the watchwords of the designers who were influenced by the Bauhaus, the de Stijl movement, the new typography of the 1920s and '30s, and by the art and design of Max Bill, Max Huber, Anton Stankowski, Emil Ruder and Armin Hofmann.

● See also Gridniks.

● P Meggs *A history of graphic design* (NY, Van Nostrand Reinhold, 1983) 379–97.

362 INUIT ART

(Also Arctic Art, Eskimo Art/Sculpture) 'Inuit' is the Eskimo word for the Eskimo people. The Eskimos have no word for art therefore 'Inuit Art' is a concept of the white culture of North America. The term was popularized via books and exhibitions organized by the Canadian Eskimo Arts Council. Although some appliqué panels, basketwork and jewellery were known previously, contemporary Inuit Art mainly consists of carvings made from soapstone, whale bone, walrus ivory, antlers and driftwood, and of prints made from carved stone panels. Typically the carvings depict hunters, animals, mothers and children; they are usually small in size since they are designed to be handled. Carving used to be a traditional skill of the Eskimos but it had fallen into disuse until revived in the late 1940s as a means of providing employment and income. Printmaking was introduced to them in 1958. Edmund Carpenter, the anthropologist, has suggested that James Houston, the man primarily responsible for promoting Inuit Art, has not preserved an indigenous art but rather created a new art which relates more to the tourist industry than to the past of the Eskimo. Even so, many Eskimo carvings exemplify high technical skill and artistic imagination. In London the Narwhal Gallery has promoted Inuit Art for a number of years.

● See also Ethnic Art, Popular Art.

● J Meldgaard *Eskimo Sculpture* (Methuen, 1960).

● G Swinton *Eskimo Sculpture* (Toronto, McCelland & Stewart, 1965).

● Canadian Eskimo Arts Council *Sculpture/Inuit–Eskimo* (Toronto, University of Toronto Press, 1971).

● C Burland *Eskimo Art* (Hamlyn, 1973).

● E Roch (ed) *Arts of the Eskimo: prints* (Toronto, Oxford University Press, 1975).

● E Carpenter *Oh, what a blow that phantom gave me!* (Paladin, 1976).

● Gerhard Hoffman (ed) *In the shadow of the sun: contemporary Canadian Indian and Inuit Art* (Canadian Museum of Civilization, 1989).

● A Houston *Inuit Art: an anthology* (Watson & Dwyer, 1990).

363 IONIST ART GROUP (IAG)

An informal, international, multi-disciplinary organization based in Wiltshire, England, founded in 1988, concerned with 'Ionism', 'Ionist Art' and 'the science–art fusion'. The terms 'Ionism / Ionist Art' were coined by the British artist–scientist Gerald Shepherd in the mid 1970s. He derived them from ionic bonding or electrovalency (the creation of a compound from mutually attracting elements such as oppositely charged atoms). Ionist Art encompassed paintings, drawings and graphics generated according to the investigative and experimental processes of science. Members of the IAG define science very broadly and produce a wide range of artworks in different materials, media and styles. (The work includes organic, process and sequential art.) Some members employ the methods of science while others treat science as subject matter. The group encourages collaborations between artists, scientists and technologists, holds public discussions, organizes thematic exhibitions – such as the 'Science–Art Fusion' show held at Bournemouth & Poole College of Art in 1990 – and publishes a newsletter *Ion Exchange* and a photocopied quarterly 'artletter' entitled *Zwitterion*.

● See also Collaborations, Process Art, Sciart.

364 IRASCIBLES

A name given to 18 American artists who sent a letter of protest to the Metropolitan Museum, New York, and who refused to participate in national art competitions because they claimed award juries were so hostile to advanced modern art. The Irascibles included the leading figures in the abstract expressionist movement. A photograph by Nina Leen depicting 15 of them appeared in *Life* magazine (January 15 1951).

In 1985 the photographer Timothy Greenfield-Sanders undertook a project called 'The New Irascibles', i.e. a series of photographs recreating the compositional format of Leen's famous image. The New Irascibles consisted of '80s American artists, critics, dealers and collectors.

● See also Abstract Expressionism.

● I Sandler *Abstract expressionism: the triumph of American painting* (Pall Mall Press, 1970) frontispiece, +213.

● R Pincus-Witten 'The New Irascibles' –in– *Postminimalism into maximalism: American art 1966–86* (Ann Arbor, Michigan, UMI Research Press, 1987) 399–418, +423.

365 ISOTYPE

Acronym standing for 'International System Of TYpographic Picture Education'. Otto Neurath, the creator of Isotype, was a Viennese philosopher of the logical positivist school who developed from the 1920s onwards a pictorial system of signs for communicating factual/statistical social and economic information. The aim was to achieve a universal or international system of communication; the assumption was that visual percep-

ISOTYPE Victor Burgin, 'Office at night' (1985-86). Three panels with photos, 183cm x 305cm. Photo: Burgin. The model is Francette Pacteau and the painting quoted in the background is by Edward Hopper.

tion was more fundamental to humanity than language. Typically, the signs took the form of schematic silhouettes of such things as human figures, telephones and cars. Statistics were presented in terms of rows of pictorial signs instead of numbers. An Isotype Institute was established in London in 1942 and Neurath was employed by the Ministry of Information on the design of films, leaflets, posters, charts and books. After Neurath's death in 1945, the Institute was run by his widow Marie until 1972. The non-profit-making organization applied the ideas of pictorial language to publications intended for children and for developing nations. Isotype was extremely influential in terms of the graphic design of the post-1945 era: it inspired such designers as Rudolf Modley, Henry Dreyfuss and Nigel Holmes. An archive – the Otto and Marie Neurath Collection – is preserved by the University of Reading, England.

During the mid '80s the British artist Victor Burgin produced a series of works combining Isotype signs, photographs and colour panels.

● See also Diagrams, Information Graphics.

○ O Neurath *Empiricism and sociology* (Dordrecht, Reidel, 1973).

○ *Graphic communication through Isotype* (Reading, Department of Typography & Graphic Design/University of Reading, 1975, rep 1981).

○ M Twyman 'The significance of Isotype' *Icographic* (10) 1976 2–10.

○ O Neurath *International picture language* (Reading, University of Reading, 1980), facsimile reprint of 1936 edition.

○ R Kinross 'On the influence of Isotype' *Information Design Journal* **2** (2) 1981 122–30.

○ E Lupton 'Reading Isotype' *Design Issues* **3** (2) Fall 1986 47–58.

366 ITALIAN CRAZE

(Also Espresso Style, Italian Line/ Style) Reconstruction in Italy after the Second World War was rapid, so that by the '50s Italian products were being exported again. In Britain during the period 1953 to '60 a mania developed for Italian design – Olivetti typewriters, Espresso coffee-making machines, Piaggio 'Vespa' scooters, Iso's 'Isetta' bubble cars, Gio Ponti furniture, Nebiolo typefaces, Italian clothes and films – especially among young, newly affluent teenagers. In 1956 Cecil

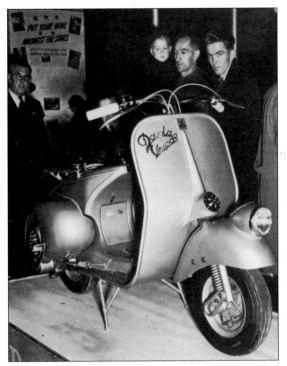

ITALIAN CRAZE CORADINO D'ASCANIO (designer), Vespa Motor Scooter, 1946, Industrie Aeronautica e Mecanica Renato Piaggio, Biagno, Italy.

Gee introduced Italian male fashions into Britain: narrow trousers, winkle-picker shoes, striped shirts and ties, short 'bum-freezer' jackets.

Design and style have been much more important in Italy than in many other countries. Indeed, design in modern Italian culture has enjoyed a high status and been subject to much intellectual debate. Manufacturing companies such as Olivetti have been enlightened patrons of art and design. In the post-1945 era Italian design benefited from interactions with avant garde art and from the high-quality craft skills provided by the artisan tradition of small workshops. Production runs tended to be small as goods were designed for a discriminating middle-class public; only a few firms such as Fiat, Pirelli and Olivetti were big enough to engage in the industrial production of consumer goods for the mass market.

Since the '50s Italian design has continued to be successful abroad both in terms of sales of products and in terms of cultural influence – witness the numerous books and exhibitions about it, and the media attention paid to such groups as Alchimia, Archizoom, Memphis, Sottsass Associates and Superstudio. These groups have been notable for their radical, experimental approach to designing. Design in Italy has undergone a number of

stylistic and ideological shifts since 1945 (documented in Penny Sparke's history listed below).

Leading post-1945 Italian designers have included: Gae Aulenti, Mario Bellini, Achille and Pier Castiglioni, Joe Colombo, Piero Fornasetti, Vico Magistretti, Alessandro Mendini, Bruno Munari, Marcello Nizzoli, Battista Pininfarina, Gaetano Pesce, Gio Ponti, Ettore Sottsass, and Marco Zanuso. Many of these designers were trained in architecture schools because Italy lacked the design colleges typical of Britain. They were particularly noted for their designs for lighting, furniture, interiors, office equipment, glassware, architecture (Gio Ponti, Vittorio Gregotti, Pier Luigi Nervi, Ernesto Rogers, Aldo Rossi, Renzo Piano), shoes (Salvatore Ferragamo), fashion (Giorgio Armani, Mariuccia Mandelli, Rosita Missoni, Gian-Franco Ferre, Elio Fiorruci, Gianni Versace), cars and scooters. Glossy magazines such as *Domus, Casabella, Casa Vogue* and *Abitare* promoted Italian design the world over. Also vital were the exhibitions mounted in Milan (a city called in 1981 'the design capital of the world'): the Triennale, furniture fairs and fashion shows.

● See also Olivetti, Programmed Art, Radical Design, Triennale.

● M Laski 'Espresso' & S Gardiner 'Coffee bars' *Architectural Review* **118** (705) September 1955 165–73.

● *Modern Italian design* (Manchester, City Art Gallery, 1956).

V Gregotti *New directions in Italian architecture* (NY, Braziller, 1968).

● E Ambasz (ed) *Italy: the new domestic landscape* (NY, MoMA, 1972).

● P Fossatti *Il disegno in Italia 1945–72* (Turin, Einaud, 1973).

● G Taborelli & V Fagone (eds) *Disegno Italiano* (Milan, Silvana, 1979).

● P Sartago (ed) *Italian re-evolution: design in Italian society in the eighties* (La Jolla, California, La Jolla Museum of Contemporary Art, 1982).

● A Branzi & M de Lucchi *Il disegno Italiano degli anni '50* (Milan, IGIS, 1983).

● A Branzi *The hot house: Italian new wave design* (Thames & Hudson, 1985).

● O Calabrese *L'Italie aujourd'hui: aspects de la création Italienne de 1970 à 1985* (Nice, Centre d'Art Contemporain, 1985).

● C Sabiono & A Tondini *Italian Style* (Thames & Hudson, 1985).

● *Italian fashion* 2 vols (Milan, Electa, 1987).

● P Sparke *Italian design: 1870 to the present* (Thames & Hudson, 1988).

367 | **JAPANESE DESIGN/STYLE**

Following Japan's traumatic military defeat in 1945, the nation turned its energies to reconstruction and success in the economic sphere. A few decades later, Japan had become one of the world's leading economic powers and its major manufacturing companies – Sony, Sharp, Hitachi, Nissan, Yamaha, Honda, Suzuki, Toyota, Daihatsu, Minolta, Sanyo, Toshiba, Canon, Olympus, Nikon, National Panasonic, etc. – had become world famous. A key ingredient in the appeal of Japanese products to both native and foreign buyers was their elegant design. Japanese consumer goods – cameras, motorcycles, small cars, transistor radios ('trannies'), TV sets, video and tape recorders, Hi-fi equipment, pocket calculators – became bywords for fine quality, innovative ideas, technical sophistication, refined visual style, reliability, low cost, convenience...and so were successfully exported around the globe. To single out just one product: in the 1980s the Sony Walkman (a lightweight portable stereo tape-cassette player with headphones)

became a cult object amongst the young around the world.

Traditional Japanese art, architecture, furniture, crafts, prints and kimonos had, of course, been admired in the West for over a century (as the European nineteenth-century vogue 'Japonisme' indicated), but what was significant about post-1945 Japanese architecture and industrial design was the way they managed to incorporate certain national cultural and aesthetic traditions, while assimilating Western influences (including modernist design theory), and exploiting new technology, new methods of manufacture/management and new markets. Penny Sparke, a design historian, cites 'miniaturization and portability, multi-functionality, attention to minute detail rather than to overall form, and the decorative use of functional components' as signs of the continuity of historical aesthetic and cultural values. She identifies two broad strands in Japanese art and design: (1) a highly decorative strand favouring complexity and ornamental detail; (2) a minimalist strand favouring extreme simplicity, natural materials and use of modules. The latter

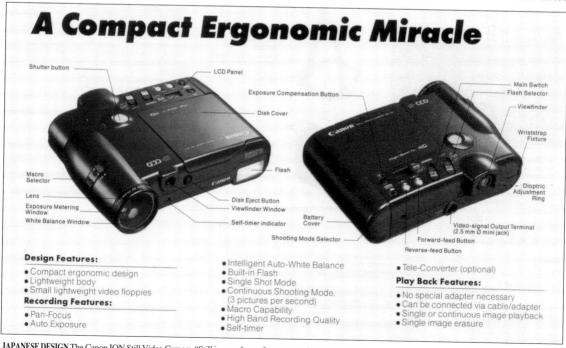

A Compact Ergonomic Miracle

Shutter button
LCD Panel
Exposure Compensation Button
Disk Cover
Main Switch
Flash Selector
Viewfinder
Wriststrap Fixture
Macro Selector
Flash
Lens
Disk Eject Button
Viewfinder Window
Exposure Metering Window
White Balance Window
Self-timer indicator
Battery Cover
Shooting Mode Selector
Dioptric Adjustment Ring
Video-signal Output Terminal (2.5 mm Ø mini jack)
Forward-feed Button
Reverse-feed Button

Design Features:
- Compact ergonomic design
- Lightweight body
- Small lightweight video floppies

Recording Features:
- Pan-Focus
- Auto Exposure

- Intelligent Auto-White Balance
- Built-in Flash
- Single Shot Mode
- Continuous Shooting Mode. (3 pictures per second)
- Macro Capability
- High Band Recording Quality
- Self-timer

- Tele-Converter (optional)

Play Back Features:
- No special adapter necessary
- Can be connected via cable/adapter
- Single or continuous image playback
- Single image erasure

JAPANESE DESIGN The Canon ION Still Video Camera "Still images for perfect presentation on TV". 1991.

strand, she argues, converged with the 'less equals more' aesthetic of the modern movement and resulted in minimalist design. There were also more popular, vulgar and violent forms of expression typified by Japanese comics called 'Manga'.

Design in Japan was primarily a team/company effort and was often undertaken by engineering and production departments. Even so, the names of certain individual architects and designers have become known internationally, e.g. Kenji Ekuan, Sori Yanagi (industrial designers), Kisho Kurokawa, Kenzo Tange, Arata Isozaki, Tadao Ando (architects), Hanae Mori, Issey Miyake, Yohji Yamamoto, Kenzo Takada (fashion designers).

The term 'Japanese Design/Style' is clearly a nationalistic one but since no country is completely self-contained, modern Japan is a mix of national and international influences, hence its culture has been characterized as 'hybrid'. During the 1980s Japanese architects and designers have contributed to the international tendency known as 'post-modernism'.

● See also Cult Objects, Hybrid Culture, Metabolist Group, Minimalist Design/Style, Post-Modernism.

◉ R Boyd *New directions in Japanese architecture* (Studio Vista, 1968).

◉ *Japan style* (Victoria & Albert Museum, 1980).

◉ Boilerhouse Project *Sony design* (Victoria & Albert Museum/Boilerhouse Project, 1982).

◉ I Buruma *A Japanese mirror: heroes and villains of Japanese culture* (Jonathan Cape, 1984).

◉ L Koren *New fashion Japan* (NY, Kodansha International, 1984).

◉ B Bognar *Contemporary Japanese architecture: its development and challenge* (NY, Van Nostrand Reinhold, 1985).

◉ H Suzuki & R Banham *Contemporary architecture of Japan 1958–84* (NY, Rizzoli, 1985).

◉ 'Japan into the future' *The Face* (83) March 1987 44–67.

◉ P Sparke *Japanese Design* (Michael Joseph, 1987).

◉ S Evans *Contemporary Japanese design* (Collins & Brown, 1991).

◉ R Thorton *Japanese graphic design* (Laurence King, 1991).

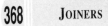

368   JOINERS

A term invented by the British artist David Hockney to describe those of his works produced in the 1980s which are composed of a series of small photographs joined together. The photographs are taken from different viewpoints and then arranged so that they link up or overlap with the result that the finished collage resembles a photographic version of cubism. Due to his fame, Hockney has come to be regarded as the inventor of this form of art but in fact artists such as Jan Dibbets and John Stezaker were making 'Joiners' long before

JOINERS JOHN STEZAKER 'Here and Now' (1977). Photo: courtesy of the artist.

Hockney.

● See also Photo-Montage, Photo-Works.

◉ D Hockney & Paul Joyce *Hockney on photography: conversations with Paul Joyce* (Jonathan Cape, 1988).

369   JUNGIAN AESTHETICS

Whereas Freudian aesthetics derives from the psychoanalytic work of Sigmund Freud, Jungian Aesthetics derives from the work of the Swiss psychologist and psychiatrist Carl Gustav Jung (1875–1961), in particular his theory of the 'collective unconscious' of humankind. Jungian theories of art, therefore, tend to stress the artist's use – consciously or unconsciously – of archetypes. Artists are assumed to be men urged into creativity (assumed to be feminine) by various types of involvement with the Mother archetype. According to Erich Neumann, creative man 'holds fast to the archetypal world and to his original bisexuality and wholeness...'. This type of analysis has been applied to the sculpture of Henry Moore. The latter wished to avoid any conscious knowledge of Jungian theory but American artists such as John Graham, Mark Rothko and Adolph Gottlieb were keen to learn all they could. For some years Jackson Pollock underwent analysis by a Jungian and produced drawings for his psychotherapist which were later published. The American examples demonstrate that not all art is a direct reflection of the unconscious; in many instances artists reflect upon contents and workings of the unconscious as revealed by the psychologists and psychoanalysts of their time.

● See also Art Therapy, Freudian Aesthetics.

◉ E Neumann *The archetypal world of Henry Moore* (Routledge & Kegan Paul, 1959).

● — *Art and the creative unconscious* (Routledge & Kegan Paul, 1959).

● M Philipson *Outline of a Jungian Aesthetic* (Evanston, Illinois, North Western University Press, 1963).

● A Jaffé 'Symbolism in the visual arts' – in – *Man and his symbols* C Jung (ed) (Aldus Books, 1964) 230–71.

● C Wysuph *Jackson Pollock: psychoanalytic drawings* (NY, Horizon Press, 1970).

● J Wolfe 'Jungian aspects of Jackson Pollock's imagery' *Artforum* **11** (3) November 1972 65–73.

● B Carter 'Jackson Pollock's drawings under analysis' *Art News* **76** (2) February 1977 58–60.

● W Rubin 'Pollock as Jungian illustrator' *Art in America* **67** (8) November 1979 72–91.

● C Jung *Word and image* A Jaffé (ed) (Princeton University Press, 1979).

● D Gordon & others 'Department of Jungian amplification...' *Art in America* **68** (8) October 1980 43–67.

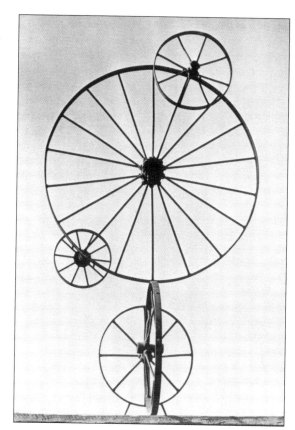

JUNK SCULPTURE Ettore Colla, 'Continuity' (1951). Iron, 230 cm high. Photo: Boccardi, Rome.

370 JUNK CULTURE/ SCULPTURE (Also Culture de Débris, Scrap Art) Two closely related terms dating from the 1950s. The British art critic Lawrence Alloway coined the term 'Junk Culture' to describe mixed-media work that rescued the waste products of city life, art that incorporated objects that accumulate in drawers and attics – discarded but still retaining the history of their human use. An essay with this title appeared in the catalogue for the 'New forms, new media' show held in New York in October 1960.

Junk Sculpture was a form of three-dimensional collage or assemblage popular in Europe and the United States during the 1950s. Metal objects, automobile parts and other debris taken from rubbish dumps were used as a basis for sculptures by such artists as Lee Bontecou, César, John Chamberlain, Ettore Colla, Eduardo Paolozzi and Richard Stankiewicz. Some artists presented objects as found, others transformed them by crushing them or by welding them together to make abstract or figurative sculptures. The method of collaging junk together marked a reaction against the carving and modelling traditions of sculpture. It derived from cubist collage and the work of Kurt Schwitters, the German dadaist who was such a great exponent of the artistic use of street debris.

● See also Assemblage Art, Combine Paintings, Creative Salvage, Mutoid Waste Co, New British Sculpture, Nouveau Réalisme.

● L Alloway 'Junk Culture' *New forms, new media 1* (NY, Martha Jackson Gallery, 1960).

● — 'Junk Culture' *Architectural Design* **31** (3) March 1961 122–3.

371 KELPRA STUDIOS A London screen printmaking studio established by the master printer Christopher Prater in 1958 which became well known during the 1960s for its posters for the Arts Council, the ICA and the Robert Fraser Gallery, and for its artists' prints by such luminaries as Richard Hamilton, Eduardo Paolozzi, R B Kitaj, Victor Pasmore, Bridget Riley and Joe Tilson. (The medium of screen-printing proved to be especially suited to the styles of op and pop in the '60s.) The prints were sold via such outlets as the Marlborough Fine Art, Editions Alecto and the Petersburg Press.

● See also Atelier 17, Collaborations, Curwen Studios, Silk-Screenprinting, Tamarind Lithography Workshop, Tyler Graphics.

● R Alley & J Tilson *Kelpra prints* (Arts Council of Great Britain/Hayward Gallery, 1970).

● P Gilmour & others *Kelpra Studio* (Tate Gallery, 1980).

372 KINETIC ARCHITECTURE In a book published in 1971 W. Zuk and R. Clark argued that the static, fixed forms of traditional architecture were incapable of responding to the rapidly changing needs of a society in a state of flux and that therefore a new type of architecture – 'Kinetic' – was required. Kinetic Architecture was dynamic, adaptable and responsive to the changing demands of its users; it also encompassed several subcategories, i.e. deformable/ disposable/ incremental/ reversible architecture. Zuk and Clark cited works and projects by R. Buckminster Fuller, Pier Luigi Nervi, the Metabolists, Archigram and others to demonstrate that examples of Kinetic Architecture already existed. A similar concept – 'mobile architecture' – was proposed in the late 1950s by Yona Friedman and the group GEAM.

● See also Archigram, GEAM, Metabolist Group, Mobile Architecture, Participatory Design.

● W Zuk & R Clark *Kinetic Architecture* (NY, Van Nostrand Reinhold, 1971).

373 KINETIC ART (Also Kineticism, the Movement Movement) The word 'kinetic' derives from the Greek for 'moving'. In the nineteenth century it was applied to movement phenomena in physics and chemistry. In the twentieth century it was used sporadically in the context of the plastic arts but Kinetic Art as a distinct movement did not really emerge until the 1950s; it then reached a climax in the '60s. This kind of art has been called 'four-dimensional' because it adds the dimension of time to sculpture.

Naum Gabo, the Russian constructivist, created the first Kinetic work in 1920 when he used a motor to

KINETIC ART: DAVID MEDALLA & PAUL DALY, 'Cloud Canyons no 12 Bubble Machine' (1989). Acrylic, galvanised steel, pvc, wood, motors, water and detergent. 460cm x 305cm diam. Installation in the Hayward Gallery. Photo: Martin Meyer & courtesy of Andrew Dempsey of the South Bank Centre.

vibrate a vertical steel rod. Shortly afterwards Marcel Duchamp, the French dadaist, invented some rotating reliefs and demi-spheres. However, before 1945 Alexander Calder's 'mobiles' were perhaps the best-known and most popular form of Kinetic Art. According to Frank Popper, various kinds of movement can be identified within Kineticism: (1) actual movement – mobiles, moving lights, machines; (2) virtual movement – a response in the viewer's eyes to static visual stimuli; (3) movement of the viewer in front of the work or manipulations of its parts by the spectator. Some theorists prefer to categorize virtual movement as 'op' or 'optical' art rather than Kinetic Art; even so, the two are obviously closely related and they have often been discussed together.

Kinetic Art generally required technical proficiency (Kinetic works owned by museums are all too frequently out of order) and therefore adherents of the movement sought a union of art, science and technology. They had a propensity to form groups (e.g. GRAV, Gruppo N, Gruppo T, Zero) and to pursue 'visual research'. Many Kinetic artists seemed to believe that static art was inherently inferior to art that moved; its critics, however, referred to it disparagingly as 'turntable art'. Kinetic Art was an international movement, but one especially favoured in Europe and South America in the 1960s. The major artists associated with it were: Yaacov Agam, Pol Bury, Frank Malina, Nicolas Schöffer, Jesus Raphael Soto, Takis, Jean Tinguely, Victor Vasarely and Yvaral. Tim Lewis is a British Kineticist whose work was much praised in 1989. A cynic might argue that the experiments of modern Kinetic artists found their social fulfilment in the light shows of the pop music discos of the 1970s and '80s.

● See also Cinétisations, Electronic Art, GRAV, Gruppo N, Gruppo T, Light Art, Nouvelle Tendance, Op Art, Programmed Art, Spatio-Dynamism, Technological Art, Zero.

● G Kepes (ed) *The nature and art of motion* (Studio Vista, 1965).

● *Kinetic and optic art today* (Buffalo, Albright Knox Gallery, 1965).

● S Bann & others *Four essays on Kinetic Art* (Motion Books, 1966).

● (Special issue on Kinetics) *Studio International* **173** (886) February 1967.

● M Compton *Optical and Kinetic Art* (Tate Gallery, 1967).

● G Brett *Kinetic Art: the language of movement* (Studio Vista, 1968).

● F Popper *Origins and development of Kinetic Art* (Studio Vista, 1968).

● W Sharp *Kineticism* (NY, Kineticism Press, 1968).

● (Six articles on Kinetics) *Studio International* **180** (926) October 1970.

● *Kinetics* (Hayward Gallery/Arts Council, 1970).

● F Malina (ed) *Kinetic Art: theory and practice, selections from the journal Leonardo* (NY, Dover, 1974).

● J Jenkins & D Quick *Motion, motion: Kinetic Art* (Salt Lake City, Utah, Gibbs Smith, 1989).

374 KITCHEN SINK SCHOOL A label applied by the British art critic David Sylvester in an article published in *Encounter* in 1954 to the artists John Bratby, Derrick Greaves, Jack Smith and Edward Middleditch, ex-students of the Royal College of Art, who normally exhibited at the Beaux Arts Gallery, London (hence they were also called the 'Beaux Arts Quartet'). These painters often depicted, in dark colours, social realist-type scenes of domestic life (interiors which included the kitchen sink). In the case of Bratby, his pictures featured tables loaded with consumer products and consequently his subject matter – if not his mode of representation – anticipated pop art. Although Sylvester provided the name, the critic who supported these artists the most was the independent Marxist John Berger. The vogue for a Kitchen Sink type of realism was not restricted to the fine arts: it was also manifested in certain novels, plays and films of the period.

In 1984 an exhibition organized by the Graves Art Gallery in Sheffield of '50s realism reopened old controversies concerning the nature and function of social realist art and prompted an acrimonious debate between

KITCHEN SINK PETER COKER (r) with one of his 'Butcher's Shop' series outside Zwemmers Gallery, January 1956. Photo courtesy of Philip Wilson Publishers.

Julian Spalding and Juliet Steyn about the issue of historical truth.

● See also Pop Art.

J Berger *Looking forward* (Whitechapel Art Gallery, 1952).
'The Beaux Arts Gallery and some young British artists' *Studio* **154** (775) October 1957 110–13.

D Cherry & J Steyn 'The moment of realism: 1952–6' *Artscribe* (35) June 1982 44–9.

J Steyn 'Realism versus realism in the '50s' *Art Monthly* (78) July–August 1984 6–8.

J Spalding *The forgotten fifties* (Sheffield, Graves Art Gallery, 1984).

F Spalding (intro) *The Kitchen Sink painters* (Mayor Gallery/Julian Hartnoll, 1991).

POP ART BEER CAN LAMP

HEAVENLY BODIES FOR YOUR WALL OR TABLE

Musical COFFIN CIGARETTE BOX

that golden touch! Mushroom Salt and Peppers

KITSCH Images from small ads in American magazines (1960s).

375 KITSCH

All intellectuals recognize Kitsch when they encounter it but defining and explaining it is much more problematical. Most writers on Kitsch believe the word derives from the German 'verkitschen' – 'to make cheap'; hence Kitsch is artistic rubbish, a low art that apes the effects of past fine art styles and in the process vulgarizes them. Gilbert Highet, however, has suggested that the word may derive from the Russian 'Kitchit'sya' meaning 'to be haughty and puffed up'. In the United States an alternative term is 'schlock art' (from the Yiddish meaning 'cheap merchandise').

Harold Rosenberg described Kitsch as the daily art of our times – all those cheap, sentimental, cute artefacts found everywhere in Western industrialized societies – a form of art that followed established rules when genuine modern artists put into question all rules in art. Clement Greenberg, in a famous essay contrasting avant garde art and Kitsch, remarked that if the former represented the forefront of art, then the latter represented the rearguard. Kitsch, then, is generally viewed as the antithesis of avant garde art and plain, functional modern design. (Most Kitsch is overloaded with colours and ornament.)

Examples of Kitsch include: the academic paintings favoured by the Nazis; many of the portraits of the British Royal Family; Indian musical films; most 'fantasy art'; Elvis Presley's stage clothes and his home 'Graceland'; telephones in the shape of Mickey Mouse; flights of plaster ducks; cheap replicas of famous artworks executed in inappropriate materials; the millions of products (most of them unnecessary for survival) associated with the gadget, gift, souvenir and tourist industries: the garden gnome, Disneyland, most birthday and Christmas cards, etc., etc. Kitsch manifests itself in every sphere: film, television, photography, sculpture, painting, interior decor, fashion, advertising, music, pornography (hence 'porno-kitsch')....

Most critics regard Kitsch as an inevitable consequence of the industrial revolution because it gave rise to a mass-produced art catering for millions who were philistine in their tastes because they lacked formal education or who had lost touch with traditional folk cultures. Mass production cannot be blamed entirely for Kitsch because fine-quality goods can be mass produced, but it has certainly magnified the problem of bad taste. Abraham Moles, a Kitsch analyst, claims that it satisfies bourgeois values of security, self-esteem, ownership, geniality and the need for daily rituals. Kitsch is normally equated with middle-class taste during its upwardly mobile phase, i.e. when it sought to imitate the opulence of the aristocracy. Now analysts would probably say that Kitsch is enjoyed by huge numbers in the lower middle and working classes.

Most critics discuss Kitsch in a tone of moral disapproval: it has been called the cultural revenge of the lower classes; however, it does have its appreciators amongst intellectuals, i.e. the camp taste that delights in the outrageously awful. Indeed, many artists and designers have been attracted to Kitsch as a contrast to the over-refined quality of much fine art, and as the last source of shock-value. These artists have included Mathius Klarwein, Yves Klein, Jeff Koons, Andrew Logan, Claes Oldenburg (his Kitsch-type rooms), Andy Warhol, Robert Warrens; also the Italian design groups Archizoom, Memphis and Superstudio, plus the American architect Morris Lapidus (Kitsch-like hotels). There are also fine artists whom some critics would regard as producers of Kitsch: Anthony Brandt, Giorgio de Chirico (late work), Leonor Fini, Salvador Dali (late work) and Vladimir Tretchikoff (dubbed 'King of Kitsch', creator of the best-known example of Kitsch: the green Chinese girl). Virtually all post-modernist art, architecture and design exhibits Kitsch-like qualities, so a sharp line between Kitsch and contemporary art/design can no longer be drawn.

● See also 'Bad' Painting, Biba, Camp, Disneyana, Fantastic Art, Nazi Art, Popular Art, Totalitarian Art.

◉ C Greenberg 'Avant garde and Kitsch' (1939) – in – *Art & culture* (Thames & Hudson, 1973) 3–21.

◉ G Dorfles (ed) *Kitsch: an anthology of bad taste* (Studio Vista, 1969).

◉ *Kitsch: the grotesque around us* (Wichita Art Museum, 1970).

◉ L Giesz *Phänomenologie des Kitsches* (Munich, Fink, 2nd ed 1971).

◉ A Moles *Le Kitsch: l'art du bonheur* (Paris, Mame, 1971).

◉ J Sternberg *Les chefs d'oeuvre du Kitsch* (Paris, Éditions Planète, 1971/London, Academy, 1972).

◉ R Steinberg (ed) *Nazi-Kitsch* (Darmstadt, Melzer Verlag, 1975).

◉ 'Kitsch issue' *Artlook* (100) April–May 1976.

◉ C Brown *Star-spangled Kitsch* (George Prior, 1976).

◉ M Calinescu *Faces of modernity: avant garde, decadence, Kitsch* (Indiana University Press, 1977).

◉ *Kitsch: an exhibition of popular art* (St Paul, Minnesota, Art Gallery College of St Catherine, 1979).

◉ R Saisselin *Bricabracomania: the bourgeois & the bibelot* (Thames & Hudson, 1985).

◉ V Romano 'Power, cult and Kitsch' *Media, Culture & Society* **8** 1986 211–21.

◉ T Kulka 'Kitsch' *British Journal of Aesthetics* **28** Winter 1988 18–27.

◉ P Ward *Kitsch in sync: a consumer's guide to bad taste* (Plexus, 1991).

376 KOMAR & MELAMID (K&M)

Vitaly Komar and Aleksander Melamid are two Russian-born artists who work collaboratively and who achieved artworld recognition in the West in the 1980s. Both trained as artists in the USSR during the '60s and took part in 'unofficial' art exhibitions in the early '70s. They then emigrated, first to Israel, then to the USA. Their work proved popular in New York when it was shown by the Ronald Feldman Gallery because it was critical of Soviet history and because it was post-modernist in its approach. And magazines like *Newsweek* welcomed them as 'dissidents'. K & M made use of historical subjects and images. They deployed a variety of pictorial styles and media – often within the same work – in order to parody and lampoon official icons of political power in both East and West, e.g. a portrait of US President Ronald Reagan as a centaur. Favourite targets for satire were socialist realist portraits of Stalin and images of the Yalta conference. The label 'sots art' – from the first syllable of the Russian for socialist realism – has been used to describe their work (e.g. it was the title of a show held at the Semaphore Gallery in New York in 1984), essentially meaning a Soviet counterpart to pop art.

Although praised by some writers for their critiques of ideology and representation, their ability to combine avant garde with kitsch via neo-academic means K & M's work has been judged harshly by others. David Brett, for instance, declared that their colours were muddy, their indecency was mean-spirited and their reputation a sham. He also considered their work suffered from exactly the same faults as that which it parodied.

● See also Collaborations, Unofficial Soviet Art.

◉ Z Zinik 'Sots art' *Syntaxis* (3) 1979.

◉ G Indiana 'Komar & Melamid confidential' *Art in America* **73** (6) June 1985 94–101.

◉ P Hill 'Komar & Melamid interviewed' *Artscribe* (54) September–October 1985 36–9.

◉ B Taylor 'Komar & Melamid' *Art Monthly* (91) November 1985 5–6.

KOMAR & MELAMID 'The origin of Socialist Realism' (1982-83). Oil on canvas 72" x 53". Photo: the artists.

● P Wollen *Komar & Melamid* (Edinburgh, Fruitmarket Gallery, 1985).

● D Brett 'Komar & Melamid' *Circa* (27) March–April 1986 38–40.

● C Ratcliff *Komar & Melamid* (NY, Abbeville, 1989).

377   KOS

(Kids of Survival) In 1980 Tim Rollins, an American artist and teacher with a strong desire to work in a community, encouraged a number of his teenage students from the poor, Hispanic populations of South Bronx, New York, to collaborate in making artworks after school. (Rollins had been associated with the conceptual art movement and he was also a member of another collaborative project called 'Group Material'.) This team was subsequently known as 'Tim Rollins and the Kids of Survival' or simply 'K. O. S.'. Somewhat surprisingly KOS became fashionable in the artworld. They set up a studio and a non-profit-making company, travelled extensively and mounted exhibitions in several countries (they had a show at the Riverside Studios in London in 1988). Works were also purchased for the Saatchi Collection. A typical KOS piece consisted of a large sheet of linen whose surface was covered with rows of pages taken from a classic work of literature upon which the group drew and painted human/animal caricatures of famous politicians or more complex combinations of imagery inspired by or commenting on the content of the text in question. (A dialogue with history was intended.)

● See also Collaborations, Community Art & Media, Group Material, Political Art.

● R Brooks 'Tim Rollins + KOS' *Artscribe International* (63) May 1987 40–7.

● W Januszczak 'Artful dodge in the Bronx' *Guardian* September 22 1987 11.

● T Hilton 'Kids' stuff' *Guardian* August 3 1988 11.

● L Nilson 'From dead end to avant garde' *Art News* **87** (10) December 1988 132–7.

378   KUNSTKOMPASS

An annual listing of the top one 100 artists of the Western world devised in 1969 by the German Dr Willi Bongard (died 1985). The Kunstkompass was not a best-seller list but a reputation scale compiled according to such factors as works purchased by museums and citations in the literature of art. Bongard edited a newsletter (available on subscription) entitled *Art Aktuell* advising collectors and investors about the art business.

● W Bongard *Kunst und Kommerz: Zwischen Passion und Spekulation* (Oldenburg & Hamburg, Gerhard Stalling Verlag, 1967).

● C Lauf 'Snakes & ladders: the archive of Dr Willi Bongard' *Artscribe* (84) November–December 1990 67–71.

379 LANGUAGE ART

A large number of artists have used language (or words, or letters) in a way that relates to the tradition of the visual arts rather than to the tradition of literature. See, for example, the entries on Art & Language, Book Art, Conceptual Art, Concrete Poetry, Lettrism, Mail Art and Story Art. This work is so diverse that it is virtually impossible to bring together under one heading. The term 'Language Art' is an attempt to provide such a heading but it is so lacking in specificity it is virtually useless.

● J Bowles & T Russell (eds) *This book is a movie: an exhibition of Language Art and visual poetry* (NY, Dell, 1971).

● *Language & structure in North America* (Toronto, Five Six Seven Gallery, 1975).

380 LASER ART

The word 'laser' is an acronym for 'light amplification by stimulated emission of radiation'. According to Dr Leon Goldman, these devices for producing coherent, high-density beams of radiation or light, provide artists and craftspersons with a new tool for use in the fields of design, etching and sculpture, e.g. they can be used to carve jade and plastic. Also, lasers can be used to generate a form of art in their own right: helium–neon lasers have been used, in association with optical and acoustic systems, to produce a type of kinetic art. Artists like Rockne Krebs and Keji Vsami have created environmental or sky artworks with pencil-thin beams of various colours up to a mile in length. During the 1970s laser light shows became commonplace at rock concerts. In 1977 the Planetarium in London presented Ivan Dryer's 'Laserium' (i.e. a light and music performance or 'cosmic laser concert' first developed in Los Angeles in 1973). A decade later commercial firms were offering for sale laser gadgets for use as home entertainment. An exhibition devoted to Laser Art was held in Cincinnati in 1969, and another show called 'Light Fantastic' (organized by John Wolff) was mounted at the Royal Academy, London, in 1977.

Laser light is integral to the generation of holograms. Laser holography enables three-dimensional sculptures to be displayed when the original is unavailable.

● See also Air Art, Conceptual Architecture, Environmental Art, Holographic Art, Light Art, Projected Art, Rock Art/Design/Fashion.

● *Laser light: a new visual art* (Cincinnati Art Museum, 1969).

● L Goldman 'Lasers – a coherent approach to art' *New Scientist* January 21 1971 146–8.

● —'Progress of Laser Art in lapidary work' *Lapidary Journal* 25 (2) May 1971 3289.

● J Burne 'Making light with lasers' *Time Out* July 1–7 1977 19.

● *Light Fantastic* (Royal Academy, 1977).

● T Kallard *Laser Art and optical transforms* (NY, Optosonic Press, 1979).

381 LATE-MODERN ARCHITECTURE

A term introduced by Charles Jencks in 1977 to distinguish buildings by architects extending the tradition of modernism despite the advent and dominance of post-modernism. Jencks argued that Late-Modern architects took the ideas and forms of the modern movement 'to an extreme, exaggerating the structure and technological image of the building'. (The word 'late' has connotations of decline and decadence – Jencks described Late-Modernism as 'an elaborated or mannered modernism'.) As examples he cited two high-tech buildings: the Sainsbury Centre designed by Norman Foster and the Pompidou Centre designed by Renzo Piano and Richard Rogers. According to Jencks, such buildings were singly coded, as against post-modern buildings which were doubly coded (i.e. half modern and half something else).

In later writings Jencks argued that a return to modernism enabled him to describe some contemporary architects as 'the new moderns'.

● See also High-Tech, Modern Movement, Pompidou Centre, Post-Modern Architecture, Sainsbury Centre.

● C Jencks *Late-Modern Architecture & other essays* (Academy Editions, 1980).

● —*The new moderns* (Academy Editions, 1990).

An extremely broad and imprecise art-historical category. Although Europeans and North Americans had shown sporadic interest in Latin American Art during the period 1945–85, it was not until the late '80s that this interest became intense – to judge from the spate of exhibitions and books, and the founding of a specialist journal. Also, in London a Latin American Arts Association – a cultural and educational charity – was established in 1985.

'Latin America', Dawn Ades argued, was 'a cultural and political designation' stemming from the period of European colonialism. It encompassed the French- and Spanish-speaking countries of Central and South America and some of the Caribbean islands. In terms of time, it concerned the modern era, i.e. the period since the wars of independence from Europe in the early nineteenth century. Previously, it was the pre-Columbian Aztec and Inca art, and the modern art of Mexico (the Mexican muralists, Frida Kahlo, José Posada) that was most familiar to Europeans and North Americans, though they were also aware of the modern architecture of Brasilia, the carnival of Rio, and the style of fantastic or magic realism typical of so much South American literature and painting. The English art critic Guy Brett was therefore somewhat exceptional in his support of the optical and kinetic art movements of South America from the '60s onwards.

The arts and crafts of the various countries of Latin America are extremely diverse and heterogeneous. They are the consequence of complex conjunctions of cultural and socio-political influences: the arts and traditions of the ancient and native peoples of the area; the imported arts and religions of the white European colonialists and the black slaves of Africa; nationalistic and popular movements plus, in the twentieth century, the international styles of modernism.

In 1989 a British reviewer dismissed Latin American Art on the grounds that it did not equal 'European museum quality' and that it represented 'the failure of all the hopes we had reposed in modern art'. According to an alternative view, Latin American culture was nothing if not 'mestizo' (mixed blood, mixed cultures), a condition it relished in order to challenge the norms of Europe.

● See also Arpilleras, Brasilia, Carnival, Fantastic Art, Indigenismo, Madí Movement, Taller de Gráfica Popular.

● S Catlin & T Grieder *Art of Latin America since independence* (New Haven, Connecticut, Yale University Art Gallery/Austin, University of Texas Art Museum, 1966).

● T Messer *The emergent decade* (NY, Guggenheim Museum, 1966).

● G Chase *Contemporary art in Latin America* (NY, Free Press, 1970).

● J Franco *The modern culture of Latin America: society and the artist* (Harmondsworth, Penguin Books, 1970).

● J Findlay *Modern Latin American Art: a bibliography* (Westport, Connecticut, Greenwood Press, 1983).

● N Richard 'The problematic of Latin American Art' *Art & Text* (21) 1986.

● H Day & H Sturges *Art of the fantastic: Latin America 1920–87* (Indianapolis Museum of Art/Bloomington, Indiana University Press, 1987/8).

● *The Latin American spirit: art and artists in the United States 1920–70* (NY, Bronx Museum of the Arts/Abrams, 1988).

● *Latin American Art* (Magazine: Scottsdale, Arizona, Spring 1989–).

● D Ades & others *Art in Latin America: the modern era 1820–1980* (Hayward Gallery/South Bank Centre, 1989).

● O Baddeley & V Fraser *Drawing the line: art and cultural identity in contemporary Latin America* (Verso, 1989).

● G Brett *Transcontinental: nine Latin American artists* (Birmingham, Ikon Gallery/Manchester, Cornerhouse Gallery/London, Verso, 1990).

LATIN AMERICAN ART Cover of *Latin American Art*, inaugural issue, Spring 1989 with painting by FERNANDO BOTERO.

383 LAURA ASHLEY STYLE

In 1953 Laura Ashley (1926-85) began to print small, Victorian-inspired floral patterns on fabrics for scarves on her kitchen table in London. From the beginning her aim was to evoke a rural, comfortable lifestyle. Since there was a demand for her designs, Laura's husband Bernard gave up his job in the City and helped to transform the craft hobby into an industry. The first Laura Ashley shop was opened in South Kensington in 1968. During the '60s there was a vogue for country and peasant clothing to which Ashley contributed. By the 1980s 'Laura Ashley' had become a multi-national design and retailing business selling co-ordinated home furnishing products and fashions.

In fact, there is not one Laura Ashley Style; the book by Gale & Irvine cited below describes five styles: rustic, country house, romantic, period and modern. Laura Ashley designs tend to be pretty, traditional, romantic and nostalgic; they reinterpret the designs and patterns of the past preserved in the company's archive. Like Habitat, the Laura Ashley shops issue illustrated catalogues. A range of books is also associated with the firm; they are celebratory and promotional rather than critical.

NB The term 'Ashley Style' has also been applied to the work of Ashley Havinden, art director for the London advertising agency W. S. Crawford from 1929-67.

● See also English Style, Habitat, Lifestyle.

● I Gale & S Irvine *Laura Ashley Style* (Weidenfeld & Nicolson, 1987).

● S Irvine *Laura Ashley bedrooms* (Weidenfeld & Nicolson, 1987).

● N Ashley *Laura Ashley at home: six family homes and their transformation* (Weidenfeld & Nicolson, 1988).

● E Dickinson & others *The Laura Ashley book of home decoration* (Hamlyn, rev ed 1988).

● K Corbett-Winder *Laura Ashley living rooms* (Weidenfeld & Nicolson, 1989).

● A Sebba *Laura Ashley: a life by design* (Weidenfeld, 1990).

LETRASET Detail from a Letraset catalogue of the 1970s. Reproduced by kind permission of Esselte Letraset Ltd.

developed 'cut-up' methods in reaction to Letraset's dominance in the field of headline lettering.

● See also Punk.

● A Wenman 'The Letraset story' *Penrose Annual* **69** 1976 173–83.

● Letraset' *Graphik* **30** (6) 1977 39–45.

● Letraset UK Ltd *Graphic design handbook* (Letraset UK Ltd, 1988).

384 LETRASET A dry transfer, instant lettering system that has been a great boon to graphic and architectural designers since it was launched in 1961. Letraset had its origins in a 1956 transfer headline typesetting process. The inventor of Letraset was the British graphic designer J. C. C. Davies; he founded the Letraset company in 1959. It rapidly expanded and became international. In Britain a new factory was opened in 1968 in Ashford, Kent. Marketing of the product was assisted by the publication of a catalogue illustrating a wide range of old and modern typefaces in various point sizes. Besides letters and display faces, the system includes colours, symbols and line drawings of figures. Sets of Letraset products are widely distributed: they are stocked by most art and design shops. Some designers in the '70s (e.g. the punk designer Jamie Reid)

385 LETTRISM (Also Lettrisme, Lettriste Movement/ International) An international, avant garde, poetry and art movement of the post-war years based in Paris. Isidore Isou, a Romanian writer who came to France in 1945, was the leading figure and promoted Lettrist ideas with 'aggressive megalomania'; other participants included Gabriel Pomerand, Guy Vallot, Maurice Lemaitre, Jean-Louis Brau, Gil Wolman, François Dufrêne and Guy-Ernest Debord. The first manifestation of Lettrism occurred in 1946 when a public demonstration was made against dada and surrealism. Isou believed that the word in poetry was exhausted and that it was the sound and appearance of letters which should be foregrounded, hence he generated a nonsense sound poetry. Lettrist principles, it was claimed, were capable of revolutionizing all the arts (Isou and Lemaitre made films in 1951) and politics (Lemaitre stood as a candidate in the French election of 1967). In terms of visual art, Lettrism focused upon letters, numbers and signs as motifs; the results often resembled concrete poetry. (In fact the term 'Lettrism' has been employed by N. and E. Calas simply to mean the use of letters and pictographs in paintings by such artists as Jasper Johns, S. Arakawa, Robert Watts and Robert Indiana.) Another term the Lettrists were fond of was 'hypergraphology' – a new science of language and sign – and their visual pieces were called 'hypergraphics'.

Between 1952 and '57 certain artists broke away from Isou and formed the Lettriste International and also Ultra-Lettrism. Participants in the former later joined with the situationists.

● See also Concrete Poetry, Hyper-graphics, Semiotics, Situationists.

● I Isou *Introduction à une nouvelle poésie* (Paris, Gallimard, 1947).

● —'The creations of Lettrism' *Times Literary Supplement* (3,262) September 1964 796–7.

● C Cutler 'Paris: the Lettrist Movement' *Art in America* **58** (1) January–February 1970 116–19.

● N & E Calas 'Lettrism' – in – *Icons and images of the sixties* (NY, Dutton, 1971) 131–48.

● G-P Broutin & others *Lettrisme et hypergraphie* (Paris, Georges Fall, 1972).

● F Dufrêne 'Le Lettrisme et toujours pendant' *Opus International* (40–41) 1973.

● J-P Curtay *La poésie Lettriste* (Paris, Éditions Seghers, 1974).

● P Ferrua (ed) *Proceedings of the First International Symposium on Lettrism 1976* (Portland, Oregon, Lewis & Clark College/Paris, Avant Garde Publishers, 1979).

● S Foster (ed) 'Lettrisme: into the present' *Visible Language* **17** (3) 1983 (special issue).

● *Lettrism and hypergraphics 1945–85* (NY, Franklin Furnace, 1985).

386   LIFESTYLE

A term which became very popular in the discourses of advertising, journalism, design, market research and sociology in the 1970s and '80s. A 'Lifestyle' is a particular mode of human existence expressed outwardly in terms of a complex of material goods, tastes and habits of consumption. Anthropologists and art historians have, for a long time, analysed the close link between visual styles and the modes of life of particular groups, tribes, and social classes but they tended to assume that styles were organic rather than artificially adopted or purchased off the peg. More recently, subcultural theorists have argued that modern consumer societies offer a diversity of Lifestyles from which affluent people can choose in the same way they choose between products. Irving Toffler has described a Lifestyle as a 'superproduct' which offers people a sense of identity and a way of organizing products and ideas. He also claims its social function is to reduce anxiety caused by value-vertigo and by the over-choice associated with consumerism. Lifestyles in the future, Toffler has argued, will be adopted and discarded at an increased rate and will become throw-away items like other consumer goods. Pierre Bourdieu, the author of an ambitious sociological study of taste and Lifestyles in France, employs a closely related term 'habitus'.

● See also Colour Supplements, Cult Objects, Filofax, Subculture.

● I Toffler *Future shock* (NY, Random House, 1970).

● A Mitchell *The nine American Lifestyles* (NY, MacMillan, 1983).

● P Bourdieu *Distinction: a social critique of the judgement of taste* (Routledge & Kegan Paul, 1984).

● J Abrams 'Lifestyles: what next? Forecasting tomorrow' *Blueprint* (20) 1985 14–15.

● M Featherstone 'Lifestyle and consumer culture' *Theory, Culture & Society* **4** 1987 55–70.

387   LIGHT ART

(Also Neon Art, Plasma Sculpture) The advent of powerful sources of artificial light in the modern era made it possible for artists to employ light directly to make works of art. The American artist Willoughby Sharp has argued that Light Art is the only totally new artform of the modern age. The term itself signifies a broad concept encompassing such diverse phenomena as colour organs, fireworks, projected light, lasers and sculptures made from neon tubes. Light Art has often been treated as a subcategory of kinetic art, but some writers have claimed that such a large movement deserved a separate status. A more pertinent reason for such a distinction was the fact that not all artists who used light were concerned with movement or changes of illumination in time; for example, Dan Flavin's austere neon installations were considered part of minimalism, while Chryssa's and Bruce Nauman's neon tube lettering related to pop art rather than to kinetics. Among the best-known kineticists exploiting light in the years since 1945 were: Lucio Fontana, Julio Le Parc, Frank Malina, Bruno Munari, Nicolas Schöffer, plus artists associated with the German group Zero and the French organization GRAV.

Neon light was invented by the Frenchman Georges Claude. By 1912 it was being used for shop advertising in France. In the 1920s and '30s neon signs became a

LIGHT ART RON HASELDEN, 'Fete' (1989). Light & sound installation, Feeringbury Manor, Essex. Photo: Edward Woodman; courtesy of Ron Haselden.

vital part of American street advertising and this is still one of neon's main applications; today, however, it is also used in films, on TV programmes and as interior decor. 'Neon art' is obviously a subdivision of Light Art. Unless readymade tubes are employed, neon art is slow to produce because circuitry has to be designed and tubes shaped by specialist glass-benders. During the 1960s artists such as Flavin, Chryssa, Martial Raysse and James Rosenquist made neon fashionable for a while but then it suffered a period of neglect which lasted until the 1980s. In Los Angeles a Museum of Neon Art (MoNA) was founded as a non-profit making institution in 1981. Lila Lakich, its director and co-founder, has been a neon artist for over 20 years. She is the creator of 'Mona', an animated, fluorescent-coloured, punning portrait after Leonardo. Besides contemporary neon art, the Museum mounts exhibitions of electric and kinetic art. It also has a permanent collection of vintage neon signs, clocks and automata. Tuition is also available for those wishing to make neon art.

One artist exhibiting at MoNA was Larry Albright. He has created so-called 'bottled lightning' or 'plasma sculptures', i.e. glass spheres containing rare gases and an antenna capable of generating fluorescent ions. When the two react as a result of a discharge of electricity, colourful, moving, three-dimensional tentacles of plasma particles are created. These forms resemble forks of lightning and are responsive to both sound and touch. Plasma sculptures are based upon nineteenth century 'Chambers of Living Lightning' invented by Nikola Tesla and they are offered for sale in gift catalogues as sophisticated home decor or as executive toys.

● See also Electrographic Architecture, GRAV, Kinetic

Art, Laser Art, Luminism, Pop Design, Zero.

● *Kunst-licht-kunst* (Eindhoven, Stedelijk Van Abbemuseum, 1966).

● N Piene 'Light Art' *Art in America* **55** (3) May–June 1967 24–47.

● A Spear 'Sculptured light' *Art International* **11** (10) Christmas 1967 29–49.

● *Light, motion, space* (Minneapolis, Walker Art Center, 1967).

● *Lumière et mouvement* (Paris, Musée d'Art Moderne de la Ville de Paris, 1967).

● F Popper 'Light & movement' – in – *Origins and development of kinetic art* (Studio Vista, 1968) 156–89.

● T Hess & J Ashbery (eds) *Light from Aten to laser* (NY, MacMillan, 1969), *Art News* Annual **35**.

● W Sharp 'Luminism and kineticism' – in – *Minimal art: a critical anthology* G Battcock (ed) (Studio Vista, 1969) 317–58.

● L Lakich *Neon lovers glow in the dark* (Los Angeles, MoNA, 1986).

● R Stern *The new Let there be neon* (NY, Abrams, rev ed 1988).

● K Marshall 'A new lease on light' *American Way* (American Airlines magazine) **22** (14) July 15 1989 48–54.

● M Donohue 'Neon in tinseltown' *Sculpture* **9** (5) September–October 1990 40–3,+ 70.

388 LIVING ART

In its straightforward sense this expression means the art of now, art by living artists; hence it has been employed as a title by periodicals dealing with contemporary art (e.g. *Living Arts* (ICA, three issues 1963–4) and *L'Art Vivant* (1968–75)). More profoundly, it refers to an attempt to overcome the gap – which Robert Rauschenberg said he worked within – between art and life by substituting 'the real for the aesthetic object' (see, for instance, Actions, Direct Art, Living Sculpture). In effect, Living Art seeks the end of art. However, Ad Reinhardt has argued that 'art is always dead ..."Living Art" is a deception'. Herbert Marcuse agrees that the notion is absurd because 'art must retain, no matter how minimally, the form of art as different from non-art, and it is the artform itself which frustrates the intention to reduce or even annul this difference...art cannot become reality, cannot realise itself without cancelling itself as art in all its forms...'. These philosophical difficulties stem from the fact that art is a cultural and material phenomenon which transcends individuals but which is made from parts of reality, extends existing reality, and requires for its production and consumption the consciousness of living human beings.

The term 'Live Arts' refers, of course, to those arts –

such as theatre and dance – which are performed in real time by real people in front of a real audience.

● H Marcuse 'Art as a form of reality' – in – *On the future of art* E Fry (ed) (NY, Viking Press, 1970) 123–34.

● A Reinhardt –quoted in– *Conceptual art* by U Meyer (NY, Dutton, 1972) 167.

● R Ayers & D Butler *Live art* (Sunderland, AN Publications, 1991).

389 LIVING SCULPTURE

An example of a persistent tendency in art since 1960 for artists to set aside the production of physical objects and to present themselves, or tableaux vivant, as the artwork. In 1961, for instance, the Italian artist Piero Manzoni signed nude models and also declared his friends to be works of art. The trajectory of Manzoni's career was towards a total identification of his body, its processes and waste products, with art. In 1962, during the Fluxus-inspired 'Festival of Misfits' held in London, the French artist Ben Vautier exhibited himself in the window of Gallery One for 15 days and nights as an example of 'Living Sculpture'. Stuart Brisley, the British performance artist, has also endured various 'life situations' in gallery settings. In Stockholm in 1969 Pi Lind provided a number of pedestals in a gallery so that real people could sit motionless pretending they were statues.

LIVING SCULPTURE GILBERT & GEORGE The Singing Sculpture. Photo courtesy of Sonnabend Gallery, New York.

The Greek artist Jannis Kounellis, who worked in Rome during the '60s, introduced parrots and even horses into his exhibitions. In London in 1972 Ann James mounted an exhibition called 'Sculpture in reverse' based on the idea that visitors constituted the show; James provided a setting of cobwebs for them to become entangled. In exhibitions of waxworks and extremely realistic sculptures, it has become a cliché to include a motionless live human in order to create uncertainty about what is, and what is not, real. The team of Gilbert & George are perhaps the most extreme example of the Living Sculpture concept.

Besides Living Sculptures, Living Paintings have also been generated. For example, in July 1965 Günter Brus carried out a 'self-painting' in which he walked the streets of Vienna (until arrested for disturbing the peace) with his head and clothes covered with white paint with a vertical black line down the middle as if his body had been cut in half.

● See also Body Art, Direct Art, Gilbert & George, Performance Art, Verist Sculpture.

390 LOS ANGELES FINE ARTS SQUAD

A group of four painters – Victor Henderson, Terry Schoonhover, Jim Frazin and Leonard Korin – founded in 1969. The artists resided in Venice, California, and specialized in the creation of large-scale murals on blank walls in a trompe l'oeil style. The images they produced had surrealistic and humorous touches. They were not really instances of community art but they did tend to have some relationship to the local context, e.g. a view of a street painted on a wall in that street so that it functioned like a mirror. A London group of muralists later parodied the Americans' name by calling themselves the 'Fine Heart Squad' (they claimed to be putting the heart back into art).

● See also Billboard Art, Community Art & Media, Street Art, Trompe L'Oeil.

● T Garver 'Venice in the snow' *Artforum* **9** (6) February 1971 91–2.

● G Glueck 'Art notes: the art squad strikes again' *New York Times* July 9 1972 16.

● W Wilson 'The LA Fine Arts Squad: Venice in the snow and other visions' *Art News* **72** (6) 1973 28–9.

391 LOW-TECH

(Also Low-impact Technology) The antithesis of high-tech. If the latter is advanced, complex and expensive, then the former is commonplace, simple and cheap. Recycling of objects and materials is a feature of Low-Tech: Victor Papanek and George Seeger once constructed radios for a few cents from old tin cans using paraffin wax as a power source. The Low-Tech approach to design – which dates from the 1960s – is appropriate to the circumstances of poor people and poor countries; it is also advocated as an alternative (hence 'alternative', 'appropriate', 'intermediate', 'utopian' technology) by those conscious of the environmental damage high-tech can cause. While some writers distinguish between high and low technology, others distinguish between hard and soft.

● See also Creative Salvage, DIY, Green Design, High-Tech, Radical Design, Reactivart, Soft Design/Tech, Technological Art.

◉ D Dickson *Alternative technology and the politics of technical change* (Fontana/Collins, 1974).

◉ R Ball & P Cox *Low Tech* (Century Publishing, 1982).

◉ M Hill & others *Low Tech: temporary furniture for next to nothing* (Architectural Press, 1982).

◉ V Papanek *Design for the real world* (Thames & Hudson, rev ed 1985).

392 LUDWIG COLLECTION

An important collection of modern art accumulated by the wealthy German businessman and powerful patron Peter Ludwig. The collection is particularly strong on American pop art. A new museum building to house the collection was opened in Cologne in 1986. There is another Ludwig Museum in Aachen. Peter Ludwig has been the subject of a critical work of art entitled 'The chocolate master' (1981) by the Left-wing artist Hans Haacke.

◉ *Hans Haacke. Vol 2: works 1978–83* (Eindhoven, Stedelijk Van Abbemuseum/London, Tate Gallery, 1984).

◉ S Gohr *Museum Ludwig, Cologne* (Munich, Prestel-Verlag, 1986).

◉ E Weiss & G Kolberg *Museum Ludwig, Cologne* (Catalogue Raisonné) 2 vols (Munich, Prestel-Verlag, 1986).

◉ The Director & senior curators *Ludwig Museum , Cologne* (Scala Books, 1991).

393 LUMINISM

A genre of American landscape painting popular in the period 1850–75 in which views were suffused with light to such an extent that light became central to the painting's meaning. This tradition persists into the twentieth century – witness the paintings shown in the 1985 exhibition held at the Henry Art Gallery in Seattle. The term 'Luminism' generally refers to depicted light but some modern writers also use it to mean artworks made from real light sources. In this text, for the sake of clarity, the latter are discussed under the heading 'Light Art'.

◉ *Sources of light: contemporary American Luminism* (Seattle, University of Washington, Henry Art Gallery, 1985).

◉ J Wilmerding (ed) *American light: the Luminist movement 1850–75* (Princeton University Press, 1989).

394 LYRICAL ABSTRACTION

A term first suggested by the French painter Georges Mathieu as the title of an exhibition held in Paris in 1947 (the show was in fact called 'The Imaginary'), featuring works by Jean Atlan, Camille Bryen, Hans Hartung, Jean-Paul Riopelle, Wols and others. Later on, Pierre Restany and other critics employed it to characterize abstract (but non-geometric) paintings by such artists as James Brooks, Helen Frankenthaler, Sam Francis and Philip Guston. Their paintings were more gentle, intuitive, painterly and decorative than those by other contributors to the abstract expressionist and l'art informel movements. The word 'lyrical' implies 'a poet's spontaneous, ardent outpouring of feeling' and also a poem or song that is 'light and graceful'.

● See also Abstract Expressionism, Art Informel, Tachisme.

◉ P Restany *Lyrisme et Abstraction* (Milan, Apolinaire, 1960).

Lyrical Abstraction (NY, Whitney Museum of American Art, 1971).

◉ M Ragon 'Lyrical Abstraction from explosion to inflation' – in – *Abstract art since 1945* by W Haftmann & others (Thames

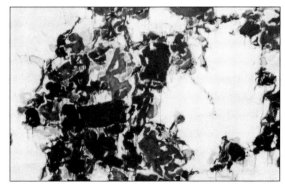

LYRICAL ABSTRACTION SAM FRANCIS 'Round the blues'. Oil on canvas 108"x 192"(1957). Martha Jackson Gallery, New York.

M

395 MACHINE AESTHETIC/ART

The Machine Aesthetic' was the title of a famous 1955 essay by the architectural critic Reyner Banham. Earlier, in 1921, Theo van Doesburg had spoken of a 'mechanical aesthetic', i.e. an aesthetic expressive of the modern era based on the new possibilities of the machine. The Machine Aesthetic consisted in the homage which certain modern artists, architects and designers paid to machines (e.g. the futurists' celebration of racing cars) and to engineering and technology in general. Machines were viewed by modernists as emblematic of the modern age of industry and manufacture – the so-called 'first machine age'. In contrast to handicrafts, machines facilitated repetition and standardization, the mass production of identical goods whose forms – Le Corbusier, the purists and the artists of the de Stijl believed – tended to be simple and geometric, and whose finish tended to be smooth. Banham's article was critical of this conception. The idea that one particular 'look' or aesthetic was implied by machines was simplistic. However, the role of machines cannot be discounted: in prefabrication, high-tech and pneumatic structures, architects depend heavily on machines and factory production for the components from which their buildings are assembled. In terms of industrial design, machines are inescapable: industrial designers have to take into account the manufacturing process and the machines employed – which now can involve automated production using computer-controlled robots. Also, in terms of the design process itself, machines such as computers and Quantel paintboxes have become crucial tools.

The term 'Machine Art' has several meanings: industrial design; works of fine art depicting machinery; works of art made with the help of machines; works of art consisting of machines. Two artists who depicted machines (ironically) were Picabia and Duchamp. Computer art and video art are two kinds of art that are heavily dependent on machines and kineticists are one group of artists who construct works of art which function mechanically.

Since Philip Johnson's 'Machine Art' show at MoMA in 1934, a number of exhibitions have been held exploring the interactions between art/design and machines/robots.

● See also Computer-Aided Design, High-Tech, Kinetic Art, Media Art, Post-Industrial Design, Quantel Paintbox, Rational Architecture, Technological Art.

P Johnson *Machine Art* (NY, MoMA, 1934/Arno Press reprint 1969).

J Richards 'Towards a rational aesthetic' *Architectural Review* **78** December 1935 211–18.

S Giedion *Mechanisation takes command: a contribution to anonymous history* (NY, Oxford University Press, 1948).

R Hamilton (curator) & R Banham (introd) *Man, machine, motion* (Newcastle Upon Tyne, Hatton Gallery/London, ICA, 1955).

R Banham 'Machine Aesthetic' (1955) – in – *Design by choice* P Sparke (ed) (Academy Editions, 1981) 44–7.

— *Theory and design in the first machine age* (Architectural Press, 1960).

K Pontus Hulton *The machine as seen at the end of the mechanical age* (NY, MoMA, 1968).

S Bayley & J Woudhuysen *Robots* (Victoria & Albert Museum, Boilerhouse Project, 1984).

R Wilson & others *The machine age in America 1918–41* (NY, Brooklyn Museum/Abrams, 1986).

396 MADÍ MOVEMENT

(Also Arte Madí) An Argentine avant garde movement founded in Buenos Aires in 1946 by Gyula Kosice, Arden Quin, Martin Blaszko, Rhod Rothfuss and others. Their first exhibition took place at the French Institute. Kosice wrote a manifesto in 1946. Several explanations of the word 'Madí' have been given: that it derived from a contraction of the cry 'Madrid!', from 'Movimento de Arte Invención', and from 'MAtérialisme DIalectique'. An initial interest in concrete art evolved into a commitment to kinetic art. (A rival group was called Arte Concreto-Invención.) Madí artists stressed invention and movement; their aesthetic principles applied to all the arts; they produced totally abstract, brightly painted wooden constructions that were irregular in shape (the rectangular shape was rejected, hence Madí art anticipated the '60s vogue for shaped canvases); also works that were articulated so that they could move and be transformed; and light works made from neon tubing. (By the late '50s Kosice had become well known in France and noted for his 'hydrokinetic art' or 'hydraulic' sculpture and architecture (i.e. constructions involving water, light and movement).)

Although the original Madí group disbanded in 1947, Kosice published a magazine entitled *Arte Madí Universal,* eight numbers of which appeared between 1947 and '54. Exhibitions of Madí Art also took place in Europe and South America during the late '40s and the '50s, e.g. 'Arte Madí Internacional' (Gallery Bonino, Buenos Aires, 1956); '15 años de Arte Madí' (Museum de Arte Moderna, Buenos Aires, 1956).

● See also Concrete Art, Kinetic Art, Latin American Art, Shaped Canvas, Total Art/Design.

● M Seuphor *Kosice* (Paris, Galerie Denise René, 1960).

● G Habasque & others *Kosice* (Paris, Hofer, 1965).

● G Kosice *Arte Hidrocinetico Movimento Luz Agua* (Buenos Aires, Paidos, 1969).

● M Ragon 'Kosice the poorly-known precursor and the Madí Movement' *Cimaise* (95/96) January–April 1970 30–45.

● J Rivera *Madí y la Vanguardia Argentina* (Buenos Aires, Mundo Moderno No 81/Paidos, 1976).

● O Chiérico Kosice: *Reportajè á una anticipación* (Buenos Aires, Taller Libre, 1979).

● G Kosice *Arte Madí* (Buenos Aires, Ediciones de Arte Gaglianone, 1982).

● V Roitman *Retrospective Arden Quin* (Paris, Galerie Franke Berndt, 1988).

● 'Arte Madí/arte concreto-invención' – in – *Art in Latin America* by D Ades & others (Hayward Gallery/South Bank Centre, 1989) 240–51, also 'Madí manifesto' 330.

397 MAGAZINE ART

Since their emergence in the eighteenth century, art magazines have been growing in numbers and influence. Their ability to establish the reputation of an artist and to promote an art movement has been particularly marked in the twentieth century. Realizing the power of art magazines, groups of artists have used existing ones or founded their own in order to publicize their work and theories. (So one can distinguish between artists' magazines and magazines of comment and criticism.) By the 1970s the power of the art magazine to define and legitimize new developments in art rivalled that of private galleries and museums. In the period 1966–76 a significant number of artists (mostly of the conceptual persuasion) adopted the use of language and/or photo-text as their primary modes of communication and, as a result, a number of new magazines appeared claiming to be art – hence the term 'Magazine Art'. Existing art magazines also began to allocate front covers and inside pages to artists so that they could present their ideas in writing, drawing or graphic form. In 1976 conferences, exhibitions and special issues of periodicals were devoted to the subject of art magazines.

● See also Book Art, Conceptual Art, The Face.

● 'Art magazines' *Studio International* **192** (983) September–October 1976.

● T Fawcett & C Phillpot (eds) *The art press* (Art Book Co, 1976).

● H Pindell 'Alternative space: artists' periodicals' *Print Collector's Newsletter* September–October 1977 96–109, 120–1.

● C Phillpot 'Art magazines and Magazine Art' *Artforum* **13** (6) February 1980 52–4.

398 MAIL ART

(Also Communication Art, Correspondence Art, Envois, Postal Sculpture) During the 1970s and '80s international communication networks (but mainly in Europe and North America) were established by thousands of individuals and small groups – artists, poets, designers, typographers, etc. – who made use of the postal system in order to generate, disseminate and exchange works of art. These works were usually mixed-media items consisting of drawings, collages, photocopied images, writings, and so forth executed on paper. In terms of their

MAIL ART 'Artists Report/ Mail-Art' Catalogue cover of IX Congress of the IAA/AIAP 1979, Stuttgart, Germany.

content, style and quality, they varied immensely. At first the label 'correspondence art' was used to describe the genre but later on 'Mail Art' gained greater currency.

Ray Johnson, an American artist, was probably the originator of Mail Art. In the late '50s he presided over the creation of a series of seminal collages: they were produced with the help of friends and strangers who posted them to each other for alterations and additions. Johnson's name for these activities was the 'New York Correspondence School'. Later, other 'schools' were formed: 'Airpress', 'Fat City School of Finds Art', 'North West Mounted Valise', 'Ace Space Company', 'a space', 'Image Bank', 'Mail Order Art', 'Sam's Cafe', plus the group Ant Farm and the international movement Fluxus. Besides Johnson, individual artists exploiting the post were Robert Watts, John Dowd and Robin Klassnik. The last-named was a British artist who organized in 1972 a 'postal sculpture' event in which he constructed a sculpture from items sent to him through the post and then displayed it in a shop window.

The emergence and popularity of Mail Art can be accounted for in several ways: the relative cheapness of paper and stamps; the widespread availability of photocopying machines; the desire of artists to collaborate in ways which involved the element of chance. Mail Art provided a means by which artists separated by vast geographical distances could communicate with one another. It indicated a creative response to the information explosion and the massive quantity of printed matter and ephemera associated with it. Some subversive artists who hoped to undermine the art establishment and other social institutions were also attracted to Mail Art because of the possibility of using public systems for the purposes of satire, criticism and misinformation. (In 1976 the British artist Genesis P. Orridge (GPO) was prosecuted by the General Post Office (GPO) and fined for sending a 'pornographic' postcard through the mail.)

In 1972 Thomas Albright claimed that Mail artists constituted an 'underground' whose work was an alternative to the museum/gallery system. However, the movement was rapidly documented; many collections of Mail Art were published; and exhibitions were mounted (e.g. the one at the Whitney Museum, New York, in 1970). The movement was fated, therefore, to become an overground, established form of art. Although this type of art had great democratic potential, it could be criticized on the grounds that much of it was trivial and that it was incestuous in the sense that most contacts were between artists rather than between artists and the public at large.

As a by-product of their Mail Art activities, many artists designed and made their own rubber stamps and postage stamps (though the latter are not valid in the eyes of the postal authorities); hence 'Stamp Art'.

● See also Ant Farm, Copy Art, Fluxus, Media Art, Postcard Art, Stamp Art, Underground Art.

◗ W Wilson 'NY Correspondence School' *Art & Artists* **1** (1) April 1966 54–7.

◗ 'The New York Correspondence School' *Artforum* **6** (2) October 1967 50–5.

◗ D Bourdon 'Notes on a letter head' *Art International* **13** (9) November 1969 78–80.

◗ T Albright 'New art school: correspondence' *Rolling Stone* (106) April 13 1972 20.

◗ —'Correspondence Art' *Rolling Stone* (107) April 27 1972 20–1.

◗ J Poinset *Mail Art* (Paris, Cedic, 1972).

◗ D Zack 'An authentik and historikal discourse on the phenomenon of Mail Art' *Art in America* **61** (1) January–February 1973 46–53.

◗ M Kozloff 'Junk mail: an affluent art movement' *Art Journal* **33** (1) Fall 1973 23–6.

◗ J Greengold & C Tanz 'Correspondences' *Visible Language* **10** (3) Summer 1976 269–76.

◗ *Correspondence: an exhibition of letters of Ray Johnson* (Raleigh, North Carolina Museum of Art, 1976).

◗ K Friedman 'Correspondence Art in perspective' *Gray Matter: Mail Art Show* (San Diego State University Art Gallery, 1978) 12 pg xerox pamphlet.

◗ G Lloyd 'The Mail Art community in Europe: a first hand view' *Umbrella* **5** (1) January 1982 1–5.

◗ M Crane & M Stofflet (eds) *Correspondence Art* (San Francisco, Contemporary Arts Press, 1984).

◗ *Mail Art* (NY, Franklin Furnace, 1984).

◗ *Works by Ray Johnson* (Roslyn Harbour, NY, Nassau County Museum, 1984).

399 MARXIST AESTHETICS

Although Marx's and Engels' scattered comments on art – generally literature – provided some initial models for Marxist Aesthetics, criticism and art history, their treatment of art was unsystematic and their references to its role in a future communist society were brief and extremely utopian. Marxist Aesthetics, therefore, developed in the twentieth-century when followers tried to explain art in ways consistent with Marxist theories of economics, ideology, politics and society. Later contributors to Marxist theory and practice, e.g. Lenin, Trotsky, Chairman Mao, Gramsci and Althusser, also wrote on art and culture and their role in the revolution; consequently their texts also influenced the work of neo-Marxist aestheticians, critics and art historians. The work and writings of communist artists such as Mayakovsky, Brecht, Rivera and John Heartfield were of particular value to theorists. (Picasso's case was far more problematical.)

During the 1930s European neo-Marxists such as Theodor Adorno, Walter Benjamin, György Lukács, Herbert Marcuse and Max Raphael explored the possibilities of a Marxist Aesthetic, but their work was subject to repression both by the rising fascist regimes and by Stalinist Russia where 'Zhdanovism' (named after Andrei Zhdanov, its main exponent) became the official approach to art until at least the late 1950s, leading to the identification of Marxist Aesthetics with prurient and anti-modernist censorship and the promotion of socialist realism. The work of Adorno *et al.* (see Frankfurt School Aesthetics) became influential in the West during the 1960s and the importance of Raphael's writings was recognized in Britain first by Herbert Read and second by John Tagg. Other notable writers on art inspired by Marxism include E. Fischer, Anthony Blunt, Christopher Caudwell, Arnold Hauser, Frederick Antal, F. D. Klingender, Stefan Morawski, John Berger, Toni del Renzio, Frederick Jameson and T. J. Clark.

Briefly, the main themes of Marxist Aesthetic enquiry are: the origins and evolution of the fine arts as material/technical practices and art as a specific historical and social institution; the origins and development of the aesthetic sense; the relation of art to the theory of dialectics and to the means and relations of production, distribution and consumption (in particular the role of patronage, collecting, the private gallery/public museum system, dealing, auction houses, etc.); the implications for art of economic and social changes and the invention of new technologies such as photography/mechanical reproduction; the relation between form and content, and the vexed question of aesthetic quality and judgements of taste; the social functions, use-values and impact of art and how art works acquire exchange-value; art's relation to the different social classes, to ideology, truth, alienation and the mass media; the question of the relative autonomy of art within society; the degree of determination exercised upon art as part of the ideological superstructure by the material base or infrastructure of society; the role of art in ideological and political struggles in bourgeois, socialist and future communist societies.

Contrary to received opinion, Marxism is not a fixed, monolithic body of dogma. Indeed, it is heterogeneous, self-critical, constantly evolving and full of unresolved problems and contradictions. However, since it is a philosophy which seeks to fulfil itself in political practice, in the revolutionary overthrow of class societies, rather than remain academic, it is a philosophy relevant to Left-wing avant garde artists because they too seek to resolve problems of theory in practice, they too seek revolutionary transformations of human consciousness.

● See also Frankfurt School Aesthetics, New Art History, Peasant Painting, Political Art.

● F Klingender *Marxism and modern art: an approach to social realism* (Lawrence & Wishart, 1943; rep 1975).

● G Plekhanov *Art and social life* (Moscow, Progress Publishers, 1957).

● E Fischer *The necessity of art: a Marxist approach* (Harmondsworth, Penguin Books, 1963).

● V Lenin *On literature and art* (Moscow, Progress Publishers, 1967).

● L Baxandall *Marxism and aesthetics: a selected, annotated bibliography* (NY, Humanities Press, 1968).

● M Raphael *The demands of art* (Routledge & Kegan Paul, 1968).

● B Lang & F Williams (eds) *Marxism and art: writings in aesthetics and criticism* (NY, David McKay, 1972).

● H Avron *Marxist Aesthetics* (Ithaca, New York, Cornell University Press, 1973).

● F Lifshitz *The philosophy of art of Karl Marx* (Pluto Press, 1973).

● M Solomon (ed) *Marxism and art: essays classic and contemporary* (NY, Knopf, 1973).

● A Vasquez *Art and society: essays in Marxist Aesthetics* (NY, Monthly Review Press, 1973).

● K Marx & F Engels *Karl Marx and Frederick Engels on literature and art: a selection of writings* L Baxandall (ed) (NY, International General, 1974).

● A Zis *Foundations of Marxist Aesthetics* (Moscow, Progress Publishers, 1977).

● P Johnston *Marxist Aesthetics* (Routledge & Kegan Paul, 1984).

● M Rose *Marx's lost aesthetic* (Cambridge University Press, 1984).

● M Sprinker *Imaginary relations: aesthetics and ideology in the theory of historical materialism* (Verso, 1987).

400 MASS ART

This term has been used by art critics such as Harold Rosenberg and Jasia Reichardt to mean any art appealing to a mass audience, e.g. Hollywood movies, pulp fiction, television shows.... The more usual term is 'Mass culture': some theorists argue that because 'art' was historically a class (i.e. aristocratic and then bourgeois) concept it is necessarily élitist, a minority taste, and therefore cannot appeal to the masses. Other theorists (e.g. Raymond Williams and Alan Swingewood) are equally critical of the concept 'mass' as it appears in 'mass culture' and 'mass media'. All in all a problematical expression.

● See also Kitsch, Media Art, Pop Art, Popular Art.

● *L'Art de Masse n'existe pas* (Paris, Union Générale d'Éditions, 1974), special issue of *Revue d'Esthétique* (3/4) 1974.

● P Barker 'Introduction: dreaming together – how to "read" the Mass Arts'– in – *Arts in society* P Barker (ed)

(Fontana/Collins, 1977) 7–16.

● A Swingewood *The myth of mass culture* (Macmillan, 1977).

401 MASS MOCA

Provisional name of a proposed Museum of Contemporary Art to be situated in the run-down industrial town of North Adams, Massachusetts. The Museum, being masterminded by Thomas Krens and financed by state funds and by rich private patrons, is planned to house the largest collection of contemporary art in the world. It will be located in the huge industrial buildings abandoned by manufacturing companies. (The aim is also to put on temporary shows rivalling those of Documenta in Germany and to exhibit large-scale works which existing city museums cannot because of lack of space.) By investing in culture, using the Museum as a focus to attract tourists and new business, it is hoped that an economic revitalization of the area will result.

● See also Documenta.

● K Johnson 'Showcase in Arcadia' *Art in America* **76** (7) July 1988 94–103.

402 MATTER ART

(Also Matière Painting, Matterism) An aspect of l'art informel and assemblage art. During the 1950s artists such as Jean Fautrier, Jean Dubuffet, Antonio Tàpies, Manolo Millares, Modesta Cuixart, Enrico Donati and Alberto Burri foregrounded their materials by producing paintings with thick, textured surfaces resembling rinds or crusts. Some of these artists also introduced 'foreign', 'unworthy' materials such as cinders, charred wood, old sacking, etc. This kind of work was an extension of the tradition which began with the cubist collages of Braque and Picasso. Matter artists wanted to incorporate 'reality' in a non-illusionistic way, thus their materials were both their means and their subject. In Britain during the 1950s painters like Leon Kossof and Frank Auerbach also produced images with very thick layers of pigment which made their paintings like relief maps. And in the Netherlands the works of artists like Jaap Wagemaker and Bram Bogart, and in Belgium Bert de Leeuw, René Guiette and Marc Mendelson, gave rise to the label 'matterism'. In Austria in the early 1960s artists associated with Vienna Aktionismus (see Direct Art) were strongly influenced by Matter Art and action painting, particularly Otto Mühl, and during this period their work developed from an art of materials to 'material actions'. In the latter half of the decade a comparable stress of materials was evident in the arte povera, earth art and anti-form movements. Later still, in the early 1970s,

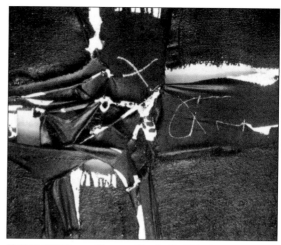

MATTER ART MANOLO MILLARES, 'Caudro No 162' (1961). Plastic paint, canvas & sacking. 39" x 32". Photo: Marlborough Fine Art, London.

the American abstract painter Larry Poons produced works with crust-like surfaces which indicated a renewed interest in Matter Painting. The origin of the term is obscure but seems to derive from French art criticism employing the word 'matière' meaning 'material', 'substance' or 'paint'.

● See also Anti-Form, Art Informel, Arte Povera, Assemblage Art, Direct Art, Earth & Land Art.

● M Seuphor 'Matière à discussion' *XXe Siècle* (5) June 1955 9–14.

● C Spencer 'Jaap Wagemaker: matière painter' *Studio* **166** (848) December 1963 244–5.

403 MAXIMALISM

According to its inventor, the American art critic Robert Pincus-Witten, this was 'a shock-value journalistic term' employed to characterize forms of art fashionable during the early 1980s. Maximalism appears to gain its specificity by contrast to minimalism. It refers to the pluralistic tendencies – 'constructionism, architecture-as-art, neo-primitivism and expressionism' – that followed hard upon the era of minimalism and post-minimalism. Pincus-Witten regarded Maximalism as a more conservative style because it privileged traditional art-forms such as painting and sculpture. The term seems to be an alternative to neo-expressionism and post-modernism. Following its appearance in the art press, the critics–curators Tricia Collins and Richard Milazzo began to employ the term 'maximal art'.

● See also Minimal Art, Neo-Expressionism, Post-Minimalism, Post-Modernism, Unexpressionism.

● R Pincus-Witten *Entries (Maximalism)* (NY, Out of London Press, 1983).

● T Collins & R Milazzo (eds) *Effects* Winter 1986.

● R Pincus-Witten *Post-Minimalism into Maximalism: Ameri-*

can art 1966–86 (Ann Arbor, Michigan, University of Michigan Research Press, 1987).

404   MEC ART

(Also Peinture Mécanique) 'Mec Art' is short for 'Mechanical Art'. It was a term employed in 1964 by the French painter Alain Jacquet and the Italian artist Mimmo Rotella to describe 'paintings' produced entirely by the creative manipulation of photo-mechanical reproduction processes. (The word 'mec' in France also has other connotations, i.e. a pimp.) It was possible to issue such works in editions of 200 or more. Mec Art reflected the influence of techniques pioneered by the Americans Robert Rauschenberg and Andy Warhol. Exhibitions of Mec Art featuring Rotella and Jacquet, with works by other artists – Nikos (Nikos Kessanlis), Pol Bury, Gianni Bertini and Serge Béguier – took place at the Galerie J in Paris in 1965, at Galeria Blu in Milan in 1966, and at the Paris Biennale in 1967.

● See also Multiples, Silk-Screenprinting.

● O Hahn 'Lettre de Paris: La Peinture Mécanique' *Art International* **9** (6) September 20 1965 70–2.

● P Restany 'Alain Jacquet: the big game of reality and fiction' *Domus* (510) May 1972 51–5.

● T Trini *Rotella* (Milan, Giampaolo Prearo Editore, 1974).

MEDIA ART JAN WANDJA, 'Sebastian (1)' (1982). Graphite wash and watercolour, 60" x 80". An image based on a sports photograph. Photo: Wandja.

405   MEDIA ART

All art is embodied in a physical medium (intermediate agency or substance) of some kind, consequently the term 'Media Art' could be regarded as superfluous and uninformative. However, in the twentieth-century the word 'media' has come to refer to those systems of mass communication and distribution – television, films, paperbacks, records, posters, magazines, etc. – which dominate the culture of developed nations. Technological progress in these fields has meant an increase in the number of media available to modern artists. They can now make art using photography, film, video, computers, copying machines and so forth.

Marshall McLuhan regarded the mass media as global extensions of our senses and consciousness which in turn influenced our view of the world (his concept of media was very broad: it included clothes, the motor car and money). The development of the mass media since the invention of photography in the 1840s has had an immense impact on the fine arts. Indeed, some theorists argue (e.g. Walter Benjamin) that the status and function of the fine arts have been fundamentally changed as a result (the story is too complex to recount here). A great deal of interaction has also taken place; e.g. pop artists ransacked the mass-media for images and the mass-media in turn made use of pop art. A key feature of the mass-media is their relay function: probably more people experience the fine arts at second-hand through the mediation of the reproductions, cinema, radio and television than through first-hand contact in galleries.

The term 'Media Art' has been employed in various senses: (a) to mean the work of commercial artists, illustrators, photographers and graphic designers employed by the mass culture industries; (b) the work of politically motivated artists who seek to turn the mass media against themselves (e.g. Thomas Albright used it in this sense to refer to the group Sam's Cafe – Marc and Terri Keyso, David Shine – engaged in 'media inversion' activities in the early 1970s); (c) the work of fine artists who undertake some critique of mass-media imagery in their work (e.g. Cindy Sherman, Barbara Kruger, Jenny Holzer, and others); (d) work by artists committed to new media such as holography, lasers, computers, etc. Perhaps the term applies most to artists such as Laurie Anderson and Jamie Reid who comment on the mass-media and at the same time make use of them to reach large audiences.

A large-scale exhibition of American media-based art entitled 'Image world' was organized by curators of the Whitney Museum during the winter of 1989–90. Exhibits were displayed inside the Museum but also outside in the streets of New York.

● See also Book Art, Copy Art, Cross-Overs, Electronic Art, Magazine Art, Mass Art, Museum Without Walls, Pictorial Rhetoric, Political Art, Pop Art, Popular Art, Rock Art/Design/Fashion, Scratch Video, Video Art.

● M McLuhan *Understanding media: the extensions of man* (Sphere Books, 1967).

● T Albright 'Visuals' *Rolling Stone* (85) June 1971 36–7.

● D Davis 'Media/art/media' *Arts Magazine* **46** Summer 1971 43–5.

● J Benthall 'The inflation of art media' *Studio International* **183** (937) October 1971 124–6.

● E Booth-Clibborn (ed) *European illustration '74,'75* (Constable, 1974).

● G Battcock 'Les Levine: media artist' *Domus* (560) July 1976 50–1.

● 'Art and the media' *Documenta 6 catalogue* (Kassel, 1977).

● J Walker *Art in the age of mass media* (Pluto Press, 1983).

● R Pelfrey & M Hall-Pelfrey *Art and mass media* (NY, Harper & Row, 1985).

● J Coldeway & others (eds) *European Media Art festival* (Osnabrück, Experimental Film Workshop EV, Film und Medienbüro Niedersachsen, EV, 1988).

● M Heiferman & others *Image world: art and media culture* (NY, Whitney Museum of American Art, 1989).

406 MEGASTRUCTURES (Also Omnibuildings) During the 1960s a number of architects, in response to the daunting urban problems of the age, proposed vast new structures (mega = great) to replace existing cities, on the grounds that large problems required large technological solutions. In the design of Megastructures individual buildings become merely components or lose their separate identity altogether; these designs also attempt to allow for the demand for universal mobility and for rapid change, their overall purpose being to provide a total environment for work and leisure. The best-known architects associated with the concept of Megastructures were Kenzo Tange (Tokyo Bay project), Leonardo Ricci, Paolo Soleri (see Arcology), Yona Friedman, and the British group Archigram. Commonly cited examples of Megastructures were Place Bonaventure, Montreal and Cumbernauld town centre, Scotland. The term 'megastructure' dates from 1964 and is credited to the Japanese architect Fumihiku Maki.

● See also Archigram, Arcology, High-Tech, Kinetic Architecture, Metabolist Group, Mobile Architecture, Pompidou Centre, Utopian Architecture.

● W Karp 'Omnibuilding' *Horizon* **12** (1) Winter 1970 48–55.

● J Burns 'Social and psychological implications of Megastructures' – in – *Arts of the environment* G Kepes (ed) (Aidan Ellis, 1972) 135–51.

● R Banham *Megastructures: urban futures of the recent past* (Thames & Hudson, 1976).

407 MEMPHIS An Italian design group whose post-modernist work was influential and fashionable in the early 1980s. The name 'Memphis' was intended to evoke both ancient Egypt and American rock 'n' roll. Memphis emerged from the radical design aspirations of earlier groups such as Studio Alchimia and the desire of designers to work outside existing firms and institutions. Founded in Milan in 1981, its membership included artists, architects and designers from several countries, the best-known of whom were Ettore Sottsass and Andrea Branzi. Memphis furniture and ceramics were brightly coloured, decorative, made from industrial materials, eccentric in form, frequently humorous and impractical, and inspired by the popular culture and kitsch of earlier decades. Their bizarre, expensive products were intended as an affront to 'good' taste/design and to the anti-ornament functionalism of modern design.

● See also Alchimia, 'Good Design', Kitsch, Italian Craze, Post-Modernism, Radical Design.

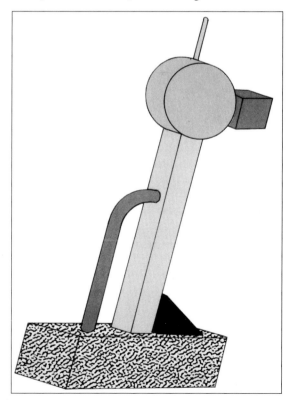

MEMPHIS Ettore Sottsass, 'Tahiti' table lamp (1981). Metal, wood, laminate. Image from *Memphis, Milano, in London* (broadsheet, 1982) designed by STAFFORD CLIFF, Conran Associates. Conran Foundation, London.

● B Radice (ed) *Memphis: the new international style* (Milan, Electa, 1981).

● S Bayley & P Sparke *Memphis in London* (Conran Foundation/Boilerhouse Project, 1982).

● P Sparke *Ettore Sottsass Jnr* (Design Council, 1982).

● B Radice *Memphis* (Thames & Hudson, 1985).

● S Paluch 'Meta-Art' *Journal of Value Inquiry* **5** (4) Winter 1971 276–81.

● A Piper 'In support of Meta-Art' *Artforum* **12** (2) October 1973 78–81.

● J Lipman & R Marshall *Art about Art* (NY, Dutton/Whitney Museum, 1978).

408 **META-ART**

(Also Art-about-Art) The prefix 'meta' (from the Greek meaning 'together with', 'after', 'behind') has been linked with the word 'art' from about 1970. The new term was formed by analogy with 'meta-language' – any language used to discuss another language. The former has also been called 'the observer's language' and the latter 'the object language' (i.e. 'object-of-study language'). These two terms are relational: French can be used to speak about English and vice versa. A meta-language can also be discussed by a third language and so there is the possibility of an infinite hierarchy: language, meta-language, meta-meta-language, etc.

Straightforward examples of Meta-Artworks are those that 'speak about' other works of art; e.g. Roy Lichtenstein's pop paintings which reinterpret paintings by Claude Monet and Pablo Picasso. An exhibition of 'art-about-art' was held at the Whitney Museum of American Art in New York in 1978. More complex examples of Meta-Artworks are those addressing the concept of art in general: Marcel Duchamp's readymades were in part a challenge to existing concepts of art; the works produced by some of the conceptual artists (e.g. Joseph Kosuth, Ian Burn and Mel Ramsden) of the late '60s were also propositions about the nature of art intended to act as both reflections about the concept and extensions of it.

● See also Conceptual Art.

● E Johnson 'Jim Dine and Jasper Johns: Art about Art' *Art & Literature* (6) Autumn 1965 128–40.

META-ART GREG CONSTANTINE, 'Van Gogh's greatest hits' (1986). Mixed-media, 57" x 77" x 9". Photo: O K Harris Gallery, New York.

409 **METABOLIST GROUP**

A Japanese experimental architectural group formed under the direction of Kenzo Tange in 1960. Members included: Norboru Kawazoe, Kisho Kurokawa, Kiyonori Kikutake, Fumihiku Maki and Masato Otaka. The Metabolists envisaged an architecture whose principles were analogous to those of biology, especially those concerning cycles of growth, change and decay. They were concerned with the design of urban systems, services and connections between buildings rather than with individual buildings themselves. Kurokawa designed a plant-like community with living space above ground and production facilities below ground. In a 1960 project for the Tokyo Bay area the Metabolists planned a linear, open system capable of responding to different rates of change. It was based on a theory of metabolic cycles – hence 'metabolic architecture', a term which Kurokawa shortened to 'meta-architecture'.

● See also Biotecture, Collective Form, Contextual Architecture.

● G Nitschke 'The Metabolists of Japan' *Architectural Design* **34** (10) October 1964 509–24.

● K Kurokawa *Metabolism in architecture* (Studio Vista, 1976).

● — & F Chaslin *Kisho Kurokawa: the architecture of symbiosis* (NY, Rizzoli, 1988).

410 **METAVISUAL**

Expression used in the title of an exhibition of abstract paintings held at the Redfern Gallery, London, in April–May 1957. The show was largely the inspiration of Patrick Heron. It included works by Gillian Ayres, Alan Davie, Robyn Denny, Patrick Heron, Roger Hilton, Gwyther Irwin, Ralph Rumney and Bryan Wynter. A gestural style of painting was evident which owed something to American action painting and something to European tachisme. The use of the term 'Metavisual' – meaning 'beyond the visual' – indicated that the artists were 'prepared to divorce their achievements from the observation of objects'.

● See also Action Painting, Tachisme.

● D Sutton (preface) *Metavisual, tachiste, abstract: abstract painting in Britain* (Redfern Gallery, 1957).

411 METRO-LAND

The collective name given in 1915 to certain London suburbs: actual places but with mythical overtones. In the period between the two World Wars parts of Buckinghamshire, Hertfordshire and Middlesex were linked to London by an extension of the Metropolitan electric railway running north-west of the capital from Baker Street station.

Suburbs were built at intervals alongside the track and the railway company advertised their creation as 'Metroland'. In the hamlets along the line are a number of houses of architectural distinction designed by such notable architects as Norman Shaw, Charles Voysey and Amyas Connell. Sir John Betjeman, poet and architectural enthusiast, nostalgic for the pre-war idyll of the British middle class, celebrated Metro-land in his poetry and in a film made for television (BBC, 1973).

● See also Subtopia, Suburban Art, Suburbia.

◦ 'All stations to Amersham: Sir John Betjeman in Metro-land' *Listener* **96** (2472) August 26 1976 240–1.

◦ O Green (introd) *Metro-land* (Harpenden, Herts, Oldcastle Books/London Transport Museum, 1987). Reprint of 1932 edition of *Metro-land*.

412 MINIMAL ART

(Also ABC Art, Anti-illusionism, Art of the Real, Bare Bones Art, Cool Art, Idiot Art, Know Nothing Nihilism, Literalist Art, Minimalism, Nart, Object Art, Primary Structures, Reductive Art, Rejective Art, Zombie Art) A major abstract art movement of the mid and late 1960s, primarily sculptural (or rather three-dimensional), and mainly American. An important exhibition of Minimal Art entitled 'Primary Structures' was held at the Jewish Museum, New York, in 1966. The major artists associated with Minimalism were: Carl Andre, Larry Bell, Ronald Bladen, Walter de Maria, Dan Flavin, Donald Judd, Sol Lewitt, John McCracken, Robert Morris, Richard Serra, Tony Smith, Robert Smithson, and William Turnbull. Apart from Turnbull, all these artists were American. Anthony Caro, another British sculptor, was included in certain Minimalist shows by some curators. The painters Kenneth Noland and Frank Stella were

MINIMAL ART View of Minimalism exhibition, Tate Gallery North, Liverpool, (1989). In the foreground CARL ANDRE's 'Equivalent 8' (1966) & in the background Robert Morris's 'Untitled' (1965/76). Photo: Ged Murray/Tate Gallery, Liverpool.

also Minimalists in the eyes of some critics. The term 'Minimal Art' dated from 1965 and was credited to the philosopher Richard Wollheim, though some writers ascribed it to Barbara Rose. (John Graham, the Russian-American painter and theorist, had used the term 'Minimalism' as early as 1937.) The use of the adjective 'minimal' signified 'minimal means' and 'a minimal aesthetic experience'.

Minimal Art was the culmination of a long process of abstraction, purification and reduction (to essentials) in twentieth-century art. Precedents can be found for it in the work of Malevich, in constructivism, basic design exercises, Barnett Newman's late work, the paintings of Ad Reinhardt and Robert Rauschenberg's monochromatic canvases of 1952. The aim of the Minimalists seemed to be to reduce art to a condition of non-art, to reduce culture to nature. The status of Minimalist objects as art depended almost totally on the artworld context, in particular the art gallery. Outside the gallery Minimalist pieces were often unrecognizable as works of art.

A cube made from steel, wood or mirror glass was the favourite form of the Minimalists because of its geometry, clarity and simplicity, and because there was no part/whole relationship. (Minimalists viewed the latter as the lingering trace of cubism, an anthropomorphic aesthetic they wished to transcend.) The viewer was expected to pay attention to the discrepancy between the perception of the cube and knowledge of its ideal form, and to attend to the literal qualities of the materials from which it was made. Such a work set up a dialogue with the gallery space it occupied: the installation became very important as did the phenomenological aspects of its perception by visitors. The object was intended to have no references to an external reality, no symbolism or figuration, i.e. no illusions or allusions.

The intention was to stress the reality and autonomy of the object as a new entity brought into existence by the decisions of the artist but not in order to express his or her feelings. Minimalist objects were made impersonally with no signs of craftsmanship or sculptural handwork; indeed, in the case of Andre readymade, commonplace materials such as bricks or metal plates were used to build or arrange simple forms; similarly, Flavin purchased readymade neon tubes and used them to mount light installations. Other pieces were fabricated in factories according to specifications supplied by the artists. The emphasis placed on a set of instructions which could be used to generate objects when and if required, was to prove influential in terms of the development of conceptual art.

In the late 1960s and in the '70s Minimal Art provoked much controversy and adverse criticism. In the artworld it was attacked by politically conscious artists and critics

for its lack of human or social content. Also, the look of Minimalism resembled the plain design of modern buildings and office interiors favoured by business and government bureaucracies: banks, multinational corporations, etc. Since it also seemed to mark an end-point of reduction beyond which it was impossible to go, artists felt that another basis for making art had to be found. Meanwhile, the general public and the popular press viewed it as the ultimate con trick of modern art and in the case of the famous furore over Carl Andre's 'bricks' at the Tate Gallery, a blatant waste of public money. However, leading Minimalists such as Richard Serra and Donald Judd continued unabashed and became extremely successful in the art market and the movement itself was accepted by major modern art museums. During the late 1980s several exhibitions of Minimalism took place, and a book by Kenneth Baker was published, which indicated that the movement was undergoing something of a revival.

● See also Anti-Form, Arte Povera, Conceptual Art, Cool Art, Earth & Land Art, Installation, Monochromatic & Monotonal Painting, Object Art, Objecthood, Post-Minimalism, Shaped Canvas.

◉ *Primary Structures: younger American and British sculptors* (NY, Jewish Museum, 1966).

◉ G Battcock (ed) *Minimal Art: a critical anthology* (NY, Dutton, 1968/London, Studio Vista, 1969).

◉ *Minimal Art* (The Hague, Gemeentmuseum, 1968).

◉ 'Aspects of an art called "Minimal"' *Studio International* **177** (910) April 1969 165–89.

◉ *The Art of the Real: an aspect of American painting and sculpture 1948–68* (Tate Gallery, 1969).

◉ W van Ness 'The Minimal era' *Arts in Society* **11** (3) Fall–Winter 1974 436–51.

◉ W Mertens *American Minimal music* (Kahn & Averill, 1983).

◉ *Art Minimal I, II* (Bordeaux, Musée d'Art Contemporain, 1985, '87).

◉ H Foster 'The crux of Minimalism' – in – *Individuals: a selected history of contemporary art 1945–86* H Singerman (ed) (Los Angeles, Museum of Contemporary Art/NY, Abbeville, 1986) 162–83.

◉ K Baker *Minimalism* (NY, Abbeville Press, 1988).

◉ M Craig-Martin (essay) *Minimalism* (Liverpool, Tate Gallery, 1989).

◉ J Watkins *Minimal means* (The Showroom, 1989).

◉ F Colpitt *Minimal Art: the critical perspective* (Ann Arbor, Michigan, University of Michigan Research Press, 1990).

413 | **MINIMALIST DESIGN/STYLE**

A vogue for extremely bare, austere interiors in offices, shops, houses and flats has recurred throughout the period from the 1940s to the 1980s. Colour, decoration and ornament tended to be forbidden and furniture kept to a minimum – possessions were stored away out of sight. In the 1940s the Mexican architect Luis Barragan applied the modernist principle 'less equals more' to interior design. His example was followed, in the late 1950s and early '60s, by the American designers Ward Bennett and Benjamin Baldwin who developed the international style of architecture to an ultimate degree of purity. Nico Zographos also designed offices according to the same aesthetic.

Minimalist architects and designers were inspired by severe examples of modern architecture (e.g. the work of Mies Van Der Rohe and Adolf Loos), but also by the simplicity and purity of medieval monasteries and by traditional Japanese architecture and Zen Buddhist garden design. Contemporary Japanese designers favouring this approach included Toyo Itoh, I. Mitsuhashi and Takao Kawasaki. A Czech émigré designer resident in Britain espousing monochrome and minimalism was Eva Jiricna. The British architectural partners John Pawson and Claudio Silvestrin achieved fame in the '80s for their monastic interiors. An office they designed for Starckmann, Marylebone, London in 1988 was described by Jonathan Glancey as 'an essay in absolute minimalism'.

In the '80s Minimalist Design for homes was a minority taste. It tended to be the wealthy who could afford the stripped-down look and who wanted to hide away their many possessions in cupboards. Such people had a horror of clutter and the overload of images and products typical of a consumer/mass-media society; minimalism offered a contrast: a calm, soothing environment. Shops adopting this style were designed to intimidate and to signify exclusiveness.

● See also Minimal Art.

◉ C Ray Smith 'Minimal interiors' (interview with Benjamin Baldwin) *Progressive Architecture* March 1967 148–55.
◉ M Cooper 'The deceptive simplicity of Eva Jiricna' *Blueprint* (1) October 1983 14–15.
◉ A Tate & C Ray Smith *Interior design in the twentieth century* (NY, Harper & Row, 1986).

414 MOBILE ARCHITECTURE

A concept primarily associated with the Hungarian-French architect and theorist Yona Friedman (b. Budapest 1923, moved to Paris in 1957). In the mid 1950s he perceived a crisis in society and architecture brought about by the static and inflexible nature of cities and buildings, their slowness in responding to rapid social and technological change. His proposal was that the future inhabitants and users of buildings and cities should be much more involved in their planning and in their alteration. Architects would become technicians supplying spatial skeletons or infrastructures (and services) raised above ground (or above existing buildings), which would be capable of being moved, and within which many possibilities would exist for users to move walls, partitions, etc. To assist laypeople Friedman produced several manuals with cartoons explaining how maximum flexibility could be achieved. Friedman's projects tended not to be fully realized but his ideas were influential in the architectural community. Although a theorist and visionary, he nevertheless advocated a scientific inquiry into design, i.e. employing objective, logical and systematic methods. In 1970 he summed up his ideas in a book whose title included the term 'scientific architecture'. Friedman's ultimate aim was to make knowledge concerning the environment available to the poorest people.

● See also Design Methods, GEAM, Kinetic Architecture, Megastructures, Participatory Design, Utopian Architecture.

◉ M Ragon 'Architecture Mobile' *Cimaise* (64) March–June 1963 106–15.
◉ — 'Mobile Architecture: prerequisite for a new urbanism' *Landscape* **13** (3) 1964 20–3.
◉ H Dudar 'Mobile Architecture' *Art in America* **54** (4) July–August 1966 70–87.
◉ Y Friedman *L'Architecture Mobile: vers une cité conçue par ses inhabitants* (Paris & Tournai, Casterman, 1970).
◉ — *Toward a scientific architecture* (Cambridge, Mass, MIT Press, 1975).

415 MODERN ART

A complex notion ignored by most dictionaries of art. In a broad sense it is a chronological concept encompassing all the art produced during the modern era (however that is periodized). Hence some writers prefer the neutral description 'twentieth-century art'. More narrowly, it is an ideological concept referring only to that art of the modern era which self-consciously exemplifies modernity (however that is defined).

No two critics or historians agree on a date for the birth of Modern Art but most locate it in the middle or late nineteenth century (i.e. the realist, impressionist or post-impressionist movements). The question of when or whether Modern Art died is also a contentious issue. Given the immense variety of styles, movements and groups making up Modern Art, it is more sensible to speak of modernisms in the plural than modernism in the singular. It is not possible therefore to sum up all Modern Art in terms of the same checklist of characteristics. Even so, certain features do recur in many of the movements of Modern Art: a break with the past or with academic art;

an experimental approach to form and content, materials, media and techniques; a rejection of ornament; a tendency towards abstraction; a desire to shock or disturb; a body of artists constituting an 'advanced guard', etc.

The intensive use of any adjective in relation to the art of a certain epoch inevitably links that word to that period. 'Modern', for instance, was most closely associated with the radical European art movements appearing between 1910 and 1938. As new generations of artists emerged after 1945, there was a search for a new label to differentiate the young from the old. In the 1950s the word 'contemporary' was tried but it suffered the same fate as 'Modern'. Periodically, critics and curators resort to the feeble label 'the new art/wave' but of course this label is of limited value because newness does not last for very long and the term itself does not indicate what is novel about the new development.

During the 1980s in Britain a university distance-learning course on Modern Art was instituted and several new surveys of Modern Art were published. Since these books coincided with an intense debate on the topic of post-modernism, they could be regarded as the obituary notices of Modern Art.

● See also Avant Garde Art, Contemporary Style, Experimental Art, Late-Modern Architecture, Post-Modernism.

● H Chipp (ed) *Theories of Modern Art: a source book* (Berkeley, University of California Press, 1968).

● R Hughes *The shock of the new* (BBC, 1980; Thames & Hudson, rev ed 1990).

● N Lynton *The story of Modern Art* (Phaidon, 1980).

● P Selz *Art in our times: a pictorial history* (Thames & Hudson, 1982).

● Open University *Modern Art and modernism: Manet to Pollock* (Milton Keynes, Open University Press, 1983), TV and radio programmes, course units, published readers.

● A Boime *Social history of Modern Art* (Chicago, University of Chicago Press, 1987).

● H Arnason *A history of Modern Art* (Thames & Hudson, rev ed 1989), revised and updated by D Wheeler.

● D Britt (ed) *Modern Art: impressionism to post-modernism* (Thames & Hudson, 1989).

● J Russell *The meanings of Modern Art* (Thames & Hudson, rev ed 1989).

● K Varnedoe *A fine disregard: what makes Modern Art modern* (NY, Abrams/London, Thames & Hudson, 1990).

416 **MODERN MOVEMENT** This term is virtually synonymous with 'modern art' but it has tended to be used about architecture and design rather than painting and sculpture. However, R. H. Wilenski's book *The Modern Movement in art*

(1927) did focus on the latter arts. Wilenski situated the origins of the Movement in 1884, i.e. the first exhibition of the Salon des Indépendants, and he identified its salient characteristics as: (1) art in the service of art rather than religion; and (2), a return to classicism. In 1936 Nikolaus Pevsner's *Pioneers of the Modern Movement* appeared (the 1960 revised edition was re-entitled *Pioneers of Modern Design*) and again the origins were located in the nineteenth century. Some scholars plumped for art nouveau as the first modern style because it avoided the eclecticism of Victorian design, while others were certain the Modern Movement was a manifestation of the period between the two World Wars. These writers equated 'modern' with the no-ornament, rational designs of the Bauhaus (Gropius, Mies van der Rohe and others) and with the work of 'heroes' like Le Corbusier. (Alison and Peter Smithson identified a 'heroic period' which lasted from 1915 to 1929.) Modern architecture also came to be known as 'the international style' (because of its claims to universality) and 'rational architecture'.

Charles Jencks' 1973 *Modern Movements in architecture* begins in 1920. Note his use of the plural rather than the singular. Jencks believed that previous histories were distorted by omissions caused by ideological bias, so instead of a single, linear tradition he proposed a series of six traditions running in parallel: logical, idealist, self-conscious, intuitive, activist and unself-conscious.

After 1945 the masters of the 'international style' continued to design fine buildings but the utopian promises of modernism for society as a whole were not fulfilled. And in Britain during the 1960s a proliferation of poorly constructed and brutal tower blocks for housing and for offices caused public disillusionment with modern architecture and its functionalist aesthetic. Committed modernists such as Richard Rogers and Norman Foster worked successfully in the high-tech mode and some of their buildings proved popular (e.g. the Pompidou Centre in Paris), but many other architects sought alternatives in pop, community, neo-Georgian and post-modern architecture. Modern architecture persisted, but lost its dominant position and became only one stylistic possibility among a range of options. In the 1970s a number of texts were published analysing the failures of modern architecture.

● See also Community Architecture, High-Tech, Late-Modern Architecture, New International Style, Pop Architecture, Post-Modern Architecture, Pluralism.

● R Wilenski *The Modern Movement in art* (Faber & Faber, 4th ed 1957).

● N Pevsner *Pioneers of modern design from William Morris to Walter Gropius* (Harmondsworth, Penguin Books, 1960).

● A & P Smithson 'The heroic period of modern architecture'

Architectural Design **35** (12) December 1965 590–639.

● C Jencks *Modern Movements in architecture* (Harmondsworth, Penguin Books, 1973).

● K Rowland *The Modern Movement in art, architecture and design* (NY, Van Nostrand Reinhold, 1973).

● B Brolin *The failure of modern architecture* (NY, Van Nostrand Reinhold, 1976).

● P Blake *Form follows fiasco: why modern architecture hasn't worked* (Boston, Little-Brown, 1977).

● A Drexler (ed) *Transformations in modern architecture* (Secker & Warburg, 1980).

● K Frampton *Modern architecture: a critical history* (Thames & Hudson, 1980).

● T Wolfe *From Bauhaus to our house* (NY, Farrar Strauss & Giroux, 1981).

● B Riseboro *Modern architecture and design: an alternative history* (Cambridge, Mass, MIT Press, 1983).

● M Tafuri & F Dal Co *Modern Architecture* (NY, Rizzoli, 2nd ed 1986).

● P Nuttgens *Understanding modern architecture* (Unwin Hyman, 1988).

● W Curtis *Modern architecture since 1900* (Oxford, Phaidon, 2nd ed 1989).

417 MODERN PAINTERS Title of an art magazine established (in 1988) and edited by the prolific British author, journalist and art critic Peter Fuller (1947–90). The title derived, of course, from the famous nineteenth-century text by John Ruskin. Fuller's aims were to stress the aesthetic and spiritual dimensions of art, to celebrate the achievements of British art, in particular the work of the neo-romantics, plus those belonging to the School of London, and figurative artists with traditional craft skills capable of creating works of high aesthetic quality. Fuller was very critical of avant garde fashions and most forms of official culture, and so he used the pages of his magazine to attack artists like Gilbert & George and Julian Schnabel. In his view great art derived from national and regional roots, not from international tendencies.

Despite his distaste for the mass media and media-based art, during the 1980s Fuller became a media-personality; he was the most strident and controversial of British critics. Previously he had written for magazines like *Seven Days, New Society* and *Art Monthly*. In the beginning his ideas were influenced by Marxism and the work of John Berger; his subsequent changes of mind regarding politics and his rejection of Berger led many on the Left to consider him a publicity-seeking reactionary; he ended by writing for the conservative newspaper *The Daily Telegraph*. His books included studies of the abstract paintings of Robert Natkin,

psychoanalysis and art, and Australian art.

Fuller coined several new terms during the course of his career: 'social functionalism', a disparaging term dating from 1978 intended to characterize Left-wing political art appearing in Britain during the late '70s which purported to serve progressive social purposes; 'kenosis', a theological term applied to the visual arts in 1980 to describe the 'self-emptying' – a process of exclusion, reduction and relinquishing of skills – which Fuller claimed typified the modernist fine art tradition since the late 1880s; 'mega-visual tradition', a phrase intended to describe the new, large-scale visual media (such as advertising) associated with the rise of monopoly capitalism (Fuller saw this development as a profound threat to the survival of the traditional fine arts); 'theoria', a term borrowed from Ruskin. According to the latter, while aesthesis is 'mere animal consciousness of pleasantness', theoria is 'the full comprehension of the Beautiful as the gift of God'. Furthermore, 'impressions of beauty are neither sensual nor intellectual, but moral'.

● See also Figurative Art, Gilbert & George, Neo-Romanticism, Political Art, School of London.

P Fuller 'On social functionalism' *Artscribe* (13) August 1978 43–7.

● —*Art & psychoanalysis* (Writers & Readers, 1980).

● —'Fine art after Modernism' *Beyond the crisis in art* (Writers & Readers, 1980) 44–67.

● T del Renzio 'Instant critic: Peter Fuller in 1980' *Block* (4) 1981 57–60.

● P Fuller *Aesthetics after modernism* (Writers & Readers, 1983).

● —*Images of God: the consolations of lost illusions* (Chatto & Windus, 1985).

● *Modern Painters* **1** (1) Spring 1988 –

● P Fuller *Seeing through Berger* (Claridge Press, 1988).

● —*Theoria: art, and the absence of Grace* ((Chatto, 1988).

● *Modern Painters: a memorial exhibition for Peter Fuller* (Manchester City Art Gallery, 1991).

418 MODERNISM A doctrine, ideology or system of ideas, principles and values subscribed to all those who consider themselves modern artists, architects, designers, musicians and writers. In fact, it is highly unlikely that all these people would share the same set of ideas because their different practices make different demands. Even so, there are certain recurrent or overlapping concerns. Ihab Hassan has identified the following conditions and features as relevant to Modernism: urbanism, technologism, 'dehumanization', primitivism, eroticism, antinomianism and experimentalism. Clement Greenberg, on the other hand, claimed that Modernism was characterized by 'inclu-

IT WAS TOM'S FIRST BRUSH WITH MODERNISM

MODERNISM GLEN BAXTER, 'It was Tom's first brush with modernism'. Copyright drawing taken from *The impending gleam* (Jonathan Cape, 1981), reproduced courtesy of Glen Baxter.

siveness, openness and indeterminateness'. He added: 'Modernism defines itself in the long run not as a "movement", much less a programme, but rather a kind of bias or tropism: towards aesthetic value as such and as an ultimate.' In this way Modernism distinguished itself from popular culture and the mass media.

Other striking characteristics of Modernism were its self-critical and reflexive attitudes: art which reflected upon itself, which advocated the 'honest' use of materials (because of the 'truth to materials' principle), which foregrounded medium, process and technique, which was committed to revolution, innovation and experiment and which put into question all artistic conventions and systems of representation. In so far as Modernism was committed to modernity, it rejected the past and it also rejected contemporary academic art. (Greenberg argued that the break with academic art was in fact a dialectical move designed to 'maintain or restore continuity ...with the highest aesthetic standards of the past'.) The rejection of the past became institutionalized in the sequence of avant garde movements each one of which tried to go beyond the one before. However, once Modernism was established, the demand to rebel against the past became a demand to rebel against Modernism itself; the result was post-modernism.

Most Modernist artists came from the middle class and their principal audience and target was the bourgeoisie. That class was duly shocked by the antics of Modernists but it was bourgeois patronage which supported them and eventually Modernism became the official culture of the ruling élites of the West – witness the founding of the Museum of Modern Art in New York. Before 1939 the word 'Modernism' had pejorative connotations of bourgeois decadence and disintegration for both the Nazis and the Stalinists. For many American conservatives, on the other hand, the word signified 'abstract art made by communists'. 'Modernistic' was often used disparagingly to refer to the dominant design style of the 1920s and '30s, i.e. art deco.

● See also Avant Garde Art, Experimental Art, Formalism & Formalist Criticism, Modern Art, Modernist Painting, MoMA, Post-Modernism.

◉ (Special issue on Modernism and post-modernism) *New Literary History* **3** (1) Autumn 1971.
◉ M Bradbury & J McFarlane (eds) *Modernism 1890–1930* (Harmondsworth, Penguin Books, 1976).
◉ (Special issue on Modernism) *New German Critique* (22) Winter 1981.
◉ F Frascina & C Harrison (eds) *Modern art and Modernism: a critical anthology* (Harper & Row, 1982).
◉ M Berman *All that is solid melts into air: the experience of modernity* (Verso, 1983).
◉ B Buchloh & others (eds) *Modernism and modernity: the Vancouver conference papers* (Halifax, Nova Scotia, Press of the Nova Scotia College of Art & Design, 1983).
◉ S Gablik *Has Modernism failed?* (Thames & Hudson, 1984).
◉ C Harrison & F Orton (eds) *Modernism, criticism, realism* (Harper & Row, 1984).
◉ B Taylor *Modernism, post-modernism, realism: a critical perspective for art* (Winchester School of Art Press, 1987).
◉ S Guilbaut (ed) *Reconstructing Modernism: art in New York, Paris & Montreal 1945–64* (Cambridge, Mass, MIT Press, 1990).

419 MODERNIST PAINTING A theory of the evolution of modern abstract painting developed by the American writer Clement Greenberg, the leading formalist art critic during the period 1943 to '65, and outlined in a famous essay first published in *Arts Yearbook* (4) 1960. Greenberg defined the essence of modernism in painting as 'the use of the characteristic methods of a discipline to criticise the discipline itself...to entrench it more firmly in its area of competence'. He regarded Modernist Painting as the mainstream of art since Manet, painting which openly acknowledged as virtues its physical constraints – flat surface, properties of pigment, shape of support – and which gradually eliminated conventions considered inessential (i.e. those shared with other arts). Although Greenberg claimed that he was simply describing a logical, inevitable historical process, his theory was seen by others as prescriptive and it influenced the practice of a number of leading painters. While Greenberg's theory may have explained the work of some painters, it was useless in respect of movements such as surrealism, neo-dada and pop art. (Movements outside of his narrow category, Greenberg tended to dismiss as 'novelty art'.) A considerable quantity of literature was generated in the 1970s by those seeking to refute Greenberg's ideas.

● See also Formalism & Formalist Criticism.

● R Krauss 'A view of modernism' *Artforum* **11** (1) September 1972 48–51.

● E Carmean 'Modernist art 1960–70' *Studio International* **188** (968) July–August 1974 9–13.

● D Kuspit *Clement Greenberg, art critic* (Madison, Wisconsin, University of Wisconsin Press, 1980).

● C Greenberg *Collected essays* 2 vols (Chicago, University of Chicago Press, 1986).

420 MODULAR ART

Paintings and sculptures based on a module, i.e. a unit of size or measurement repeated throughout the artwork. Architects have used the modular concept for centuries and especially since the development of standardized building components. Le Corbusier devised a scale of proportions he called 'Le Modulor' based on such distances as the height of a man with his arm raised, but architectural writers insist that 'modular' (unit of standardization) should not be confused with 'modulor' (scale of proportion). Furniture designers too have been fond of modules, witness so-called 'unit furniture'.

The explicit use of modules in painting and sculpture only developed in the 1960s, i.e. the severe, abstract paintings of Robert Mangold and Brice Marden and the minimalist sculptures of Carl Andre, Tony Smith and Sol Lewitt. An exhibition of 'Modular Painting' curated by Robert Murdock was held at the Albright-Knox Gallery, Buffalo, in 1970.

● See also Grids, Minimal Art, Serial Art.

● G Kepes (ed) *Module, symmetry, proportion* (Studio Vista, 1966).

● R Murdock *Modular Painting* (Buffalo, New York, Albright-Knox Gallery, 1970).

421 MoMA

Initials standing for 'Museum of Modern Art', New York. MoMA performs a public service but it is nevertheless a private institution controlled by a board of trustees. It was founded in 1929 by wealthy patrons (e.g. the Rockefellers) and its first director was Alfred H. Barr Jr. A building in the international style designed by Edward Durrell Stone and Philip Goodwin was opened in 1939. MoMA is one of the world's most influential cultural institutions noted for its collections of modern art, architecture, design, prints, films, photographs and videos and for its programme of exhibitions and publications. It is regarded by some theorists as the prototypical modern art museum and its arrangement, policies and function have been subject to many analyses and critiques (including an Open University TV programme scripted by Griselda Pollock and Fred Orton).

● See also Modern Art, Modernism.

● A Goodyear *The Museum of Modern Art: the first ten years* (NY, Goodyear, 1943).

● A Drexler *The design collection* (NY, MoMA, 1970).

● R Lynes *Good old Modern: an intimate portrait of the Museum of Modern Art* (NY, Atheneum, 1973).

● J Masheck 'Embalmed objects: design at the Modern' *Artforum* **13** (6) February 1975 49–55.

● C Duncan & A Wallach 'MoMA: ordeal and triumph on 53rd St' *Studio International* **194** (988) January 1978 48–57.

● 'The Museum of Modern Art at fifty' *Art News* **78** (8) October 1979.

● S Hunter *The Museum of Modern Art, New York: the history and the collection* (NY, Abrams, 1988).

● A Goldfarb Marquis *Alfred H Barr Jr: missionary for the Modern* (NY, Contemporary Books, 1989).

422 MoMI

Museum of the Moving Image. A mixed-media museum devoted to the history of motion pictures and television situated on the South Bank of the Thames in London. It was opened in 1988 after a ten-year struggle by Leslie Hardcastle (controller of the British Film Institute, South Bank), David Francis (curator of the National Film and Television Archive) and Anthony Smith (director of the BFI from 1979) to raise the £10m from private sources needed to fund it. MoMI is notable for its populist mode of exposition intended to encourage audience involvement, e.g. there is a reconstruction of a Bolshevik agitprop train with an actor playing the part of a red guard. Neal Potter was in charge of design. An American Museum of the Moving Image in Queens, New York was also opened in 1988.

● A Turner *Museum of the Moving Image* (MoMI/BFI, 1988).

● S Bode 'MoMI dearest' *City Limits* Sept., 1-8 1988 14–15.

● J Wyver *The moving image: an international history of film, television and video* (Oxford, Blackwell, 1989).

423 MONO - HA

A short-lived (1968–70) but influential Japanese movement which had affinities with the Western post-minimalist tendencies arte povera and process art. The name means 'thingism' or 'school of things'. Typical examples included: a 'structure' consisting of a loose assembly of sheets of iron and stones placed on the floor; a hole in the ground plus the cylinder of displaced earth; a heavy stone dropped on a sheet of glass. Mono-Ha's main theoretician was Ufan Lee. Other artists associated with the movement were: Susumu Koshimizu, Katsuhiko Narita, Kishio Suga and Katsuro Yoshida. An exhibition of the work of Mono-Ha was mounted in Tokyo in 1987 and in Rome a year later.

● See also Arte Povera, Post-Minimalism, Process Art.

○ *Mono-Ha* (Tokyo, Seibu Museum of Art, 1987).

○ *Mono-Ha: la scula delle cose* (Rome, Palazzo de Rettorato, Citta Universitaria, 1988).

● E Gomez 'Rome: Mono-Ha' *Art News* **88** (3) March 1989 191.

424 MONOCHROMATIC & MONOTONAL PAINTING

Since 1945 a number of painters have followed Malevich's and Rodchenko's example by producing sets of abstract paintings in a single colour or tone. The artists in question include: Piero Manzoni, Lucio Fontana, Yves Klein, Frank Stella, Robert Rauschenberg, Robert Mangold, Robert Ryman, Ad Reinhardt, William Turnbull, Bob Law and Marcia Hafif. Monochromatic canvases can be regarded as extreme instances of the reductivist aesthetic. Perhaps the most famous series was that generated by Klein in the 1950s for which he devised and patented special pigments: International Klein Blue, Rose and Gold. The German curator Udo Kultermann organized a show of Monochromatic paintings in 1960. As the painter Marcia Hafif explained in 1981, this type of painting has also been called 'pure', 'real', 'concrete', 'absolute', 'painting-painting', and 'aniconic' (i.e. no imagery).

● See also All-Over Painting, Colour-Field Painting, Fundamental Painting, Minimal Art.

○ U Kultermann *Monochrome Malerei: eine neue Konzeption* (Leverkusen, Schloss Morsbroich, 1960).

○ *White on white: the white monochrome in the twentieth century* (Chicago, Museum of Contemporary Art, 1971–2).

● M Hafif 'Getting on with painting' *Art in America* **69** (4) April 1981 132–9.

● C Ratcliff 'Mostly monochrome' *Art in America* **69** (4) April 1981 111–31.

425 MOORES, JOHN

An open exhibition of British painting sponsored by Sir John Moores (reported in 1986 to be 'the richest man in England'), held every two years since 1958 at the Walker Art Gallery, Liverpool. Entries are normally selected by a panel of experts and a number of prizes awarded. Over the years many leading British artists have gained wider public recognition by being awarded prizes at the John Moores which is probably the most prestigious art exhibition to take place outside of London. Winning paintings join the modern collection of the Walker Art Gallery. Catalogues are issued and the shows are reviewed at length in the press.

● M Lothian 'Every egg a bird...' (profile of Sir John Moores) *Guardian* January 25 1986 7.

426 MÜLHEIMER FREIHEIT

(Mulheim Freedom) A group name adopted in 1981 by six German artists who lived in Cologne: Peter Bommels, George Jiri Dokoupil, Gerard Kever, Hans Peter Adamski, Walter Dahn and Gerhard Naschberger. The name derived from the street in which their studio was located. Paintings by these artists were generally placed in the broad category of 'neo-expressionism' but they were also called 'new subjectivism', 'new savages', 'young fauves' and 'freestyle art'. Driven by 'a hunger for pictures' and an 'anything goes' attitude comparable to that of punk, this group produced a tremendous number of crude, aggressive paintings with the conventions and content of painting treated with irreverence and bitter irony.

● See also Neo-Expressionism, Punk.

○ C Oliver 'The second bombing...' *Artscribe* (44) December 1983 22–6.

○ *Mülheimer Freiheit* (London, ICA, 1984).

427 MULTIPLES

An extension of the ancient practice of producing works of art in editions (etchings, cast bronzes, lithographs, etc.). They were objects created by artists that could be repeated – multiplied – in production via a design or matrix. The idea of Multiples was first suggested by the artists Agam and Jean Tinguely to the Parisian dealer Denise René in 1955 but none was issued until 1962. René tried, unsuccessfully, to patent the word 'multiple' for the exclusive use of her stable of artists. Her artists' Multiples were always issued in strictly limited editions though industrial manufacturing techniques, such as vacuum forming, made unlimited editions possible. During the '60s many artists designed Multiples, e.g. Joseph Beuys, Richard Hamilton, Julio Le Parc, Claes Oldenburg, Daniel Spoerri and Joe Tilson. Usually, the Multiples were a minor stylistic version of the artist's painting or sculpture. Many hoped that Multiples would bring about a democratization of art by making it available to a

MULTIPLES RICHARD HAMILTON, 'The critic laughs' (1972). Mixed-media multiple, edition of 60.

mass public at a cheap price through non-art outlets such as supermarkets, but the idea failed because it undermined the ideological and economic basis of the art-world: as commonplace, shop commodities, Multiples would have lost their fine art status as special, exclusive objects. They did have a certain vogue in the late 1960s; what they represented was an extension of the market in prints.

● See also Silk Screen-printing.

◉ 'Multiples supplement' *Art & Artists* **4** (3) June 1969 27–65.
◉ *New Multiple art* (Whitechapel Gallery, 1970).
◉ J Reichardt 'Multiples' *Architectural Design* **41** (2) February 1971 71.
◉ *Multiples: the first decade* (Philadelphia Museum of Art, 1971).
◉ 'Multiples supplement' *Studio International* **184** (947) September 1972 94–108.
◉ J de Sanna 'I Multipli: esistono veramente?' *Domus* (528) November 1973 1–4.
◉ J Schellmann (ed) *Joseph Beuys: Multiples* (catalogue raisonné) (Munich: Edition Schellmann, 6th rev ed 1985).
◉ P Gilmour 'Claes Oldenburg and the Multiple' – in – *Ken Tyler, master printer and the American print renaissance* (NY, Hudson Hills, 1986) 69–76.
◉ *Panamarenko: Multiples* (Amsterdam, Galerie Ronny van der Velde, 1988).
◉ D Ripley 'From candy to kool: the joy of multiple' *Artscribe International* (87) Summer 1991 94–5.

(Also Musée Imaginaire) An expression dating from the 1950s invented by the French writer André Malraux. He argued that in the modern age of printed imagery, reproductions of works of art on cards, in magazines and books constituted a 'musée imaginaire', an imaginary museum, i.e. one without walls. He also maintained that museums conditioned the way we experienced works of art: style became all important because the objects were seen divorced from their original contexts. It followed that the Museum Without Walls extended the process set in motion by the physical museums. It made available to the private individual the art of all times and peoples but at the costs of removing their socio-historical contexts and replacing the originals with substitutes. In 1963 the British sculptor Reg Butler made a work consisting of 39 bronze figures placed in a wooden display cabinet entitled 'Musée Imaginaire'.

◉ A Malraux *The voices of silence* (Secker & Warburg, 1954).

In the twentieth century new, experimental kinds of music have required the development of new forms of musical notation. The latter, called 'Musical Graphics', 'eye music' and 'implicit notation', are drawings or designs whose purpose is to stimulate the musician to produce sounds equivalent in some way to the quality of the visual marks. Composers who have made use of Musical Graphics include Earle Brown, John Cage, Malcolm Carder, Cornelius Cardew, R. Haubenstock-Ramati, Mauricio Kagel and Robert Moran. Some examples of Musical Graphics have been regarded as works of art in their own right and have been exhibited in art galleries.

● See also Sound Art.

◉ E Karkoschka *Notation in new music: a critical guide to interpretation and realisation* (Universal Edition, 1972).
◉ H Cole *Sounds and signs: aspects of musical notation* (Oxford University Press, 1974).

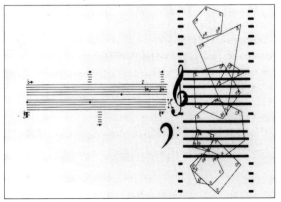

MUSICAL GRAPHICS JOHN CAGE, 'Page 8 of the 63 page "Solo for piano" from *Concert for piano and orchestra* (1957-58). Ink on paper, 11" x 17". Northwestern University Music Libary, John Cage 'Notations' collection. Photo: Anthony D'Offay Gallery, London.

● P Griffiths *Eye Music: the graphic art of new musical notation* (Arts Council of Great Britain, 1986), catalogue of a touring exhibition.

430 **MUTOID WASTE CO**

A British mixed-media group founded in London in 1984 by Robin Cooke, Joe Rush and Joshua Bowler as a creative response to post-industrialism, unemployment and inner city decay. Later the group expanded to include Richie Bond, Ricky Lee, Ivan Tarassenko and others. None of the founders had received a formal art training but this did not stop them making bizarre sculptures, robot costumes, 'skull buses' and 'furniture' from urban junk such as broken machines, cars and motorbikes. They also constructed environments, organized performances, 'road trains' and warehouse parties which attracted audiences of thousands. They encouraged public participation and their activities represented a challenge to museum and gallery art though they did show work at the International Art Fair, Olympia, in 1985 and sell pieces via the Crucial Gallery. It was also featured in magazine articles, TV programmes, music festivals and a lager commercial.

An expression of underground street culture, the Mutoids' work was characterized as 'anarcho-punk art', 'creative salvage', 'scrap-heap or waste art' and 'skip culture'. In terms of style, MWC artefacts recalled the fantastic, nightmarish future depicted in the Australian 'Mad Max' movies. The aesthetic also embodied the influence of rock 'n' roll, Judge Dredd comics, and a post-apocalypse sensibility. For members of MWC life and art were one: they lived in the vehicles they built or customized and, like a band of gypsies, moved around from waste site to waste site. Constant mobility was one key idea of the group; another was the idea of evolving, adapting to survive, hence – mutation, mutoid.

● See also Assemblage Art, Creative Salvage, Customizing & Custom Painting, Junk Culture/Sculpture, Low-Tech, New British Sculpture, Punk.

● D Sharrock 'King's Cross Mutoids reach end of the line' *Guardian* October 28 1988 5.

MUTOID WASTE CO 'Car crash?', Mixed-media installation.London (1987). Photo: Heather Strutt.

431 **MYTHOLOGIES**

Title of an influential collection of essays (French edition 1957) by the French literary and cultural theorist Roland Barthes (1915 –80). His essays provided a semiotic and ideological critique of the myths of daily life in France, especially those of mass culture. During the 1960s the word 'mythologies' began to appear in the discourse of the visual arts, e.g. the exhibition 'Mythologies Quotidiennes' organized by Marie-Claude Dane and others at the Musée d'Art Moderne, Paris, in 1964. Artists featured included Pierre Bettencourt, Dado, Peter Klasen, Jacques Monory, Martial Rayasse, Öyvind Fahlström, Jean-Pierre Raynaud and Peter Saul. Critics employed the terms 'everyday mythologies' and 'individual' or 'personal mythologies' to characterize the work of artists whose subject matter was the myths of modern life (as against the myths of ancient Greece and Rome), or the work of artists like Joseph Beuys who developed a mythology of their own, i.e. a 'private' symbolic system or iconography.

● See also Semiotics.

● R Barthes *Mythologies* (Jonathan Cape, 1972).

● G Gassiot-Talabot 'Everyday mythologies...' – in – *Figurative art since 1945* by J Hodin & others (Thames & Hudson, 1971) 272–302.

● H Szeemann *Individuelle mythologien* (Berlin, GFR, Merve, 1985).

432 N E Thing Co (NETCO)

A satirical, conceptual or post-object art 'group' founded by Iain and Elaine/Ingrid Baxter in Vancouver in 1966 and active in the late '60s and early '70s. 'Anything' was structured like a business with a 'president' – Iain Baxter – and a number of 'departments' – Research, Things, Accounts, ACT (Aesthetically Claimed Thing), ART (Aesthetically Rejected Thing), Photography, Films, Projects, Consultations and COP. The last department was concerned with 'cop art', i.e. the appropriation and use of the work of other artists, e.g. extending one of Kenneth Noland's chevron images by 15 feet. N E Thing was not interested in the production of art objects, but acting as a provider of alternative cultural information.

● See also Conceptual Art, Copy Art, Information, Plagiarists, Post-Object Art.

● *Report on the activities of the N E Thing Co of North Vancouver, British Columbia* (Ottawa, National Gallery of Art, 1969).
● L Lippard *Six years: the dematerialization of the art object from 1966 to 1972* (Studio Vista, 1973).

433 NAIVE ART

(Also Innocent Art, Peintres Naïfs, Primitive Art) A taste for exotic and 'primitive' cultures was a key characteristic of modernism. This taste encompassed the work of talented peintres naïfs who were contemporaneous with the masters of modern art, the most famous example being 'Le Douanier' Rousseau who was known to Picasso. Many, many modern artists have sought to imitate or reproduce the directness and simplicity of Naive Art in their own work; the paintings of L. S. Lowry are a case in point. Recognition of Naive Art beyond a local sphere generally depends upon the appreciation of professional modern artists and critics even though the Naive artists themselves remain ignorant of the theory and practice of modernism while at times influencing it. For instance, in St Ives the paintings of the amateur Alfred Wallis were admired by the artists Ben Nicholson and Christopher Wood and by the critic Adrian Stokes; Wallis influenced Wood but he remained free of influences from contemporary British art.

Naive Art is difficult to define. The term 'primitive' is unsatisfactory because it leads to a confusion with tribal art; the description 'non-professional' meaning 'without a formal art training, not employed full-time as an artist' is inadequate because some Naive artists do make a living from their art; nor is the term 'Laienmalerei' ('layman's painting') adequate because although Naive artists are often elderly men and women who turn to art as a hobby in their retirement, it is necessary to distinguish them from the majority of amateur, Sunday, sparetime or do-it-yourself artists who lack the intense and obsessional character of the true Naive artist. There is clearly an overlap between Naive Art and the categories of l'art brut and outsider art.

The word 'naive' derives from the Latin 'nativus' meaning 'acquired through birth', hence the typical Naive artist is naturally gifted and his/her work has a childlike innocence; it is spontaneous, ingenuous, unaffected. The paradox of the genre is that it is an artless type of art. Naive artists generally favour painting as a medium, they like bright colours and revel in meticulous detail and precise delineations, they play havoc with the rules of perspective, almost invariably treat figurative subjects and paint from their immediate experience or knowledge. Their pictures tend to be small in scale, flat, highly finished and decorative, static and crowded. Naive artists ignore the historical stage of development of their chosen medium; their view of art is uncritical, unreflective, anachronistic and provincial. They address themselves to matters of private import rather than to issues of public concern; they suffer from an excessive narrowness in imagination and are limited in terms of methods and techniques; their art is frequently sentimental and ingratiating in its appeal. Schools of Naive Art have tended to flourish in underdeveloped countries with strong peasant and folk art traditions, e.g. Yugoslavia and Spain. Besides Rousseau and Wallis, well-known Naive artists include: André Bauchant, Camille Bombois, Ivan Generalić, Morris Hirshfield, Grandma Moses, Joseph Pickett, Séraphine de Senlis and Louis Vivin.

Clement Greenberg has argued that Naive Art began with the industrial age: 'Amid the decay of folk art, picture making...provided a new outlet for plebeian "artistic energy'". He claimed that Naive artists belonged to the petit bourgeoisie and that it was 'temperamental and psychic factors rather than social ones' that prevented them from acquiring artistic sophistication. In his view, it was 'bungled realism' that was the hallmark of Naive Art.

● See also Art Brut, Hobby Art, Outsider Art, Peasant Painting, Popular Art.

● C Greenberg '"Primitive" painting' (1942, '58) – in – *Art & culture* (Thames & Hudson, 1973).

● O Bihalji-Merin *Modern primitives* (Thames & Hudson, 1971).

● R Nacenta *Les Naïfs* (Paris, Nouvelles Éditions Françaises, 1973).

● D Larkin *Innocent Art* (Pan/Ballantine, 1974).

● G Gamulin *Les Peintres Naïfs: école de Hlebine* (Paris, Robert Laffont, 1976).

● A Jakovsky *Peintres Naïfs: lexicon of the world's Naive painters* (Basel, Basilus Press, 2nd ed 1976).

● I Niggli (ed) *Naive Art: yesterday and today* (Niederteufen, Niggli, 1976).

● J Vallejo-Nagera *Naïfs Españoles contemporaneos* (Madrid, Mas Actual, 1976).

● E Lister & S Williams *Twentieth century British Naive and Primitive artists* (Astragal/Architectural Press, 1977).

● O Bihalji-Merin & E-B Tomasevic *World encyclopedia of Naive Art: one hundred years of Naive Art* (Bracken Books, 1984).

● J & M Leman *A world of their own: twentieth century British Naive painters* (Pelham Books, 1985).

434 NARRATIVE FIGURATION/PAINTING

Following the 'misuse' of narration by Victorian genre and history painters, it remained out of favour as far as modern artists were concerned until 1963 when a number of painters, mostly European, developed a new form of Narrative Figuration. The French critic Gerald Gassiot-Talabot organized a show of this work at the Galerie Europe in Paris in 1965 to define the new tendency. 1960s' narrative art represented events in time – with or without a storyline – on a single canvas. It blended aspects of pop art with illustration and reflected the influence of films and comic strips. The major artists associated with it were: Öyvind Fahlström, Gianfranco Baruchello, David Powell, Dado, Hervé Telemaque and Bernard Rancillac.

Since the '60s the issue of narration in art has continued to fascinate artists and curators – witness the following exhibitions: 'Narrative painting in Britain in the 20th century' (Camden Arts Centre, 1970); 'Narrative painting' (Bristol, Arnolfini Gallery, 1979); 'Narrative/Humanist painting in Los Angeles in the '70s' (Los Angeles, Art Center College of Design, 1981); 'The image employed: the use of narrative in black art' (Manchester, Cornerhouse, 1987).

Timothy Hyman, a painter and critic inspired by the example of modern figurative artists like Max Beckmann, Edward Hopper and Balthus, organized a show of British Narrative Paintings at Bristol in 1979. The show featured works by Hyman, Michael Andrews, Paul Butler, Jeffrey Camp, Peter de Francia, R. B. Kitaj, Howard Hodgkin, David Hockney, Ken Kiff, Anthony Green, Maggi Hambling, Peter Sylveire and others. Hyman's conception of 'narrative' was somewhat imprecise. He did not mean pictures which told stories in an illustrational or literary sense but which had 'subjects' and which demonstrated 'an imaginative vision of life', i.e. art that was more than a comment on other art. The paintings were not generally painted direct from the motif; they were invented or imagined scenes showing people in situations of social interaction. Some critics doubted that such pictures could count as narratives.

Narration is normally concerned with the actions of human beings, consequently narrative art is generally figurative. However, some critics have argued that the category could also include those abstract paintings that involve successive transformations of an image such as one might find in systemic paintings.

● See also Bande Dessinée, Comic Art, Comix, Equipo Crónica, Figurative Art, Graphic Novels, Humanist Art, New Image Painting, Story Art, Superhumanism, Systemic Painting.

● P Couperie & others *Bande Dessinée et Figuration Narrative* (Paris, Musée des Arts Décoratifs, 1967).

● G Gassiot-Talabot 'Everyday mythologies...' – in– *Figurative art since 1945* (Thames & Hudson, 1971) 272–302.

● T Hyman *Narrative Painting: figurative art of two generations* (Bristol, Arnolfini, 1979).

● —'Narrative Painting 1'; G Volsky 'Narrative Painting 2' *Art Monthly* (30) October 1979 17–21.

● M Rees-Roberts 'Polemic: a note on Narrative Painting' *Art Monthly* (38) July–August 1980 33–4.

● W Gabrielson 'Narrative/Humanist Painting in Los Angeles in the '70s' *Decade: Los Angeles painting in the '70s* by P. Plagens & others (LA, Art Center College of Design, 1981).

● *The image employed: the use of narrative in black art* (Manchester, Cornerhouse, 1987).

● C Jencks 'Narrative classicism' *Art & Design* **3** (9/10) 1987 45–64.

435 NATIONAL ARTISTS ASSOCIATION (NAA)

A British organization founded in Birmingham in 1985 in order to represent and further the interests of visual artists. The NAA is run by working artists and there is no selection procedure for new members. It came into being as a result of a realization that there was no collective voice able to speak for artists to local and national decision-making bodies. Its administrative costs are funded by members' subscriptions and its management committee is democratically elected. Issues of concern to the NAA include: art education, copyright, disabled artists, insurance of artworks, exhibition and resale rights payments, social security, taxation, legal problems, the policies of funding bodies, racism and sexism in the artworld. NAA has organized a series of national conferences and publishes a bi-monthly newsletter. It is clearly similar to the earlier body, the British Artists' Union. The difference between them appears to be that the NAA sees itself as a professional organization rather than a trade union.

● See also Artists' International, Artists' Unions, International Artists' Association.

R Miller 'National Artists Association' *Variant* (Glasgow) (3) Autumn 1987 14.

436

NATIONAL CAMPAIGN FOR THE ARTS (NCA)

A British organization/pressure group founded in 1984 in order 'to mobilise public opinion in support of the arts and to win political recognition of their importance in Britain'. The NCA was prompted by the conviction that the British Government and its agency the Arts Council were cutting back on public funding. NCA's first president was the novelist and TV personality Melvyn Bragg and its first director was Simon Crine.

● See also Arts Councils.

The Arts – a growing concern (NCA, 1985).

437

NATIONAL MUSEUM OF WOMEN IN THE ARTS (NMWA)

An American museum founded in 1981 by Wilhelmina Holladay in response to the lack of representation of women artists in existing museums and galleries. The NMWA opened in May 1987 and the building (a former Masonic temple) is situated in Washington D C. Its aim is to preserve and celebrate women's achievements in the visual arts. It is funded by membership fees, foundation and corporate patronage. It has over 500 works in its permanent collection, and it maintains a library and a schedule of temporary exhibitions. From the outset this gender-based institution aroused controversy and it has been criticized by many writers – both male and female – in terms of its conception, association with the very rich, policies, staffing, and so on.

● See also Feminist Art, Hobby Art, Women Artists Slide Library.

National Museum of Women in the Arts (NY, Abrams, 1987), illustrated guide.

A Higonnet 'Woman's place' *Art in America* **76** (7) July 1988 126–31, +149.

438

NATO

Not the North Atlantic Treaty Organization but a British group of radical architects founded at the Architectural Association in London in July 1983. NATO emerged from the Unit 10 course at the AA taught in the 1970s by the architectural scholar Bernard Tschumi and, later, by Nigel Coates. Its members were: Coates, Mark Prizeman, Catrina Beevor, Martin Benson, Peter Fleissig, Melanie Sainsbury, Carlos Villaneuva and Robert Mull; and the writer who did most to publicize its activities was the architectural critic Brian Hatton. The name 'NATO' stood for 'Narrative Architecture Today'. Narrative did not mean storytelling but incorporating a time dimension and creating fictions (fantastic design scenarios that might happen). The experimental approach of NATO was influenced by the situationists and by such theorists as Robert Venturi and Jean Baudrillard, and by the chaotic, decaying/developing, media-saturated urban environment of London where everything signifies, even the rubbish. NATO attempted to respond positively to the complexities of the

NATO 'Gamma City' Issue of NATO Magazine (3) which doubled as a catalogue for the show held at the AIR Gallery London. (1985).

new post-industrial, post-modern condition. It was as if Archigram had cross-fertilized with punk.

What NATO proposed was not a completely new beginning but a reworking of what already existed – embracing the contrasts and contradictions of modern life with pleasure, combining local primitivism with global high technology. They produced conceptual architecture in the form of energetic, expressionist free-style drawings and publications (for a time they issued a large -format magazine). They also mounted exhibitions such as the 'Gamma City' show at the AIR Gallery, London, in 1985. The shows generally consisted of complex collages of found objects and waste materials because NATO found chaos stimulating, they also appreciated the value of ugliness and the absurdity of the way things were. Other realizations took the form of interiors and set designs for films. There were no NATO buildings as such, but Coates (in partnership with Doug Branson) designed several shops and nightclubs; his work was popular in Japan (e.g. the 1987 Caffe Bongo, Tokyo). The design critic Jonathan Glancey has labelled Coates' architecture as 'industrial baroque'.

● See also Archigram, Post-Modernism, Situationists.

◐ N Coates 'Ghetto and globe' *AA files* **5** 1984 60–8.

◐ B Hatton *Nigel Coates: ARKALBION and six other projects* (Architectural Association, 1984).

◐ 'Gamma City issue' *NATO Magazine* 1985.

◐ B Hatton 'Who is Slyvia? What is NATO?' *ZG* (13) Spring 1985 12–13.

◐ —'Industrial Capriccio' *Artscribe* (56) February–March 1986 50–3.

◐ N Coates 'Street signs' – in – *Design after modernism: beyond the object* J Thackara (ed) (Thames & Hudson, 1988) 95–114.

◐ R Poynor *Nigel Coates: the city in motion* (Fourth Estate/Wordsearch, 1989).

439 **NAZI ART** (Also Total Kultur) Like Nazism itself, Nazi Art has proved to be an embarrassment to those espousing the values of Western civilization. During the 1970s a renewed interest was shown in the visual propaganda and art of the Third Reich. On the one hand there were collectors of Nazi regalia motivated by nostalgia, or by a sympathy for fascism, and on the other hand there were art historians who wished to situate Nazi Art in the general history of art from which it had been excluded on the grounds of its politics and/or low quality. There were also neo-Marxists who wished to display Nazi Art in a critical context in order to forestall its uncritical rehabilitation. The latter group hoped to expose the ideology of fascism, as embodied in Nazi Art, as a way of countering

NAZI ART FRITZ ERLER 'Portrait of the Fuhrer' (1939). Photo: *Kunst im Dritten Reich.*

contemporary revivals of fascism. A major exhibition designed for this purpose – 'Art of the Third Reich: documents of oppression' – toured Germany in 1974–5. As a follow-up, Gustav Metzger organized the AGUN Symposium on Nazi Art in 1976.

Major Nazi artists included: Albert Speer and Ludwig Troost (architects), Fritz Erler, Paul Padua, Werner Peiner, Ivo Saliger, Johannes Schult, and Adolf Ziegler (painters), and Arno Breker and Josef Thorak (sculptors). Realizing the importance of art as a cultural weapon, the Nazi leadership encouraged the above-named artists and suppressed radical and modernist art. Expressionist and abstract art was attacked as 'degenerate, Jewish and Bolshevik' and held up to public ridicule in the infamous 'Degenerate Art' exhibition of 1937 which opened at the same time as the official 'Haus der Deutschen Kunst'. Nazi Art celebrated the 'soul, yearning, and beauty' of the Volk, the heroism of the German soldier, the German land and the peasantry, the near pornographic nakedness of Aryan men and women. Countless portraits served the cult of the Führer, the leader of the master race, Adolf Hitler – a man who was, ironically, a failed artist and frustrated architect. Monumental architectural schemes proclaimed the awesome power and authority of the Nazi state. The dominant style was neo-classicism because the Nazis believed the master race originated with ancient Greece and Rome.

Bess Hormats has pointed out that only a small proportion of the art produced in the 1930s and '40s was Nazi, the majority of German art was academic, conservative. Nevertheless, the conservatives did not oppose Nazism in their art and they benefited from the suppression of modern art. There was also the anomalous case of Emile Nolde, an expressionist painter who was a card-carrying member of the Nazi party. He was one of those forbidden to paint by the regime.

Nazi 'culture' encompassed far more than the traditional fine arts: the design of flags, symbols and uniforms, mass paramilitary street and stadium spectacles, radio broadcasts, films both fictional and documentary, photography, caricature...all means of communication were made subservient to the state and were used to propagate the vile racist doctrines of the Nazi party.

● See also Holocaust Art, Political Art, Prop Art, Totalitarian Art.

● *Die Kunst im Dritten Reich* (1937–44).

● F Roh *'Entartete' Kunst: Kunstbarbarei im Dritten Reich* (Hanover, Fackeltrager, 1962).

● H Brenner *Die Kunstpolitik des Nationalsozialismus* (Hamburg, Rowohlt, 1963).

● J Wulf *Die Bildenden Kunst im Dritten Reich: eine Dokumentation* (Gutersloh, Sigbert Mohn Verlag, 1963).

● G Mosse (ed) *Nazi culture* (W H Allen, 1966).

● A Speer *Inside the Third Reich* (Weidenfeld & Nicolson, 1970).

● *Art in the Third Reich* (Frankfurt, Kunstverein, 1974).

● R Taylor *The world in stone: the role of architecture in the National Socialist ideology* (Berkeley, University of California Press, 1974).

● M Hoelterhoff 'Art of the Third Reich...' *Artforum* **14** (4) December 1975 55–62.

● G Metzger 'Art in Germany under National Socialism' *Studio International* **191** (980) March–April 1976 110–11.

● B Hormats 'Whatever happened to the German war art collection?' *Art Monthly* (2) November 1976 6–9.

● B Phillips *Swastika: cinema of oppression* (Lorrimer, 1976).

● J Heskett 'Modernism and archaism in design in the Third Reich' *Block* (3) 1980 13–24.

● B Hinz *Art in the Third Reich* (Oxford, Blackwell, 1980).

● H Grosshans *Hitler and the artists* (NY, Holmes & Meir, 1983).

● S Sontag 'Fascinating fascism' – in – *Under the sign of Saturn* (Writers & Readers, 1983).

● J Walker 'Total Kultur: Nazi Art and media' *AND Journal of Art & Art Education* (9) 1986 3–11.

● T Smith 'A state of seeing' *Block* (12) 1986–7 50–70.

● B Taylor & W van der Will (eds) *The Nazification of art: art, design, music, architecture and film in the Third Reich* (Winchester, Hants, Winchester Press, 1990).

440 NEGRITUDE

Originally, the name of a literary movement associated with two African poets Léopold Senghor and Aimé Césaire who had links with the surrealists in Paris. Black artists and intellectuals living in Europe in the 1930s discovered that the Western habits and knowledge they had acquired did not prevent them from suffering from racism and discrimination. In reaction they turned to their African roots in search of an alternative culture based on blackness. Negritude has been called 'hybrid' because it involved both Western and African cultures, e.g. the poets continued to write in French and to be modernists. The term has also been applied to the work of the Cuban surrealist painter Wilfredo Lam and the French designer Jean-Paul Goude.

● See also Black Art, Hybrid Culture.

● J-P Goude *Jungle fever* H Hayes (ed) (Quartet Books, 1982).

● T Colless & P Foss 'Demolition man' *Art & Text* (10) Winter 1983 37–46.

● R Linsley 'Wilfredo Lam: painter of Negritude' *Art History* **11** (4) December 1988 527–44.

441 NEO-DADA

Dada was a highly critical, iconoclastic and anti-art phenomenon first manifested in Zürich during the First World War. 'Neo-' or 'New Dada' is, therefore, a term designating subsequent developments perceived as having some affinity with the original movement. In fact, as the examples cited below indicate, it is a term which has been used about several different kinds of art.

The label 'Neo-Dada' was applied by *Art News* in January 1958 to the work of Jasper Johns. It was later extended to encompass the art of Robert Rauschenberg. Johns painted with Duchampian irony banal, 'ready-made' images – targets, flags, maps and numbers – filling the whole surface of the canvas, thus raising a question in the spectator's mind as to the ontological status of the object displayed. Rauschenberg incorporated industrial refuse and mass-media images into his 'combine paintings' in a manner which reminded some critics of Kurt Schwitters' *merz* collages. Because Johns and Rauschenberg drew upon popular imagery, their work was later seen as heralding the arrival of pop art; hence it was also called 'proto-pop'. In certain respects Neo-Dada was an inappropriate term because the two Americans did not share the political intentions of the original Dadaists. Indeed, in a later article about the politics of the art of the 1950s, the critic Moira Roth identified an 'aesthetic of indifference'.

In Europe the equivalent to Neo-Dada was the movement called 'nouveau réalisme', orchestrated by the critic Pierre Restany. The work of this group of artists was also categorized as 'Neo-Dada' but in this instance there was more justification because one exhibition of the group held in Paris in 1961 was entitled 40 degrees above Dada'.

In Japan a group of artists active between 1958 and '63 called themselves the 'Neo-Dada Organizers'. Members included: Shusaku Arakawa, Genpei Akasegawa, Tomio Miki and Shijiro Okamoto. The work of this group had close affinities with Western destructive art and junk sculpture.

In London in the 1970s James Holiday devised a 'hoax bureaucracy' (named the 'New Dada Agency') for the purpose of 'assassinating art'. Holiday's anti-art activities were manifested in the occasional publication *The Agent*.

The term 'Dada' was revived yet again in the 1980s in the title of a Washington show featuring critical works by artists like Chris Burden, Lyn Foulkes and Hans Haacke.
● See also Anti-Art, Combine Paintings, Destructive Art, Junk Culture/ Sculpture, Nouveau Realisme, Pop Art.

● P Restany *À 40° au-dessus de Dada* (Paris, Galerie J, 1961).

● L Steinberg *Jasper Johns* (Milan, Editoriale Metro, 1963).

● M Roth 'The aesthetic of indifference' *Artforum* **16** (3) November 1977 46–53.

● J Newland (ed) *No! Contemporary American Dada* 2 vols (Washington, Henry Art Gallery, 1985).

NEO-EXPRESSIONISM Rainer Fetting, 'Van Gogh and wall' (1978). Powder paint on cotton, 195 x 200 cm. Photo: Anthony d'Offay Gallery, London.

442 NEO-EXPRESSIONISM
(Also Energism, Il Nuove Nuove, Naive Nouveau, New Fauves, New Wave, Violent, Wild or Vehement Painting) During the late 1970s and early '80s painting in the West, and to a lesser extent sculpture, was dominated by a new stylistic tendency called 'Neo-Expressionism' because it appeared to owe a debt to the German expressionist movement of the early twentieth century. It was an unsatisfactory label because much of the new work was not expressionist in appearance or intention. After the media pluralism of the '70s, Neo-Expressionism signalled a 'return' to the more traditional artforms of painting and sculpture. It was therefore welcomed by art dealers, curators and collectors. While much of the art of the '70s had been politically motivated, Neo-Expressionism on the other hand emphasized the imagination and personal, subjective experience; many of the artists involved adopted an apolitical or post-political attitude; as a result their work was judged by Left-wing critics as reactionary both artistically and politically.

Typically, the Neo-Expressionist work was large, figurative, fragmentary and crudely, rapidly executed. Paintings often had embedded in their surfaces peculiar objects or materials, e.g. straw, broken plates, antlers, etc. There was a desire to shock viewers and to overwhelm them by sheer size and aggression. Although the works were figurative, they contained such a mish-mash of images, quotations and narratives that coherent stories or statements were hard to discern. Certain images were, indeed, painted and exhibited upside-down (Baselitz). In some respects Neo-Expressionism exemplified postmodernist characteristics – historicism, eclecticism, non-utopianism, etc. – in other respects it reproduced modernist tactics (e.g. novelty, shock-value, making strange, primitivism). While supposedly transcending the concept of the avant garde, it nevertheless turned out to be 'the next big thing'.

Neo-Expressionism had many supporters and advocates in the artworld but its critical reception was very mixed. Much of the work seemed deliberately bad, i.e. conventional notions of skill and quality were ignored. This resulted in several critical attacks evaluating the work as 'inauthentic', 'ersatz expressionism', 'fashionable trash'. Donald Kuspit, the American art critic, was one writer who provided thoughtful and ingenious defences of the German branch of Neo-Expressionism.

Paradoxically, the tendency was at once national and international, i.e. it was an international phenomenon with nationalistic inflections. Three countries contributed most: Germany, Italy and the United States. German artists included: Georg Baselitz, Walter Dahn, Georg Jiri Dokoupil, Rainer Fetting, Jörg Immendorff, Anselm Kiefer, Markus Lupertz, A. R. Penck, Salomé, and Bernd Zimmer. Italians included: Sandro Chia, Francesco Clemente, Enzo Cucchi, Nino Longobardi and Mimmo Paladino. Americans included: Robert Kushner, Susan Rothenberg, David Salle and Julian Schnabel. This list indicates the masculine bias of Neo-Expressionism. Two major exhibitions at the beginning of the decade signalled the canonization of the tendency: 'The new spirit of painting' (London, Royal Academy, 1981) and 'Zeitgeist' (West Berlin, 1982). A further seal of approval was the large sum of money spent by the Saatchis acquiring works for their collection.

● See also 'Bad' Painting, Mülheimer Freiheit, New Image Painting, Post-Modernism, Saatchi Collection, Trans-Avant Garde, Zeitgeist.

● E Busche 'Violent painting...' *Flash Art* (101) January–February 1981 27–31.

● W Faust '"Du hast keine chance. Nutze sie!" With it and against it: tendencies in recent German art' *Artforum* **20** (1) September 1981 33–9.

● D Kuspit 'The new(?) expressionism: art as damaged goods' *Artforum* **20** (3) November 1981 47–76.

● *A new spirit in painting* (Royal Academy, 1981).

● J Walker 'Julian Schnabel at the Tate' *Aspects* (20) Autumn 1982 4–5.

● W Faust & Gerd de Vries *Hunger nach Bildern: Deutsche Malerei der Geganwart* (Cologne, Dumont, 1982).

● *Expressions: new art from Germany* (St Louis, Art Museum, 1983).

● T Godfrey *The new image: painting in the 1980s* (Oxford, Phaidon, 1986).

443 NEO-GEO

(Also Fakism, Neo-Conceptualism, Neo-Futurism, Neo-Minimalism, Neo-Op, Neo-Pop, New Abstraction, Poptometry, Post-Abstraction, Simulationism, Smart Art) 'Neo-Geo' is short for 'Neo-Geometric'. The label originally referred to a group of young American abstract painters using hard edges and flat, dayglo colours; it was then extended to include certain sculptors. The artists concerned exhibited in New York's East Village in the mid 1980s: Ashley Bickerton, Ross Bleckner, Robert Gober, Peter Halley, Jeff Koons, Tim Rollins and KOS,

NEO-GEO ASHLEY BICKERTON, 'Le Art' (1987) Silkscreen, acrylic and bronze powder, laquer, anodied aluminum, 34" x 72" x 15". Photo: Saatchi Collection, London.

Heim Steinbach, Philip Taaffe and Meyer Vaisman. The interest of the collector Michael Schwartz and the bulk-buying of the Saatchis ensured the fashionability of Neo-Geo. As the several alternative labels suggest, the work of these artists derived from a variety of earlier art movements. Koons revamped the readymades of dada by presenting consumer products such as vacuum cleaners as art and by exhibiting stainless steel replicas of kitsch objects; Taaffe supplied a rehash of optical art and parodies of Barnett Newman's abstract paintings; Bickerton recalled pop art by fabricating aluminium wall constructions ('wall sculptures') displaying a range of corporate logos; Halley simulated hard-edge abstraction by painting diagrams of prison cells and computer circuits; Steinbach built shelving from formica and placed objects such as baskets and footballs upon them to generate kitsch-like still lives.

For the most part the art was intellectual, calculated, impersonal and 'cool', hence it formed a complete contrast to the melodrama of the preceding dominant tendency, neo-expressionism. Neo-Geo artists were also aware of the critique of the art market, commodities and the consumer society which had been current since the mid 1970s; consequently their art included ironic (and some claimed critical) comments on these issues. A cynicism (or realism) pervaded the work in the sense that none of the artists believed in the transcendental power of art or in a political art capable of changing society; as a result they were accused of being 'complicit with capitalism' ('complicity' became a fashionable word). Several art critics dismissed Neo-Geo artists as careerists and opportunists ('artists of the next 15 fifteen minutes') and Donald Kuspit, judging that the art lacked any moral or spiritual substance, declared it 'dead on arrival'.

● See also Business Art, KOS, Media Art, New Futurism, Political Art, Simulation/Simulacra/Hyperreality.

● E Heartney 'Neo-Geo storms New York' *New Art Examiner* **14** (1) September 1986 26–9.

● — 'Simulationism: the hot new cool art' *Art News* **86** January 1987 130–7.

● P Taylor 'My heart belongs to Dada' *Observer Magazine* September 6 1987 36–8.

● C Hart 'Intuitive sensibility: Meyer Vaisman & Peter Halley interviewed' *Artscribe International* (66) November–December 1987 36–9.

● *Art & its double: a New York perspective* (Madrid, Sale de Exposiciónes de la Fundación Caja de Pensiónes, 1987).

● D Cameron *NY art now: the Saatchi collection* (Milan, Giancarlo Politi, 1987).

● G Oosterhof *Horn of plenty: 17 artists from New York* (Amsterdam, Stedelijk Museum, 1989).

444 NEO-LIBERTY

During the 1950s there occurred a revival of interest in the art nouveau style, especially in Italy. Architects such as M. D. Bardeschi, Vittorio Gregotti, Raffaello Lelli and Leonardo Savioli came under its influence, as did the furniture designer Gae Aulenti. Their work was described as 'sensuous, decorative, with flowing lines and flower-like profiling'. Reyner Banham criticized it as 'infantile regression', a retreat from the ideals of the modern movement. The term 'Neo-Liberty' was first used by Paolo Portoghesi in 1958. It derived from 'stile Liberty', the Italian name for art nouveau, after the British firm of Liberty's which had supplied art nouveau style goods to Italy.

● See also Historicism, Modern Movement.

● R Banham 'Neo-Liberty: the Italian retreat from modern architecture' *Architectural Review* **125** (747) April 1959 231–5.

● — 'Neo-Liberty: the debate' *Architectural Review* **126** (754) December 1959 341–4.

● T del Renzio 'Neo-Liberty' *Architectural Design* **30** (9) September 1960 375–6.

445 NEO-PICTURESQUE

In Britain during the mid 1940s a revival of interest in the picturesque developed among architects and writers associated with the journal *Architectural Review*. As a result of the wartime bombing, Britain's towns had many ruins and in accordance with the picturesque taste for crumbling remains, architects were encouraged to retain some of them. For instance, Basil Spence retained the bombed-out shell of the old Coventry Cathedral as part of his design for a new complex including a brand new cathedral.

● See also Coventry Cathedral, Neo-Romanticism.

446 NEO-ROMANTICISM

(Also Neo-Romantic Painting) A dominant strand within British art that developed during the mid 1930s and continued up until the early 1950s. In terms of content, Neo-Romanticism was concerned with the human body, the land of Britain, and a spiritual quest: 'the body and sexuality; nostalgia and anxiety; myth making; organic fantasies; the threat of war and extinction' (David Mellor). It owed something to the native romantic, visionary, landscape painting tradition (e.g. Samuel Palmer) and something to surrealism. (Neo-Romanticism's relationship to modern art was problematical; some critics viewed it as anti-modernist kitsch, a reactionary, provincial movement.) Images produced tended to be highly emotional and theatrical. Some critics regarded them as literary and illustrational (indeed many were created to illustrate books). The artists – mostly painters and water-colourists – associated with the movement included: John Piper, Henry Moore, Paul Nash, Graham Sutherland, Cecil Collins, John Craxton, David Jones, John Minton, Michael Ayrton, Robert Colquhoun and Keith Vaughan. The film director Michael Powell was also dubbed a Neo-Romantic. The artists listed above never belonged to an identifiable group but were seen as similar in their themes and style; the term itself was coined by the critic Raymond Mortimer and later used by Robert Ironside in a 1946 British Council brochure. After decades of neglect, Neo-Romantic art became fashionable again amongst dealers and art historians in the 1980s – witness the major exhibition held at the Barbican Art Gallery in 1987.

● R Ironside 'Painting since 1939' – in – *Since 1939* (Phoenix House, 1948) 147–81.

● *The British Neo-Romantics 1939–45* (Cardiff, National Museum of Wales, 1983).

● D Mellor (ed) *A paradise lost: the Neo-Romantic imagination in Britain 1935–55* (Lund Humphries/Barbican Art Gallery, 1987).

● M Yorke *The spirit of place: nine Neo-Romantic artists* (Constable, 1988).

447 NEO-VERNACULAR

(Also called Realism & New Realism in Europe; Shed Aesthetic & Neo-Shingle Style in the United States) A term employed by Charles Jencks in the 1980s to name an anti-modernist tendency in architectural design of the '70s and '80s which, he claims, began in the '50s. British architects such as Andrew Derbyshire, Jeremy Dixon, and Darbourne & Darke, and American architects such as Edward Larabee Barnes designed brick-and-shingle housing with pitched roofs and traditional urban details. Neo-Vernacular, Jencks maintained, was the sign of an 'instant community'. A major British example of the Neo-Vernacular style applied to a public building was the Civic Offices at Hillingdon, Uxbridge (1973–8) designed by Robert Matthew, Johnson-Marshall & Partners. Because of its bulk, Jonathan Glancey has described this building as 'monumental vernacular'. According to the *Architectural Review,* buildings which adopt a vernacular vocabulary but retain the functional plan ideal of modernism may be termed 'romantic pragmatism'. An example of this style was the Sainsbury Building, Worcester College, Oxford (1983) designed by MacCormac, Jamieson, Pritchard & Wright.

American vernacular architecture of the 1980s has also been described as 'unvernacular' and 'consumerist' by

NEO-VERNACULAR DARBOURNE & DARKE, Lillington Gardens Estate, Lillington St, London SW1 (1961-71). Photo: Roderick Coyne.

John Chase. In respect of contemporary motels, shopping malls and so on, Chase observed: 'What distinguishes contemporary consumerist architecture from earlier forms is that it is consciously conceived of as imagery, as a form of environmental psychology based on marketing.'

● See also Pop Architecture.

● J Chase 'Unvernacular vernacular: contemporary American consumerist architecture' *Design Quarterly* (131) 1986, thematic issue.

● C Jencks *Architecture today* (Academy Editions, 1988) 150–7.

448 NEOISM

(Also Neoist Cultural Conspiracy)A term used by Monty Cantsin and others. Cantsin was previously Istvan Kantor, b. Budapest 1949. He moved to Montreal in 1977 after meeting David Zack, the founder of a mail art information network in the early '70s. Neoism refers to art and anti-art activities – graffiti, video installations, rituals and musical performances, screenings – taking place in Montreal in 1979. A magazine called *The Neo* was also published in Montreal from '79 to '80. An international network of Neoists was established which attracted people influenced by the punk movement. Dada/Fluxus-type events and apartment festivals later took place in Baltimore, Berlin, Wurzburg and Ponte Nossa (Italy) featuring work by Cantsin and Pete Horobin. The term 'Neoism' appears to signal an unprecedented identification with the idea of newness or novelty associated with avant garde art. Cantsin observed that at first Neoism was so new it didn't have a definition, then it acquired thousands; the best one, he says, 'is always the next one'.

NEOISM MONTY CANTSIN, Various graphics and stickers (1990). Supplied by the artist.

● See also Anti-Art, Avant Garde Art, Fluxus, Graffiti, Mail Art, Performance Art, Punk.

◦ P Horobin & P Below *The Neoist network's first European training camp* (Wurzburg, West Germany, Kryptic Press, 1982).

◦ *The 9th Neoist festival* (Ponte Nossa, Italy, Arte Studio, 1985).

◦ M Cantsin (ed) *Neoism now* (Berlin, Artcore Editions, 1987).

◦ S Home *The assault on culture: utopian currents from lettrisme to class war* (Aporia Press & Unpopular Books, 1988).

◦ P Scott 'Neoism' – in – *Rapid Eye 1* S Dwyer (ed) (Brighton, R E Publishing Ltd, 1989) 48–51.

449 NEW ART HISTORY

During the 1970s and '80s the intellectual discipline of art history was changed radically in Europe and the United States through the contributions of a younger generation of scholars who were influenced by such external systems of thought and method as Marxism, anthropology, social history, feminism, linguistics, psychoanalysis, Russian formalism, semiotics, structuralism, reception theory and deconstruction. These contributions appeared in such journals as *Block, Screen* and *Art History*. In Britain the expression 'New Art History' was originally used jokingly but it was soon taken seriously by publishers.

● See also Association of Art Historians, Deconstruction, Design History Society, Marxist Aesthetics, Reception Theory/Aesthetics, Semiotics, Structuralism & Art/Design.

◦ A Rees & F Borzello (eds) *The New Art History* (Camden Press, 1987).

◦ N Bryson (ed) *Calligram: essays in New Art History from France* (Cambridge University Press, 1988).

◦ S Bann (ed) 'The New Art History' *History of the Human Sciences* **2** (1) February 1989.

◦ D Preziosi *Rethinking art history: meditations on a coy science* (New Haven/London, Yale University Press, 1989).

450 NEW BRITISH SCULPTURE

(Also Bricolage Sculpture) A somewhat uninformative term used to categorize the work of such sculptors as Edward Allington, Kate Blacker, Tony Cragg, Anish Kapoor, David Mach, Julian Opie, Jean-Luc Vilmouth (French, resident in London) and Bill Woodrow. Their work was exhibited internationally during the early 1980s and achieved an unexpected degree of success that was at once critical, popular and commercial. Although the art of these sculptors was stylistically diverse, there were certain characteristics that tended to recur, namely a

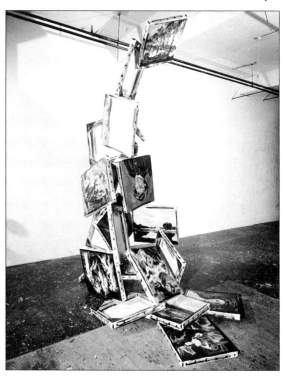

NEW BRITISH SCULPTURE JULIAN OPIE, 'Tate Collection' (1985). Oil paint on steel, 9' x 6' x 5'. Photo: Lisson Gallery, London.

bricolage approach related to the decaying urban environment in Britain and the waste generated by the consumer society (pieces constructed from discarded consumer products, playful transformations and combinations of such objects); an interest in content as much as form with objects being treated as signs as well as things; imagery (broken fragments assembled in the shape of the British Isles, for example); a dispersed Gestalt; a synthesis of pop and kitsch elements with more purely sculptural concerns; colour (the use of pigments on cement or metal); wit and humour; an association with the Lisson Gallery, London. This kind of work was analysed and praised by such critics as John Roberts and Michael Newman, was the subject of a film/TV arts programme, and was shown at the 1982 Venice Biennale and at the 1983 São Paulo Bienal in 1983.

● See also Adhocism, Assemblage Art, Creative Salvage, Junk Culture/Sculpture, Mutoid Waste Co.

◉ *Objects and sculpture* (London, ICA, 1981).
◉ J Roberts 'Urban renewal' *Parachute* (30) March 1983.
◉ M Vaizey 'Taking art off the streets' *Sunday Times Magazine* 14 August 1983 46–9.
◉ *Transformations: new sculpture in Britain* (São Paulo Bienal, British Council, 1983).
◉ M Newman 'Discourse and desire: recent British sculpture' *Flash Art* (110) January–February 1984 48–55.
◉ T Ness (ed) *A quiet revolution: British sculpture since 1965* (Thames & Hudson, 1987).

451 NEW BRUTALISM

A tendency in British architecture primarily associated with Alison and Peter Smithson – especially their work during the period 1953-5 – and the critical writings of Reyner Banham. New Brutalism was not so much a style as 'a programme or an attitude to architecture' or, as the Smithsons put it, 'an ethic, not an aesthetic'. Above all, the New Brutalists waged a moral crusade against the diluted versions of modern architecture produced in England in the post-1945 period, and against the compromises they felt even the masters of the modern movement were making. The Smithsons set out to re-establish the original strength and integrity of modern architecture, in buildings like the Hunstanton secondary school, by expressing structure and services honestly, and by using materials truthfully, sensuously in the manner of Le Corbusier, Mies van der Rohe and Japanese architecture.

The term 'New Brutalism' derived from 'Neo-Brutalist' coined by the Swedish architect Hans Asplund. It had connotations of 'béton brut': Le Corbusier's rough, tex-

NEW BRUTALISM London County Council/Greater London Council, Architects Dept., Sir Hubert Bennett & Jack Whittle. Detail of Hayward Gallery, South Bank Arts Centre, London (1964-8). Photo: Roderick Coyne.

tured building surfaces – concrete imprinted with the grain of the wooden shuttering. In London this kind of architecture was exemplified by two buildings made from grey concrete, the Hayward Gallery and the National Theatre, which are part of the South Bank arts complex. The style may have been popular with radical architects, but as far as the public was concerned this particular variety of New Brutalism was simply brutal. The term 'New Brutalism' was not limited to architecture: it also encompassed the art brut of Jean Dubuffet, the paintings of Magda Cordell and the sculptures of Eduardo Paolozzi.

● See also Art Brut, Modern Movement.

● R Banham 'Brutalism' – in – *Encyclopedia of modern architecture* G Hatje (ed) (Thames & Hudson, 1963) 61–4.

● — *The New Brutalism: ethic or aesthetic?* (Architectural Press, 1966).

● R Boyd 'The sad end of New Brutalism' *Architectural Review* **142** (845) July 1967 9–11.

452 NEW CLASSICISM Since the classical style's origins in ancient Greece and Rome, it has been revived many times. In order to distinguish later revivals from the original, the terms 'new/neo-classicism', 'neo-neo-classicism', 'modern classicism' and 'post-modern classicism' have been devised. The advent of the era of post-modernism gave architects permission to raid the past; consequently during the 1980s classical devices – Corinthian columns, porticos and pediments – were deployed by such post-modern architects as Philip Johnson, Michael Graves, James Stirling, Charles Moore, Terry Farrell, Ricardo Bofill and John Outram. Two highly traditional British architects – Raymond Erith and Quinlan Terry – were convinced classicists long before the '80s fad. From their

NEW CLASSICISM QUINLAN TERRY Whittaker House, Richmond Riverside Development, London (1983-88). Photo: Roderick Coyne.

perspective, post-modern classicism was a form of packaging applied to the surfaces of buildings that were modern underneath.

Classicizing tendencies were also evident during the '80s in the arts of painting and sculpture – witness the vogues for arcadian and cultured painting and the ironic monuments of Ian Hamilton Finlay (a sculptor who parodied the neo-classical buildings of Nazi architects like Albert Speer).

Charles Jencks, in a 1988 book about post-modernism, appeared to equate it with the New Classicism. Jencks, an obsessive classifier, identified numerous sub-varieties of modern classicism: free style, metaphysical, narrative, allegorical, realist, classical sensibility, fundamentalist, revivalist, urbanist and eclectic!

● See also Arcadian Painting, Cultured Painting, Nazi Art, Post-Modern Architecture.

● H Searing & H Reed *Speaking a New Classicism: American architecture now* (Northampton, Mass, Smith College Museum of Art, 1981).

● C Jencks *Post-Modern Classicism* (Academy Editions, 1980).

● — (ed) *Free Style Classicism* (Academy Editions, 1982).

● D Kuspit & others *Neo-Neo-Classicism: the uses of tradition in the late twentieth century* (Annadale on Hudson, Bard College, Edith C Blum Art Institute, 1986).

● 'The Classical sensibility in contemporary painting and sculpture' *Art & Design* **4** (5/6) 1988.

● C Jencks *Post-Modernism: the New Classicism in art and architecture* (Academy Editions, 1988).

● 'The New Classicism in architecture and urbanism' *Architectural Design* **58** (1/2) 1988.

● R Stern *Modern Classicism* (Thames & Hudson, 1988).

● A Papadakis & H Watson *New Classicism, omnibus volume* (Academy Editions, 1990).

453 NEW CONTEMPORARIES (Previously Young Contemporaries) Annual exhibitions of work by British fine art students generally organized by committees of students. A panel of artists often assisted in the selection process. The first Young Contemporaries took place in 1949 at the Royal Society of British Artists (the RBA galleries) in London. The exhibitions rapidly established themselves as showcases for new talent. The shows of 1961 and '62 were particularly notable for the appearance of pop art pictures by Derek Boshier, Allen Jones, R. B. Kitaj, David Hockney and Peter Phillips (all students at the Royal College of Art). Periodically the exhibition failed to take place because of lack of energy, funds or organization. In 1974 the name 'New Contemporaries' was adopted. Catalogues are usually produced and the one listed below contains a history of the exhibition.

● See also Art Schools, Pop Art.

◗ Z Mathews & A Lambirth *New Contemporaries 1986: recent work from Britain's art schools* (London, ICA/Newcastle upon Tyne, Hatton Gallery/Liverpool, Bluecoat & Hanover Galleries, 1986).

454 NEW EMPIRICISM (Also New Humanism) A term applied by British writers to the new Swedish architecture – houses, town halls, hotels, sports facilities, etc. – designed in the mid 1940s by such architects as Ralph Erskine (British-born, resident in Sweden since 1939), Sture Frölen, Sune Lindström, Sven Markelius, Kjell Odeen and Gunnar Wejke. Their work was also described as 'gentle and self-effacing', 'new humanism', 'pragmatic' and 'welfare state architecture'.

● See also Scandinavian Style.

◗ 'The New Empiricism: Sweden's latest style' *Architectural Review* **101** (606) June 1947 199–204.

◗ E de Mar & others 'The New Empiricism' *Architectural Review* **103** (613) January 1948 8–22.

455 NEW FUTURISM (Also Neo-Futurism, Nuovo Futurismo) A label applied in the mid 1980s to the work of several Italian artists who resided in Milan and who exhibited at the Galleria Luciano Inga-Pin and at the Studio Pelligrino in Bologna. The artists were: Gianantonio Abate, Clara Bonfiglio, Innocente, Marco Lodola, Luciano Palmieri, Plumcake and Umberto Postal. Their work tended to take the form of eccentric objects and bas-reliefs made from a variety of materials which resembled gadgets and consumer goods more than conventional sculpture. The objects drew upon the craft/design flair of Milan and made reference to the popular culture of comics and rock music. Apparently, what this group shared with the original Futurists was a desire to break with the art of the past.

● See also Italian Craze, Object Art.

◗ F Haks & others *Nuovo Futurismo* (Groningen, Groninger Museum, 1985).

◗ G Verzotti 'New Futurism' *Flash Art* (127) April–May 1985 57–9.

◗ —'New Futurism' *Flash Art* (136) September–October 1987 81–5.

456 NEW GENERATION Title of a series of four influential exhibitions sponsored by the Peter Stuyvesant Foundation (established 1963) which took place at the Whitechapel Gallery in East London between 1964 and '68. These shows served to introduce young British painters and sculptors to the public. The main tendencies represented were pop and op art, colour or fun sculpture.

● See also Business Sponsorship, St Martin's School of Art Sculptors.

◗ *The New Generation* (Whitechapel Gallery, 1964/5/6/8).

457 NEW GEORGIANS An anti-modernist tendency in British architecture, interior design, clothing and lifestyle fashionable in the 1980s involving a revival and celebration of historical styles. New Georgians ('Georgies' for short) were keen conservationists with a passion for restoring old houses in run-down inner city zones. The houses were treated as 'antiques for living in'. Rooms were filled with period furniture and the Georgies themselves frequently dressed up in period costumes.

● See also Heritage Industry, Historicism, Retro.

◗ A Artley 'Home is where the art is' *Sunday Times Colour Supplement* October 27 1985 56–60.

◗ J Martin Robinson & A Artley *The New Georgian handbook* (Ebury Press, 1985).

458 NEW IMAGE PAINTING A vague and broad term used by several critics and curators to categorize the work of certain painters of the 1970s and '80s for whom imagery took on a new importance.

An exhibition with the title 'New Image Painting' was held at the Whitney Museum of American Art, New York, in 1979. It featured the work of ten painters who 'utilize imagery in non-traditional and innovative ways...the images fluctuate between abstract and real...they are presented as isolated.... drastically abbreviated or exaggerated'. Among the artists represented were Jennifer Bartlett, Neil Jenney, Susan Rothenberg and Joe Zucker.

Tony Godfrey's book about new painting in the '80s surveyed work from Europe and America in many different styles including those described in this text under the headings Neo-Expressionism, Cultured Painting and Figuration Libre. Godfrey observed that New Image Painting was 'content-heavy'. In some instances imagery resulted from direct observations of nature or daily life but in many cases it was derived from history, myth, the art of the past and the artists' imaginations. Some artists simply made up images as they went along or they emerged from the unconscious during the process of painting. In yet other instances, imagery was appropriated from existing sources such as the mass media. The

NEW IMAGE PAINTING ADRIAN WISZNIEWSKI, 'British sculptor, British painter, British critic' (1987). Oil on canvas, 213.5cm x 213.5cm. Collection: Aberdeen Museum & Art Gallery. Photo: Nigel Greenwood Gallery, London.

interest in content/imagery amongst younger artists was prompted by a reaction against preceding forms of abstract/minimal and conceptual art, and by a re-evaluation of such major twentieth-century figurative painters as Max Beckmann, Otto Dix, George Grosz, Diego Rivera, Francis Picabia, Giorgio de Chirico and Pablo Picasso. Philip Guston's switch in the late 1960s from abstract expressionism to a funky, cartoon-like, highly personal mode of figuration was also an important example/influence.

In Britain the term 'New Image Painting' was also applied to the work of a new generation of Scottish painters living and exhibiting in Glasgow, i.e. Steven Campbell, Ken Currie, Peter Howson, Adrian Wiszniewski and others. The art critic Waldemar Januszczak labelled these artists 'Glasgow pups'.

● See also Figurative Art, Media Art, Neo-Expressionism.

● R Marshall *New Image Painting* (NY, Whitney Museum of American Art, 1979).

● L Casadio & others *New Image: a generation (and a half) of young international artists* (Milan, Gabriele Mazzotta Editore, 1980).

● A Moffat *New image: Glasgow* (Glasgow, Third Eye Centre, 1985).

● T Godfrey *The New Image: painting in the 1980s* (Oxford, Phaidon, 1986).

● J Picardie 'Shock of the noo' *The Face* (87) July 1987 92–7.

(Also Beautiful Painting, Lyrical Colourism, New Colourists) In the late 1960s a wave of American painters – David Cummings, David Diao, Robert Duran, Donald Lewallen, Alan Shields, Ken Showell, James Sullivan and others – challenged the view that painting was dead by producing large scale pictures using acrylic pigments sprayed or stained onto canvas. These works were abstract and extremely decorative. The influence of process art was evident in the way paint was applied in multiple layers, a method said to imitate 'a natural way of forming matter'. Critics compared these new works to the painting styles of the '50s, i.e. action painting or painterly abstraction, l'art informel, lyrical abstraction, tachisme – especially the more decorative aspects of these idioms. The label 'New Informalists' was devised by the critic Carter Ratcliff who argued that the painters sidestepped the 'formalist' concerns of American art of the previous decade. He also noted a connection between their use of colour and texture and certain stylistic mannerisms associated with the youth cult of drugs, rock concert light shows, and tie-dye fabrics. Another critic dismissed the paintings as 'visual muzak'.

● See also Art Informel, Formalism & Formalist Criticism, Process Art, Psychedelic Art.

◉ L Aldrich 'Young lyrical painters' *Art in America* **57** (6) November–December 1969 104–13.

◉ D Ashton 'Young abstract painters: right on' *Arts Magazine* **44** (4) February 1970 31–5.

◉ C Ratcliff 'The New Informalists' *Art News* **68** (10) February 1970 46–50.

◉ R Channin 'New directions in painterly abstraction' *Art International* **14** (7) September 20 1970 62–5.

(Also Neo-Modern Design) In 1981 at the Milan furniture fair, the Italian design group Memphis issued a catalogue in which the claim was made, somewhat mischievously, that the work on display represented a 'New International Style' (the work of Alessi, Alchimia, and several non-Italian designers also appeared). The claim was provocative because Memphis design with its colour, decoration and popular culture references was very different from the purism of 1930s International Style architecture and design.

The term 'International Style' dates from 1932; in that year an international survey exhibition of modern architecture was held at MoMA, New York and a book written by Henry-Russell Hitchcock and Philip Johnson was published which used the term as a title.

● See also Alchimia, Memphis.

◉ A Barr, H-R Hitchcock & P Johnson *Modern architecture, international exhibition* (NY, MoMA, 1932).

◉ H-R Hitchcock & P Johnson *The International Style: architecture since 1922* (NY, W W Norton, 1932).

● J Woudhuysen & D Sudjic 'The New International Style' *Design* (395) November 1981 54–7.

● C Jencks 'The...New...International...Style...e altre Etichette' *Domus* (623) December 1981 41–51.

● R Stern 'International Style: immediate effects' *Progressive Architecture* **63** February 1982 106–9.

● R Wilson 'International Style: the MoMA exhibition' (of 1932) *Progressive Architecture* **63** February 1982 92–101.

461 NEW MATERIALISM

An extremely broad label used by the British art critic William Feaver to describe art of the late 1960s that was part painting, part sculpture and part stage prop, art that was made of 'unworthy' materials such as dirt, slag and perishables. His category included works by such artists as Stephen Buckley, David Medella, Keith Milow, Jeff Nuttall and Kenneth Price. Further details of the kind of art Feaver was referring to can be found under the headings of Arte Povera, Food Art and Funk Art.

Robert Janjigian has also employed the term 'New Materialism' in order to characterize 1980s artist-designer furniture and jewellery in which the tactile and visual qualities of materials were emphasized. For example, a table by Bruce Tomb and John Randolph with legs of rough concrete and a top of thick, sandblasted glass; a stereo system by Ron Arad encased in concrete; a couch by Jody Norskag and Sherry Stein made from the boot of a Cadillac car.

● See also Artists' Furniture, Creative Salvage, High-Touch, Matter Art.

● W Feaver 'The New Materialism' *London Magazine* **10** (8) November 1970 77–85.

● *Material pleasures: furniture for the post-modern age* (NY, Queens County Art & Cultural Center, 1985).

● R Janjigian *High touch: the New Materialism in design* (Columbus Books, 1987).

462 NEW MUSEOLOGY

Museology is the branch of knowledge concerned with museums. Museologists – who may be curators or scholars employed in higher education – study their histories, their collecting, conservation, de-accessioning and research policies, their methods of arrangement and display, their social/political functions and their publics. New Museology, a term that emerged in the late 1980s, indicated: (a) a sense of dissatisfaction with old museology; and (b) a radical questioning of the ideologies, values and methodologies of existing museum culture.

During the '80s museums experienced, on the one hand, expansion and popularity, and on the other, crises of funding, management and direction. Many new muse-ums were opened and attendance figures grew until they exceeded those for certain popular sports. New buildings were constructed and some were highly praised for their architectural quality, e.g. James Stirling's 'Staatsgalerie' (1977-84) in Stuttgart. In Britain curators argued about the issues of entrance charges and the commercialization of services, while the Victoria & Albert was wracked by organizational disputes. In the United States museums found it very difficult to match sky-high auction prices and some resorted to controversial practices such as de-accessioning (i.e. selling off existing works in order to raise funds to buy new works). A much-debated public issue was that of the return of cultural property, acquired by Western museums during the era of colonialism, to its place of origin.

● See also Heritage Industry, Museum Without Walls.

● D Horne *The great museum: the representation of history* (Pluto Press, 1984).

● H Klotz & W Krase *New museums of the Federal Republic of Germany* (Academy Editions, 1986).

● J Coolidge *Patrons and architects: designing art museums in the twentieth century* (Fort Worth, Texas, Amon Carter Museum, 1989).

● B Lumley (ed) *The museum time machine* (Routledge, 1989).

● P Vergo (ed) *The New Museology* (Reaktion Books, 1989).

● D Wilson *The British Museum: purpose and politics* (BM Publications, 1989).

● P Weiss 'Selling the collection' *Art in America* **78** (7) July 1990 124–31.

463 NEW ROMANTICS

(Also Blitz Culture/Kids, Cult with no name, Futurists, New Dandies, Now Crowd) A trend in the worlds of British fashion and pop music around 1980-81 which marked a reaction against the aggression and crudity of punk. London night-clubs such as Blitz and Hell attracted young people and art students who delighted in dressing up and posing in make-up, weird hair-styles and fancy clothes, and listening to electro-disco music. Steve Strange and Rusty Egan organized 'Music for Heroes' nights at which clothes of an eclectic, extravagant and historicist kind were worn: cravattes and crinolines, frilly shirts and knickerbockers. Stephen Jones, fashion graduate of St Martin's School of Art, devised the hats worn by many of the New Romantics.

The response of the New Romantics to the nation's economic decline was to dress up like peacocks, Regency dandies and Prince Charming rather than to dress down. The clothes have been called 'fantasy wear' because often they were inspired by films such as Hollywood costume dramas. Steve Strange, Boy George and

Philip Sallon were three of the style's leaders, while precursors included David Bowie, Gary Glitter, Bryan Ferry and Andrew Logan. In 1981 the fashion designer Vivienne Westwood created pirate and highwayman looks for Adam Ant which then reached a mass audience via concert tours, magazine spreads and rock videos. Other pop bands associated with the New Romantics were Culture Club, Duran Duran, Spandau Ballet and Visage.

New Romantics indulged in 'the art of posing', the self-conscious, short-term adoption of readymade images and body postures: the self presented as an art object. (A similar tendency was discernible in the visual arts, i.e. in the work of Gilbert & George, Bruce Mclean/Nice Style and Cindy Sherman.) Some critics objected to the lack of social and political consciousness shown by the narcissistic, fashion-obsessed New Romantics and accused them of 'fiddling while Rome burned'.

In the late '80s renewed interest was evinced by curators and critics in Romanticist tendencies in the visual arts (particularly British painting) and the label 'New Romantics' was applied to several European artists, e.g. Enzo Cucchi, Andy Goldsworthy, Anslem Kiefer, Christopher Lebrun, Hughie O'Donoghue, Thérèse Oulton and Michael Porter.

● See also Camp, Gilbert & George, Neo-Romanticism, Nice Style, Punk, Subculture.

◉ 'The Cult with no name' *The Face* (7) November 1980.

R Brooks 'Blitz Culture' *ZG* (1) 1980 4–5.

◉ I Birch & others 'You look fantastic...' *Time Out* (563) January 30 – February 5 1981 12–15.

◉ I Birch (ed) *The book with no name* (Omnibus Press, 1981).

K Patrick 'Romantic roots: British painting in the 1980s' *Modern Painters* **1** (2) Summer 1988 47–50.

◉ — *The Romantic tradition in contemporary British painting* (Birmingham, Ikon Gallery, 1988).

◉ 'The New Romantics' *Art & Design* **4** (11/12) 1988.

◉ J White 'Strange but true' (Steve Strange) *Independent (Weekend)* August 4 1990 27.

464 NEW SENSUALISM A broad movement in modern architecture identified by *Progressive Architecture* in 1959, and essentially the post-1945 work of the architects Le Corbusier, Paul Rudolph, Eëro Saarinen, Minoru Yamasaki, Felix Candela, Pier Luigi Nervi, Jorn Utzon and others. The buildings concerned were sculptural in design and possessed a sensuous plasticity of form different from the rectilinear, modular or flat-surfaced style normally thought of as typical of modern architecture.

◉ T Creighton 'The New Sensualism I' *Progressive Architecture* **40** (9) September 1959 141–7; 'The New Sensualism II' *Progressive Architecture* **40** (10) October 1959 180–7.

465 NEW SPIRIT (Also New Wave, New Romanticism) A term popular in the 1980s, witness the 1981 Royal Academy exhibition 'The New Spirit of painting' and the 1986 special issue of *Architectural Review*. According to E. Farrelly, editor of the latter, post-modernism in art and design was dead and had been replaced by a 'New Spirit' that was romantic, aggressive, iconoclastic, dynamic and streetwise. The new tendency was influenced by dada and punk; in architecture it involved the energetic use of space, movement and 'raw' materials (the New York work of Elias Moser and William Godwin was cited as was the work of Coop. Himmelblau). Neville Brody was considered a 'New Spirit' graphic designer.

● See also Coop. Himmelblau, Post-Modernism, Punk.

◉ E Farrelly (ed) 'The New Spirit' *Architectural Review* **CLXXX** (1074) August 1986.

466 NEW YORK FIVE (Also, 'The Whites') Label applied to five American architects – Peter Eisenman, Michael Graves, Charles Gwathmey, John Hejduk and Richard Meier – who constituted a loosely connected group and who dominated avant garde American architecture in the 1960s and '70s. They were the subject of a meeting of CASE (Conference of Architects for the Study of the Environment) held at MoMA in 1969 and subsequently a book first published in 1972. The work of these architects was judged to be neo-rationalist, i.e. refined reworkings of the so-called 'white architecture' of the 1920s.

● See also Cardboard Architecture, Rational Architecture.

◉ K Frampton & others *Five architects: Eisenman...* (NY, Oxford University Press, 2nd ed 1975).

467 NEW YORK SCHOOL This term dates from the 1940s. The United States emerged from the Second World War as the world's most powerful nation politically, militarily and economically; consequently it was logical that it should dominate culturally too. The emergence of the abstract expressionist movement in the 1940s and '50s signalled the superiority of America in the realm of fine art and since this movement was centred on New York it became synonymous with the New York School. Paris was replaced by New York as the world's art capital and the School of Paris was displaced by the New York School. Whether or not the character of the city itself influenced the type of painting produced within it was difficult to judge. Harold Rosenberg suggested that a largeness of scale, a direct and crude method of execution and a hardness of light were some of the characteristics of New York painting.

New York remained pre-eminent until around 1980 when a more equitable balance was achieved between the art cities of America and Europe.

● See also Abstract Expressionism, East Village Art, School of London, SoHo.

● B Friedman (ed) *School of New York: some younger artists* (NY, Grove Press, 1959).

● 'The New York School' *Artforum* **4** (1) September 1965, special issue.

● H Geldzahler *New York painting and sculpture 1940–70* (Pall Mall Press, 1969).

● M Tuchman *The New York School: abstract expressionism in the '40s and '50s* (Thames & Hudson, 1970).

● H Rosenberg 'Ecole de New York' – in – *The de-definition of art: action art to pop to earthworks* (Secker & Warburg, 1972) 188–200.

● D Ashton *The life and times of the New York School* (Bath, Adams & Dart, 1973).

● I Sandler *The New York School: the painters and sculptors of the fifties* (NY, Harper & Row, 1978).

● P Rosenzweig *The fifties: aspects of painting in New York* (Washington DC, Hirshhorn Museum, 1980).

● 'Brand New York' *Literary Review* October 1982, special issue.

● L Phillips *The third dimension: sculpture of the New York School* (NY, Whitney Museum of American Art, 1985).

● J Saltz & others *Beyond boundaries: New York's new art* (NY, Alfred van der Marck Editions, 1986).

● D Crane *Transformation of the avant garde: the New York artworld 1940–85* (Chicago, University of Chicago Press, 1987).

● L Walloch (ed) *New York: cultural capital of the world* (NY, Rizzoli, 1988).

468   NICE STYLE

The name of a short-lived British performance art group billed as 'the world's first pose band'. The group consisted of Garry Chitty, Robin Fletcher, Bruce McLean and Paul Richards and it was active between 1971 and '75. Performers executed violent and acrobatic movements 'with style' and then froze into poses for viewers to appreciate with judgements such as 'nice' and 'sharp'. Nice Style shows were highly entertaining, amusing and satirical: the pretensions of the artworld and art education were favourite targets.

● See also Body Art, Camp, Gilbert & George, Performance Art.

● 'Nice Style' *Studio International* **186** (960) November 1973 190–1.

● 'Nice Style at the Hanover Grand' *Audio Arts* **1** (2) 1974, sound recording.

● C Tisdall 'Nice Style' *Guardian* October 30 1974 p. 12.

● M Hartney 'Nice Style at Garage' *Studio International* **188** (971) November 1974 1, 9–10 (review section).

● 'Nice Style at Garage' *Audio Arts* (supplement) 1974.

● 'Nice Style' *Studio International* **189** (974) March–April 1975 p. i, xiv–xv (advertisement section).

469   NO ART

(Also Doom / Shit Art) Paintings, sculptures and assemblages by a group of American artists – Michelle and Stanley Fisher, Sam Goodman and Boris Lurie – exhibiting in New York between 1959 and '64. Their mixed-media installations at the March and Gertrude Stein galleries had provocative titles: 'The Doom/Involvement/No/Vulgar Show'. They consisted of chaotic assemblages of rubbish, bloody dismembered toys, excrement and sexual fetishes designed to shock and disturb the viewer. No Art occurred during the McCarthy era of American politics; it was essentially a form of social and political protest. No artists disliked uncommitted art, especially pop art (though their work was featured in one history of pop). They said 'no' in their art to exploitation, pollution, poverty, the arms race, religion and so on.

● See also Assemblage Art, Political Art, Pop Art.

● L Lippard & others *Pop art* (Thames & Hudson, 1966) 102–3.

● B Lurie 'No Art' (statements) – in – *Aktionen: Happening und Demonstrationen seit 1965* by W Vostell (Hamburg, Rowohlt, 1970).

● G Glueck 'The non gallery of No Art' *New York Times* (section 2) January 24 1971.

● E & R Schwarz 'No Art: an American psycho-social phenomenon' *Leonardo* **4** (3) Summer 1971 245–54.

● —'Violence and caprice in "No Art"' *Leonardo* **7** (4) Autumn 1974 34–34.

● —B Lurie 'Shit no! Ten years after' – in – *Something Else Yearbook* (Barton, Something Else Press, 1974) 63–73.

470   NON-RELATIONAL ART

(Also Wholistic/ Holistic Painting) Paintings with hierarchies of forms – small, medium, large – part/whole relations and figure/ground contrasts have been described as 'relational'. In contrast, 'Non-Relational' paintings – such as the 1960s 'shaped canvas' paintings of Frank Stella – had a single uniform space, they avoided depth effects because forms stretched across the whole canvas from edge to edge. Other painters achieved a similar result by uniform fields of colour (e.g. Yves Klein) or by an even distribution of brushmarks. Since such works lacked internal relationships, the viewer's attention was drawn to the whole canvas as a unit which itself became a figure on the field of the gallery wall. The lack of an illusionistic pictorial space also encouraged a lateral reading of the canvas. 'Non-relational' was also a term applied to minimal art objects because they related to nothing outside of themselves.

● See also Abstract Impressionism, All-Over Painting, Colour-Field Painting, Hard-Edge Painting, Minimal Art, Shaped Canvas.

● L Alloway 'Systemic painting' – in – *Minimal art: a critical anthology* G Battcock (ed)(NY, Dutton/London, Studio Vista, 1968) 37–60.

471 **NOUVEAU RÉALISME** (New Realism, also Les Nouveaux Réalistes or New Realists, Factualists) A movement in European art dating from the early 1960s. It was centred in Paris and promoted by the critic Pierre Restany. The term 'Nouveau Réalisme' was first used by Restany in a manifesto published in April 1960 and in October of the same year the Nouveaux Réalistes group was formally constituted at the home of Yves Klein in the presence of the artists Arman, François Dufrêne, Raymond Hains, Klein, Martial Raysse, Daniel Spoerri and Jean Tinguely. Several others – César, Christo, J. M. de la Villeglé, Gerard Deschamps, Mimmo Rotella and Niki de Saint-Phalle – participated later on.

The work of the artists who took part in the movement was disparate (see, for instance, Affiches Lacérées, Destructive Art, Kinetic Art, Monochromatic & Monotonal Painting, Packaging, Performance Art, Snare Pictures), consequently it is hard to identify a common denominator. A number of the artists worked in the idiom of assemblage and they were 'realists' or 'factualists' because they accumulated and employed actual objects and materials acquired from the urban environment. Nouveau Réalisme was contemporaneous with the neo-dada movement in the United States and in fact joint shows were organized in Paris and New York in 1962. Both movements were also viewed, in hindsight, as having contributed to the development of pop art.

● See also Assemblage Art, Junk Culture/Sculpture, Neo Dada, Pop Art.

● P Restany *Nouveaux Réalistes* (Milan, Galleria Apollinaire, 1960).

● J Ashbery, P Restany & S Janis *New Realists* (NY, Sidney Janis Gallery, 1962).

● P Restany *Les Nouveaux Réalistes* (Paris, Éditions Planète, 1968).

● —'The New Realism' – in – *Figurative art since 1945* by J Hodin & others (Thames & Hudson, 1971) 242–71.

● P Trigano 'Les Nouveaux Réalistes' *Realities* (367) September 1976 56–65, + 84.

● M Giroud 'Le Nouveau Réalisme' *Art Press International* (3) December 1976 30–1.

● P Restany 'Le Nouveau Réalisme' *Flash Art* (105) December–January 1981–2 26–37.

● *1960: Nouveau Réalisme* (Paris, Musée d'Art Moderne de la Ville de Paris, 1986).

NOUVEAU RÉALISME Yves Klein, 'Imprint ANT 66' (Anthropmétrie 66, 1960). Blue paint on paper on canvas, 157cm x 312 cm. Photo: Gimpel Fils Gallery, London.

472 NOUVELLE TENDANCE

(New Tendency, Neue Tendenzen, Nove Tendencje) Expressions used during the early 1960s by artists from Europe, Japan and South America associated with the kinetic and constructivist movements. These artists admired the art of Yves Klein and Piero Manzoni (who died in 1962 and 1963 respectively) and opposed the loose painterly styles of abstract expressionism and tachisme. They banded together into groups in order to produce collective or anonymous work, to exploit new materials and techniques, and to explore the use of light, movement and spectator participation in art. The loose association of these groups and their shared attitudes constituted the Nouvelle Tendance. The term itself derived from the title of an exhibition organized by Matko Mestrovic in Zagreb in 1961. Later the French group GRAV helped to mount another show at Frankfurt (1963) entitled 'European avant garde: Arte Programmata, Neue Tendenzen, Anti-Peinture, Zero'. A further major exhibition was held in 1964 in Leverkusen and Paris.

● See also Constructivism, GRAV, Kinetic Art, Light Art, NUL, Participatory Art, Programmed Art, Zero.

Nouvelle Tendance (Paris, Musée d'Art Décoratifs, 1964).

● F Popper *Origins and development of kinetic art* (Studio Vista, 1968).

473 NUCLEAR ART

(Arte Nucleare, Movimento Nucleare) A short-lived movement of the early 1950s dedicated to the renewal of painting, associated primarily with the Italian artists Enrico Baj (whom Italian critics later hailed as the 'father of pop art') and Sergio Dangelo. Their first manifesto was issued in 1952 on the occasion of a show at the Gallery Apollo in Brussels; it declared 'Forms disintegrate: man's new forms are those of the atomic universe'. A further statement dated 1957 declared its opposition to all forms of geometric abstraction and indeed any fixed style of art. It proposed instead experimentation with tachist, calligraphic and automatic painting techniques. The language employed by the Nuclearists referred to 'atomized situations', 'states of matter' and 'heavy water' colours, but exactly what connection was intended with nuclear physics remains unclear.

The British abstract relief artist Mary Martin has also used the term 'nuclear' to describe her method of working, i.e. building up part by part around a central core.

● See also Art Informel, Tachisme.

● T Sauvage *Art Nucléaire* (Paris, Éditions Vilo, 1962).

● 'The end of style' *Leonardo* **3** (4) October 1970 465–6.

● *Arte Nucleare 1951–7. Opere, testimonianze, documenti* (Milan, Galleria San Fedele, 1980).

474 NUL

The name of a group of Dutch artists founded in 1961 by Henk Peeters, Jan Schoonhoven, Hermann de Vries and Armando. It was a development of the Nederlandse Informale Groep which had been in existence since 1958. 'Nul' was the Dutch equivalent of the German group 'Zero' and its aims were similar: the promotion of abstract art of a kinetic, light, or constructivist kind. Peeters made collages from white, cottonwool balls and lenses. De Vries adopted chance procedures and preferred to describe his work as 'visual information' rather than 'art'. Schoonhoven made objects from papier mâché and white panel reliefs. Nul members took part in the nouvelle tendance exhibitions in the early '60s and published a magazine *Nul=0* from 1961 to '63.

Exhibitions featuring Nul were held in Amsterdam (1962, 1965), in London (New Vision Centre, 1963) and in the Hague (1964).

● See also Constructivism, Kinetic Art, Light Art, Nouvelle Tendance, Zero.

● H Peeters & H de Vries (eds) *Nul=0, magazine devoted to the new tendency* (Arnhem, Holland, 1961–3).

● *Nul: Armando, de Vries, Peeters, Schoonhoven* (The Hague, Gemeentmuseum, 1964).

● *Vertrekpuntnul: Nul, zero, nieuwe realisten* (Utrecht Centraal Museum, 1988–9)

475 OBAALA

Initials standing for 'Organization for Black Arts Advancement and Learning Activities'. OBAALA was founded in 1981 by artists and others belonging to the African–Caribbean community in Britain. It was located in London and committed to fostering the interests of black people in particular artists. An exhibition space and shop – the Black Arts Gallery – was opened in Finsbury Park in 1983. OBAALA organized exhibitions and summer schools, and issued posters, reproductions and publications. Its director in 1988 was Shakka Dedi.

● See also Black Art, Carnival, Negritude, Orature.

○ S Dedi 'Brief background to OBAALA' *Artrage* (21) Autumn 1988 26-7.

476 OBJECT ART

(Also Objekt Kunst) Objects are visible tangible things, hence the use of the words 'art objects' to encompass such material entities as paintings and sculptures. 'Object Art', however, generally has a narrower reference, i.e. works literally incorporating non-art objects rather than simply depicting them. 'Object sculptures' for instance was used before 1945 to describe three-dimensional collages by the futurists, dadaists and surrealists; essentially it was an alternative to 'assemblage'. Since 1945 numerous artists have exploited as raw material the huge quantity of goods modern industry generates. (Some artists prefer to use goods that are brand-new, while others prefer those discarded as waste.) In the 1950s Jasper Johns and Robert Rauschenberg began to incorporate found objects into their paintings. In Britain John Latham began to construct reliefs from old books, while simultaneously in Europe the nouveaux réalistes devised many works consisting of accumulations of everyday products. And in 1965 the French critic Alain Jouffroy labelled a group of artists making art from objects or taking casts of them, 'Objecteurs'; the artists concerned were Antonio Recalcati, Jean Pierre Raynaud, Tetsumi Kudo and Paul van Hoeydonck. Also in the '60s the Greek-American sculptor Lucas Samaras created a series of striking mixed-media boxes and sculptures made from such things as pins and nails. American minimalists in the mid 1960s spoke about their three-dimensional constructions as 'specific objects'. In 1970 a book about an exhibition of craft objects which had toured the United States was entitled 'Objects USA'. In the early 1980s several British sculptors made a public impact with works and installations consisting of recycled junk. During the mid 1980s several American sculptors associated with the neo-geo movement featured objects – readymade consumer goods – in their work.

Both 'art object' and 'object art' imply that art always consists of material things. However, from the late 1960s onwards this idea was challenged by various avant garde tendencies which caused people to speak of 'anti-' and 'post-object art'.

● See also Assemblage Art, Combine Paintings, Junk Culture/Sculpture, Neo-Dada, Neo-Geo, New British Sculpture, Nouveau Réalisme, Post-Object Art, Tableau.

○ A Jouffroy 'Les Objecteurs' *Quadrum* (19) 1965 5–32, 185–9.

○ H Rosenberg *The anxious object: art today and its audience* (Thames & Hudson, 1965).

○ F Mathey 'L'objet de notre temps' *Quadrum* (20) 1966 121–36, + 180.

○ D Ashton 'Furnishing an objective world: the role of objects in modern art' – in – *A reading of modern art* (Cleveland, Press of the Case Western Reserve University, 1969) 167–76.

○ L Nordness (ed) *Objects USA* (NY, Viking Press, 1970). *Métamorphose de l'objet: art et anti-art 1910–70* (Brussels, Palais des Beaux Arts, 1971).

○ W Rotzler *Objekt-Kunst von Duchamp bis Kienholz* (Cologne, Dumont, 1972).

○ J Weightman 'The obsessive object' – in– *The concept of the avant garde: explorations in modernism* (Alcove Press, 1973) 38–60.

○ E Johnson *Modern art and the object: a century of changing attitudes* (Thames & Hudson, 1976).

○ H Finkelstein *Surrealism and the crisis of the object* (Ann Arbor, Michigan, University of Michigan Research Press, 1980).

○ D Adrian 'Rummaging among twentieth- century objects' *Art Journal* **45** (4) Winter 1985 344–9.

○ H Foster '(Dis)agreeable objects' – in – *Damaged goods: desire and the economy of the object* (NY, New Museum of Contemporary Art, 1986).

● M Livingstone *British object sculptors of the 1980s* (2 vols) (Japan, Kyoto, Art Random, 1989).

346–81.
● S Kircherer *Olivetti* (Trefoil, 1988).

477 OBJECTHOOD

A term that frequently occurred in American formalist criticism during the 1960s, especially in the writings of Michael Fried. It was Fried's contention that there was a conflict between our perception of physical works of art as art, and as real objects; he claimed that viewing a painting as an object was to perceive it as a non-art entity. He believed that modernist painting, to be valid, had to defeat or suspend its own objecthood but without resorting to the illusionistic means of the past. The problem was complicated by the fact that the whole trend of art since post-impressionism had been to stress the literal, object qualities of painting. For instance, in the '60s Frank Stella emphasized the box-like quality of the support by using thick stretchers. Minimal artists banished illusion and stressed the objectness of their 'primary structures'. This caused Clement Greenberg to accuse them of cultivating a 'non-art look'.

● See also Formalism & Formalist Criticism, Minimal Art, Modernist Painting, Presence.

● M Fried 'Art and Objecthood' – in – *Minimal art: a critical anthology* G Battcock (ed) (Studio Vista, 1968) 116–47.

478 OLIVETTI

An Italian manufacturing company founded in the town of Ivrea, Piedmont, by the engineer Camillo Olivetti (1868–1943) in 1908. Camillo was succeeded by his son Adriano (1901–60). By 1958 Olivetti had established several factories in Italy and controlled 17 allied foreign companies. Olivetti designs and makes typewriters, computers, office furniture, and other office equipment. It became famous in the design world because of its encouragement of high-quality design in terms of its products and publicity graphics, and its innovations in social welfare and design management. It has employed such well-known designers as Aldo Magnelli, Marcello Nizzoli (responsible for the elegantly styled Lettera 22 portable typewriter of 1950), Mario Bellini and Ettore Sottsass. Olivetti has been the subject of celebratory exhibitions at MoMA, New York, in 1952 and the ICA, London, in 1957. The company has been art-conscious: it has employed artists, commissioned sculptures and sponsored travelling exhibitions of art (see Programmed Art).

● See also Italian Craze.

● A Olivetti *Olivetti 1908–58* (Ivrea, Olivetti, 1958).
● R Zorzi 'Olivetti concept and form' *Graphis* (150) 1971–2

479 OP ART

(Short for Optical Art. Also Art Cinétique, Art Visuel, Perceptual Abstraction, Retinal Art) This term was first used by *Time* magazine in 1964 and popularized by James Canaday, art news editor of the *New York Times*. It described an international movement in painting, fashionable in the mid 1960s, specializing in the production of powerful optical responses within the visual system of the viewer. Op paintings were abstract and geometric. They made use of parallel lines, or patterns of squares or circles, and periodic structures, all painted with sharp precision, and employing strong colour contrasts, or black/white contrasts, to generate optical shimmer or flicker, after-images, moiré patterns, multi-stable images or ambiguous spatial effects, and so forth. Many of the devices employed by Op artists were derived from the diagrams found in psychology of perception textbooks. Op artists reworked this source material in order to offer a more intense visual experience. Since Op Art was concerned with virtual movement, it was closely aligned with kinetic art and the two tendencies were often discussed together. Op also shared certain formal characteristics with hard-edge painting. However, not all Op Art consisted of paintings – there were also reliefs and environmental constructions.

A large-scale exhibition of Op Art called 'The Responsive Eye' was held at MoMA, New York, in 1965. The best-known practitioners were Agam, Richard Anuskiewicz, Wolfgang Ludwig, François Morellet, Reginald Neal, Larry Poons, Bridget Riley, Jesús Raphael Soto, Jeffrey Steele and Victor Vasarely. Some critics considered Joseph Albers a precursor of Op Art but he objected strongly to the term, arguing that since all pictorial art was 'optical' it was nonsensical. He proposed instead 'perceptual painting' but this does not seem any improvement. Other possible precursors were: Duchamp, Mondrian, the futurists and the Bauhaus basic course exercises. The founding father of Op was surely Vasarely who was painting such images as early as 1935. Since Op Art required 'visual research', it appealed to those European artists interested in light, movement and colour who formed groups for research purposes, e.g. Equipo 57, GRAV, Gruppo N, Nul, Zero.

For a short period in the mid '60s Op Art became very popular. Its eye-dazzling patterns appealed to designers, advertisers and business people (much to the disgust of Bridget Riley) and appeared on textile fabrics, clothes (e.g. the fashions of Getulio Alviani), interiors, trademarks (e.g. the 'Woolmark'), film and TV stage sets. As

OP ART FRANCIS CELENTANO 'Kinetic Painting no.3' 121cm diameter, 1967. Photo: Courtesy of Howard Wise Gallery, New York.

a result of over-exposure and dilution, the style was quickly exhausted. In any case, it was a form of art that appealed to the retina rather than to the mind. During the 1980s a revival of interest in Op Art occurred amongst painters associated with the neo-geo tendency (see the article 'Poptometry' listed below).

● See also Cinétisations, Hard-Edge Painting, Kinetic Art, Neo-Geo, Programmed Art.

● 'Op Art: pictures that attack the eye' *Time* October 1964.

D Beyfus 'Op Art rooms' *Telegraph Magazine* September 17 1965 40.

● W Seitz *The Responsive Eye* (NY, MoMA, 1965).

● R Carraher & J Thurston *Optical illusions and the visual arts* (Studio Vista, 1966).

● M Compton *Optical and kinetic art* (Tate Gallery, 1967).

● R Parola *Optical Art: theory and practice* (NY, Van Nostrand Reinhold, 1969).

● C Barrett *Op Art* (Studio Vista, 1970).

● — *An introduction to Optical Art* (Studio Vista, 1971).

● L Lippard 'Perverse perspectives' – in – *Changing: essays in art criticism* (NY, Dutton, 1971) 167–83.

● J Lancaster *Introducing Op Art* (Batsford, 1973).

● C McCormick 'Poptometry' *Artforum* **24** (3) November 1985 87–91.

● K Türr *Op Art: Stil, Ornament oder Experiment?* (Berlin, Gebr Mann Studio, 1986).

480 OPEN COLLEGE OF THE ARTS (OCA)

A British, private educational charity with headquarters in London which offers practical courses in art and design – painting, photography, textiles and sculpture – for students working mainly at home on a part-time basis. The OCA was the brainchild of Lord Young of Dartington (who also helped to found the Open University in the 1960s) and a pilot scheme was launched in 1987. OCA is thus a distance-learning organization; however, students are given monthly, face-to-face tutorials in local art colleges and they can attend summer schools. In 1988 the Chairman of OCA was Lord Young and the Director was I. Tregarthen Jenkin. Lord Young has stated: 'The aim is to use new educational methods and technologies to make Britain a nation of doers.' At a time of constriction in the publicly funded sector of British art education, some observers regard the emergence of a privately funded initiative such as the OCA with suspicion.

● See also Art Schools.

● I Tregarthen Jenkin 'Studying art and design at home' *The Artist* July 1988.

● C Jennings 'The Open College of Art – a new option' *Art Monthly* (119) September 1988 30.

● J Brown 'Open learning in the arts' *Education Now* September–October 1988.

481 ORATURE

A term used by black writers to identify the distinctive characteristics of black art and culture. Some writers define it as a return to the oral traditions which existed before European colonialism but, according to Kwesi Owusu, 'Orature is an *aesthetic*, a multi-levelled, multi-process fusion of the political and the cultural, of art forms and languages, which is grounded in the experience, traditions and aspirations of black people'. Orature implies a recognition of the fundamental unity of all the various artforms and media (exemplified in phenomena like carnivals) and is based on the concept of the circle.

● See also Black Art, Carnival, Ethnic Art, Negritude.

● K Owusu *The struggle for black arts in Britain* (Comedia, 1986).

482 ORGANIC ARCHITECTURE/ ART/ DESIGN

An influential notion in the discourse of twentieth-century art and design. The concept of Organic Architecture is credited to Louis Sullivan in 1915 but it was later advocated as a modern, humane ideal by Frank Lloyd Wright in the 1930s; later still, in 1950, it was discussed by Bruno Zevi. According to Wright (who considered his own buildings exemplified Organic Architecture), it depended upon an organic society. It was associated with a love of beauty and natural processes of formation: 'organic architecture is a natural architecture – the architecture of nature, for nature'. In practical terms the harmonious human–nature relation was realized by low-level houses interpenetrating nature: 'we are ground loving animals...garden and building may now be one'. Being natural, intuitive, irregular and so on, Organic Architecture was implicitly the antithesis of rational, geometric, academic and stylistic architecture (in short, inorganic architecture). Zevi provides a checklist of 15 oppositions in his text. He also quotes from a New York catalogue of an exhibition of 'Organic Design': 'A design may be called organic when there is an harmonious organization of the parts within the whole...' Zevi's own conclusion was: 'Architecture is organic when the spatial arrangement of room, house, city is planned for human happiness, material, psychological and spiritual. The organic is based therefore on a social idea not a figurative idea. We can only call architecture organic when it aims at being human before it is humanist.'

A contemporary architect whose work has been dubbed 'organic' (and also 'regionalist') by several critics is the Hungarian Imre Makovecz, especially his 'Cultural Centre' at Sárospatak (1979–83), a mound-like building half buried in the ground. Another such architect is the Belgian Lucien Kroll. A radical and controversial figure, Kroll prefers the word 'landscape' to 'architecture'; he has designed a Metro station resembling a wood. He favours natural materials and curved/irregular forms. Kroll does not mind if his buildings take a long time to construct, because this allows for an organic evolution and a thorough consultation process. In fact, participation by users or 'the community' in the design process is essential to his vision of Organic Architecture which is inseparable from humane architecture. Conflicting demands from a heterogeneous body of users has resulted in buildings that are 'anarchic' in their forms, materials and styles, e.g. the 1970s medical centre at the University of Louvain. (The contradictions and complexities of life are thus retained.) A broad brief is also given to artisans and builders so that they too can contribute to the creative process. Kroll rejects what he calls 'easel' or 'art gallery architecture' – ideal works of art that ignore contexts and people.

In 1971 a special issue of the magazine *The Structurist* was devoted to the theme of Organic Art. It discussed such topics as humanity's relation to ecosystem, the golden section, the spiral in art, fragmentation and wholeness.

● See also Biotecture, Community Architecture, Participatory Design, Rational Architecture, Structurism.

● E Noyes *Organic Design* (NY, MoMA, 1941).

● B Zevi *Towards an Organic Architecture* (Faber & Faber, 1950).

● F Wright *An Organic Architecture: the architecture of democracy* (Lund Humphries, 1970), 1st published in 1939.

● 'An Organic Art: ecological views of Man/Nature' *The Structurist* (11) 1971.

● C Jencks *Architecture today* (Academy Editions, 1988) 328–9.

A term used by various scholars to describe the conceptions and images of the Orient (i.e. the Arab Near East rather than China) propagated by Western artists and intellectuals. The taste for representing the Orient dates primarily from the nineteenth century when artists such as Gros, Delacroix, Gérôme, Gleyre, Tissot, Ingres, Renoir, Bonington and Lewis delighted in the exotic appeal of scenes set in North Africa, Turkey and the Middle East: paintings of harems, odalisques, despots, the desert, mosques, and so on. Several twentieth-century artists too have been intrigued by the same kind of subjects, Matisse and Brangwyn for instance. Some artists visited the Orient in order to make first-hand observations but others simply relied on their imaginations and existing records. Critics of Orientalism argue that the representations were mythical and an aspect of European colonialism. In the 1980s a number of visual artists explored the theme of Orientalism in an analytical fashion in their work, e.g. Olivier Richon, an artist employing the medium of photography, and Deanna Petherbridge, an artist employing the medium of drawing. Beginning in 1979, Petherbridge visited India several times and created a series of meticulous, architectonic drawings as metaphoric responses to the temples she studied in India.

● E Said *Orientalism* (Routledge & Kegan Paul, 1979).

● *The Orientalists: Delacroix to Matisse, European painters in North Africa and the Near East* (Royal Academy, 1984).

● O Richon 'Representation, the harem and the despot' *Block* (10) 1985 34–47.

● G Michell & J McEwen *Temples and tenements: the Indian drawings of Deanna Petherbridge* (Calcutta, Seagull Books/London, Fischer Fine Art, 1987).

● C Tawardos 'Foreign bodies: art history and the discourse of nineteenth-century Orientalist art' *Third Text* (3/4) Spring–Summer 1988 51–68.

● J Sweetman *The Oriental obsession* (Cambridge University Press, 1988).

● J Thompson *The East imagined, experienced, remembered: Orientalist nineteenth-century paintings* (Liverpool, Walker Art Gallery/Dublin, National Gallery of Ireland, 1988).

 484   ORNAMENTALISM

(Also New Ornamentalism) According to Robert Jensen and Patricia Conway, a revival of interest in ornament and decoration occurred in the United States and Europe from the mid 1960s onwards. This 'new ornamentalism' was manifested in architecture, interior design, glassware, ironwork, ceramics, furniture and even painting. Its appearance marked a reaction to the machine aesthetic of modernism and the minimalist art of the '60s. Amongst the architects cited were Michael Graves, Ralph Erskine, Charles Moore, Robert Stern and Robert Venturi. Arguably, the resurgence of ornament was simply one characteristic of post-modernism.

● See also Machine Aesthetic/Art, Minimal Art, Pattern Painting, Post-Modern Architecture/Design, Supergraphics, Symbolic Architecture.

● B Auger 'A return to ornament?' *Architectural Review* **CLX** (954) August 1976 77–80.

● E Gombrich *The sense of order: a study in the psychology of decorative art* (Phaidon, 1979).

● P Fuller 'Ornamentation: should products be decorated?' *Design* (416) August 1983 33–45.

● R Jensen & P Conway *Ornamentalism: the new decorativeness in architecture and design* (Allen Lane, 1983).

● B Brolin *Flight of fancy: the banishment and return of ornament* (Academy Editions, 1985).

● S Durant *Ornament* (MacDonald, 1986).

OUTSIDER ART Photograph by NEK CHAND of a figure from the rock garden Chandigarh, India, featured on the front cover of *Raw Vision* (1) March/April 1989. Photo: courtesy of the editor John Maizels.

485 OUTSIDER ART

(Also Art of the Alienated, Alternative/ Anti-Cultural/ Non-Conformist and Autistic Art) A term devised by Robert Cardinal to describe artworks that represented an alternative to the academic, official, professional and cultural art of the museums and galleries. He included in his category many examples drawn from the art brut collection established by Jean Dubuffet: paintings, drawings and sculptures by schizophrenics; also works by uneducated, innocent artists such as hermits and mediums. Such beings, Cardinal maintained, existed outside normal society and evaded its cultural conditioning; consequently they remained free to create highly original works of art which satisfied their own psychic needs rather than those of the public. For this reason, Cardinal excluded peasant or folk art, popular art, naive and Sunday painters, tribal and child art, and the work of prisoners.

Artists identified as 'outsiders' included: Aloise, Ferdinand Cheval, Abbé Fouéré, Madge Gill, Augustin Lesage, Francis Marshall, Joel Negri, Simon Rodia, Clarence Schmidt, Oskar Voll, Scottie Wilson, Adolf Wölfli and Joseph Yoakum. Identifying what such artists have in common is problematic because they are vaunted as the epitome of individuality. Even so, many of them produce images with obsessive detail in which the whole paper is covered with intricate patterns and designs. Those that favour three dimensions frequently spend their lives constructing elaborate decorations and structures (using cement and waste materials) around their homes.

In the 1980s Monika Kinley established an Outsider Art archive in South London and in 1989 a magazine was founded entitled *Raw Vision* (London & New York) devoted to Outsider Art (and also grassroots art, visionary art and l'art brut). Some theorists would argue that the very category is suspect because if human beings are regarded as social beings by definition, then no one can exist outside society. The idea that Outsider artists are always social outcasts or mentally sick has been rejected by Victor Musgrove.

● See also Art Brut, Art Therapy, Naive Art, Popular Art, Prison Art, Visionary Art.

● R Cardinal *Outsider Art* (Studio Vista, 1972).

● —*Outsiders* (Hayward Gallery, 1979), broadsheet to accompany an Arts Council exhibition.

● V Musgrove 'Insider Outsiders' (letter) *Art Monthly* (75) April 1984 20.

● L Navratil 'The artists' house: Outsider Art in Austria' *Art Monthly* (108) July–August 1987 7–9.

● M Gooding 'On Outsider Art' *Art Monthly* (110) October 1987 14–16.

● V Willing (intro) *In another world: Outsider Art from Europe and America* (Arts Council of Great Britain, 1987).

P

486 PACKAGED FURNITURE (Also Demountable/Knock-down/ Nomadic Furniture) Furniture designed for sale in a package, for self-assembly at home. During the Second World War the Stockholm retail store Nordiska Kompaniet experimented with chairs and tables designed by Elias Svedberg in sections so that they could be packed into cardboard cartons. The aim was to reduce prices by cutting the costs of furniture storage, handling and distribution. An exhibition of Svedberg's work was shown at the Building Centre in London in 1947. Since the 1940s, Packaged Furniture has become commonplace and the practice has been adopted by stores in many countries (e.g. Habitat in Britain); items can be taken away by customers from the shops or acquired by mail order. The term 'Nomadic Furniture' refers to any domestic furniture that folds, stacks or deflates in order to facilitate easy transportation – it has been estimated that the average American family moves every three to four years.

● See also Habitat, Scandinavian Style.

● H Dunnett 'Packaged Furniture' *Architectural Review* **111** (664) April 1952 240–9.

● J Hennessey & W Papanek *Nomadic Furniture* (NY, Pantheon Books, 1973).

487 PACKAGING (Also, Bagging, Emballages, Wrapping) It was Man Ray, the surrealist, who introduced this technique into the fine arts with his mysteriously shrouded object entitled 'The enigma of Isidore Ducasse' (1920). Later on, in the 1950s and '60s it was to become an activity indulged in by artists internationally. At least one post-1945 artist – Christo (Bulgarian/School of Paris sculptor b. 1935) – devoted his whole *oeuvre* to this idea: his so-called 'empaquetages' included wrapped chairs, nude women, whole buildings, bridges and even stretches of coastline. Meanwhile in Poland the painter, sculptor and theatre director Tadeusz Kantor (1915-90) made 'emballages' from the mid 1950s onwards. (The word 'emballage' is French for packing and package.) Kantor used clothes, bandages, paper etc. to wrap things and people. The practice was formalized in a manifesto published in

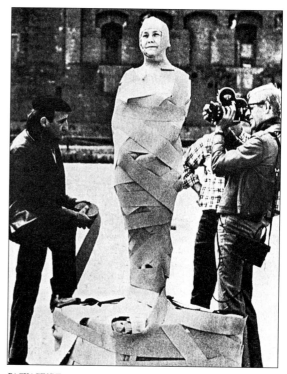

PACKAGING TADEUSZ KANTOR (left) with Emballage, Nurenberg, 1968.

1963. In Britain during the '60s Yoko Ono promoted 'bagism', i.e. enclosing herself and John Lennon in white bags at public events to make the point 'what is essential is not visible to the eye'. The Canadian artist Iain Baxter also wrapped or bagged whole rooms and all their contents using transparent polythene; the result he called a 'bagged place'.

Perhaps the significance of this technique is indicated by market research findings which show that the packaging of a product is almost as important to consumers as the product itself. Robert Opie, a British market researcher, has claimed that his museum of packaging – bottles, boxes, tins, packets – and advertising ephemera, opened in 1984, was the first in the world. The collection (Albert Warehouse, Gloucester Docks, Gloucester) contains some 300,000 items. In 1975 Opie organized an exhibition with the punning title 'The Pack Age' at the Victoria & Albert Museum, London.

● See also Assemblage Art.

Tadeusz Kantor: Emballages 1960–70 (Whitechapel Art Gallery, 1976).

J Schellmann & J Benecke (eds) *Christo: prints and objects 1963–87* (Munich, Editions Schellmann, 1988).

R Opie *Packaging source book: a visual guide to a century of Packaging design* (MacDonald/Orbis, 1989).

H David 'A package deal preserved for posterity' *Independent on Sunday* August 5 1990 18.

H Milton *Packaging design* (Design Council, 1991).

488 PADDINGTON PRINTSHOP

A community-conscious visual arts organization / workshop located in West London, established in 1974. PP is supported by local and state arts funding and registered as a non-profit-making Friendly Society. Its purpose is to advance the arts of printmaking, graphic design, photography, and education in these arts. It provides access and training to printmaking and graphic design facilities for visual artists and members of the public. The printshop has a design studio, a darkroom, silkscreen and slide copying facilities. PP also mounts poster exhibitions and publishes and markets artists' prints.

● See also Community Art & Media.

Annual report 87–88 (Paddington Printshop, 1988), leaflet.

489 PAINTERLY PAINTING

(Also Painterliness) A concept first introduced into art theory by Heinrich Wölfflin in 1915. He applied the term 'Malerische' (painterly) to the baroque style in order to distinguish it from the classical style. The latter was predominantly linear and hence was equated with the tactile sense, while the former was equated with the optical sense or pure visibility. Much later the American critic Clement Greenberg used the term 'painterly abstraction' as a synonym for abstract expressionism. Other artists who foregrounded the materials and techniques of painting – e.g. Jules Olitski, the new informalists – were also considered painterly.

● See also New Informalists.

H Wölfflin *Principles of art history: the problem of the development of style in later art* (NY, Dover, 1950).

C Greenberg 'After abstract expressionism' – in – *New York painting and sculpture 1940–70* by H Geldzahler & others (Pall Mall Press, 1969) 360–70.

G Muller 'Materiality and Painterliness' *Arts Magazine* **46** (1) September–October 1971 34–7.

T Hess & J Ashbery (eds) *Painterly Painting* (NY, Newsweek, 1971), *Art News* annual **37**.

J Elderfield 'Painterliness redefined: Jules Olitski and recent abstract art', part 1 *Art International* **16** (10) December 1972 22–6; part 2 *Art International* **17** (4) April 1973 36–41, + 101.

490 PAINTERLY REALISM

A term employed by Gerrit Henry to characterize the work of a number of American painters active during the period 1950–80: Fairfield Porter (1907–75) – dubbed 'the father of Painterly Realism' – John Button, Robert Dash, Jane Freilicher, George Nick and Neil Welliver, whose careers developed alongside those of the abstract expressionists. The acclaim received by the latter overshadowed the achievements of the former. As the term indicates, these figurative artists were committed to the truthful representation of the natural world, but they were also fully aware of the plastic character of the medium they were using, consequently, they avoided photo-realistic renditions of surface appearances. Henry also identified a second generation of Painterly Realists: Bill Sullivan, Frederick Church, Robert Berlind, Darragh Park and others. Painterly Realism was a conservative style that also permitted a degree of modernist experimentation. This, Henry claimed, was the reason for its longevity.

● See also Abstract Expressionism, Figurative Art, Perceptual Realism, Photo-Realism.

G Henry 'Painterly Realism and the modern landscape' *Art in America* **69** September 1981 112–19.

491 PAINTERS ELEVEN

Canadian abstract painters who formed a group in Toronto in 1953 and who exhibited together at the Roberts Gallery in February 1954. A neutral name was chosen because apart from their commitment to abstraction the artists had little in common. The best-known members of the group were Jack Bush and Harold Town. After showing across Canada and in the United States, Painters Eleven finally disbanded in 1960.

K Woods *History of Painters Eleven* (Oshawa, Ontario, Robert McLaughlin Gallery, 1971).

492 PANORAMAS

Large-scale painted or photographic scenes displayed on the inner walls of circular buildings so as to provide all-round vistas analogous to natural vision when seen from a central point. Aerial views of major cities were perhaps the favourite subjects of Panoramas. The word itself derives from the Greek 'pan', for 'all' and 'orama' for 'see'. Robert Baker, a Scottish painter, is credited with the invention of the first true panorama which he patented in 1787. Panoramas became popular in the nineteenth century along with peepshows, dioramas, cos-

PANORAMAS WERNER TÜBKE, detail from his panorama 'The early bourgeois revolution in Germany' i.e. the Battle of the Rainbow during the peasants' war of 1525 (1977-89). Oil on canvas, 400' x 50'. Interior of a rotunda near Bad Frankenhausen, Thuringia, East Germany. Photo: Channel 4 television.

moramas and moving Panoramas. Such illusionistic devices are generally ignored by mainstream histories of fine art because few major artists were involved in their manufacture and because they catered for a popular desire for entertainment and spectacle. These devices can, in fact, be regarded as the precursors of such modern mass media as the cinema and television.

An entry on Panoramas is justified in this text because of the scholarly attention that has been paid to them in recent years and because there are some artist–photographers (e.g. the Briton Simon Read) and some painters who continue to experiment with the form. In 1989 the East German painter Werner Tübke completed an enormous and highly detailed 360° mural located in Bad Frankenhausen, Thuringia, on the subject of the peasants' war.

● *Panoramic photography* (NY, New York University Grey Art Gallery, 1977).

● C Westerbeck 'Taking the long view' *Artforum* **16** (5) January 1978 56–9.

● *The Panoramic image* (Southampton, John Hansard Gallery, 1981).

● *The world is round: contemporary Panoramas* (NY, Hudson River Museum, 1987).

● R Hyde *Panoramania! The art and entertainment of the 'all-embracing' view* (Trefoil/Barbican Art Gallery, 1988).

493 PANZA COLLECTION A large and important collection of contemporary art assembled by the Italian Count, scientist and philosopher, Giuseppe Panza di Biumo from 1957 onwards. His collection was first housed in the Panza Villa, Varese. Panza began by collecting the abstract expressionists but later became interested in the minimal and conceptual work of the 1960s and '70s, especially large-scale installation pieces. Unable to persuade the Italian authorities to take over his collection, Count Panza decided in 1990 to make a combined gift and sale of 300 works to the Guggenheim Museum in New York.

● See also Abstract Expressionism, Conceptual Art, Installation, Minimal Art.

● T Trini 'At home with art: the villa of Count...' *Art in America* **58** (5) September–October 1970 102–9.

● B Kurtz 'Interview with Giuseppe Panza di Biumo' *Arts Magazine* **46** (5) March 1972 40–3.

● *Art of the '60s and '70s: the Panza Collection* (NY, Rizzoli, 1988).

● *Colección Panza* (Madrid, Centro de Arte Reina Sofia, 1988).

● S Morgan 'Past, present, future' *Artscribe International* (76) Summer 1989 53–6.

494 PARAESTHETICS A neologism coined by the American scholar David Carroll and used as the title of a study of the issue of art in the work of three French theorists: Foucault, Lyotard and Derrida. Paraesthetics means an approach to art 'in terms of its relations with the extra aesthetic...in the philosophical, historical and political issues raised by the question of form or the problem of beauty... Paraesthetics indicates something like an aesthetics turned against itself or pushed beyond or beside itself, a faulty, disordered, improper aesthetics – one not content to remain within the area defined by the aesthetic...a critical approach to aesthetics for which art is a question not a given...'

● D Carroll *Paraesthetics: Foucault, Lyotard, Derrida* (NY, Methuen, 1987).

495 PARTICIPATORY ART (Also Change Paintings, Fun Art, Option Art, Part Art, Polymorphic Paintings, Transformables, Variable

Painting) All works of art require the intellectual and emotional involvement of a spectator before they are complete – a point emphasized by Marcel Duchamp at a discussion session on the creative act held in Houston, Texas, in 1957 – and to this extent all art is participatory. However, there are degrees of participation: a viewer contemplating a painting is not so actively involved as someone target-shooting at a funfair. From the late 1950s onwards many avant garde artists wanted to increase the extent of audience participation and so they created objects, machines, games or structured situations explicitly to encourage adult play. In a sense the artists tried to make the creative act more democratic by sharing decision-making as to the final result with the audience.

The participation tendency was evident in op art (which involved vision more actively than traditional oil painting); in some forms of kinetic art (those that made use of spectator movement); in cybernetic sculptures (those that responded to sounds made by spectators); in happenings, environmental, community or street art (where the public was integral to the event). In 1968 an exhibition entitled 'Options', held in Milwaukee and Chicago, was designed specifically to encourage spectator participation. This gave rise to the label 'option art' which encompassed the 'variable paintings' of the Swedish artist Öyvind Fahlström with their detachable elements attached to the picture surface by hinges and magnets which permitted endless permutations; the 'change paintings' of the British artist Roy Ascott; the 'transformables' or 'polymorphic paintings' of the Israeli artist Yaacov Agam; and the contour shapes that Timothy Drever, a British sculptor, spread out on floors and lawns for spectators to manipulate.

From this general tendency there emerged a specific genre 'Part Art' (short for Participatory Art). An exhibition – 'Pioneers of Part Art' – featuring works by Li Yuan Chia, Lygia Clark, John Dugger, David Medalla and Helio Oiticica was held at the Museum of Modern Art, Oxford, in 1971. Medalla advocated the use of the word 'art' as in 'articulation', not as in 'art object'. Also in 1971, the American sculptor Robert Morris presented a series of heavy objects for visitors to play with and upon – described by one critic as 'an assault course' – at the Tate Gallery. In this instance the work was too successful: visitors participated over- vigorously and the authorities closed this section of the exhibition for fear that spectators would injure themselves.

In the United States Part Art was often called 'fun art'. Thomas Meehan, writing in 1970, claimed that it was a new artform that had excited large crowds in American museums and galleries. Such art was often expensive because of its technical requirements – inflatables, air currents, sounds/lights, electronics, and so forth – hence

it tended to be created by artists with engineering skills. Artists noted for this kind of work included Howard Jones, Stanley Landsman and Jean Tinguely. Clearly the name 'fun art' stresses spectator enjoyment but, arguably, the pleasure provided by this kind of art was not primarily aesthetic.

Experimental art groups such as the GRAV, the Haus-Rucker-Company, the Eventstructure Research Group, and community arts organizations such as Action Space and Inter-Action were all committed to audience participation and achieved a considerable measure of success. However, the idea had its critics. Michael Billington argued that physical participation was one of the great myths of contemporary art and that it was a substitute for spiritual involvement. In retrospect it can be seen that Part Art was a facet of 1960s counter-culture. With the decline of that culture in the '70s and '80s, a reversion to more conservative modes of making and appreciating art occurred.

● See also Community Art & Media, Cybernetic Art, Environmental Art, Eventstructure, Game Art, GRAV, Happenings, Haus-Rucker-Co, Inter-Change, Kinetic Art, Op Art, Technological Art.

◉ M Duchamp 'The creative act' – in – Marcel Duchamp by R Lebel (Paris, Trianon Press, 1959) 77–8.
◉ Directions 1: Options (Milwaukee Art Center, 1968).
◉ L Alloway 'Interfaces and options: Participatory Art in Milwaukee and Chicago' Arts Magazine 43 (1) September–October 1968 25–9.
◉ —'Options' Art & Artists 4 (7) October 1969 16–21.
◉ T Meehan 'Fun Art' Daily Telegraph Magazine (276) January 30 1970 18–23 + cover.
◉ A Forest 'Popa at MoMA' Art & Artists 6 (3) June 1971 46–7.
◉ E Lucie-Smith 'Art and playpower: a new philistinism' Encounter (8) August 1971 58–60.
◉ M Billington 'Life copying art' Guardian June 2 1972 8.
◉ J Wintle The Fun Art bus (Methuen, 1973).
◉ S Kranz 'Toward environmental art...' – in – Science and technology in the arts (NY, Van Nostrand Reinhold, 1974) 155–62.
◉ F Popper Art – Action – Participation (Studio Vista, 1975).

496 PARTICIPATORY DESIGN (Or Design Participation) During the late 1960s and early '70s certain architects, planners and designers (mainly those concerned with the public rather than the private sector) became disenchanted with the results they were achieving and looked for ways in which to involve users more so that their social needs could be better satisfied. Groups of ordinary people too reacted against the idea that the experts always knew best. They began to demand a say in the environmental, housing and product design decisions that influenced their lives so significantly and, in a number of instances, a degree of participation was achieved. Participation in design processes depended on the willingness of experts to consult users and to establish research organizations, mechanisms and channels through which people were enabled to contribute to the design of their dwellings, to the planning of the redevelopment of a neighbourhood, and so forth. Pressure groups such as the Consumers Association could also influence designers to generate better, safer products. There was a gap between experts and laypersons to be bridged, but there was also a need to reconcile different interests within communities, to overcome conflicts between the community as a whole and the various families, individuals and factions from which it was made up. The political implication of Participatory Design is indicated by Henry Sanoff's observation that it is a 'methodological intent which stems from the assumption that designing ought to be a collective decision-making effort operating on the principles of a democracy'.

In 1971 the DRS (Design Research Society) sponsored an international conference in Manchester on the theme of design participation. Some of the professionals attending conceived of participation in a technological way, i.e. in terms of 'responsive' environments that, through the agency of computers, could react according to the needs and desires of their human users. The continuing relevance of the concept of participation was indicated by another international conference which took place at Eindhoven in April 1985.

● See also Advocacy Planning, Community Architecture, Design Research Society, Mobile Architecture, Participatory Art, SAR, Social Architecture/Design, Soft Architecture.

◉ N Cross (ed) *Design Participation* (Academy Editions, 1972).

◉ S Nicolson & B Schreiner *Community participation in city decision-making* (Milton Keynes, Open University Press, 1973).

◉ F Becker *User participation, personalization and environmental meaning* (Ithaca, NY, Cornell University Program in Urban & Regional Studies, 1977).

◉ M Francis (ed) *Participatory planning and neighborhood control* (NY, CUNY/Center for Human Environments, 1978).

◉ A Wrona *Participation in architectural design and urban planning* (Warsankry, Poland, Politechniki, 1981).

◉ M Beheshti (ed) *Design Coalition Team vol 2* (Eindhoven, Proceedings of the International Design Participation Conference, 1985).

◉ 'Design Participation' *Design Studies* **7** (3) July 1986, special issue.

◉ 'Integrating research and Design Participation' *Design Studies* **9** (1) January 1988, special issue.

◉ *Tenant participation in housing design: a guide for action* (RIBA/IOH, 1988).

497 PATTERN PAINTING

(Also Decorative Painting, Dekor) A vogue in American art during the mid and late 1970s involving such artists as Robert Kushner, Cynthia Carlson, Joyce Kozloff, Brad Davis, Joseph Zucker, Mario Yrissary, Valerie Jaudon, Kendall Shaw, Kim MacConnel, Robert Zakanitch, Miriam Shapiro and Jerry Clapsaddle. Exhibitions of Pattern Painting were mounted at the P.S.1 Gallery, New York, Project Studios One, Long Island City, in 1977 and at the Museum of Modern Art, Oxford, in 1980.

As its name makes clear, this kind of painting celebrated patterns whether geometric (grids, nets, lattices) or non-geometric. Much of the work was abstract but some pieces featured figurative, floral and plant motifs. Pattern Painting marked a reaction to the puritanism of formalist abstraction, minimal and conceptual art; it also signalled a re-evaluation of the pleasures of colour, brushwork, the decorative in art, and craft/design processes. Items often resembled rugs and quilts more than traditional paintings and this led to a debate as to whether they were fine art or fabric design. Certain pieces involved off-stretcher, shaped wall hangings and costumes constructed like collages from printed fabrics, while others resembled wall-

PATTERN PAINTING KIM MACCONNEL, 'A new design' (1975). Acrylic, cotton & printed fabric, 7' x 6'. Photo: Project Studios One, Long Island.

paper in the sense that designs covered all the walls in some gallery installations. Influences upon the work included the late Matisse, Celtic and Islamic art, native American art, Ballet Russes, Persian and Indian miniatures, and patchwork.

Critics argued that Pattern Painting had its roots in modernist art but that in certain key respects it contradicted that tradition. It was also said to have a feminist dimension (i.e. the re-evaluation of craft and the decorative arts produced mainly by women). Pattern Painting was judged 'fun, gaudy, vulgar, jocular, hedonistic'. However, some critics considered it a short-lived fashion designed for the art market while others detected a lack of intellectual substance.

● See also Feminist Art, Grids, Installation, Ornamentalism, Shaped Canvas, Surface Design.

◉ A Goldin 'Patterns, grids and painting' *Artforum* **14** (1) September 1975 50–4.

◉ J Perreault 'Issues in Pattern Painting' *Artforum* **16** (3) November 1977 32–6.

◉ K Geirlandt *Pattern Painting* (Paris, Palais des Beaux Arts, 1979).

◉ T Godfrey 'Dekor: the marriage of reason and squalor (?!)' *Art Monthly* (36) May 1980 15–16.

◉ D Elliott & C Rickey *Dekor: decor and ornamentation in recent American art* (Oxford, MoMA, 1980).

498   **PEASANT PAINTING**   (Huxian & Masses Paintings, Spare-Time Art) In China during the communist rule of Chairman Mao the bourgeois conception of art as the concern of an educated élite and specialized professionals called 'artists' was challenged by the idea that art was an activity in which all members of society ought to participate as producers or consumers.

In the late 1950s and again in the wake of the Cultural Revolution of 1966 (a revolution in which many artistic treasures of the past were destroyed), workers and peasants (many of them women) were encouraged to begin painting in their spare time and thousands of works were generated as a result. They depicted the social and technological progress of the nation, illustrating scenes of agricultural labour, construction work, political meetings and village recreations, and so on. Travelling exhibitions of these paintings (particularly those from Huxian province) made them known to Western viewers in the early 1970s and they excited interest because they contrasted so strongly with the norms of Western avant garde art.

What was striking about them was their high level of technical proficiency (given that they were supposed to be by untrained peasants) and also their stylistic uniformity: bright, flat, emblematic colours; muscular drawing with precise outlines; an all-over decorative effect; cellular, decentralized compositions foregrounding group or collective activities (only party officials tended to be painted as individuals). The pictures seemed be a blend of Western comic-book art (the source was actually Chinese folk art, particularly new year, good luck pictures) and traditional Chinese painting with its tipped-up perspectives. Socialist realist stereotypes were on the whole avoided.

In China art was considered an ideological weapon in the class struggle, therefore peasant paintings were wholly public in their appeal and function; i.e. they did not present the personal visions or private obsessions of gifted individuals. Unlike the avant garde art of the West, much of which was decadent, narcissistic, sex-obsessed (what Rosetta Brooks called 'ego art'), Chinese art radiated pride and optimism. 'They are pictures of Utopia made by people who believe they inhabit one', wrote Brooks. Just as in the West it was advertising that celebrated the joys of capitalism, so in China it was art that celebrated the joys of communism. A cynic might say a huge amount of kitsch was generated by both systems.

A display of Chinese peasant paintings was shown at the 9th Paris Biennale in 1975. In a review Brooks argued that Mao's demand for a unity of art and politics, content and form, was achieved in the realist style of the peasant pictures but this realism was not 'a Western version of realism in the sense of paring away rhetoric and connotation to achieve a pure denotative reference of reality, but one which accepts its rhetorical orientation and denotes social relations as its reality'. Another Western art critic who wrote sympathetically and perceptively about this type of art was Guy Brett.

● See also Mass Art, Naive Art, Political Art, Popular Art, Totalitarian Art.

◉ Mao Tse-Tung *Talks at the Yenan forum on literature and art* (Peking, Foreign Languages Press, 4th ed 1967).

◉ *Chinese graphic art* (Fribourg University, 1973).

◉ *Peasant Paintings from Huhsien county* (Peking, Foreign Languages Press, 1974).

◉ G Brett 'China's Spare-Time artists' *Studio International* **189** (973) January–February 1975 12–15.

◉ P Pacey 'The art of red China: a note on the literature' *ARLIS Newsletter* (22) March 1975 19–21.

◉ R Brooks 'France: 9th Paris Biennale' *Studio International* **190** (978) November–December 1975 230–3.

◉ R Skoggard 'Report from China: Chinese art, from Tao to Mao' *Art in America* **64** (6) November–December 1976 52–5.

◉ G Brett 'A lesson in the fields'– in – *Through our own eyes: popular art and modern history* (London, Heretic-GMP Publishers/Philadelphia, New Society Publishers, 1986) 55–81.

499 PENTAGRAM

A pentagram is a star shape with five points. It is also the name of one of Britain's leading design partnerships formed in London in 1972 by five mature designers – Theo Crosby, Colin Forbes, Alan Fletcher, Mervyn Kurlansky and Kenneth Grange – each of whom had international reputations in their own fields. Pentagram blended graphic, product and architectural design skills in order to provide a comprehensive service for large companies.

● See also Consultant Design.

● H Spencer 'Pentagram: a London design group' *Graphis* **27** (158) 1971-2 550–67.

● Pentagram Design Partnership *Pentagram: the work of five designers* (Lund Humphries, 1972).

● P Gorb (ed) *Living by design: Pentagram* (Lund Humphries, 1978).

● Pentagram *Ideas on design* (Faber & Faber, 1987).

500 PERCEPTUAL REALISM

(Also Perceptualism) A term used by the Canadian painter and film-maker John or Jack Chambers (1931–78) to characterize a particular group of realistic paintings based on coloured photographs produced from 1969 onwards. The paintings seemed straightforward enough but they were accompanied by verbose, obscure statements. The theory of Perceptual Realism appeared to depend upon the assumption that there are moments of disinterested vision which precede our normal recognition of the world – a kind of pure perception before culture intervenes – it is this experience Chambers attempted to capture in his paintings and films.

● See also Photo-Realism.

● J Chambers 'Perceptual Realism' *ArtsCanada* (136/137) October 1969 7–13.

● M Amaya 'Jack Chambers' *Art in America* **58** (5) September–October 1970 118–21.

● D Shadbolt 'On the evolution of John Chambers' "Perceptual Realism"' *ArtsCanada* (148/149) October–November 1970 57–62.

● R Woodman 'The realism of John Chambers' *Art International* **14** (9) November 1970 37–41.

● *Jack Chambers* (Vancouver Art Gallery, 1970).

● J Chambers 'Perceptualism' *Art & Artists* **7** (9) December 1972 28–33.

501 PERFORMANCE ART

An extremely broad category of contemporary art encompassing a variety of activities and behaviours, different styles and aesthetic intentions, having as a common denominator the execution of prescribed courses of action before live audiences. Performance Art is an international phenomenon but tends to be called by different names in different countries. Also, it overlaps with several other kinds of art, i.e. actions, body art, community art, happenings, process art, street art and video art, and with popular forms of entertainment, e.g. busking, stunts, children's games (e.g. dressing up), rock music, and with ancient or 'primitive' culture, e. g. shamanism, tribal rituals.

Because of its diversity, transience and geographic dispersal, no single critic is in a position to give a complete account of Performance Art. For the same reasons it is hard to define. Definitions tend to specify the ways in which it differs from performing arts such as dance and theatre. Performance Art is normally created by people with a fine art training; consequently it relates to the history of painting and sculpture not the history of the theatre, and it takes place in art galleries rather than in theatres. For the most part, it ignores the conventions of the performing arts. Some artists object to the idea of a genre called 'Performance Art'. Stuart Brisley, for instance, once declared his work to be 'anti-Performance Art'.

Public performances or demonstrations were a feature of several early modern art movements – dada, futurism, surrealism – but the post-1960 vogue for Performance tended to derive more from the emphasis on the painter's creative act in action painting: Jackson Pollock's behaviour in the studio was made public via photographs

PERFORMANCE ART NIGEL ROLFE, 'Work with fan & dust' (1989). Photo: Stuart Smyth, courtesy of Nigel Rolfe.

and films; Georges Mathieu painted canvases before live audiences according to a time schedule; Yves Klein used live naked models as paintbrushes to generate a series of canvases he called 'anthropometrics' – these too were made in front of an invited audience.

Fine artists were attracted to Performance because it provided an alternative to the isolation of the studio: there was a live situation, an immediate public response. Furthermore, it enabled them to collaborate with other artists. In New York three American artists – John Perreault, Majorie Strider and Scott Burton – formed the 'Association for Performance' to promote, present and preserve new forms of 'artists' theatre'. Other American artists noted for Performance included: Vito Acconci, Laurie Anderson, Eleanor Antin, Chris Burden (who organized situations in which his life was put at risk), John Cage, Richard Foreman (founder of the Ontological-Hysteric Theatre), Dan Graham, Joan Jonas, Alison Knowles, Robert Longo, Yoko Ono, Dennis Oppenheim, Yvonne Rainer, Robert Rauschenberg and Robert Wilson.

In Britain the popularity of Performance in the 1960s and '70s was evident from the proliferation of groups: the Bow Gamelan Ensemble, Coum Transmissions, Fine Artists, Gilbert & George, Hesitate & Demonstrate, John Bull Puncture Repair Kit, Nice Style, the People Show, the Phantom Captain, Situations & Real Lifescapes, Station House Opera, Ting-Theatre of Mistakes, Words Actions & Situations, etc., etc. British artists (and artists resident in Britain) noted for their Performances included: Anna Bean and Paul Burwell, Stuart Brisley, Shirley Cameron and Roland Miller, Rob Con, Rose Finn-Kelcey, Mona Hatoum, Susan Hiller, Anthony Howell, Sonia Knox, Robbie Kravitz, Bruce Lacey and Jill Bruce, John Latham, Richard Layzell, Bruce Mclean, Denis Masi, David Medalla, Jeff Nuttall, Hannah O'Shea, Carlyle Reedy, Nigel Rolfe, Marty St James and Anne Wilson, Alistair Snow, Kerry Trengrove and Silvia Ziranek.

In Europe key figures in Performance included: from Germany Joseph Beuys and Wolf Vostell; from France Yves Klein; from Italy Piero Manzoni; from Austria the Wiener Aktionismus artists Nitsch, Brus and Mühl; and from Spain the spectacular group La Fura dels Baus (Vermin of the Sewers). International, national and annual festivals of Performance Art were held in several countries. One which took place in Britain was organized by the South Hill Park Arts Centre in Bracknell (from 1983 onwards). Performance became one of the most documented genres of contemporary art: amongst the magazines devoted to it were *High Performance* (Los Angeles), *Performance* (London) and *P. S. Primary Sources* (Brighton & London). A selection of articles, histories and anthologies is listed below.

● See also Actions, Behavioural Art, Body Art, Cross-Overs, Direct Art, Environmental Art, Fluxus, Gilbert & George, Happenings, Living Sculpture, Nice Style, Participatory Art, Shamanism, Time-Based Arts, Video Art.

● E Robbins 'Performing art' *Art in America* **54** (4) July–August 1966 107–10.

● V Acconci 'Some notes on activity and Performance' *Interfunctionen* (5) November 1970 138–42.

● 'Performance at the limits of Performance' *Drama Review* **16** (1) March 1972 70–86.

● A Henri 'The artist as performer' – in – *Environments and happenings* (Thames & Hudson, 1974) 133–85.

● R Goldberg 'Space as praxis' *Studio International* **190** (977) September–October 1975 130–5.

● M Chaimowicz 'Performance' (irregular column) *Studio International* **191** (979) January–February 1976–.

● C Tisdall 'Performance Art in Italy' *Studio International* **191** (979) January–February 1976 42–5.

● A Kaprow 'Non-theatrical Performance' *Artforum* **14** (9) May 1976 45–51.

● 'Performance' *Studio International* **192** (982) July–August 1976, special issue.

● 'Actions/Performance issue' *Musics* (9) September 1976.

● M Benamou & C Caramello (eds) *Performance in post -modern culture* (Madison, Wisconsin, Coda Press, 1977).

● A Bronson & P Gale (eds) *Performance by artists* (Toronto, Art Metropole, 1979).

● C Loeffler & D Tong (eds) *Performance anthology: a source book for a decade of California Performance Art* (San Francisco, Contemporary Art Press, La Mamelle Inc, 1980).

● J Nuttall *Performance Art* 2 vols (John Calder, 1980).

● A Melzer *Latest rage the big drum: dada and surrealist Performance* (Ann Arbor, Michigan, University of Michigan Research Press, 1981).

● M Roth (ed) *The amazing decade: women's Performance Art in America 1970–80* (Los Angeles, Astro Artz, 1983).

● G Battcock & R Nickas (eds) *The art of Performance: a critical anthology* (NY, Dutton, 1984).

● R Goldberg *Performance Art: from futurism to the present* (Thames & Hudson, rev ed 1987).

● R Miller 'Performance Art from the '70s to the '80s' *Variant* (Glasgow) (4) Winter–Spring 1987–88 8–12.

● H Sayre *The object of Performance: the American avant garde since 1970* (Chicago University Press, 1989).

502 PHASES MOVEMENT

In the early 1950s the French poet Edouard Jaguer presided over an international movement centred on Paris devoted to the art of the imaginary, i.e. continuing the principles of surrealism. The movement was called 'Phases' after an irregular review of that name first published in 1954. Jaguer organized a number of exhibitions which featured work by artists as various as Enrico Baj, Pierre Alechinsky, Antonio Tàpies and Öyvind Fahlström.

● E Jaguer *Phases of contemporary art* (Paris, Galerie Creuze, 1955).

● *Parfois c'est l'inverse* ('Phases' exhibition) (Amsterdam, Stedelijk Museum, 1957).

● A Pellegrini *New tendencies in art* (NY, Crown, 1966) 283–92.

● G Ollinger-Zingue 'Phases'– in– 'The Belgian contribution to surrealism' *Studio International* **183** (937) October 1971 155.

● *Rétroviseur* (Nice, 1972).

503 PHENOMENOLOGY & ART

Phenomenology is a school of philosophy mainly associated with the writings of Edmund Husserl and Maurice Merleau-Ponty. It is concerned with the description and analysis of subjective processes and it stresses the primacy of perception. It is, therefore, particularly suited to the appreciation and critical evaluation of visual works of art. In his paper 'Eye and mind' Merleau-Ponty explored the relationship between vision and consciousness with special reference to the painter's way of seeing; in addition he produced a profound study of Cézanne's paintings. Attempts have been made by Dufrenne and Kaelin to construct a phenomenological aesthetics and various concepts from Phenomenology have been applied in a piecemeal fashion to 1960s art by certain American critics. Minimal art, for instance, was interpreted in terms of Phenomenology because it eschewed internal formal relations and thus emphasized the spectator's perceptual experience as he or she moved around the work considering its relationship to the space of the gallery. Bruce Nauman's work even gave rise to the pun 'phenNaumanology' (Marcia Tucker) because he isolated sensory phenomena such as light and sound for our contemplation. Another crucial feature of Phenomenology was its emphasis on intentionality. A similar emphasis on the artist's intentions implied a shift away from the art object, a break with formalist criticism.

● See also Existentialism & Art, Formalism & Formalist Criticism.

● M Merleau-Ponty 'Eye and mind' – in – *The primacy of perception* J Edie (ed) (North Western University Press, 1964) 159–90.

● —'Cézanne's doubt' *Art & Literature* (4) Spring 1965 106–24.

● E Kaelin *Art & existence: a phenomenological aesthetics* (Lewisbury, Buckness University Press, 1970).

● N Calas 'The phenomenological approach' – in – *Icons and images of the sixties* by N & E Calas (NY, Dutton, 1971) 249–57.

● J Place 'Merleau-Ponty and the spirit of painting' *Philosophy Today* **17** (414) Winter 1973 280–91.

● D Kuspit 'A phenomenological approach to artistic intention' *Artforum* **12** (5) January 1974 46–53.

● L Borden 'The new dialectic' *Artforum* **12** (7) March 1974 44–51.

● M Dufrenne *The Phenomenology of aesthetic experience* 2 vols (North Western University Press, 1974).

504 PHOTO-MONTAGE

(Also Composite Imagery, Critical Montage, Fotomontage, Photo-collage) Essentially a subcategory of collage. The term 'Photo-montage' is itself a montage, i.e. a conjunction of two terms with different meanings which, when brought together, generate a third meaning. 'Photo' obviously derives from photography, the medium par excellence for recording the appearance of reality. 'Montage', a French word meaning 'mounting', had industrial overtones in German usage: 'fitting' and 'assembling'. The artist cuts up photographs and reassembles them, like a mechanic or engineer, in order to produce a composite image with new meanings. (The analytical/constructive method of Photo-montage is considered by Left-wing artists to provide a means of penetrating deceptive surface appearances to reveal underlying truths.) Other methods for producing composite images and the so-called 'third effect' include: superimposing one image on another, adding colours or captions. Photo-montage has been called 'static film' because it is a still equivalent of the montage techniques used by film editors when they are assembling a movie. Because montage is so crucial in the cinema, the most sophisticated theories of montage are to be found in the writings of film directors and critics.

Although the first examples of Photo-montage date from the nineteenth century, it only became a technique employed seriously by fine artists at the time of the First World War when German and Russian artists began to use it for aesthetic and political purposes. For instance, the dadaists of Berlin: Hannah Höch, Raoul Hausmann, Georg Grosz, Johannes Baader and, of course, John Heartfield. In the Soviet Union El Lissitzky, Rodchenko and Gustav Klutsis exploited the technique. Later the surrealists used it: Max Ernst and Man Ray in particular, In the years since 1945 a host of artists working within several different styles have made Photo-montages: Carol Condé and Karl Beveridge, Peter Dunn & Loraine Leeson, Gilbert & George, Vaughan Grylls, R. B. Kitaj, Hans Haacke, Richard Hamilton, Chris Jennings, Ray Johnson, Peter Kennard, Barbara Kruger, the Film and

PHOTO-MONTAGE PETER KENNARD, 'Anti-nuclear photo-montage' (1982). Photo: Peter Kennard.

Poster Collective, London, Jamie Reid, Klaus Staeck, John Stezaker and Chris Themptander. While many of these artists were Left-wingers or feminists employing Photo-montage as a political and ideological weapon of propaganda and persuasion, the technique is not intrinsically a tool of the Left – it is also used daily by press illustration and commercial advertising.

One reason for the appeal of Photo-montage to artists on the Left is that it lends itself to mass reproduction via posters, photo-murals, newspapers, book covers/ illustrations and magazines; hence it has a democratic and popular potential far greater than traditional forms of art. When employed for the purposes of agit-prop and satire, Photo-montage has close connections with cartoons and caricatures.

● See also Assemblage Art, Factography, Gilbert & George, Joiners, Mail Art, Photo-works, Pictorial Rhetoric, Political Art, Prop Art, Punk, Situationists.

● A Scharf *Art and photography* (Allen Lane, The Penguin Press, 1968).

● *John Heartfield* (Arts Council of Great Britain, 1969).

● J Berger 'The political uses of Photo-montage' – in – *Selected essays and articles: the look of things* (Harmondsworth, Penguin Books, 1972) 183–9.

● L Kuleshov 'The origins of montage' – in – *Cinema in revolution: the heroic era of the Soviet film* L & J Schnitzer & M Martin (eds) (Secker & Warburg, 1973) 67–76.

● R Diederich & R Grubling *'Unter die Schere mit den 8 Geiern!' : Politische Fotomontage in der Bundesrepublik und WestBerlin: Documente und Materialien* (Berlin, Elefanten Press Galerie, 1977).

● J Heartfield *Photo-montages of the Nazi period* (Gordon Fraser/Universe Books, 1977).

● J Holtenfreter *Politische Fotomontage* (Berlin, Elefanten Press Galerie, 1977).

● E Siepmann & others *Montage: John Heartfield* (Berlin, Elefanten Press Galerie, 1977).

● R Sobieszek 'Composite Imagery and the origins of Photomontage. Part I the naturalistic strain' *Artforum* **17** (1) September 1978 58–65; Part II October 1978 40–5.

● A Jurgens-Kirchhoff *Technik und Tendenz der Montage in der bildenden Kunst des 20. Jahrhunderts* (Geissen, Anabas Verlag, 1978).

● J Stezaker *Fragments* (Photography Gallery, 1978).

● G Patti & others *Fotomontaggio: storia, tecnica ed estetica* (Milan, Gabriele Mazzotta Editore, 1979).

● D Kahn *John Heartfield: art and mass media* (NY, Tanam Press, 1985).

● D Ades *Photo-montage* (Thames & Hudson, rev ed 1986).

● D Evans & S Gohl *Photo-montage: a political weapon* (Gordon Fraser, 1986).

● J Reid & J Savage *Up they rise: the incomplete works of Jamie Reid* (Faber & Faber, 1987).

● D Evans & J Roberts *Critical Montage* (Gunnersbury Park, Small Mansion Art Centre, 1988).

● P Kennard *Images for the end of the century: Photo-montage equations* (Journeyman Press, 1990).

505 PHOTO-REALISM (Also Artificial / Cool / Extreme/ Hyper/ New/ Post-Pop / Radical / Super / Sharp-focus Realism, Inhumanists, New Academicians, New York Naturalism.) Periodically a fresh generation of artists finds it necessary to confront that great nineteenth-century rival of painting, photography. Photo-Realism – short for Photographic Realism – was one such response dating from the 1960s and early '70s. It came to public notice when shown in force at the Documenta 5 exhibition of 1972. In Europe, 'hyperrealism' was the generally preferred term.

Artists included in this category were: Robert Bechtle, Claudio Bravo, John Clem Clarke, Chuck Close, Robert Cottingham, Don Eddy, Richard Estes, Bruce Everett, Malcolm Morley, Frank Gertsch, Ralph Goings, Michael Gorman, John Kacere, Alfred Leslie, Richard McLean and John Salt. This list indicates the internation-

PHOTO-REALISM ROBERT BECHTLE, '61 Pontiac' (1968-9). Oil on canvas 60" x 84". Photo: Geoffrey Clements/Whitney Museum of American Art, New York.

al character of the genre, though the majority of the names are American.

Most Photo-Realists used photographs as an impersonal source of visual imagery. Because their attitude to subject matter was neutral, they preferred reportage photographs and postcards of banal motifs – automobiles, suburban scenes, shop fronts, horses, ships and faces. Clarke and Morley also revamped reproductions of old masterpieces. The source images were meticulously copied in acrylic paint to generate paintings of high illusionism and extreme verisimilitude, hence the prefixes 'super', 'radical', 'hyper', etc. Often the scale of these canvases was monumental, e.g. Chuck Close's portraits. Their inflated size and cold, mechanical finish endowed them with a disturbing quality resembling surrealist paintings.

In a sense Photo-Realists were not realists. They did not want to depict reality directly, only to copy visual signs that conventionally stand as truthful records of reality. Their attitude to photographs recalled the way that Jasper Johns had used flags and the pop artists had used mass-media images, i.e. as flat images to be used on flat surfaces. They were intrigued by the technical problems of rendering tones across a surface and capturing highlights and reflections. Morley treated his source photos as if they were abstractions: he turned the photos sideways to negate their subject matter and copied them square by square. Arguably, Photo-Realism was more akin to formalist abstraction than realism. Photo-Realist pictures fulfilled their destiny when reproduced as photographs in art magazines: the viewer looked at a photo of a painting of another photograph and felt uncertain about the identity of what was being reproduced. Many critics reacted negatively to this genre and condemned it as 'a late bourgeois edition of salon painting'.

Some sculptures were also produced in the same vein as Photo-Realism: see Verist Sculpture.

● See also Superhumanism, Zebra.

◉ U Kultermann *New realism* (Mathew Miller Dunbar, 1972).

◉ L Alloway *Photo-Realism: paintings, sculpture and prints from the Ludwig Collection and others* (Serpentine Gallery, 1973).

◉ L Chase *Les Hyperréalistes Américains* (Paris, Filipacchi, 1973).

◉ *Hyperréalisme: maîtres Américains & Européens* (Brussels, Isy Brachot Éditeur, 1973).

◉ G Battcock (ed) *Super-Realism: a critical anthology* (NY, Dutton, 1975).

◉ E Lucie-Smith *Super Realism* (Oxford, Phaidon, 1979).

◉ J Arthur *Realism/Photo-Realism* (Tulsa, Oklahoma,

Philbrook Art Center, 1980).

● C Lindey *Superrealist painting and sculpture* (NY, Morrow, 1980).

● L Meisel *Photo-Realism* (NY, Abrams, 1980).

● S Booth-Meredith & others *Real, really real, super-real: directions in contemporary American realism* (San Antonio, Texas, Museum of Art, 1981).

● F Goodyear *Contemporary American realism since 1960* (Philadelphia, Pennsylvania Academy of Fine Arts/Boston, New York Graphic Society, 1981).

506 PHOTO-THERAPY (Also Psychic Realism) A term invented by the British feminist photographers Jo Spence and Rosy Martin in the mid 1980s to describe the use of the medium of photography as an aid to healing and self-understanding. Camera sessions were employed in order to act out scenes from the past and to explore the various images of the self from which their social identities were constructed. Photo-Therapy was devised as a radical alternative to conventional portraiture.

● See also Art Therapy, Auto-Art, Body Art, Feminist Art, Photo-Works, Story Art.

● R Martin & J Spence 'New portraits for old: the use of the camera in therapy' *Feminist Review* (19) Spring 1985 66-92.

● J Spence *Putting myself in the picture: a political, personal and photographic autobiography* (Camden Press, 1986).

● — & R Martin 'Photo-Therapy: Psychic Realism as a healing art?' *Ten 8* (30) Autumn 1988 2–17.

507 PHOTO-WORKS (Including Photo-Grams & Photo-Sculptures) Although there are still some conservatives who refuse to accept that photography can be art, the fact is that the medium has been adopted by many fine artists in the twentieth century. They use it to do more than simply record sculptures or paintings. Art galleries, museums and auction houses also display, preserve and sell photographs. 'Photo-Works' is a term that has come to be used about photographs by artists, or about photographs by others that fall outside the wider categories of photo-journalism, social documentary, amateur photography, fashion photography, etc. Its limitation is that it is a neutral, blanket term which gives no indication of the differences (in aesthetic intentions) between the artists concerned. Amongst those who have employed photography in a substantial way since the 1960s are: Keith Arnatt, John Baldessari, Victor Burgin, James Collins, Jan Dibbets, Hamish Fulton, Gilbert & George, David Hockney, John Hilliard, Richard Long, Yve Lomax, Sarah McCarthy, Arnulf Rainer, Klaus Rinke, Cindy Sherman, Andy Warhol and Paul Wombell. These artists have contributed to a dozen different tendencies: feminist art, land art, conceptual art, story art, and so on. Most conceptual artists had little interest in the medium of photography as such nor did they want to take beautiful pictures; photography was simply a means by which certain ideas or concepts could be visualized.

One characteristic typical of much Photo-Work has been the use of a sequence of images to record a process or event, or to generate new meanings. In the latter case, the montage did not take place within a single frame (as in the photo-montages of John Heartfield) but, as in film, by abutting a number of distinct images. Frequently, the meanings were also the result of textual additions, consequently in many instances a more precise label would be 'Photo-Text Works'. Some artists used photos and words to produce a kind of photo-journalism while others preferred to employ readymade mass-media images rather than taking their own photos, and combined them with drawings, words and so forth in order to effect a critique of the material and to exploit the pleasures of intertextuality. And others, like Sherman, imitated an existing photographic genre; in her case, Hollywood film still portraiture.

'Photo-Sculpture' is a term with several meanings. In the 1860s it was used by François Willème to refer to

PHOTO-WORKS ANDY GOLDSWORTHY, 'Polished to catch the light, creased and folded, pinned with thorns'. Castres, October 18 1989. Photo: the artist & Watershed Media Centre, Bristol.

portrait sculptures produced semi-mechanically with the aid of a camera (a person was photographed from many viewpoints), projected silhouettes, a pantograph and a clay model. The term has also been used in 1989 by Rupert Martin to refer to artworks by Hannah Collins, Andy Goldsworthy, Mari Mahr, Ron O'Donnell, Gary Miller, Boyd Webb and others resulting from the intersection of sculpture and photography, two media in which light is crucial. Fragile sculptures made from ephemeral materials such as leaves were given permanence by being photographed. Photo-Sculptures can also be generated without cameras: i.e. 'Photo-Grams' produced by placing objects on light-sensitive paper.

● See also Anonymous Sculpture, Concerned Photography, Joiners, Photo-Montage, Photo-Therapy, Projected Art, Staged Photography, Story Art.

● V Haffer *Making Photo-Grams: the creative process of painting with light* (Focal Press, 1969).

● L Alloway 'Artists and photographs' *Studio International* **179** (921) April 1970 162–4.

● 'Special issue on Photo-Works' *Flash Art* (52/53) February–March 1975.

● 'Art & photography' *Studio International* **190** (976) July–August 1975.

● V Kahmen *Photography as art* (Studio Vista, 1975).

● 'Kunst-fotografie...' *Magazine Kunst* **16** (4) 1976 60–124.

● J Reichardt (ed) *Time, words, and the camera: Photo-Works by British artists* (Graz, Kunstlerhaus, 1976).

● P Hill & others *Three perspectives on photography: recent British photography* (Hayward Gallery/Arts Council of Great Britain, 1979).

● M Bogart 'Photo-sculpture' *Art History* **4** (1) March 1981 54–65.

● M Vaizey *The artist as photographer* (Sidgwick & Jackson, 1982).

● D Davis *Photography as fine art* (Thames & Hudson, 1983).

● F Neusüss (ed) *Fotogramme: die Lichtreichen Schatten* (Kassel, GFR Fotoforum, 1983).

● V Burgin *Between* (Oxford, Blackwell/London, ICA, 1986).

● A Grundberg & K Gauss *Photography as art: interactions since 1946* (NY, Abbeville Press, 1987).

● M Lumley (curator) *Shadow of a dream* (contemporary French Photo-Works) (Cambridge, UK, Cambridge Darkroom, 1989).

● R Martin *Photo-Sculpture: from object to image* (Bristol, Watershed Media Centre, 1989).

PICTORIAL RHETORIC

(Also Rhetoric of the Image, Visual Poetics/Rhetoric) The art of rhetoric – using speech or writing to persuade, exhort and instruct – dates back to ancient Greece. Various skills were associated with the second of the seven liberal arts – invention, arrangement, style, memory and delivery – plus a host of literary devices – metaphor, simile, synecdoche, personification, etc. Such devices can also be found in images, particularly those of caricature and advertising, hence the validity of the terms 'Visual' or 'Pictorial Rhetoric'. Systems of mass communication like advertising rely upon conventions, stereotypes and clichés known to millions. Avant garde art, on the other hand, has tended to be appreciated by a minority audience because of its intellectual difficulty due to the repeated attempts to transcend meaning altogether or to devise new 'private' languages or codes different from those of mass communication systems. (It should be acknowledged that what one generation finds difficult and incomprehensible the next may understand easily.)

In the 1960s theorists in Germany, France and Italy revived the study of the rhetoric of images. For teachers at Ulm, the German school of design, the aim was to influence future design by raising the level of understanding of designers and communicators as to how images worked. The aim of French theorists, on the other hand, was to increase the understanding of consumers of images so that they would be armed against the 'mother of lies', as rhetoric has been called.

During the 1970s a number of fine artists in Britain and the United States, prompted by a desire to reach a wider public and influenced by theoretical analyses of imagery by French semioticians, began to employ the Pictorial Rhetoric of the mass media in their work. Victor Burgin, for instance, adopted the mass medium of photography in order to make photo-text works and he also taught and wrote articles about the rhetorical devices of photography. 'Guerrilla Rhetoric' was a term employed about work which undertook a politically motivated critique of mass-media imagery.

● See also Information Graphics, Photo-Montage, Photo-Works, Prop Art, Semiotics, Situationists, Ulm.

● G Bonsiepe 'Persuasive communication: toward a Visual Rhetoric' *Uppercase* (5) 1961 19–34.

● J Durand 'Rhétorique et image publicitaire' *Communications* (Paris) (15) 1970 70–95.

● R Barthes 'Rhetoric of the image' *Working Papers in Cultural Studies* Spring 1971 36–50.

● V Burgin 'Photographic practice and art theory' *Studio International* **190** (976) July–August 1975 39–51.

● R Brooks 'Please, no slogans' *Studio International* **191** (980) March–April 1976 155–61.

● V Burgin 'Art, common sense and photography' *Camerawork* (3) July 1976 1–2.

● 'Visual Poetics' *Twentieth Century Studies* (15–16) December 1976, special issue.

● H Evans *Pictures on a page: photo-journalism, graphics and picture editing* (Heinemann, 1978).

● 'The language of images' *Critical Inquiry* **6** (3) Spring 1980, special issue.

509 PIN-UPS

(Including Calendar Girls, Cheesecake) Mark Gabor has defined a Pin-Up as 'a sexually evocative image, reproduced in multiple copies, in which either the expression or attitude of the subject invites the viewer to participate vicariously in, or fantasize about, a personal involvement with the subject'. Pin-Ups overwhelmingly depict women and are almost exclusively appreciated by men. They enable men to dominate women – in their imaginations – in a manner impossible in reality. Pin-Ups hover on the edge of soft pornography. Many feminists regard them as pornographic, as degrading to women, and exhibitions of calendar girls, such as the one at the ICA, London, in 1976, have been defaced by women's liberationists.

Although the term itself dates from the Second World War – it derived from the habit of American GIs of pinning up on lockers and walls pictures of nubile females and famous Hollywood stars – the concept of the Pin-Up is much older. A great boost to Pin-Ups was given by the advent of photography and they appeared on postcards in vast numbers during the First World War. In the 1930s and '40s Hollywood film stars added glamour to the genre and during the same period cartoonists began to incorporate Pin-Up girls in their strips, e.g. Al Capp's 'Daisy Mae', Norman Pett's and Mike Hubbard's 'Jane'. The '50s and '60s were marked by ever-growing permissiveness and greater sophistication in colour photography. The artistry of 'art photographs' served as an alibi for near-pornographic nudes. The famous series of Pirelli Calendars became collector's items and were sold for high prices in fine art auctions.

Pin-Up images found their way into fine art during the '60s when pop artists such as Peter Blake, Allen Jones, Tom Wesselmann and Mel Ramos made use of them. In the following decade it was photo-realist painters such as John Kacere who transposed them into the fine art realm. A book was also published about the well-known commercial illustrator specializing in Pin-Ups – Vargas. Also, in the '70s Pin-Ups attracted the attention of feminist art historians and social critics. Via glossy magazines such as *Playboy, Men Only* and *Mayfair,* Pin-Ups invaded virtually every newsagent. During the '80s Pin-Ups appeared at the breakfast table via the 'page three girls' in the British tabloid press. Measures to outlaw such images proposed by women members of Parliament were met with derision by most male MPs. A Tory minister even claimed they were the poor man's

equivalent of the erotic female nudes of the Western European oil-painting tradition.

● See also Erotic Art, Gay Art, Photo-Realism, Pop Art.

● M Gabor *The Pin-Up: a modest history* (Andre Deutsch, 1972).

● J Sternberg & P Chapelot *Pin-Up* (Academy Editions, 1972).

● 'Pin-Up and icon' – in – *Women as a sex object* T Hess (ed) (Allen Lane, 1973), *Art News* Annual **38**.

● M Casalis 'The discourse of *Penthouse:* rhetoric and ideology' *Semiotica* **15** (4) 1975 355–91.

● *The complete Pirelli Calendar book* (Pan Books, 1975).

● M Colmer *Calendar Girls* (Sphere Books, 1976).

● A Vargas & R Austin *Vargas* (NY, Crown, 1978).

● R Cranshaw 'The object of the centrefold' *Block* (9) 1983 26–33.

● *Lost Venus: the history of the Pin-Up* (Plexus, 1983).

● R Bradbury *The art of Playboy* (NY, Van der Marck, 1985).

● M Pye & D Forsyth *The Pirelli Calendar album* (Pavilion Books, 1989).

510 PLAGIARISTS

In early 1988 a number of radical artists organized a 'Festival of Plagiarism', i.e. a series of critical mixed-media exhibitions and events at off-beat locations in London and San Francisco. Those taking part included: Ed Baxter, Shaun Caton, Malcolm Dickson, Graham Harwood, Steve Perkins, Ralph Rumney, Karen Strang and Stefan Szczelkun. Theoretical back-up was supplied by Stewart Home. Plagiarism – the appropriation and passing off as one's own the work of others – is generally regarded as a bad thing, theft even, but paradoxically copying other artists and borrowing from them has been commonplace in the history of art. This was especially true of the pop artists who plundered mass culture and of the New York 'appropriation' artists of the 1980s (e.g. Sherrie Levine).

The self-proclaimed 'New Plagiarists' promoted the activity as an 'anti-capitalist, revolutionary tool'; they saw it as a necessary response to mass-media image glut, as an attack on private property rights, and upon artworks as commodities. To facilitate the act of copying, liberal use was made of photocopying machines. In fact, pure plagiarism rarely took place because in most cases transformations of the originals occurred. The art featured was extremely disparate in character and uneven in quality; no single medium or style predominated. Echoes of dada, Fluxus and happenings were discernible but also post-modern concerns with 'image scavenging' and the pop musical practice of 'sampling'.

● See also Commodity Aesthetics, Copy Art, Post-Modernism, Simulation/ Simulacra/ Hyperreality.

● S Home (ed) *Plagiarism: art as commodity and strategies for*

PLAGIARISTS GRAHAM HARWOOD, detail of treated xerox image from *John & other storys* (sic) (Graham Harwood, 1987). Photo: Harwood.

its negation (Aporia Press, 1987).

J Walker 'Perspective: living in borrowed time' *Times Higher Educational Supplement* February 26 1988 13.

E Baxter 'A footnote to the Festival of Plagiarism' *Variant* (Glasgow) (5) Summer–Autumn 1988 26–30.

511 PLASTICIENS, LES A group of Canadian artists established in Montreal in 1954, consisting of the painter–critic–mathematician Rodolphe de Repentigny, and the painters Louis Belzile, Jean-Paul Jerome and Fernand Toupin. These four were later joined by Fernand Leduc. Les Plasticiens reacted against the vogue for gestural painting and produced a style of geometric abstraction continuing the neo-plasticism of Mondrian and the abstract art of Malevich. Their paintings also had affinities with the international mode known as 'hard-edge painting'. Guido Molinari – a painter who was to become internationally known – exhibited with the group in 1959 and in the same year he and three others formed the group called 'Nouveaux Plasticiens'.

● See also Geometric Abstraction, Hard-Edge Painting.

F Saint-Martin 'Le dynamisme des Plasticiens de Montreal' *Vie des Arts* (44) Autumn 1966 44–7, + 98.

P Théberge 'Les Plasticiens' – in – *Canadian art today* W Townsend (ed) (Studio International, 1970) 25–6, + 86.

512 PLASTICS A group of natural and synthetic materials which can be shaped and moulded when soft. (The word 'plastic' derives from the Greek 'plastikos' meaning 'mouldable', hence 'the plastic arts' are those involving substances that can be shaped and moulded.) Modern plastics are extremely versatile; they are light, strong and durable; they can take on a tremendous variety of forms: sheets, rods, tubes, elastomers, films, gel, and so on. Also, plastic products can be hard and rigid, or pliable and foamlike. When synthetic plastics were first introduced into design they tended to be used as substitutes for traditional materials, with the consequence that the word 'plastic' acquired a pejorative association (i.e. 'not the real thing') which is no longer appropriate. Materials such as Celluloid and Parkesine were developed in Britain and the United States during the nineteenth century but the first synthetic plastic – Bakelite – was patented by Dr Leo Baekeland in 1907. However, it was not until the 1930s that a modern plastics industry came into being. (Polystyrene became commercial in 1937.) From then on, the expression 'the plastics age' began to be used.

Plastics are materials which have been employed in the twentieth century by artists, architects and designers in a multitude of ways; consequently a complete history or survey is impossible here. What follows are some examples to indicate the variety of uses to which different kinds of plastics have been put. Antoine Pevsner and Naum Gabo were the first artists to use celluloid sheets from which to construct sculptures in the 1920s. The material enabled them to open up the interior space of sculptures and to make their structures transparent. In the 1950s Dr A. Fleischmann carved figures from acrylic blocks in order to take advantage of the material's translucency. In the following decade Claes Oldenburg made soft sculptures from shiny PVC (vinyl) stuffed with kapok, while Piero Gilardi devised 'nature carpets' painted with lacquer made from expanded polyurethane.

PLASTICS PACAMAC & QUANT, Black & white mac by Pacamac, bag by Mary Quant, and other items (c 1966). PVC plastic. Photo: Fischer Fine Art Ltd., London.

poured on to the floors of galleries – they formed strange shapes and set rigid in minutes. The British sculptors Michael Sandle and Philip King constructed sculptures from GRP – glass fibre-reinforced plastic – because they could be built up in layers to yield a tremendous variety of shapes. Meanwhile Arman exploited the transparency of GRP resin by embedding objects in it. Kinetic artists such as Agam, Le Parc, Moholy-Nagy, Schöffer, Soto and Yvaral found acrylic sheets useful because they could be engraved and because they lent themselves to coloured light and optical illusion effects.

Painters too benefited from developments in plastics technology. The introduction in the '60s of acrylic pigments which could be diluted with water speeded up drying times and gave rise to a new kind of colour and paint quality as exemplified in the '60s work of David Hockney. Acrylics also enabled paintings to be built up from dilute colour washes that were allowed to flood and stain unprimed canvases.

Certain companies found plastics ideal for producing editions of those objects half-way between art and furniture, e.g. the 'lips' sofa designed by Studio 65 and manufactured by the Italian firm of Gufram (derived from a 1936 piece by Salvador Dali). Also in the '60s there was a vogue for transparent, blow-up chairs designed by Scolari, Lomazzi, D'Urbino & De Pas, Quasar Khanh, Paul Woods and Gernot Nalbach. Fashion designers such as Courrèges, Mr Freedom, Daniel Hechter, Mary Quant and Paco Rabanne designed clothes from plastic materials such as see-through PVC. Architectural instances of blow-up structures are discussed under the heading of Pneumatic Architecture. Readers seeking surveys of the use of plastics in the design of radio and TV cabinets, telephones, crockery, etc., should refer to the books by John Gloag and Sylvia Katz listed below.

Interest in plastic products has developed in recent decades amongst design historians and collectors (plastics antiques are called 'plastiquities'). The Plastics Historical Society was founded in Britain in 1986 and an ambitious exhibition about the role of plastics in design was held at the Victoria & Albert Museum in 1990. One disadvantage of plastic goods is that they have a very long life and hence pose a danger to the planet in terms of litter.

● See also Air Art, Artists' Furniture, Pneumatic Architecture, Pop Design, Stain Painting.

◉ J Gloag *Plastics and industrial design* (Allen & Unwin, 1945).

◉ J Mills *Acrylic painting* (Pitman, 1965).

◉ *Plastic as Plastic* (NY, Museum of Contemporary Crafts, 1968).

◉ R Barthes 'Plastic' – in – *Mythologies* (J Cape, 1972).

◉ T Newman *Plastics as design form* (Philadelphia, Chilton, 1972).

◉ N Roukes *Sculpture in Plastics* (Pitman, 1972).

◉ T Newman *Plastics as an artform* (Pitman, 1973).

◉ A Quarmby *The Plastics architect* (Pall Mall Press, 1974).

◉ *Plastics antiques 1850–1950s* (Wolverhampton Polytechnic, 1976).

◉ S Katz *Plastics: designs and materials* (Studio Vista, 1978).

◉ — *Classic Plastics: from Bakelite to high-tech* (Thames & Hudson, 1984).

◉ A DiNoto *Art Plastic* (NY, Abbeville Press, 1985).

◉ N Whiteley *Classic Plastic: a look at design 1950–74* (Fischer Fine Art, 1989).

◉ P Sparke *The Plastics age: from modernity to post-modernity* (Victoria & Albert Museum, 1990).

◉ S Lewin *Formica & design: from the countertop to high art* (NY, Rizzoli, 1991).

513 **PLURALISM** This word became highly fashionable in the artworld during the 1970s and was regarded by many as the defining characteristic of post-modernism. Borrowed from the discourse of politics where it represents a liberal-democratic ideal, the term 'Pluralism' signified a situation in which a number of different styles of art co-existed. No one style or movement was considered dominant, hence the single-strand, progressive development of art model associated with modernism was rejected as erroneous and authoritarian. (In fact, such a description of modern art was very dubious.) The word was also applied to artists and architects who combined several styles in a single work. A number of American art critics discussed the concept of Pluralism in November 1978 at the School of Visual Arts, New York. A symposium entitled 'Pluralism in architecture' was also held at the

Architecturmuseum, Frankfurt, in October 1988.

Many critics approved of Pluralism because it signified heterogeneous cultures with lots of variety and choice. However, sceptics perceived that diversity could also produce confusion, conflict and relativism. Herbert Marcuse, writing in 1964, viewed it as a sign of repressive tolerance: 'The absorbent power of society depletes the artistic dimension by assimilating its antagonistic contents. In the realm of culture, the new totalitarianism manifests itself precisely in a harmonizing pluralism, where the most contradictory works and truths peacefully co-exist in indifference.' (*One-dimensional man* (Routledge, 1964) pp 60–1.)

● See also Modernism, Post-Modern Architecture, Post-Modern Art, Post-Modern Design, Post-Modernism.

● C Jencks 'Introduction: the plurality of approaches' – in – *Modern movements in architecture* (Harmondsworth, Penguin Books, 1973) 11–27.

● John Perreault & others 'Pluralism in art and in art criticism' *Art Journal* **40** (1/2) Fall–Winter 1980 377–9.

● W Mitchell '*Critical Inquiry* and the ideology of Pluralism' ● *Critical Inquiry* **8** (1) Summer 1982 609–18.

● H Janne 'Cultural Pluralism' *Cultures* **8** (3) 1982 26–37.

● H Foster 'Against Pluralism' – in – *Recodings: art, spectacle, cultural politics* (Port Townsend, Washington, Bay Press, 1985) 13–32.

● C Robins *The Pluralist era: American art 1968–81* (Harper & Row, 1985).

● 'Pluralism and its discontents' *Critical Inquiry* **12** (3) Spring 1986, thematic issue.

● 'Art in the age of Pluralism' *Art & Design* **4** (7/8) 1988, (A & D Profile 10).

● A Papadakis (ed) *The architecture of Pluralism* (Academy Editions, 1989).

514 PNEUMATIC ARCHITECTURE

(Also Airdomes, Airhouses, Inflatable Structures) The examples of balloons and airships indicates that pneumatic technology has existed for some time. However, it was not until 1917 that the first patent for 'Pneumatic Architecture' – a field hospital – was filed by a British engineer F. W. Lanchester, and despite the appearance of Stomeyer inflatable tents in the 1930s, it was not until the Radomes of the late 1940s that large-scale pneumatic structures were erected. By 1957 there were 50 firms in the United States producing pneumatics. A decade later the first international colloquium on the subject was held at Stuttgart. Contemporary architects who have designed pneumatic structures include Jean-Paul Jungmann, Yutaka Murata and Cedric Price.

In traditional architecture it was the structure of the buildings which determined their internal environments, whereas in Pneumatic Architecture structural stability is the result of the release of internal energy (air or gas pressure) with a membrane or bag (often made of PVC-coated nylon). This kind of architecture is, therefore, a subcategory of pressurized construction (water or other liquids can also be used to pressurize). Three main types of pneumatics have been identified: air-inflated, air-supported and air-controlled. Because of their mode of construction, pneumatics generally consist of curved forms such as domes or half-cylinders. Their rounded forms, organic and responsive characteristics, have prompted some writers to compare them to the human body.

Pneumatics have been used as tents, warehouses, offices, arts centres, exhibition pavilions, greenhouses, swimming pool and stadium covers, and for various military purposes. Their advantages are said to be: speed of erection and dismantling, lightness, portability, flexibility, cheapness in terms of materials. They can be used in the short term to provide shelters against the weather while more conventional buildings are put up inside them. They can also be used in the construction process itself: concrete domes have been built using inflated domes as formworks.

● See also Air Art, Plastics, Utopie Group.

● F Otto *Tensile structures* vol 1 (Cambridge, Mass, MIT Press, 1967).

● *Proceedings of the 1st International Colloquium on Pneumatic Structures* (Stuttgart, University of Stuttgart, 1967).

● R Dent *Principles of Pneumatic Architecture* (Architectural Press, 1971).

● C Price & others *Air structures: a survey commissioned by the Ministry of Public Buildings and Works* (HMSO, 1971).

515 POLITICAL ART

(Also Activist Art, Agit-Prop, Angry Art, Art Dirigé, Art Engagé, Critical Art, Dialectical Art, Didactic Art, Dissident Art, Leftist Art, Marx Art, Progressive Art, Protest Art, Radical Art, Revolutionary Art, Socart, Social Functionalism, Socialist Formalism, Subversive Art, Utilitarian Art) Some Left-wing theorists maintain that all art is political, that all art either affirms or challenges the status quo. (Victor Burgin has argued that it is not possible to politicize art because it is already political. What the artist can do is to change its politics.) In most societies art has been a conservative force because it has served the interests and ideologies of the ruling powers: religion, the state, royalty, aristocrats, the bourgeoisie. A clear-cut case in the twentieth century was the art produced at the behest of the Nazis. However, in art criticism the term 'Political Art' is normally limited to those works of art that have an explicit political content and purpose, e.g. the agitation–propaganda work of the Soviet artists in the wake of the Russian Revolution, the anti-Nazi photo-montages of the German dadaist and communist John Heartfield, the public history paintings of the Mexican muralists, Picasso's 'Guernica', the films of Jean-Luc Godard, the posters of the Atelier Populaire, the paintings about torture by Leon Golub, and so on.

With the advent of the French Revolution of 1789 artists faced a new choice – to side with the forces of reaction or with the forces of revolution (Jacques-Louis David served both during his career). The emergence of the political ideologies of anarchism and socialism in the nineteenth century and the sharpening of the class struggle between the middle and working classes, caused some artists (e.g. Courbet, Camille Pissarro) to become politically committed. From then on the link between art and politics became inescapable and it was manifested in the major movements of dada, futurism and surrealism.

In the immediate post-1945 period French artists such as André Fougeron and Boris Taslitzky responded to Louis Aragon's demand for a politically engaged art (Aragon was the literary spokesman for the French Communist Party). At the same time, the Italian artist Renato Guttuso, a communist since 1935, emerged as the leading socialist realist painter in Europe. The dominant

movements of the 1950s were, however, abstract. Even so, these movements could be used for political purposes as subsequent analyses of the cultural propaganda role of abstract expressionist travelling exhibitions has demonstrated. Whatever the internal political content of a work of art, its political significance very much depends on the cultural context of display: during the 1950s an exhibition of abstract art in the West would have signified tolerance and freedom, whereas in the Soviet Union the same show would have been considered an act of provocation against the State. Another problem is estimating the social impact of Political Art. Often, the only signs are negative ones, i.e. censorship or vandalism.

During the 1960s a significant number of political works of art were made in Europe and the United States commenting upon the war in Vietnam and other issues of the day (e.g. civil rights, sexual politics). The emergence of the community art movement also signalled a concern with the politics of limited localities and groups. In the mid 1970s, for various reasons, there was a shift to the Left amongst many artworld intellectuals in Europe, South and North America; witness the founding of such magazines as *Artery, Black Graphics International, Block, Cultural Studies, The Fox, Left Curve, Ostrich,*

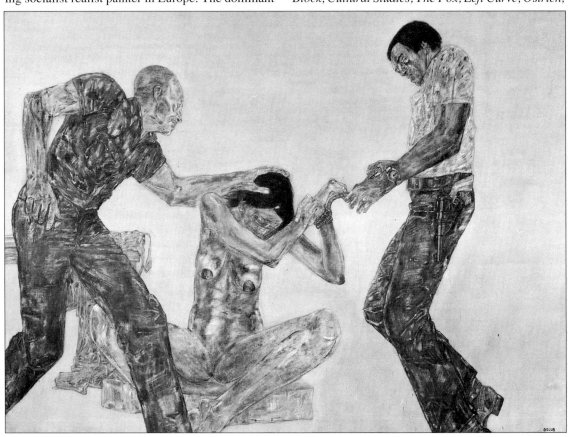

POLITICAL ART Leon Golub, 'Interrogation (III)' (1981). Acrylic on canvas, 120" x 166". Photo: Alan Zindman, New York.

Praxis, the contents of which were influenced by Marxism. Marking the culmination of this phase in Britain were the 1978 exhibitions 'Art for society' (Whitechapel Art Gallery) and 'Art for whom?' (Serpentine Gallery). In Germany the particularly strong tradition of Political Art – Heartfield, Grosz, Kollwitz *et al.* – was renewed in the '70s by Joseph Beuys, Hans Haacke, Klaus Staeck and many others.

Many politically conscious artists distrusted the label 'Political Art' because it implied that only some art was political and because they feared it heralded the recuperation of their work by museums and private galleries. During the 1980s the latter did indeed appear to happen especially in New York, i.e., after initial resistance, Political Art was accepted by dealers and curators as one type of art among a plurality of types, and artists like Golub, Terry Atkinson, Conrad Atkinson, Nancy Spero, Barbara Kruger, May Stevens etc. found that rich collectors were acquiring their work, that it was being accepted as art, but not contributing to social change to the extent the artists had hoped. Some of the most effective Political Art was that which undertook a critique of the art system from within the art system (e.g. certain works by Hans Haacke).

● See also Atelier Populaire, Banners, Black Art, Capitalist Realism, Community Art & Media, Disinformation, Feminist Art, Frankfurt School Aesthetics, Gay Art, Geometry of Rage, Guerrilla Art Action Group, Marxist Aesthetics, Nazi Art, Photo-Montage, Prop Art, Punk, Situationists, Totalitarian Art.

● H Rosenberg 'The politics of art' – in – *The anxious object: art today and its audience* (Thames & Hudson, 1965) 214–23.

● 'Art & politics...' (section 8) – in – *Theories of modern art* H Chipp (ed) (Berkeley, University of California Press, 1968) 456–500.

● D Egbert *Social radicalism and the arts: Western Europe* (Duckworth, 1970).

● *Kunst und Politik* (Karlsruhe, Badischen Kunstvereins, 1970).

● L Baxandall (ed) *Radical perspectives in the arts* (Harmondsworth, Penguin, 1972).

● *Kunst im Politischen Kampf* (Hanover, Kunstverein, 1973).

● *Art into society: society into art* (ICA, 1974).

● *Art: politics: theory: practice* (Royal College of Art, 1974), conference papers.

● 'Art and social purpose' *Studio International* **191** (980) March–April 1976, special issue.

● B Taylor (ed) *Art & politics* (Winchester School of Art Press, 1977), conference papers.

● *Art for society: contemporary British art with a social or political purpose* (Whitechapel Art Gallery, 1978).

● R Cork *Art for whom?* (Serpentine Gallery/Arts Council, 1978).

● H Millon & L Nochlin (eds) *Art and architecture in the service of politics* (Cambridge, Mass, MIT Press, 1978).

● R Philippe *Political graphics: art as a weapon* (NY, Abbeville Press, 1982).

● L Lippard *Get the message? A decade of art for social change* (NY, Dutton, 1984).

● *Politics in art, the art of politics* (NY, Museum of the Borough of Brooklyn, 1984).

● H Foster 'For a concept of the political in art' – in – *Recodings: art, spectacle, cultural politics* (Port Townsend, Washington, Bay Press, 1985) 139–55.

● D Kahn & D Neumaier (eds) *Cultures in contention* (Seattle, Real Comet Press, 1985).

● *Art history* (Hayward Gallery, 1987).

● D Wye *Committed to print: social and political themes in recent American printed art* (Thames & Hudson, 1988).

● A Goldstein & others *A forest of signs: art in the crisis of representation* (Cambridge, Mass, MIT Press/LA, MOCA, 1989).

● B Rolston *Politics and painting: murals in Northern Ireland* (Associated University Press, 1991).

516 POMPIDOU CENTRE

(Also Beaubourg Centre) A huge art and culture complex situated on the site of Les Halles, Paris, initiated by Georges Pompidou (President of France) in 1969 and opened in 1977. Its full title is 'Centre National d'Art et de la Culture Georges-Pompidou'. One aim of this complex was to re-establish Paris as the world's art capital. Housed in the Centre are: Le Musée National d'Art Moderne; a cinema; public library and information service; a documentation archive on contemporary art; L'Institut de Recherche et de Co-ordination Acoustique/ Musique (IRCAM); spaces for prestigious temporary exhibitions; Le Centre de Création Industrielle. The first visual arts director of the Centre was Pontus Hultèn.

The colourful, high-tech steel-and-glass structure with an external moving staircase has been called a 'megastructure'. It was designed by the English/Italian architects Richard Rogers and Renzo Piano. Despite or because of its uncompromisingly modern design, the Centre proved extremely popular with tourists and the public. However, intellectuals criticized it on a variety of grounds. The most trenchant critique was the Open University's Modern Art and Modernism course TV programme (1983) with a commentary by Michael Baldwin influenced by the ideas of Jean Baudrillard.

● See also CNAC, High-Tech, Megastructures.

● 'Centre Pompidou' *Architectural Design* **42** (2) February 1977.

● 'Centre National...' *Domus* (566/575) 1977 (special compilation).

● Cultural Affairs Committee, Parti Socialiste Unifié

'Beaubourg: the containing culture in France' *Studio International* **194** (988) January 1978 27–36.

J Baudrillard 'The Beaubourg-effect: implosion and deterrence' *October* (20) Spring 1982 3–13.

Masterpieces from the Pompidou Centre (Thames & Hudson, 1983).

R Rogers *Richard Rogers & architects* (Academy Editions, 1985).

R Piano & R Rogers *Du plateau Beaubourg au Centre Georges-Pompidou* (Paris, Éditions du Centre Pompidou, 1987).

517 POP ARCHITECTURE

This expression, short for 'popular architecture', has been employed by architectural writers to refer to several different categories of building:

(1) Structures popular with large sections of the general public and/or spec builders and property developers, e.g. SPAN housing, shopping malls and centres; this kind of architecture has also been called 'commercialized modern'.

(2) Structures whose shape or form depicts their function, e.g. a shoe repair shop built in the shape of a shoe. Such 'eccentric' or 'roadside architecture' was especially prevalent in the United States in the 1920s and '30s. It has also been called 'programmatic architecture' and been documented by J. J. C. Andrews and studied by the Society of Commercial Archaeology. In the case of a roadside curio shop built in the form of a dinosaur in order to delight and to attract attention, the expression 'fantasy architecture' is appropriate. Charles Jencks has employed the term 'bizarre architecture' to describe such 'bastard' or 'illegitimate' buildings. Also included in the category of 'autoscape architecture' (Robert Venturi's term) are the huge illuminated signs typical of Las Vegas (so-called 'electrographic architecture'); such structures are clearly conceived as communication or sign systems rather than as arrangements of forms.

(3) Schemes and buildings by professional architects influenced or inspired by popular architecture in the same way that pop artists were inspired by popular culture, e.g. the work of SITE, and post-modernist architects such as Venturi, Terry Farrell and Minoru Takeyama.

(4) Bizarre or futuristic projects by experimental architectural groups such as Archigram incorporating popular culture characteristics like expendability. Also proposals by pop artists like Claes Oldenburg for public sculptures on an architectural scale.

● See also Archigram, Electrographic Architecture, Hiway Culture, Pop Art, Popular Art, Post-Modern Architecture, SITE, Utopian Architecture.

R Banham 'On trial 5: the spec builders, towards a Pop Architecture' *Architectural Review* **132** (785) July 1962 43–6.

G Broadbent 'Towards a Pop Architecture' *RIBA Journal* **72** (3) March 1965 142–3.

R Venturi *Complexity and contradiction in architecture* (NY, MoMA, 1966).

P Reilley 'The challenge of Pop' *Architectural Review* **142** (848) October 1967 255–9.

G Lehmann 'Pop Architecture' *Architecture Canada* **45** (6) (issue no 513) June 1968 69–71.

'Pop Architecture' *Architecture Canada* **45** (10) (issue no 517) October 1968, special issue.

C Jencks 'Pop non Pop' part 1 *AAQ* **1** (1) Winter 1968–9 48–64; part 2 *AAQ* **1** (2) April 1969 56–74.

F Vostell & D Higgins *Fantastic architecture* (NY, Something Else Press, 1969), German edition published as 'Pop architektur'.

F Schulze 'Chaos in architecture' *Art in America* **58** (4) July–August 1970 88–96.

R Venturi *Learning from Las Vegas* (Cambridge, Mass, MIT Press, 1972).

F Schulze 'Toward "impure" architecture' *Dialogue* **7** (3) 1974 54–63.

C Jencks *Bizarre architecture* (Academy Editions, 1979).

J Andrews *The well-built elephant and other roadside attractions: a tribute to American eccentricity* (NY, Congdon & Weed, 1985).

518 POP ART

(Also Commodity Art, Commonism, Consumer Style, Consumerist Realism, Factualist Art, Gag Art, Industrial Art, New Sign Painting, New Super Realism, O K Art, Reactionary Realism) The term 'Pop Art' dates from the 1950s. It has been credited to the British art critic Lawrence Alloway, though when he first used it at meetings of the Independent Group in London, it referred to popular or mass culture rather than works of fine art based on popular culture.

Pop Art emerged in the mid and late 1950s in Britain – the work of Peter Blake, Richard Hamilton and Eduardo Paolozzi – and it flourished in the 1960s in both Europe and the United States. British Pop artists of the 1960s included Clive Barker, Derek Boshier, Pauline Boty, Patrick Caulfield, David Hockney, Allen Jones, Peter Phillips and Joe Tilson. The Americans included Jim Dine, Jann Haworth (who worked in Britain), Robert Indiana, Roy Lichtenstein, Claes Oldenburg, Mel Ramos, Larry Rivers, James Rosenquist, Andy Warhol and Tom Wesselmann. R. B. Kitaj – American but resident in London – was also associated with the movement though he has refused the label 'Pop artist'. Some histories of Pop also encompass the work of the European nouveaux réalistes.

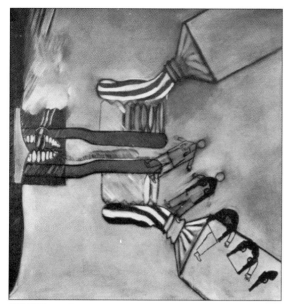

POP ART DEREK BOSHIER, 'So Ad men became depth men' (1962). Oil on canvas, 72" x 72". Photo: Grabowski Gallery, London.

The 1950s neo-dada work of Jasper Johns and Robert Rauschenberg was a major influence on the development of Pop Art which was part of a widespread reaction against the dominant, gestural abstract painting styles of the 1950s. Pop was 'cool', analytical, detached in its manner. Not only did it draw its subject matter from the mass media and the affluent, consumer society, it also simulated the mechanistic, graphic styles and techniques of the mass media, e.g. Lichtenstein's paintings based on comic-strip images imitated the ben day dots and hard-edge lines of the source material. Transformations of sources did occur in Pop Art – as material was transposed from 'low' to 'high' culture – but the extent to which a critical or moral comment was involved proved controversial. Warhol (1928–87) – who began as a commercial illustrator – was the quintessential Pop artist. He became a media celebrity and a successful, wealthy businessman, head of an enterprise marketing products in a dozen different media. His art spanned the division between fine art and mass culture. Pop Art did, in fact, reach a far wider audience than previous avant garde movements and it fed back into the mass media themselves. Peter Blake too, through his record cover commissions for rock groups like the Beatles, managed to reach mass audiences.

During the 1960s most of the literature on Pop was descriptive and celebratory but from the mid 1970s onwards more theoretical and critical assessments began to appear in which the movement was condemned as 'reactionary/consumerist realism'.

Critics and curators writing in the late 1980s and early 1990s have argued that Pop has 'a continuing history'; some of the founders of Pop are still working and younger artists like Jeff Koons are said to be working in the tradition of Pop Art, hence the increasing use of the term 'neo-pop'.

● See also Capitalist Realism, Comic Art, Cool Art, Cross-Overs, Independent Group, Neo-Dada, Nouveau Réalisme, Pop Design, Rock Art/Design/Fashion.

● M Amaya *Pop Art: a survey of the new super realism* (Studio Vista, 1965).

● J Rublowsky *Pop Art: images of the American dream* (NY, Nelson, 1965).

● L Lippard & others *Pop Art* (Thames & Hudson, 1966).

● C Finch *Pop Art: object and image* (Studio Vista, 1968).

● — *Image as language: aspects of British art 1950–68* (Harmondsworth, Penguin Books, 1969).

● J Russell & others *Pop Art redefined* (Thames & Hudson, 1969).

● M Compton *Pop Art* (Hamlyn, 1970).

● G Melly *Revolt into style: the Pop Arts in Britain* (Allen Lane, The Penguin Press, 1970).

● L Alloway *American Pop Art* (NY, Collier-Macmillan, 1974).

● D Kuspit 'Pop Art: a reactionary realism' *Art Journal* **36** (1) Fall 1976 31–8.

● *Pop Art in England* (Hamburg, Kunstverein, 1976).

● J Pierre *An illustrated dictionary of Pop Art* (Woodbury, Barron, 1978).

● A Warhol & P Hackett *Popism* (Hutchinson, 1981).

● R Hamilton *Collected words 1953–82* (Thames & Hudson, 1982).

● D Hebdige 'In poor taste: notes on Pop' *Block* (8) 1983 54–68.

● D Kunzle 'Pop Art as consumerist realism' *Studies in Visual Communication* **10** (2) Spring 1984 16–33.

● H Geldzahler *Pop Art 1955–70* (Australia, Art Gallery of New South Wales, 1985).

● D Boland 'Pop Art – a reflection' *Aspects* (33) Winter 1986 10–11.

● L Alloway & others *Modern dreams: the rise and fall of Pop* (NY, ICA Clocktower Gallery/Cambridge, Mass, MIT Press, 1988).

● C Mashun *Pop Art and the critics* (Ann Arbor, Michigan, University of Michigan Research Press, 1988).

● M Livingstone *Pop Art: a continuing history* (Thames & Hudson, 1990).

● — (ed) *Pop Art* (Royal Acaemy/Weidenfeld & Nicolson, 1991).

● — & others *Objects for the ideal home, the legacy of Pop Art: artists of the 1980s and 1990s* (Serpentine Gallery, 1991).

An aspect of British design which emerged in the 1950s and reached a climax in the '60s; the equivalent in design of pop architecture, pop music and pop Art. Pop Design, as exemplified in the mini-skirt and the products sold in Carnaby Street and the boutiques of the Kings Road, departed from the 'good design' ideal associated with the modern movement and its theory of functionalism. (For this reason it has been labelled 'post-modern'.) The word 'pop' signified 'popular' but this type of design appealed mainly to young people, not the whole populace. (In the 1950s and 1960s teenage consumers constituted a large and affluent market.) Pop Design involved expendability, bold designs, bright colours, eye-dazzling patterns, the use of new materials such as transparent plastic, external influences from such countries as Italy and India, and stylistic revivals such as Victoriana, art deco and art nouveau. Above all it was characterized by a hedonistic attitude to consumption and an ironic use of mass-culture references, e.g. the satiric/affectionate quoting of the Union Jack flag motif ('camp patriotism' – Whiteley).

Pop Design was visible across a range of fields: graphics, fashion, furniture and furnishings. It was associated with such designers and illustrators as Mary Quant, Vidal Sassoon, Alan Aldridge, Nigel Weymouth and Michael English, Martin Sharp, Kenneth Grange, Barbara Hulanicki, John Stephen, Terence Conran, Roger and Martin Dean. However, the styles of the 1960s were also determined by models, fashion photographers, film directors, TV programmes, magazines, rock bands and by subcultural groups such as the Mods and the Hippies.

Nigel Whiteley, a historian of Pop Design, claims there were three varieties: intellectual, conscious and unselfconscious; and three phases: early Pop (1952–62), high Pop (1962–6), and late or post-Pop (1966–72). It was certainly the case that the style of the early 1960s was quite different from that of 1967–68; consequently there was not a single style of the decade.

POP DESIGN PAULINE BUTLER (designer), 'Floral tin tray' (1967). From the 'Lazy Daisy' co-ordinated range produced by Xlon. Sold in Harrods & Peter Jones, London.

● See also Archigram, Biba, Carnaby Street, Colour Supplements, The Fool, 'Good Design', Habitat, Italian Craze, Op Art, Post-Modern Design, Psychedelic Art, Rock Art/Design/Fashion, Subculture, Underground Art.

● K & K Baynes 'Behind the scene' *Design* (212) August 1966 18–29.
● J Aitken *The young meteors* (Secker & Warburg, 1967).
● B Bernard *Fashions in the 1960s* (Academy, 1978).
● J Harris & others *1966 and all that: design and the consumer in Britain 1960–9* (Trefoil Books/Manchester, Whitworth Art Gallery, 1986).
● N Whiteley 'Interior design in the 1960s: arenas for performance' *Art History* **10** (1) March 1987 79–90.
● —— *Pop Design: modernism to mod* (Design Council, 1987).
● 'The Sixties' *Oxford Art Journal* **10** (2) 1987, special issue.
● P Powell & L Peel *50s and 60s style* (Apple Press, 1988).

(Also Everyday Arts, Indigenous Art, Unsophisticated Arts, Vernacular Art) This is a complex and problematical concept because, arguably, the two words making up the term contradict one another. The word 'popular' derives from the Latin 'popularis' meaning 'belonging to the people'. Popular Art would, therefore, be an art made by the people for the people, i.e. the common people as against the ruling classes (who in fact have been throughout history the patrons of most fine art) – in pre-industrial or peasant societies what is generally called 'folk art'. Popular Art in this sense could be seen as persisting in industrial societies in such forms as hobbies, amateur or spare-time art/photography and in such expressions as graffiti, though in these cases they are the expressions of only a small part of the people. In Paris a National Museum has been established to preserve the material culture of the French people: Musée National des Arts et Traditions Populaires. The concept 'the people' is itself problematical since it suggests a homogeneous and undifferentiated mass; the term 'working-class culture' immediately introduces another dimension.

G. Fletcher and other writers have used the term 'Popular Art' in an untheoretical way to encompass those minor artforms produced anonymously which are enjoyed by ordinary people, e.g. Christmas cards, Valentines, pictorial tiles, souvenirs, tattoos, ship models in bottles, children's peepshows, fairground and barge painting. Fletcher characterizes these arts as 'escapist' and regretfully admits that they are now largely anachronisms. Many of these types are now part of industrial manufacture (e.g. Christmas cards) and would be categorized by many theorists as 'kitsch'. Societies in transition from agricultural/rural to industrial/urban economies, e.g. France in the nineteenth century, often produce intermediary forms such as popular prints which make use of ancient themes and are at the same time manufactured in large editions.

In poor, developing societies types of culture can arise which recall folk art in certain respects but which are new, not a timeless reiteration of traditional forms. Guy Brett, a British critic and historian sympathetic to the problems of oppressed people and developing countries, has argued that in periods of overwhelming historical change groups of 'ordinary' people have resorted to art to externalize their experiences. His 1986 book on Popular Art discusses such topics as Chilean patchworks, Chinese peasant painting, images made by Japanese survivors of atom bombs, urban amateur paintings from Africa, fence collages and actions by Greenham Common anti-nuclear weapons women protesters.

In developed societies, Popular Art or rather popular culture has ceased, in the main, to be produced by the people; instead it has become the province of a cadre of specialists – professional designers, photographers, filmmakers, etc. – who work directly for media industries and indirectly on behalf of the people or mass audiences (hence the term 'mass culture' is often preferred to 'popular culture' though some writers use these terms interchangeably). Richard Hamilton in a famous letter written in 1957 offered a checklist of the characteristics of pop art (in the sense of popular or mass culture): 'Popular (designed for a mass audience), transient (short-term solution), expendable (easily forgotten), low cost, mass produced, young (aimed at youth), witty, sexy, gimmicky, glamorous, big business'.

If 'popular' is simply taken to mean 'enjoyed by large numbers', then some fine artists have achieved this goal, e.g. Salvador Dali, David Hockney, Andy Warhol, David Shepherd, Pietro Annigoni, Andrew Wyeth. In seeking to account for the popularity of artists like Wyeth to 'middle America', Andrew Brighton pointed to such characteristics as sentimental rustic nostalgia, photographic detail, and themes of universal significance such as birth and death.

Twentieth-century artists committed to modernism, realism and socialism have frequently wrestled with the problem of producing an art that is simultaneously modern, realist and popular (or at least capable of becoming popular). Bertolt Brecht, for instance, wrote of the need for 'an art for the broad masses, for the many who are oppressed by the few.... Our concept of what is popular refers to a people who not only play a full part in historical development but actively usurp it, force its pace, determine its direction. We have in mind a fighting people and therefore an aggressive concept of what is *popu-*

lar.... Popular means: intelligible to the broad masses, adopting and enriching their forms of expression, assuming their standpoint, confirming and correcting it, representing the most progressive section of the people so that it can assume leadership, and therefore intelligible to other sections of the people as well, relating to traditions and developing them...' (see Bloch listed below).

● See also Arpilleras, Atelier Populaire, Community Art & Media, Democratic Art, Fairground Art, Graffiti, Hobby Art, Kitsch, Mass Art, Naive Art, Orature, Peasant Painting, Pin-Ups, Pop Art, Public Art, Spitting Image, Township Art.

▣ B Jones *The Unsophisticated Arts* (Architectural Press, 1951).

▣ G Fletcher *Popular Art in England* (Harrap, 1962).

▣ B Jones & B Howell *Popular Arts of the First World War* (Studio Vista, 1972).

▣ C Bigsby (ed) *Approaches to popular culture* (Edward Arnold, 1976).

▣ E Bloch & others *Aesthetics and politics* (NLB, 1977).

▣ A Brighton 'Andrew Wyeth: Popular painting and populism' *Art Monthly* (37) 1980 3–6.

▣ *Popular culture* (Milton Keynes, Open University Press, 1981), 14 course booklets.

▣ G Brett *Through our own eyes: Popular Art and modern history* (Heretic/GMP Publishers, 1986).

▣ C Ford (ed) *The Kodak Museum: the story of popular photography* (Century Publishing, 1989).

▣ M Lambert & E Marx *English Popular Art* (Merlin Press, 1989), first published Batsford 1951.

▣ A Durr & H Martin (eds) *A common tradition: Popular Art of Britain and America* (Brighton Polytechnic Gallery, 1991).

521 **POPULUXE** A term devised by Thomas Hine to encapsulate aspects of American architecture, design, advertising and lifestyle during a period that was for many middle-class families a golden age of affluence, consumerism and hedonism, i.e. 1954–64. 'Populuxe', he says, is 'a synthetic word created in the spirit of many coined words of the time'; 'it derives from populism and popularity, with just a fleeting allusion to pop art...it has luxury for all...with a thoroughly unnecessary "e" to give it class'. Hine's book explores the modernistic design of 1950s' cars with tailfins, adverts, interior decor, TV dinners, Barbie dolls, fall-out shelters, motels, the hotels of Morris Lapidus, freeform/boomerang/amoeboid furniture, etc. Populuxe was fantasy, colour and styling applied to practical objects; it was 'an attitude', not merely having material goods but 'an expression of vulgar joy in being able to live so well'.

● See also Art Ultra, Contemporary Style, Free Forms,

Pop Design, Styling.

● T Hine *Populuxe* (Bloomsbury Press, 1987).

522 POST-FEMINIST ART

According to Kathi Norklun, a 'phase in which the feminist (modernist) discourse has been assimilated by the culture it critiques'. She claimed the term was 'neither negative nor positive but rather descriptive'. American artists whom she counted as Post-Feminist included Barbara Kruger, Dara Birnbaum, Sherrie Levine, Martha Rosler and Jenny Holzer. In the case of Kruger, the work was said to be Post-Feminist because it posited 'a prior knowledge of feminist discourse'. Dan Cameron's list of Post-Feminist artists included Nancy Dwyer, Vicky Alexander, Annette Lemieux and Sarah Charlesworth besides some of those already cited. According to Cameron, these artists initiated 'an art of sceptical bemusement, one which challenged the viewer to question art's moral authority'; they hearkened 'back to Lacan, who joined Freud in proclaiming the revolutionary power of women's laughter'.

● See also Feminist Art.

● K Norklun 'Courage' *Real Life* (10) Summer 1983 18–21.

● D Cameron 'Post-Feminism' *Flash Art* (132) February–March 1987 80–3.

523 POST-FORMALIST ART

(Also Anti-Formalist Art) A term used by the American writer Jack Burnham from 1968 onwards. While formalist art emphasized the formal properties of the artwork, made a fetish of craft skills and aimed for total hermeticism, Post-Formalist Art stressed systems rather than objects, procedures rather than end-products, and sought an interactive relationship with the world. Some observers considered the influence of Marcel Duchamp contributed most to the reaction against formalist art in the late 1960s, hence the introduction of the term 'post-Duchampian art' employed by Burnham and the British artist John Stezaker to encompass both systems and conceptual art. In 1990 Robert C. Morgan employed the term 'Anti-Formalist Art' to characterize works produced in the 1970s by a number of individuals. These works ranged from the conceptual to the decorative; what they had in common was a rejection of the restrictive aesthetic of formalism.

● See also Conceptual Art, Formalism & Formalist Criticism, Ornamentalism, Process Art, Systems Art.

● J Burnham *Great Western Saltworks: essays on the meaning of Post-Formalist Art* (NY, Braziller, 1974).

● R Morgan *Concept–décoratif: Anti-Formalist Art of the '70s* (NY, Nahan Contemporary, 1990).

524 POST-INDUSTRIAL DESIGN

This expression was used by several writers on design in the 1980s. Obviously it was dependent upon the idea that a society based on heavy industry, manufacture and production had been supplanted by one based on either (a) hyper-expansion, an information revolution, automation, advanced technology, consumption and mass media, or (b) ecological consciousness, intermediate technology, small-scale production of quality artefacts. These two models of post-industrial society clearly give rise to two different conceptions of the role of design in the future. According to Nigel Cross, Post-Industrial Design based on the second model involves a design process that is more democratic and participatory, designers who are collaborative and anonymous, and products that are multi-purpose, long-lived, repairable and short run. One person Aldo Tanchis considered in 1986 to be a Post-Industrial designer was the veteran Italian artist–designer Bruno Munari.

● See also High-Tech, Participatory Design, Post-Modern Design, Radical Design, Soft Design/Tech.

● D Bell *The coming of post-industrial society: a venture in social forecasting* (NY, Basic Books, 1973/London, Heinemann, 1974).

● 'The post-industrial interior' *Architectural Review* **168** (1004) October 1980 202–7.

● N Cross 'The coming of post-industrial design' *Design Studies* **2** (1) January 1981 3–8.

● Aldo Tanchis *Bruno Munari: from futurism to post-Industrial Design* (Milan, Idea Books, 1986/London, Lund Humphries, 1987).

● M Poster *The mode of information: towards a theory of post-industrial society* (Cambridge, Polity Press, 1988).

525 POST-MINIMALISM

(Also Anti-Minimalism) This term was coined by the American art critic Robert Pincus-Witten in the early 1970s to encompass those developments in American art of the late 1960s – 'from process orientated experience to an art of purely intellectual activity such as we find in the conceptualist movement' – which succeeded minimalism and reacted against it. 'Anti-Minimalism' refers to those modes of art – fetishistic, obsessional sculptures by Lucas Samaras, Eva Hesse and others – that appeared at the same time as minimal art but departed from its aesthetic principles.

● See also Conceptual Art, Funk Art, Maximalism, Minimal Art.

● R Pincus-Witten *Post-minimalism: essays 1966–76* (NY, Out of London Press, 1977).

● —*Post-minimalism into maximalism: American art 1966–86*

(Ann Arbor, Michigan, University of Michigan Research Press, 1987).

526 POST-MODERN ARCHITECTURE (Also Jukebox Architecture, New Classicism, Supermannerism) A term which gained currency in the mid 1970s, primarily as a result of the voluminous writings of the architectural critic Charles Jencks. However, the American architect and theorist Robert Venturi was the pioneering advocate of an alternative to the purism of the modern movement. Since that alternative was first conceived of as pop architecture, it was this mode which was first thought of as Post-Modern. But pop, it transpired, was simply one option available to Post-Modern architects.

Disillusionment with modern architecture dated from the 1960s and Post-Modernism was said to have been born on July 15 1972 when Minoru Yamasaki's award-winning housing estate Pruitt-Igoe, St Louis, was blown up because of its failure to please its inhabitants. As the prefix 'post' indicates, the term referred to what came after modernism but did not describe it. In fact, Post-Modern architecture inverted many of the principles of modernism: the latter was against ornament, so P-M A was for it; the latter was against mixing styles, so P-M A was in favour of stylistic eclecticism; the latter made a radical break with the past, so P-M A was historicist or combined the old and the new; the latter stressed function, whereas P-M A conceived of buildings as metaphoric statements or signs; the latter was serious, so P-M A indulged in humour and pastiche; the latter was exclusive, so PM A was inclusive; the latter was white or grey in colour, so P-M A delighted in vivid hues.

The broadest definition of P-M A would be 'all building taking place after the death of modern architecture'. However, Jencks argued that modern architecture did not die altogether; it lost its dominant position as 'the one true style of the age' but remained as one stylistic option among a range of options. (Hence the label 'late-modernism'. High-tech architecture was one development of modernist principles which did prove successful in many instances.) It also remained as a style Post-Modernists could parody. A narrower definition would

POST-MODERN ARCHITECTURE JAMES STIRLING, Clore Gallery, Tate Gallery extension, Millbank, London (1982-6). Photo: Roderick Coyne.

restrict the label to those buildings whose design evinced an awareness of the Post-Modern condition of stylistic pluralism. P-M A proved very popular with large commercial corporations. According to Jencks, the dual coding of P-M buildings meant that they could be appreciated by two publics: their popular elements meant they could be enjoyed by ordinary people and their intertextual references to other architecture meant that they could also be enjoyed by architectural experts.

The main P-M architects were Ricardo Bofill, Peter Eisenmann, Terry Farrell, Michael Graves, Lucien Kroll, Charles Moore, Philip Johnson (most notably his New York AT & T skyscraper of 1978–84, an international-style building but with a Chippendale-type broken pediment), Robert Stern and John Hagmann, Minoru Takeyama, Stanley Tigerman and Ben Weese. Stephen Gardiner, architectural critic of the *Observer* (in an article dated October 17 1982), predicted the imminent demise of Post-Modern Architecture.

● See also High-Tech, Late-Modern Architecture, Modern Movement, NATO, Ornamentalism, Pluralism, Pop Architecture.

● R Venturi *Complexity and contradiction in architecture* (NY, MoMA, 1966).

● C Jencks *The language of Post-Modern Architecture* (Academy Editions, 1977; 5th ed 1987).

● C Ray Smith *Supermannerism: new attitudes in Post-Modern Architecture* (NY, Dutton, 1977).

● C Jencks & W Chaitkin *Current architecture* (Academy Editions, 1983).

● P Portoghesi *Post-modern: the architecture of the post-industrial society* (NY, Rizzoli, 1983).

● H Klotz (ed) *Post-modern visions: drawings, paintings and models by contemporary architects* (NY, Abbeville, 1985).

● C Jencks *What is Post-Modernism?* (Academy Editions, 1986).

● C Jencks *Post-Modernism: the New Classicism in art and architecture* (Academy Editions, 1988).

● H Klotz *History of Post-Modern Architecture* (Cambridge, Mass, MIT Press, 1988).

527 | **POST-MODERN ART**

Broadly, all the visual fine art produced after the 'death' of modern art considered to have occurred during the 1960s. In this case the term would encompass all the various strands within the art of the '70s and '80s: pattern painting, neo-expressionism, neo-geo, new British sculpture, etc. More narrowly, art that exemplified in its form and content the Post-Modern condition of post-history and stylistic pluralism, e.g. the paintings of Duggie Fields; or the multi-media work of Laurie Anderson, an artist aware of and taking advantage of the new mass-communication technologies. One could also include in this category the work of artists influenced by the ideas of fashionable Post-Modern theorists such as Lyotard and Baudrillard.

By the 1960s modern art had become the official culture of the West. The modernist dictum 'rebel against the past' thus applied to modern art itself. This kind of art had always had its critics on the Right and among philistines but in the 1960s it also began to be criticized from within by artists unhappy with the seemingly inevitable, single-strand sequence of movements which resulted in reductive styles like minimalism. These artists were also concerned by the lack of social content and lack of relation to ordinary people typical of so much avant garde art.

Pop Art in the 1950s and 1960s departed in some respects from the ideals of modern art and consequently was considered Post-Modern. However, it was the critique of art undertaken by the conceptualists in the second half of the '60s which opened the way for various kinds of political art in the 1970s (e.g. feminist art, community art), but unfortunately it also opened the door to all kinds of other art not desired by the anti-modernists (e.g. academic and historicist works, a resurgence of traditional forms such as painting and sculpture). Subsequently, some writers argued that there existed two kinds of P-M Art: a Post-Modernism of reaction and a Post-Modernism of resistance. Included in the former were artists like Carlo Maria Mariani who cynically recycled worn-out styles like neo-classicism. Included in the latter were Left-wing and feminist artists making work about political issues and undertaking critiques of the art-world, patriarchy, and so forth.

● See also Minimalism, Modern Art, Pop Art, Simulation/Simulacra/Hyperreality.

● P Miran *Manifesto for Post-Modern Art* (NY, American Art Gallery, 1951).

● B O'Doherty 'What is Post-Modernism?' *Art in America* **59** May–June 1971 19.

● C Tomkins *The scene: reports on Post-Modern Art* (NY, Viking Press, 1976).

● P Fuller 'Fine art after modernism' *New Left Review* (119) January–February 1980 42–59.

● H Kramer 'Post-Modern: art and culture in the 1980s' *New Criterion* **1** (1) September 1982 36–42.

● H Foster (ed) *The anti-aesthetic* (Port Townsend, Washington, Bay Press, 1983); reprinted as *Post-Modern culture* (Pluto Press, 1985).

● B Wallis (ed) *Art after modernism: rethinking representation* (NY, New Museum of Contemporary Art/Boston, David Godine, 1985).

● H Foster *Recodings: art, spectacle, cultural politics* (Port Townsend, Washington, Bay Press, 1986).

● M Newman 'Revising modernism...' – in – *Post-Modernism*

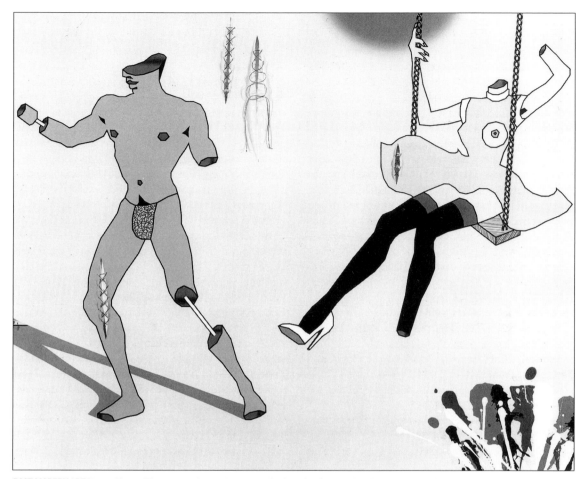

POST-MODERN ART DUGGIE FIELDS, 'The conceptual meets the perceptual at the point of perpetual motion' (1978). Acrylic on canvas, 76" x 60". Photo: Prudence Cuming Assoc., London.

L Appignanesi (ed) (ICA Documents, 1986).

⬤ S Trachtenberg (ed) *The Post-Modern movement: a handbook of contemporary innovation in the arts* (Westport, Connecticut, Greenwood Books, 1986).

⬤ S Nairne *State of the art* (Chatto, 1987), book of TV series.

⬤ B Taylor *Modernism, Post-Modernism, realism: a critical perspective for art* (Winchester School of Art Press, 1987).

⬤ K Levin *Beyond modernism* (Harper & Row, 1988).

⬤ H Risatti (ed) *Post-Modern perspectives: issues in contemporary art* (Englewood Cliffs, NJ, Prentice Hall, 1990).

⬤ J Roberts *Post-Modernism, politics & art* (Manchester University Press, 1990).

528 **POST-MODERN DESIGN**

In brief, design after modernism. Design contradicting the central principles of modern design or 'good design'. P-M D cannot be described or defined easily because it encompasses such a range of disparate styles, design which mixes styles from different periods, or which refers to or quotes from both high and low culture sources. Since the pop design of the 1960s was viewed as the first major departure from the ideals of modernism, this mode was the first to be called 'Post-Modern'. The kind of furniture designed by Ettore Sottsass and the Memphis group in the early 1980s exemplified some common characteristics of P-M D: humour, parody, pastiche, colour and ornament, impracticality, the use of kitsch and popular culture.

⬤ See also 'Good Design', Memphis, Pop Design.

⬤ P York *Style wars* (Sidgwick & Jackson, 1980).

⬤ J Thackara (ed) *Design after modernism: beyond the object* (Thames & Hudson, 1988).

⬤ M Collins & A Papadakis *Post-Modern Design* (Academy Editions, 1989).

529 **POST-MODERNISM**

(Also P-M, Po-Mo, and 'the Post') A topic endlessly discussed by intellectuals in the 1970s and '80s. These debates generated a vast literature impossible to summarize adequately here. (Writings on P-M ranged from scholarly tomes to A–Z guides in fashion magazines.) The emergence of the term signified a major paradigm shift in Western culture: a new situation resulting from the end of modernism. Writers such as Lyotard identified not an 'ism' but a 'Post-Modern condition' which necessarily influenced all the architecture, design, art, literature, etc., produced within it. This condition was associated with a loss of faith in the 'grand narratives' of the modern era (i.e. faith in science, rationality and the idea of social and technological progress); with a post-industrial society (hence the term 'post-Fordism'); with a global society dominated by commodities, images, signs and mass-media systems to a degree never experienced before. (Baudrillard's writings were of crucial importance in relation to the latter.) According to Jameson, author of perhaps the best summary article, P-M was in essence 'the cultural logic of late capitalism'.

While P-M was welcomed by many artists and theorists because it permitted a thousand different styles and genres to flourish in the ruins of modernism, others regarded it as a culture of the fragment, a philosophy of nihilism, pessimism and political quietism.

● See also Globalization, Modernism, Pluralism, Simulation/ Simulacra/ Hyperreality.

◉ I Hassan 'Post-Modernism: a paracritical bibliography' *New Literary History* **3** (1) Autumn 1971 5–30.
◉ 'Special issue on modernism' (and Post-Modernism) *New German Critique* (22) Winter 1981.
◉ F Jameson 'Post-Modernism, or the cultural logic of late capitalism' *New Left Review* (146) July–August 1984 53–93.
◉ 'Modernity and Post-modernity' *New German Critique* (33) Fall 1984.
◉ J-F Lyotard *The Post-Modern condition* (Manchester University Press, 1984).
◉ C Dilnot 'What is Post-Modernism?' *Art History* **9** (2) June 1986 245–63.
◉ 'Modernism and Post-Modernism' *Guardian* December 1, 2, 3 1986, a series of articles.
◉ F Owen & C Brown 'An A–Z of Post-Modernism' *i-D* (38) 1986.
◉ L Appignanesi (ed) *Post-Modernism* (ICA Documents, 1986).
◉ D Hebdige 'A report from the Western Front' *Block* (12) 1986–7 4–26.
◉ 'Post-Modernism issue' *Theory Culture & Society* **5** (2/3) June 1988.
◉ 'New times' *Marxism Today* October 1988 (Post-Fordism issue).
◉ J Baudrillard *Selected writings* M Poster (ed) (Cambridge, Polity Press, 1988).
◉ J Fekete (ed) *Life after Post-Modernism* (Macmillan, 1988).
◉ E Grosz & others *Futur-fall: excursions into Post-Modernity* (Sydney, Power Institute Publications, 1988).

530 POST-OBJECT ART

(Also Anti- or Non-Object Art) A broad category dating from the late 1960s that encompassed various tendencies within avant garde art which had in common the desire to go beyond the art object, e.g. conceptualism and time-based arts such as performance, video and film. Post-Object Art was often ephemeral rather than permanent and appealed to the intellect rather than to the senses of sight or touch. The advent of an art – conceptualism – foregrounding concepts and employing language as a medium rather than sensuous physical materials caused some critics to herald 'the dematerialization of the art object'. However, the material basis of art can never be eliminated because even mental concepts have to be embodied physically in order to exist or to be communicated.

An exhibition organized by Donald Brook and Jim Allen entitled 'Australian and New Zealand Post-Object Show – a survey' held at the Experimental Art foundation in Adelaide in May 1976 provoked hostile press reaction including the accusation that it was 'non-art'.

● See also Conceptual Art, Experimental Art Foundation, Information, Object Art, Time-Based Arts.

◉ D Karshan 'Post-Object Art – in – *Conceptual art & conceptual aspects* (NY, Cultural Center, 1970).
◉ L Lippard *Six years: the dematerialization of the art object...* (Studio Vista, 1973).
◉ C Newman (ed) 'Anti-Object Art' *Triquarterly* (32) Winter 1975, special issue.
◉ D Brook 'Flight from the object' (1969) – in – *Concerning contemporary art* B Smith (ed) (Oxford, Clarendon Press, 1975) 16–34
◉ — 'Post-Object Art in Australia and New Zealand' (1976) – in – *A decade at the EAF; a history of Experimental Art Foundation 1974–84* S Britton (ed) (Adelaide, EAF, 1984) 20–5.

531 POST-PAINTERLY ABSTRACTION

(Also New Abstraction) Title of a major exhibition of abstract paintings, selected by Clement Greenberg, held in Los Angeles in 1964. The term 'painterly abstraction' was an alternative for 'abstract expressionism' and so Greenberg's show was intended to define an aspect of American art in the wake of that movement. The artists concerned included Paul Feeley, Sam Francis, Helen Frankenthaler, Al Held, Ellsworth Kelly, Alexander Liberman and Frank Stella. Many of these painters reacted against the gestural, romantic style of the previous generation: their work was cooler, hard-edge, more geometric and systematic. An alternative term, even less informative, was 'New Abstraction'. This derived from a show mounted in New York in 1963. It featured many of the same artists. In his catalogue introduction, Ben Heller claimed the New Abstractionists shared 'a conceptual approach to painting'. Subsequently, the term 'New Abstraction' was adopted by other critics, amongst them John Coplans.

● See also Hard-Edge Painting, Painterly Painting, Stain Painting, Systemic Painting.

◉ B Heller *New Abstraction* (NY, Jewish Museum, 1963).

◉ C Greenberg *Post-Painterly Abstraction* (Los Angeles, County Museum of Art, 1964).

◉ J Coplans 'The New Abstractionists on the West Coast, USA' *Studio International* **169** (865) May 1965 192–9.

532 POSTCARD ART

(Or Artists' Postcards) Postcards are visual, printed artefacts that cut across the divide between high and low culture, fine art and popular culture. Whether photographs, photo-montages or drawn images, picture postcards are a long-established form of communication; millions of designs have been published since the nineteenth century and many have since become collector's items. The master-illustrator of the saucy English seaside postcard (published by Bamforths of Holmfirth) was Arnold Taylor.

Today, postcards reproducing works of art are sold in huge numbers from bookshops in art galleries and museums. Postcards have also been created as one-offs by fine artists and a number of exhibitions of such works have been mounted in private and public galleries; in 1979, for example, the ICA in London put on a show entitled 'Postcard as Art'. In these cases postcards are a form of edition art, an extension of the idea of prints. Furthermore, a number of artists, designers and cartoonists have made the production of postcards a major means of expression; these artists are generally motivated by humour, feminism or politics. In the 1980s British practitioners included: John Stalin, Chic Pix (Peta Coplans and Stanley Becker), Cath Tate, Jill Posener, Peter Kennard and Biff. Postcard Art often relied upon the vast image bank accumulated by the mass media; artists gave dated images a new lease of life by recycling them and by changing their meanings.

● See also Copy Art, Mail Art, Mass Art, Multiples, Photo-montage, Popular Art, Stamp Art.

◉ E Mullins 'The postcard: instant communication and lasting art' *Daily Telegraph Magazine* December 4 1970 70–1, + 74, + 78.

◉ G Wietek & others *Kunst und Postkarte* (Hamburg, Altonaer Museum, 1970).

◉ W Domingo 'Artists' Postcards' *Art Monthly* (27) June 1979 20–1.

◉ S Taylor 'The card sharp (John Stalin)' *The Face* (10) February 1981 16–17.

◉ Chic Pix *I walked with a zombie* (Sidgwick & Jackson, 1985).

533 POWER INSTITUTE

The Power Institute of Fine Arts is part of the University of Sydney, Australia. It was founded in 1965 as a result of a bequest given in 1961 by the widow of Dr John Power (1881–1943), a wealthy individual who had been an artist in Europe in the 1920s and 1930s. The Institute has three components: a fine art department teaching the history of art; a gallery of contemporary art; and a research library. It also maintains a studio in Paris for the use of Australian artists. A prestigious public lecture – The John Power Lecture in Contemporary Art – is sponsored by the Institute annually. Past speakers have included Donald Brook, Peter Fuller, Clement Greenberg, Patrick Heron, Lucy Lippard and Richard Wollheim.

◉ B Smith 'Sydney's Power Institute of Fine Arts' *Studio International* **180** (926) October 1970 142–4.

◉ B Smith (ed) *Concerning contemporary art: the Power Lectures 1968–73* (Oxford, Clarendon Press, 1975).

◉ *Dr John Power & the Power bequest* (Sydney, Power Institute, 1977).

◉ J Kavanagh 'Fifteen years on – the Power Institute in review' *Art Network* (8) Summer 1983 14–16.

534 PREFABS

(Also Emergency Housing) Prefabricated houses that were built in large numbers in Britain immediately after the Second World War as temporary dwellings to replace those destroyed by bombing. (A similar initiative had followed the First World War.) In 1944 the Government passed the Housing (Temporary Accommodation) Act as a result of which 11 types of Prefab were designed by

POSTCARD ART TOM PHILLIPS, 'Time is a great dealer' (1988). Watercolour 30 x 42.5cms. Reproduced as a postcard by Flowers East Gallery, London. Reproduced courtesy of Tom Phillips & Angela Flowers.

different architectural groups. Three of the most significant were the ARCON, the Aluminium bungalow and the Uni-Seco. Prefabs were manufactured in factories from lightweight materials; the various parts and units were then transported to prepared sites for speedy assembly. Between 1945 and 1948 160,000 were erected. They were intended to last for 10 or 15 years but a proportion of them survived much longer – in 1989 approximately 10,000 were still in use. In terms of their design, Prefabs were in advance of much existing housing: they had built-in furniture, fitted bathrooms and kitchens. They were also detached, single-storey houses surrounded by light and gardens. For these reasons they proved to be comfortable, popular homes.

Prefabrication as a building method was, of course, a much older idea dating back to at least Joseph Paxton's Crystal Palace of 1851. Also, prefabricated houses were common in the United States both before and after the Second World War. Although prefabrication implies large-scale production in order to gain the benefit of the economy of scale, it can also be used to generate one-off houses. A case in point was the highly praised Boat House, Poole, Dorset (1982) by Richard Horden Associates, a high-tech, modular grid construction exploiting standard yacht components. Apparently, the architect Horden was a keen yachtsman.

● See also CLASP, High-Tech, Systems Architecture.

A Bruce & H Sandbark *A history of prefabrication* (NY, John B Pierce Foundation, 1944).

R Graff & others *The prefabricated house: a practical guide for the prospective buyer* (Garden City, NY, Doubleday, 1947).

B Kelly *The prefabrication of houses* (Cambridge, Mass, Technology Press/Wiley, 1951).

R White *Prefabrication: a history of its development in Great Britain* (HMSO, 1965).

B Russell *Building systems, industrialization and architecture* (John Wiley, 1981).

N Morris 'All live in little boxes' *Design* (480) December 1988 36–9.

535 PRESENCE

According to several American critics, an attribute of minimal art. William S Rubin defined it as 'the ability of a configuration to command its own space'; Michael Fried argued that it was basically theatrical: a stage presence. Clement Greenberg, the first writer to analyse Presence, claimed it was not an artistic quality, merely the consequence of the size and non-art look of minimal objects.

● See also Installation, Minimal Art, Objecthood.

M Fried 'Art and objecthood' – in – *Minimal art: a critical anthology* G Battcock (ed) (Studio Vista, 1969) 127.

W Rubin *Frank Stella* (NY, MoMA, 1970) 37.

536 PRIMATE AESTHETICS

Some primates – monkeys and chimpanzees – enjoy painting and are capable of a degree of pictorial control, e.g. balancing a composition. The paintings they generate are abstract and calligraphic, resembling in style action painting and tachisme. The scientific study of ape 'art' and the investigation of the visual preferences of apes and monkeys has been called 'Primate Aesthetics'. It was popularized by the artist–scientist Desmond Morris in the early 1960s. The aim of such research is to discover if there are any biological principles common to both ape and human art.

M Levy 'Chimpanzee painting: the roots of art' *Studio* **161** (818) June 1961 203–7.

D Morris 'Primate Aesthetics' *Natural History* **70** 1961 22–9.

— *The biology of art* (Methuen, 1962).

T Osman 'The aesthetic ape' *Sunday Times Magazine* January 14 1973 30–2.

A Whiten 'Primate perception and aesthetics' – in – *Beyond aesthetics: investigations into the nature of visual art* D Brothwell (ed) (Thames & Hudson, 1976) 18–40.

537 PRINTED ART

Title of an exhibition of works by over a hundred artists held in New York in 1980. A broad category, Printed Art encompassed illustrated books, artists' books, postcards and, of course, prints.

● See also Book Art, Copy Art, Mail Art, Media Art, Postcard Art.

R Castleman *Printed Art: a view of two decades* (NY, MoMA, 1980).

538 PRISON ART

(Also Penal Art, Prisoners' Art) For centuries, whenever conditions have permitted, the inmates of prisons have engaged in creative activities by producing drawings, paintings, carvings, graffiti, writings, craftwork and even photographs. Such artistic expressions are generally considered beneficial – therapeutic – for prisoners and for the smooth running of the institutions. Sales of works can be a means of raising money for such purposes as ex-prisoners' charities. Portraits of prisoners can also be of help to their families outside. Some prison authorities have encouraged inmates to be creative by providing facilities, materials and outside tuition. A well-known example was the Special Unit of the Barlinnie prison in

PRISON ART RITA DONAGH, 'Long Meadow' (1982). Oil on canvas, 152cm x 152cm. Photo: Rita Donagh

work has been deeply concerned with Northern Ireland; she has explored the theme of the H-Block prisons in a whole series of paintings and drawings.

● See also APG, Art Therapy, Artist-in-Residence, Hard Architecture, Holocaust Art.

● G Brandreth 'Prison Art' *Art & Artists* **4** (4) July 1969 58–60.
● M Kozloff 'Conversations with the dead' *Art News* **69** (8) December 1970 24–7, 70–2.
● G Brandreth *Created in captivity* (Hodder & Stoughton, 1972).
● A Anderson 'Art from the inside' *Art in America* **61** (2) March–April 1973 14–15.
● Groupe de Cinq 'La Roquette, women's prison' *Heresies* (1) January 1977 36–41.
● G Szekely 'Art education in correctional settings' *Studies in Art Education* (USA) **24** (1) 1982 33–42.
● *The Special Unit* (Glasgow, Third Eye Centre, 1982).
● M Quanne, introd J Berger *Prison paintings* (John Murray, 1985).
● *Prison Art: artwork by prisoners from Norwich Prison complex and Wayland Prison, Norfolk* (Norwich, Contact Gallery, 1989).

Glasgow where the aggression of the hardman Jimmy Boyle was transformed partly through the practice of sculpture. Boyle was visited and encouraged by the famous German artist Joseph Beuys. Hugh Collins, serving a sentence for murder in Barlinnie, also produced a notable statue of Jesus Christ in the mid 1980s which excited artworld interest. Some recalcitrant prisoners have even used prison pottery workshops for criminal purposes, e.g. producing fake Bernard Leach pots.

Numerous exhibitions of prisoners' art have been held in galleries since 1945. Sometimes the aim of such shows was to make a political point, i.e. to call attention to unsatisfactory conditions inside prisons. However, images showing prison scenes are normally not permitted for security reasons. Arthur Koestler, the writer, was once a prisoner himself and consequently he took an interest in the welfare of prisoners and instituted a prize for prisoners' art. According to David Cohen's TV programme 'Art behind bars' (*Signals,* Channel 4, November 1988), the Home Office, in association with the Arts Council, intends to undertake a survey of all the art in British prisons.

The term 'prison art' could also be taken to mean works about imprisonment made by professional artists who were themselves prisoners (e.g. Gustave Courbet) or who were in residence/placement inside prisons. For instance, the British artist Ian Breakwell made a film about Broadmoor while on a placement there. A controversial painting about the IRA prisoners' 'dirty protest' in Northern Ireland was Richard Hamilton's 'The Citizen' (1984). Rita Donagh is another British artist whose

539 PROCESS ART

(Also Procedural Art) In the practice of action painting and tachisme in the 1940s and 1950s particular stress was laid on the creative act of the artist; the making process became as important as the end result. Pollock's drip paintings and, later on, Morris Louis's stain paintings were records of the technical procedures employed to produce them, hence process became both the means and the subject of the works. Process Art, as a specific minor genre within avant garde art, emerged in the late 1960s and represented a formalization and systematization of the earlier work of Pollock and Louis. It also marked the introduction of time, chance and change into minimal art.

Artists regarded as belonging to the category included both painters and sculptors: Robert Morris, Bernard Cohen, Mark Lancaster, Keith Sonnier, Rafael Ferrer and Richard Serra. A typical example (by Morris) consisted of the artist firing a shotgun at a wall, photographing the result, placing an enlarged print of the first mark on the wall, then firing the gun again, then photographing the result, etc. Since Process Art tended towards the generation of a series of similar artefacts, systemic painting was included in the category by some critics. A number of exhibitions held in 1969 made the vogue for Process Art public: 'Ant-Illusion: procedures/materials' (NY, Whitney Museum); 'Place & Process' (Edmonton Art Gallery); 'When attitudes become form' (London, ICA).

Carl Andre welcomed the fact that his open-air pieces made from steel rusted because the work became 'a record of everything that happened to it'. The critic Thomas Albright defined Process Art as 'the act of change, the process of creation itself' and distinguished two kinds: performance or body art and 'force art', i.e. art making use of nature's forces or elements (see Ecological Art).

● See also Action Painting, Anti-Form, Body Art, Minimal Art, Performance Art, Post-Minimalism, Systemic Painting, Tachisme.

● W Sharp 'Place and Process' *Artforum* **8** (3) November 1969 46–9.

● *When attitudes become form* (ICA, 1969).

● T Albright 'Visuals' *Rolling Stone* (85) June 14 1971 36–7.

● J Burnham *The structure of art* (NY, Braziller, 1971).

● *Robert Morris* (Tate Gallery, 1971).

540 PRODUCT ENVIRONMENT

A term devised by the American design historian Victor Margolin. He defined it as: 'all the necessary conditions for acquiring the product, learning to use it, following its changes and improvements, providing components for it, keeping it in good repair. The term "environment" denotes everything that surrounds the product and becomes part of its identity and value.' Margolin argued that many modern artefacts – e.g. personal computers and video recorders – were technologically complex, multi-purpose and permitted a high degree of user participation, hence the need for designers to consider the product's 'environment' as well as its physical form and technical functioning. As automobiles increase in complexity, maintenance and service contracts and reliability become more important to buyers of new cars – another instance of the shift of emphasis away from the product's form or style to its 'environment'.

● See also Customizing & Custom Painting, Participatory Design, Reception Theory/Aesthetics.

● V Margolin 'Expanding the boundaries of design: the Product Environment and the new user' *Design Issues* **4** (1/2) 1988 59–64.

541 PRODUCT SEMANTICS

An expression fashionable amongst American design theorists and designers in the 1980s. Semantics is the branch of linguistics concerned with meaning; consequently Product Semantics is based on the assumption that all designed goods involve meanings and symbolism for those who buy, use and see them. The term itself was originated by Klaus Krippendorff and Reinhart Butter in 1984. They defined it as 'a study of the symbolic qualities of man-made forms in the cognitive and social contexts of their use and the application of the knowledge gained to objects of industrial design'. Instead of designing enigmatic black boxes which concealed what a product was and did, American designers of the '80s looked for visual metaphors, ornament, and ways of styling products that would enrich their appearance and express their function. For instance, the Chicago consultancy Design Logic (founded 1985) employed grid patterns on a number of products 'to express the digital electronic nature of their functioning'.

● See also Commodity Aesthetics, Semiotics, Styling, Symbolic Architecture.

● M Csikszentmihaly & E Rochberg-Halton *The meaning of things: domestic symbols and the self* (Cambridge, Cambridge University Press, 1981).

● K Krippendorff & R Butter '"Product Semantics": exploring the symbolic qualities of form' *Innovation* **3** (2) 1984 4–9.

● H Aldersey-Williams *New American design: products and graphics for a post-industrial age* (NY, Rizzoli, 1988).

● 'Product Semantics' (special issue) *Design Issues* **5** (2) Spring 1989.

● K Krippendorff 'On the essential context of artifacts...' *Design Issues* **5** (2) Spring 1989 9–39.

● S Vokeva (ed) *Product Semantics 1989 conference* (Helsinki, University of Industrial Arts, 1990).

542 PROGRAMMED ART

(Also Arte Programmata) A description applied by the Italian artist–designer Bruno Munari to certain of his own works produced since 1945. They took the form of small viewing screens displaying changing combinations of colour and shape. The transformations were achieved by electric motors turning movable parts. Programming, a word derived from computer terminology, consisted in deciding operating speeds and length of time required to complete a cycle of transformations. Munari's declared aim was to 'show forms in the process of becoming'. His work seemed to be a type of kinetic art but he denied it. Nevertheless, the label 'Arte Programmata' was used to describe the kinetic works produced by the Italian Gruppo N of Padua. During the early 1960s the Italian company Olivetti sponsored exhibitions of 'Arte Programmata' in Europe and the United States. One, featuring the work of Gruppo N and Gruppo T, appeared at the Royal College of Art, London, in 1964.

Certain movements of the 1960s – op art, systemic painting, serial art – were also described as 'programmed' because their forms and relationships were often predetermined by mathematical series. The term 'Programmed Art' would seem to be ideal for computer art because it is literally programmed.

● See also Computer Art, Gruppo N, Gruppo T, Kinetic Art, Multiples.

● U Eco *Arte Programmata* (Milan, Societa Olivetti, 1962).

● B Munari 'Programmed Art' *Times Literary Supplement* (3262) September 3 1964 793.

● J Healy, Group N & Group T *Luminous pictures and Arte Programmata* (Royal College of Art/Olivetti, 1964).

● P Selz 'Art Programmata' *Arts Magazine* **9** (6) March 1965 16–21.

● B Munari *Design as art* (Harmondsworth, Penguin, 1971) 174.

● J Hlavacek 'About the interpretation of Programmed Art' *BIT International* (7) 1972 67–74.

543 PROJECTED ART

Title of an exhibition held at Finch College Museum in the winter of 1966–7. 'Projected Art' simply meant works of art requiring projecting equipment to be seen, e.g. films, slides and video enlargements. During the late 1960s much use was made of slide imagery projected during rock music concerts (see Psychedelic Art) and in mixed-media performances. John Latham's 'skoob' films, for instance, were projected during early Pink Floyd gigs and during his own stage events taking place at the Mercury Theatre as part of the Destruction in Art Symposium in 1966.

In the following decade Projected Art emerged as a minor genre of avant garde art in its own right. The British artist Tim Head devised several installations in which photos of objects in gallery spaces were projected on to those same objects and spaces. During the 1980s the Polish émigré artist Krzysztof Wodiczko specialized in site-specific, xenon-arc projections taking place at night, out of doors in public places. By projecting large-scale images on to significant examples of architecture, monuments and war memorials he was able to generate ironic and political meanings via the montage juxtapositions between the content of his images and their 'screens'; for example, in 1985 he projected an image of a swastika on to the South African embassy in central London. These works were called 'counter monuments'.

Works of art consisting of laser beams could also be counted as examples of Projected Art.

● See also Destructive Art, Installation, Laser Art, Performance Art, Public Art, Site-Specific Art.

● E Varian *Projected Art* (NY, Finch College Museum of Art, 1966–7).

● L Carney 'The revival of the slide' *Art Magazine* (Canada) **19** (6) Fall 1974 22–3.

● J Tagg 'In camera...' *Studio International* **190** (976) July–August 1975 55–9.

● K Wodiczko 'The Wall' *Circa* (Belfast) (24) September–October 1985 17–22.

● E Lajer-Burcharth *Krzysztof Wodiczko: counter monuments* (Cambridge, Mass, MIT Visual Arts Center, 1986).

● 'Krzysztof Wodiczko in conversation with William Furlong' *Art Monthly* (120) October 1988 11–12.

● P Wood 'Projection' *Artscribe* (73) January–February 1989 12–13.

544 PROP ART

(Also Persuasive Art) Short for 'Propaganda Art', the kind exemplified by the political posters of Cuba. 'Agitprop' (agitation–propaganda) was a term which gained currency during the Russian Revolution and its aftermath. The word 'propaganda' derives from a Catholic organization of 1622 charged with propagating the faith. In spite of this religious origin, the term is normally taken to mean 'lies, distortions, information intended to deceive or mislead'. Propaganda is a phenomenon most liberal-humanists associate with repressive and totalitarian regimes such as Nazi Germany but in fact all nations indulge in it, especially when they are at war. In consumer societies commercial advertising can be regarded as a relentless flow of propaganda in favour of a particular economic and social system.

Many writers on fine art maintain that art and propaganda are mutually exclusive categories (because art is devoted to truth and high spiritual values while propaganda is ideological and partisan?) but, arguably, they are not because: (1) many distinguished and recognized fine artists have been employed to produce political posters; (2) visual propaganda often relies upon aesthetic devices and pleasure to ensure the successful communication of its messages; (3) the idea that art is non-ideological is naive.

PROJECTED ART KRZYSZTOF WODICZKO, 'The Grand Army Plaza projection, Brooklyn' (1985). Photo: Wodiczko.

In the United States a quarterly publication entitled *Journal of Decorative and Propaganda Arts* was established in 1986 by the Wolfson Foundation of Decorative and Propaganda Arts, Miami. The period covered by the journal was 1875 to 1945. In view of the negative connotations of the word 'propaganda' the journal disclaimed any political stance. It defined Prop Art as 'art in the service of an idea or an ideology'. Articles have been published on such subjects as WPA murals, Soviet posters and Nazi postage stamps.

● See also Atelier Populaire, Banners, Disinformation, Nazi Art, Pictorial Rhetoric, Political Art, Totalitarian Art.

● D Stermer *The art of revolution: 96 posters from Cuba* (Pall Mall, 1970).

● G Yanker *Prop Art: international political posters* (Studio Vista, 1972).

● A Rhodes *Propaganda: the art of persuasion World War II* (Angus & Robertson, 1976).

● S Neale 'Propaganda' *Screen* **18** (3) Autumn 1977 9–40.

● (Special issue on Propaganda) *Oxford Art Journal* **3** (2) 1980.

545 PROVINCIALISM PROBLEM

An issue named by the Australian writer Terry Smith in 1974 and much discussed since. The 'problem' arises from the fact that certain countries and cities are dominant in the field of art (e.g. USA/New York) and others are subordinate (e.g. Australia/Sydney). The dominance arises from concentrations of wealth, power (economic, military, political) and cultural capital. Within a single country the power relation favours the major city as against the provinces (to be called 'provincial' is generally considered an insult). Internationally, the power relation favours dominant nations as against subordinate nations. Peter Fuller, the British art critic, opposed internationalism in art and quoted John Ruskin to the effect that 'all great art, in the great times of art, is *provincial*'.

For artists, the question is one of a relationship to place, whether locality, region or country: should artists seek to develop indigenous styles or traditions or should they follow international styles (which although called 'international' are usually the styles of the dominant city or nation)? Should they live and work where they are born or should they emigrate to Paris or London or New York? (Artists from the margins are generally drawn to the centres of power because they cannot make a living as artists where they are born.) Or should they train in these cities and then return to their homes? Today, all artists are exposed to both local and global influences, hence their problem is to find a convincing resolution which takes account of both. International trade and travel, plus the worldwide mass-media systems are rapidly producing a global market and culture. If this trend continues, there may come a time when art styles bear no relation to any particular place.

● See also Critical Regionalism, Global or World Art, Globalization.

● T Smith 'The Provincialism Problem' *Artforum* **13** (1) September 1974 54–9.

● A Van Den Bosch 'Ten years on: the Provincialism Problem' *Art Monthly* (86) May 1985 9–13.

● D Brett 'From the local to the global: the place of place in art' *Circa* (Belfast) (29) July–August 1986 17–21.

● P Fuller 'Against internationalism' *Art Monthly* (100) October 1986 12–14.

546 PSYCHEDELIC ART

(Also Acid Art, Dayglo Art) A tendency in the painting and light art of the mid and late 1960s coincident with the Hippie/Flower Children drug culture, international in scope but primarily an American West Coast phenomenon. Techniques of sensory deprivation and drugs such as LSD ('acid') can produce states of consciousness very different from normal waking experience. Drugs, it is claimed, enhance perception, increase aesthetic sensitivity, improve creativity and unlock the unconscious mind. Psychedelic artists were those whose works were influenced by their altered consciousnesses. Often they attempted to communicate, via a visual analogue, the drug experience itself. Admirers of this kind of work postulated a psychedelic sensibility to account for the stylistic precedents they discovered in the art of Hieronymus Bosch, William Blake and in art nouveau and surrealism, and in the work of the Fantastic Realists of Vienna. (Psychedelic Art also encompassed images drug users enjoyed looking at while on a trip.) In fact, drug-influenced art was not exclusive to the '60s: the decadent and symbolist painters of the late nineteenth century sought inspiration from similar substances.

Common characteristics of modern Psychedelic Art were: obsessively detailed images, all-over decorative patterns (some close to op art), a mélange of abstract and figurative motifs, snaky dissolving forms, ambiguous spatial effects, iridescent or acidic colours. Their impact was summed up by Timothy Leary as 'retinal orgasm'. Other observers found the style 'tedious', its forms 'niggling' and its colours 'emetic'. No major artist emerged from the movement; perhaps the best known were Isaac Abrams and Allen Atwell.

Psychedelia was not confined to the art of painting: it was a style that flourished in terms of interior decor, fashion design and tie-dye textiles, posters and record covers (e.g. the Beatles' 'Sergeant Pepper' LP with cover design by Peter Blake and Jann Haworth; plus the work of the group The Fool, and the Australian Martin Sharp), underground magazines, indeed the whole lifestyle associated with the Hippie subculture.

The kaleidoscopic effects, amoebic forms ('pulsating protoplasmic blobs') sought by the painters were more successfully achieved via light shows and these became obligatory for a time at rock music discos, concerts and dances. In the United States the USCO commune organized a mixed-media happening at the Riverside Museum in 1966 which has since been described as the first Psychedelic show. Also in America, Don Synder projected organic images from painted slides on to the bodies of naked performers and Andy Warhol collaborated with the rock band The Velvet Underground to present a multi-media disco called the Exploding Plastic Inevitable (EPI). Meanwhile in London the Scottish artist Mark Boyle devised 'liquid light' shows for rock groups such as Soft Machine at the UFO club in 1967. Multimedia performances of this kind attempted to induce synaesthesia by employing sounds, strobe lights, smoke to assault several senses at once. The extreme loudness of the music and the intensity of the light oscillations were designed to produce sensory overload, a disorientation of normal consciousness, in short a synthetic trip.

During the 1980s there were several attempts to revive the Psychedelic style in terms of fashion and music, e.g. the magazine *Encyclopedia Psychedelica* founded by Fraser Clark in 1986, the London shop Planet Alice, the vogue for Acid House music/parties in 1987–9, the rock groups Stone Roses, Happy Mondays and All About Eve.

● See also Cosmic Art, Fantastic Realism, The Fool, Light Art, Projected Art, Rock Art/Design/Fashion, Underground Art, USCO, Visionary Art.

● 'Psychedelic Art' *Life* September 9 1966.
● M Duckett 'Are we suffering from Psychedelic fatigue?' *Design* (229) January 1968 21.
● R Masters & others *Psychedelic Art* (Weidenfeld & Nicolson, 1968).
● N Gosling 'Snakes in the grass' *Art & Artists* **4** (9) December 1969 26–31.
● D Shears 'When I shut my eyes I see many rings' *Daily Telegraph Magazine* (314) October 23 1970 50–6.
● D Synder *Aquarian odyssey: a photographic trip into the Sixties* (NY, Liveright, 1979).
● S Wilson 'Psychedelic revival' *Time Out* September 25–October 1 1981 10–17.
● G O'Brien 'Psychedelic Art: flashing back' *Artforum* **22** (7) March 1984 72–8.
● V Joynson *The acid trip: a complete guide to Psychedelic music* (Todmorden, Lancs, Babylon Books, 1984).
● *Encyclopedia Psychedelica* (1) 1986–.
● N Whiteley *Pop design: modernism to mod* (Design Council, 1987) 168–74.
● C Salewicz 'Heavy Petal' *20/20* (12) March 1990 50–3.

547   PUBLIC ART

This term encompasses various kinds of art – sculptures, fountains, mosaics, reliefs, stained glass windows, slide-image and laser projections, works on billboards, murals, performances – having in common the fact that they were designed to be sited or to take place in public places. (Some theorists make a distinction between Public Art and studio/gallery art which is simply deposited in a public space; the latter has been referred to as 'the turd in the plaza'!) These spaces may be urban or rural, they may be in the open air – parks, woods, streets, squares, walkways, etc. – or indoors – inside churches, hospitals, the foyers of public buildings, the concourses of railway stations, underground tube stations, subways, etc. Because Public Art often occupies unprotected sites (i.e. this kind of art is not guarded to the same extent as museum objects) it is sometimes subject to vandalism or protest by people who resent the works concerned, feeling that they represent unwarranted intrusions into familiar territories. For this reason, and for reasons of resistance to the weather, most traditional forms of Public Art – statues of the famous, war memorials, and so on – were made from marble or bronze and were set on plinths or columns high above the heads of pedestrians.

Making a modern public work of art poses far more challenges to the artist than a purely private work because there is the vexed question of the 'language' or symbolism employed: will it be understood by those who see it? Can it be difficult, critical and challenging, or must it aim to please as many as possible? (A huge steel sculpture by Richard Serra provoked much controversy in the 1980s because its minimalist idiom was detested by so many New Yorkers; finally it was removed. However, a similar work located in the new Broadgate development in London was accepted without protest.) In fact, the very concept of 'the public' is highly problematical. (Passers-by in the street are not a homogeneous body of educated and informed citizens.) The artist normally has to please a client too, whether a business or an agency of local or national government. Then there is the further issue of the physical context: the work must relate successfully to what surrounds it, in particular the architecture. Or, in the case of new developments, the artist has to be able to collaborate with the architect. Many public projects are on a much larger scale than those the artist normally tackles and so there are also more technical and logistical problems to solve. In Britain during the 1980s much emphasis was placed on Public Art: what was called 'the public sculpture problem' was debated at length, more money was spent on commissions, and art college courses devoted to it were started or revamped. On the one hand, this emphasis represented an attempt on the part of the artworld to reduce the alienation of the contemporary artist from society as a whole, on the other hand it marked an ideological shift on the part of arts authorities away from the more politically sensitive issue of community art ('public' was a more nebulous concept than 'community' and hence implied a blander, less partisan kind of art). One artist who successfully combined Public Art with a sense of community, locality and history was the witty Scottish sculptor George Wyllie: in 1987 he made a full-size steam locomotive from straw as a tribute to the train builders of Glasgow; it was later ritually burnt. In 1989 he constructed a large paper boat as a homage to the shipworkers of Clydeside; at night it floated on the water illuminated from within. Wyllie once defined Public Art as 'art the public can't avoid'; he favoured 'people-specific art' rather than 'site-specific art'. His simple but memorable sculptures evoked a popular response because they were presented with showmanship and served as the foci for public festivities.

● See also Art & Architecture, Artangel Trust, Billboard Art, Community Art & Media, Environmental Art, Free Form Arts Trust, Graffiti, Hospital Arts, Popular Art, Projected Art, Sculpture Parks, Site-Specific Art, Street Art, Town Art/Artist.

● P Damaz *Art in European architecture* (NY, Reinhold, 1968).

● L Redstone *Art in architecture* (NY, McGraw-Hill, 1968).

● L Alloway 'The public sculpture problem' *Studio International* **184** (948) October 1972 122–5.

● 'Public Art, special issue' *Art in America* **62** (3) May–June 1974.

● R Mace *Trafalgar Square* (Lawrence & Wishart, 1976).

● M Robinette *Outdoor sculpture: object and environment* (NY, Watson-Guptil, 1976).

● D Thalacker *The place of art in the world of architecture* (NY, Chelsea House, 1980).

● B Diamonstein (ed) *Collaboration artists and architects* (NY, Architectural League, 1981).

● L Redstone & R Ruth *Public Art, new directions* (NY, McGraw-Hill, 1981).

● P Davies & T Kripe (eds) *A sense of place: sculpture in landscape* (Sunderland Arts Centre, 1984).

● P Townsend (ed) *Art within reach: artists and craftworkers, architects and patrons in the making of Public Art* (Thames & Hudson, 1984).

● A Elsen *Rodin's 'thinker' and the dilemmas of modern public sculpture* (New Havens/London, Yale University Press, 1985).

● *Public Art and artists* (Birmingham, Ikon Gallery, 1985).

PUBLIC ART KEVIN ATHERTON, 'Platforms piece' (1986). One of three lifesize bronze sculptures, Brixton British Rail Station, London. Photo: Atherton.

● D Petherbridge (ed) *Art for architecture* (HMSO, 1987).

● J Cruikshank & P Korza *Going public: a field guide to developments in art in public places* (Washington, DC, Arts Extension Program/NEA, 1988).

● P Hook (introd) *Art for the public: new collaborations* (Dayton, Ohio, Dayton Art Institute, 1988).

● 'Art in public places' *Circa* (45) May–June 1989, special issue.

● G McCue *Sculpture city: St Louis* (NY, Hudson Hills, 1989).

M Miles & others *Art for public places* (Winchester School of Art Press, 1989).

● D Joselit 'Public Art and the public purse' *Art in America* **78** (7) July 1990 142–50, + 183.

548 **PUBLIC ART DEVELOPMENT TRUST (PADT)** A British charitable organization established in 1983 and based in London which seeks to encourage the siting of works of art in public places by initiating and organizing commissions, by fostering the collaboration of developers, architects, local authorities and artists, by providing a consultative and advisory service, and by maintaining a slide index. It also encourages school workshops, artists' residences and artists working on site. Achieving an integration between the work of art and the physical location and local community is a key concern. Projects undertaken so far include: bronze figurative sculptures by Kevin Atherton on Brixton railway station platforms; murals and sculptures in various hospitals and schools; an abstract stained glass window by Alexander Beleschenko at Stockley Park. Financially PADT has been supported by the Greater London Arts (GLA) and by the Calouste Gulbenkian Foundation. In 1988 the director of PADT was Lesley Greene and the chairman of the trustees Tom Bendham.

● See also Artangel Trust, Public Art.

G Darley 'PADT' *Crafts Magazine* March–April 1986.

L Greene 'Going public' *Arts Express* March 1986 14–15.

Public Art Development Trust (PADT, 1988). booklet.

---

549 PUBLIC DESIGN

(Also Civic Design, Sociable Architecture) A term used by British design journalists to refer to design for publicly owned housing or nationalized industries such as British Rail, and also design for those items such as street furniture which are located in public spaces. A closely related term is 'civic design' ('civic' means 'pertaining to the city and to citizenship' as in the groups of public buildings called 'civic centres'). Philadelphia is an American city which has become noted for the attention it pays to civic design. An organization – the Foundation for Architecture – established by Leslie Gallery in 1980 enables citizens to influence the architecture and planning of the city. The Foundation takes conservation initiatives, mounts educational programmes and publishes a magazine called *CitySites;* generally it seeks to encourage a consensus by involving politicians, developers, architects, planners, community groups, etc. in design issues. In Charleston, South Carolina there is a similar organization called the Mayor's Institute for Civic Design while in Britain there is the Urban Design Group (UDG, 1978–). In March 1990 a special issue of *Architects' Journal* argued that London was in dire need of a civic design vision for the future.

● See also Community Architecture, Participatory Design, Social Architecture/Design.

L Young 'Trashing Public Design's old image' *Design* (485) May 1989 40–1.

R Cowan & L Gallery (eds) 'A vision for London' *Architects' Journal* **191** (11) March 14 1990.

---

550 PULSA

An American art, research and technology group formed in 1967 by ten artists but by 1970 consisting of seven: Michael Cain, Patrick Clancy, William Crosby, William Duesing, Peter Kindlmann, David Rumsey and Paul Fuge. PULSA, based in New Haven, Connecticut, made use of electronic technology to generate sensory phenomena in programmed environments. For instance, in a sculpture court at the 'Spaces' exhibition (NY, MoMA, 1969–70) they devised an environment of computer-controlled light, sound and heat systems responsive to human behaviour and the noise of the urban setting. The group was active from the mid '60s to the early '70s.

● See also Computer Art, Environmental Art, Technological Art.

W Sharp 'PULSA: sound, light and seven young artists' *New York Times* December 24 1970.

J Burns *Arthropods: new design futures* (NY, Praeger, 1972) 138–42.

PULSA 'The city as an artwork' – in – *Arts of the environment* G Kepes (ed) (Aidan Ellis, 1972) 208–21.

---

551 PUNK

(Also New Wave) An aggressive, angry, rebellious subcultural movement which erupted in the United States and Britain in the mid 1970s. 'Punk' is an old word; it is slang for someone who is worthless, degraded or bad. Although primarily associated with rock music, visual and design aspects – clothing and graphics – were also crucial to the Punk style. (Photography and films also played a part in publicizing the movement.) Furthermore, Punk had a revitalizing impact upon the visual arts since many young artists (e.g. Robert Longo) and artschool graduates (e.g. Adam Ant, David Byrne and Jamie Reid) participated in, or were energized by, the Punk scenes in London and New York. A key stylistic influence on Punk was the 1960s band The Velvet Underground and Nico which for a time collaborated with Andy Warhol.

In Britain the leading Punk bands were the Sex Pistols, the Clash, the Damned, the Jam, Generation X, the Buzzcocks, Siouxsie and the Banshees, Poly Styrene and X Ray Spex, Subway Sect, the Slits, Sham 69, the Vibrators and Adam and the Ants. American bands included the Ramones, the New York Dolls, Johnny Thunders and the Heartbreakers, Television, Void-Oids, the Dead Kennedys and Blondie. Many Punk musicians had little or no musical training or skill: there was a do-it-yourself, improvisational philosophy, plus energy, rawness, loudness and a feeling that attitude counted more than musicianship. Punks reacted against the remote, rich supergroups of the early 1970s; they also despised the 'peace and love' ethos of the Hippies. It was a cynical, pessimistic response to unemployment and urban decay. The Punk movement mounted attacks on good taste, tourism, authority, the British Royal family, and record

PUNK JAMIE REID, 'Pretty vacant' (1977). Artwork for sleeve of single by the Sex Pistols & for poster. Photo: Reid.

companies. It set out to shock and outrage and succeeded in its aim. A collage or cut-up aesthetic characterized the Punk style. In terms of fashion, second-hand clothes and recycled junk and images borrowed from the mass media were used: black leather jackets with lots of zips, slashed T-shirts, with rude or political slogans ('Destroy', 'Money from chaos', 'No future'), string vests, old school ties, torn jeans or bondage trousers tied at the knees, studded dog-collars, bin liners, chains and straps, razor-blade decor and safety pins attached to flesh, ripped Union Jacks, swastikas, close-cut or spiky hair dyed lurid colours, white corpse-like make-up on faces plus primitivistic decorations. Parodies of bondage and sado-masochism were typical of the dress style and song lyrics. Any participant in the movement could contribute ideas but there were certain taste-makers, e.g. Malcolm McLaren (ex-artschool and manager of the Sex Pistols) and Vivienne Westwood who designed Punk clothing and sold it via a shop in the Kings Road.

In terms of graphics, the key figure was Jamie Reid (ex-artschool, follower of the situationists, designer for the Sex Pistols). His posters and record sleeve designs were notable for their harsh imagery, brash colours and ransom-note style of lettering. A collection of his artwork was later purchased for the Theatre Collection in London and in 1986 another body of work was exhibited at Hamilton's Gallery in Mayfair. An additional visual dimension was supplied by the cheaply and crudely produced 'fanzines', the most famous of which was *Sniffing Glue* devised by a teenager called Mark P. (Mark Perry).

Design and visual arts responses to Punk were soon forthcoming. The English pop painter Derek Boshier illustrated a songbook for the Clash. In the spring of 1978, in the United States, the designer Richard Mauro claimed to be making 'Punk furniture', and at the Washington Project for the Arts, an exhibition of Punk art was mounted.

● See also Art schools, Situationists, Subculture.
◉ P Marsh 'Dole-queue rock' *New Society* January 20 1977 112–14.
◉ A Carter 'Year of the Punk' *New Society* December 22–9 1977 14–16.
◉ E Lucie-Smith & others 'Does Punk art exist?' *New Style* (7) 1977 26–7.
◉ D Laing 'Interpreting Punk rock' *Marxism Today* **22** (4) April 1978 123–8.
◉ A Kagen 'Most wanted men: Andy Warhol and the anti-culture of Punk' *Arts Magazine* **53** (1) September 1978 119–21.
◉ J Burchill & T Parsons *'The boy looked at Johnny' : the obituary of rock and roll* (Pluto Press, 1978).
◉ V Hennessy *In the gutter* (Quartet Books, 1978).
◉ D Hebdige *Subculture: the meaning of style* (Methuen, 1979).
◉ M Shore 'Punk rocks the artworld...' *Art News* **79** (9) November 1980 78–85.
◉ P Belsito & others *Street art: the Punk poster in San Francisco* (San Francisco, Last Gasp, 1981).
◉ F & J Vermorel *The Sex Pistols: the inside story* (W H Allen/Star, rev ed 1981).
◉ C Coon *1988: the New Wave Punk rock explosion* (Omnibus, 2nd. ed. 1982).
◉ J Savage 'Guerrilla graphics: the tactic of agit pop art' *The Face* (42) October 1983 26–31.
◉ T Henry 'Punk and the avant garde' *Journal of Popular Culture* **17** (4) Spring 1984 30–7.
◉ D Laing *One chord wonders: power and meaning in Punk rock* (Milton Keynes, Open University Press, 1985).
◉ J Reid & J Savage *Up they rise: the incomplete works of Jamie Reid* (Faber & Faber, 1987).
◉ J Savage *England's dreaming: the Sex Pistols & Punk rock* (Faber & Faber, 1991).

552 PUSH PIN STUDIO An influential American graphic design organization of 20 artists founded in 1954 by Milton Glaser and Seymour Chwast. Admirers of the Push Pin style claimed that it combined wit, superb draughtsmanship and diverse imagery. The Studio issued a magazine entitled *Push Pin Graphic*.

◉ A Ferebee & M Genehell 'Revivalism revisited' *Design* (242) February 1969 32–7.
◉ E Stephano 'The Push Pin Studio' *Art & Artists* **5** (6) September 1970 26–7.
◉ *The Push Pin style* (Palo Alto, California, Communication Arts Magazine, 1970).
◉ *Push Pin Studios: Idea extra issue 1972* (Tokyo, Orion Books, 1972).
◉ S Tora 'The twentieth anniversary of Push Pin Graphic Inc' *Idea* **25** (145) November 1977 68–71.

553 **QUADRIGA** (Also Die Quadriga, Frankfurt Quadriga) A two-wheeled chariot drawn by four horses. Also the name of a group of German tachist painters founded in Frankfurt in 1952. The four founder members were: Karl Otto Götz (editor of the magazine *Meta,* 10 issues 1948–53), Heinz Kreutz, Otto Greis and Bernard Schultze; Emil Schumacher joined later. Their work was influenced by the examples of Wols, Jackson Pollock and Jean-Paul Riopelle. Quadriga's first exhibition, held at the Zimmergalerie Franck, Frankfurt, in December 1952 was entitled 'neo-expressionists'; French writers dubbed them 'New German Romantics'.

● See also Art Informel, Free Abstraction, Neo-Expressionism, Tachisme.

● R Hinds *Quadriga* (Frankfurt, Zimmergalerie Franck, 1953).

● *Tachismus im Frankfurt: Quadriga 52: Kreutz, Götz, Greis, Schultze* (Frankfurt, Städisches Historischen Museums, 1959).

554 **QUANTEL PAINTBOX** A digital 'paintbox' of immense value to graphic artists working for television, developed by the international company Quantel in 1982. A TV set replaces paper or canvas, hence colours are mixed and painted in light directly on the television screen via a touch tablet

QUANTEL PAINTBOX Advertisement issued by Quantel 1991.(Detail).

upon which the artist or designer can draw with an electronic stylus. Facilities include: painting, graphics, text, cut and paste, stencil operations and picture library. The machine has been instrumental in helping to produce sophisticated TV graphics to introduce programmes and special effects in advertisements and rock videos. It has also been used by some fine artists: in 1987 David Hockney, Sidney Nolan, Howard Hodgkin and others experimented with the machine for the BBC 2 TV series 'Painting with light'.

● See also Computer-Aided Design, Computer Art, Rock Video.

● W Feaver 'Screen debut' *Observer Magazine* April 19 1987 22–5.

● 'David Hockney's paintbox pictures' *Art & Design* **3** (7/8) 1987 37–44.

● D Merritt *Television graphics, from pencil to pixel* (Trefoil, 1987).

Name describing the early 1960s work of two German artists: Winfred Gaul, a painter, and Hans Peter Alvermann, a sculptor. Gaul's pictures were schematic; they blended abstraction and figuration, and took as their motifs everyday devices such as traffic signs (hence 'signal art'). Alvermann constructed bizarre metal sculptures from readymade objects such as chairs and taps. Critics considered their art a German version of pop art, junk sculpture, or nouveau réalisme; the artists, however, were concerned to distance themselves from such tendencies in their 'First Quibb Manifesto' (Düsseldorf, January 1963) because they thought their work was different, more critical than pop art.

● See also Junk Culture/Sculpture, Nouveau Réalisme, Pop Art.

● 'Quibb quack' *Vernissage* **3** (3) June 1963 9.

● L Lippard & others *Pop art* (Thames & Hudson, 1966).

● *Winfred Gaul: Signaux, Signalen* (Brussels, Palais des Beaux Arts, 1967).

R

556 RADICAL DESIGN

During the late 1960s and early '70s it became fashionable to link the word 'radical' to the words 'architecture', 'art' and 'design'. In some instances it denoted art that was extreme in its form or technique (e.g. photorealist painting was also called 'radical realism'), while in other instances it denoted art based on extreme political principles (generally those of the Left). Many believed it was vital to produce an art that was radical in both its form and its politics.

The concept of Radical Architecture/Design was heavily promoted in Italy. *Casabella* (Milan, 1928–) described itself as 'the magazine of radical design'. In practice Radical Architecture often consisted of the graphic presentation of fantastic and utopian projects by small groups of architects and designers (e.g. Archizoom, Superstudio, UFO, etc.). Their aim was to challenge established notions of what architecture/design was and to this end they also published theoretical critiques of the economic and ideological dimensions of 'normal' architecture and industrial design. For Radical designers and architects, the built environment was primarily a system of meanings. They viewed architecture as a 'language' whose statements served the interests of the dominant social classes, consequently they considered it essential to change people's consciousnesses rather than to add new buildings to the existing urban fabric. Although a form of 'paper design', the ideas of the Radicals were eventually to influence Italian commercial design.

The terms 'negative', 'critical' and 'oppositional' were also applied to their activities but Radical Design was perhaps distinguished from 'alternative' or 'counter' design by its greater awareness of politics and ideology. Penny Sparke, in her writings on Sottsass and Italian design, has employed the expression 'anti-design movement': 'a blurring of the boundaries between design practice and design criticism' resulting in a kind of 'meta-design'.

● See also Alchimia, Community Architecture, Conceptual Architecture, Italian Craze, Memphis, Political Art.

◉ A Mendini 'Radical Design' *Casabella* (367) July 1972 5.

◉ A Branzi 'A long-term strategy' *Casabella* (370) October 1972 13.

◉ C Celant 'Radical architecture' – in – *Italy: the new domestic landscape* E Ambasz (ed) (NY, MoMA, 1972) 380–7.

◉ 'Architecture and design' *Contemporanea* (Florence, Centro Di, 1973) 289–334.

◉ P Navone & B Orlandini *Architettura 'radicale'* (Milan, Documenti di Casabella, 1974).

◉ P Sparke *Italian design: 1870 to the present* (Thames & Hudson, 1988) 185–95.

◉ L Binazzi 'Radical chic' *Design* (501) September 1990 20–3.

557 RANDOM ART

(Also Aleatory Art, Stochastic Painting) A concept announced by the Dutch artist Hans Koetsier in 1969, referring to art based on the laws of probability or chance. In fact, many artists have been willing to take advantage of happy accidents or to incorporate random factors into their creative procedures, e.g. Marcel Duchamp's 'Standard stoppages', Hans Arp's collages made from pieces of paper allowed to fall to the ground, Jackson Pollock's drip painting technique. During the 1960s chance procedures became more formalized. Science-orientated artists employed statistical techniques derived from probability and information theory, giving rise to such terms as 'Aleatory Art' and 'Stochastic Painting'. Artists using computers can always surprise themselves by building in random factors into their programs.

● See also Computer Art, Programmed Art.

◉ A Bork 'Randomness and the twentieth-century' *ICA Bulletin* (175) November–December 1967 7–16.

◉ F Whipple 'Stochastic Painting' *Leonardo* **1** (1) January 1968 81–3.

◉ R Pincus-Witten *Against order: chance and art* (Philadelphia, ICA, 1970).

◉ M Challinor 'Change, chance and structure: randomness and formalism in art' *Leonardo* **4** (1) Winter 1971 1–11.

558 RATIONAL ARCHITECTURE

A term used sporadically in the history of twentieth-century architecture. Those architects deemed to belong to this tendency have been called 'Rationalists' and even 'the Rats'. Rational Architecture appears to be an alternative description of the modern architecture of such figures as Walter Gropius, Mies van der Rohe and Peter Behrens. Rationalists subscribed to a machine aesthetic, i.e. truth to materials, functionalism, rational as against irrational design, geometric as against organic forms, impersonality as against expression, grids and right angles, exactness, cleanness, precision of form and finish. (Art nouveau architects who did not follow these dicta were therefore dubbed 'anti-Rationalists' by J. M. Richards and Nikolaus Pevsner.)

Italian Rationalism began in 1926 when seven young architects formed 'Gruppo 7'. Two years later they organized an exhibition of Rational Architecture and in 1931 formed MIAR (Movimento Italiano per l'Architettura Razionale). These architects proposed to serve Mussolini's fascism. The group included Luigi Figini and Giuseppe Terragni. The latter's 'Casa del Fascio' at Como (1932–6), a severe half-cube, is considered to be a key example of the tendency.

In the post-1960 era the term 'Neo-Rationalists' has also been applied to such figures as Aldo Rossi, Robert Krier and Ricardo Bofill. Rossi organized a show of contemporary Rational Architecture at the Milan in 1973. Charles Jencks identified several different strands: Critical Rationalism, Historicist Rationalism and Surrationalism. According to Jencks, the latter stemmed from the fact that when 'rationalism' was pushed to an extreme it became 'irrational'.

● See also Machine Aesthetic/Art, Modern Movement, Organic Architecture/Art/Design, Tendenza.

◉ J Richards 'Towards a rational aesthetic' *Architectural Review* **78** December 1935 211–18, reprinted in Sharp (below).

◉ R Giolli *L'Architettura Razionale: antologia* C de Seta (ed) (Bari, Editori Laterza, 1972).

◉ J Richards & N Pevsner (eds) *The anti-Rationalists* (Architectural Press, 1973).

◉ A Rossi (organizer) *Architettura Razionale, XV di Milano* (Milan, Franco Angeli Editore, 1973).

◉ A Colquhoun 'Rational Architecture' *Architectural Design* **45** (6) 1975 365–70.

◉ S Danesi & L Patteta (eds) *Il Razionalismo e l'architettura in Italia durante il fascismo* (Venice, Edizioni La Biennale di Venezia, 1976).

◉ D Sharp (ed) *The Rationalists: theory and design in the modern movement* (Architectural Press, 1978).

◉ W Lesnikowski *Rationalism and romanticism in architecture* (NY, McGraw-Hill, 1982).

559 REACTIVART

(Also Eco-Art, New Ecology, Recycled Art) The name of an apolitical, informal network of over 100 British artists, designers and craftspersons who make bizarre clothes, furniture, sets, etc., from recycled materials in order to draw attention to environmental issues. The use of old things is intended to encourage people to adapt and recycle what they already possess rather than buying new. Reactivart was founded in 1988–9 by Janette Swift and others. Swift is noted for her three-dimensional clothes made from latex, painted images and plastic flowers which are half sculpture and half fashion. Other participants include: Vicky Hawkins, Lennie Lee, Bridget Tapp, Chris Holland, Johnny Ford, Lucy Shuker, and the duo Fin Savant and Jason Atomic ('Technotribe'). One critic described the work of Reactivart as 'Blade Runner meets Mad Max'. Fashion shows and exhibitions have been held in London shops and galleries such as the Submarine Gallery, but projects have also been organized in schools to educate the next generation.

● See also Assemblage Art, Creative Salvage, Ecological Art, Green Design, Junk Culture/Sculpture, Mutoid Waste Co, New British Sculpture.

◉ G Rudge 'The New Ecology' *City Limits* April 7–14 1988 90–2.

◉ A Garland 'Reaction against rubbish' *Guardian* July 7 1989 17.

◉ J Alexander 'Make do and mend' *City Limits* October 26 – November 2 1989 93–5.

560 RE/ARCHITECTURE

A term employed by Sherban Cantacuzino to refer to the re-use and re-furbishment of old buildings. Many such buildings are of solid construction and pleasing design but no longer serve their original function. A vogue for conversion rather than demolition occurred in the 1970s and '80s in order to preserve worthwhile architecture and townscapes. A noted British example was the conversion of Liverpool's nineteenth century cotton warehouses at Albert Dock. One was transformed into an art gallery – Tate Gallery North – by James Stirling.

● See also Heritage Industry.

◉ S Cantacuzino *Re/architecture: old buildings/new uses* (Thames & Hudson, 1989).

561 RECEPTION THEORY/ AESTHETICS

A branch of criticism and history-writing concerned with the impact works of art and design make upon viewers, the way texts, images and objects are differentially 'read', interpreted, evaluated, used and 'consumed'. Hence this kind of research marks a shift away from the production side (artists, the making of art) to the side of consumption; clearly, it is closely related to the study of taste. Reception Theory tends to concern itself with the ideal reader implied by a text, while Reception History tends to be concerned with actual readers. This type of theoretical work has been particularly associated with German literary studies since the 1960s, i.e. scholars such as Hans Jauss and Wolfgang Iser; however, there are equivalent studies in the field of the visual arts, as the following four examples demonstrate. Phillipe Boudon undertook a survey of the history of a housing settlement at Pessac, France, designed by Le Corbusier in the 1920s. He interviewed residents as to their experiences of the buildings and recorded the way in which the architect's designs had been adapted and changed ('customized') by the inhabitants. Carol Zemel examined critical writings about the work of Van Gogh in the years after his death in order to explain how the Van Gogh legend came into being. Juan Bonta traced the reception of Mies van der Rohe's 1929 Barcelona Pavilion in the discourses of journalism, criticism and history-writing in order to discover exactly how it came to join the canon of 'great' modern buildings. Dick Hebdige looked at the way Italian design in the form of scooters was received in Britain during the 1950s and '60s.

● See also Customizing & Custom Painting, Italian Craze.

● P Boudon, *Lived-in architecture: Le Corbusier's Pessac revisited* (Lund Humphries, 1972).

● P Hohendahl 'Introduction to Reception Aesthetics' *New German Critique* (10) Winter 1977 29–63.

● J Bonta *Architecture and its interpretation* (Lund Humphries, 1979).

● D Hebdige 'Object as image: the Italian scooter cycle' *Block* (5) 1981 44–64.

● C Zemel *The formation of a legend: Van Gogh criticism 1890–1920* (Bowker, 1981).

● H Jauss *Toward an aesthetic of reception* (Minneapolis, University of Minnesota Press, 1982).

● R Holub *Reception Theory: a critical introduction* (Methuen, 1984).

562 RELATED STUDIES

(Also Complementary/ Contextual/ Critical/ General/ Historical/ Liberal Studies) Academic courses supplementary to studio courses introduced into British artschools during the 1960s in order to broaden the understanding of art and design students and to make their education more academically respectable. Such courses were taught by sociologists and art historians. They did provide social and historical contextual information but they also proved highly controversial. Many students resented book-learning, lectures, slide tests, writing essays and theses. They asked: 'what relevance does a study of Renaissance religious painting have to my training as an industrial designer?'

How exactly theory and history related to practice remained, in most institutions, an unresolved problem. Related Studies departments were intended to stimulate ideas and discussion. In 1968 the General Studies staff at Hornsey College of Art, London, participated in the student occupation and the debates about art education which took place; as a result they were blamed for the occupation and lost their jobs. In the late 1980s, as a consequence of the emergence of an 'enterprise culture', Related Studies staff were increasingly required to teach business studies.

● See also Art Schools.

◉ Students & Staff of Hornsey College of Art *The Hornsey affair* (Harmondsworth, Penguin Books, 1969).

◉ B Nunn & C Locke *Related Studies for art & design students* (Longman, 1984).

◉ D Thistlewood (ed) *Critical Studies in art and design education* (Longman & NSEAD, 1989).

563 RETAIL CULTURE/ DESIGN/ REVOLUTION

In Britain during 'the design decade' of the 1980s a credit/consumer boom occurred which resulted in an expansion in shopping and retailing. Existing supermarkets, shopping centres and malls were redesigned and new, larger ones were built. The new out-of-town shopping malls such as the MetroCentre, Tyneside (developer John Hall; designers International Design Group) in particular provided total, 'themed' environments and 'leisure experiences' for their visitors.

British malls were often inspired by the American

RETAIL CULTURE JOCK MCFADYEN, 'Born to shop' (1987). Oil on canvas, 80" x 80". Owned by the Scottish Gallery, London. Photo: courtesy of the artist.

ones designed by the architect Victor Gruen. High street shops and chain stores were also revamped (interiors and exteriors) along with signs and logos by such people as Rodney Fitch and Eva Jiricna. Clothes shops such as the Next chain (the brainchild of George Davies with design by David Davies Associates) were founded which catered for the affluent group known as 'yuppies'; for a time such shops were highly successful. The '80s were also significant for the success of retail specialists such as Sock Shop and Tie Rack: so-called 'niche marketing/retailing'.

● See also Carnaby Street, Habitat, Street Fashion/Style, Styling.

● V Barr & C Broudy *Designing to sell: a complete guide to retail store planning and design* (NY, McGraw-Hill, 1986).

● G Michell *Design in the high street* (Architectural Press, 1986).

● C Gardner & J Sheppard *Consuming passion: the rise of Retail Culture* (Unwin Hyman, 1989).

● A Hallsworth *The human impact of hypermarkets and superstores* (Aldershot, Gower, 1989).

● N Scott *Shopping centre design* (NY, Van Nostrand Reinhold/London, Spon, 1989).

● R Fitch & L Knobel *Fitch on Retail Design* (Oxford, Phaidon, 1990).

564 RETRO

(Also La Mode Rétro, Retro Style, Retrochic) A term made fashionable in the mid 1970s by French writers commenting on the trend for artists, designers, television producers and film-makers to look back to the past for inspiration and to revive the styles of the recent past. The word 'retro' is a prefix meaning 'backwards'; it has connotations of 'retrograde', 'retrogressive' and 'retrospective'. Such historicism was considered one of the defining characteristics of the post-modern condition. (The modern movement in contrast had been obsessed with the future.) A shop exploiting the vogue for nostalgia, located in London's Tottenham Court Road, adopted the term as its name in 1975. Attacking Retro Style in the French cinema, Pascal Bonitzer and Serge Toubidua dismissed it as a 'cynicism... a snobbish fetishism of the old fashioned...a ridiculing of history'.

In 1979 the American feminist art critic Lucy Lippard used the term 'Retrochic' to describe a sensibility of the mid 1970s, associated with 'retrograde' punk artists, of which she disapproved. She defined it as 'a reactionary wolf in countercultural sheep's clothing', e.g. works of art presenting racist material in an uncritical manner in order to titillate, created by artists who assumed they had the right to do so because 'it was only art'.

A 1990 article in *Design* reports that Sanyo, a Japanese company, has designed crockery and kitchen appliances intended to appeal to those nostalgic for the 1950s. Sanyo markets it as 'Retro Modern Collection'.

● See also Heritage Industry, Historicism, Post-Modernism, Punk.

● P Bonitzer & S Toubidua 'Anti-Retro' (Interview with Michel Foucault) *Cahiers du Cinema* (251–2) July–August 1974. (Trans: 'Film & popular memory' *Radical Philosophy* (11) Summer 1975 24–9.)

● L Lippard 'Rejecting Retrochic' (1979) – in – *Get the message? A decade of art for social change* (NY, Dutton, 1984) 173–8.

● B Fether 'Points of style' *Design* (500) August 1990 32–3.

565 ROBOT ART

A form of kinetic art developed in the 1960s by the Israeli artist P. K. Hoenich making use of the forces of the sun, the wind and the movement of the Earth to activate mobiles and to structure light and shadow. In some cases the operating period for such works was as long as six months.

Jack Burnham, the American artist and art historian, in his 1968 book on the impact of science and technology on modern sculpture, also employed the term 'Robot Art' to describe works combining robotic and human

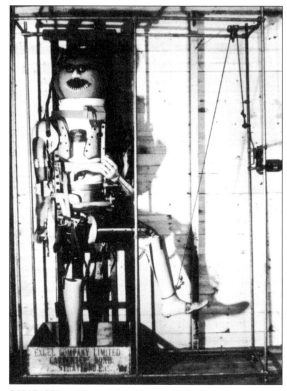

ROBOT ART Bruce Lacey 'Boy, oh boy, am I living!', wood, metal, plastic, electrics, 183cm x 122cm x 91.5cm. (1964). Photo:Tony Evans.

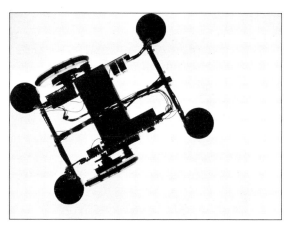

ROBOT ART JOHN KAINE, 'M E L 12'. Darkness seeking robot which continuously explores any dark area bounded by light. Perspex, steel, aluminium, with various chips and electronic components based around the MEL 12 light sensitizing resistor. (l)290 x (w)216 x (h)120mm. (1985). Photo: Kaine.

forms produced by artists like Eduardo Paolozzi and Ernest Trova. These 'mock-robot' sculptures he discussed as a preliminary to a full examination of working robots operating according to cybernetic principles.

● See also Computer Art, Cybernetic Art, Kinetic Art, Light Art.

● M Myers & P Hoenich 'Robot Art' *Ark* (35) Spring 1964 30–3.

● J Burnham *Beyond modern sculpture...* (Allen Lane, Penguin Press, 1968).

● P Hoenich 'Kinetic art with sunlight' *Leonardo* **1** (2) April 1968 113–20.

● — '"Robot Art" using the rays of the sun' *Studio International* **175** (901) June 1968 306–9.

● — *Sonnen-Malerei* (Cologne, Dumont, 1974).

566 ROCK ART/ DESIGN/FASHION

Various kinds of visual art and design are associated with rock 'n' roll and pop music: paintings and sculptures depicting famous singers and groups; illustrations in comics, fanzines, magazines and songbooks and on record sleeves; posters advertising records or concerts or simply depicting bands. (NB. the term 'rock art' is also used to refer to paintings appearing on the walls of caves.) Although the majority of people contributing to this field are 'commercial artists' or graphic designers – Alan Aldridge, Roger Dean, Michael English, Rick Griffin, Martin Sharp, Hipgnosis, etc. – fine artists such as Peter Blake, Derek Boshier, Richard Hamilton, David Oxtoby, Andy Warhol and Karl Wirsum, have also been involved. Also, the imagery of album covers and posters frequently pays homage to the history of art by reproducing or quoting from famous paintings and by imitating the major styles of art. Arguably, there are times when music industry products attain the high aesthetic quality associated with fine art, e.g. late '60s San Francisco psychedelic posters (which have been honoured with an exhibition at the San Francisco Museum of Modern Art) and the Beatles' 'Sgt Pepper' LP of 1967.

In addition to graphics, design takes place in respect of musical instruments, stage sets, lighting and the interiors of discos, stage costumes, make-up and hair-styles. Leading British fashion designers such as Zandra Rhodes, Vivienne Westwood and Anthony Price have created costumes for a number of rock bands. The media of photography, film and video are also crucial to the dissemination of images of rock groups and stars. In fact, this is a domain of culture that almost always involves teamwork and the combination of several media.

Many fruitful collaborations have taken place between visual artists and rock musicians as the exhibition 'Interaction: art–music–art' held at the Camden Art Centre, London, in the winter of 1986 demonstrated. A notable 1980s example of collaboration was that between the French graphic designer Jean-Paul Goude and the American singer Grace Jones.

Increasingly, museums, archives and collections of rock and pop materials are being founded and sales of rock 'n' roll memorabilia are now commonplace at major auction houses; consequently the tradition of connoisseurship associated with the fine arts is now beginning to be associated with the visual culture of rock music.

ROCK ART HENRY KONDRAKI, 'Holly days' (1985). Oil on canvas, 42" x 31". Photo: Blond Fine Art, London.

● See also Cross-Overs, The Fool, Hipgnosis, Psychedelic Art, Punk, Rock Video, Scenography, Sub culture, Underground Art.

● A Aldridge (ed) *The Beatles illustrated lyrics* 2 vols (Mac-Donald, 1969, '71).

● M Farren *Get on down: a decade of rock and roll posters* (Futura, 1976).

● W Medeiros *San Francisco rock poster art* (San Francisco, Museum of Modern Art, 1976).

● B Benedict & L Barton *Phonographics: contemporary album cover art and design* (NY, Collier-Macmillan, 1977).

● D Saleh (ed) *Rock Art: the golden age of record album covers* (NY, Comma/Ballantine, 1977).

● M English *3-D eye: the posters, prints and paintings of Michael English 1966–79* (Limpsfield, Paper Tiger, 1979).

● A Errigo & S Leaning *The illustrated history of the rock album cover* (Octopus, 1979).

● J-P Goude *Jungle fever* (Quartet Books, 1982).

● J Walker 'They all live in a yellow hi-tech shed' (Beatle City, Liverpool) *Building Design* October 5 1984 18–20.

● R Dean *Album cover album* vol 3 (Limpsfield, Paper Tiger, 1984).

● M Evans *The art of the Beatles* (A Blond, 1984).

● T Polhemus & L Proctor *Pop styles: where fashion meets rock & roll* (Hutchinson, 1984).

● C Bromberg 'Design live!' *Industrial Design* **32** (2) March–April 1985 42–7, + 74.

● P Grushkin *The art of rock: posters from Presley to punk* (NY, Abbeville, 1987).

● M Jones *Getting it on: the clothing of rock and roll* (NY, Abbeville, 1987).

● R Taylor *Elvis in art* (Elm Tree Books, 1987).

● J Walker *Cross-overs: art into pop, pop into art* (Comedia/Methuen, 1987).

● K & T Ohrt *Rockens Billeder: images of rock* (Odense, Denmark, Kunsthallen Brandts Klaedefabrik, 1990).

ROCK VIDEO KEVIN GODLEY AND LOL CREME, two leading rock video makers of the British pop industry.

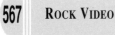

ROCK VIDEO

(Also Music Video, Pop Video, Promo Video, Video Clips) Short films or videos designed to promote the sales of records of rock and pop music singers and bands. Filmed adverts have been produced by the record industry since the 1930s but it was only in the period 1975–83 that Rock Video developed into a major form of expression when a massive financial and creative investment was made following a decline in record sales. Although this development was regretted by those whose first loyalty was to music and live performance, Rock Video represented a long-awaited synthesis of sound and image and the two dominant forms of youth culture entertainment: rock music and television. Technological and marketing innovations were of crucial importance: video-cassettes, home video-recorders, sophisticated TV editing suites, computer graphics machines, cable TV stations providing specialist services such as MTV (Music TeleVision) around the clock.

Artistically, the key development was treating the video's visual images in the same way as musical sounds, so that what started life as a TV commercial became an aesthetic commodity in its own right. (Collections of music videos could be bought on video-cassettes from record shops instead of records.) Images began to assume as much importance as sounds, and since constant formal innovation was demanded, the whole history of cinema and avant garde art was cannibalized by video-makers. They also exploited to the hilt the extraordinary special effects the new computer and video technologies made possible.

An entry on Rock Video is warranted here on two grounds: the high aesthetic quality of some of the videos and the involvement of artists or artschool graduates in their making. Kevin Godley and Lol Creme, for instance, were trained as graphic designers in British art colleges, then had success in the pop group 10cc, and then became famous as the directors of videos for the Police, Culture Club, Herbie Hancock and many others. Laurie Anderson, the New York performance artist, made her own promo video for her hit record 'O Superman'. David Byrne of Talking Heads was also at artschool in North America and the distinctive videos associated with this band reflected an acute awareness of the achievements of modern art. Video directors were also willing from time to time to make use of the works of fine artists, e.g. the jerky robots built by the British sculptor Jim Whiting. That Rock Videos can count as art is indicated by the fact that they are collected by museums and galleries such as MoMA, New York and the ICA, London.

● See also Cross-Overs, Rock Art/Design/Fashion, Scratch Video, Video Art.

◉ M Shore *The Rolling Stone book of Rock Video* (Sidgwick & Jackson, 1985).

◉ V Bódy & P Weibel (eds) *Clip, Klapp, Bum: von der visuelle Musik zum Musikvideo* (Cologne, Dumont, 1987).

◉ E Kaplan *Rocking around the clock: music television, post-modernism and consumer culture* (NY, Methuen, 1987).

◉ J Walker *Cross-overs: art into pop, pop into art* (Comedia/Methuen, 1987).

568 ROSC

An international exhibition of contemporary art held in Dublin every four years from 1967 onwards. 'Rosc' is, apparently, an old Gaelic word meaning 'the poetry of vision'. The Irish architect Dr Michael Scott and the American James Johnson Sweeney had the idea for this show, and the name was devised by Fr Frank Shaw. Each show is limited to only 50 artists and they cannot appear in consecutive Roscs. There are in fact two Rosc exhibitions, one dealing with modern art and one dealing with ancient art; the purpose being to reveal connections between the old and the new.

◉ C Barrett 'Rosc: coming of age' *Art Monthly* (120) October 1988 4–6.

569 ROTHKO CHAPEL

A plain brick, octagonal-shaped chapel located in Houston, Texas, designed by the architect Philip Johnson as a religious setting for 14 abstract paintings by Mark Rothko (1903–70). Rothko's large, colour-field canvases are dark purple and wine in hue; the building has no windows – illumination is provided by a central skylight. The patrons for the paintings and building were John and Dominique de Menil. The chapel was opened in 1971. It is ecumenical in character and has been used for religious ceremonies, private meditation, musical performances, and weddings. Outside the chapel, set in a pool of water, is Barnett Newman's 1963–7 metal sculpture 'Broken Obelisk'.

● See also Abstract Expressionism, Colour-Field Painting.

◉ B O'Doherty 'The Rothko Chapel' *Art in America* **61** (1) January–February 1973 14–20.

◉ A Holmes 'The Rothko chapel six years later' *Art News* **75** (10) December 1976 35–7.

◉ S Barnes *The Rothko Chapel: an act of faith* (Austin, Texas, Rothko Chapel Book/University of Texas Press,1989).

570 RUBBISH THEORY

An ingenious attempt by Michael Thompson, a social anthropologist who has taught in art and design colleges, to explain how value is created and destroyed, i.e. how manufactured objects – including works of art and craft – lose or gain in value as time passes, come to be thought of as rubbish, are then perhaps rediscovered to acquire value again. Objects, he argued, fall into two categories: (1) transient (because they have finite lifespans and they decrease in value over time); (2) durable (they have 'infinite' lifespans and increase in value over time). What interested him was the social process by which objects transferred from one category to the other. Emphasis was placed on rubbish because Thompson considered it a zone of zero value, a covert category, upon which the whole process depended. Seeking a mathematical model of change, he turned to a theorem in topology – catastrophe theory – first stated by René Thom.

Two case studies were discussed by Thompson in some detail: the history of Stevengraphs and the gentrification of Georgian terrace houses in London.

◉ M Thompson *Rubbish Theory: the creation and destruction of value* (Oxford University Press, 1979).

571   SAATCHI COLLECTION

By spending millions of pounds derived from the profits of the advertising group Saatchi & Saatchi, Charles and Doris Saatchi rapidly established, in the 1980s, a massive collection of contemporary art. A public gallery such as the Tate could not afford such expenditure, hence private wealth exposed the relative poverty of the public sector in Britain. In 1985 the Saatchis opened a gallery in North London (a warehouse refurbished by the architect Max Gordon (1931–90)) to display the collection to the public. A notable characteristic of the gallery was the care and sensitivity with which works of art were presented.

Artists whose work was acquired included Frank Auerbach, Georg Baselitz, Lucien Freud, Peter Halley, Donald Judd, Anslem Kiefer, Jeff Koons, Robert Longo, David Salle, Julian Schnabel, Frank Stella, Andy Warhol and Bill Woodrow. Such a variety of styles was represented, it was hard to detect any logic to the collection. Furthermore, the work of some artists was bought in bulk and then, later on, resold. Most of the collection consists of paintings and sculptures – some very large – hence it could be argued that the more radical developments in art – video, media art, performance, community art, etc. – were ignored by the Saatchis. Such was their purchasing power that whole movements could be bought, e.g. neo-geo. While most artists welcomed the patronage of the Saatchis, some were critical of such wealth and power. Hans Haacke, for instance, featured the Saatchis in his satiric portrait of Mrs Thatcher 'Taking stock' (1983–4) and in another work he attacked Saatchi & Saatchi's business links with South Africa.

● *Art of our time: the Saatchi Collection* 4 vols (Lund Humphries, 1985).

● D Hawthorne 'Saatchi & Saatchi go public' *Art News* **84** (5) May 1985 72–81.

● S Morgan & others 'The Saatchi Museum' *Artscribe* (54) September–October 1985 45–50.

● R Walker 'The Saatchi factor' *Art News* **86** (1) January 1987 117–21.

● D Cameron *New York art now: the Saatchi Collection* (Milan, G Politi, 1987).

● H Haacke *Global marketing* (Victoria Miro Gallery, 1987), booklet.

● P Kleinman *The Saatchi story* (Weidenfeld & Nicolson, 1987).

● I Fallen *The brothers: the rise and rise of Saatchi and Saatchi* (Hutchinson, 1988).

● A Graham-Dickson 'Saatchi sneezes and the artworld shivers' *Independent* October 14 1989 8.

● C Bennett 'Mrs Saatchi's minimalism' *Sunday Correspondent magazine* December 17 1989 20–7.

● A Hicks *New British art in the Saatchi Collection* (Thames & Hudson, 1989).

572   SAINSBURY CENTRE

A centre for the study and appreciation of the arts opened in 1978 situated on the campus of the University of East Anglia, Norwich. It houses the Sainsbury Collection which was begun in the 1920s by Sir Robert Sainsbury (of the Sainsbury chain of supermarkets). The collection (plus an endowment to sustain it) was presented as a gift to the University by Robert and Lisa Sainsbury. It consists of international modern art – primarily sculptures – plus examples of 'primitive' African, Oceanic, and pre-Columbian art. There is a study collection which enables the University art historians and their students to examine works of art at close quarters. The building in which the collection is housed is itself notable: a high-

SAINSBURY CENTRE Interior view of the Sainsbury Centre. Photo: John Donat Photography, London.

tech metal and glass structure resembling an aircraft hangar designed by Norman Foster, one of Britain's leading modern architects. A new extension to the Sainsbury Centre - 'the Crescent Wing'- was also designed by Foster. The multi-purpose extension - an arc-shaped building half-buried in the ground - was opened in 1991.
● See also High-Tech.

● R Sainsbury (ed) *Robert & Lisa Sainsbury collection: exhibition for the opening of the Centre, April 1978* (Norwich, University of East Anglia, 1978).

● S Williams 'Journey into space: the Sainsburys' supermarket of art' *Sunday Times Magazine* April 2 1978 76–9.

● 'East Anglia arts' *Architectural Review* **CLXIV** (982) December 1978 345–62.

● R Miller 'Playing to the gallery' *Sunday Times Magazine* June 23 1991 16-24.

573 ST IVES SCHOOL (Also Cornish School, West Country School) St Ives, Cornwall, is a fishing/ tourist village situated in a part of England noted for the quality of its light and the beauty of its landscape. Artists were attracted to it in the nineteenth century. In the twentieth century it has been one of the few significant centres for the production of visual art outside of London. However, the word 'school' is misleading because there has been a series of different styles and movements represented. Before 1945 a mixture of abstract and naive art prevailed: artists who resided there included Ben Nicholson, Barbara Hepworth, Naum Gabo, Alfred Wallis, Christopher Wood, and the potter Bernard Leach. During the late 1940s and early '50s a number of younger artists, working in a wide variety of idioms, took up permanent residence in St Ives or visited for the summer months: John Wells, Bryan Wynter, Terry Frost, Victor Pasmore, William Scott, Roger Hilton, Robert Adams and Merlyn Evans. Patrick Heron, the abstract painter, has lived and worked in St Ives for decades. Peter Lanyon (1918–64) was perhaps the quintessential St Ives artist because he was born there and his lyrical, semi-abstract paintings reflected his experience of the physical environment: the sea, sky and moors.

In 1976 Hepworth's Trewyn Studio and garden was opened to the public as a memorial to her sculpture. A new gallery, designed by Eldred Evans and David Shalev, focusing upon the art of the St Ives School is due to open in 1992. It has been dubbed 'the Tate of the West' because it will house the St Ives collection of the Tate Gallery, London.

● D Val Baker *Britain's art colony by the sea* (George Rowland, 1959).

● 'Notes on the St Ives School. Peter Davies talks to four leading members' *Art Monthly* (48) July–August 1981 3–8.

● T Cross *Painting the warmth of the sun: St Ives artists 1939–75* (Guildford, Hodge & Lutterworth, 1984).

● P Davies *The St Ives years* (Wimbourne Bookshop, 1984).

● *St Ives 1939–64: twenty-five years of painting, sculpture and pottery* (Tate Gallery, 1985).

ST IVES SCHOOL Garden of Trewyn Studio, St Ives with sculptures by Barbara Hepworth. Photo: Barbara Hepworth Museum/Tate Gallery, London.

574 ST MARTINS SCHOOL OF ART SCULPTORS A description applied to a number of talented British sculptors – David Annesley, Michael Bolus, Philip King, Tim Scott, William Tucker and Isaac Witkin – all of whom (except Tucker) studied under the modernist artist Anthony Caro in the late 1950s and early '60s at St Martin's School of Art, London. Like Caro, they rejected the carving and modelling traditions of sculpture represented in Britain by Henry Moore and Barbara Hepworth. They also avoided the 'geometry of fear' style, submitting instead to the influence of American artists like the sculptor David Smith and the abstract painter Kenneth Noland.

The British sculptors first attracted public attention at the 'New Generation' exhibition held at the Whitechapel Gallery, London, in 1965. Their works were generally open in format and stood directly on the floor rather than on plinths (hence 'floor art'). They were made up of basic elements in the constructivist tradition but also stressed qualities such as hue, surface texture, volume and topology. Most of the sculptures were abstract but a vein of surrealistic imagery was discernible in some works. Industrial-type materials such as sheet steel, metal pipes and netting, fibreglass and acrylic plastics were employed rather than wood, marble or bronze.

Since the sculptures were covered with vivid commercial gloss paints they were called 'colour sculpture', and since they presented a cheerful appearance 'fun sculpture'. Works by many of the sculptors cited above were bought by Alistair McAlpine who subsequently gave them to the Tate Gallery.

Since the halcyon days of the '60s, the sculpture course at St Martin's has undergone many changes and during the 1980s it experienced a severe crisis (see the articles by Scott and Gouk, and Jones).

● See also Geometry of Fear, Modernist Painting, New Generation.

◗ *The New Generation: 1965* (Whitechapel Gallery, 1965).

◗ 'Some aspects of contemporary British sculpture' *Studio International* **177** (907) January 1969 10–37.

◗ *The Alistair McAlpine Gift* (Tate Gallery, 1971).

◗ T Hilton *Sculpture at St Martin's* (Martin Brian & O'Keefe, 1979).

◗ T Scott & A Gouk 'The St Martin's affair: "gone too far"' *Artscribe* (42) August 1983 30–8.

◗ G Jones 'The "A" course' *AND Journal of Art & Art Education* (1) Winter 1984 25–8.

575   SAR

(Stichting Architecten Research) A foundation for architectural research and design established at the Technical University of Eindhoven in 1965 by Nicholas John Habraken with the aim of developing the architectural and institutional means by which control over urban housing could be returned to users at the level of both the community and the individual. Houses were to become individual dwellings again as against the standardized mass housing for standard families supplied by bureaucrats. Initially the emphasis was on what Habraken called 'supports': prefabricated infill components and residential structures that permitted many variations. Residents were then encouraged to design their own dwelling plans and to participate in larger-scale planning decisions. According to Habraken, the most successful example of SAR principles was the housing complex Molenvliet, Papendrecht, Holland whose architect was Frans van der Werf. John Carp succeeded Habraken as director of SAR. In the 20 years following its foundation, SAR's ideas were to prove influential amongst architects and planners throughout Europe and North America.

● See also Community Architecture, Participatory Design, Social Architecture/Design.

◗ N Habraken *Supports: an alternative to mass housing* (Architectural Press, 1972).

◗ J Carp 'SAR: supports for participation' – in – *The scope of social architecture* C Hatch (ed) (NY, Van Nostrand Reinhold, 1984) 22–39, plus several other articles on SAR projects.

576   SCANDINAVIAN STYLE

(Also Nordic Design) During the 1950s a vogue for Swedish, Norwegian, Danish and Finnish products – furniture, ceramics, glassware, silverware, textiles, jewellery and enamels – occurred in Britain and their style was quickly copied by British manufacturers. Scandinavian designers who became internationally known included Alvar Aalto, Eward Hald, Arne Jacobson, Nils Landberg, Bruno Mathsson, Egil Rein and Tapio Wirkkala. Design in Scandinavia developed along the lines laid down by the arts and crafts movement of the nineteenth century, but it also pioneered new research techniques such as anthropometrics in the period between the two World Wars. 'Swedish modern', in fact, had achieved international recognition in the 1930s. Unlike their British counterparts, Scandinavian artist–designers were highly regarded by their employers and by the general public; their higher professional status permitted greater creative freedom. Also, the relatively small scale of Scandinavian industries enabled designers to be closely involved in the production process. As a result of these factors, Scandinavian design achieved a union of the handicraft tradition and mass-production methods.

In terms of high-quality industrial design, the streamlined SAAB motor cars designed by Sixten Sason in the 1950s and '60s were a commercial and critical success. The Swedish SAAB company (Svensk Aeroplan Aktiebolaget) had its origins in the aircraft industry and the design of the car benefited from this high-tech connection.

Scandinavian domestic products were both attractive and functional. Furniture designers made sensitive use of natural woods and woven fabrics. Generally speaking, Scandinavian designers sought purity and simplicity of form, so their products tended to be perceived as safe and unexciting when compared to Italian goods of the '50s and British pop design of the '60s.

● See also 'Good Design', Italian Craze, New Empiricism, Packaged Furniture, Pop Design.

◗ A Boe *Norsk/Norwegian industrial design* (Oslo, Kunstindustrimuseet, 1963).

◗ U Hard af Segerstad *Modern Scandinavian furniture* (Studio Vista, 1963).

● E Zahle (ed) *Scandinavian domestic design* (Methuen, 1963).

● E Beer *Scandinavian design: objects of a lifestyle* (NY, Farrar, Straus, Giroux, 1975).

● M Donovan (ed) *Scandinavian modern design 1880–1980* (NY, Cooper-Hewitt Museum/Abrams, 1982).

● J Opie *Twentieth century Scandinavian ceramics and glass* (Victoria & Albert Museum, 1989).

SCENOGRAPHY Set designed by da Gama, London, for a Pop video 'When all's well' by Everything but the Girl, directed by Tim Pope (1985). Photo: Jean Louis Gregoire.

577 SCENOGRAPHY

(Including Set & Theatre Design) Painting scenery and designing sets for the performing arts – drama, ballet, opera, musicals, rock concerts and puppet shows – are skills with long histories, but the scope for scenic artists was greatly expanded in the modern era by the advent of film and television. BBC Television, for instance, has a department which undertakes the painting of landscapes, architecture and decorative work on backcloths and scenery; actor's portraits; copies of paintings of all periods; glass/matte and video paintbox images.

Scenography is a complex artform because it normally depends upon the successful collaboration of a team of specialists and because it usually involves several elements: backdrops, props, lighting and costumes. It is also a difficult art to judge and appreciate because it is ephemeral and because it is part of a larger whole: by itself a brilliant set cannot rescue a badly written and acted play.

Two categories of stage designers can be identified: (1) full-time professionals such as Sue Blane, Maria Björnson, Lucio Fanti, David Fielding, Ezio Frigerio, Nicholas Georgiadis, Karl Herrmann, Vladimir Ivanov, Sean Kenny, Yannis Kokkos, Ralph Koltai, Stefanos Lazaridis, Anthony MacDonald and Tom Cairns, Alex Manthey, Phillip Prowse, Josef Svoboda, Volodya Serebrovskii, Robert Wilson, and Tassos Zographos; and (2) fine or graphic artists who occasionally contribute to the theatre, e.g. Karel Appel, Eduardo Arroyo, Jean Dubuffet, David Hockney, Picasso, Robert Rauschenberg, Bridget Riley, David Salle and Gerald Scarfe. Tadeusz Kantor, (1915–90) the avant garde Polish artist–designer and leader of the troupe 'Cricot 2', overlapped both categories. In 1988 the Linbury Prize for stage design was instituted in Britain. The 1989 winner was Kenny MacLellan, a graduate of the Almeida Theatre design course. Many British theatre designers have received their training at the Slade School of Fine Art in London. Examples of set design are preserved in the Theatre Museum in Covent Garden.

In the cinema the related terms 'film' or 'production design' and 'art direction' are employed. In 1979 Thames Television organized an exhibition paying tribute to the important but little recognized work of Hollywood's art directors. To cite just one example of an artist's influence upon the look of a film: the disturbing and cruel imagery of Hans Rudi Giger, the Swiss fantasy artist, played a crucial role in the success of the science fiction/horror film 'Alien' (Twentieth Century Fox, 1979).

If the term 'Scenography' can be stretched to include the design of outdoor street festivals and parades, then it is worth citing Jean-Paul Goude's spectacular designs for the 1989 celebrations in Paris to commemorate the 1789 French Revolution.

● See also Carnival, Installation, Performance Art, Rock Video, Staged Photography, Street Art, Tableau.

● H Rischbieter (ed) *Art & the Stage in the 20th century* (NY, Graphic Society, 1970).

● *The art of Hollywood: fifty years of art direction* (Thames Television/Victoria & Albert Museum, 1979).

● H Giger *Giger's Alien* (Big O Publishing, 1979).

● P Scanlon & M Gross *The book of Alien* (Star Book/W H Allen, 1979).

● M Vaizey 'The theatrical genius of Tadeusz Kantor' *Sunday Times Magazine* August 24 1980 26–9.

● C Owens 'The proscenic event' *Art in America* **69** (10) December 1981 128–33.

● A de Angelis *Scenografia: il disegno dell' ambiente* (Naples, Fratelli Fiorentino Editore, 1981).

● 'Art on stage' *Art International* (7) Summer 1989 11–44.

● J Goodwin (ed) *British theatre design* (Weidenfeld & Nicolson, 1989).

578 SCHOOL OF LONDON

An expression first used in 1976 by R. B. Kitaj, the American-born artist resident in London, and subsequently employed as the title for a British Council exhibition which toured Europe in 1987. The exhibition featured paintings by six figurative artists: Kitaj, Francis

SCHOOL OF LONDON FRANK AUERBACH, 'E. O. W. on her blue eiderdown 6' (1962). Oil on canvas, 44cm x 51cm. Collection Dr S. Charles Lewsen. Photo: Beaux Arts Gallery, London.

(Also Cover Art, Futurate Art, SF Art) A subcategory of fantastic art which is also closely related to space art and visionary art. The term 'science fiction' was coined in 1929 by Hugo Gernsback, editor of the first science fiction magazine *Amazing Stories*. The label 'Sci-Fi Art' refers to the highly detailed, lurid, fanciful images of space travel, aliens, future societies, etc., appearing on the covers of sci-fi paperbacks, on posters for sci-fi films, and to the illustrations appearing in sci-fi magazines and comics. Paintings and limited edition prints are also sold via specialist galleries. Well-known artists of the genre include: Chesley Bonestell, Patrick Woodroffe, Virgil Finlay, Edd Carter, Roger Dean, Earle Bergey, Alex Raymond and Frank Hampson (of Dan Dare fame). Although dismissed as 'surrealistic kitsch' by some observers, Sci-Fi Art has acquired many admirers. In fact, during the 1970s Sci-Fi Art became something of a cult as histories began to be published and as large-format magazines such as *Science Fiction Monthly,* founded in 1974, began to feature it in full-colour layouts, and as original artwork began to be acquired by fans and collectors.

In December 1989 the gallery Abandon Art was opened in Richmond, Surrey. It claimed to be the first art gallery devoted to the genres of visionary, fantasy and Sci-Fi Art. Abandon Art was founded by Steve Jackson, a collector of such art, an author and an inventor of fantasy games.

● See also Comic Art, Fantastic Art, Mass Art, Popular Art, Space Art, Visionary Art.

● L Alloway 'Technology and sex in science fiction: a note on Cover Art' *Ark* (17) Summer 1956 19–23.

● B Aldiss *Science Fiction Art* (New English Library, 1975).

● L Del Rey (ed) *Fantastic Science Fiction Art 1926–54* (NY, Ballantine Books, 1975).

● F Rottensteiner *The Science Fiction book: an illustrated history* (Thames & Hudson, 1975).

● J Sadoul *2000 AD: illustrations from the golden age of Science Fiction pulps* (Souvenir Press, 1975).

● D Kyle *A pictorial history of Science Fiction* (Hamlyn, 1976).

● J Sacks (ed) *Visions of the future* (New English Library, 1976).

● A Adler (ed) *Science Fiction and horror movie posters in full colour* (NY, Dover, 1977).

● B Ash *The visual encyclopedia of Science Fiction* (Pan, 1978).

● R Weinberg *A biographical dictionary of Science Fiction and fantasy artists* (Westport, Connecticut, Greenwood Press, 1988).

Bacon, Frank Auerbach, Lucien Freud, Leon Kossof and Michael Andrews. Since all these artists were highly individualistic, the term 'school' was dubious. What these painters shared besides individuality, according to Michael Peppiatt, was (a) a commitment to the human figure as the proper subject for art; (b) a disregard for short-term fashions in art; (c) personal and gallery links; (d) long-term residences in London (the city was also part of the subject matter of some of these painters); and (e) a monastic sense of vocation. (One could also add, a high level of artistic achievement.) In a book published in 1989 Kitaj's concept was extended by Alistair Hicks to include artists such as Howard Hodgkin, Gillian Ayres and John Walker. In a review of Hicks' book the art critic Tim Hilton flatly denied there was any such thing as a 'School of London'. The purpose of the label seems to be to do for London's artists what the label 'New York School' did for the artists of that city.

NB The 'School of London' should not be confused with the 'London Group', an exhibiting society functioning in the 1980s but founded at the time of the First World War.

● See also Figurative Art, New York School.

● R Kitaj *The human clay* (Hayward Gallery/Arts Council of Great Britain, 1976).

● M Peppiatt *A School of London: six figurative painters* (British Council, 1987).

● A Hicks *The School of London: the resurgence of contemporary painting* (Oxford, Phaidon, 1989).

● T Hilton 'Unknotting the old school tie' *Guardian* July 26 1989 46.

580 SCIART

A merger of science and art proposed by the American physicist, poet and art gallery dealer Bern Porter in 1971. In a manifesto appended to his book *I've left*, Porter listed a number of scientific discoveries – polarized light, nuclear particle beams, etc. – which, he argued, should be exploited by artists.

Leonardo is an art magazine publishing articles with a strong scientific emphasis. The common ground between science and art was a theme explored by various writers during the 1980s.

● See also Technological Art.

● B Porter *I've left* (NY, Something Else Press, 1971).

● J Reichardt 'Art at large: the union of science and art' *New Scientist* January 6 1972 46.

● M Pollock (ed) *Common denominators in art and science* (Aberdeen University Press, 1983).

● A O'Hear *The element of fire: science, art and the human mind* (Routledge, 1988).

581 SCOPOPHILIA

Title of an anthology of photographs and statements by their producers about their attitudes to looking and photography. Among the 30 artists and photographers featured were John Baldessari, Elliott Erwitt, Duane Michals, Ed Ruscha and Andy Warhol. 'Scopophilia' is a Freudian/psychoanalytic term describing the instinctual gratification to be derived from looking (voyeurism is the erotic version of scopophilia) or being looked at (exhibitionism is the mirror image of scopophilia). The role of the scopic drive in the creation and appreciation of the visual arts is obviously crucial but appears to have been little discussed by art theorists.

● See also Erotic Art, Gay Art, PhotoTherapy.

● L Eidelberg *Encyclopedia of psychoanalysis* (NY, Free Press, 1968).

● G Malanga (ed) *Scopophilia: the love of looking* (NY, Van der Marck Editions, 1985).

582 SCRATCH VIDEO

A form of video popular during the early 1980s, especially in Britain. The word 'scratch' derived from the practice of scratching records, i.e. a manual method of altering the sounds of records associated with the black, hip hop culture of New York. In terms of video, existing material (generally recordings pirated from mainstream TV broadcasts) was 'deconstructed' or cut up and then 'reconstructed' or treated in various ways via video editing suites in order to generate a new tape with new meanings. Scratch was the video equivalent of collage or photo-montage.

Scratch Video was generally the work of independent video-makers, some of whom had been to artschool. It owed something to the rock videos of the music business and something to the avant garde videos made by artists since the late '60s. Motivations for the manipulations of existing TV images varied: some like George Barber sought abstract decorative effects; some like the Duvet brothers sought a left-wing political critique; some like Sandra Goldbacher and Kim Flitcroft were intent on a feminist reinterpretation; while still others like Jeffrey

SCRATCH VIDEO Three stills from the DUVET BROTHERS' video featured on 'Scratch video: the greatest hits of Scratch video', Vol 1 1984, London.

Hinton were engaged in a parody of mass culture. Scratchers employed special effects such as repeat edits, superimpositions, etc., as poetic devices in their own right so that the naturalism of mainstream TV was subverted. However, the vogue for Scratch Video was short-lived because its oppositional relation to TV was undermined when Scratch began to appear on TV and when its formal innovations were imitated by TV commercials and rock videos.

● See also Photo-montage, Plagiarists, Rock Video, Video Art.

A Lipman 'Scratch and run' *City Limits* October 5–11 1984 18–19.

M O'Pray 'Scratch Video' *Art Monthly* (87) June 1985 32–3.

C Elwes 'Through deconstruction to reconstruction' *Independent Video* (48) November 1985 21–3.

A Lipman *Video: the state of the art* (Channel 4 Television/Comedia, 1985).

M O'Pray 'Scratching deeper' *Art Monthly* (95) April 1986 34–5.

M Dunford 'Video art: the dark ages' *Undercut* (16) Spring–Summer 1986 6–8.

J Walker *Cross-overs: art into pop, pop into art* (Comedia/Methuen, 1987).

583 SCULPTURE PARKS

Outdoor zones specifically set aside for displaying sculptures. Placing sculptures – statues, monuments, fountains, follies, inscriptions – in parks and gardens is, of course, an ancient practice but the vogue for Sculpture Parks (in Britain at least) dates from the 1970s. Large-scale pieces require plenty of space which may not be readily available inside buildings or in city streets. Also, some (not all) sculpture benefits from a relationship to natural light, sky, trees, water, etc. Precursors were the temporary exhibitions of sculpture held in London parks in Battersea and Holland Park during the '50s. A curator and other staff plus sufficient funding to acquire or commission new work are required if a Sculpture Park is to thrive. There is generally a permanent collection but temporary shows, conferences, workshops and technical demonstrations can also take place. Besides giving aesthetic pleasure and breathing new life into an underused rural environment, such parks often serve economic purposes by acting as magnets for tourists. They have proved a highly successful way of increasing the appreciation of modern sculpture amongst the general public. Against them it could be argued that they are simply open-air museums, sanitized reservations where a 'sculpture for sculpture's sake' ideology is propagated.

In England the 'Yorkshire Sculpture Park' at Bretton Hall College, West Bretton (nr Wakefield), was inaugu-

SCULPTURE PARKS BARBARA HEPWORTH, 'The family of man (nine figures on a hill), Ancestor II and Ultimate Form'. (1970). Two bronze sculptures in the permanent collection of the Yorkshire Sculpture Park. Photo: Yorkshire Sculpture Park.

rated in 1977 and in Scotland the 'Landmark Sculpture Park' at Carrbridge, Inverness-shire, was opened in 1978. Some Sculpture Parks present pieces as punctuations on a nature trail; see, for instance, the 'Welsh Sculpture Park' at Margam County Park (nr Port Talbot), Glamorgan. Sculptors can be invited to make site-specific works: this was the case at the outset of the 'Portland Clifftop Sculpture Park' at Tout Quarries, Isle of Portland, in 1983. An example of a one-man Sculpture Park is Ian Hamilton Finlay's 'Garden Temple' at Stonypath, Little Sparta, Dunsyre, Lanarkshire, which took 20 years of labour to construct.

In North America during the '80s many so-called 'theme parks' were opened and these included 'Artparks', e.g. one at Lewiston, New York, a public park where in the summer over 30 artists executed works *in situ* and in public view.

● See also Earth & Land Art, Public Art, Site-Specific Art.

Murray 'The development of Sculpture Parks in Britain' *Studio International* **196** (1001) August 1983 44–5.

J Oille 'Canada's Wonderland and Artpark, USA' *Art Monthly* (71) November 1983 3–4.

C Rowe 'Portland Clifftop Sculpture Park' *Studio International* **196** (1003) February 1984 43–4.

● S Lawrence & others *Music in stone: great sculpture gardens of the world* (NY, Train/Branca Books, 1984; London, Frederick Muller, 1985).

● K Spencer 'A field guide to Sculpture Parks, gardens and landscape sites' *The Green Book* **3** (1) 1989 50–3.

● B Redhead *The inspiration of landscape: artists in national parks* (Oxford, Phaidon, 1989).

584 SEMANTIC PAINTING

A type of painting dating from the 1950s and early '60s in which quasi-meaningful signs or calligraphic symbols – crosses, circles, squares, zig-zags, etc. – were employed as motifs in order to generate pattern-like abstractions. Paradoxically, in the process of rhythmical repetition across the picture surface, the semantic nature of the signs was normally negated. Three artists producing this kind of work were the Italians Luciano Lattanzi and Giuseppe Capogrossi (1900–72), and the German Werner Schreib (1925–69). Lattanzi wrote a 'manifesto of Semantic Painting' in 1957, and with Schreib he issued a second manifesto in 1961 entitled 'On the Semantic picture'.

● L Lattanzi *La peinture sémantique* (1962).

585 SEMIOLOGICAL SCHOOL

(Or Semiotic School) Charles Jencks, the architectural critic, and others have argued that the urban environment is a 'communicating system, a tissue of signs and symbols' and that therefore the science of semiology or semiotics (see the next entry) is of fundamental importance to the art of architecture. Semiotics is a science that can be used to analyse how architectural signs function; this knowledge can then be taken into account in the design of buildings. Writing in 1971, Jencks forecasted the emergence of a 'Semiological School' committed to making 'a complex environment significant' and he discussed the work of Robert Venturi and José Luis Sert in terms of this theory.

● See also Pop Architecture, Post-Modern Architecture.

● C Jencks & G Baird (eds) *Meaning in architecture* (Barrie & Rockliff, 1969).

● C Jencks *Architecture 2000: predictions and methods* (Studio Vista, 1971).

● D Preziosi *Semiotics of the built environment* (Bloomington, Indiana University Press, 1979).

● G Broadbent & others (eds) *Signs, symbols and architecture* (Chichester, John Wiley, 1980).

586 SEMIOTICS

The general science of signs; the science that studies the life of signs in society; an important mode of analysis that became fashionable (along with structuralism) in academic circles during the 1960s and '70s, especially in France and Italy. An international association of Semiotics was founded in 1969 and several scholarly journals were established including *Semiotica* and *Versus*. Other magazines featuring articles applying Semiotics to different kinds of material were *Communications, Tel Quel* (Paris), *Cultural Studies* (Birmingham), *Screen* (London).

The word 'semiotic' derived from the Greek 'semeion' meaning 'sign'. Initially, on the continent of Europe, 'semiology' was preferred to 'semiotic' but international agreement was later reached in favour of the latter term. Various thinkers have made use of the term: John Locke in the seventeenth century, C S Peirce and F. de Saussure in the late nineteenth century. However, the majority of Semiotic studies date from the second half of the twentieth century.

According to Peirce, 'a sign is something which stands to somebody in some respect or capacity'. Hence a sign can stand for something which exists but which is absent (i.e. the sign has a real referent) or which exists only in human imagination (e.g. angels). A key feature of signs is that they can be used to lie or to construct fictional worlds. Any process of communication or experience of meaning involves signs, consequently Semiotic research encompasses such diverse subjects as gestures, language, clothes, facial expressions, diagrams, films, photographs, buildings, etc., etc. Some theorists considered Semiotics as the science best qualified to disclose 'the logic of culture' – they regarded it as a crucial discipline because all other forms of human knowledge depended upon the use and interpretation of signs.

Since human language was the sign system most fully studied by scholars in the twentieth century, linguistics tended to function as the model for all other branches of Semiotics even those concerned with visual signs. Various scholars have focused upon visual signs, e.g. Eco has studied architecture and television, Bertin diagrams, Barthes photography and fashion, Metz the cinema, Williamson advertising, and Fresnault-Deruelle comics. Many art historians and critics welcomed Semiotics because it provided them with a sophisticated analytical methodology with which to decode images. The British artist Victor Burgin valued the science because it increased his understanding of the mechanisms of photographic signs and the pictorial rhetoric of advertising, thus enabling him to deconstruct and construct signs for educational and critical purposes. At one time Semiotics was also considered a tool of use to trainee designers and so became part of the curriculum at the German school of design known as Ulm.

● See also Diagrams, Pictorial Rhetoric, Political Art, Structuralism & Art/Design, Ulm.

● R Barthes *Elements of semiology* (Jonathan Cape, 1967).
● 'L'analyse des images' *Communications* (15) 1970.
● P Fresnault-Deruelle *La bande dessinée...* (Paris, Hachette, 1972).
● F de Saussure *Course in general linguistics* (Fontana/Collins, 1974).
● C Metz *Film language: a Semiotics of the cinema* (NY, OUP, 1974).
● —*Cinema and language* (The Hague, Mouton, 1974).
V Burgin 'Photographic practice and art theory' *Studio International* **190** (976) July–August 1975 39–51.
● J Paris *Painting and linguistics* (Pittsburgh, Colonial Press, 1975).
● U Eco *A theory of Semiotics* (Bloomington, Indiana University Press, 1976).
● L Matejya & I Titunik (eds) *Semiotics of art: Prague School contributions* (Cambridge, Mass, MIT Press, 1976).
● J Williamson *Decoding advertisements* (Marion Boyars, 1978).
● R Barthes *The fashion system* (Jonathan Cape, 1985).
● R Innis (ed) *Semiotics: an introductory anthology* (Hutchinson, 1986).

587 SERIAL ART

This term appears to have been invented in the 1930s by Amédée Ozenfant when advocating the production of works of art in large editions (see also Multiples). However, with a different meaning it gained artworld currency in the 1960s as a result of two exhibitions held in the United States: 'Art in series' (Finch College Museum, 1967) and 'Serial Imagery' (Pasadena Art Museum, 1968). Dictionaries define a series as 'a number of things, events, etc., ranged or occurring in spatial or temporal, or other succession'. Traditionally, artists attempted to perfect a single, unique work – what John Coplans called 'the masterpiece concept' – but since the 1880s, when Claude Monet painted his 'Haystack' series and Eadweard Muybridge published his sets of photographs revealing animal and human locomotion, many modern artists have chosen to work in series. Artists employing the serial method have belonged to different art movements – geometric abstraction, pop and minimal art – hence it does not result in a single style of art.

Artists working in series generally wished to explore an idea until it was exhausted, and to play variations on a theme. These aims were achieved in various ways: Monet painted the same motif at different times of day under different conditions of light; Andy Warhol repeated the same image many times within a single canvas and also across several canvases. The images were applied via photo-screenprinting and individual variations (equivalent to the 'handwriting' of traditional painting) achieved by 'errors' in the printing process. Josef Albers became famous for a series of paintings called 'Homage to the square', in which one formal device – squares within other squares – was held constant while another – colour – was varied. Jasper Johns' 'American flag' series of the 1950s was another example of the Albers approach: the subject matter remained constant while Johns altered colours, placement of flag-image, and brushwork.

Serial Art, to be appreciated, required the viewing of a complete set since individual canvases were simply parts of a larger whole. The latter was often called 'the system' (see Systemic Painting). When single canvases appeared in mixed shows, therefore, they tended to seem thin and shallow, but they gained in impact when encountered in the context of one-person shows.

During the '60s minimal artists such as Mel Bochner, Sol Lewitt, Donald Judd and Carl Andre embraced the serial idiom. Bochner characterized Serial Art as 'highly abstract', an 'ordered manipulation of thought...self-contained and non-referential'. Serialism, he claimed, was premised on the idea that the succession of terms (divisions) within a single work were based on a numerical or otherwise predetermined derivation (progression, permutation, rotation or reversal) from one or more of the preceding terms in that piece. The idea was carried out to its logical conclusion without regard to taste or chance. Bochner drew an analogy with music and cited Lewitt's 'Series A' (1967) as a prime instance of Serial Art.

Some minimal sculptures consisted of a number of identical units spaced at regular intervals like the teeth of a comb (e.g. Judd's wall piece 'Untitled', 1968). They gave the impression of being segments of a continuum, works whose beginnings and ends were arbitrary. Variety was provided by the interaction of such objects with their environments and by the spectator's perceptual experience as he or she moved around the gallery.

In 1989 an exhibition entitled 'En série' was held in Southampton. It featured works by three artists – Arturo Di Stefano, Tim Maguire and Matthias Mansen – who made lithographs and woodcuts but not with the usual intention of producing editions of the same image; rather, their aim was to generate a series of prints, each of which was unique but closely related to the others in the same series.

● See also Geometric Abstraction, Minimal Art, Pop Art, Silk-Screenprinting.

● A Ozenfant 'Serial Art' *The painter's object* M Evans (ed)

(Gerald Howe, 1937) 43–51.

● L March 'Serial Art' *Architectural Design* **36** (2) February 1966 62–3.

● M Bochner 'The Serial attitude' *Artforum* **6** (4) December 1967 28–33.

● D Lee 'Serial rights' *Art News* **66** (8) December 1967 42–5, 68–9.

● L Alloway 'Serial forms' – in – *American sculpture of the sixties* (Los Angeles, County Museum of Art, 1967) 13–14.

● J Coplans *Serial Imagery* (NY, Graphic Society, 1968).

● M Bochner 'Serial Art, systems, solipsism' – in – *Minimal Art* G Battcock (ed) (Studio Vista, 1969) 92–102.

● N Calas 'Art and strategy' – in – *Icons and images of the sixties* by N & E Calas (NY, Dutton, 1971) 218–21.

● I Johnston & J Watkins *En Série* (Southampton, University of Southampton/John Hansard Gallery, 1989).

● P Hayes Tucker *Monet in the '90s: the series paintings* (New Haven & London, Yale University Press, 1990).

588 SHAMANISM

According to Joan Halifax: 'an ecstatic religious complex of particular and fixed elements with a specific ideology that has persisted through millennia and is found in many cultural settings'. The word 'Shaman' derives from the Vedic 'scram', to heat oneself or to practise austerities. Shamans were associated with the hunting/gathering way of life found in Northern and Central Asia, Africa, Australia, Oceania, the Americas and Northern and Eastern Europe. Shamanism was particularly prevalent in the prehistoric cultures of Siberian hunters. Shamans are healers, seers and visionaries who are said to have mastered death. The encounter with death and the subsequent rebirth and illumination are the traditional initiation processes of the Shaman, who is believed to be in communication with a world of spirits and to have the power to separate from his earthly body and go to 'unearthly realms'.

The term is included in this glossary because several important modern artists have cast themselves in the role of Shamans: Joseph Beuys, Yves Klein and Denis Oppenheim for instance. As a Stuka pilot in World War II, Beuys was shot down over the Crimea and then 'warmed' back to life by nomadic Tartars. He later interpreted this experience as one of Shamanistic 'transforming' pain. The materials fat and felt used by the Tartars to restore the artist's health were to play a key part in his artworks. Emulating the Shaman, Beuys designed installations and performances in order to unify nature, spirit, cosmos and the intellect.

Klein was also said to function Shamanistically. In 1958 he declared the empty space of the Iris Clert gallery in Paris to be a 'zone of immaterial pictorial sensibility'

and offered it for sale for pure gold. Some of the abstract expressionists were influenced by the primal imagery of the native Americans. Jackson Pollock, for instance, was aware of native American Shamanic art and ritual. His 1943 canvas 'Guardians of the secret' depicts two 'Shamans' protecting a ritual painting made for healing purposes. More generally, it could be argued that the turn to abstraction in modern art was Shamanistic in that it was often motivated by a desire to transform materials into symbols of the supernatural.

Shamans employ songs, costume, dance, magic tricks and even hallucinogenic drugs to induce ecstatic states in themselves and their audiences. Rogan Taylor has claimed that rock and pop music performances play a comparable ritualistic function in contemporary society and that therefore the star performers are akin to Shamans.

Shamanism in art can be viewed as an instance of the vogue for primitivism. Given that the social context of the modern artist is so very different from that of actual Shamans, the idea that such artists can perform a similar social function seems a dubious one.

● See also Performance Art.

● M Eliade *Shamanism: archaic techniques of ecstasy* (NY, Bollingen Foundation/Pantheon Books, 1964).

● A Lommel *Shamanism: the beginnings of art* (NY, McGraw-Hill, 1967).

● J Burnham 'The artist as Shaman' – in – *Great western saltworks* (NY, George Braziller, 1974) 139–46.

● J Halifax *Shamanic voices: a survey of visionary narratives* (Harmondsworth, Penguin, 1980).

● *Yves Klein (1928–62): a retrospective* (NY, Guggenheim Museum, 1982).

● T McEvilley 'Art in the dark' *Artforum* **21** (10) June/Summer 1983 62–71.

● R Taylor *The death and resurrection show: from Shaman to superstar* (Anthony Blond, 1985).

● C Tisdall *Joseph Beuys* (Thames & Hudson, rev ed 1987).

● N Kaye 'Ritualism and renewal' *Performance* (59) Winter 1989–90 31–45.

589 SHAPED CANVAS

(Also Constructed Painting, Dimensional Painting, Sculptural/ Topological Canvas) Traditionally, the shape of portable oil paintings was rectangular so as to match the walls from which they derived and upon which they were displayed. Even so, other shapes – diamond, cross and tondo – were employed by painters from time to time. In the twentieth century Giorgio de Chirico used triangular and trapezoid shapes, Jackson Pollock worked on exceptionally long horizontal rectangles, and Barnett Newman produced very narrow verti-

SHAPED CANVAS FRANK STELLA, Installation view of a show, (1964). Leo Castelli Gallery, New York.

cal paintings, but despite these examples there was comparatively little experimentation with shape of support before the 1960s.

Different artists have been credited with the 'invention' of the modern Shaped Canvas: H. Arnason cites Lucio Fontana, W. Rubin cites Barnett Newman; one could also cite the artists of the South American Madí movement. Since 1960 painters as various as Rodolfo Arico, Trevor Bell, Derek Boshier, Bernard Cousinier, Anthony Green, Charles Hinman, David Hockney, Allen Jones, Kenneth Noland, Harvey Quaytman, James Rosenquist, John Stezaker and Joe Tilson have created Shaped Canvases, but the chief exponent of the genre was Frank Stella. His famous series of notched canvases with their external forms determined by the pattern of the stripes of pigment crossing their surfaces, dated from 1960. Subsequently he explored in a systematic fashion the reciprocal relation between internal pattern and external profile. (Michael Fried, the art critic, used the term 'deductive structure' to describe pictorial forms 'deduced' from the painting's external format.) Shaped Canvases emphasized the objecthood of paintings. In Stella's case this tendency was reinforced by the use of thick stretchers. In non-relational painting the 'figure on the field' effect was banished from the interior of the picture. This tended to emphasize the external shape of the canvas which itself became a figure against the back-ground wall of the gallery.

In 1989 John Stezaker exhibited in London a series of irregularly shaped canvases featuring screenprinted images. Some of these works had pieces 'cut out' from them in such a way as to slice human figures in half. In this instance the shaping impulse appeared to derive from the photo-montage practice of cutting up and cutting into images. (Stezaker made hundreds of photo-montages in the 1970s.)

Although Stella's and Stezaker's canvases were shaped, they conformed to the convention of flatness in painting. Other artists, however, have devised three-dimensional forms covered with canvas for painting on, e.g. Richard Smith and Justin Knowles; hence the labels 'sculptural' and 'dimensional painting'.

● See also Madí Movement, Non-Relational Art, Objecthood, Photo-Montage.

◉ L Alloway *The Shaped Canvas* (NY, Guggenheim Museum, 1964).

◉ D Judd 'The Shaped Canvas' *Arts Magazine* **39** February 1965 56.

◉ M Fried 'Shape as form: Frank Stella's new paintings' *Artforum* **5** (3) November 1966 18–27.

◉ P Overy 'Justin Knowles: Dimensional Paintings' *Studio International* **173** (885) January 1967 32–3.

◉ W Rubin *Frank Stella* (NY, MoMA, 1970).

◉ K Moffett 'Kenneth Noland's new paintings and the issue of

Shaped Canvas' *Art International* **20** (45) April–May 1976 8–15, + 74.

● I Jeffrey *John Stezaker: the new work* (Salama-Caro Gallery, 1989).

● C Barnes (ed) 'Constructed painting' *Art Journal* **50** (1) Spring 1991 (thematic issue).

<table>
<tr><td>**590**</td><td>**SIGNALS**</td></tr>
</table>

An influential London gallery directed by Charles and Paul Keeler assisted by David Medalla, devoted to the international kinetic art movement, operative in the mid 1960s. Its name derived from the title given by the Greek artist Takis to a series of 'tensile' (i.e. vibrating metal) sculptures he began making in 1955. Besides the 'Signals' of Takis, the gallery featured the work of Sergio de Carmargo, Lygia Clark, Liliane Lijn, Medalla, Helio Oiticica and Jesus-Raphael Soto. It acted, therefore, as a showcase for many Latin American artists. A newspaper-style bulletin edited by Medalla was issued to accompany each exhibition. Signals also dubbed itself 'The Centre for Advanced Creative Study'; one of its prime concerns was the relationship between modern art and modern science.

● See also Kinetic Art.

● *Signals Bulletin* August 1964 – March 1966.

● D Medalla 'Memories of the sixties' *AND Journal of Art & Art Education* **17** 1988 8–17.

● — 'Signals' – in – *The other story: Afro-Asian artists in postwar Britain* by R Araeen & others (Hayward Gallery, 1989) 115–20.

<table>
<tr><td>**591**</td><td>**SILK-SCREENPRINTING**</td></tr>
</table>

(Also Photo-Screenprinting) A technique commonly employed in the textile and graphic arts which has been adopted by many painters since the heyday of pop art in the 1960s. By squeegeeing ink across photo-stencils made from silk, mass-media images can be transferred to canvas thus eliminating the need to construct an image by means of drawing or painting. Oil or acrylic paint can however be applied by brush to the support before printing the image, or it can be applied afterwards. (Silk screened paintings often involve a disjunction or 'misregistration' between their images and their colours.) Variations of colour can also be achieved by using printing inks of different hues. The silk-screen process multiplies the image-making capacity of the artist: the same

SILK-SCREENPRINTING JOHN STEZAKER, 'Frame', Diptych (1988). Silk-screen on shaped canvas, 178cm x 127 cm. Photo: Friedman-Guiness Gallery, Frankfurt.

image can be repeated again and again either within the same canvas or across a number of separate canvases. Although in the applied arts and in fine art print-making, the aim is normally to generate a limited edition consisting of a series of identical prints, painters often encourage printing 'errors' in order to generate a series of similar but unique pictures.

In the post-1945 era thousands of artists have created screenprints usually in association with skilled printers such as Chris Prater and Stanley Hayter. Artists particularly noted for their prints include Richard Hamilton, R. B. Kitaj, Eduardo Paolozzi, Richard Smith and Gerd Winner (Smith made three-dimensional screenprints as multiples in the '60s). Painters employing the process of photo-screenprinting on to canvas have not been so numerous but they include: Alain Jacquet, Robert Rauschenberg, John Stezaker and Andy Warhol.

● See also Atelier 17, Copy Art, Curwen Studio, Kelpra Studio, Mec Art, Media Art, Multiples, Pop Art, Serial Art, Tamarind Lithography Workshop, Tyler Graphics.

◉ P Gilmour *Modern prints* (Studio Vista, 1970).
◉ R Field 'Silkscreen, the media medium' *Art News* **70** (9) January 1972 40–3, 74–5.
◉ P Gilmour *The mechanised image: an historical perspective on twentieth-century prints* (Arts Council of Great Britain, 1978).
◉ M Livingstone 'Do it yourself: notes on Warhol's technique' – in – *Andy Warhol: a retrospective* K McShine (ed) (NY, MoMA, 1989) 63–78.

SIMULATION/ SIMULACRA/ HYPERREALITY

Three terms associated with the difficult but thought-provoking writings of the French theorist Jean Baudrillard which proved highly influential in 1980s art and art theory. Simulating is pretending, imitating something real or a possible future event. Simulations are increasingly being used for training purposes, as a way of testing the properties of a system, and as a design technique. Computer simulations can model actual events but they can also model fictional events, hence one can have simulations with no real referents. Baudrillard's controversial argument is that simulations – in the form of images, media – have replaced reality, creating a new hyperreality. He outlines a series of phases of the development of the image: (1) it is a reflection of a basic reality; (2) it is a mask and perversion of a basic reality; (3) it is the mask of the absence of a basic reality; (4) it bears no relation to any reality whatsoever, it is its own pure simulacrum.

The relevance of Baudrillard's ideas to art is the issue of representation in a hyperreal, media-saturated environment. (One could argue that simulation is another word for art in that artists have been supplying simulated or fictional realities for centuries.) An exhibition selected by the critic Michael Newman with the title 'Simulacra' was held in London in 1982. It featured the work of Jonathan Miles, John Stezaker, Jan Wandja and John Wilkins, four artists whose starting-point is a fascination with the imagery of the mass media.

Eleanor Heartney, a critic writing for *Art News,* used the terms 'Simulation art' and 'Simulationism' to describe the work of young American artists like Ashley Bickerton, Meyer Vaisman, Jeff Koons and others exhibiting in New York in the mid 1980s because the art so often mimicked the outward appearance of consumer goods. In this text this kind of art is discussed under 'neo-geo'.

Another meaning of the word 'simulacra': the 'found' or 'chance' images encountered in nature (e.g. seeing faces in rocky cliffs) or the figures and faces 'hidden' in the drawings and paintings of such artists as Mantegna, Durer, Courbet and Dali.

● See also Media-Art, Neo-Geo.

◉ J Michell *Simulacra: faces and figures in nature* (Thames & Hudson, 1979).
◉ M Newman *Simulacra: a new art from Britain* (Riverside Studios, 1982).
◉ G Celant 'From Alpha Trainer to subway' *Art & Text* (9) Autumn 1983 60–9.
◉ J Baudrillard 'The precession of Simulacra' *Art & Text* (11) 1983 3–47.
◉ — *Simulations* (NY, Foreign Agent series, Semiotext(e), 1983).
◉ A Frankovits (ed) *Seduced and abandoned: the Baudrillard scene* (Glebe, Australia, Stonemoss Services, 1984).
◉ R Brooks 'From the night of consumerism to the dawn of Simulation' *Artforum* **23** (5) February 1985 76–81.
◉ *Endgame: reference & Simulation in recent painting & sculpture* (Boston, Mass, ICA/MIT Press, 1986).
◉ E Heartney 'Simulationism: the hot new cool art' *Art News* **86** January 1987 130–7.
◉ E Burden *Design Simulation: use of photographic and electronic media in design and presentation* (Mitchell, 1988).
◉ S Shepherd *Visualizing future landscapes through Simulation: a user's guide for architects, planners and designers* (NY, Van Nostrand Reinhold, 1989).

SITE

(Also Anti-Architecture, Arch-Art) Acronym for 'Sculpture In The Environment', a multi-disciplinary organization founded in New York in 1970 following a number of environmental art projects undertaken in 1969 by a group of five artists. Ten years later the principal members of SITE were James Wines, Alison Sky, Emilio Sousa and Michelle Stone. SITE functioned like an architectural team, working collectively and individually on different projects seeking a synthesis of sculpture and architecture. They had no preconceived aesthetic or style; they responded to the characteristics of each site, hence the name of the group.

SITE treated architecture as a form of public art rather than as design, indeed as the subject matter or raw material of art. From 1972 onwards SITE employed the terms 'de-architecture' and 'de-architecturization' to describe their philosophy. De-architecture was 'a frame of reference for questioning the nature and practice of architecture'. What this entailed was a subversion, or inversion, of the rational and functional postulates of modern design. SITE's creations – particularly those for the Best showrooms in the United States – generated much public attention because of their bizarre and surrealistic character, e.g. showrooms with walls peeling away from the structure or with indeterminate and tilted façades; a car park with 'ghost' vehicles buried in concrete. SITE's interventions into the built environment and their transgressions of the norms of architecture were often funny and amazing; they served, in fact, as a highly successful form of advertising for the owners of the buildings concerned.

Besides their architectural work, SITE produced a series of books on the environmental arts under the collective title 'ON SITE'.

● See also Environmental Art, Public Art, Radical Design, Street Art.

◉ SITE *SITE: projects and theories* (Bari, Italy, Dedalo Libri, 1978).

◉ SITE, P Restany & B Zevi *SITE: architecture as art* (Academy Editions, 1980).

◉ J Wines *De-architecture* (NY, Rizzoli, 1987).

◉ — & others *SITE* (NY, Rizzoli, 1989).

594 **SITE-SPECIFIC ART**

(Also Post-Studio Sculpture, Site-Related Art) Works of art created in relation to particular physical places – either indoors or out of doors – to such a degree that their character and meaning would be lost or changed if they were moved somewhere else. A 1989 British example was Richard Wilson's three-dimensional construction in Matt's Gallery, London, which involved cutting out the gallery's large window and displacing it to the centre of the room.

The term 'Site-Specific Art' dates from the 1960s and appears to have been popularized by the American land artist Robert Smithson (1938–73) whose work from 1968 was concerned with the dialectic between 'site' and 'non-site'. Land artists in particular responded to the character of rural sites; they frequently made their works

from the natural materials found at those sites. Another American artist whose minimalist works and writings have been influential is Robert Irwin. He has distinguished between site-dominant, site-adjusted, site-specific and site-determined works. His own installations have also been called 'conditional art'.

An exhibition entitled 'Sitings' held at La Jolla in 1986 featured the work of four 'post-studio' sculptors: Alice Aycock, Richard Fleischner, Mary Miss and George Trakas.

● See also Correalism, Earth & Land Art, Environmental Art/Design, Installation, Projected Art, Public Art, SITE.

◉ R Smithson *The writings of Robert Smithson* N Holt (ed) (NY, New York University Press, 1979).

◉ R Irwin *Being and circumstance. Notes towards a conditional art* (Larkspur Landing, California, Lapis Press, 1985).

◉ H Davies & R Onorato *Sitings* S Yard (ed) (La Jolla, California, La Jolla Museum of Contemporary Art, 1986).

◉ M Lewandowska (ed) *Sight works volume one: several enquiries* (Chance Books, 1988).

◉ K Wagenknecht-Harte *Site + sculpture: the collaborative design process* (NY, Van Nostrand Reinhold, 1989).

595 **SITUATION**

This word became fashionable in the post-1945 era as a result of the existentialist philosophy of Jean-Paul Sartre (a philosophy of extreme situations). 'Situations' was employed as the title of a magazine founded in 1959 by the Canadian painter Guido Molinari and others, while 'Situation' was employed as the title of two important exhibitions of painting held in London in 1960 and '61. The work in these shows represented the British version of post-painterly abstraction: it was very large in size, abstract and made use of flat fields of colour or gestural marks (but without the violence of action painting). 'Situation' was a loose association of 20 artists including Gillian Ayres, Bernard and Harold Cohen, Robyn Denny, John Hoyland, Henry Mundy, Richard Smith and Peter Stroud. (In the second show 'New London Situation' the sculptor Anthony Caro also participated.) Artists belonging to the St Ives School were excluded because their work still had references to nature. One aim of the Situation exhibitions was to construct environments which would involve spectators by filling their whole field of vision.

In 1971 a short-lived London gallery, or bureau, called 'Situation' was established by the dealer Robert Self and Anthony de Kerdrel to encourage 'openness, new directions', to act as an outlet for films, videos and performance. Impermanent forms of art such as performance were discussed in the art press in 1980 under the heading 'situation esthetics'. Earlier, in 1969, Victor Burgin had employed the similar term 'situational aesthetics' to characterize the kind of quasi-conceptual pieces he was devising at the time.

● See also Environmental Art, Hard-Edge Painting, St Ives School, Site-Specific Art.

● R Coleman *Situation: an exhibition of British abstract painting* (RBA Galleries, 1960).

● L Alloway 'Situation in retrospect' *Architectural Design* **31** (2) February 1961 82–3.

● *New London Situation: an exhibition of British abstract art* (New London Gallery, 1961).

● '"Situation": the British abstract scene in 1960' *Isis* (1468) June 6 1964 6–9.

● V Burgin 'Situational aesthetics' *Studio International* **178** (915) October 1969 118–21.

● 'Exhibitions: Situation' *Time Out* (103) February 4–10 1972 36.

● V Acconci & others 'Situation esthetics: impermanent art and the '70s audience' *Artforum* **18** (5) January 1980 22–9.

SITUATIONISTS Two frames from a Situationist comic. Source: C. Gray *Leaving the twentieth century* (1974).

596 SITUATIONISTS

A playful, volatile alliance of avant garde artists, architects, poets, art historians and political theorists who were active in several European countries during the 1950s and '60s. In spite of their small number (70), the Situationists were to prove remarkably influential amongst Left-wing intellectuals, activists and graphic designers. The 'Internationale Situationiste' (IS) was formed at a conference in Italy in 1957 by amalgamating two existing organizations: 'Lettriste Internationale' (see Lettrism) and the 'International Union for a Pictorial Bauhaus'. It disbanded in 1972 when the project seemed no longer viable. The ideas of the Sits were drawn from surrealism, the anti-art of dada, existentialism, Marxism and anarchism. They generated countless radical pamphlets and magazines, and coined many memorable slogans. Situationist theory evolved into a kind of intellectual terrorism directed against bourgeois society and sought its overthrow by means of revolution. In the meantime everyday life was to be transformed by creativity, by experiments in behaviour. Soon a conflict emerged between those members committed to art as a profession and those who sought 'the supersession of art'. The latter were convinced there could not be any such thing as 'Situationist art' because art/culture was 'the ideal commodity, the one which helps sell all the others'.

Members of IS included the writer and film-maker Guy Debord, the architect Constant, the poet Jörgen Nash, the painters Asger Jorn, Giuseppe Pinot-Gallizio, Ralph Rumney and the art historian T. J. Clark. One of the aims of IS was to overcome the specialization of the different arts and indeed the separateness of art from life. IS was male dominated; one of the few female participants was Michèle Bernstein. Debord was editor of the main journal of the Sits – *Internationale Situationiste* (Paris, 12 issues 1958–69) – and he introduced the key ideas of 'constructing situations' and attacking the character and passivity of 'the society of the spectacle', i.e mass media/consumer capitalism. Other important concepts were psychogeography, dérive or drifting, détournement or deflection, and unitary urbanism (i.e. a criticism of town planning).

Détournement involved the re-use of existing material as a means of propaganda, e.g. adding a slogan to an advert to change its meaning; defacing (by overpainting) academic or kitsch images in order to give them a new lease of life (Jorn's 'nouvelle disfigurations'). Pinot-Gallizio undertook a critique of the art of painting and the art business by producing abstract expressionist 'industrial paintings' by the roll. (These activities of the '50s anticipated Warhol's Factory methods of the '60s.) He also created a total environment with his violent canvases called 'the chamber of anti-matter'. Constant designed and built models for future utopian environments that fulfilled his theory of 'unitary urbanism'. Debord's films rejected all conventional cinema by containing no images at all.

The IS was subject to regular splits and expulsions. One breakaway faction, called 'Bauhaus Situationiste Drakabygzet' based on Kierkegaard's philosophy of situations, was established in Sweden in 1961. Another branch existed in Germany – Gruppe Spur. The Situationists achieved their greatest triumph during the May 1968 revolt in Paris when their ideas were put into practice by the students. During the mid 1970s their ideas were again influential within the British punk rock and graphics movement. Many other individuals and groups have been inspired by Situationist theory. In 1989–90 their historical importance was confirmed by an exhibition held at the Pompidou Centre in Paris and at the ICAs in London and Boston (Mass.). Followers of the Situationists saw this show as a sign of the power of official culture and museums to absorb all radical initiatives.

● See also CoBrA, Lettrism, Political Art, Punk, Spur.

◉ *Internationale Situationiste 1958–69* (Amsterdam, Van Gennap, 1972 reprint).

◉ *Situationist Times* (Copenhagen, 1963–4).

● G Debord *Society of the spectacle* (Detroit, Black & Red, 1970).

◉ *Situationister 1957–71* (Lund, Sweden, Skanska P Konstmuseum, University of Lund, 1971).

◉ M Bandini 'Pinot-Gallizio' *Data* (9) Autumn 1973 16–26, 82–5, 94–5.

◉ C Gray (ed) *Leaving the 20th century: the incomplete work of the Situationist International* (Free Fall Publications, 1974).

◉ R Vaneigem *The revolution of everyday life* (Practical Paradise Publications, 1975).

◉ M Bandini *L'estetico, il politico: da CoBrA all'Internationale Situazionista 1948–57* (Rome, Edizione Officina, 1977).

◉ K Knabb (ed) *Situationist International: anthology* (Berkeley, Bureau of Public Secrets, 1981).

◉ 'A little Situationism...' *Artscribe International* (66) November–December 1987 50–62.

◉ (Special issue on Situationists) *Yale French Studies* (73) 1987.

◉ J Barrot *What is Situationism?* (Unpopular Books, 1987).

● G Robertson 'The Situationist International: its penetration into British culture' *Block* (14) Autumn 1988 38–53.

◉ I Blazwick (ed) *An endless adventure...an endless passion...an endless banquet: a Situationist scrapbook* (ICA/Verso, 1989).

◉ J Martos *Histoire de l'Internationale Situationiste* (Paris, Les Éditions Lebovici, 1989).

597 SLOAP

Acronym standing for 'Space Left Over After Planning' devised by the American Leslie Ginsburg. Modern planners and architects are notorious for generating oddly shaped patches of ground as by-products of their schemes. In 1989 the British architectural critic Martin Pawley employed the term 'Sloap culture' to describe people such as skateboarders who took advantage of areas of concrete (such as those found under London's South Bank arts complex) which were otherwise unsightly and useless.

● See also Subtopia.

◉ M Pawley 'Repelling boarders' *Guardian* March 20 1989 38.

598 SNARE PICTURES

(Tableaux Pièges; also Trap Pictures) A name given by the Swiss sculptor Daniel Spoerri (b Romania 1930, has lived in Switzerland and Paris) to his own three-dimensional works dating from the 1960s. Accumulations of common objects, such as those remaining on a table at the end of a meal, were 'snared' by Spoerri, i.e. glued to a board or the seat of a chair and then turned on their sides and hung on a wall. These literal still lives were Spoerri's contribution to the nouveau réalisme movement.

● See also Assemblage Art, Nouveau Réalisme, Object Art.

◉ S Williams 'Stilled lives' *Art & Artists* **7** (4) July 1972 28–33.

◉ C Bremer & M Bloem *Daniel Spoerri* (Zürich, Helmhaus, 1972).

599 SOCIAL ARCHITECTURE/ DESIGN

(Including Alternative & Counter Design, Design for Need) These concepts were discussed in at least three texts published in the 1980s. In the previous decade, the terms 'alternative' and 'counter' design were more fashionable. What the latter signified were attempts by socially aware designers living in affluent Western countries to use their skills and knowledge for the benefit of those most in need either in their own societies (e.g. disadvantaged minorities such as the disabled) or for the poor in the developing world. Alternative designers sought a mode of practice that was different from the industrial and consultant design required by commerce and big business. They were concerned about the social and ecological implications of mass production, industrialization and consumerism and hoped to ameliorate their adverse effects by means of better, more appropriate design. The British SIAD (Society of Industrial Artists and Designers) set up an Alternative Design Group and the ICSID (International Council of Societies of Industrial Design) organized a conference entitled 'Design for Need' which was held at the Royal College of Art in London in 1976. Victor Papanek was perhaps the best-known advocate and practitioner of 'integrated, comprehensive, anticipatory design' aside from Buckminster Fuller. Papanek refused to patent his designs, so anyone was free to use them.

The terms 'social' architecture and design marked a reaction against architecture and design concerned mainly with form and style, and with serving the needs of the wealthy and powerful in society. In a 1983 book the American behavioural psychologist Robert Sommer argued that designers of buildings and urban environments should pay far more attention to the needs of the mass of people as social beings. He advised architects to reject formalism and to take note of the findings of psychology so that they could be more effective in the future. Social Design also implied a redistribution of design services, i.e. away from the rich towards the poor and other disadvantaged minorities, plus a concern for environmental issues such as pollution and the need to conserve energy. Sommer wrote: 'The goal of social design is to produce buildings and neighbourhoods that suit the occupants...The culture of the people tends...to be conservative...Social designers are distinguished from their more traditional counterparts by an explicit and primary commitment to the occupants...The term "social design" reflects the combination of participatory planning methods and social science concepts.'

In 1984 C. Richard Hatch, an American architect and teacher, edited a book describing 26 projects from 12 countries which shared a conception of architecture as 'an instrument for transforming the environment and the people who live in it'. According to Hatch, Social Architecture implied that (1) public participation was essential; (2) architecture was a public discourse and it should aim for 'rational transparency' (i.e. it should be more legible, able to reveal the social forces that condition it); (3) present society was not immutable but subject to historical change; (4) buildings should encourage critical reflection and develop the many-sidedness of humanity; cities should be redesigned so as to avoid the separation of functions typical of zoning – they could then provide a rich and complex experience for citizens.

Three years later the term 'Social Architecture' was used in the title of a book by Andrew Saint. The text recounted the history of the building of new schools in England during the post-1945 welfare state period. The schools were intended for the benefit of the whole of society and they were the result of a team effort by offi-cials, planners, architects, industrialists and educationists; two leading figures were Stirrat Johnson-Marshall and Charles Aslin, architects for the County of Hertfordshire. This generation of decision-makers believed that social problems could be solved by the application of scientific methods, by technological innovation, and by rational planning. Inspired by the functionalist/modular principles of modern architecture, they constructed schools from standardized, prefabricated parts – light steel frames, glass and concrete cladding – made in the factories of Hills & Co., West Bromwich. Despite the standardized parts, the schools were not identical in design because the units were capable of being assembled in different configurations.

● See also Advocacy Planning, ARCH, CLASP, Community Architecture, Environmental Design, Participatory Design, Radical Design, SAR.

● A Mondini 'The land of good design' – in *Italy: the new domestic landscape* (NY, MoMA, 1972) 370–9.

● V Papanek *Design for the real world: human ecology and social change* (Thames & Hudson, 1972; rev ed 1985).

● 'Alternative design issue' *Designer* September 1976.

● H Fathy *Architecture for the poor: experiment in rural Egypt* (Chicago, University of Chicago Press, 1976).

● J Bicknell & L McQuiston (eds) *Design for need: the social contribution of design* (Oxford, Pergamon Press, 1977).

● R Sommer *Social Design: creating buildings with people in mind* (Englewood Cliffs, New Jersey, Prentice-Hall, 1983).

● C Hatch (ed) *The scope of Social Architecture* (NY, Van Nostrand Reinhold, 1984).

● A Saint *Towards a Social Architecture: the role of school building in post-war England* (New Haven & London, Yale University Press, 1987).

600 SOCIOLOGICAL ART GROUP (Collectif Art Sociologique) A group of French artists – Hervé Fischer, Fred Forest and Jean-Paul Thénot – founded in Paris in 1974. Influenced by the critical theory of the Frankfurt School and the radical ideas of the situationists, the members of CAS developed an artistic practice whose aim was to question and criticize bourgeois society and the concept of art. Their work was called 'sociological' because it utilized certain ideas and research methods from the social science of sociology, e.g. questionnaires. CAS sought to transform society and differed from the sociology of art in being an active practice rather than an academic study.

● See also Frankfurt School Aesthetics, Political Art, Situationists.

● *Collectif Art Sociologique: théorie – pratique – critique* (Paris, Musée Galliera, 1975).

● P Restany 'Sociological Art' *Domus* (548) July 1975 52–3.

● H Fischer 'Manifesto no. 2 for Sociological Art' *Control* (9) December 1975 8.

● — 'Sociological Art as utopian strategy' *The Fox* **1** (3) 1976 166–9.

● F Forest *Art Sociologique* (Paris, Union Générale, 1978).

● M Blanchette *Hervé Fischer* (Quebec, Ministère des Affaires Culturelles/Musée d'Art Contemporain, 1981).

601 SOFT ARCHITECTURE

(Also Architecture Douce, Adaptable & Responsive Architecture) Several proposals for 'soft' architecture were made during the 1960s. The Japanese architect Arata Isozaki and his studio meant by it a living space with as few fixed elements and permanent divisions as possible; shelter and services would be provided by an inflated dome, light and sound machines, and plug-in units.

In 1967 Warren Brodey (an American physician) proposed an artificial man–machine system, a computer-programmed, intelligent environment that would be capable of responding to the moods and needs of its users, e.g. changing the colour of the lighting if certain changes in heartbeat were registered. The word 'soft' stemmed from the 'concept of an intelligent environment softened by a gentle control'. Alternatively, it could have been derived from 'software'. In 1989 the Japanese computer expert Ken Sakamura unveiled in Tokyo his 'Tron Intelligent House', the first working prototype of a fully computerized home. An automated home or intelligent house is also referred to as a 'smart house' or, in France, a 'domotique' (in Paris in 1988 a conference entitled 'Domotique '88' was held). In Britain Leslie Haddon (of RMDP Brighton) edits a newsletter called 'The Intelligent Home' to encourage the application of information and communications technology to the domestic realm.

Certain French critics writing in *Architecture d'Aujourd' hui* spoke of 'architecture douce' (from 'doucement' – gently, softly) meaning low-energy, low-tech dwellings – a new kind of self-build/folk architecture. This term has also been used to describe two 1980s harbour developments (one in France and one in the United States) designed by François Spoerry.

● See also Architecture Machine, Environmental Design, Hard Architecture, Low-Tech, Soft Design/Tech.

● W Brodey 'Soft Architecture: the design of intelligent environments' *Landscape* (USA) **17** (1) 1967 8–12.

● R Boyd *New directions in Japanese architecture* (NY, Braziller/London, Studio Vista, 1968).

● N Negroponte *Soft Architecture machines* (Cambridge, Mass, MIT Press, 1974).

● F Spoerry *Spoerry: L'Architecture Douce: de Port Grimaud à Port-Liberté* (Paris, Édition Robert Laffont, 1989).

● C Hardyment 'Rising out of the dust' *Weekend Guardian* August 11–12 1990 8.

602 SOFT ART

(Also Soft Painting/ Sculpture) In the past, finished works of sculpture were normally made from hard, rigid materials – wood, marble, bronze – in order to ensure permanence. Making sculptures durable has not been such an important consideration as far as many artists of the post-1945 period were concerned (see Expendable Art). They have been attracted to other, softer (or more flexible) materials such as cloth, vinyl, rubber, latex, feathers, felt, hair, rope and sand. The interest in softer materials was particularly evident in the 1960s: Claes Oldenburg's 'Soft typewriter' of 1963 being just one of a series of bizarre objects made from vinyl, canvas and kapok held together by sewing or lacing. His sculptures reversed the normal properties of certain everyday objects: hard, rigid wash-basins became soft and floppy. They were prefigured by the soft watches found in the surrealist paintings of Dali. Children's stuffed toys were another obvious precedent for certain kinds of Soft Sculpture. John Chamberlain was another American sculptor of the 1960s who worked with soft materials, in his case polyurethane foam. One reason for the appeal of limp, pliable materials was that they permitted forms that were more organic and visceral in their connotations.

In Britain during the same decade the American pop artist Jann Haworth constructed life-sized human figures from fabric filled with stuffing, while the sculptor Barry Flanagan designed installations employing such flexible materials as rope, felt and sand. In 1969 Felicity Youett

SOFT ART VERA SZKEKELY, 'Installation Budapest' (1981). String and fabric. Photo: Barbican Centre, London.

began to specialize in the production of padded or stuffed satin objects and animals, including a giant toothbrush, fish, simulated windows, and even a model train.

Since the late '60s various survey exhibitions of Soft Art have been mounted: at the New Jersey State Museum (1969); at the New York Cultural Center (1973); at the Camden Arts Centre, London (1974); at the Kunsthaus, Zürich (1979–80); and at the Barbican Centre Gallery, London (1988–9). The latter show featured large, abstract, textile sculptures by eight French artists (seven of them women). The artists included Daniel Graffin who made cell structures from cloth; Marinette Cueco who made hangings from woven grass; and Vera Szekely who made sail-like structures from string and fabric. This type of work has in the past attracted the label 'fibre art'. It often emerged from an applied arts/interior decor context rather than a fine art context and the resulting objects were hybrids of art and craft. The use of lightweight materials such as string and cloth enabled some artists to create environments big enough to enclose the visitor. Several works indeed were intended to function in the open air and to respond to light and wind.

The term 'Soft Painting' has been used by Nancy Marmer to designate American and European paintings dating from the 1970s characterized by the absence of stretchers. Canvases were simply pinned or taped to walls; they were also often irregular in shape.

● See also Air Art, Anti-Form, Arte Povera, Environmental Art, Matter Art, Shaped Canvas.

● R Pomeroy 'Soft objects at the New Jersey State Museum' *Arts Magazine* **43** (5) March 1969 46–8.

●—'New York: Soft Art' *Art & Artists* **4** (1) April 1969 26–7.

● *Soft Art* (Trenton, New Jersey State Museum, 1969).

● M Kozloff 'The poetics of softness' – in – *Renderings: critical essays on a century of modern art* (Studio Vista, 1970) 223–35.

● *Soft as Art* (NY, New York Cultural Center, 1973).

● D Meilach *Soft Sculpture and other soft artforms with stuffed fabrics, fibers and plastics* (Allen & Unwin, 1974).

● *Soft Art* (Camden Arts Centre, 1974).

● N Marmer 'Report from Los Angeles: "Unstretched surfaces"' *Art in America* **66** (3) May–June 1978 56–7.

● E Billeter & others *Weich und plastisch: Soft Art* (Zürich, Kunsthaus, 1979).

603 SOFT DESIGN/TECH

According to Julian Gibb, the word 'soft' became very popular in the discourse of Italian design in the mid 1980s. He cites its use by the colour consultant Clino Castelli. Workspaces were humanized by attending to 'soft phenomena', i.e. subjective, sensual aspects such as light, sound, colour, texture, pattern and microclimate. Soft Design was thus evolved to ameliorate the impact of 'hard' or high-tech design: soft was 'a bridge between artificial, mechanical order and natural variety' – hence the equal popularity of 'Soft-Tech'. Castelli also ran a postgraduate course at the Domus Academy, Milan, with the title 'Primary Design' (Disegno Primario) defined as 'a way of working within existing design methodologies to compensate for the inhuman, alienating aspects of technology'.

Soft-Tech was a concept fashionable with many designers and journalists in the 1980s – the Italian architect Renzo Piano for instance. Writers used it to describe ptfe-coated glass fibre fabrics with light-transmission qualities from which buildings, exhibition tents or canopies could be constructed, and to refer to furniture made from tubular metal frames with fabric stretched across them.

● See also High-Tech, Italian Craze, Low-Tech.

● S Braidwood 'Soft-Tech: the style of the '80s' *Design* (410) February 1983 47.

● L Relph-Knight 'Soft-Tech style' *Design* (414) June 1983 48–51.

● J Gibb 'Soft: an appeal to common sense' *Design* (433) January 1985 27–9.

604 SoHo

In the artworld this word denotes not the district of central London, but SoHo, New York, i.e. South Houston, a business district that became a centre for artists' lofts and art galleries in the 1970s. In 1984 the pretensions of the SoHo art scene were mocked by the critic Robert Hughes in a satire written in heroic couplets.

● See also East Village Art, New York School.

● P Gardner 'SoHo, brave new bohemia' *Art News* **73** (4) April 1974 56–7.

● *SoHo: downtown Manhattan* (Berlin, Kunst und Berliner Festwochen, 1976).

● C Simpson *SoHo: the artist in the city* (Chicago, University of Chicago Press, 1981).

● Junius Secondus 'The SoHoiad: or, the masque of art' *New York Review of Books* March 29 1984 17–19.

● P Gardner 'SoHo: downtown boomtown' *Art News* **86** (3) March 1987 128–33.

● S Zukin *Loft living: culture and capital in urban change* (Radius, 1988).

605 SOUND ART

(Also Audio Art, Aural Art, Sonic or Sound Sculpture, Sound Poetry, Soundworks, Text–Sound Compositions) Sounds organized into meaningful patterns are crucial to several arts – music, opera, poetry, theatre, film and television – but until the twentieth century sounds played no part in the fine arts of painting and sculpture. This situation began to change in 1913 with the publication of the futurist manifesto 'The art of noises' by Luigi Russolo, a painter who also generated 'noise music' (also called 'bruitism'). As the century progressed and the visual arts became more mixed-media and receptive to all kinds of experimental activities, the distinctions between painting, sculpture, music, video, film, poetry and performance began to blur. Modern technological inventions such as the development of radio, disc and tape recording, multi-track studio facilities and so forth were also vital in encouraging those from a fine art background to experiment with sounds and the dimension of time which, of course, sequences of sounds foreground.

By the 1950s it was possible for an experimental musician such as John Cage to be as well known in fine art circles as in music circles. It was also possible for Robert Rauschenberg to add a collage of sounds to the normally silent artform of painting by incorporating a radio into one of his combines. Since then many visual artists have employed sounds. Some have used them as an adjunct to their main activity, some as one element in a mix of media, and some have specialized in the production of Soundworks. The way in which artists have made use of sound has tended to vary according to the particular art movement they subscribed to; for example, Robert Morris's 'Box with the sound of its own making' (1961), a wooden box with a three-hour tape recording of its construction, was a clear example of process art. During the 1960s British artschools provided a fertile context for the exploration of sounds and rock music; Brian Eno, an art student himself, later described them as 'the cradles of experimental music'.

The machines devised by kinetic artists during the '60s normally produced some noise as a by-product whether desired by the artist or not. The phrase 'audio-kinetic sculpture' was coined to describe those works in which sound and movement were deliberately linked.

Sound Sculpture implied a different, more environmental approach, i.e. employing recordings and loudspeakers in a gallery in order to use sounds to 'sculpt' the space as the visitor moved within it. The British artist John Anderton engaged in this kind of work. He pointed out that sound could be experienced from within as well as outside the pattern formed by the speakers. This kind of work clearly relied upon the active participation of visitors, especially if their movements influenced the character of the sounds. For the 'Magic Theatre' exhibition held at the Nelson Art Gallery, Kansas City in 1969 the American artist Howard Jones devised a 'sonic games chamber' in which changes in sound patterns were produced by the movements of the visitors. Tom Marioni, an artist who combined conceptual and performance art, employed amplifiers to pick up the sounds of his actions and by a process of feedback made those sounds persist in the room space for as long as there was any movement.

In 1969 Dennis Oppenheim produced a 'sculpture' consisting of a tape recording of the sound of his footsteps as he walked a particular route. A year later at the Museum of Conceptual Art in San Francisco, a show was mounted entitled 'Sound sculpture as'. It featured the sounds of guns being fired, telephones ringing, and an artist urinating into a bucket.

In 1970 the Museum of Contemporary Crafts, New York, organized the first major exhibition to focus entirely on sound. Three years later a show entitled 'Sound/Sculpture' was held at the Vancouver Art Gallery, Canada. It featured works by François and Bernard Baschet, Harry Bertoia, David Jacobs, Reinhold Marxhausen, Charles Mattox, Stephen von Huene and Walter Wright. The 'catalogue' consisted of a 30 minute recording. This reminds us that many artists working in the visual arts have made recordings, e.g. Kurt Schwitters uttering his *merz* poetry. The printed catalogue to the exhibition 'Record as artwork 1959–73' lists over 50 examples of such recordings. Another 'catalogue' in the form of disc was that for the 1969 'Art by telephone' exhibition mounted in Chicago. Clearly, sound recording can be used to produce primary material (artworks) or secondary material (documentation). A magazine presenting both types of material is *Audio Arts,* a British venture dating from 1973, which has presented the discourse of conceptual artists, interviews with artists, recordings of performance pieces, etc., in the form of an audio tape cassette. *Audio Arts* was founded and is edited by William Furlong.

Since the late '70s sound experimentation by artists has increased considerably. Perhaps the most notable example was the American performance artist Laurie Anderson who achieved popular success with her record 'O Superman' and then went on to entertain large theatre audiences with mixed-media concerts in which the electronic manipulation of live and recorded sounds played a key role. Exhibitions and festivals – too numerous to describe in detail – have also been held internationally, focusing on the many different facets of Sound Art. The extreme diversity of the artistic activities involving sounds has prevented 'Sound Art' from becoming a restrictive category.

● See also Concrete Poetry, Cross-Overs, Environmental Art, Fluxus, Game Art, Participatory Art, Performance Art, Process Art, Rock Art/Design/Fashion, Time-Based Arts, Video Art.

● L Russolo *The art of noises* (NY, Something Else Press,

1967).

● *Sound, light and silence* (Kansas, William Rockhill Art Gallery, 1967).

● *Art by telephone* (Chicago, Museum of Contemporary Art, 1969).

● A McMillan 'The listening eye' *Craft Horizons* **30** (1) January–February 1970 14–19.

● *Record as artwork 1959–73* (Royal College of Art, 1973).

● C Celant 'The record as artwork' *Domus* (520) March 1973 51–3.

● J Lowndes 'Sound/Sculpture' *ArtsCanada* (180/181) August 1973 66–9.

● S Melikan 'The Baschet brothers: the sounds of sculpture' *ArtNews* **72** (8) October 1973 70–1.

● M Eastley *Sonic Sculpture* (Dartington Hall Press, 1973).

● M Neuhaus 'Sound in public places' *Domus* (562) September 1976 50–2.

● J Grayson (ed) *Sound Sculpture* (Vancouver, ARD Publications, 1976).

● *Airwaves* (a two-record anthology of artists' aural works and music) (NY, One Ten Records, 1978).

● *Soundings* (Purchase, NY, State University of New York, 1981).

● H Charlton 'Max Eastley: sonurgist and sound sculptor' *Art Monthly* (60) October 1982 6–7.

● J Gordon (producer) *Revolutions per minute (the art record)* (NY, Ronald Feldman Fine Arts, 1982).

● L Anderson *United States* (NY, Harper & Row, 1984).

● L Wendt 'Sound poetry...' *Leonardo* **18** (1) 1985 11–23.

● M Archer & others *Sound/Vision* (Plymouth Arts Centre, 1985).

● *Audio by artists festival* (Halifax, Nova Scotia, 1985).

● *A noise in your eye! An international exhibition of Sound Sculpture* (Bristol, Arnolfini Gallery, 1985).

● S Pedersen 'Audio by artists' *Vanguard* **15** (1) February–March 1986 31–3.

● P Panhuysen & others *Echo: the image of sound* (Eindhoven, Apollohuis, 1987).

● *Sound re-visited* (Amsterdam, Void Editions, 1987).

● A Van Barneveld & A de Vries (eds) *Geluidkunst Nederland* (Amsterdam, Time-Based Arts, 1988).

● D Lander & M Lexier (eds) *Sound by artists* (Toronto, Art Metropole & Walter Phillips Gallery, 1990).

606   SPACE

Acronym for Space Provision (Artistic Cultural & Educational) Ltd, a London organization founded in 1968 by Maurice de Sausmarez, Bridget Riley, Peter Sedgley, Peter Townsend, Professor West and Irene Worth for the purpose of providing studio space for artists. The organization stemmed from an awareness that (a) there were many artists who needed large working areas, and (b) there existed many disused factories and warehouses in London. Within a year SPACE managed to accommodate 90 artists in St Katherine's Dock, a derelict warehouse. Exhibitions of SPACE artists have often been mounted for publicity and fund-raising purposes.

● See also ACME, AIR.

● 'A proposal to provide studio workshops for artists' *Studio International* **177** (908) February 1969 65–7.

● 'Notes on SPACE' *Catalyst* January 1971 56.

● S Braden 'AIR RA RIP? SPACED' *Time Out* (84) September 24–30 1971 20–1.

607   SPACE ART

(Also Space Age Art) The Belgian artist Paul Van Hoeydonck was once described as 'the Giotto of the age of space exploration' because the subject matter and forms of his paintings and sculptures were inspired by the Soviet and United States space programmes. For this reason his work was dubbed 'Space Art'.

Frank J. Malina (1912–81), the scientist and kinetic artist, preferred the expression 'Space Age Art' and identified three types: (1) 'art made on Earth with new techniques or materials developed by astronautical technology, incorporating visual experiences provided by space flight and exploration'; (2) 'art made on Earth to express either the resulting new psychological experiences or the new philosophical experiences of man and of the universe'; (3) 'art made and used on the moon and on other planets'. One could also add works of art made on Earth but included as part of the cargo of spacecraft. Other kinds of work utilizing space include: transmitting radio messages and TV images to outer space; reworking satellite photographs and video recordings; designing satellites as artworks. In 1986 a 'Sky and Space artists' manifesto' was written by Otto Piene and others as a consequence of 'sky art' conferences held in the United States – at the Center for Advanced Visual Studies – and in Europe. The manifesto was presented in November 1986 in Paris at a conference on the theme of culture in space.

The visualizing ability of artists has played a role in space research. For example, artists have been employed to create pictures or models of conditions on planets as yet unvisited by camera-equipped spacecraft. A specialist in this kind of art was the architect and astronomer Chesley Bonestell whose first book illustrations on space themes date from the early 1950s.

● See also Air Art, Center for Advanced Visual Studies, Sci-Fi Art.

● 'Personal profile: Chesley Bonestell, Space artist' *Spaceflight* **11** (82) 1969.

● J van der Marck 'Paul van Hoeydonck's ten year Space Art program' *Art International* **14** (2) February 1970 41–3.

● F Malina 'On the visual fine arts in the space age' *Leonardo* **3** (3) July 1970 323–5.

● D Hardy 'The role of the artist in astronautics' *Spaceflight* **12** (14) 1970.

● L Pesek 'An artist in modern times: on extraterrestrial land-scapes' *Leonardo* **5** (4) Autumn 1972 297–300.

● A Clarke 'Beyond Jupiter' *Sunday Times Magazine* April 21 1974 30–9.

● 'Sky and Space artists' manifesto'– in – *Otto Piene und das CAVS* (Karlsruhe, Badischer Kunstverein, 1988) 36–7.

● D Hardy *Images in space* (Limpsfield, Surrey, Dragon's World, 1989).

608 | **SPACE STRUCTURE WORKSHOP**

A British group based in London founded in 1968 as the culmination of ideas that had been developing from the early 1960s. Members included Maurice Agis, Peter Jones and Terry Scales. SSW was concerned with collaborations with industry, staging public events and providing environments using air structures with the aim of integrating space, colour and sound. By providing alternative aesthetic experiences, SSW hoped to liberate the senses of the public, to heighten their awareness of a dehumanized urban environment and thus stimulate social and political change. SSW was active in Britain and Holland during the late '60s and early '70s.

● See also Air Art, Community Art & Media, Environmental Art, Political Art.

● 'Spaceplace: selections from the notes of Agis, Jones, Marigold and Pitt' *Studio International* **183** (940) January 1972 34–7.

609 | **SPADEM**

(Société de la Propriété Artistique et Dessins et Modèles.) A non-profit-making organization founded in France in 1954 in order to negotiate, authorize and recover copyright fees on behalf of artists, designers and photographers. It is managed by a committee made up of artists and artists' agents and its aims are to defend visual artists' legal and economic rights. By the 1980s SPADEM represented over 30,000 artists through a network of sister societies in more than 20 countries. In Britain DACS – Design and Artists Copyright Society – formed in 1983 fulfils the same function as SPADEM.

610 | **SPATIALISM**

(Also Movimento Spaziale, Spazialismo) An aesthetic doctrine associated with the Argentine-Italian artist Lucio Fontana (1899–1968) first expounded in his

SPATIALISM LUCIO FONTANA in his studio with 'slit' canvases called 'Attese'. (1962?). Photo: Ugo Mulas, Milan, courtesy of Gimpel-Hanover Gallerie, Zürich.

'Manifesto blanco' of 1946.

Fontana advocated a radical break with the past: he thought artists should embrace modern technology such as neon light and television in order to project colour into real space. He wanted to end the separation of architecture, painting and sculpture by synthesizing all physical elements – colour, sound, space, motion and time – into a new kind of total art. Fontana had been trained as a sculptor and this encouraged him to introduce literal space – as opposed to depicted space – into his canvases by means of holes and slits. He also introduced relief elements so that cast shadows would be created.

During the 1950s he became interested in matter art and added pebbles, glass and other foreign materials to the painted surface. At the same time he evolved a form of environmental art making use of ultraviolet and neon light in black-painted rooms. 1951–2 seems to have been the climax of the Spatialist movement; some other artists who participated were Roberto Crippa, Enrico Donati and Ettore Sottsass.

● See also Concrete Poetry, Environmental Art, Light Art, Matter Art, Total Art/Design.

◉ A Pica *Fontana e lo Spazialismo* (Venice, Edizioni Cavallino, 1953).

◉ G Giana *Spazialismo...* (Milan, Edizioni Conchiglia, 1956).

◉ G Balla *Lucio Fontana* (Pall Mall Press, 1971).

◉ *Lucio Fontana* (Milan, Palazzo Reale, 1972).

◉ E Crispolti *Lucio Fontana* catalogue raisonné, 2 vols (Milan, 1986).

◉ B Blistène (ed) *Lucio Fontana* (Paris, Centre Pompidou, 1987).

◉ *Fontana* (Whitechapel Art Gallery, 1988).

611 SPATIO-DYNAMISM

A form of kinetic art practised from 1948 onwards by the Hungarian/School of Paris artist Nicolas Schöffer, whose work continued the space/motion/light tradition established by László Moholy-Nagy. Schöffer's vertical metal and plexiglass towers of the early 1960s were electronically guided mobiles or robots. Light was reflected from highly polished surfaces and the spectacle of their movement was accompanied by tape recordings of urban sounds. Like most kinetic artists, Schöffer believed in the fruitful co-operation of art and science; he made use of the vocabulary of science when he called his towers 'cybernetic'. He also coined the term 'luminodynamism' to express the idea of a union of light and motion.

● See also Kinetic Art, Light Art, Sound Art.

◉ J Ernest 'Nicolas Schöffer' *Architectural Design* **30** (12) December 1960 517–20.

◉ M Joray (ed) *Nicolas Schöffer* (Neuchâtel, Éditions du Griffon, 1963).

◉ N Schöffer *La ville cybernetique* (Paris, Tchou, 1969).

◉ —*Le nouvel esprit artistique* (Paris, Gonthier, 1970).

612 SPITTING IMAGE

Title of a popular comedy series transmitted on ITV television in Britain from 1984 onwards. John Lloyd was the producer of the programmes for Central Television in Birmingham. (A series also appeared on NBC TV in the USA in 1986.) In terms of content the programmes were savagely critical and anti-establishment. The characters – politicians, members of the British Royal Family, film and pop music stars, TV personalities and so on – satirized in the programmes were animated puppets made from foam or latex rubber. They were devised and made by a team of designers headed by Peter Fluck and Roger Law who had previously studied commercial art together at Cambridge School of Art in the late 1950s. *Spitting Image* was a brilliant development of the ancient art of caricature, an extension of that art into three dimensions, movement and the medium of television. An exhibition of the puppets was held at the Norwich School of Art in June 1985.

● See also Media Art, Political Art.

◉ I Starsmore 'Bodies politic' *Crafts* (65) November – December 1983 22–7.

◉ D MacPherson 'Cruel to be cruel' *The Face* (57) January 1985 32–7.

◉ J Lloyd & others *The Spitting Image book (The appallingly disrespectful Spitting Image book)* (Faber & Faber, 1985).

◉ I Starsmore *Spitting Image* (Norwich School of Art, 1985), broadsheet.

◉ L Chester *Tooth & claw: the inside story of Spitting Image* (Faber & Faber, 1986).

613 SPUR

The German word 'Spur' means 'trace' or 'trail'. Gruppe Spur was founded in Munich in 1957 by the sculptor Lothar Fischer and the painters Heimrad Prem, Josef Senft (J. Hohburg), Helmut Sturm and Hans Peter Zimmer. Other artists joined later. They favoured the collective, non-competitive production of art and organized several mixed exhibitions in the late '50s and early '60s. A radical group, it was in certain respects an outpost of the Situationist International. Spur's views on art and society were highly political and critical: 'Art is the dung heap upon which kitsch grows...we demand kitsch, dirt, primaeval slime, the desert'. A Spur text called 'Spur im Exil' provoked a Munich court case on the grounds of pornography and blasphemy. Between 1960 and '62 the group published a magazine *Spur,* with funds supplied by Asger Jorn, featuring aggressive graphics and articles on 'unitary urbanism'. Spur disbanded in 1965.

● See also CoBrA, Kitsch, Situationists.

○ *Spur* 1–7 (Munich, 1960–2).

○ J Roh *Deutsche Kunst der 60er Jahre: Malerei, Collage, Op Art, Graphik* (Munich, Bruckmann, 1971).

○ V Loers (ed) *Gruppe Spur 1958–65* (Regensberg, Stadtische Galerie, 1986).

○ H Platschek 'Einer der Ungern Nachgibt' *ART: Das Kunst-magazin* part 11, November 1987 62–74.

614 STAGED PHOTOGRAPHY

(Also Congealed Theatre, Constructed Photography, Photofictions, Simulated Realities, Tableau Photography) The medium of photography has the reputation of being able to record reality truthfully, objectively, but since scenes and events can be invented specially for the camera, what it records can be fictional situations. (This is especially obvious in the case of advertising photographs.) In the 1970s and '80s many contemporary artists and photographers deliberately staged narrative tableaux, or still lifes, or 'self'-portraits involving disguises, for the purpose of making photographs. The American Les Krims, for instance, delighted in shooting bizarre and humorous situations; he also enjoyed producing fake murder scenes in emulation of police crime photos. Cindy Sherman generated a series of images of herself playing the roles of women in imitation of Hollywood film stills. Other Americans involved in this kind of work were William Wegman, Barbara Kasten, James Casebere, Joyce Neimanas, Ralph Eugene Meatyard, Joel-Peter Witkin and Laurie Simmons.

Three British practitioners working within the fine art context were Boyd Webb, Calum Colvin and Ron O'Donnell. In the Netherlands Staged Photography proved popular during the '80s especially in Rotterdam. Ger van Elk was a pioneer. Other Dutch practitioners included: Teun Hocks, Dominique Pelletey, Henk Tas and Rommert Boonstra.

As Ralph Hughes points out, in contrast to manipulated images, the staged photo 'keeps the integrity of the print which, as a photograph, conveys a persuasive reality as well as having a rationally appreciated falsity'.

● See also Installation, Photo-Therapy, Photo-Works, Scenography, Simulation/Simulacra/Hyperreality, Tableau.

○ E Dines *Anxious interiors: an exhibition of Tableau Photography and sculpture* (Laguna Beach, California, Laguna Beach Museum of Art, 1984).

○ P Ter Hofstede (ed) *Fotografia Buffa: Staged photography in the Netherlands* (Groninger Museum, 1986).

○ A Hoy *Fabrications: staged, altered and appropriated photographs* (NY, Abbeville, 1987).

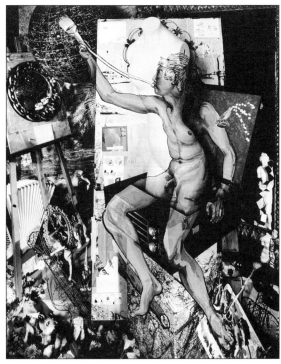

STAGED PHOTOGRAPHY CALUM COLVIN, 'Deaf man's villa' (1989). Cibachrome colour photograph, 96"x 77", central panel of a triptych, edition of 3. Photo: Salama-Caro Gallery, London.

○ *True stories and Photofictions* (Cardiff, Ffotogallery, 1987). R Hughes 'Photography...' *Alba* (Scotland) (9) 1988 26–30.

615 STAIN PAINTING

(Also New Aestheticism) In 1952 the American painter Helen Frankenthaler, inspired by Jackson Pollock's drip technique, devised a similar method of painting that involved soft stains or blots of pigment on unsized canvas. Two years later Morris Louis (1912–62) was in turn impressed by Frankenthaler's work and he adopted and developed the stain technique. The abstract paintings that he, Paul Jenkins, Kenneth Noland, Jules Olitski and others produced in the late 1950s and early 1960s made this method famous internationally.

Stain painters normally employed very diluted acrylic pigments, such as Magna, which they applied to unprimed, unstretched cotton duck canvas. The liquid paint was spilt, poured or flooded on to the surface. (In the case of Louis these facts are presumed since he was secretive about his working methods.) Olitski also applied paint with a spray gun and rollers. The unstretched canvas was sometimes folded or pleated to yield design variations. On completion the canvases were stretched and it was then the artists were faced with the problems of placement, i.e. relating 'image' to framing edge and shape of support. A characteristic of much

Stain Painting was the use of large areas of blank canvas to offset the zones of colour. Diluted paints soaked into the canvas so that the results resembled dyed fabrics rather than traditional oil paintings. In some of Louis' works successive washes of paint combined to produce translucent veils of colour which achieved a merger of figure and ground.

To an extent the method was automatic. Art critics claimed that certain 'advantages' followed from this: since no hand or arm movements were involved the painter was freed from the linear quality of drawing and the whole tradition of painting with brushes; since the stained areas of paint existed as pure colour the problem of tonal modulation was overcome; since the paintings were a record of the process by which they were made, they exemplified the unity of pictorial structure and mode of production.

Opinions as to the merits of Stain Paintings varied. Some critics thought they were extremely seductive to the eye (hence the 'new aestheticism' label), while others found their beauty 'cosmetic' and identified a lack of intellectual substance.

● See also Automatic Art, Colour-Field Painting, Drip Painting, Process Art, Washington Colour School.

M Fried *Morris Louis* (NY, Abrams, 1970).

B Rose *Frankenthaler* (NY, Abrams, 1971).

J Elderfield *Morris Louis* (Arts Council of Great Britain/Hayward Gallery, 1974).

616　STAMP ART

(Also Marginal Media, Rubber Stamp Art) A facet of mail art that developed in the 1950s and '60s, and expanded during the early '70s. The term does not refer, as one might expect, to the design of official postage stamps – though these are sometimes designed by artists of significance – but to unofficial stamps and rubber stamp images, emblems and slogans created by artists contributing to the international mail art network. Stamp Art appealed to concrete poets and to many of those taking part in Fluxus activities. Rubber stamps were easy and cheap to make and they could print images quickly and in large numbers. The creation of such devices was often regarded as a subversive gesture directed against the bureaucratic and official use of rubber stamps. Kurt Schwitters was considered the father figure of the movement because of his series of 'stamp drawings'. Other artists who have made stamps include Arman, Joseph Beuys, George Brecht, Ken Friedman, Ray Johnson, J. Kocman, Carol Law, Dieter Roth, Saul Steinberg, Ben Vautier and Emmett Williams. Many collections of Stamp Art by individuals and groups have been published in book or catalogue form. Hervé Fischer claims to have organized the first Stamp Art show in Paris in 1974. (He employed the term 'marginal communication'.) An international survey was also held at La Mamelle Arts Center, San Francisco, in April–May 1976.

● See also Concrete Poetry, Fluxus, Mail Art, Media Art, Postcard Art.

J Kocman *Stamp activity* (Brno, Czechoslovakia, Selbstverlag, 1972).

H Fischer *Art et communication marginale. Tampons d'artistes* (Paris, Éditions Andre Balland, 1974).

T Ulrichs 'Stempel, zur Kunst gestempelt' *Magazin Kunst* **15** (1) 1975 66–82.

J Brand & P van Beveren *Stempelboek* (Middleburg, Netherlands, Brummense Uitgeverij van Luxe Werkjes, 1975).

'International Rubber Stamp Exhibition: special catalog edition' *Front* (San Francisco) **1** (4) May 1976 (includes essay: 'The stamp and Stamp Art' by K Friedman & G Gugelberger).

H Fischer *Art et communication marginale 2* (Geneva, Écart, 1981).

617　STIL-MALEREI

(Also Stil-Bild, Style-Painting) A term devised by the German neo-expressionist painter Markus Lüpertz to characterize his own work of the 1970s. His art evolved through several phases: dithyrambic (1963–9), a wild or Dionysian process whereby abstract marks were transformed during the process of painting into forms with representational connotations; motiv-bild or motif painting (1969–75) in which motifs such as German military helmets served as forms, as an excuse for painting; and style-painting (1975–80s) in which the styles of other twentieth-century artists were treated as forms or motifs to be explored and transmuted.

● See also Neo-Expressionism, Post-Modern Art.

M Lüpertz *Dithyrambische Manifest* (Berlin, 1966).

Dithyrambische und Stil-Malerei (Berne, Kunsthalle, 1977).

S Gohr *Markus Lüpertz: 'Stil' paintings 1977–9* (Whitechapel Gallery, 1979).

Markus Lüpertz: Bilder 1970–83 (Hanover, Kestner Gesellschaft, 1983).

618　STOCKWELL DEPOT SCULPTORS

Roland Brener, David Evison, Roger Fagin, Gerard Hemsworth, Peter Hide, Roelof Louw, Alan Barkley and John Fowler: eight British sculptors who worked and exhibited in the late 1960s in a Victorian industrial building in South London called 'Stockwell Depot'. The artists were not a group in the sense of sharing a common aesthetic but their work did have two points of similarity: it was generally abstract and large in scale. Annual exhibitions were held throughout the '70s in which other artists, including some painters, participated. According to Peter Fuller, Stockwell sculpture was 'synonymous with third generation Caroism'.

● A Seymour *Stockwell Depot 2* (Stockwell Depot, 1969).

● —'London commentary: sculpture at Stockwell Depot' *Studio International* **178** (916) November 1969 173–4.

● P Fuller 'Stockwell Depot' (12th annual exhibition) *Art Monthly* (30) October 1979 14–17.

619 STORY ART

(Also Diaristic Art, Journalistic Art, Narrative Art, Post-Conceptual Theatre) A minor genre of avant garde art which appeared in the United States and Europe during the first half of the 1970s. The term itself derived from a show mounted by the John Gibson Gallery, New York in 1973. Story Art encompassed works by such artists as David Askevold, John Baldessari, Didier Bay, Bill Beckley, Robert Cumming, Peter Hutchinson, Jean le Gac, Italo Scanga, William Wegman and Roger Welch. These artists received critical support from the artist–critic James Collins. Story artists employed various media and mixes of media – photographs, drawings, texts, tape recordings, wooden models – to recount anecdotes and fantasies, to document their environments, and to record biographical and autobiographical histories.

According to Collins, Story Art was 'a breakaway tendency from the catholic wing of conceptual art' but unlike the latter its aim was to please and entertain. Story Art gave the impression of being lightweight, amateurish and escapist but the low-key, dead-pan approach was deliberate. It had an ironic, quirky character due in part to the presentation of humorous and trivial incidents in a high art context.

● See also Auto-Art, Conceptual Art, Narrative Figuration/Painting.

● J Collins 'Story...John Gibson Gallery' *Artforum* **12** (1) September 1973 83–7.

● R Pincus-Witten 'Theater of the conceptual: autobiography and myth' *Artforum* **12** (2) October 1973 40–6.

● J Collins 'Narrative 2' *Artforum* **13** (1) September 1974 75–6.

● *Narrative Art* (Brussels, Palais des Beaux Arts, 1974).

● B Radice 'Story Art' *Data* (16/17) July–August 1975 81–109.

● 'Narrative Art: photo & parole' *Domus* (555) February 1976 48–51.

● *American Narrative/Story Art* (Houston, Texas, Contemporary Arts Museum, 1978).

620 STREET ART

(Including Contact Art, Façade Art, Gable-End Art, Mural Art, Outdoor Art, Skyline Painting, Strassen Kunst, Streetworks, Town Painting) An extremely broad category encompassing the many different kinds of visual art that can be encountered in the streets, squares and vacant lots of towns and cities, e.g. mosaics, graffiti, murals, projected images and reliefs on the façades of buildings, static free-standing monumental sculptures and memorials made from stone and bronze or impermanent materials, pavement drawings, posters and other artworks on billboards, displays in shop windows, plus temporary live activities such as actions, busking, carnivals, dancing, festivals, games, happenings, music, performance, processions, and street theatre. All these works and activities can be further divided into two types: (1) those which are authorized and approved by the state or other official bodies; (2) those emanating from the will of artists who make use of the streets without the knowledge or approval of the authorities. Official statues and monuments generally encapsulate dominant ideologies, whereas unofficial streetworks are frequently critical of those ideologies.

Artists often place works of art in the public domain of the street because they want to reach a wider audience than that which attends art galleries. Also, the decision frequently implies a political intention or effect. The New York artist Tosun Bayrak, for instance, in 1971 made works with great shock-value and put them in the street in order to call attention to the social problems of the urban environment. Street Art as a form of political propaganda and mass spectacle can be traced back to the Festivals of the Supreme Being at the time of the French Revolution designed by the painter Jacques-Louis David. Similar activities took place in the wake of the Russian Revolution; the poet Vladimir Mayakovsky urged his fellow artists 'to make the streets our brushes, the squares our palette'.

● See also Actions, Alternative Arts, Billboard Art, Carnival, City Walls, Community Art & Media, Graffiti, Happenings, Los Angeles Fine Arts Squad, Performance Art, Projected Art, Public Art, SITE, Town Art/Artist.

● J Perreault 'Street works' *Arts Magazine* **44** (3) December–January 1969–70 18–20.

● J Thwaites 'Street Art one: Hanover' *Art & Artists* **5** (10) January 1971 10–15.

● G Wise 'Art on the street' *Studio International* **184** (948) October 1972 122–5.

● T Street-Porter 'Skyline Painting' *Design* (300) December 1973 56–9.

● D Kunzle 'Art in Chile's revolutionary process: guerrilla muralist brigades' *New World Review* **41** (3) 1973 42–53.

● A Seide 'Strassen Kunst fur wen?' *Magazin Kunst* **14** (1) 1974 33.

● R Sommer *Street Art* (NY, Links, 1975).

● G Oosterhof '"Town Painting", een bericht uit Rotterdam' *Museumjournaal* **21** (2) April 1976 64–7.

● L Lippard 'The geography of street time: a survey of Streetworks downtown' – in – *Get the message? A decade of art for social change* (NY, Dutton, 1984) 52–66.

● E Heartney 'Street scenes' (the work of Dennis Adams) *Art in America* **77** (4) April 1989 230–7, + 277.

● V Tolstoy & others (eds) *Street Art of the Revolution: festivals and celebrations in Russia 1918–33* (Thames & Hudson, 1990).

621 **STREET FASHION/ STYLE**

Two expressions which became extremely popular amongst designers and design journalists in the 1970s and '80s. The extent to which the clothes people wear and how they look is determined by themselves or by professional designers is problematical. The term 'Street Fashion' implies that what people wear on the street reflects their own creativity and individuality; hence Street Fashion (SF) was seen by Vivienne Westwood as an alternative to what she called 'Establishment Fashion' (EF). The word 'street' also occurs in 'high street fashion' but of course refers to mass-market, designed clothes sold via chainstores.

Some styles of dress do emerge to a significant extent from the grassroots (punk, for example) and even when clothes are bought readymade from shops, individual taste can still be manifested in the way the various items of attire are selected/combined. An influential magazine devoted initially to British Street Fashion was *i-D* (turned sideways the logo resembles a winking/smiling face, it also suggests 'identity') founded in 1981 by Terry Jones. Early issues of this magazine included many photographs of teenagers taken on the street who were not therefore fashion models wearing the latest collection of designer clothes. In fact, their clothes often derived from second-hand shops. The graphic design of *i-D* was also intended to evoke a cheap, amateur, spontaneous, energetic impression.

'Street Style' has been employed by the design historian Catherine McDermott as the title of a book about British youth culture and innovative, eccentric, anarchic design produced in the aftermath of punk. Her book surveyed the work of Simon Forbes, Ron Arad, Neville Brody, Barney Bubbles, Bodymap, The Cloth, Nigel Coates, Scott Crolla, Malcolm Garrett, Katherine Hamnett and others. Since most of these designers were trained in art and design colleges and operated as professional designers, the 'Street Style' label was, arguably, misleading.

● See also New Romantics, Punk, Zoot Suits.

● K Sampson & D Rimmer 'Ellesse...the ins and outs of high street fashion' *The Face* (39) July 1983 22–5.

● C McDermott *Street Style: British design in the '80s* (Design Council, 1987).

622 **STRUCTURAL/ MATERIALIST FILM**

A term devised by the filmmaker and theorist Peter Gidal in 1974 to describe his own work and that of other avant garde film-makers such as Hollis Frampton, Kurt Kren, Peter Kubelka, Malcolm LeGrice and Michael Snow. Earlier, in 1969, the adjective 'structural' had been applied to film in Britain by Gidal and in the United States by P. A. Sitney. According to the latter, 'the structural film insists on its shape, and what content it has is minimal and subsidiary to the outline...Four characteristics of the structural film are: a fixed camera position...the flicker effect, loop printing and rephotography off of a screen'. 'Elongation' was another characteristic identi-

STREET FASHION/ STYLE Double page spread of *iD* magazine (4) (1983?).

fied by Sitney. Gidal regarded Sitney's use of the term 'structural' as unsatisfactory, hence his efforts to substitute 'structural/materialist'. 'Structural' was a word used by minimal artists ('primary structures') and it also had overtones of the anthropological theory of structuralism. The word 'material' evoked both the physical nature of film (a 'truth to materials' aesthetic) and the Marxist notion of dialectical materialism.

Much avant garde art derives its polemical zeal from a distaste for mass culture/media. This was the case with S/M Film which repudiated the values, pleasures and visual conventions of the commercial cinema, i.e. illusionism, narrative, plot, stars, entertainment, and so forth. Instead it foregrounded the structural elements and the material character of film (duration – a piece of time – became the basic unit), and took as its subject matter the process of film-making itself. The self-imposed task of S/M Film was to deconstruct the nature of film by means of film in order to demystify it. S/M Film claimed to be reflexive: a cinema in which viewers watched themselves watching.

● See also Fundamental Painting, Marxist Aesthetics, Minimal Art, Process Art, Structuralism & Art/Design.

◉ P Sitney 'Structural film'– in – Film culture: an anthology P Sitney (ed) (Secker & Warburg, 1971) 326–49.

◉ P Gidal 'Definition and theory of the current avant garde: Materialist/Structural Film' Studio International **187** (963) February 1974 53–6.

◉—'Theory and definition of Structural/Materialist Film' Studio International **190** (978) November–December 1975 189–96.

◉—(ed) Structural film anthology (BFI, 1976).

◉ P Wollen '"Materialism" and "ontology" in film' Screen **17** (1) Spring 1976 7–23.

◉ A Cotringer 'Critique of Peter Gidal's theory and definition of Structural/Materialist Film' After/Image (6) Summer 1976 86–95.

◉ P Gidal Materialist film (Routledge, 1989).

623 STRUCTURALISM & ART/DESIGN

Structural anthropology – a discipline indebted to structural linguistics – treats human culture and social behaviour as if they were articulated like a language (with surface and deep structures). Hence it studies human kinship systems, myths, sign systems and so on, in order to reveal the hidden structures and the rules of transformation governing them. The doyen of Structuralism was the French scholar Claude Lévi-Strauss. His writings were extremely influential during the 1960s and '70s and, as the items listed below indicate, had a significant impact on theorists in the spheres of advertising, art, architecture, art history, fashion and popular culture.

● See also Semiotics.

◉ C Lévi-Strauss Structural anthropology (NY, Basic Books, 1963).

◉ A Moles 'Vasarely and the triumph of Structuralism' Form (UK) (7) March 1968 24–5.

◉ M Pleynet 'Peinture et "Structuralisme"' Art International **12** (9) November 20 1968 29–34.

◉ G Charbonnier Conversations with Claude Lévi-Strauss (Jonathan Cape, 1969).

◉ G Dorfles 'Structuralism and semiology in architecture' – in – Meaning in architecture C Jencks & G Baird (eds) (Barrie & Rockliff, 1969) 38–49.

◉ A Michelson 'Art and the Structuralist perspective' –in –On the future of art E Fry (ed) (NY, Viking Press, 1970) 37–59.

◉ S Nodelman 'Structural analysis in art and anthropology' – in – Structuralism J Ehrmann (ed) (NY, Doubleday, 1970) 7993.

◉ J Burnham The structure of art (NY, Braziller, 1971).

◉ P Heyer 'Art and the Structuralism of Claude Lévi-Strauss' The Structurist (12) 1972–3 32–7.

◉ R Barthes Mythologies (Jonathan Cape, 1972).

◉ P Bourdieu 'The Berber house' – in – Rules and meanings: the anthropology of everyday knowledge M Douglas (ed) (Harmondsworth, Penguin Books, 1973) 98–110.

◉ W Vazan & P Heyer 'Conceptual art..' Leonardo **7** (3) Summer 1974 201–5.

◉ V Leymore Hidden myth: structure and symbolism in advertising (Heinemann, 1975).

◉ E Leach 'Michelangelo's "Genesis": Structuralist comments on the Sistine Chapel ceiling' Times Literary Supplement March 18 1977 311–13.

◉ R Barthes The fashion system (Jonathan Cape, 1985).

◉ D Francis 'Advertising and Structuralism: the myth of formality' International Journal of Advertising **5** 1986 197–214.

624 STRUCTURISM

A theory and method of creation developed by the American artist Charles Biederman (author of Art as the evolution of visual knowledge (1948)). He coined the term in 1952 to describe his own work from the late 1930s onwards and in order to distinguish it from his earlier concept 'constructionism'. Biederman made brightly coloured abstract reliefs in an attempt to synthesize certain qualities of painting, sculpture and architecture. His reliefs came into being, he claimed, in accordance with the structural processes of nature.

Pre-1939 traditions of abstract art were continued in the post-1945 era by a number of other artists living in Europe and North America, all of whom admired Biederman. They included the English artist Anthony Hill who used the expression 'structural art' to characterize his own work; the Dutch artist Joost Baljeu, founder of the magazine Structure (1958–); and the Canadian artist

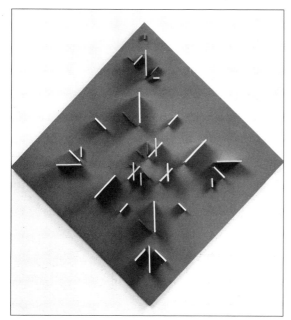

STRUCTURISM Charles Biederman, 'Work no 1, (4), NR' (1984-6). Painted aluminum 28"x 28"x 3". Photo: Grace Borgenenicht Gallery, New York.

Eli Bornstein who called his reliefs 'structurist' and who was the editor of an art annual entitled *The Structurist* (University of Saskatchewan, 1960–).

During the '60s American art critics also employed the labels 'structural' and 'structuralist' to refer to objects more generally known as minimal art. The reason for this was an exhibition of minimalism held in New York in 1966 entitled 'Primary Structures'.

● See also Constructionism, Minimal Art.

○ *Charles Biederman: the structurist relief 1935–64* (Minneapolis, Walker Art Center, 1965).

○ G Kepes (ed) *Structure in art and science* (Studio Vista, 1965).

○ E Bornstein 'Structurist art and creative integration' *Art International* **11** (4) April 20 1967 31–6.

○ A Hill (ed) *Data: directions in art, theory and aesthetics* (Faber & Faber, 1968).

○ E Bornstein 'Notes on Structurist vision' – in – *Canadian art today* W Townsend (ed) (Studio International, 1970) 52–6.

625 STYLING

A style is normally thought of as the visual expression of unconscious factors; however, the words 'styling' and 'stylization' imply a self-conscious process. Stylists are designers who deliberately create a new style or who exaggerate the typical characteristics of an existing style or who borrow styles indiscriminately in order to apply them to products for which they are unsuited. Realizing that all styles have a limited lifespan, they try to induce stylistic change and to accelerate the rate of stylistic turnover. One motive for this is the desire for the new; another is economic: if consumers can be persuaded that the style of their clothes or car is outmoded, then they will be induced to buy new products in the latest style even before the old ones have worn out (hence the expression 'consumer engineering'). The technique of 'artificial' or 'psychological obsolescence' was pioneered by the women's fashion industry and then adopted by the American automobile industry from the late 1920s onwards, in particular the annual model changes introduced by General Motors and their chief designer Harley Earl. 'Detroit Machiavellismus' was how the Germans expressed their distaste for this kind of American design.

Since stylists are primarily concerned with the look of products, their activities have been called 'shroud design' and criticized as 'superficial'. (It is easier to alter the external appearance of a product than to redesign it fundamentally.) Styling is despised by many designers and engineers because it contradicts the modernist principle 'form should follow function'. A striking example of the absurdity of styling was the application of aerodynamic streamlining to static products such as ashtrays. What had been functional for aircraft became non-functional for ashtrays. Streamlining is perhaps the best-known instance of styling in the history of design. Gifford Jackson has identified five different style changes in American product design since the 1920s: stepform, streamform, taperform, sheerform and sculptureform.

'Car styling' was one of the topics discussed at the Independent Group meetings at the ICA during the 1950s and the British pop artist Richard Hamilton later produced writings and paintings paying homage to the styling of American automobiles.

● See also Expendability in Design, Independent Group, Pop Art, Surface Design.

○ G Jackson 'Analysis – design styles and clichés' *Industrial Design* **9** (9) September 1962 59–67.

○ R Hamilton 'Urbane image' *Living Arts* (2) 1963 44–59.

STYLING Ford Motor Company, Detroit, Michigan. The ill-fated Edsel car, 1957-59.

● V Packard *The waste makers* (Harmondsworth, Penguin, 1963).

● R Nader *Unsafe at any speed. The designed in dangers of the American automobile* (NY, Grossman, 1965).

● J de Syllas 'Streamform...' *AAQ* **1** (2) April 1969 32–41.

● G Muller-Krauspe 'Design Ideologien 2: Styling – das Prinzip der Diskontinuität' *Form* (47) September 1969 31–5.

● K Plummer 'Streamlined moderne' *Art in America* **62** (1) January–February 1974 46–54.

● M Arceneaux *Streamline: art and design of the '40s* (San Francisco, Troubadour Press, 1975).

● D Bush *The streamlined decade* (NY, George Braziller, 1975).

● J McLellan *Bodies beautiful: a history of car styling and craftsmanship* (Newton Abbot, David & Charles, 1975).

● A Nahum 'Streamlining, function and style' *Studio International* **196** (1000) July 1983 52–5.

● J Tipler *The world's greatest automobile stylists* (Apple Press, 1990).

626 SUBCULTURE

A sociological term meaning any distinctive pattern of behaviour, set of values, beliefs and attitudes associated with a limited group of people living within a larger or dominant culture. Subcultures became a major field of academic research in Britain in the 1970s by staff and students of 'cultural studies' courses in British polytechnics and universities. Scholarly interest focused upon youth Subcultures (mainly, groups of male teenagers) because of their variety, intrinsic appeal and historical evolution. They are relevant to this text because of their visual or design/style aspects, i.e. each Subculture has a distinctive 'look', body language, clothes, hair-styles, mode of transportation (e.g. scooters or motorbikes) and musical tastes. From 1950 onwards Britain witnessed a sequence of youth Subcultures: Teddy Boys, Beats, Rockers, Mods, Hippies, Punks, Skinheads, Rockabillies, New Romantics, etc. Some of these occurred in the United States too. Certain groups, like the Hell's Angels, persist for decades and others, like the Rudies and Rastas, are specific to the children of black immigrant minorities. In the view of some theorists, the political significance of Subcultural styles is that they are a form of 'resistance through ritual', a symbolic or magical way subordinate groups have evolved to compensate for their lack of status and power in society.

Although members of a Subculture can and do contribute to the invention of a style, there are also usually tastemakers and specialist shops and professional designers who supply particular fashion commodities – clothes, jewellery, etc. Furthermore, Subcultural styles are often exploited and recuperated by the fashion industry, i.e. imitated and watered down for wider consumption.

● See also New Romantics, Punk, Street Fashion/Style, Styling.

● S Hall & T Jefferson (eds) *Resistance through ritual: youth Subcultures in post-war Britain* (Hutchinson, 1976).

● D Hebdige *Subculture: the meaning of style* (Methuen, 1979).

● P York *Style wars* (Sidgwick & Jackson, 1980).

● M Brake *Comparative youth cultures* (Routledge & Kegan Paul, 1985).

● H Rees *14–24: British youth culture* (The Boilerhouse/Victoria & Albert Museum, 1986).

627 SUBTOPIA

This word is a combination of 'suburb' and 'utopia' and means 'making an ideal of suburbia...visually speaking, the universalization and idealization of our town fringes...philosophically, the idealization of the Little Man who lives there'. It was coined in the mid 1950s by the architectural writer Ian Nairn who was upset by the blurring of the identities of town and country: 'a witless chaos – a dumping down of every kind of man-made object, urban, suburban and subrural with no relationship to each other or to the site...a desert of wire, concrete roads, cosy plots and bungalows'. The attack on Subtopia mounted by Nairn and the *Architectural Review* had the character of a moral crusade. In the United States the similar word 'slurb' was coined, i.e. a combination of 'slum' and 'suburb'.

● See also SLOAP, Suburban Art, Suburbia.

● I Nairn *Outrage* (Architectural Press, 1955).

● — *Counter attack against Subtopia* (Architectural Press, 1959).

● — *Your England revisited* (Hutchinson, 1964).

'Public opinion versus "Slurb"' *Design* (232) April 1968 24.

628 SUBURBAN ART

A term used by Susan Freudenheim in 1987 to characterize the work of such American artists as Eric Fischl, Cheryl Laemmie and Nic Nicosia. She regarded them as the heirs of Edward Hopper; they were 'suburban' artists because their work focused upon the interior life considered typical of the suburbs. An exhibition presenting a spectrum of artistic responses to the American suburb was held at the Whitney Museum of American Art, Fairfield County, Stamford, Connecticut in 1989. It included paintings by Fischl and Robert Bechtle, photographs by Diane Arbus, Laurie Simmons, Stephen Shore and Judy Dater, sculpture by Duane Hanson, videos by Dan Graham and Todd Haynes, feature films

1987 134–40.

M Kwon, S Bayliss & C Hoover (essays by) *Suburban home life: tracking the American dream* (Stamford, Connecticut, Whitney Museum of American Art, 1989).

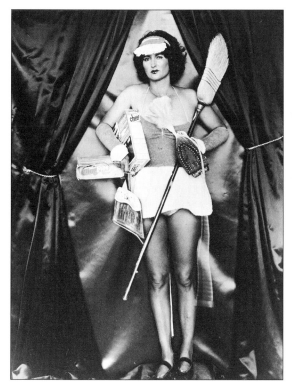

SUBURBAN ART JUDY DATER, 'Ms Clingfree' (1982). Colour Photograph 24" x 20". Photo: the artist and Whitney Museum of American Art, Fairfield County, Stamford.

by Tobe Hooper and George Romero, and material about suburban architecture. In terms of painting the mode of representation best suited to capturing the banality and detail of suburbia was probably photo-realism. Suburbia has come to exemplify a set of middle-class values: a highly conventional lifestyle in which man is the provider and woman the housewife, a calm safe environment, a private home within which resides a happy nuclear family. The consequence has been that fears, anxieties and tensions between people have been repressed. For this reason certain male American film directors have regarded suburbia as the ideal locale for violent horror movies. Women artists, on the other hand, have generally preferred to undertake a critique of the roles women are expected to play in suburbia. Exceptionally, the movie 'Suburbia' (1983), directed by Penelope Spheeris, focused on the plight of a group of teenagers at odds with suburban society.

In Britain scenes of suburbia frequently appear at the Royal Academy's summer exhibition. Carel Weight, a British painter and Royal Academician, recorded the minor incidents and scenes of London's suburban streets and gardens for several decades.

● See also Hobby Art, Metro-land, Photo-Realism, Subtopia, Suburbia.

S Freudenheim 'Suburban hamlets' *Artforum* **25** (9) May

629 SUBURBIA

According to Arthur Edwards, 'Suburbia' is 'a dirty word' indicative of everything dull and hideous. Suburbs – the low-rise residential districts encircling the cores of major cities – have their origins in ancient times but their growth was particularly marked in the nineteenth and twentieth centuries as a result of the development of railways and motor cars which enabled millions to live a long way from their workplaces. Suburbs provide their populations with a predominantly middle-class, commuter lifestyle that attempts to combine the advantages of the urban with those of the rural. 'Suburbia' refers to the totality of suburbs and the suburban ideal or way of life. Cosmopolitans normally consider the latter to be anti-intellectual, conformist and conventional but the suburbs can be places where eccentricity flourishes.

Suburban houses also have their defenders amongst architectural historians even though most of the housing making up Suburbia consists of private estates designed by spec builders or council estates designed by local authority architects. Objections to suburbs have been listed by Edwards as follows: they are socially sterile and lack neighbourliness; they are wasteful of space and of time for commuters and shoppers; they are weak in terms of scale and spatial design; town and country are different – it is worth preserving the contrast – consequently they should not be fused into a hybrid.

Robert Fishman, an American writer, has argued that in recent times a decentralization of businesses (particularly new high-tech companies) from city centres to peripheries has occurred which has resulted in what he terms 'technoburbs' such as Silicon Valley in California. Another reason for Fishman's invention of this neologism was the fact that more and more office workers resident in the suburbs work at home using computers, fax machines and so on to keep in touch with co-workers and head office.

● See also High-Tech, Metro-land, Subtopia, Suburban Art.

L Masotti & J Hadden (eds) *The urbanization of the suburbs* (Sage Publications, 1973).

J Richards *The castles on the ground: the anatomy of Suburbia* (John Murray, 2nd ed 1973).

D Thorns *Suburbia* (Paladin, 1973).

A Edwards *The design of Suburbia: a critical study in environmental history* (Pembridge Press, 1981).

P Oliver & others *Dunroamin: the suburban semi and its enemies* (Barrie & Jenkins, 1981).

R Stern (ed) *The Anglo American suburb* (Architectural Design profile, 1981).

F Thompson (ed) *The rise of Suburbia* (Leicester University Press, 1981).

H Barrett & T Phillips *Suburban style: the British home 1840–1960* (MacDonald, 1987).

R Fishman *Bourgeois utopias: the rise and fall of Suburbia* (NY, Basic Books, 1987).

J Stilgoe *Borderland: origins of the American suburb 1820–1939* (New Haven & London, Yale University Press, 1989).

630 SUPERGRAPHICS

A new type of environmental design which appeared in Western countries from 1966 onwards. The invention of Supergraphics has been credited to Charles Moore and Barbara Stauffacher while working on the West Coast of the United States. Supergraphics were akin to fine art in that they dispensed with the communication of direct information; they were generally abstract designs covering internal walls, ceilings and exteriors of shops, offices, restaurants and homes. They were huge in scale and made use of vivid, rainbow colours. Supergraphics were a form of decoration providing a cheap means of enlivening dull architecture.

● See also Environmental Design, Street Art, Supermannerism.

C Ray Smith 'Supergraphics' (Charles Moore) *Progressive Architecture* November 1967 132–7.

C Bouyeure 'Le Supergraphisme' *Jardin des Arts* (198) May 1971 70–1.

T Albright 'Visuals' *Rolling Stone* (93) October 14 1971 39–40.

I Wiegrand 'Painted walls' *Graphis* **28** (163) 1972–3 388–97.

'Supergraphics' *Art Directions* **25** (12) March 1974 56–8.

631 SUPERHUMANISM

A slightly tongue-in-cheek term invented by the British art dealer Nicholas Treadwell in 1980 to characterize the work of many of his stable of painters and sculptors. Assiduously promoted at art fairs, this type of art was invariably figurative because it was 'an art about people...living the ordinary life of an urban society'. The favourite mode of pictorial representation was a slick, photographic illusionism. According to Treadwell, Superhumanism was a 'mongrel art movement' because it was the result of interbreeding by earlier movements such as symbolism, surrealism, abstraction and pop art.

Individual pieces were often erotic, eccentric and humorous. One of the best artists represented by Treadwell in 1989 was Lloyd Gibson, a specialist in wall sculptures of poignant figures.

● See also Art Fairs, Figurative Art, Humanist Art, Naive Art, Photo-Realism, Popular Art, Verist Sculpture.

N Treadwell & M Shepherd *Superhumanism: a British art movement* (Nicholas Treadwell Books, 1980).

632 SUPERMANNERISM

A trend in American interior design and decoration of the late 1960s identified by *Progressive Architecture* magazine. Supermannerism or 'mega-decoration' opposed tasteful design. It was characterized by largeness, the use of transparent, reflective, synthetic materials, and perverse trickery both optical and intellectual. As the term indicated, the resulting style was mannerist; by including the name 'Superman' the term also revealed popular culture as a major source of inspiration. During the 1970s the label was extended to encompass certain architecture of the post-modern era.

● See also Post-Modern Architecture, Supergraphics.

'Revolution in interior design: the bold new poly expanded mega-decoration' *Progressive Architecture* (10) October 1968 148–208.

C Ray Smith *Supermannerism: new attitudes in post-modern architecture* (NY, Dutton, 1977).

633 SUPERSENSUALISTS

In the early 1970s architectural and design journalists described a number of European designers and groups – Gae Aulenti, Ettore Sottsass, Hans Hollein, Archizoom, Haus-Rucker-Co, Superstudio – as 'Supersensualists' because their work from 1960 onwards manifested a common approach to design characterized, according to Charles Jencks, by extravagant sensuality, metaphysical angst, beauty, advanced technology and, piquantly enough, Marxism. Many of the designers created fantasy worlds in which ideas were taken to extreme conclusions. Their actual commissions – provided by the urban middle class – were usually for furniture and the interior design of boutiques, apartments and restaurants. Supersensualism was particularly marked in the case of Italian designers who were also dubbed the 'Dolce Vita School' because their approach to aesthetics echoed the permissiveness of the characters in Fellini's famous film.

● See also Archizoom, Haus-Rucker-Co, Italian Craze, Superstudio.

C Jencks 'The Supersensualists' *Architectural Design* **XLI** June 1971 345–7.

—'The Supersensualists Part II' *Architectural Design* **XLII**

January 1972 18–21.

634   **SUPERSTUDIO**

An Italian experimental architecture and design group formed in 1966 and based in Florence. Members included: Adolfo Natalini, Cristiano Toraldo di Francia, Piero Frassinelli, Alessandro and Roberto Magris. Superstudio specialized in extravagant, futuristic conceptions, e.g. the anti-functional, visionary project called 'continuous monument' intended to span the globe; spaceship cities; continuous production/conveyor belt cities; and so forth. Members of Superstudio and the similar group Archizoom were called 'supersensualists' and their work was variously described as 'conceptual', 'alternative' and 'radical'. Images of their projects were regularly featured in magazines such as *Domus, Casabella,* and *Architectural Design.*

● See also Conceptual Architecture, Italian Craze, Radical Design, Supersensualists.

◉ 9999 & Superstudio *S-Space: life, death and miracles of architecture* (Florence, Separate School for Expanded Conceptual Architecture, 1971).

◉ G Pettena *Superstudio 1966–82: storie, figure, architettura* (Florence, Electa Editrice, 1982).

SUPPORTS/SURFACES LOUIS CANE, 'Painting' (1972). 243cm x 243 cm (wall), 202cm x 185cm (floor). Private Collection, Paris.

635   **SUPPORTS/ SURFACES**

In the period of cultural change which followed the revolutionary events of May 1968 in France, a number of French painters began to rethink their practice and established a group entitled 'Supports/Surfaces' which had its first show in Paris in 1970. Founder members included Vincent Bioules, Louis Cane, Marc Devade, Daniel Dezeuze and Claude Viallat, but by 1973 only Cane and Devade remained of the original membership. S/S wished to make a break with the linear sequence of avant garde movements by re-evaluating the history of modern painting since Cézanne with particular reference to the work of Matisse. As well as making paintings, the artists engaged in theoretical work. They were influenced by the writings of the poet and critic Marcelin Pleynet on painting and by other fashionable theories: linguistics, Marxism, structuralism and psychoanalysis. To provide an outlet for their writings they founded, in 1971, the journal *Peinture, Cahiers Théoriques.*

S/S's restitution of the art object (painted canvas) marked a reaction against the conceptual art of the late 1960s and the tendency for politically conscious artists to substitute actions, performances, etc. for making works of art. However, what was surprising about the paintings of the group was that they contained no explicit political subject matter. In sharp contrast to the intricate and sophisticated theory of their writings, the paintings were large, plain abstractions concerned with colour and process very much in the manner of the American stain painting. As far as S/S were concerned, the 'signifying practice' of painting was only one part of a threefold programme also consisting of ideological struggle and theoretical practice. S/S artists were criticized by J-L. Perrier on the grounds that their understanding of Marxist–Leninist theory was superficial and that they made paintings based on the bourgeois notion of classless art.

● See also Fundamental Painting, Political Art, Stain Painting.

◉ *Supports/Surfaces* (Paris, Musée d'Art Moderne de la Ville de Paris (ARC), 1970).

◉ M Pleynet 'Support/Surface' *Art International* **14** (10) December 1970 63, 70.

◉ —*L'enseignement de la peinture* (Paris, Éditions du Seuil, 1971).

◉ 'Supports/Surface' *VH 101* (5) Spring 1971.

◉ J-L Perrier 'Un château dans les nuages' *VH 101* (6) Summer 1972 38–44.

◉ 'Extracts from *Peinture, Cahiers Théoriques*' *Studio International* **185** (953) March 1973 110–11.

◉ M Devade & L Cane 'The avant garde today' *Studio International* **186** (959) October 1973 145–6.

◉ L Cane 'Marc Devade plongé dans la couleur' *Art Press* (9) February 1974 12–13.

◉ M Devade 'Painting and its double' *Tracks* **2** (2) Spring 1976

50–65.

● J-L Pradel 'La strategie de Supports/Surfaces' *Opus International* (61/62) January–February 1977 63–7.

● P Rogers 'Contemporary painting in France' *Artscribe* (13) August 1978 22–8.

● — 'Towards a theory/practice of painting in France' *Artforum* **17** (8) April 1979 54–61.

636 SURFACE DESIGN

A term used in the United States to encompass the various kinds of two-dimensional design typical of the decorative and applied arts, e.g. the designs and patterns adorning dress and furnishing fabrics, textiles, ceramics and walls. In 1977 a national, non-profit-making organization – the Surface Design Association – was established 'dedicated to the promotion, communication and education of Surface Design'. Its membership included independent studio artists, designers for industry and people involved in design education. The SDA mounted regional meetings and national conferences. It also established regional slide banks, a newsletter and a full-colour quarterly entitled the *Surface Design Journal.*

● See also Pattern Painting.

637 SURVIVAL RESEARCH LABORATORIES (SRL)

An American artists' collective based in the San Francisco area specializing in 'spectacular mechanical presentations'. Mark Pauline is the founder and director; he has been assisted by Matthew Heckart and Eric Werner plus numerous volunteers. SRL began staging their events in the late 1970s at the time of punk. The name of the collective derived from an advert for a survivalist organization in a magazine for mercenaries. Part of their aim was to mimic such extremist paramilitary groups, while simultaneously emphasizing their destructiveness by mounting outdoor shows with home-made weapons, animal corpses, radio-controlled mobile robots and bombs that shower the audience with leaflets. SRL favour useless destruction rather than 'useful' destruction. Their manic machines and grotesque events normally provoke a mixture of amazement and fear. They have often been banned or censored. In 1988 SRL made a tour of Europe; their work tends to be disseminated via magazines (such as *Re/Search*) and video recordings (directed by Jonathan Reiss) rather than via conventional art galleries. SRL have also appeared on news broadcasts, produced work for Hollywood films and for Music Television. Critics have detected the influence of stock-car racing, horror movies, the Destruction in Art movement of the 1960s, and seen an affinity with heavy metal pop music stage performances. The activities of SRL have also been characterized as 'industrial culture' and 'post-industrial romanticism'.

● See also Destructive Art, Happenings, Media Art, Mutoid Waste Co, Performance Art, Political Art, Punk, Robot Art.

● 'Mark Pauline' *Re/Search* (6/7) 1983 20–41 (Industrial Culture Handbook issue).

● M Kelley 'Mekaník Destruktïv Kommandöh: Survival Research Laboratories and popular spectacle' *Parkett* (21) 1989 122–9.

638 SUSPENDED PAINTINGS

Canvases without stretchers hung from walls or ceilings at various points and then draped, pleated or twisted to create three-dimensional forms. (The results somewhat resembled curtains or washing hanging on a line.) An American artist particularly noted for this type of work during the late 1960s was Sam Gilliam. His paintings were extremely colourful and decorative because they were abstractions produced by dripping and staining canvas with fluid acrylic pigments. The idea of suspending canvases appeared to combine three tendencies of '60s art, namely anti-form, stain painting and process art. Several other artists made use of this display tactic, e.g. Robert Ryman, Phillip Lewis, David Stephens and Derek Southall.

● See also Anti-Form, Process Art, Shaped Canvas, Stain Painting.

● J Applegate 'Paris Letter' *Art International* **15** (1) January 20 1971 33.

● G Jones 'Paintings on unstretched canvas' *Leonardo* **5** (4) Autumn 1972 337–8.

639 SYMBOLIC ARCHITECTURE

A term employed by the American-born architectural writer Charles Jencks in 1985 in relation to the redesign/decoration of the façades, interiors, fixtures and furniture of three of his own properties which he undertook between 1978 and 1985. Jencks was assisted by the architects Terry Farrell, Michael Graves and Piers Gough, and by the all-purpose material MDF (medium density fibreboard). The artist Eduardo Paolozzi also contributed a mosaic. Symbolic Architecture was a facet of post-modernism. It marked a return to pre-modern ways of conceiving of architecture as forms, structures and ornament personifying ideas and representing cultural systems such as astrology, as against merely performing practical functions. For instance, in Jencks' West London Victorian villa (dubbed 'The Thematic House') the design was determined by two major themes: cosmic time and cultural time. The ground floor

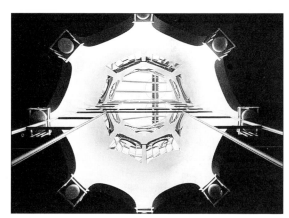

SYMBOLIC ARCHITECTURE CHARLES JENCKS, 'Interior view of the Thematic House, Lansdowne Walk, West London: the Moonwell with its real and virtual phases of the moon' (1984). Photo: Charles Jencks.

rooms were refurbished to symbolize the four seasons while the spiral stairs formed a symbolic calendar (with 52 steps). Visual jokes and puns abounded: e.g. a window seat made out of framed glass. Farrell also indulged in symbolism when he incorporated a series of egg-cups on the roof of the TV-AM building in Camden Town, i.e. a breakfast-time television station.

● See also Analogical Architecture, Cosmic Architecture, Figurative Architecture, Post-Modern Architecture.

○ C Jencks *Towards a Symbolic Architecture* (Academy Editions, 1985).

○ D Sudjic 'No place like home' *Sunday Times Magazine* November 17 1985 52–7.

640 SYN

(Also Groupe Syn) Name of a German group founded in 1965. 'Syn' was a Greek word for 'together'. Members included Erwin Bechtold, Bernd Berner, Rolf-Gunter Dienst, Klaus Jürgen-Fischer and Eduard Micus. Earlier, in 1963, Jürgen-Fischer had published a manifesto entitled 'Was ist komplexe Malerei?' which formed the theoretical basis of Groupe Syn. He also edited a journal entitled *Syn*. The artists of this group were abstractionists but they rejected both geometric and gestural kinds of painting and espoused instead a form of modern classicism based on 'pure plastic principles'.

○ K Jürgen-Fischer 'Thoughts on the idea of complex painting and sculpture' *Syn* (1) 1965 38–44.

○ *Syn: Bechtold, Berner...* (Weisbaden, Nassauischer Kunstverein, 1967).

○ M Fath *Groupe Syn* (Kassel, Kunstverein, 1969).

641 SYNERGETICS

The culminating concept of R. Buckminster Fuller's design philosophy. The word 'synergy' means 'combined action'; 'synergetic' means 'working together'. Fuller (1895–1983) argued that the universe was a total system whose behaviour could not be predicted by considering any part in isolation, hence the need for a holistic approach to decision-making. Fuller's concept was similar to that of gestalt psychologists who emphasized that the whole was greater than the sum of its parts.

● See also Dymaxion.

○ R Buckminster Fuller *Synergetics: explorations in the geometry of thinking* (Collier-macMillan, 1975).

○ A MacKay 'Spaceships to Xanadu' *Architectural Design* **46** (4) April 1976 197–8.

○ K Critchlow 'R Buckminster Fuller' *Architectural Review* **46** (5) May 1976 296–7.

○ R Buckminster Fuller & E Applewhite *A Synergetics dictionary* 2 vols (NY, Garland, 1989).

642 SYSTEMIC PAINTING

An aspect of post-painterly abstraction defined by Lawrence Alloway in an exhibition held in New York in 1966. On display were works by 28 American artists including Kenneth Noland, Ellsworth Kelly, Larry Poons, Al Held, Frank Stella and Paul Feeley. A number of these artists employed a given pictorial device – chevron, cross, quatrefoil – again and again in a series of canvases. (Alloway also suggested the label 'one-image art'.) However, the images were subject to transformations of colour and variations of form from canvas to canvas and therefore required to be read in time as well as space. Viewers were invited to seek 'variety within conspicuous unity'. According to the curator, the sequence of any particular image constituted a system – 'a whole composed of parts in orderly arrangement according to some scheme or plan' – hence the term 'Systemic'. The category was extended to encompass works consisting of a single field of colour, or to groups of such works, and also to paintings based on modules. Repetition of motifs was also characteristic of much pop art of the '60s; consequently the silk-screenprinted canvases of Andy Warhol showed close affinities with Systemic paintings. The fact that Alloway's essay was later reprinted in an anthology devoted to minimal art indicated that Systemic Painting was viewed as part of the minimal movement of the '60s.

● See also Minimal Art, Modular Art, Pop Art, Post-Painterly Abstraction, Serial Art.

○ L Alloway *Systemic Painting* (NY, Guggenheim Museum, 1966).

○ —'Background to Systemic' *Art News* **65** (6) October 1966 30–3.

○ R Pincus-Witten '"Systemic Painting"' *Artforum* **5** (3) November 1966 42–5.

● L Alloway 'Systemic Painting' – in – *Minimal art* G Battcock (ed) (Studio Vista, 1969) 37-60.

643 SYSTEMS ARCHITECTURE

(Also Performance Design) In relation to architectural design, the word 'systems' has three possible meanings (listed here in increasing order of complexity): (1) system building, i.e. designing a range of components to be pre-fabricated in factories and combined on site in various ways to generate different types of structure; (2) systems analysis, i.e. problem-solving by means of rigorous analysis and the use of logical procedures (useful in respect of the supply of materials and in the construction process, also essential as a preliminary to computerization); (3) architecture conceived as a system within larger systems, i.e. individual buildings perceived as parts of urban complexes, architecture perceived as a subsystem of cultural and social systems. In 1967 the American journal *Progressive Architecture* devoted a special issue to the topic of systems. The editors proposed the term 'performance design': 'design based on a scientific method of analysing functional requirements, including the psychological and aesthetic needs of people'.

In the 1960s, when design methods were fashionable, systems analysis appealed to many architects despite its technocratic and scientistic overtones. However, in the following decade it became somewhat discredited because it had not yielded all the benefits promised. Nevertheless, systems analysis has become one of the tools used by architects, and systems analysts are now employed to support the work of architects and town planners involved in large-scale urban redevelopment projects.

● See also Computer-Aided Design, Contextual Architecture, Design Methods.

● 'Performance Design' *Progressive Architecture* August 1967.

● B Handler *Systems approach to architecture* (NY, American Elsevier, 1970).

● 'SBI: system building for industry, for the Milton Keynes Development Corporation' *Architectural Design* **42** (9) September 1972 546–52.

● 'Whatever happened to the systems approach?' *Architectural Design* **46** (5) May 1976.

● E Ehrenkrantz *Architectural systems: a needs, resources and design approach* (NY, McGraw-Hill, 1989).

● B Finnimore *Houses from the factory: system building and the welfare state* (Rivers Oram Press, 1989).

644 SYSTEMS ART

During the late 1960s and early '70s the word 'system' became extremely fashionable in the artworld of the West. In some instances it was employed in the straightforward dictionary sense of 'a whole composed of parts in orderly arrangement according to some scheme or plan' (see Systemic Painting and Systems Group). In other instances, its use reflected a more scientific awareness, one demonstrating the influence of Ludwig von Bertalanffy (a scientist associated with General Systems Theory) and the phenomenal growth of the science of systems analysis since 1945. The latter was concerned to understand processes involving subsystems, their interrelationships, and their relation to whatever context or environment they existed within. Systems Art was, therefore, work by artists like Robert Morris, Hans Haacke and Dennis Oppenheim involving a shift of emphasis from objects to processes, and work which interacted with its real environment (natural or social). Jack Burnham, a North American writer, published several articles on Systems Art in the late '60s while in 1974 Jorge Glusberg, a South American, employed the term to describe artworks by Latin American artists with socio-political ambitions, i.e. works regarded as systems of signs representing in a critical manner the larger social, economic and political system within which they were generated.

● See also Conceptual Art, Ecological Art, Media Art, Political Art, Process Art.

● J Burnham 'Systems and art' *Art in Society* Summer–Fall 1969.

● W Feaver 'Art: system' *Listener* **87** (2250) May 11 1972 633.

● J Burnham 'Systems aesthetics' (1968) & 'Real time systems' (1969) – in – *Great Western Saltworks: essays on the meaning of post-formalist art* (NY, George Braziller, 1974) 15–38.

● J Glusberg *Art systems in Latin America* (ICA, 1974).

645 SYSTEMS GROUP

An informal association of British artists including Richard Allen, John Ernest, Malcolm Hughes, Colin Jones, Michael Kidner, Peter Lowe, James Moyes, David Saunders, Geoffrey Smedley, Jean Spencer, Jeffrey Steele and Gillian Wise-Ciobotaru exhibiting and discussing together in the late 1960s and early '70s. These artists did not sign a joint manifesto nor did they collaborate in the production of works of art, but they were indebted to the constructivist tradition and shared an interest in structuralism, semiotics and such formal issues as order, sequence, structure and rhythm. They

SYSTEMS GROUP MALCOLM HUGHES, "White Relief No. 1" (of a series of four) (1972). Wood, hardboard, acrylic, 210cm x 105cm x 10cm. Photo: courtesy of the artist.

advocated a modern classical art based on 'order within endless variety'. Systematic procedures – often based on mathematics – were used to generate artworks that were totally abstract and geometric. Since this kind of art was concerned with syntax – 'orderly or systematic arrangement of parts or elements' – it was also dubbed 'syntactic' and 'systematic art'. In June 1971 a more rigorously defined group of Systems artists exhibited at the Arnolfini Gallery, Bristol, under the name 'Matrix'.

● See also Constructionism, Constructivism, Semiotics, Structuralism & Art/Design, Structurism, Systems Art.

● M Hughes 'Notes on the context of "Systems"' *Studio International* **183** (944) May 1972 200–3.

● S Bann *Systems* (Whitechapel Art Gallery, 1972), Arts Council touring exhibition.

● P Steadman *Systems 2: Richard Allen...* (Polytechnic of Central London, 1973).

T

(Also Tee-Shirts) Reasonably priced, lightweight, close (or loose) fitting, collarless shirts with short (or long) sleeves. These popular garments had a humble beginning: they developed from nineteenth-century male underwear; in the twentieth-century they were streamlined by the United States Navy and then made internationally fashionable by being worn by film-stars such as Marlon Brando and James Dean. During the 1970s and '80s T-Shirts with pictures and names of rock bands became part of the merchandise sold by the record industry. T-Shirts are usually made from white cotton and used as casual wear by young people. Besides being cult design objects, they are significant because they so often serve as grounds for silkscreened images, symbols, abstract decoration or slogans. T-Shirts can be mobile billboards. Via political slogans, designers and wearers can make public statements or through bad taste and erotic images they can shock the general public. Some images reproduced on T-Shirts have, in fact, prompted prosecution on the grounds of obscenity. The British fashion designer Katherine Hamnett became famous in 1984 for wearing an anti-nuclear weapons 'message' T-Shirt to a meeting with Mrs Thatcher, the British Prime Minister. T-Shirts can be purchased with readymade images and statements of all kinds but many people prefer to devise and print their own. The British artist Simon Miles has specialized in hand-painting original designs on T-Shirts with screenprinting ink. Two British firms noted for their T-Shirt designs in the '80s were Modzart and State Arts.

● See also Cult Objects, Pop Design.

◉ J Strapp 'State of the Arts' *The Face* (10) February 1981 48–9.

◉ G Dorfles & D Fiori *T-Shirt T-Show* (Milan, Electa, 1984).

◉ J Gordon & A Hiller *The T-Shirt book* (Ebury Press, 1988).

◉ J Rumbold 'Imagery out of the trashcan' *Guardian* May 29 1989 11.

A term used by several artists to describe their sculptures or assemblages. Dictionaries define a 'tableau' as 'a group of persons and accessories producing a picturesque effect'. In France the term 'tableau vivant' means 'living picture', i.e. people posing as if in a picture. A theatrical tradition of such scenes dates back to the Middle Ages and three-dimensional representations based on them are familiar to us from waxworks, museums and shop-window displays. In the early 1960s the American sculptor Edward Kienholz extended his reliefs from walls to the floor. These constructions generally consisted of real objects, full-size figures and recorded sounds. (Normally, living people were not included; see Living Art, Performance Art.) He called them 'Tableaux' after the costumed, 'stop-action' presentations he had witnessed in rural churches in his youth. Tableau sculpture was a half-way house between the single isolated work of tradition and the total enclosure of environmental art. In general the spectator remained outside the Tableaux, preserving the impression of looking into a picture or a window. Exceptionally, some of Kienholz's Tableaux were complete rooms visitors could enter, e.g. 'Roxy's' (1961) and 'The Beanery' (1965). Other artists who made Tableaux in the '60s and '70s were George Segal, Claes Oldenburg, Paul Thek, Colin

TABLEAU Ed Kienholz, 'Five card Stud' (1972). Mixed-media tableau. Exhibited: Documenta 5, Kassel, Germany.

Self and Duane Hanson.

● See also Assemblage Art, Environmental Art, Installation, Living Art, Performance Art, Scenography, Sound Art, Staged Photography, Verist Sculpture.

◉ *Edward Kienholz: 11 Tableaux* (Zürich, Kunsthaus/London, ICA, 1971).

TACHISME Jean-Paul Riopelle, 'Repaire' (1957). Oil on canvas, 25" x 32". Photo: Hanover Gallery, London.

648 TAC

(The Architects Collaborative) A famous and influential American architecture and design partnership. It was established in Cambridge, Massachusetts, in 1945 by Walter Gropius (1883–1969) and seven others of a younger generation. (It later grew to an office of over 200.) The use of the word 'collaborative' in the name signalled Gropius' belief in the value of teamwork in architectural design. Over the decades TAC designed a tremendous range of buildings: offices, banks, schools, houses, university departments, laboratories, libraries, etc., both in the United States and abroad. Two of their notable buildings were the Pan Am skyscraper in New York (1958) and the American Embassy in Athens (1961). In the mid 1960s a department of Interior Architecture and Graphic Communication was added to TAC. From 1974 onwards it was under the direction of Klaus E. Muller. Collaboration within TAC and with clients and the wider community were still priorities, but also design that conserved energy. TAC Interiors undertook many large-scale projects; the planning process was assisted by the TAC computer-based system for building design called Facilities Information System. According to David Morton, what characterized the work of TAC Interiors was 'clean space with dramatic but subtle use of colours'.

● See also Collaborations, Computer-Aided Design.

◉ W Gropius & others (eds) *The Architects Collaborative* 1945–65 (Teufen, Switzerland, A Niggli, 1966).

◉ D Morton 'Bold discretions: the work of TAC Interiors' *Progressive Architecture* **59** (9) September 1978 86–9.

649 TACHISME

(Tachism in English) An aspect of l'art informel that emerged in Europe during the late 1940s and remained fashionable for a decade. 'Tachisme' is a French word derived from 'tache' meaning 'stain, blot or speckle'. The term was first used by art critics in the nineteenth century in relation to artists who foregrounded the touch or brushstroke of painting. Different art historians credit different critics – Pierre Guéguen, Michel Tapié and Charles Estienne – with the first use of the term 'Tachisme' in the modern sense to describe a type of abstract painting that was expressive, spontaneous, intuitive and lyrical rather than rational and geometric. Tachist techniques involved dripped paint, pigment squirted from tubes, gestural and calligraphic brushmarks, and emphasized the materials, process and ritual act of painting, hence it was the European equivalent of American action painting but its practitioners were judged – by English-speaking critics – to be less talented and profound than their American counterparts. The major Tachist painters were Wols, Pierre Soulages, Hans Hartung, Jean-Paul Riopelle, Georges Mathieu, Henri Michaux, H. H. Sonderborg, Marcelle Loubchansky and Arnulf Rainer. Sam Francis can be regarded as a link between the Tachists and the action painters because he was an American who worked in Paris in the 1950s and because his style blended aspects of both.

● See also Action Painting, Art Autre, Art Informel, Drip Painting, Free Abstraction, Lyrical Abstraction, Quadriga.

◉ P Guéguen 'Tachisme et désintégration' *Aujourd'hui* **5** (26) April 1960 4–5.

◉ G Mathieu *Au-delà du Tachisme* (Paris, Julliard, 1963).

650 TACTILE SCULPTURE

Sculpture is an artform in which the tactile sense plays a vital role, yet visitors to galleries are not normally allowed to touch exhibits. Visitors have, therefore, to experience the sense of touch via the sense of sight and via the memory of what carved surfaces feel like. The blind are doubly penalized because they can neither see nor touch sculptures. To remedy this situation some curators have organized sculpture shows especially for the blind: at the Museum of Contemporary Crafts, New York and at the Modern Museet, Stockholm in 1969; at the Tate Gallery in 1976. The latter exhibition featured works by established modern sculptors such as Edgar

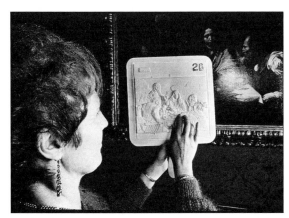

TACTILE SCULPTURE 'The supper at Emmaus' by Carravagio, as a thermoform (a plastic relief) provided in conjunction with audio-cassette tapes by The National Gallery, London, for use by the blind. Photograph: David Mansell.

Degas and Henry Moore but also specially commissioned new pieces by Lawrence Burt, Malcolm Hughes and Tim Mapston. A touring show of sculpture for the visually handicapped was also organized by the Nottingham Castle Museum in 1985. That blind people can be trained in the 'visual' art of sculpture has been demonstrated by the fact that some blind students have studied sculpture in British art colleges.

A remarkable initiative of the late '80s was undertaken by Alison Oldland, founder of the charity the Living Paintings Trust: blind people were enabled to 'see' famous paintings in the collection of the National Gallery, London, via braille-like bas-relief representations ('thermoforms'). A commentary recorded on a tape cassette directed the blind person's exploration of these 'tactile pictures'.

● I Horovitz 'Feel it...' *Craft Horizons* **29** (2) March 1969 14–15.
● L Adamson 'Blind eye' *Guardian* June 11 1976 9.
● *Sculpture for the blind* (Tate Gallery, 1976).
● M Butter & others *Beyond appearances: sculpture for the visually handicapped and sighted to share* (Nottingham Castle Museum/Arts Council, 1985).

651 TALLER DE ARQUITECTURA An influential and successful Spanish architectural practice established in Barcelona in 1962 by Ricardo Bofill, one-time Marxist and activist. The practice later opened an office in Paris as a result of several French commissions. Bofill's aim was to assemble a multi-disciplinary team (it included a poet and an economist) in order to reconsider issues of form within a broader political–cultural context so as to avoid the failures of modern, international-style architecture based on technology rather than on culture. His team consisted of people from several countries including Peter Hodgkinson from Britain. The Studio undertook research on architectural structures as signs and symbols. The work of Antonio Gaudi was an important inspiration. Since the '60s the Studio has designed many housing projects which have proved popular because of their boldness and their unusual combination of the methods of the present (e.g. prefabrication) and the styles of the past (e.g. Walden 7, Barcelona, which resembled the fortresses of the Middle Ages). While the early work was considered to belong to the so-called 'School of Barcelona' – neo-realist, brutalist – the later work owed more to classicism (e.g. the 'poor man's Versailles' – Palacio de Abraxas, Marne-la-Vallée, 1979–82).

An exhibition celebrating the work of El Taller de Arquitectura was held at the Architectural Association, London in 1981.

● See also New Classicism, Post-Modern Architecture.
● G Broadbent 'The Taller of Bofill' *Architectural Review* **154** (921) November 1973 289–97.
● P Guedes *Taller de Arquitectura: Ricardo Bofill* (Architectural Association, 1981).
● W James *Ricardo Bofill: Taller de Arquitectura, buildings and projects 1960–85* (NY, Rizzoli, 1988).

652 TALLER DE GRÁFICA POPULAR (TGP) The People's Graphics Workshop. A printmaking organization and workshop established in Mexico City in 1937 by Leopoldo Méndez, Luis Arenal and Pablo O'Higgins. These Left-wing artists were socially and politically committed. They advocated collective and functional production in the service of the people of Mexico. They taught printmaking and produced lithographs, woodcuts, linocuts, publications and posters that were mainly critical in their content and propagandist in intent.

● See also Atelier Populaire, Latin American Art, Paddington Printshop, Political Art, Prop Art.
● J Keller *El Taller de Gráfica Popular* (Austin, University of Texas, Archer M Huntington Art Gallery, 1985).
● *50 Años Taller de Gráfica Popular* (Mexico City, Museo de Palacio de Bellas Artes, Museo Nacional de la Estampa & Galería José María Velasco, 1987).

653 TAMARIND LITHOGRAPHY WORKSHOP A famous and extremely influential American print workshop founded by June Wayne in 1960. Its name derived from the name of an avenue in Hollywood where it was first located. The aim of Tamarind, a non-profit-making organization funded largely by the Ford Foundation, was to promote the art and craft of lithography by bringing fine artists and master printers together and to

TAMARIND LITHOGRAPHY WORKSHOP JUNE WAYNE in her studio. Photo: Shiva artists' materials advertisement, *Art News* March 1973.

train the printers of the future. By 1970 103 artists had participated in the project and 2,900 images had been produced. In that year Tamarind became part of the University of New Mexico, Albuquerque.

● See also Atelier 17, Collaborations, Curwen Studio, Tyler Graphics.

● J Wayne *About Tamarind* (Los Angeles, Tamarind Lithography Workshop, 1969).

● V Allen *Tamarind: homage to lithography* (NY, MoMA, 1969).

● M Tabak 'Tamarind Lithography Workshop' Part 1 *Craft Horizons* **30** (5) October 1970 28–33; Part 2 *Craft Horizons* **30** (6) December 1970 50–3.

● G Antreasian & C Adams *The Tamarind book of lithography: art and techniques* (NY, Abrams, 1971).

● L Gedeon *Tamarind: from Los Angeles to Albuquerque* (Los Angeles, Grunwald Center for the Graphic Arts, University of California, 1985).

654   TANTRA ART

(Also Meditative Art) A category of Indian art identified by Ajit Mookerjee (1915–90), a collector of Tantra Art and author of two lavish books on the subject. The word 'tantra' is derived from the Sanskrit 'tan' meaning 'to expand in continuing, unfolding process' and 'tra' meaning 'tool'. It refers to a means of extending spiritual knowledge. The Tantra religion is a blend of Buddhist, Hindu and Yoga ideas and spans the period from the fourth century AD to the present. A variety of Tantric artefacts exist: ceremonial vessels, sculptures, icons, paintings, woven fabrics, diagrams and illuminated manuscripts. A vogue for this kind of art developed in the West during the 1960s amongst those belonging to the counter culture who were attracted by the ecstatic and erotic characteristics of Eastern mysticism. Other Westerners became fascinated by Tantra's diagrammatic images because they resembled modern geometric abstract paintings. Fans of Tantra Art included the British art dealer Robert Fraser who spent a year in India.

● See also Cosmic Art, Diagrams, Erotic Art.

● A Mookerjee *Tantra Art* (Paris, Ravi Kumar, 1967).

● V Whiles 'Tantric imagery: affinities with twentieth century abstract art' *Studio International* **181** (931) March 1971 100–7.

● R Fraser 'Tantra revealed' *Studio International* **182** (939) December 1971 25–23.

● A Mookerjee *Tantra Asana* (Paris, Ravi Kumar, 1971).

● *Tantra* (Hayward Gallery, 1971).

● O Garrison *Tantra: Yoga of sex* (Academy Editions, 1972).

● P Rawson *Art of Tantra* (Thames & Hudson, 1973).

655   TEAM 10

(Also Team X) An international alliance of young, radical architects who admired each other's work and who shared certain ideas about the future of architecture. They were called 'Team 10' because they were given the task of preparing a programme for the tenth gathering of the 'Congrès Internationaux d'Architecture Moderne' (CIAM, founded 1928) at Dubrovnik in 1956. During the Congress it became evident that a wide difference of

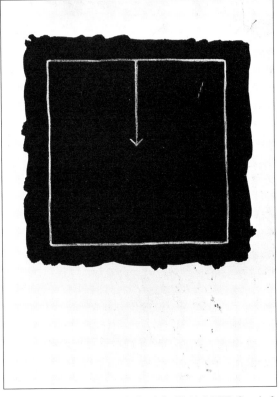

TANTRA ART Tantra artist from Rajasthan, India, 'Untitled' (1990). Goauche & gold leaf on handmade paper, 23cm x 17cm. Photo: Frith Street Gallery, London.

opinion existed between Team 10 and the older founder members of CIAM concerning the purpose of the meeting. Team 10 believed the Congress had become too large, too diffuse and only generated vague generalizations about how the problems of urban planning should be solved. The disagreements led to the dissolution of CIAM but Team 10 continued to meet. The original members were Georges Candilis, R. Gutmann, William Howell, Alison and Peter Smithson, Aldo van Eyck and John Voelcker.

● A Smithson (ed) 'Team 10 primer 1953–63' *Architectural Design* **32** (12) December 1962 559–602.

● R Banham *The new brutalism: ethic or aesthetic?* (Architectural Press, 1966) 70–2.

656 TECHNO-FUNCTIONALISM

(Also Techno-Aesthetic) A term used by several Italian design critics in the 1960s to characterize the design philosophy of such designers as Achille and Pier Giacomo Castiglioni and Marco Zanuso. Techno-functionalism required that 'the appearance of an object be dictated solely by its technological and utilitarian constraints, with nothing included that did not have a vital functional purpose'.

Writers on Japanese architecture in the '70s also employed the similar term 'Techno-Aesthetic' meaning buildings designed to look like items of technology rather than architecture and incorporating industrial principles in their construction. One example cited was Yoji Watanabe's 'New Sky building' of 1971.

● See also High-Tech, Italian Craze, Machine Aesthetic/Art.

● M Ross *Beyond metabolism: the new Japanese Architecture* (NY, McGraw Hill, 1978) 85–8.

● P Sparke *Italian design: 1870 to the present* (Thames & Hudson, 1988).

657 TECHNOLOGICAL ART

(Also Corporate Art, Tech/Tek Art) As most art requires some kind of technology to bring it into being, the adjective 'technological' in this term might appear redundant. However, the label and the concept date from the 1960s when 'technology' came to mean far more than the materials and tools of the traditional, craft-based artforms. 'Technology' denoted the techniques and methods of the applied sciences combined with the massive resources of materials, machines, plant, capital and labour deployed by modern industry; while 'advanced technology' denoted such fields as lasers, aerospace, plastics, electronics and computers.

As Jack Burnham explains in his book *Beyond modern sculpture,* twentieth-century artists have adopted many different attitudes towards the machine age, ranging from the ironic detachment of Marcel Duchamp to the enthusiasm of the futurists. Kinetic art underwent a boom in the '60s and this form of art made use of mechanical and electrical engineering but it hardly tapped the potential of modern technology. It was only in the middle 1960s that there was a significant impetus amongst artists, especially in the United States, towards collaboration with scientists, engineers and modern industry; it was the results of that collaboration that were called 'Technological Art'.

Examples of this impetus were: the development of computer art; the founding of a series of new art and technology organizations – EAT, PULSA, IRAT (Institute for Research in Art & Technology); the New York festival of art and technology called 'Nine evenings: theatre and engineering' organized by Billy Kluver in 1966; the 'Art & Technology' exhibition held at the Los Angeles County Museum of Art in 1971. The curator of this show was Maurice Tuchman; it was the culmination of a five-year programme of collaboration between artists and Californian industries. Artists taking part included Newton Harrison, R. B. Kitaj, Claes Oldenburg, Robert Rauschenberg, Tony Smith, Andy Warhol and Robert Whitman. They selected corporations with whom they worked for many months to achieve a genuine collaboration (hence the label 'corporate art').

Tuchman's project was, in its own terms, a success but the exhibition coincided with a change in attitude on the part of artists and many others towards technology, from interest and enthusiasm to disillusionment and apprehension. Some artists feared they would become subservient to industry and business as they had once been subservient to the church, while others considered industrial modes of production 'dehumanizing' and likely to generate only 'interior design art'. Suspicion of technology was also fuelled by the involvement of high-tech companies in military research and the manufacture of weapons of destruction, and also by the pollution of the environment that was one by-product of technological development. It was for these reasons that many artists began to question the political neutrality of technology within art and to turn towards ecology in the late 1960s (see Ecological Art). Theorists too began to demand 'alternative' and 'appropriate' technologies.

● See also APG, Collaborations, Computer Art, EAT, Electronic Art, Expanded Cinema, High-Tech, Holographic Art, Kinetic Art, Laser Art, Low-Tech, Machine Aesthetic, PULSA, Quantel Paintbox, Space Art, Telematics, Video Art.

● J Burnham *Beyond modern sculpture...* (Allen Lane, The Penguin Press, 1968).

● G Youngblood *Expanded cinema* (NY, Dutton, 1970).

● M Tuchman & others *A report on the Art & Technology program of the Los Angeles County Museum of Art 1967–71* (LA County Museum of Art, 1971).

● A Goldin 'Art and technology in a social vacuum' *Art in America* **60** (2) March–April 1972 46–51.

● J Benthall *Science and technology in art today* (Thames & Hudson, 1972).

● D Davis *Art and the future: a history/prophecy of the collaboration between science, technology and art* (Thames & Hudson, 1973).

● D Dickson *Alternative technology and the politics of technical change* (Glasgow, Fontana/Collins, 1974).

● S Kranz *Science and technology in the arts: a tour through the realm of science/art* (NY, Van Nostrand Reinhold, 1974).

● J Benthall *The body electric: patterns of Western industrial culture* (Thames & Hudson, 1975).

● J Wosk 'The impact of technology on the human image in art' *Leonardo* **19** (2) 1986 145–52.

658   TELEMATICS

(Also Informatic Art) A term devised by Simon Nora to describe the new electronic technology derived from the convergence of computers and telecommunication systems. His 1978 report to the French Government – *L'informatisation de la société* – led to the establishment of the 'Programme Télématique'. The term was subsequently adopted by the British artist and art educator Roy Ascott who with others around the globe has used international computer–telecommunication systems to generate interactive artworks. (The first live two-way satellite video transmission by artists took place between the East and West Coasts of the USA in 1977.) Such networking had implications for traditional conceptions of authorship: 'in telematic networking, authorship of images can be dispersed throughout the system'. Besides Ascott, artists involved in this kind of activity included Eric Gidney (Australian), Tom Sherman (Canadian) and Robert Adrian X (Austrian). Without participating in these networks it is difficult to judge the nature and quality of the art produced. However, it has been claimed that a new, collaborative type of art was produced which involved 'many individuals in the creation of meaning', art that dealt 'with the flux and flow of images and forms within shifting creative strategies'.

● See also Collaborations, Computer Art, Electronic Art, Global or World Art, Mail Art, Technological Art.

● H Grundmann (ed) *Art telecommunication* (Vancouver, Western Front/Vienna, Blix, 1984).

● R Ascott 'Arte, tecnologia e computer' *Arte e scienza, biologia, tecnologia e informatica* (Venice, Edizioni La Biennale, 1986).

● *Beuys, Warhol, Higashiyama: Global-Art-Fusion* (Bern, Art-Fusion-Edition, 1986).

● R Ascott 'On networking' *Leonardo* **21** (3) 1988 231–2.

● — 'Art education in the telematic culture' – in – *Synthesis: visual arts in the electronic culture* M Eisenbeis & H Hagebölling (eds) (Offenbach am Main, Hochschule für Gestaltung, 1989) 184–203.

● R Ascott & C Loeffler (eds) 'Connectivity: art and interactive communications' *Leonardo* **24** (2) 1991 (thematic issue).

659   TENDENZA

(Also Ticinese School) An Italian neo-rationalist architectural movement which emerged in the 1960s and came to prominence in the '70s. The term – stemming from a 1975 exhibition organized by Martin Steinmann – referred to the theory and work of such architects as Aldo Rossi, Carlo Aymonino, Giorgio Grassi, Bruno Reichlin, Fabio Reinhart and Mario Botta. These architects were Italian and Swiss. Tendenza was best exemplified in buildings erected in the Swiss canton of Ticino. According to Kenneth Frampton, the movement resisted the tendency to reduce architecture to a commodity, instead, it stressed: (1) 'the relative autonomy of architecture and the need for its re-articulation as a discourse in terms of *types* and *rules* for the logical combination of its elements; (2) the socio-cultural importance of existing urban structures...and (3), the resource of historical form as a fertile legacy...'.

● See also Analogical Architecture, Rational Architecture.

● M Steinmann *Tendenzen: neuere Architektur im Tessin* (Zürich, ETH catalogue, 1975).

● I Rota (ed) *Mario Botta: architecture and projects in the '70s* (Academy Editions, 1981).

● G Brown-Manrique *The Ticino guide* (ADT, Architecture, Design & Technology Press/Longman, 1989).

● G Grassi *Architecture: dead language* (NY, Rizzoli, 1989).

660   TENSILE ARCHITECTURE

(Also Objective/Skin Architecture) Structures made rigid by cables or rods held under tension. Examples of such structures have been known for centuries (e.g. tents), but it was only during the 1950s and '60s that modern architects began to exploit them on a large scale. The chief exponent of Tensile Architecture was the German Frei Otto. He designed vast canopies composed of steel netting held under tension which Peter Cook called 'membranes' and 'skin architecture'. Otto's work became known to a worldwide audience when he designed the German Pavilion for Expo '67, Montreal, and sports facilities for the Olympic Games held in

TENSILE ARCHITECTURE CEDRIC PRICE, LORD SNOWDON & FRANK NEWBY, Bird Cage, London Zoo, Regents Park, London (1961-2). Photo: Roderick Coyne.

Munich in 1972. He was also appointed director of the Stuttgart Institute for Lightweight Structures (founded in 1964), a body which organized conferences and published research papers on such topics as 'adaptable' and 'pneumatic' architecture. A famous British example of a tensile structure is the Bird Cage in London Zoo designed by Cedric Price, Lord Snowdon and Frank Newby in 1961–2. More recent British examples have been designed by the high-tech architect Michael Hopkins, e.g. the Schlumberger Research Laboratories, Cambridgeshire (1985) and the Mound Stand, Lord's Cricket Ground, London (1987).

● See also High-Tech, Pneumatic Architecture.

R Body 'Under tension' *Architectural Review* **134** (801) November 1963 324–34.

G Minke 'Tensile structures' *Architectural Design* **38** (4) April 1968 179–82.

W Blaser *Objektive Architektur* (Krefeld, Scherpe Verlag, 1970).

'Tensile, space, pneumatic structures' *Zodiac* (21) 1972, special number.

L Glaeser *The work of Frei Otto* (NY, MoMA, 1972).

J Park 'Lightweight heavies' *Architectural Design* **46** (9) September 1976 518–21.

P Drew *Frei Otto: form and structure* (Crosby Lockwood, 1976).

J Glancey *New British architecture* (Thames & Hudson, 1989).

661 TEXTRUCTION

In France a number of artists – Georges Badin, Gérard Duchêne, Gervais Jassaud, Jean Mazeaufroid and Michel Vachey – who came from various provincial towns – founded in 1971 a group called 'Textruction'. The works they produced were made from cut-up books and blown-up texts, some with calligraphic-style superimpositions; the results were similar in certain respects to concrete poetry. Motivated by radical political ideas and the desire to refuse the choice between writing or painting, their declared aim was to subvert and dissolve language by transgressing literary legibility. They also worked collaboratively because they opposed the myth of the author-creator. An exhibition of their work at the École Speciale d'Architecture in Paris was totally vandalized. Textruction also participated in a French festival held at the ICA, London in March 1973.

● See also Book Art, Concrete Poetry, Lettrism, Political Art.

J Lepage 'Lettres: Textruction' *L'Art Vivant, Chroniques de* (41) July 1973 23.

P Faveton 'La syntaxe d'un langage' *ArTitudes International* (15/17) October–December 1974 29–30.

662 THIS IS TOMORROW (TIT)

An influential and popular mixed-media exhibition held at the Whitechapel Art Gallery, London, in 1956. The original idea for the show came from the French Groupe Espace. It was an attempt to integrate the various arts and to foster collaboration between painters, architects and sculptors. Under the direction of Theo Crosby, 12 independent teams devised installations exemplifying contrasting aesthetics and visions of the future. British constructivist artists such as Victor Pasmore and Anthony Hill participated and so did ex-members of the Independent Group like Richard Hamilton, John McHale and Eduardo Paolozzi. One display was composed of images and artefacts derived from popular culture and the catalogue/poster featured Hamilton's seminal collage 'Just what is it that makes today's homes so different, so appealing?'. The popular culture section proved the most memorable and as a result TIT later came to be regarded as a landmark in the development of British pop art.

● See also Collaborations, Groupe Espace, Independent Group, Installation, Pop Art.

L Alloway *This is Tomorrow* (Whitechapel Art Gallery, 1956).

THIS IS TOMORROW RICHARD HAMILTON, 'This is tomorrow' (1956). Collage, 30.1cm x 47.2 cm. Photo: Graphics Collection, Staatsgalerie Stuttgart.

● T Crosby 'This is Tomorrow' *Architectural Design* September 1956 302–4; *Architectural Design* October 1956 334–6.

● L Alloway 'The development of British pop' – in – *Pop Art* by L Lippard & others (Thames & Hudson, 1966) 26–67.

● — & others *Modern dreams: the rise and fall of pop* (NY, ICA Clocktower Gallery/Cambridge, Mass, MIT Press, 1988).

● M Belford & J Herman *Time and space concepts in art* (NY, Pleiades Gallery, 1980).

● *Signs of the Times: a decade of video, film and slide-tape installation in Britain, 1980-90* (Oxford, MoMA, 1990).

663 **TIME-BASED ARTS**

This expression dates from the 1960s and probably derives from the Eventstructure theory of the British artist John Latham. All art involves a temporal dimension (in the making and appreciation processes) but the expression is normally applied to artforms other than painting and sculpture which take place over a set period of time, e.g. music/sound art, film, video, tape-slide, and performance. Just as some sculptors think of their works as being about space, some artists conceive of their works as being about time.

Time-Based Arts is also the title of a Dutch, artist-run foundation and exhibition centre situated in Amsterdam. It was established by a group of visual artists in 1983 in order to serve as a showcase for Time-Based Art by Dutch and by foreign artists. The foundation presents installations, exhibitions, concerts, performances, lectures, TV and radio programmes; it also encourages research and issues publications.

● See also Eventstructure, Performance Art, Sound Art.

664 **TOTAL ART/DESIGN**

(Also Totalism) In the twentieth century a number of artists and theorists have used the terms 'Total Architecture/Art/Design' and 'Totalism' in various ways. The basic idea stems from the German 'Gesamtkunstwerk' (total art work) associated with the multi-media music-dramas of Richard Wagner. The ideal Total work is one in which several constituent arts co-operate in order to produce a unified result, one that provides viewers with an overwhelming sensory experience. Both Bruno Taut and Walter Gropius advocated Total Architecture in the 1920s; this implied that the crafts, painting and sculpture would achieve synthesis within a new conception of architecture. Gropius also produced designs in 1926 for Erwin Piscator's 'Total Theatre'.

Ben Vautier, a French artist also known simply as 'Ben', claims to have invented Total Art. He was one of several artists who took part in the Fluxus Festival of Total Art held in Nice during July-August 1963.

For Adrian Henri 'Total Art' served as a synonym for 'environments' and 'happenings'. For the German artist Timm Ulrichs it meant exploring the frontiers of art by exhibiting himself in a glass box as a living sculpture. For the Swiss-Viennese action painter Alfons Schilling 'Total Malerei' (1961) indicated a frenzied, bodily commitment to the act of painting. For Jim Reynolds 'Total Design' meant a truly popular type of design in which people fully participated in the design process in order to meet their own social needs. ('Total Design' was also the name adopted in 1963 by a group of Dutch designers for their Amsterdam practice because their skills encompassed industrial, architectural and graphic design.)

For Logie Barrow 'Totalism' signified the end of art; artists were to become 'super-cybernetic environmentalists' working as equals with technicians and town planners for the sake of all. For the British artist Ray Arnatt 'Totalism' characterized his own '70s sculptures – they attempted to draw together as many disparities as possible and then implode them into a unified whole.

In 1983 an exhibition organized by Harald Szeemann exploring the theme of Total Art was held in Zürich. It featured a wide range of examples, in particular the work of Kurt Schwitters. The recurrent desire for Total Art can be viewed as an attempt to restore a lost unity of the arts which in the modern era have tended to develop independently and to value their autonomy.

● See also Environmental Art/Design, Happenings, Inter-Media.

● W Gropius *The scope of Total Architecture* (NY, Harper & Row, 1955).

● L Barrow 'A summary of Totalism' *Control* (1) 1965 2–3.

● J Thwaites 'Total Art' *Art & Artists* **8** (2) May 1973 20–3.

● A Henri *Total Art* (NY & Toronto, Oxford University Press, 1974).

● J Reynolds 'Total Design, or, design for the people by the people' *DIA Yearbook* (DIA, 1976) 5–6.

● R Demarco 'Towards the Total Art work: Europeans searching for Utopia' *Studio International* **196** (1001) August 1983 10–11.

● H Szeemann *Der Hang zum Gesamtkunstwerk* (Zürich, Kunsthalle, 1983).

● K Broos *Design: Total Design* (Utrecht, Reflex, 1985).

● F Dieckmann 'Vom Gesamtkunstwerk' *Bildende Kunst* **36** (7) 1988 298–9.

665 TOTALITARIAN ART

This term has been used by such scholars as John Elderfield and Igor Golomstock. It refers to the officially approved art favoured by totalitarian regimes, i.e. those ruled by dictators, centralized governments or parties which do not tolerate other parties or political movements. Key examples of such regimes were: fascist Italy under Mussolini, fascist Germany under Hitler, communist Soviet Union under Stalin, and communist China under Chairman Mao. Iraq under Saddam Hussein is a more recent example. Golomstock has argued that the forms of art fostered by such regimes have many similarities and that therefore Totalitarian Art can be considered an international style. Common features include: tight control of all cultural production; the imposition of a main style of representation, an accessible style based on nineteenth-century realism; a cult of personality centred on the leader expressed in terms of flattering portraits and statues; a penchant for massive state monuments and monumental styles of architecture (which in the case of Iraq has been called the 'Architecture of Fear'); images celebrating national traditions, the achievements of the Party and the army, plus technological and economic achievements; idealized domestic and rural genre scenes.

Art critics in liberal democracies often attack Totalitarian Art on the grounds that it is kitsch or propaganda, not art. Critics of the concept point to the differences between the political ideologies and aesthetic programmes of the various totalitarian regimes and query the notion of a common style.

● See also Democratic Art, Kitsch, Nazi Art, Peasant Painting, Political Art, Prop Art, Unofficial Soviet Art.

● J Elderfield 'Total and Totalitarian Art' *Studio International* **179** (921) April 1970 149–55.

● I Golomstock *Totalitarian Art* (Collins Harvill, 1990).

● Samir al-Khalil *The monument: art, vulgarity and responsibility in Iraq* (Andre Deutsch, 1991).

666 TOWN ART/ARTIST

This term was coined by Paul Millichip *circa* 1970 to describe the work of the artist David Harding (b. 1937) who was employed full-time from 1968 to 1978 by the development corporation of the town of Glenrothes in Scotland. Harding was a member of the archi-

TOWN ART DAVID HARDING, 'The Henge' (1970). Concrete set in granite spiral, 1.9 m to 3 m high. Glenrothes, Scotland. Photo: Peter & Aase Goldsmith, courtesy of the artist.

tecture and planning department. His role was to contribute creatively to the design of the urban environment. Although he produced sculptures, monuments, play structures and surface designs on walls, often with the help of residents and their children, his function was not limited to the traditional ones of sculptors and painters. (A precedent for Town Art was Victor Pasmore's involvement with the planning and visual appearance of the new town of Peterlee, County Durham, in the mid 1950s.) Harding also helped to create similar posts in the towns of Livingston, East Kilbride, Rochdale, Peterborough and Milton Keynes.

● See also Artist-in-Residence, Community Art & Media, Environmental Design, Public Art, Street Art.

● D Harding *Glenrothes Town Artist* (Glenrothes, Fife, Glenrothes Development Corporation, 1975).

●— *Artists and buildings* (Edinburgh, Scottish Arts Council, 1977).

● D Petherbridge 'The Town Artist experiment' *Architectural Review* **166** (990) August 1979 125–9.

● D Thorpe *Town Artist report* (Edinburgh, Scottish Arts Council, 1980).

667 TOWNSCAPE

This word, coined by analogy with 'landscape', was employed during a campaign waged by the *Architectural Review* in the late 1940s for an improvement in the planning of the British urban environment. Of particular concern was the need to reduce the quantity of street furniture and to improve its design and disposition. Successful Townscapes such as those achieved in certain historic towns involved a sequential revelation of space, contrasts of scale and function as the observer moved about them. It was hoped that lessons drawn from the past could be applied to the composition of new towns and redevelopments. Later writers on architecture dismissed the Townscape philosophy as 'picturesque' and claimed that by focusing on the surface appearance of towns it dealt only with the symptoms of urban blight not their root causes.

Adding '-scape' to existing words is also a practice which occurs in the United States – witness the awkward term 'vacationscape' used by Clare Gunn as the title of a book about designing the landscape of tourist areas.

● See also Contextual Architecture, Ekistics, SLOAP, Subtopia, Urbanism.

● G Cullen *The concise Townscape* (Architectural Press, 1973).

● R Maxwell 'An eye for an I, the failure of the Townscape tradition' *Architectural Design* **46** (9) September 1976 534–6.

● G Burke *Townscapes* (Harmondsworth, Penguin Books, 1976).

● A Tugnutt & M Robertson *Making Townscape: a contextual approach to building in an urban setting* (Mitchell, 1987).

● C Gunn *Vacationscape: designing tourist regions* (NY, Van Nostrand Reinhold, 2nd ed 1988).

668 TOWNSHIP ART

(Also Resistance Art, Transitional Art) During the 1980s, despite conditions of poverty, oppression and censorship, artists emerged from amongst the black inhabitants of such South African townships as Soweto and Sebokeng. Some of these artists received a formal art training or were taught by their elders but many did not. David Koloane, an oil painter, was trained (in part at Birmingham Polytechnic in Britain); he became curator of the Federated Union of Black Artists (FUBA), an organization and gallery founded in 1980 in Johannesburg.

Township artists employed several forms and media: Suzanne Louw, Billy Mandinidi and David Hlongwane produced lino- and woodcuts; Phutuma Seoka, Nelson Mukhuba and Jackson Hlungwan carved figures out of wood and then painted them; Noria Mabasa made figures from clay, fired them and painted them; Tito Zunga and Derrick Nxumalo drew highly detailed scenes with ball-point and felt-tip pens; Johannes Phokela painted murals on cement; Paul Sibisi drew and painted in pen and wash; many women decorated the exteriors of their houses with vivid patterns. Probably the artist best known outside of South Africa was the printmaker John Muafangejo (1943–87). These artists worked in several different styles which reflected the influence of both African and European art traditions, but their content was similar: subjects drawn from everyday life; the political struggle against apartheid. According to Gavin Younge, the term 'Township Art' was offensive to some artists

TOWNSHIP ART DAVID HLONGWANE, 'Where to go?' (1986). Lino cut print, 380mm x 295mm. Photo: Gavin Younge.

and stylistically indefensible, even so, it gained currency.

Steven Sack describes how, in the mid '80s, a spontaneous public or people's art developed as one consequence of widespread unrest and protest against apartheid. Crude, improvised sculptures or monuments were assembled from found objects and waste materials in the people's parks by groups of youngsters. Signs made from painted pebbles and little 'gardens of Eden' were also created and murals depicting scenes of daily life (which in one instance attracted the label 'self-pity art'). Since these cultural expressions were popular in origin and often political in content, they were suppressed by the white authorities.

● See also Artists Against Apartheid, Black Art, Political Art, Popular Art, Public Art.

● G Younge *Art of the South African Townships* (Thames & Hudson, 1988).

● S Sack 'Art in black South African Townships' *Art Monthly* (127) June 1989 6–9.

● C Richards *Art from South Africa* (Oxford, MoMA, 1990).

● S Williamson *Resistance Art in South Africa* (Cape Town & Johannesburg, David Philip/London, Catholic Institute for International Relations, 1990).

669 TRANS-AVANT GARDE

(Beyond the Avant Garde) This term was devised and popularized by the Italian critic Achille Bonito Oliva (with the help of the magazine *Flash Art*) in the early 1980s. It denoted that art of the 1970s and '80s which aimed to transcend the linear sequence of avant garde movements. Trans-Avant Garde artists rejected the idea of evolution and progress in art. They adopted a 'nomadic' attitude which enabled them to exploit any of the styles of the past or present, and to draw upon fine art and mass culture sources – hence their art was historicist and eclectic. Oliva's category was first applied to the work of certain Italian artists and then extended to the work of artists from the United States and other countries in Europe. Most of the artists concerned were figurative painters and sculptors of the 'new image' and 'neo-expressionist' varieties. Essentially, 'Trans-Avant Garde' is a synonym for 'post-modernism'.

● See also Avant Garde Art, Historicism, Neo-Expressionism, New Image Painting, Post-Modern Art, Post-Modernism.

● A Oliva *The Italian Trans-Avant Garde* (Milan, Giancarlo Politi Editore, 1982).

● —*The international Trans-Avant Garde* (Milan, Giancarlo Politi Editore, 1982).

670 TRIENNALE

(Triennali di Milano) An important industrial design fair held in Milan, Northern Italy every three years. The first Triennale took place in 1933. It developed from a series of biennial international exhibitions devoted to the decorative arts held at Monza from 1923 onwards. By the 1950s the Triennale had become the main showcase for modern Italian design. Two decades later the city of Milan had become, in the opinion of some design critics, the fashion and design capital of the world.

● See also Italian Craze.

● A Pansera *Storia cronache della Triennale* (Milan, Fabbri, 1978).

● —'The Triennale of Milan: past, present and future' *Design Issues* **2** (1) Spring 1985 23–32.

671 TROMPE L'OEIL

A French expression meaning 'deceive the eye'. In the discourse of art criticism, either a particular genre of illusionistic images (usually still lifes) intended to trick viewers into thinking they are seeing something real instead of something painted, or the technique of painting employed to achieve such illusionistic images. (Trompe L'Oeil paintings are paradoxical in the sense that if they do succeed in fooling the viewer, then they cease to be recognized as art at all.) This term pre-dates 1945 but an entry has been included here because despite the opposition of most modern artists to illusionism, this type of art has continued to thrive in the twentieth century. Trompe L'Oeil techniques were employed by the surrealist painter Salvador Dali and by the fantastic realists of Vienna; they were also part of the stock in trade of the commercial artists who painted high illusion billboards in the United States; the tradition was also kept alive by unfashionable artists exhibiting at the annual summer exhibitions of the Royal Academy; in the 1960s and '70s illusionism played a key role in photo-realist painting and in verist sculpture; many interior designers, community muralists and other wall painters were fond of Trompe L'Oeil effects (causing Charles Jencks to speak of 'superdeception' and 'Trompe L'Oeil counterfeit'); finally, the advent of post-modernism in the '70s and '80s resulted in a reversal of the values of modernism and hence illusionistic images and techniques achieved a new legitimacy and popularity.

● See also Billboard Art, Community Art & Media, Fantastic Realism, Los Angeles Fine Arts Squad, Photo-Realism, Superhumanism, Verist Sculpture.

● A Frankenstein *The reality of appearance; Trompe L'Oeil tradition in American painting* (NY, New York Graphic Society, 1970).

R Gregory & E Gombrich (eds) *Illusion in nature and art* (Duckworth, 1973).

M Battersby *Trompe L'Oeil: the eye deceived* (Academy Editions, 1974).

C Jencks 'Trompe L'Oeil counterfeit' *Studio International* **190** (977) September–October 1975 108–14.

M d'Otrange Mastai *Illusion in art: Trompe L'Oeil, a history of pictorial illusionism* (Secker & Warburg, 1976).

J Baudrillard 'The Trompe L'Oeil' *Signs of Change* **1** (1) December 1977 4–19.

C Dars *Images of deception: the art of Trompe L'Oeil* (Oxford, Phaidon, 1979).

M Milman *Trompe L'Oeil* (Macmillan/Skira, 1983).

C Cass *Grand illusions: contemporary interior murals* (Oxford, Phaidon, 1988).

672 TYLER GRAPHICS

A print workshop/publishing house established by Ken Tyler (b 1931), an American master printer, who advocated a creative collaboration between artists and printmakers. Tyler studied and worked at the Tamarind Lithography Workshop in the 1960s and subsequently made a significant contribution to the so-called 'print renaissance' in the United States. He worked on the West Coast from 1963 to '73, and then on the East Coast from 1974 to '85. In 1966 he founded Gemini G.E.L. (Graphic Editions Ltd) in Los Angeles, and in 1975 Tyler Graphics Ltd, Bedford Village, New York State. Artists with whom Tyler collaborated in the making of prints and multiples included Josef Albers, David Hockney, Jasper Johns, Roy Lichtenstein, Robert Motherwell, Robert Rauschenberg and Frank Stella. Critics described Tyler's West Coast lithographs as exemplifying an 'industrial aesthetic'. Tyler has been a commercially successful printmaker but he has also encouraged technical experimentation, especially in the realm of hand-made papers (e.g. Hockney's 1978 'Paper pools' series). Archives of Tyler Graphics exist in the collections of the National Gallery of Art, Washington, the Walker Art Center, Minneapolis, and the Australian National Gallery, Canberra.

● See also Atelier 17, Collaborations, Curwen Studio, Paddington Printshop, Tamarind Lithography Workshop.

P Gilmour *Ken Tyler, master printer and the American print renaissance* (NY, Hudson Hills Press/Canberra, Australian National Gallery, 1986).

M Friedman *Tyler Graphics: the extended image* (Minneapolis, Walker Art Center/NY, Abbeville Press, 1987).

K Tyler & P Gilmour *Tyler Graphics: catalogue raisonné, 1974–85* (Minneapolis, Walker Art Center/NY, Abbeville Press, 1987).

U

ULM

(Also HfG Ulm, New Bauhaus) Because of its cumbersome title, 'Die Hochschule für Gestaltung', this influential German school of design was referred to throughout the design world as 'Ulm' after the town where it was situated. The idea for a design school to continue the principles of the pre-war Bauhaus was proposed in 1948 and the school opened in 1955. Its first director was the Swiss concrete artist Max Bill, who also designed its buildings. In 1956, after policy disputes, Bill was replaced by the Argentine painter and industrial designer Tomas Maldonado. Ulm was closed in 1968 when its funds were cut off. Charles Jencks says that this was because the school's combination of systematic methods ('parametric design') and New Left politics offended the conservative government of Baden-Württemberg. The school was noted for its rational approach to design education and its emphasis on scientific and mathematical techniques; semiotics was also one of the topics studied. Reyner Banham described Ulm as 'a cool training ground for a technocratic elite'.

● See also Art Schools, Semiotics.

● *Ulm* (1-21 issues) 1958–68.

● R Hamilton 'Ulm' *Design* (126) June 1959 53–7.

● J Albers 'My courses at the Hochschule für Gestaltung at Ulm' *Form* (UK) 4 April 15 1967 8–10.

● 'Homage to Ulm' *BIT International* (4) 1969.

● K Frampton 'Apropos Ulm: curriculum and critical theory' *Oppositions* (3) May 1974 17–36.

● H Jacob 'HfG Ulm: a personal view of an experiment in democracy and design education' *Journal of Design History* **1** (3/4) 1988 221–34.

● R Kinross 'Hochschule...recent literature' *Journal of Design History* **1** (3/4) 1988 249–56.

● H Lindinger (ed) *Ulm design: the morality of objects* (Cambridge, Mass, MIT Press, 1990).

674 ULTIMATE PAINTING

(Also Black/ Invisible/ Quietistic/ Timeless Painting) During his lifetime the American artist Ad Reinhardt (1913–67) claimed that the paintings he produced from 1960 onwards were the 'ultimate abstract paintings'. He believed that the possibilities of abstract painting were finite and that his late works represented the climax of the easel painting tradition beyond which it would be impossible to proceed. The paintings consisted of a series of almost identical canvases, square in format (60" x 60"), divided into nine squares and painted in slightly varying shades of grey or black (hence 'black paintings'). Values were so closely attuned that they appeared at first sight to be uniform areas of paint with no image or motif (hence 'invisible painting'). In fact, the painting's squares – once detected – could be read as overlapping bands or even as a cross. William C. Seitz was the American curator who used the term 'invisible' in 1965.

● See also Op Art.

● W Seitz *The responsive eye* (NY, MoMA, 1965).

● B Rose 'The Black Paintings' – in – *Ad Reinhardt: Black Paintings 1951–67* (NY, Marlborough Gallery, 1970) 16–22.

● A Reinhardt *Art-as-art: the selected writings of Ad Reinhardt* B Rose (ed) (NY, Viking Press, 1975).

● G Inboden & T Kellein *Ad Reinhardt: Timeless Painting* (Thames & Hudson, 1985).

675 UNDERGROUND ART

Visual expressions created during the 1960s and early '70s by relatively unknown or amateur artists and designers belonging to the anti-establishment movement variously known as 'the underground', 'alternative society', 'flower power', 'counter/freak/hippie' or 'youth culture'. (The word 'underground' implied a non-official, secret, subversive movement.) Underground Art was predominantly graphic in character, i.e. posters, photographs, cartoons, comics, record cover illustrations, experimental and animated films, newspaper and magazine layouts. However, Underground culture also encompassed certain modes of behaviour, body language, dress, speech, craft activities, light shows, interior decor and styles of rock music. Poster artists working for rock music venues and record companies exploited op art effects and simulated drug delirium (books were published with titles like 'Pot Art') and illustrators evolved an eclectic style by plundering French symbolist painting, art nouveau and surrealism. The advent of the

UNDERGROUND ART MARTIN SHARP, 'Van Gogh poster' (1970?). Big O Posters, 28" x 19". Collection: J. Walker, London.

Underground or 'fringe' or 'free' press, in particular the magazines *Oz, It, Friendz,* and *Ink,* provided many artists and graphic designers with new outlets for their work. Offset lithography and the IBM typesetting machine enabled them to create complex effects by means of overprinting texts with colours and images. (As a result the print was often unreadable.) The word 'freaky' was used because Underground comics and cartoons tended to delight in the grotesque, the obscene and the pornographic.

Among the Underground artists who subsequently became known to the overground world were: Ron Cobb, Robert Crumb, Mal Dean, Michael English, Rick Griffin, John Hurford, Mike McInnerry, Victor Moscoso, Martin Sharp and S. Clay Wilson.

NB The term 'Underground Art' has also been employed to refer to posters designed for the London Underground tube system. Since 1908 London Transport has commissioned posters from distinguished contemporary artists. An archive of the posters is preserved in the London Transport Museum, Covent Garden.

● See also Comix, The Fool, Hapshash and the Coloured Coat, Light Art, Psychedelic Art, Rock Art/Design/Fash-ion, Visionary Art.

● G Melly 'Poster power' *Observer Magazine* December 3 1967 17.

● P Selz 'The hippie poster' *Graphis* **24** (135) 1968 70–7.

● J Nuttall *Bomb culture* (MacGibbon & Kee, 1968).

● G Keen & M La Rue (eds) *Underground graphics* (Academy, 1970).

● D Ellis 'The Underground press in America 1955–1970' *Journal of Popular Culture* **5** (1) Summer 1971 102–24.

● T Albright 'Cartoon visions on Muni walls' *Rolling Stone* (95) November 11 1971 10.

● D Blain 'The fringe press' *Design* (285) September 1972 66–71.

● D Fenton (ed) *Shots: photographs from the Underground press* (Academy, 1972).

● R Lewis *Outlaws of America: the Underground press and its context* (Pelican, 1972).

● N Skurka & O Gili *Underground interiors: decorating for alternative lifestyles* (MacDonald, 1972).

● H Jones 'Don't overlook the Underground press' *Penrose Annual* **66** 1973 49–62.

● M Estren *A history of Underground comics* (San Francisco, Straight Arrow Books, 1974).

● S Heller 'The Underground (press) revisited' *Print* March–April 1985 35–43, + 110.

● A Peck *Uncovering the '60s: the life and times of the Underground press* (NY, Pantheon, 1985).

● N Fountain *Underground: the London alternative press 1966–74* (Comedia/Routledge, 1988).

● O Green *Underground Art: London Transport posters 1908 to the present* (Studio Vista, 1990).

676 **UNDERGROUND FILM** Imprecise label employed by several film historians and critics which became popular in the 1960s. In fact, the invention of the term is credited to Manny Farber who used it in the 1940s to describe low-budget masculine adventure films of the 1930s and '40s. It is closely related to the terms 'avant garde', 'experimental', 'visionary' and 'art' film and also 'independent', 'free' and 'new American' cinema. Underground films acquired their specificity by contrast with 'overground', 'mainstream', 'commercial' cinema: they were normally made by single individuals (some of whom came from a fine art background), who funded them out of their own pockets in order to make 'personal statements'; the films were generally radical in both their form and content (the intention was to subvert the conventions of Hollywood films and the expectations of audiences used to such films). Mainly, the films were shot on 8mm and 16mm. They were normally seen by small, specialist audiences and shown at happenings, multi-media discotheques, festivals, at minority venues such as arts labs and film co-ops. (A narrower definition of 'Underground Films' would limit them to films made by people closely identified with the Underground subculture of the '60s.) American film-makers categorized as 'Underground' included Andy Warhol, Kenneth Anger, Bruce Conner, Stan Brakhage, Maya Deren, Robert Breer, and Stan VanDerBeek.

● See also Arts Lab, Expanded Cinema, Happenings, Structural/Materialist Film.

● G Battcock (ed) *The new American cinema: a critical anthology* (NY, Dutton, 1967).

● S Renan *The Underground Film: an introduction to its development in America* (Studio Vista, 1967).

● 'Avant garde film in England & Europe' *Studio International* **190** (978) November–December 1975, special issue.

● S Dwoskin *Film is...the international free cinema* (Peter Owen, 1975).

● S Luginbuhl (ed) *Cinema Underground oggi* (Padova, Mastrogiacomo Editore, 1975).

● H Scheugl & E Schmidt *Eine Subgeschichte des Films: Lexicon des Avantgarde – experimental – und underground films* 2 vols (Frankfurt, Suhrkamp, 1975).

● P Sitney *Visionary film* (NY, Oxford University Press, 1975).

● S Brakhage *Film at its wit's end: eight avant garde film-makers* (NY, McPherson & Co, 1989).

677 UNEXPRESSIONISM

A term coined by the Italian critic Germano Celant to designate those artists of the 1980s whose work rejected the mystifications of the expressionistic style of painting dominant in the first half of the decade (see Neo-Expressionism). Celant first used the label in Italian – 'Inespressionismo' – in 1981 and then in English as the title of a book published in 1988. The Unexpressionists Celant had in mind were both men and women, both American and European. They worked in various media: photography, performance, video, sculpture and mixed-media installations, so this was not a common factor. They also addressed different subject matter though many of them did create works in response to mass-media imagery and as comments on issues of authorship, ownership, and commodification (see Media Art, Neo-Geo, Simulation/Simulacra/Hyperreality). According to Celant, what distinguished their work from the neo-expressionists, was an 'analytical and critical investigation of banality and its deficiencies'. Among the artists Celant cited were: Gretchen Bender, Tony Cragg, Jenny Holzer, Jeff Koons, Sherrie Levine, Robert Longo, Gerhard Merz, Cindy Sherman, Ettore Spalletti and Jeff Wall.

● G Celant *Inespressionismo Americano* (Genoa, Bonini, 1981).

● — *Unexpressionism: art beyond the contemporary* (NY, Rizzoli, 1988).

678 UNIVERSAL LIMITED ART EDITIONS (ULAE)

An American 'lithographic institution', i.e. a print workshop/publishing house established by Tatyana Grosman (1904–82) at West Islip, New York in the mid 1950s. ULAE was noted for its pioneering efforts on behalf of lithography, its slow production times and its reliance on traditional craft skills and technologies. Amongst the artists who worked with Grosman and her printers were Jim Dine, Helen Frankenthaler, Jasper Johns, Robert Motherwell, Barnett Newman, Larry Rivers and James Rosenquist. An archive of ULAE prints forms part of the collection of the Art Institute of Chicago.

● See also Atelier 17, Collaborations, Curwen Studio, Kelpra Studio, Paddington Printshop, Tamarind Lithography Workshop, Tyler Graphics.

● M Bloch *Words and images – Universal Limited Art Editions* (Los Angeles, Wright Art Gallery, University of California, 1978).

● E Sparks & A Wallach *Universal Limited Art Editions: a history and catalogue, the first 25 years* (Chicago, Art Institute/NY, Abrams, 1989).

679 UNOFFICIAL SOVIET ART

(Also Non-Conformist/ Red/ Samizdat/ Underground Art & Sovart) In the USSR under the totalitarian rule of Stalin, the doctrine of socialist realism was formulated and imposed upon artists in the early 1930s. Avant garde and modernistic forms of art were discouraged and in 1932 independent artistic organizations were abolished and the visual arts were brought under state control via the Ministry of Culture and the Union of Soviet Artists. Later an Academy of Arts was established to control art education. Any art produced by amateurs or ex-professionals (i.e. those expelled from the Union) outside the official system thus became 'unofficial' and had to be subsidized by the artists themselves. (They had to find and pay for their own materials and studio spaces.) Because Unofficial Soviet Art refused to serve the goals laid down by the Communist Party, criticism of the Soviet system was implied even if the content of the work did not actively attack it in the same way that so-called 'dissident' art and literature did.

Unofficial Soviet Art began to appear in public during the early 1960s during the era of Khrushchev. A famous confrontation took place between Khrushchev and the sculptor Ernst Neizvestny concerning the validity of

UNOFFICIAL SOVIET ART ALEKSANDR DUDIN, 'Demonstration' (1989). Oil on canvas, 100cm x 130 cm. Photo: Camden Arts Centre.

modern art. Unofficial Soviet Art tended to be highly individualistic, stylistically diverse and uneven in quality. There were abstract, kinetic, surrealistic, neo-expressionist, and pop pictures, religious images, scenes from Jewish life, erotic, nostalgic, escapist and fantasy subjects. Artists and groups included: Neizvestny, Lydia Masterkova, Leonhard Lapin, Boris Sveshnikov, Oskar Rabin and the Liazonovo Group, Mikhail Shemyakin and the Petersburg Group, Lev Nusberg and the Dvizhenie or Movement Group.

Numbers of artists banded together to mount unauthorized apartment and open-air exhibitions. A notorious one – the 'Bulldozer' show – took place in a field near Moscow (September 1974) which the authorities broke up with bulldozers and water cannon. Gradually, Unofficial artists achieved more freedom and became better known internationally. Exhibitions of their work even began to take place in the West, e.g. a show at the ICA, London, in 1977 and a show at the Arts Club, Washington, in the same year. Many Western art critics were disappointed by the small scale, derivativeness and low quality of art featured in these exhibitions. However, some Westerners became fans: the American collector Norton Dodge for instance, a specialist in smuggled Unofficial Soviet Art, had assembled a collection of over 3,000 items by the 1980s.

Also during the 1970s a number of Unofficial artists left the USSR and began to practise abroad – hence the label 'émigré art'. Alexander Glezer, another collector of Unofficial Soviet Art, emigrated in 1975 and established a Russian Museum in Exile in France (it was later relocated to Jersey City). Some émigré artists managed to achieve critical and commercial success in the West, e.g. Neizvestny, Komar & Melamid. By 1981 about 100 ex-Soviet artists were living in or near New York.

In the 1980s, following the advent of the new glasnost and perestroika policies of Gorbachev, the prospects for artistic freedom and expansion in the USSR improved dramatically. Many informal artists' associations and clubs were established and experimental shows/happenings organized. Yurii Albert, a conceptual painter, claimed that Soviet art had entered a new phase which he called 'Soviet eclecticism'. In 1987 Sotheby's organized a sale of Soviet art in Moscow which included works by Unofficial artists (an indication that the label 'Unofficial' was becoming outmoded). The show of the paintings of Francis Bacon held in Moscow in 1988 also augured well for a flow of cultural exchanges between East and West. A year later the ICA in London gave shows to the avant garde painter Erik Bulatov and the installation artist Ilya Kabakov. The USSR eventually perceived the financial and cultural benefits of exporting Soviet art to the West, consequently they permitted Volkert Klaucke to form a company called 'Sovart' for the purpose of placing Soviet artists with Western galleries.

● See also Diasporist Painting, Dvizhenie, Komar & Melamid, Totalitarian Art.

◉ P Sjeklocha & I Mead *Unofficial Art in the Soviet Union* (Berkeley & Los Angeles, 1967).

◉ J Berger 'The Moscow underground' *Realities* March 1969 40–3, 92.

◉ I Golomshtock 'The mechanism of control: Unofficial Art in the USSR' *Studio International* **188** (972) December 1974 239–44.

◉ — & A Glezer *Unofficial Art from the Soviet Union* (Secker & Warburg, 1977).

◉ A Hilton & N Dodge 'Soviet "Unofficial Art" in the U.S.' *Art in America* **65** (6) November–December 1977 113–19.

◉ N Dodge & A Hilton (eds) *New art from the Soviet Union: the known and the unknown* (Washington DC, Arts Club, 1977).

◉ M Tupitsyn *Russian new wave* (NY, Contemporary Russian Art Center, 1981).

◉ J Gambrell 'Report from Moscow: Soviet Art today' *Art in America* **73** (11) November 1985 31–7.

◉ S Bojko & others *Russian Samizdat Art* C. Doria (ed) (NY, Willis Locker & Owens, 1986).

◉ M Cullerne-Brown & R Permar 'Russian reports' *Art Monthly* (102) December–January 19867 7–11.

◉ 'L'art au pays des Soviets 1963–88' *Les Cahiers du Musée d'Art Moderne* (26) Winter 1988.

⬤ J Gambrell 'Notes on the underground' *Art in America* **76** (11) November 1988 126–36, 193.

⬤ R Walker 'The making of a market' *Art News* **88** (3) March 1989 138–43.

⬤ A Wallach 'Import/export: marketing perestroika' *Art in America* **77** (4) April 1989 53–67.

⬤ M Cullerne-Brown *Contemporary Russian Art* (Oxford, Phaidon, 1989).

⬤ D Thorp *Transformation: the legacy of authority. Recent art from the Soviet Union* (The Showroom/Camden Arts Centre, 1989).

⬤ M Tupitsyn *Margins of Soviet Art* (Milan, Giancarlo Politi, 1989).

⬤ *Von der Revolution zue Perestroika* (Cologne, Ludwig Collection, 1990).

⬤ M Cullerne-Brown *Art under Stalin* (Oxford, Phaidon Press, 1991).

⬤ A Solomon *The irony tower: Soviet artists in a time of Glasnost* (NY, Knopf, 1991).

680 URBANISM

This term became fashionable in architectural circles during the 1980s. It was often used as a synonym for urban or town planning. The derivation seems to have been from the French: 'urbanisme'; Le Corbusier published a text with this title in 1926. However, the term has also been used by sociologists: Louis Wirth wrote an essay on Urbanism in 1938; he intended by it a specific mode of life associated with city life (as against rural life). For architects and planners, the suffix '-ism' suggests a practice or doctrine, a positive philosophy of urban design. European neo-classical architects such as Leon Krier certainly took an interest in the history of cities and in the renewal of urban values during the '80s. His brother Robert wrote a key text providing a detailed analysis of urban space. The Kriers and others saw the need for a contextual approach to infill and the need to design not merely striking individual buildings but whole streets, squares, crescents, arcades and even towns. They also argued against zoning (i.e. organization of cities in terms of zones defined by function: residential areas, industrial areas, etc.). The traditional conveniences and pleasures of urban life were to be restored by human-scale buildings constructed from similar materials and sharing a common style, designing quarters with a mix of functions, and by providing communal spaces; the motor car and commuting were to be resisted. Many of these ideas had previously been broached in the 1960s by Jane Jacobs in her critique of American town planning.

Krier has designed a master-plan for the redevelopment of Spitalfields in London, a project for a new city in the Canary Islands called Atlantis and a new town – Poundbury, Dorset – on land owned by Prince Charles. The latter has hailed Seaside, a neo-classical style resort in Florida built according to an urban code laid down by the developer Robert Davis, as a highly successful example of Urbanism. Quinlan Terry's neo-classical, Richmond riverside development in West London has also been highly praised.

● See also Contextual Architecture, New Classicism, Townscape.

⬤ L Wirth 'Urbanism as a way of life' *American Journal of Sociology* **44** 1938 1–24.

⬤ P Lavedan *Histoire de l'Urbanisme* 3 vols (Paris, Henri Laurens Édition, 1952–60).

⬤ J Jacobs *The death and life of great American cities: the failure of town planning* (NY, Random House, 1961/London, J Cape, 1962).

⬤ R Krier *Urban space (Stadtraum)* (NY, Rizzoli/London, Academy Editions, 1979).

⬤ 'American Urbanism 1' *Architectural Design* **56** (9) September 1986.

⬤ C Jencks 'Ad hoc and Urbanist: toward a city with memory' – in – *Architecture today* (Academy Editions, 1988) 158–77.

⬤ J Glancey 'Urbanism' – in – *New British architecture* (Thames & Hudson, 1989) 164–80.

⬤ R Hertz & N Klein *Twentieth-century art theory: Urbanism, politics & mass culture* (Englewood Cliffs, NJ, Prentice Hall, 1990).

681 USABLE ART

A concept devised by the American critic John Perreault to describe works selected for a 1981 exhibition. Artists whose works appeared in this show included Chris Burden, Scott Burton, Cynthia Carlson, Robert Kushner, Arlene Slavin and George Sugarman. 'Usable Art' referred to objects made by fine artists that served practical functions as against purely aesthetic ones: e.g. vehicles, kites, furniture, greenhouses, lights, tiles, pots, jewellery, clothes. Artist-designed fashions have also been called 'wearable art'. Such terms appear to be alternatives to 'applied' or 'decorative arts'.

● See also Artists' Furniture, Conceptual Clothing.

⬤ J Perreault *Usable Art* (Plattsburgh, New York, State University College, Myers Fine Arts Gallery, 1981).

⬤ — 'Usable Art' *Portfolio* (USA) **3** (4) July–August 1981 60–3.

⬤ J Dale *Art to wear* (NY, Abbeville Press, 1986).

682 USCO

(Us Company) An American artists' collective founded in 1963 by Steve Durkee, Gerd Stern and Michael Callahan that was based in an abandoned church at

USCO Double page spread from *Image* magazine, Spring 1967.

Garnerville, New York. The fluctuating membership of USCO included poets, film-makers, engineers and visual artists. USCO were committed to a mixed-media approach and designed kinetic environments, happenings called 'Be Ins' and a multi-media discotheque. They also established an organization called the 'Intermedia Systems Corporation' in conjunction with a number of behavioural scientists from Harvard University. USCO was a characteristic cultural phenomenon of the '60s and did not survive beyond the end of the decade.

● See also Environmental Art, Inter-Media, Kinetic Art, Light Art.

● R Masters & others *Psychedelic art* (Weidenfeld & Nicolson, 1968).

● R Kostelanetz *The theatre of mixed means* (Pitman, 1970) 243–71.

● G Youngblood *Expanded cinema* (NY, Dutton, 1970).

683 **UTILITY** (Including Emergency Furniture, Home Front Furniture) As a result of the Second World War, a system of government controls was imposed on British industry and a system of rationing on the British people. From 1941 to '51 the Board of Trade supervised the manufacture of furniture, fabrics, clothes and certain household goods in order to ensure the maximum use of scarce raw materials and labour, and also to ensure a fair allocation of goods. In 1941 'emergency furniture' was produced which was poor in comparison to the Utility furniture which appeared from 1943 onwards. Utility furniture and fashions were practical, well made, economical with materials and plain and simple in design. Established furniture designers like Gordon Russell – head of the Utility furniture design team – seized the opportunity of the wartime emergency to fulfil a design philosophy, i.e. to raise the whole standard of design for the mass of the people by providing them with modern, functional furni-

UTILITY Utility bedroom furniture. Board of Trade Exhibition, 1943.

ture. From 1948 onwards controls on the furniture industry began to be lifted, hence the introduction of the term 'freedom furniture'.

Enid Marx was responsible for Utility fabric designs and Hardy Amies, Norman Hartnell, Captain Molyneux and Victor Steibel designed the prototypes for women's austere dresses and suits. Writing in 1987, Sarah Mower predicted a Utility look revival in 1988.

● See also Austerity/Binge, G Plan Furniture.

◉ (Utility fashions) *Vogue* October 1942.

◉ *CC41: Utility furniture and fashion* (Geffrye Museum/ Inner London Education Authority, 1974).

◉ S Mower 'Forties glam' *Observer* December 20 1987 37.

◉ H Dover *Home Front Furniture: British Utility design 1941-51* (Aldershot, Scolar Press, 1991).

◉ F Choay *L'urbanisme, Utopies et réalités* (Paris, Éditions du Seuil, 1965).

◉ M Nicoletti 'Flash Gordon and the twentieth century Utopia' *Architectural Review* **140** (834) August 1966 87–91.

◉ C Jencks *Architecture 2000: predictions and methods* (Studio Vista, 1971).

◉ M Tafuri *Architecture and Utopia: design and capitalist development* (Cambridge, Mass, MIT Press, 1976).

◉ R Fishman *Urban Utopias in the twentieth century* (NY, Basic Books, 1977).

684 UTOPIAN ARCHITECTURE

The concept of Utopia ('no place') – an imaginary island where a perfect society existed – was originated by Sir Thomas More in 1516. During the nineteenth century Utopia became a future goal striven for by many anarchists and socialists. 'Utopian Architecture' then refers to designs and projects for future cities and megastructures that provide ideal living spaces for their inhabitants. Many leading modern architects have shared the social vision of Left-wing political theorists and have envisaged structures that would assist in the realization of that vision. Their drawings of future cities of towers have often evoked the label 'utopian' in the negative sense of 'impractical', yet some did come to fruition. However, the failure of so many modern architectural housing schemes in the post-1960 era has made people much more sceptical of the abilities of architects as social engineers. Indeed, it could be argued that vast Utopian schemes are a sign of megalomania on the part of architects seeking to impose their designs on a passive and ignorant populace (hence the alternatives of social architecture, community architecture and participatory design). Such schemes also normally envisage a *tabula rasa,* an empty site, whereas in most cases new architecture has to relate to what already exists, a complex urban fabric. What is valuable about dreams of a Utopian Architecture is that they allow architects to question existing solutions and to think beyond current constraints.

NB Some writers use the words 'utopian', 'fantastic' and 'visionary' interchangeably.

● See also Conceptual Architecture, Experimental Architecture, Fantastic Architecture, Visionary Architecture.

685 UTOPIE GROUP

A French, Marxist, experimental architectural group formed in Paris in 1967. Members included J. Aubert, Jean-Paul Jungmann, A. Stinco and H. Tonka. Utopie was concerned with the social utility of architecture, with expendability and the use of mobile, pneumatic structures. It also produced a magazine in 1967 entitled *Utopie* and collages satirizing the futurist visions of other architects.

● See also Expendability in Design, Experimental Architecture, Pneumatic Architecture.

◉ 'Voyage aux alentours d'Utopie' *L'Architecture d'Aujourd'hui* **9**, December 1967.

◉ J Aubert & others 'Utopie' *Architectural Design* **38** (6) June 1968 255.

◉ 'La pneumatique' *Architectural Design* **38** (6) June 1968 273–7.

UTOPIE GROUP Satirical collage of futurist architectural ideologies from Archigram and Mies van der Rohe to Le Corbusier.

686 VENICE BIENNALE

One of the world's largest and most important avant garde art exhibitions held every two years in a number of permanent pavilions in the Giardini di Castello, Venice, Italy. The exhibition was instituted by the city of Venice in 1895 and an autonomous agency was created to organize it in 1928. The Biennale is international in scope – over 40 nations take part and their pavilions have distinctive architectural styles. Obviously, if an artist is chosen to represent his or her country at Venice it is an honour and a benefit to their career. Prizes are also awarded. In 1964 Robert Rauschenberg was the artist chosen to represent the United States and he was also awarded a prize. Four years later, at the time of student unrest in Europe, the Biennale was criticized and disrupted by protesters. In recent years a thematic exhibition has also been mounted; in 1986 the theme was 'art and science'. Catalogues are issued and the Biennale is extensively reviewed in the art press.

● See also Documenta.

● R Bazzioni *60 anni della Biennale di Venezia* (Venice, 1962).

● L Alloway *The Venice Biennale 1895–1968: from salon to goldfish bowl* (Faber & Faber, 1969).

● C Pirovani (ed) *Arte e scienza, biologia, tecnologia e informatica* (Venice, Edizioni La Biennale, 1986).

● G Burn 'Anyone for Venice?' *Sunday Times Magazine* July 15 1990 42–6.

687 VERIST SCULPTURE

A three-dimensional equivalent of photo-realist painting. To achieve verisimilitude, Verist Sculpture depended upon the technique of making casts from the human body in fibreglass and polyester resin. In the period 1967 to 1970 American practitioners such as John de Andrea and Duane Hanson devised narrative tableaux, with social and political themes, composed of groups of life-sized figures dressed in genuine clothes and supported by other props. Like waxworks these petrified figures occupied a twilight zone between artifice and reality. The illusionism of most Verist Sculptures, like that of most photo-realist paintings, was more effective in reproduc-

tion than 'in the flesh'.

● See also Photo-Realism, Tableau, Trompe L'Oeil.

● J Masheck 'Verist Sculpture: Hanson and de Andrea' *Art in America* **60** (6) November–December 1972 90–7.

● U Kultermann *New realism* (Mathews Miller Dunbar, 1972).

688 VIDEO ART

(Including Alternative & Community Television, Artists' Video, Guerrilla Television, Satellite Art, Street Video, TV Art, Video Sculpture) Videotape recordings or video sculptures and installations made by fine artists. The Latin word 'video' meaning 'I see' was employed in the United States in the 1950s to refer to television. As TV became a mass medium in that decade one of the first artistic responses was to attack it by erasing programmes, burying TV sets, using magnets to distort its images, etc. Technological developments in the second half of the 1960s made portable video equipment (portapaks, cameras plus videotape recorders) available to artists who could then play back their recordings via TV monitors. Videotape cassettes could then be produced for sale in the same way as records and sound tapes. In the 1970s a number of art galleries began to market videotapes by artists in the same way as prints and multiples, e.g. Gerry Schum's 'Videogalerie' in Germany and Castelli-Sonnabend in New York. Museums and art centres (such as MoMA in New York and the ICA in London) began to collect artists' tapes in order to establish video archives.

Video's significance was that it broke the monopoly of broadcast television. Individuals and small groups could afford to make TV 'programmes' and in doing so could challenge and subvert the norms and conventions of broadcast TV. Much early Video Art was a self-reflexive exploration of the medium itself and it usually had a love–hate relationship with mainstream television. In the United States some artists gained access to broadcast TV facilities and had their electronic experiments transmitted to the public as early as 1968, but in Britain it was not until the 1980s that Artists' Video began to appear regularly on TV arts programmes.

Although at first picture and sound qualities were poor, images were only black and white, and there were limit-

VIDEO ART SIMON ROBERTSHAW & MIKE JONES, 'Great Britain' (1989). National Videowall Project, organized by Merseyside Moviola and L.B Camden (Arts & Entertainment). Shown at the Tate Gallery, Liverpool & the Diorama, London. Photo: courtesy of Paul Collett.

ed editing facilities, video artists were attracted by the immediacy of the medium, its instant record, erase and playback facilities. Community artists seeking an alternative to the gallery system employed video in the streets to communicate local news to the people of a neighbourhood or they established Video workshops so that nonartists could acquire video skills and produce their own television. This 'alternative television' movement was part of the counter culture of the late 1960s and its ideas were explored in the journal *Radical Software* ((1) 1970). Producing social change rather than art was the principal goal of 'alternative' or 'community television'. As the counter culture lost impetus in the years that followed, video became more and more a genre of fine art.

Video had a particular appeal to artists working in the live arts and time-based genres of dance, performance and body art because it enabled them to watch themselves on TV monitors in real time and to record their actions for posterity. Video's mirror-like capacity plus its time-shift possibilities enabled artists to devise strange installations in gallery spaces which involved the artist's and spectator's self-image in various ways. Other artists emphasized the TV monitor as an object and constructed robot-like sculptures and environments from them. Multiple sets arranged as a 'videowall' could all show the same image or different images in sequences controlled by computers. The term 'Satellite Art' refers to the use of communication satellites in space as a means of bringing together live, video work by artists from different countries.

The video medium lends itself to many different aesthetics – minimalist, structural/material, feminist, formalist, political, etc. – hence there is no common stylistic denominator in work of the list of artists who have made use of it since the '60s: Laurie Anderson, Joseph Beuys, Dara Birnbaum, Catherine Elwes, Gilbert & George, Dan Graham, David Hall, Mick Harvey, Susan Hiller, Les Levine, Stephen Littman, Stuart Marshall, Bruce Nauman, Nam June Paik, Klaus Rinke, Keith Sonnier, Stan VanDerBeek, Stana Vasulka, Bill Viola and William Wegman.

● See also Community Art & Media, Expanded Cinema, Installation, Rock Video, Scratch Video,Time-Based Arts, Underground Art.

◐ G Youngblood *Expanded cinema* (NY, Dutton, 1970) 257–344.

● M Shamberg *Guerrilla Television* (NY, Holt, Rinehart & Winston, 1971).

● 'The issue of Video Art' *ArtsCanada* **30** (4) October 1973.

● *Video Show* (Serpentine Gallery, 1975).

● 'Video Art' *Studio International* **191** (981) May–June 1976, special issue.

● P Gale (ed) *Video by artists* (Toronto, Art Metropole, 1976).

● J Gill (ed) *Video: state of the art* (NY, Rockefeller Foundation, 1976).

● I Schneider & B Korot (eds) *Video Art; an anthology* (NY, Harcourt Brace Jovanovich, 1976).

● D Davis & A Simmons (eds) *The new television: a public/private art* (Cambridge, Mass, MIT Press, 1977).

● G Battcock (ed) *New Artists' Video: a critical anthology* (NY, Dutton, 1978).

● B London 'Independent Video: the first fifteen years' *Artforum* **9** (11) September 1980 38–41. (See also the chronology of video activity in the USA 1965–80, pp. 42–5.)

● H Nigg & G Wade *Community media* (Zürich, Regenbogen, 1980).

● G Wade *Street Video* (Leicester, Blackthorn Press, 1981).

● J Hanhardt *Nam June Paik* (NY, Whitney Museum of American Art/Norton, 1982).

● W Herzogenrath (ed) *Videokunst in Deutschland 1963–82* (Stuttgart, Verlag Gerd Hatje, 1982).

● B Gruber & M Vedder *Art & Video: international development and artists* (Cologne, Dumont, 1983).

● K Huffman (ed) *Video; a retrospective 1974–84* (Long Beach, California, Long Beach Museum of Art, 1984).

● 'Video: the reflexive medium' *Art Journal* **45** (3) Fall 1985, special issue.

● D Boyle *Video classics: a guide to Video Art* (Oryx Press, 1986).

● P Podesta (ed) *Resolution: a critique of Video Art* (Los Angeles Contemporary Exhibitions, 1986).

● *Scanners: Video Art now* (London Video Arts, 1986).

● 'Special issue on Video Art' *High Performance* Spring 1987.

● K Huffman & D Mignot (eds) *The arts for television* (Los Angeles, Museum of Contemporary Art/Amsterdam, Stedelijk Museum, 1987). Exhibition also shown at the Tate Gallery in 1989.

● D Mignot (ed) *Revision: art programmes of European television stations* (Amsterdam, Stedelijk Museum, 1987).

● P Ryan 'A genealogy of video' *Leonardo* **21** (1) 1988 39–44.

● W Herzogenrath *Nam June Paik: video works 1963–88* (Hayward Gallery, 1988).

● R Perrée *Into Video Art: the characteristics of a medium* (Rotterdam/Amsterdam, Con Rumore, 1988).

● L Haskel (ed) *Video positive '89* (Liverpool, Merseyside Moviola, 1989).

● W Herzogenrath *Video-Skulptur: retrospektiv und aktuell* (Cologne, Kunstverein, 1989).

● S Cubitt *Timeshift: on video culture* (Comedia/Routledge, 1991).

689 VISIONARY ARCHITECTURE A description applied to the work of a number of architects both modern and pre-modern. (Two pre-modern visionaries were Etienne-Louis Boullée and Claude-Nicolas Ledoux.) The term became current primarily as a result of an exhibition organized by Arthur Drexler at MoMA, New York in 1960. Since then several books have been published and exhibitions mounted devoted to the topic. Visionary Architecture consists of imaginary, possible or impossible structures; consequently in physical terms such 'architecture' normally takes the form of collages, drawings and models. (Presumably, once such architecture is constructed it ceases to be visionary.)

Drexler's show included designs by Louis Kahn, William Katavolos, Frederick Kiesler, Le Corbusier, Hans Poelzig, Paolo Soleri, and Michael Webb. Drexler identified three categories of designs: (1) those based on mountains/caves; (2) those based on the image of the road including bridges and floating suspended structures; and (3), those with forms derived from geometry. In some cases architects' visions were exaggerations or distortions of structures that already existed, in other cases they were speculations about, or anticipations of, the future. Visionary Architecture has often flourished in repressive societies where conservative tastes prevail: young architects with little prospect of seeing their radical designs built expend their energies on drawings of imaginary cities and buildings.

There is clearly an overlap between utopian/fantastic and Visionary Architecture; however, the term 'visionary' suggests a more individualistic kind of imagining than 'utopian' while much 'fantastic' architecture has been built.

● See also Conceptual Architecture, Experimental Architecture, Fantastic Architecture, Utopian Architecture.

● 'Opinion: Visionary Architecture at the Museum of Modern Art, New York' *Architectural Design* **31** (5) May 1961 181–2.

● *Visionary architects: Boullée, Ledoux, Lequeu* (Houston, University of St Thomas, 1967).

● A Sky & M Stone *Unbuilt America: forgotten architecture in the United States from Thomas Jefferson to the space age* (NY, McGraw-Hill, 1976).

● V Lampugnani *Visionary Architecture of the twentieth century: master drawings from Frank Lloyd Wright to Aldo Rossi* (Thames & Hudson, 1982).

● M Belov & others *Nostalgia of culture: contemporary Soviet Visionary Architecture* (Architectural Association, 1988).

● G Feuerstein *Visionare Architektur, Wien 1958–88* (Berlin, Ernst & Sohn, 1988).

Writing in 1971 the American critic Thomas Albright identified a new movement he called 'Visionary Art'. (Of course, the term 'visionary' as applied to art was not new because such British painters as William Blake and Samuel Palmer had long been described as 'visionaries'.) It emerged from the mystical, symbolic and religious undercurrents of early psychedelic art in San Francisco. The paintings and drawings of the movement were characterized by the use of vivid colours, a graphic sensibility and an emphasis on content. Its influences and sources were surrealism, Oriental religions such as Zen, Yoga and Sufism, and the drug experience of peyote and LSD. Visionary artists included John Almond, Michael Bowen, Philip Hocking and Bill Martin.

● See also Cosmic Art, Fantastic Art, Fantastic Realism, Psychedelic Art, Sci-Fi Art.

○ T Albright 'Visuals' Part 1 *Rolling Stone* (88) August 5 1971 34–5; Part 2 *Rolling Stone* (90) September 2 1971 34–7; Part 3 *Rolling Stone* (91) September 16 1971 40–2.

○ *Visions* (Corte Madera, California, Pomegranate Publications, 1971).

An extremely broad category encompassing such phenomena as pictorial advertisement, television, photography, films, comics, illustrated magazines, typography and computer graphics. The term generally refers to the modern mass media rather than to the traditional fine arts though, arguably, they too communicate via the sense of sight. The stress on the word 'communication' (implying a signifying process involving a sender, medium/message and receiver rather than an art object) was probably due to the influence of post-1945 communications theory.

In the 1960s many colleges of art and design in Britain and Europe introduced Visual Communication courses. Often the term replaced 'graphic design' which in turn had replaced 'commercial art'. In the United States the preferred term seemed to be 'Communication Arts'. In Germany 'Visuelle Kommunikation', a label used as the title of a 1972 anthology edited by Herman Ehmer and employed from 1970 by contributors to such periodicals

VISUAL COMMUNICATION Paperback cover design, *Visuelle Communication* (Dumont Aktuell).

as *Aesthetik und Kommunikation* (centred on the Institute for Experimental Art & Aesthetics, Frankfurt), designated a field of study concerned with raising the level of political awareness. Contemporary mass communications were seen as controlling consciousness in order to preserve the status quo. To achieve social change it was thought vital for critics to expose the repressive ideologies embedded in mass-media imagery. Traditional aesthetics were considered suspect and were rejected along with the heirarchical distinction between high and low culture.

● See also Commodity Aesthetics, Information Graphics, Media Art, Pictorial Rhetoric, Semiotics.

○ J Muller-Brockman *A history of Visual Communication* (Alec Tiranti, 1971).

○ H Ehmer (ed) *Visuelle Kommunikation* (Cologne, Dumont, 1972).

692 WASHINGTON COLOUR SCHOOL

Two abstract painters from Washington (DC, USA) noted for their use of acrylic paint and emphasis on colour – Morris Louis and Kenneth Noland – achieved international recognition in the late 1950s and as a result drew attention to Washington as a centre for contemporary art. The colour tendency initiated by Louis and Noland was developed by several other Washington artists: Gene Davis, Tom Downing, Howard Mehring and Paul Reed. Their immaculately executed canvases were usually very large, totally abstract, with repetitive hard-edge patterns and devices. These 'colour painters' attracted critical attention in the early 1960s, but not everyone was impressed by the optical appeal of their work: some sceptics judged their post-painterly abstractions 'gutless' and 'cosmetic'.

● See also Colour-Field Painting, Hard-Edge Painting, Op Art, Post-Painterly Abstraction, Stain Painting.

● L Ahlander 'The emerging art of Washington' *Art International* **6** (9) November 25 1962 30–3.

● E Stevens 'The Washington Color painters' *Arts Magazine* **XL** November 1965 30–3.

WASHINGTON COLOUR SCHOOL THOMAS DOWNING, 'Rapt red' (1963). Oil on canvas, 96" x 96". Collection of Mr & Mrs James Harithas, New York.

● G Nordland *Washington Color painters* (Washington DC, Washington Gallery of Modern Art, 1965).

● G Davis 'Starting out in the '50s' *Art in America* **66** (4) July–August 1978 88–94.

693 WEST COAST SCHOOL

(Also Pacific School) Since 1945 many artists have emerged from or settled in the cities of the Western seaboard of the United States: Seattle, San Francisco and Los Angeles. From time to time critics write articles and curators mount exhibitions posing the question 'Is there a West Coast School?'. The answer is usually 'No, but...'. Of course, many national and international movements in art have had their followers amongst West Coast artists, but often they were given a distinctive inflection there because of the area's climate, lifestyle, history, links with the Orient, and so forth. Important West Coast artists and movements have included: Mark Tobey and Morris Graves (two artists associated with abstract expressionism who lived in Seattle and were influenced by Oriental art); Bay Area figuration; hard-edge painting; pop art (represented by Mel Ramos, Wayne Thiebaud, Ed Ruscha and the British painter David Hockney); assemblage and tableau (Ed Kienholz who moved to LA in 1953); naive art (Simon Rodia, creator of the famous Watts Towers); the funk art ceramicists; the customizing and finish fetish cults of Los Angeles; San Francisco rock poster art in the psychedelic style and underground comix. According to an article by Richard B. Woodward published in the *New York Times* in 1989, the differences between the East and West coasts of the United States in terms of art diminished in the 1980s as New York galleries opened branches in Los Angeles and artists on both coasts worked in very similar ways, and travelled back and forth. California curators, Woodward reported, no longer bothered with regional shows.

● See also Bay Area Figuration, CalArts, Comix, Customizing & Custom Painting, Finish Fetish, Freestyle, Funk Art, Hard-Edge Painting, Los Angeles Fine Arts Squad, Psychedelic Art, Underground Art, Visionary Art.

● *Eleven Los Angeles artists* (Hayward Gallery, 1971).

● P Plagens *Sunshine muse: contemporary art on the West*

Coast (NY, Praeger, 1974).

● *Painting and sculpture in California: the modern era* (San Francisco Museum of Modern Art, 1976).

● (Special issue on Californian art) *Data* (27) July– September 1977.

● P Plagens & others *Decade: Los Angeles painting in the 1970s* (Los Angeles, Art Center College of Design, 1981).

● *Southern California artists 1940–80* (Laguna Beach, California, Laguna Beach Museum of Art, 1981).

● M Tuchman & others *Art in Los Angeles: seventeen artists in the '60s* (Los Angeles, County Museum of Art, 1981).

● P Tuchman 'The sunshine boys' *Connoisseur* (USA) February 1987 62–9.

● R Woodward 'For art, coastal convergence' *New York Times* July 16 1989 1, +33, Arts & leisure section.

694 WESTKUNST (West or Western Art) Title of a large-scale exhibition held at the Rheinhallen, Cologne, in 1981 which provided an international survey of contemporary art in Europe and North America since 1939. The show was sponsored by the city of Cologne and organized by Kasper Koenig, a freelance curator. According to Koenig, the term 'Westkunst' was intended as a 'geographical definition' of radical art rather than a 'political constellation'. Approximately 250 artists were included and over 850 works were exhibited (all but eight were by men). One notable feature of the exhibition was the starting date of 1939 which enabled the wartime period to be considered. Another was the reconstruction of certain famous installations such as Claes Oldenburg's 'The store' and the Pop component of the 1956 'This is Tomorrow' exhibition. Westkunst was criticized for being 'too American' and for its omission of '70s art, a fact that was due to the premature exhaustion of the budget. British critics also complained about the inadequate/patchy representation of British art.

● See also Installation, This is Tomorrow.

● L Glozer *WestKunst: Zeitgenossische Kunst seit 1939* (Cologne, Dumont Buchverlag, 1981).

● K Koenig & L Glozer 'Westkunst' *Art Monthly* (49) September 1981 2.

● N Marmer 'Isms on the Rhine' *Art in America* **69** (9) November 1981 112–23.

WOMEN ARTISTS SLIDE LIBRARY HANNAH O'SHEA, still from performance section of 'A visual Time Span (A visual diary)' (1974-6). Super 8 mixed media/performance film. Photo: O'Shea.

695 WOMEN ARTISTS SLIDE LIBRARY (WASL) A British organization (a registered charity) founded in 1982 and located in London whose aim is to provide a national resource of information about the art of women, past and present, in the form of slides of works, exhibitions and events, plus a collection of books, theses, catalogues, press cuttings, tape-recorded interviews and posters. The Library seeks to represent all women artists not simply feminist ones.

Financial support has been provided by Greater London Arts and local councils; WASL also relies on the efforts of volunteers. Any women practising visual art in any medium can join WASL, as can female art historians, critics and curators. The collection is available (reference only) to publishers, dealers, curators, teachers, etc. WASL organizes exhibitions and it also publishes a bi-monthly journal, an illustrated diary, catalogues and postcards.

● See also Feminist Art, National Museum of Women in the Arts.

● P Barrie 'A projection of visual parity' *AND Journal of Art & Art Education* (7) 1985 16–17.

696 **ZEBRA**

(Also Gruppe Zebra) Name of a German group founded in Hamburg in 1965 by four painters: Dieter Asmus, Peter Nagel, Nikolaus Störtenbecker and Dietmar Ullrich. Their figurative images often depicted stop-action events. Figures and objects were generally set against flat backgrounds and executed in a precise, graphic or poster-like manner that excluded subjective expression. The style had some affinities with photo-realism but the use of commercial art techniques to solidify or metalicize organic forms produced a non-realistic result. Critics described the style as 'harsh','sleeky' and 'repellent'. Following a series of shows in Germany in the late '60s, Zebra exhibited in London in the spring of 1975.

● See also Photo-Realism, Trompe L'Oeil.

R-G Dienst *Gruppe Zebra* (Badischer Kunstverein EV, 1969).

ZEBRA (Fischer Fine Art, 1975).

697 **ZEITGEIST**

A German word meaning 'spirit of the age'. It was popularized by the idealist philosopher Georg Hegel and utilized by generations of art historians. Each age is considered to have a distinctive 'spirit' or mentality and it is this which (supposedly) accounts for perceived stylistic affinities between, say, buildings, clothes and systems of thought.

A term also used as the title of a large-scale exhibition of neo-expressionist painting and sculpture held at the Martin-Gropius-Bau, West Berlin in 1982. The show was organized by Christos Joachimides and Norman Rosenthal.

ZG – the title of a small-circulation, but highly influential art/mass-media/theory magazine edited by Rosetta Brooks – also derives from 'Zeitgeist'. The magazine was first published in London in 1980 but later it moved to New York. The adoption of this word as the title indicated a double claim: to reflect the spirit of the times and to exemplify the spirit of the times.

● See also Neo-Expressionism.

Zeitgeist (Berlin, Verlag Frolich & Kaufman, 1982).

R Harre 'What is the Zeitgeist?'– in –*Common denominators*

ZEITGEIST Front cover of *ZG* magazine (7) 1982, Desire Issue, with Cindy Sherman simulating Marilyn Monroe. The image was originally devised for a poster advertising 'Marilyn', an opera by Lorenzo Sevrero, Kassel, Germany.

in art and science M Pollock (ed) (Aberdeen University Press, 1983) 1–8.

698 **ZEN 49**

(Or Zen Group) A group of German abstract painters founded in Berlin in 1949. Members included Willi Baumeister, Hans Trier, Emil Schumacher, Bernhard Schultze, Theodor Werner, Fritz Winter and Rupprecht Geiger. These artists represented the German wing of tachisme or l'art informel; they favoured a calligraphic style of painting influenced by the art and cosmology of Zen Buddhism. Several of the artists concerned aspired to create 'absolute painting'. Zen 49 was also the title of a survey exhibition of German art produced during the ten years after the Second World War held at Baden-Baden in the winter of 1986–7.

● See also Art Informel, Tachisme.

○ *Zen 49: die ersten zehn Jahre – Orientierungen* (Baden-Baden, Staatliche Kunsthalle, 1986).

699   ZERO

(Also Group / Gruppe Zero, Group 0) An influential German experimental art group formed in Düsseldorf in 1957 by Otto Piene and Heinz Mack, both of whom had been members of Gruppe 53; a third member, Günther Uecker, joined in 1960. The word 'zero' derived from the countdown sequence of a rocket take-off, i.e. it signified 'a zone of silence for a new beginning'. Zero artists were influenced by the work of the nouvelle tendance, especially artists like Yves Klein, Jean Tinguely and Lucio Fontana. They reacted against the fashion for gestural abstraction (abstract expressionism and tachisme) and developed as an alternative a form of kinetic art exploiting light and movement with the aim of achieving a harmonious relationship with the forces of nature. They sought an art exemplifying 'purity, beauty, and silence'. White was emphasized because it contained all the other colours. Piene devised smoke and fire pictures, and also balloons filled with coloured gases; Mack created light reliefs from aluminium and glass; and Uecker made nail reliefs. The artists also engaged in happenings and demonstrations of various kinds and published three issues of a magazine *Zero* from 1958 to '61. They disbanded in 1966.

● See also Düsseldorf School, Experimental Art, Kinetic Art, Light Art, Nouvelle Tendance, Nul.

○ *Group Zero* (Philadelphia, University of Pennsylvania Institute of Contemporary Art, 1964).

○ J Thwaites 'The story of Zero' *Studio International* **170** (867) July 1965 2–9.

○ W Schmied *Heinz Mack, Otto Piene, Günther Uecker* (Hanover, Kestner-Gesellschaft, 1965).

○ C Barrett 'Group Zero' *Art & Artists* **1** (9) December 1966 54–7.

○ W Sharp *Uecker, Zero and the kinetic spirit* (NY, Kineticism Press, 1966).

○ O Piene & H Mack *Zero* (Cambridge, Mass, MIT Press, 1973), reprint of magazine.

○ S von Weise '1958–1966: Zero Group' – in – *German art in*

ZERO GÜNTHER UECKER 'New York City', nail relief, 1965. Photo: Volker Kramer.

the twentieth century: painting and sculpture 1905-85 C Joachimides & others (eds) (Royal Academy/Prestel Verlag, 1986) 468–9.

700   ZOOT SUITS

A mode of male dress popular with young blacks and chicanos in the United States in the 1930s and '40s: jackets with padded shoulders, a drape-shape and rear pleats, plus baggy trousers narrow at the ankles. In the eyes of some theorists, the emphasis on style and the extravagant use of material signified a protest against ghetto poverty and the austerity of the war years. This style provoked much antagonism and so-called 'Zoot Suit riots' took place in Los Angeles in 1943. The style is thought to have originated in the urban jazz culture of Harlem. In 1981 the style was revived and parodied in the pop music realm by the English band called 'Blue Rondo à La Turk'.

● See also Street Fashion/ Style, Subculture.

○ R Turner & S Surace 'Zoot Suiters and Mexicans' *American Journal of Sociology* **62** 1956 14–20.

○ R Elms 'Rise of the young Turk' *The Face* (20) December 1981 8–12.

○ S Cosgrove 'The Zoot Suit and style warfare' *History Workshop Journal* (18) 1984 77–91.

○ S Chibnell 'Whistle & Zoot: the changing meaning of a suit of clothes' *History Workshop Journal* (20) 1985 56–81.

○ A McRobbie (ed) *Zoot Suits and second hand clothes* (Macmillan, 1988).

BIBLIOGRAPHY

Books, catalogues and periodical articles consulted during the preparation of the A–Z entries have been listed at the foot of each entry. Readers seeking further references are advised to search the following published indexes: *ADP: Art Design Photo* (1969–77), *Art Index* (1929–), *Artbibliographies Modern* (1973–), *British Humanities Index, Répertoire d'Art et d'Archéologie, API: Architectural Periodicals Index* (RIBA, 1972–), *RILA; Répertoire International de la Littérature de l'Art* (1973–), *DAAI: Design & Applied Arts Index* (1987–). These indexes tend to employ different subject headings; consequently readers are advised to browse through them to see how they are arranged.

There is generally a time delay of months or even years before published items appear in indexes. For up-to-the minute information concerning new books and exhibition catalogues, readers should obtain the periodic lists issued by specialist art and design bookshops such as Zwemmer, Artsbibliographic, Nigel Greenwood, London Art Bookshop, and the RIBA bookshop (all in London).

Whenever possible I have indicated the major architects, artists and designers associated with each style, movement or group; consequently readers should be able to trace further information via biographical dictionaries, monographs and catalogues of one-person shows. Other key sources of information are the published catalogues to major art libraries such as those of the Victoria and Albert Museum and the Museum of Modern Art in New York.

The following bibliographies (listed in date of publication order) are restricted to books which provide general international, national and period surveys.

ARCHITECTURE

J Jacobus *Twentieth century architecture: the middle years 1940–65* (Thames & Hudson, 1966).

R Banham 'Revenge of the picturesque: English architectural polemics 1945–65' – in – *Concerning architecture* J Summerson (ed) (Allen Lane, The Penguin Press, 1968).

J Joedicke *Architecture since 1945* (Pall Mall, 1969).

P Cook *Experimental architecture* (Studio Vista, 1970).

A Jackson *The politics of architecture...* (Architectural Press, 1970).

L Benevolo *History of modern architecture* 2 vols (Routledge, 1971).

C Jencks *Architecture 2000: predictions and methods* (Studio Vista, 1971).

J Dahinden *Urban structures for the future* (Pall Mall Press, 1972).

C Jencks *Modern movements in architecture* (Harmondsworth, Penguin Books, 1973).

A Whittick *European architecture in the 20th century* (NY, Abelard-Schuman, 1974).

L Burton *A choice over our heads: architecture and design since 1830* (Talisman Books, 1978).

M Ross *Beyond metabolism: the new Japanese architecture* (NY, McGraw-Hill, 1978).

K Frampton *Modern architecture: a critical history* (Thames & Hudson, 1980).

U Kultermann *Architecture in the seventies* (Architectural Press, 1980).

S Lyall *The state of British architecture* (Architectural Press, 1980).

B Bognar *Contemporary Japanese architecture: its development and challenge* (NY, Van Nostrand Reinhold, 1985).

H Suzuki & R Banham *Contemporary architecture of Japan 1958–84* (NY, Rizzoli, 1985).

M Tafuri & F dal Co *Modern architecture* (NY, Rizzoli, 2nd ed 1986).

C Jencks *The language of post-modern architecture* (Academy Editions, 5th ed 1987).

— *Architecture today* (Academy Editions, 1988).

— *Post-modern architecture: the new classicism in art and architecture* (Academy Editions, 1988).

Charles, Prince of Wales *A vision of Britain: a personal view of architecture* (Doubleday, 1989).

W Curtis *Modern architecture since 1900* (Oxford, Phaidon, 2nd ed 1989).

J Glancey *New British architecture* (Thames & Hudson, 1989).

H Klotz & L Sabau (eds) *New York architecture* (Munich, Prestel, 1989).

A Krafft (ed) *Contemporary architecture Vol 10 1988–9* (Chapman & Hall, 1989).

J Lucan *France, architecture 1965–88* (Paris, Electa-Moniteur, 1989).

B Russell *Architecture and design 1970–90: new ideas in America* (NY, Abrams, 1989).

M Tafuri *History of Italian architecture 1944–85* (Cambridge, Mass, MIT Press, 1989).

E Coad *Spanish design & architecture* (Studio Vista, 1990).

D Davis *Museum impossible: architecture and culture in the post-Pompidou age* (NY, Abbeville Press, 1990).

J Glancey *The new moderns: interior design & architecture for the 1990s* (Mitchell Beazley, 1990).

C Jencks *The new moderns* (Academy Editions, 1990).

D Yarwood *The architecture of Europe: nineteenth & twentieth centuries* (Batsford, 1990).

ART

P Heron *The changing forms of art* (Routledge, 1955).

M Brion & others *Art since 1945* (Thames & Hudson, 1958).

N Ponente *Modern painting: contemporary trends* (Geneva, Skira, 1960).

H Rosenberg *The tradition of the new* (Thames & Hudson, 1962).

— *The anxious object...* (Thames & Hudson, 1965).

G Battcock (ed) *The new art: a critical anthology* (NY, Dutton, 1966).

W Grohmann (ed) *Art in our time: painting and sculpture throughout the world* (Thames & Hudson, 1966).

A Pellegrini *New tendencies in art* (NY, Crown, 1966).

N Calas *Art in the age of risk and other essays* (NY, Dutton, 1968).

U Kultermann *The new sculpture* (Pall Mall Press, 1969).

—*The new painting* (Pall Mall Press, 1969).

E Lucie-Smith *Movements in art since 1945* (Thames & Hudson, 1969).

M Kozloff *Renderings...* (Studio Vista, 1970).

D Ashton *A reading of modern art* (NY, Harper & Row, rev ed 1971).

N & E Calas *Icons and images of the sixties* (NY, Dutton, 1971).

W Haftmann & others *Abstract art since 1945* (Thames & Hudson, 1971).

J Hodin & others *Figurative art since 1945* (Thames & Hudson, 1971).

U Kultermann *Art events and happenings* (Mathews Miller Dunbar, 1971).

L Lippard *Changing...* (NY, Dutton, 1971).

H Ohff *Galerie der neunen Kunst* (Gütersloh, Bertelsmann, 1971).

J Roh *Deutsche Kunst der 60er Jahre...* (Munich, Bruckmann, 1971).

H Rosenberg *Art works and packages* (NY, Dell, 1971).

K Groh (ed) *Aktuelle Kunst in Osteropa* (Cologne, Dumont, 1972).

G Muller *The new avant garde...* (Pall Mall Press, 1972).

H Ohff *Kunst ist Utopie* (Gütersloh, Bertelsmann, 1972).

H Rosenberg *The de-definition of art...* (Secker & Warburg, 1972).

G Woods & others (eds) *Art without boundaries 1950–70* (Thames & Hudson, 1972).

G Battcock (ed) *Idea art: a critical anthology* (NY, Dutton, 1973).

C Greenberg *Art and culture* (Thames & Hudson, 1973).

S Hunter & J Jacobus *American art of the 20th century* (NY, Abrams, 1973).

H Kramer *The age of the avant garde...* (NY, Farrar, Strauss & Giroux, 1973).

L Lippard *Six years...* (Studio Vista, 1973).

A Oliva *Il territorio magico...* (Florence, Centro Di, 2nd ed 1973).

M Ragon & M Seuphor *L'art abstrait Vol 3: 1939–70* (Paris, Maeght Éditeur, 1973).

J Burnham *Great Western Saltworks...* (NY, Braziller, 1974).

G de Vries (ed) *Über Kunst – on art* (Cologne, Dumont, 1974).

A Henri *Total art* (NY & Toronto, Oxford University Press, 1974).

M Ragon & M Seuphor *L'art abstrait Vol 4: 1945–70* (Paris, Maeght Éditeur, 1974).

H Rosenberg *Discovering the present...* (Chicago, University of Chicago Press, 1974).

L Alloway *Topics in American art since 1945* (NY, Norton, 1975).

W Dyckes (ed) *Contemporary Spanish art* (NY, Art Digest, 1975).

B Smith (ed) *Concerning contemporary art...* (Oxford, Clarendon Press, 1975).

J Walker *Art since pop* (Thames & Hudson, 1975).

G Celant *Senzo titolo/1974* (Roma, Bulzoni, 1976).

C Gottlieb *Beyond modern art* (NY, Dutton, 1976).

D Honisch & J Jensen (eds) *Americanische Kunst von 1945 bis heute* (Cologne, Dumont, 1976).

S Hunter & J Jacobus *Modern art from post-impressionism to the present* (NY, Abrams, 1976).

E Johnson *Modern art and the object...* (Thames & Hudson, 1976).

H Rosenberg *Art on the edge...* (Secker & Warburg, 1976).

C Tompkins *The scene: reports on post-modern art* (NY, Viking Press, 1976).

G Auty *The art of self-deception: an intelligible guide* (Libertarian Books, 1977).

W Becker *The artist exhibited: art for the museum since '45* (Aachen, Neue Galerie, Sammlung Ludwig, 1977).

A Brighton & L Morris (eds) *Towards another picture* (Nottingham, Midland Group, 1977).

D Davis *Artculture: essays on the post modern* (NY, Harper & Row, 1977).

B Diamonstein (ed) *The artworld: a seventy-five year treasury of Art News 1902–77* (NY, Art News, 1977).

R Krauss *Passages in modern sculpture* (NY, Viking Press, 1977).

E Lucie-Smith *Art today: from abstract expressionism to superrealism* (Oxford, Phaidon, 1977).

A Oliva *Europe–America: the different avant gardes* (NY, Rizzoli, 1977).

A Sondheim (ed) *Individuals: post–movement art in America* (NY, Dutton, 1977).

H Adams *Art of the sixties* (Oxford, Phaidon, 1978).

H Bassett *Painting and sculpture today, 1980* (Indianapolis, Museum of Art, 1978).

Paris–New York (Paris, Musée National d'Art Moderne/Centre Georges Pompidou, 1978).

P Cummings *Artists in their own words* (NY, St Martin's Press, 1979).

B Rose *American painting: the eighties, a critical interpretation* (NY, New York University Art Gallery & Study Center, 1979).

S Wilson *British art from Holbein to the present day* (Tate Gallery & Bodley Head, 1979).

Actual Art Skira annual '70–80 (NY, Rizzoli, 1980).

P Fuller *Beyond the crisis in art* (Writers & Readers,

1980).

E Lucie-Smith *Art in the seventies* (Oxford, Phaidon, 1980).

J Spalding *Aspects of Canadian painting in the seventies* (Calgary, Alberta, Glenbow Museum, 1980).

S Buettner *American art theory 1945–70* (Ann Arbor, Michigan, University of Michigan Research Press, 1981).

J Chalumeau *Lectures de l' art* (Paris, Chêne/Hachette, 1981).

L Glozer *Westkunst: Zeitgenössische Kunst seit 1939* (Cologne, Dumont, 1981).

C Joachimides *A new spirit in painting* (Royal Academy of Arts, 1981).

J Russell *The meaning of modern art* (Thames & Hudson, 1981).

D Ashton *American art since 1945* (Thames & Hudson, 1982).

J Busch *Decade of sculpture: the 1960s* (Art Alliance Press, 1982).

F Caroli *Magico primario: l' arte degli anni ottanta* (Milan, Gruppo Editoriale Fabbri, 1982).

Commune di Milano *Arte Italiano 1960–82* (Hayward Gallery & ICA, Arts Council/Milan, Electa International, 1982).

E Johnson *American artists on art from 1940 to 1980* (NY, Icon Editions/Harper & Row, 1982).

J Pradel (ed) *World art trends* (NY, Abrams, 1982).

60–80 (Amsterdam, Stedelijk Museum, 1982).

P Selz *Art in our times: a pictorial history 1890–1980* (Thames & Hudson, 1982).

M Viatte & others *Aftermath: France 1945–54* (Barbican Art Gallery, 1982).

D Waldman & others *Italian art now: an American perspective* (NY, Guggenheim Museum, 1982).

R Pincus-Witten *Entries (maximalism)* (NY, Out of London Press, 1983).

H Smagula *Currents: contemporary directions in the visual arts* (NY, Prentice Hall, 1983).

J Walker *Art in the age of mass media* (Pluto Press, 1983).

L Alloway *Network: art and the complex present* (Ann Arbor, Michigan, University of Michigan Research Press, 1984).

N Bennett (ed) *The British art show: old allegiances and new directions* (Arts Council of Great Britain/Orbis, 1984).

B Haskell *Blam! The explosion of pop, minimalism and performance 1958–64* (NY, Whitney Museum, 1984).

L Lippard *Get the message? A decade of art for social change* (NY, Dutton, 1984).

J Masheck *Historical present: essays of the 1970s* (Ann Arbor, Michigan, University of Michigan Research Press, 1984).

— *Smart art* (NY, Willis, Locker & Owens, 1984).

K McShine *International survey of contemporary painting and sculpture* (NY, MoMA, 1984).

R Pincus-Witten *Eye to eye: twenty years of art criticism* (Ann Arbor, Michigan, University of Michigan Research Press, 1984).

B Wallis (ed) *Art after modernism: rethinking representation* (NY, New Museum of Contemporary Art & David Godine, 1984).

T Copplestone *Modern art* (Hamlyn, 1985).

H Foster *Recodings: art, spectacle, cultural politics* (Port Townsend, Washington, Bay Press, 1985).

E Lucie-Smith *American art now* (Oxford, Phaidon, 1985).

A Oliva *The international trans avant garde* (Milan, Giancarlo Politi Editore, 1985).

J Pradel (ed) *World art trends 83–84* (NY, Abrams, 1985).

C Robins *The pluralist era: American art 1968–81* (NY, Harper & Row, 1985).

J Siegel (ed) *Artwords: discourse on the '60s and '70s* (Ann Arbor, Michigan, University of Michigan Research Press, 1985).

R Alley *Forty years of modern art 1945–85* (Tate Gallery, 1986).

R Hughes *The art of Australia* (Harmondsworth, Penguin Press, 1986).

M Ragon *25 ans d' art vivant...* (Paris, Galilée, rev ed 1986, 1st ed 1969).

Reconstructions: avant garde art in Japan 1945–65 (Oxford, MoMA, 1986).

J Saltz & others *Beyond boundaries: New York's new art* (NY, Alfred van der Marck Editions, 1986).

H Singerman (ed) *Individuals: a selected history of contemporary art 1945–86* (Los Angeles, MoCA/NY, Abbeville, 1986).

K Thomas *Bis heute* (Cologne, Dumont, 1986).

D Ashton *Out of the whirlwind: three decades of arts commentary* (Ann Arbor, Michigan, University of Michigan Research Press, 1987).

L Falk & B Fisher (eds) *The event horizon* (Banff, Canada, Banff Center & Walter Phillips Gallery/Toronto, Coach House Press, 1987).

H Fox *Avant garde in the eighties* (Los Angeles, County Museum of Art, 1987).

P Frank *New, used, improved: art for the '80s* (NY, Abbeville, 1987).

E Lucie-Smith *Sculpture since 1945* (Oxford, Phaidon, 1987).

S Nairne & others *State of the art: ideas and images in the 1980s* (Chatto & Windus/ Channel 4 TV, 1987).

J Walker *Cross-overs: art into pop, pop into art* (Comedia/Methuen, 1987).

A Barzel (ed) *Europe now: contemporary art in Western Europe* (Milan, Electa, 1988).

G Celant *Unexpressionism: art beyond the contemporary* (NY, Rizzoli, 1988).

B Ford (ed) *Cambridge guide to the arts in Britain: Vol 9 since the Second World War* (Cambridge University Press, 1988).

T Godfrey *The new image: painting in the 1980s* (Oxford, Phaidon, 1988).

P Halley *Collected essays 1981–87* (Zürich, Bruno Bischofberger, 1988).

K Honnef *Contemporary art* (Cologne, Benedict Taschen Verlag, 1988).

C Jencks *Post-modernism: the new classicism in art and architecture* (Academy Editions, 1988).

E Laing *The winking owl: art of the People's Republic of China* (Berkeley, University of California Press, 1988).

K Levin *Beyond modernism* (NY, Harper & Row, 1988).

E Lucie-Smith & others *The new British painting* (Oxford, Phaidon, 1988).

B Rose *Auto-critique: essays on art and anti-art* (NY, Weidenfeld & Nicolson, 1988).

I Sandler *American art since the 1960s* (NY, Harper & Row, 1988).

J Siegel (ed) *Artwords 2: discourse on the early '80s* (Ann Arbor, Michigan, University of Michigan Research Press, 1988).

W Ali (ed) *Contemporary art from the Islamic world* (Buckhurst Hill, Essex, Scorpion, 1989).

H Arnason *A history of modern art* (Thames & Hudson, rev ed 1989), revised and updated by D Wheeler.

Battle of images: contradiction, unity and fragmentation in art from 1960 (Cologne, Ludwig Museum Rheinhallen, 1989).

J Brea *72–1992: before and after the enthusiasm: Spanish art* (The Hague, SDU Publishers/Amsterdam, Contemporary Art Foundation, 1989).

W Campschreur & J Divendal *Culture in another South Africa* (Zed Books, 1989).

J-L Daval *History of abstract painting* (Art Data, 1989).

M Friedman & others *Sculpture inside out* (NY, Rizzoli, 1989).

K Hartley *Scottish art since 1900* (Lund Humphries, 1989).

A Hicks *British painting now* (Oxford, Phaidon, 1989).

— *New British art in the Saatchi Collection* (Thames & Hudson, 1989).

D Kuspit *The new subjectivism: art of the 1980s* (Ann Arbor, Michigan, University of Michigan Research Press, 1989).

M Lovejoy *Post-modern currents: art and artists in the age of electronic media* (Ann Arbor, Michigan, University of Michigan Research Press, 1989).

N Lynton *The story of modern art* (Oxford, Phaidon, 2nd ed 1989).

A Oliva *Superart* (Milan, Giancarlo Politi Editore, 1989).

D Reid *A concise history of Canadian painting* (Don Mills, Ontario, Oxford University Press, 2nd ed 1989).

T Sokolowski & others *Against nature: Japanese art in the '80s* (San Francisco, Museum of Modern Art, 1989).

P Taylor (ed) *Post-pop art* (Cambridge, Mass, MIT Press, 1989).

J Ward *American realist painting 1945–80* (Ann Arbor, Michigan, University of Michigan Research Press, 1989).

D Wheeler *Art since mid century* (Thames & Hudson, 1989).

R Armstrong & R Marshall (eds) *The new sculpture 1965–75: between geometry & gesture* (NY, Whitney Museum, 1990).

Art et Publicité (Paris, Éditions du Centre Pompidou, 1990).

J Ashbery *Reported sightings: art chronicles 1957–87* (Manchester, Carcanet, 1990).

D Elliott & M Jaaukkuri *Northlands: new art from Scandinavia* (Oxford, MoMA, 1990).

J-L Ferrier (ed) *Art of our century: the story of Western art 1900 to the present* (Longman, 1990).

P Freeman & others *New art* (NY, Abrams, 1990).

S Guilbaut (ed) *Reconstructing modernism: art in New York, Paris and Montreal 1945–64* (Cambridge, Mass, MIT Press, 1990).

R Hewison *Future tense: a new art for the nineties* (Methuen, 1990).

R Hughes *Nothing if not critical* (Collins Harvill, 1990).

— *Shock of the new* (Thames & Hudson, rev ed 1990).

C Lindey *Art in the Cold War from Vladivostok to Kalamazoo, 1945–62* (Herbert Press, 1990).

E Lucie-Smith *Art in the eighties* (Oxford, Phaidon, 1990).

R Martin (ed) *The new urban landscape* (NY, Rizzoli, 1990).

D Pirie & others (eds) *Polish realities: the arts in Poland 1980–89* (Glasgow, Third Eye Centre, 1990).

K Varnedoe & A Gopnik *High & low: modern art & popular culture* (NY, MoMA/Abrams, 1990).

S Bann & W Allen *Interpreting contemporary art* (Reaktion Books, 1991).

R Castleman (ed) *Art of the forties* (NY, MoMA/London, Thames & Hudson, 1991).

J Howell (ed) *Breakthroughs: avant garde artists in Europe and America 1950-90* (NY, Rizzoli, 1991).

C Joachimides & N Rosenthal (eds) *Metropolis* (Berlin, Martin Gropius - Bau/ NY, Rizzoli, 1991).

L Lerner & M Williamson *Art and architecture in Canada* (2 vols) (Toronto, University of Toronto Press, 1991).

A Papadakis & others (eds) *New art: an international survey* (Academy Editions, 1991).

A Renton *Technique Anglaise: current trends in British art* (Thames & Hudson, 1991).

DESIGN

M Farr *Design in British industry: a mid century survey* (Cambridge University Press, 1955).

R Banham 'Design by choice, 1951–61, an alphabetical chronicle...' *Architectural Review* **130** (773) July 1961 43–8.

E Moody *Modern furniture* (Studio Vista, 1966).

D Joel *Furniture design set free: the British furniture revolution from 1851 to the present day* (Dent, 1969).

'Anniversary issue: a visual record of 21 years, 1949–70' *Design* (253) January 1970.

J Doblin *One hundred great product designs* (NY, Van Nostrand Reinhold, 1970).

A Ferebee *A history of design from the Victorian era...* (NY, Van Nostrand Reinhold, 1970).

E Ambasz (ed) *Italy: the new domestic landscape...* (NY, MoMA, 1972).

J Burns *Arthropods: new design futures* (NY, Praeger, 1972).

F MacCarthy *All things bright and beautiful...* (Allen & Unwin, 1972), also published as *A history of British design 1830–70* (Allen & Unwin, 1979).

C Meadmore *The modern chair classics in production* (Studio Vista, 1974).

N Carrington *Industrial design in Britain* (Allen & Unwin, 1976).

T Faulkner (ed) *Design 1900–60: studies in design and popular culture of the twentieth century* (Newcastle upon Tyne Polytechnic, 1976).

'25 years of British design' *Architectural Review* **969** November 1977.

Leisure in the twentieth century (Design Council, 1977), (Proceedings of the 1976 Design History Society Conference).

G Selle *Die Geschichte das Design in Deutschland von 1870 bis heute* (Cologne, Dumont, 1978).

S Bayley *In good shape: style in industrial products 1900 to 1960* (Design Council, 1979).

American Institute of Graphic Arts *Graphic design USA* Vols 1–8 (NY, Watson Guptil, 1980–7).

P Garner *The contemporary decorative arts from 1940 to the present day* (Oxford, Phaidon, 1980).

— *Twentieth century furniture* (Oxford, Phaidon, 1980).

J Heskett *Industrial design* (Thames & Hudson, 1980).

I Vercelloni *1970–80: dal design al post-design* (Milan, Casa Vogue, 1980).

P York *Style wars* (Sidgwick & Jackson, 1980).

V Gregotti *Il Disegno del prodotto industriale: Italia 1860–1980* (Milan, Electa, 1982).

P Sartago (ed) *Italian re-evolution: design in Italian society in the eighties* (La Jolla, California, Museum of Contemporary Art, 1982).

K-J Sembach *Contemporary furniture* (NY, Architectural Book Publishing, 1982).

Design in America: the Cranbrook vision 1925–50 (Detroit Institute of Arts/NY, Metropolitan Museum, 1983).

K Hiesinger & G Marcus (eds) *Design since 1945* (Philadelphia, Museum of Art/London, Thames & Hudson, 1983).

P Meggs *A history of graphic design* (NY, Van Nostrand Reinhold, 1983).

A Pulos *American design ethic* (Cambridge, Mass, MIT Press, 1983).

I Anscombe *A woman's touch: women in design from 1860 to the present day* (Virago, 1984).

British art and design 1900–60 (Victoria & Albert Museum/Zwemmer, 1984).

P York *Modern times: everybody wants everything* (W Heinemann, 1984).

C Greenberg *Mid-century modern* (Thames & Hudson, 1985).

N Hamilton (ed) *From Spitfire to microchip: studies in the history of design from 1945* (Design Council, 1985).

L Phillips & others *High styles: twentieth century American design* (NY, Whitney Museum of American Art/Summit Books, 1985).

R Stern (ed) *The international design yearbook 1985–6* (Thames & Hudson, 1985).

S Bayley & others *Twentieth century style and design*

(Thames & Hudson, 1986).

P Dormer *The new ceramics: trends and traditions* (Thames & Hudson, 1986).

A Forty *Objects of desire: design and society 1750–1980* (Thames & Hudson, 1986).

G Clark *American ceramics: 1876 to the present* (NY, Abbeville, rev ed 1987).

M Collins *Toward post-modernism: design since 1851* (British Museum Publications, 1987).

P Dormer *The new furniture: trends and traditions* (Thames & Hudson, 1987).

C McDermott *Street style: British design in the 1980s* (Design Council, 1987).

C Ray Smith *Interior design in twentieth century America* (NY, Harper & Row, 1987).

P Sparke *Design in context* (Bloomsbury, 1987).

G Stael & H Wolters (eds) *Holland in Vorm: Dutch design 1945–87* (Amsterdam, Stedelijk Museum, 1987).

H Aldersey-Williams *New American design: products and graphics for a post-industrial age* (NY, Rizzoli, 1988).

S Casciani *Industrial art: objects, play & thought in Danese production* (Milan, Arcadia Edizioni, 1988).

N Coleridge *The fashion conspiracy* (Heinemann, 1988).

M Collins & A Papadakis *Post-modern design* (Academy Editions, 1988).

Design Français 1960–90 trois décannies (Paris, Éditions du APCI/Centre Georges Pompidou, 1988).

A Pulos *The American design adventure 1940–75* (Cambridge, Mass, MIT Press, 1988).

J Thackara (ed) *Design after modernism: beyond the object* (Thames & Hudson, 1988).

G Albera & N Monti *Italian modern* (NY, Rizzoli, 1989).

P Atterbury (ed) *Interior design yearbook 1989* (Weidenfeld & Nicolson, 1989).

J Attfield & P Kirkham (eds) *A view from the interior: feminism, women and design* (Women's Press, 1989).

S Bayley *French design* (Fourth Estate, 1989).

S Bayley & H Rees *Design* (Design Museum, 1989).

— (eds) *Commerce and culture* (Design Museum, 1989).

C Buckley *Women designers in the pottery industry 1870–1955* (Women's Press, 1989).

V Fischer (ed) *Design now: industry or art?* (Munich, Prestel Verlag, 1989).

M Friedman (ed) *Graphic design in America: a visual language history* (Minneapolis, Walker Art Center, 1989).

F Huygen *British design* (Thames & Hudson, 1989).

R Martin & H Koda *Jocks and nerds* (NY, Rizzoli, 1989).

R Remington & B Hodik *Nine pioneers in American graphic design* (Cambridge, Mass, MIT Press, 1989).

B Russell *Architecture and design 1970–1990: new ideas in America* (NY, Abrams, 1989).

D Sudjic (ed) *From matt black to Memphis and beyond & back again: 1980s – the design decade* (ADT Press/Longman, 1989).

A Bangert & K Armer *80s style: designs of the decade* (Thames & Hudson, 1990).

N Bellati *New Italian design* (NY, Rizzoli, 1990).

E Coad *Spanish design and architecture* (Studio Vista, 1990).

P Dormer *The meaning of modern design: towards the 21st century* (Thames & Hudson, 1990).

M Erlhoff (ed) *Designed in Germany since 1949* (Munich, Prestel Verlag, 1990).

J Glancey *The new moderns: interior design & architecture for the 1990s* (Mitchell Beazley, 1990).

G Howell *Sultans of style: 30 years of fashion & passion 1960–90* (Ebury Press, 1990).

V Margolin (ed) *Design discourse* (Chicago, University of Chicago Press, 1990).

A Massey *Interior design in the 20th century* (Thames & Hudson, 1990).

S Minick & J Ping *Chinese graphic design in the twentieth century* (Thames & Hudson, 1990).

R Craig Miller *Modern design 1890–1990: the design collection of the Metropolitan Museum* (NY, Abrams, 1990).

G Raimondo *Italian living design: three decades of interiors* (Tauris Parke, 1990).

J Woodham *Twentieth century ornament* (Studio Vista, 1990).

C Pearce *Twentieth century design classics* (The Green Wood Publishing Co, 1991).

ENCYCLOPEDIAS, GLOSSARIES, BIOGRAPHICAL DICTIONARIES, CUMULATED BIBLIOGRAPHIES

J Barron *Language of painting: an informal dictionary* (NY, World Publishing Co, 1967).

P Cabanne & P Restany *L'avant garde au XX ^{e} Siècle* (Paris, Balland, 1969).

B Sani & W Pennestri *Nuovi termini di referimento per il linguaggio artistico* (Florence, Centro Di, 1971).

'Dizionario dei nuovi termi d'arte' *Casa Vogue* (14) May–June 1972.

R Charmet *Concise encyclopedia of modern art* (Glasgow, Collins, 1972).

M de Molina *Terminos de arte contemporanea* (Colombia, Bienal de Arte Coltejer 3, 1972).

G Ashworth *Encyclopedia of planning* (Barrie & Jenkins, 1973).

A Hill (ed) *A visual dictionary of art* (Greenwich, Connecticut, New York Graphic Society, 1973).

Phaidon dictionary of twentieth century art (Phaidon, 1973).

K Thomas *Dumont's Kleines Sachwörtebuch zur Kunst des 20. Jahrhunderts von Anti-Kunst bis Zero* (Cologne, Dumont Schauberg, 1973).

A Lemke & R Fleiss *Museum companion: a dictionary of art terms and subjects* (NY, Hippocrene Books, 1974).

B Myers *Dictionary of twentieth-century art* (NY, McGraw-Hill, 1974).

T Richardson & N Stangos (eds) *Concepts of modern art* (Harmondsworth, Penguin, 1974).

G Bazin *Les languages des styles: dictionnaire des formes artistiques et des écoles d'art* (Paris, Somogy, 1976).

P Cummings (ed) *Dictionary of contemporary American artists* (NY, St Martin's Press, 3rd ed 1977).

J Lewinski *Photography: a dictionary of photographers' terms and techniques* (Arrow Books, 1977).

A Coulsham *Bibliography of design in Britain 1851–1970* (Design Council, 1979).

C Parry-Crooke *Contemporary British artists* (Bergstrom & Boyle Books, 1979).

J Ehresmann (ed) *The pocket dictionary of art terms* (John Murray, rev ed 1980), revised by J Hall.

W Hunt *Encyclopedia of American architecture* (NY, McGraw-Hill, 1980).

R Huyghe (general editor) *Larousse encyclopedia of modern art* (Hamlyn, updated ed 1980).

D Bell *Contemporary art trends: 1960 – 80, a guide to sources* (Metuchen, New Jersey, Scarecrow Press, 1981).

H Osborne (ed) *The Oxford companion to twentieth century art* (Oxford University Press, 1981).

A Placzek (ed) *Macmillan encyclopedia of architects* 4 vols (NY, Free Press/Macmillan, 1982).

Who's who in graphic art (Dübendorf, Switzerland, De Clivo Press, 1982).

Art books 1980–84 (NY, Bowker, 1984).

S Jervis *The Facts on File dictionary of design and designers* (NY, Facts on File, 1984).

— *The Penguin dictionary of design and designers* (Harmondsworth, Penguin, 1984).

E Lucie-Smith *Art terms: an illustrated dictionary* (Thames & Hudson, 1984).

C Marks *World artists 1950–1980* (NY, H. W. Wilson Co, 1984), biographical dictionary.

A McCulloch *Encyclopedia of Australian art* 2 vols (Melbourne, Hutchinson, 1984).

R Siegal *American graphic designers* (NY, McGraw-Hill, 1984).

V Smith *Design* (Oxford, Clio Press, 1984), cumulated bibliography.

L von Bamford *Design resources: a guide to architecture and industrial design information* (Jefferson, NC, McFarland & Co, 1984).

S Bayley (ed) *The Conran dictionary of design* (Octopus Conran, 1985).

A Morgan & C Naylor (eds) *Contemporary designers* (Chicago & London, St James Press, 1985).

— *International contemporary art directory* (Chicago & London, St James Press, 1985).

V Lampugani (ed) *The Thames & Hudson encyclopedia of twentieth-century architecture* (Thames & Hudson, 1986).

P Marcan *Arts address book* (High Wycombe, Bucks, Peter Marcan Publications, 2nd ed 1986).

G O'Hara *Encyclopedia of fashion* (Thames & Hudson, 1986).

V Margolin *Design history bibliography* (ICOGRADA, 1987).

A Morgan & C Naylor (eds) *Contemporary architects* (Chicago & London, St James Press, 2nd ed 1987).

J Fleming & H Honour *The Penguin dictionary of decorative arts* (Viking, new ed 1989).

Groupes, mouvements, tendances de l'art contemporain depuis 1945 (Paris, École Nationale Supérieure des Beaux Arts, 1989).

International dictionary of art and artists 2 vols (Chicago & London, St James Press, 1989).

C Naylor (ed) *Contemporary artists* (Chicago & London, St James Press, 3rd ed 1989).

J Watson & A Hill *A dictionary of communication and media studies* (E Arnold, 2nd ed 1989).

R Atkins *Artspeak: a guide to con-temporary ideas, movements and buzzwords* (NY, Abbeville Press, 1990).

Dictionary of British twentieth century painters, sculptors and other artists (Woodbridge, Sussex, Antique Collectors',Club, 1990).

Getty Art History Information Program *Art & architecture thesaurus* 3 vols (Oxford University Press, 1990).

J Godfrey (ed) *A decade of i-deas: the encyclopedia of the '80s* (Penguin Books, 1990).

J Pile *Dictionary of twentieth century design* (NY, Facts on File/Roundtable Press Book, 1990).

American art directory 1991-92 (Sevenoaks, Kent, Bowker-Saur, 53rd ed 1991).

M Bideault & M Rinehart (eds) *BHA: bibliography of the historyof art vol 1* (Williamstown, Mass, Getty Art History Programme/Vandoeuvre-lès-Nancy, Institut de l'Information program Scientifique et Technique, 1991).

Designers International Directory (Sevenoaks, Kent, Bowker-Saur, 1991).

P Dormer & others *The illustrated dictionary of designers* (Headline, 1991).

Who's who in American art 1991-92 (Sevenoaks, Kent, Bowker-Saur, 19th ed 1991).

INDEX

INSTRUCTIONS FOR USE
Numbers refer to the A–Z entries not pages.
Numbers in bold and in brackets indicate a main entry for the term in question.
Alphabetical filing is word by word not 'all through'.

Marfa (Texas), the Marfa project, 211

Margam (Glamorgan, Wales), County Park, 583

Margerin, Frank, 102

Marginal communication/media, 616

Margolies, J., 162

Margolin, Victor, 540

Mariani, Carlo Maria, 195, 527

Marinetti, Filippo Tommaso, 168

Marioni, Tom, 163, 605

Marisol, 147, 270

Markelius, Sven, 454

Market, in art, 378

Market research, 487

Markets, global, 306

Marle, Del, 320

Marmer, Nancy, 602

Marne-le-Vallée (France), Palacio de Abraxas, 651

Marr, Leslie, 119

Marseilles (France), Unite d'Habitation, 326

Marshall, Francis, 485

Marshall, Stuart, 688

Marsil, Tancrede, 99

Martin, Agnes, 270, 290, 317

Martin, Bill, 690

Martin, Jean-Hubert, 305

Martin, Kenneth, 170, 171,

Martin, Mary, 170, 473

Martin, Rosy, 506

Martin, Rupert, 507

Marx, Enid, 683

Marx, Karl, 399

Marx art, 515

Marxhausen, Reinhold, 605

Marxism, 280, 283, 417, 449, 515, 596, 622, 633, 635, 685

Marxist aesthetics, 156, 283, (**399**)

Mas, 136

Masi, Denis, 110, 303, 501

Masks, 324

Mason, John, 4

Mason, Stewart, 350

Mass art, (**400**)

Mass communication systems, 354

Mass culture, 31, 193, 202, 216, 248, 283, 400, 520, 622

Mass media, 86, 182, 256, 352, 355, 405, 439, 504, 508, 510, 518, 524, 529, 532, 592, 677, 691

Mass Moca, (**401**)

Mass produced art, 375

Massachusetts Institute of Technology, 22, 46, 138

Masses' painting, 498

Massironi, Manfredo, 321

Masterkova, Lydia, 679

Masterpiece concept, The, 587

Material actions, 214, 402

Material culture, 520

Materialism, in art/design, 461

Materialist film, 622

Mathematics, 167, 180, 282, 542, 645

Mathieu, Georges, 56, 62, 394, 501, 649

Mathsson, Bruno, 576

Matière painting, 402

Matisse, Henri, 103, 118, 483, 497, 635

Matriarchies, 270

Matrix, 269

'Matrix', exhibition, 645

Matter art, 62, 199, (**402**), 610

Matthew, Robert, 447

Mattox, Charles, 198, 605

Mauro, Richard, 551

Maximalism, (**403**)

Mayakovsky, Vladimir, 263, 399, 620

Mayfair magazine, 509

Maymont, Paul, 297

Mazeaufroid, Jean, 661

MDF, 639

Mead, Dorothy, 119

Meadows, Bernard, 302

Meals, 278

Meaning, in design, 541

Meatyard, Ralph Eugene, 614

Mec art, (**404**)

Mechanical aesthetic/art, 395, 404

Mechanical reproduction, 182, 404, 504

Medalla, David, 22, 232, 461, 495, 501, 590

Media art, (**405**), 677

'Media burn', event, 35

Media bus, 358

Media inversion, 405

Meditative art, 654

Medium density fibreboard, 639

Meehan, Thomas, 495

Mega-decoration, 632

Mega-visual tradition, 417

Megastructures, 49, 262, (**406**), 516, 684

Meggs, Philip, 361

Mehring, Howard, 692

Meir, Richard, 466

Meister, Howard, 59

Melamid, Aleksander, 148, 376

Melbourne (Australia), Museum of Modern Art, 351; Victoria Artists Society, 39

Melchert, James, 4

Mellis, Margaret, 221

Mellor, David, 446

Membranes, in architecture, 660

Memorials, 620

Memphis (Italian design group), 23, 366, 375, (**407**), 460, 528

Men, images of, 270

Men Only magazine, 509

Mendelson, Marc, 402

Mendez, Leopoldo, 652

Mendini, Alessandro, 23, 366

Menswear, 134, 700

Mental institutions, 64

Mercer, Frank, 172

Merleau-Ponty, Maurice, 503

Merz, Gerhard, 677

Merz, Mario, 69, 170

Merz collages, 441

Merz poetry, 605

Merzbauten, 241

Message T-shirts, 646

Mestizo culture, 382

Mestrovic, Matko, 472

Meta magazine, 553

Meta-architecture, 409

Meta-art, (**408**)

Meta-design, 556

Metalanguage, 408

Metabolists, 258, 372, (**409**)

Metal Hurlant, 102

Metal sculpture, 302, 370

Metamatics, 98

Metaphors, in architecture, 526

Metaphysical art, 186

Metaphysical classicism, 452

Metavisual, (**410**)

Methods, in design, 206, 207

Metro-land, (**411**)

Metz, Christian, 586

Metzger, Gustav, 119, 210, 439

Mexican art, 3, 353, 382, 515, 652

Miami (Florida), Wolfson

New television, 688
New tendency, 472
New typography movement, 361
New wave, 101, 465, 551
New wave architecture, 287
New wave art, 415, 442
New wave comics, 310
New wave graphics, 287
New York (City), A T & T
    skyscraper, 526; Architectural
    League, 148; Art et Industrie *see*
    Art et Industrie; Castelli-
    Sonnabend Gallery, 688; Center
    for Book Arts, 118; City Walls *see*
    City Walls; Civilian Warfare, 229;
    Cultural Center, 602; Deborah
    Sharpe Gallery, 229; East Village,
    229; Fashion Moda, 309; Finch
    College Museum, 543, 587;
    Franklin Furnace, 118; Fun
    Gallery, 229; Gertrude Stein
    Gallery, 469; Guggenheim
    Museum, 493; Harlem, 43, 700;
    International Society of Copier
    Artists, 182; Jewish Museum, 412;
    John Gibson Gallery, 619; March
    Gallery, 469; Metropolitan
    Museum, 364; Museum of
    American Graffiti, 309; Museum
    of Contemporary Crafts, 605, 650;
    Museum of Contemporary
    Hispanic Art, 249; Museum of
    Holography, 342; Museum of
    Modern Art *see* MoMA;
    P.P.O.W., 229; Pan Am
    skyscraper, 648; Pat Hearn
    Gallery, 229; Razor Gallery, 309;
    School of Visual Arts, 513;
    Semaphore Gallery, 376; Shafrazi
    Gallery, 309; SoHo *see* SoHo;
    Subway, 309; Virtual Garrison,
    229; Whitney Museum of
    American Art, 398, 405, 408, 458;
    Worldwide Plaza Building, 268
New York (State), Lewiston Artpark,
    583
New York Correspondence School,
    398
New York Dolls, rock group, 551
New York Five, 133, (**466**)
New York naturalism, 505
New York school, 3, 229, 443, (**467**),
    578, 604
New York Strike, 66
New York Telephone, 347
New York Times, 479, 693
New Zealand art, 530
Newby, Frank, 660
Newcastle upon Tyne
    (Northumberland), Byker, 158
Newman, Barnett, 3, 4, 6, 10, 151,
    241, 330, 412, 443, 569, 589, 678
Newman, Michael, 450, 592
Newman, Oskar, 201
Newman, Paul, 342
Newspaper design, 675
Newspeak, 83
Newsweek, 376
Next, shops, 563
Nice Style, 463, (**468**), 501
Niche marketing, 306, 563
Nicholson, Ben, 433, 573
Nick, George, 490
Nickolls, Trevor, 1
Nico, 551
Nicosia, Nic, 628
Niemeyer, Oskar, 120
Nihilism, 100, 529
Nikon, Japanese company, 367
Nikos, 404
Nilsson, Gladys, 140, 345
'Nine evenings', festival, 230, 657
Ninth art, The, 102
Nissan, Japanese company, 367
Nitsch, Hermann, 214, 501
Nixon, David, 292
Nixon, Richard, 278
Nizzoli, Marcello, 366, 478
NMWA *see* National Museum of
    Women in the Arts,
No art, (**469**)
No rules architecture, 287
Noigandres group, 168
Noise music, 605
Nolan, Sidney, 30, 554
Noland, Kenneth, 6, 151, 178, 412,
    432, 574, 589, 615, 642, 692
Nolde, Emil, 439
Nomadic furniture, 486
Non-art, 530
Non-conformist art, 485, 679
Non-conscious design, 33
Non-object art, 530
Non-pedigreed architecture, 47
Non-relational art, (**470**), 589
Non-site, 594
Nordic design, 576
Nordic expressionism, 146
Norklun, Kathi, 522
Norman & Hill, Ilford, 274
Norskag, Jody, 461
North Adams (Mass), Museum of
    Contemporary Art *see* Mass
    Moca,
North West Mounted Valise, 398
Northern Ireland, prisons, 538
Norton, Tom, 182
Norwegian design, 576
Norwich (Norfolk), University of
    East Anglia, Sainsbury Centre *see*
    Sainsbury Centre,
Nostalgia, 564
Notation, musical, 429
Notting Hill (London), carnival, 136
Nottingham (Nottinghamshire),
    Castle Museum, 650
Nouveau réalisme, 20, 441, (**471**),
    555, 598
Nouveaux plasticiens, 511
Nouveaux réalistes, 471, 476, 518
Nouvelle disfigurations, 596
Nouvelle peinture, 290
Nouvelle tendance, 244, 312, 321,
    (**472**), 474, 699
Nova, Simon, 658
Novelty art, 419
Novy Lef group, 263
Now crowd, The, 463
Nowhere architecture, 162
Nuclear art, (**473**)
Nuclear weapons, 210
Nude, paintings of, 270, 296, 509
NUL, (**474**), 479
Nuova Secessione Artistica Italiana,
    289
Nuove nuove, 442
Nuovo futurism, 455
Nusberg, Lev, 225, 679
Nutt, James, 140, 345
Nuttall, Jeff, 461, 501
Nxumalo, Derrick, 668

O M Theatre, 214
'O Superman', song/record, 567, 605
O'Connor, Francis, 222
O'Doherty, Brian, 27, 357
O'Donnell, Ron, 507, 614

T

Vostell, Wolf, 20, 210, 277, 501
Voulkos, Peter, 4, 291
Vowles, Hannah, 61
Voyeurism, 247, 267, 509, 581,
Voysey, Charles, 411